The Douglas DC-1/DC-2/DC-3 75 Years

Volume 3

Jennifer M Gradidge
in collaboration with John M Davis,
David W Lucabaugh, Peter J Marson,
Matt Miller & Douglas D Olson

An AIR-BRITAIN Publication

The Douglas DC-1 / DC-2 / DC-3
Volume Three: 75 Years

Published in the United Kingdom by

Air-Britain (Historians) Ltd

Sales Dept:
41 Penshurst Road, Leigh,
Tonbridge, Kent TN11 8HL, England

Website: www.air-britain.co.uk

Correspondence regarding this publication to:

Jennifer M Gradidge
32 Meadow Way, Rickmansworth,
Herts WD3 7PA, England

or to our dedicated email address: **dc3@air-britain.co.uk**

Regd Office address:

Victoria House, Stanbridge Park,
Staplefield Lane, Staplefield,
West Sussex RH17 6AS, England

ISBN 978 085130 429 8

Printed in the UK by
Henry Ling Ltd, The Dorset Press,
Dorchester DT1 1HD

Origination by Howard Marks, Icklesham

Front cover photograph:
Visiting EAA AirVenture at Oshkosh, Wisconsin on 26 July 2010 from "The Last Time Douglas DC-3 & C-47 Reunion" was N728G (c/n 4359), painted in an attractive scheme reminiscent of the Douglas Super DC-3 prototype. The aircraft is owned by K W Plastics Inc. (Karl Krämer)

Back cover photographs:
Above: The Museum of Flight Foundation's "Boeing" Douglas DC-2 N1934D (c/n 1368), marked as "NC13711" (which was Transcontinental & Western Air's first DC-2 in 1934) touches down after arrival from California at Rock Falls, Illinois at "The Last Time Douglas DC-3 & C-47 Reunion" on 24 July 2010. The Fleet number "322" currently carried actually belonged to NC13784 (c/n 1294). (Ralph M Pettersen)

Below: N5106X (c/n 9058), a former C-47-DL in USAAF colours marked as "232832" (its genuine original serial number), is seen parked at "The Last Time Douglas DC-3 & C-47 Reunion" at Rock Falls, Illinois after arrival on 23 July 2010. (Ralph M Pettersen)

CONTENTS

Two 16-page Colour Galleries are to be found following pages 96 and 192.

INTRODUCTION

When American Airlines first ordered the Douglas DST, the sleeper version of what was to become the DC-3, no-one could have predicted that the airframe would still be in production ten years later, after a World War that changed so much. Even less could anyone have predicted that seventy-five years on there would still be several hundred DC-3s flying, some fitted with turboprop engines, but many still with the original Pratt & Whitney R-1830s. Many predictions have been made as to how long the type would keep flying, but despite huge increases in fuel prices and shortages, and difficulty in finding engines, DC-3s continue to fly – more often kept airworthy for airshow work or in areas where their ability to operate out of short airstrips is valuable. Indeed a fly-in at Oshkosh in 2010 had thirty-five DC-3s in the air.

When Volumes 1 and 2 of "The First Seventy Years" were published, space restricted our ability to cover everything we had hoped to include, and it has been decided that a further Volume should be published to coincide with and commemorate the Seventy-fifth Anniversary of the first DC-3 flight and to use it, first of all, to include the changes that have taken place and the new material that has come to light since Volumes 1 and 2 were published. In addition, the opportunity is now being taken to cover further topics for which there was no room in the original two volumes. For example, Arthur Pearcy's widow, Audrey, gave us much of his photographic archive and included in this was material on the Antarctic operations of the United States Navy. This material is now being used in an extended article on these operations.

We also have details of the DC-3 conversions and overhauls carried out by Scottish Aviation between 1945 and 1955, and while this has some data missing, it is of considerable interest in illustrating the huge amount of work carried out by such organizations for other operators during these early post-war years. Other notable companies undertaking such conversion work over the years, included Remmert Werner in the USA, Fokker in the Netherlands, Field Aircraft Services at Nottingham, England, Hindustani Aviation in India and others. Some airlines did their own overhauls, and we look forward to hearing from readers with stories of these companies' many exploits.

Peter Marson has been delving into the British Airways archives and has unearthed details of BOAC's use of the DC-3, much of which has not hitherto been published. The opportunity is also being taken to include a selection of timetables and other memorabilia for operators using the type – though this can never be comprehensive. There is also a short note on the hybrid aircraft produced for the USAAF, and details of the USAAF units in India.

Much new information has come out of Russia and China in recent years, both on C-47s and Li-2s, and we present extensive updates on C-47 and Li-2 operations in these two countries. From these it is obvious that there is much more information to come in the future from the long-hidden archives of both countries.

Finally we are including a comprehensive survey of the surviving airframes, subdivided into those that are airworthy, those preserved in museums, the aircraft currently stored and perhaps awaiting overhaul or better times, and the many airframes that may never fly again because of their derelict state.

DEDICATION

This volume is dedicated to the memory of one of our co-authors in Volumes 1 & 2 of "The DC-1/2/3, The First Seventy Years", Allen 'The Rat' Bovelt who died, suddenly, in June 2007.

On these two pages are a selection of photographs of named C-47s in Australia during World War Two, provided by Al Bovelt.

42-23582 (c/n 9444) "Honeymoon Express" of 41 TCS. This aircraft was destroyed by a time bomb at Manila on 11th March 1945.

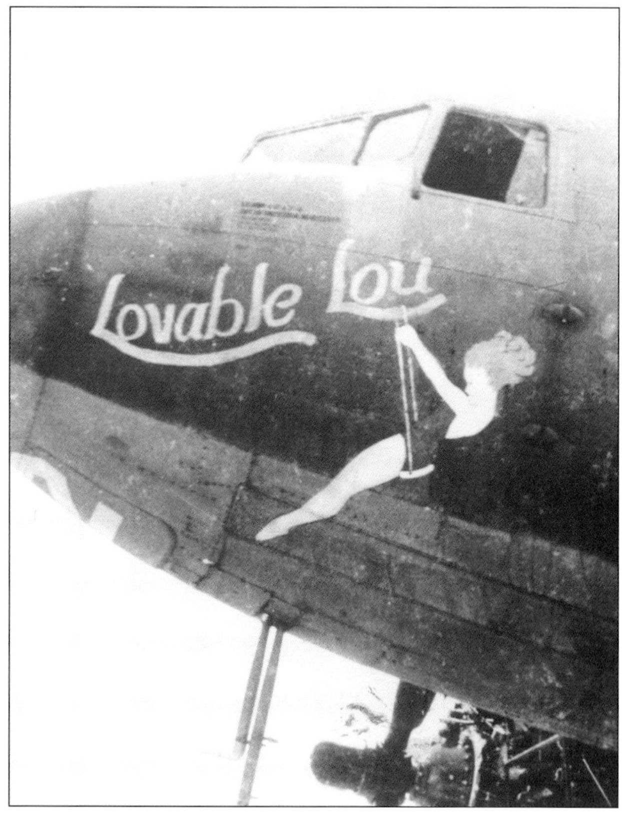

42-23958 (c/n 9820) "Lovable Lou" of 39 TCS, which suffered an accident on 4th August 1945.

PREFACE

The Author would like to thank all those who have contributed information to the DC-3 Website and also to her personally, by mail. This has certainly added very much to this Volume 3, but it is very clear that there is much more to come. Various internet websites have been set up in the last few years, and these have been a source for some of the USAAF/USAF and US Navy casualty reports, but the picture is still incomplete. In particular we formally thank Matt Miller who has copied onto disc files available on the internet, covering recently unearthed Form 14 casualty reports which give details of accidents, however small, to C-47s, C-53s etc serving with the USAAF and USAF. Despite these additions there remain many C-47s for which no accurate fate is known.

The Dedication on these pages is brief, but I must pay tribute to Al Bovelt's work in building up our knowledge of the C-47s and C-53s which saw service in the SW Pacific and Australia regions. It is obvious from the rosters of Troop Carrier Squadrons that recent work has failed to add anything to what Al unearthed – so thorough was he. Al was very much a mystery man. He worked for New Zealand National Airways Corp before going to Australia. He probably learned to fly there, but later moved to New Guinea where he is reported to have flown for Mandated Airlines before its take-over by Ansett. He once told me that he had been responsible for the write-off of a DC-3 at one of the difficult strips in New Guinea, though which aircraft was involved is uncertain, possibly VH-MAE. He operated Allan's Petroleum Service in New Guinea to check the quality of fuel supplied to airlines. Al retired to Sydney in 1992 but continued to fly with Jack Curtis of Dakota National Air (later Discovery Air Tours). Jack willingly volunteered to scatter Al's ashes from one of his DC-3s.

Al formed the Pacific Islands Aviation Society in the 1950s and 60s to record happenings in the area. He helped Peter Berry with 'The Douglas Commercial Story' in 1971 and this continued with the 1984 'Douglas DC-3 and its Predecessors'. He remained in contact and helped considerably with 'The First Seventy Years'. My first verbal contact with Al was a 'phone call on 1st January 2000 to wish me a Happy New Year. Later he phoned that he had not received 'The First Seventy Years' and when this was rectified he called again – for the last time. He told me he that he had been in hospital with encephalitis, a virus infection of the brain, and although he recovered, it left him weakened. He will be sorely missed.

The following have contributed to this present Volume:- Lennart Andersson, Brian Austria-Tomkins (decd), Roger Besecker (decd) (USA), Martin Best, Al Bovelt (decd), V Cedrio, John Chapman, Chris Chatfield, John Davis (USA), Herman Dekker, William G Dougherty, Mike Draper, Bill Fisher, Paul Giblin, Dick Gunnell, Toby Gursanscky (Australia), Karl Hayes (Eire), Leif Hellstrom (Sweden), Willy Henderickx (Belgium), Peter Hillman, Niels Larsen (Denmark), Ruud Leeuw (Holland), Dave Lucabaugh (USA), Sean Meagher, Marcelo Magalhaes (Brazil), John Matthews, Tom Macfadyen, Jack McKillop, Matt Miller (USA), Peter Marson, Tony Morris, Doug Olson (USA), Dave Partington, Pierre Parvaud, Michael Prophet (Holland), L. Roffer, Laurence Safir (decd), Manuel Santaner, R.A.Scholefield, Terry Smith, Barrie Towey, Aad van der Voet, Jimmy Wadia (India), John Wegg, M West, Maurice Wickstead, Tom Woodhouse, and Air-Britain News, Aviation Letter, LAAS, Propliner and Scramble. Mention should also be made of all those who have contributed small items of news of a current or historical nature that have richly enhanced the contents of Chapter 16.

It should also be recorded that Air-Britain artist Cliff Minney, who provided some of the drawings used in the first two volumes of the Book, passed away during the course of the preparation of Volumes 1 & 2.

Jennifer M Gradidge
March 2011

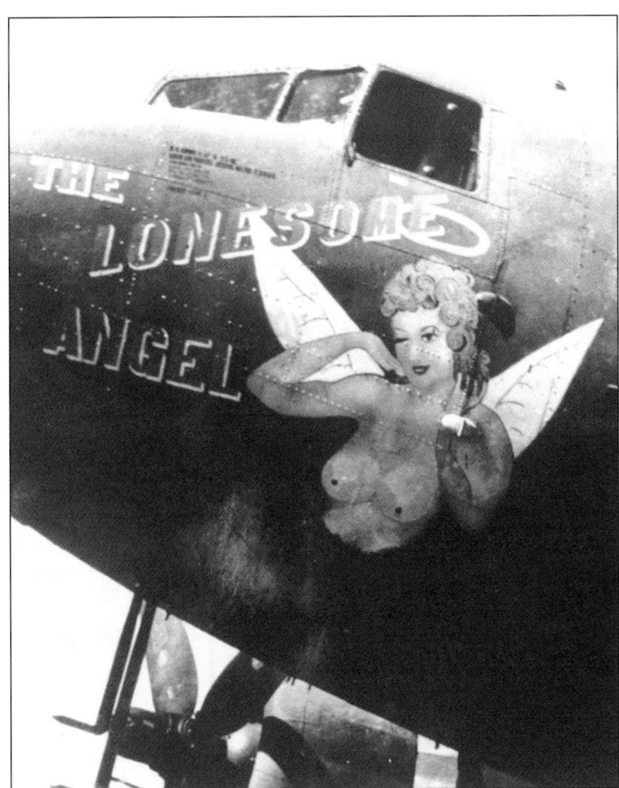

42-23955 (c/n 9817) "The Lonesome Angel" of 39 TCS. This aircraft crashed on 2nd August 1944 and was condemned the following day as "salvage".

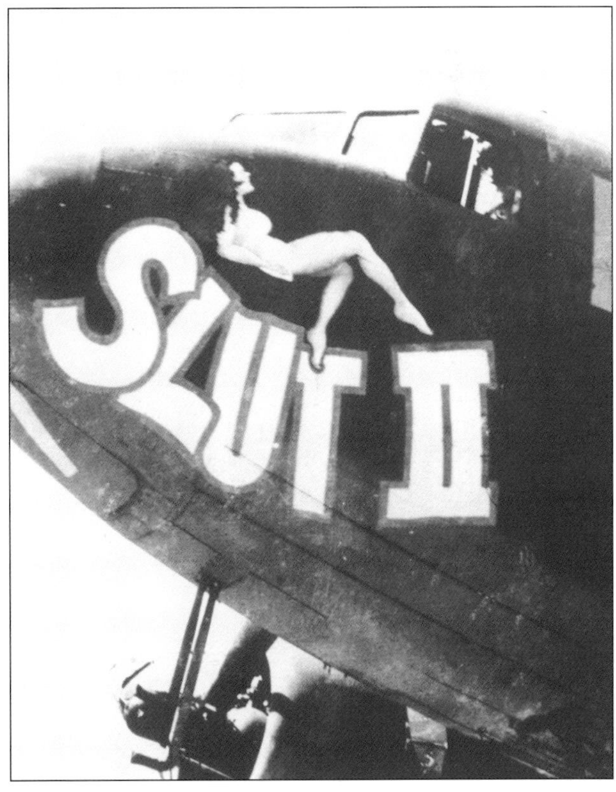

41-18498 (c/n 4590) "Slut II" field number 17 of 6 TCS. This aircraft had an accident on 31st October 1943, but was not condemned until 26th March 1945 as "salvage".

The left-hand side of a Dakota cockpit – in this case British European Airways' G-ALYF, shown in 1950. Items to be seen are: left – radio compass, ASI, altimeter, rate of turn indicator; centre – compass, rate of climb indicator, turn & slip indicator, ILS display; right – compass, fire-warning light, automatic control panel (with direction indicator and artificial horizon), with the engine RPM, boost gauge and oil temperature gauge below. At the bottom, to the left of the throttle quadrant with the throttle and mixture control levers can be seen the elevator trim tab control wheel and the propeller speed control. *(Flight via Stephen Piercey, no.25216s)*

The right-hand side of the same Dakota (G-ALYF) cockpit. Items to be seen are: left – automatic control panel (as on previous picture) with engine gauges, throttle quadrant; centre – clock, airspeed indicator, turn & bank indicator, altimeter and compass. Below are the starboard engine fuel selector cock with oil and fuel pressure gauges. To the right are the rate of turn indicator and engine temperature gauge, and on far right the landing gear and hydraulic system pressure gauges. *(Flight via Stephen Piercey, no.25214s)*

Close-up of the engines (Wright R-1830s) and the Hamilton Standard propellers on a Swissair DC-3. *(Swissair)*

Chapter 1
Flying the DC-3

by Andrew Dixon

It's 3 AM, my feet are two solid blocks of ice, and the rest of my body is not a lot better, outside the windscreen a few feet in front of me it's raining – hey in the cockpit it's raining - now you know why we buy the laminated copies of the topographical charts. My arms ache after hours of fighting the moderate chop associated with winter weather in Europe with heavy and ineffective ailerons . . .

It's 3 PM, the day is lovely, warm and sunny not a cloud in the sky on this beautiful calm summer's day. In the cabin 36 happy passengers are enjoying the delights of 1940s airline travel with the wonderful views of the English country side passing by below . . .

This is "Flying the DC-3" - OK you could add charging across the North Sea at 25 feet dispersing oil, or cruising across the North Atlantic with the cabin loaded with AVGAS on a ferry flight from Israel to Canada – what has this aircraft not done?

To fully "enjoy" the experience let's assume you are a new commercial pilot just starting on your first airline job and by luck, chance or otherwise you find yourself flying the DC3 rather than a Boeing 737, and I have the job of teaching you how to fly it.

So you have successfully completed the ground school and passed the technical examination and therefore you have a good idea of how the "old lady" works. Now is the time to find out the practicalities.

Our steed today officially started life as a Douglas C47B-10-DK delivered in November 1944 from the Douglas factory at Oklahoma City, however in this day and age all the variants are known as DC-3s or Daks and that will do for us. Firstly a careful pre-flight or A Check as it is known in the commercial flying world. This can be a very pleasant experience on a nice summer's afternoon, and a somewhat different task in the depths of winter. It is also the time to learn about "Pratt and Whitney medals". The Pratt and Whitney R1830 radial engines fitted to our aircraft hold up to 26 Imperial Gallons of oil and no matter how good your engineers are, the engines have a wonderful habit of leaking some of this from various orifices. They also seem to know when you are wearing a new clean shirt and are only too happy to drip all

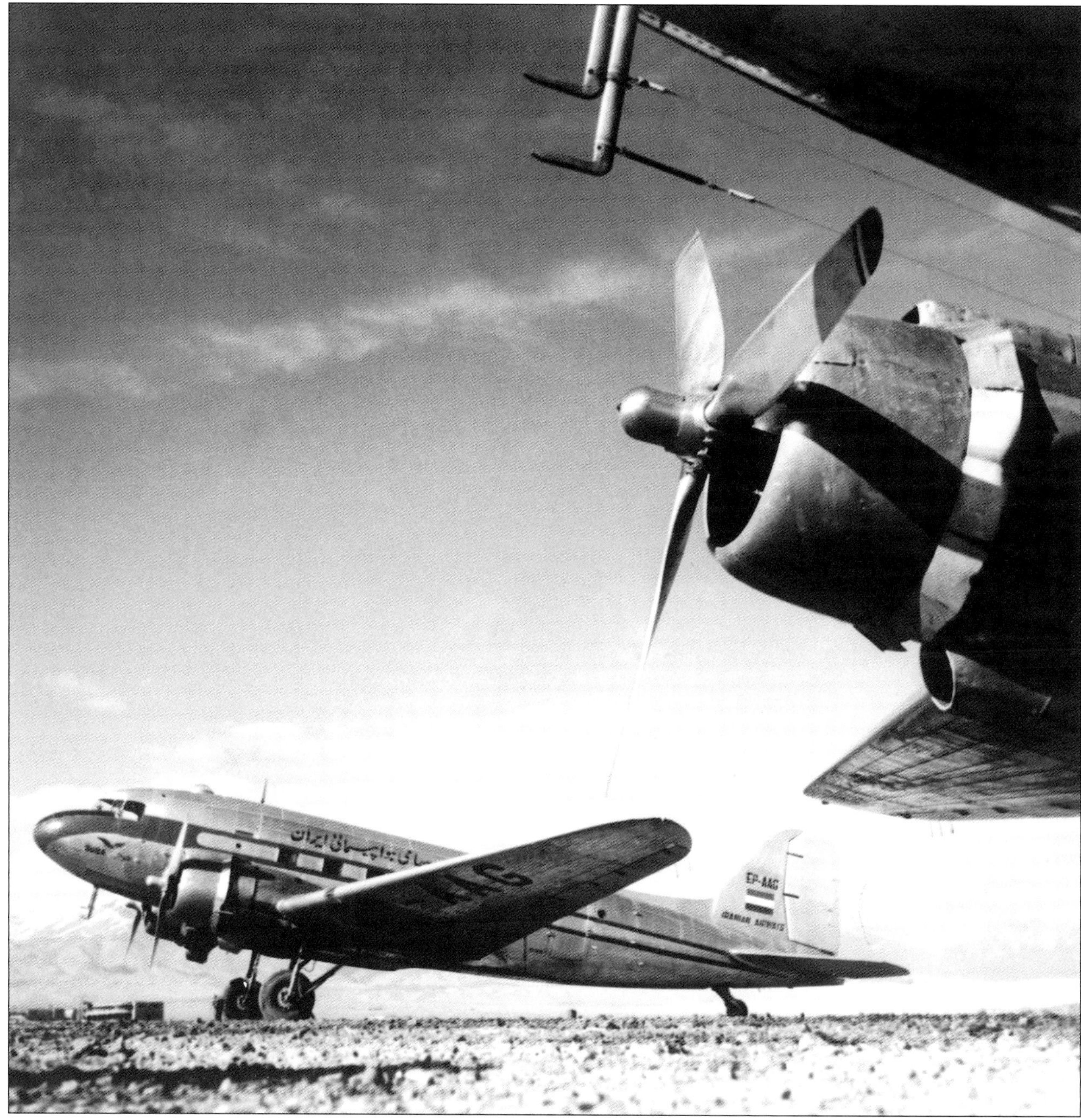

Close-up of the engine of a DC-3/Dakota showing the cowl-gills in the open position. The aircraft in the background is EP-AAG (c/n 9453) of Iranian Airways. *(via Jennifer Gradidge)*

over it. I did once know a Captain who could keep immaculately clean around a Dak but never could find out how he did it.

Leaking oil of course requires replacement and this is where a good ground crew come into their own, however they are not always around so at times a little mountaineering is required. Young keen new pilots are very adept at leaping on the wing to top up the oils and to dip the fuel tanks. As one becomes a little more experienced a small step ladder makes things a little easier – nothing to do with getting older of course.

Whilst talking of the ground crew, hopefully they have also pulled through the propellers. Unless one is flying a DC-3 that has been converted to turbine power like the Basler conversion or suchlike your aircraft will be fitted with a couple of radial engines – either Wright R1820s or as in our case the more usual Pratt and Whitney R1830s. These engines if left for any period of time longer than about two hours, can lock solid with oil or fuel draining into the bottom cylinders. If you attempt to start the engine with such a hydraulic lock one of two things is going to occur. Either the cylinder will be torn out of the crankcase or the connecting rod will bend, neither good for extended engine life. Therefore before starting, the engine must be pulled through by hand to check for any lock so the offending liquid can be removed if necessary. You only need to pull it through nine blades per engine but – well it helps keep you fit.

Having completed the external check we climb aboard and make sure we have five locks, two pins and a pitot cover. This refers to the external locking devices for the controls and undercarriage. The retractable undercarriage on the Dak was one of the first such systems and as such is not as automated as some more modern systems – more of this later. One of the things it does not run to is a "squat switch" designed to prevent the inadvertent retraction of the gear on the ground, instead two metal pins are installed in the undercarriage when the aircraft is parked, they don't look much but they will stop the gear retracting on the ground or in flight. It is therefore somewhat important to remove them before flight – they say there are the Dak pilots who have taken off with the pins in and those who are going to – so as a standard operating practice the last thing we do before getting in the aircraft is for one pilot to remove the gear pins before he also removes the external rudder lock. That way either the pins will be removed before departure or hopefully the difficulty in taxiing the aircraft with the rudder lock still in should give a clue that all is not right.

We now climb up the aircraft to the cockpit which is surprisingly compact and bijou. There again pilots are non-fare-paying passengers so don't get a lot of room. However once installed with the seat adjusting up and down as well as fore and aft and with adjustable rudder pedals it is actually really quite comfortable. We run through the checklist which is very similar to that of the light twin-engine aircraft you will have been flying up until now. Then we come to starting the engines and here things get a little different again. No two aircraft are the same these days as various modifications and improvements have been made to the systems over the years but we will go through the procedure most common these days. To start the engine we need a starter, a primer, fuel booster pump, magneto switch and mixture control all manipulated in the correct order at the correct time and you still only have two hands.

So throttle set, battery master switch on 'flight' unless we are using ground power but that is something of a rarity. Ignition master 'on', check the propeller is clear and depress the starter switch once the engine is turning and not before, we don't want a leaking idle cut-off valve to cause a hydraulic lock, 'on' with the booster pump, check the fuel pressure and prime the engine as required, after nine blades have passed on with the magnetos and hopefully the engine will fire up at this point hold the prime, advance the mixture to auto rich and when you think the engine has settled release the prime, check the oil pressure and job's done – easy really. Now we just repeat it for the other side.

With the magic of Pratt and Whitney warming up on both sides we run through the 'after start' checklist whilst waiting for a minimum of 40 degrees oil temperature and 120 degrees cylinder head temperature. Once these have been achieved it is safe to increase the engine RPM over 1200 without any danger of poor lubrication due to overly cold and thick oil. Now we can taxi, out with the tailwheel lock so the aircraft will turn, off with the parking brake – remembering this only works from the left-hand seat so if you are sitting in the right get the other guy to do it – and away we go.

Gentle applications of power along with coarse use of the rudder and gentle differential braking will allow you to guide the aircraft along the taxiway - just remember the inertia, it can all get away from you very easily. If it does, just come to a halt and start again.

Once at the hold it's time for the engine run-up. Firstly check the magnetos for a dead cut below 1000 RPM just in case one magneto is completely dead at least the resulting backfire won't blow the exhaust system into the next county. If this is OK then power up to 1700 RPM on both engines whilst your colleague in the cockpit holds the control column fully back for all he's worth to stop the tail rising. At this power both generators should be on line and giving a balanced output. Now we check the propeller Constant Speed Units (CSUs) through their range. One check if it's a warm day, a couple on a cold day to get some warmer oil around the system. We then test the propeller feathering system. By pushing in the appropriate feather button we should see a rise in the generator output as the electric feathering pump runs, then a drop in the engine RPM as the propeller moves toward feather. At this point unless we need to fully check the system we can pull the feathering button out to stop the process. As the propeller moves move towards fine pitch we will see a drop in engine oil pressure as the oil is used to move the propeller blades by the CSU. Then another check of the CSU to make sure that they have control of the prop again and not the feathering pump as this could lead to a massive overspeed on take-off which is not recommended. Whilst you have been doing the propeller checks your colleague will have checked the carburettor heat system to make sure this is working as it should. Once the propeller checks are completed we pull both throttles back to check the idle, then one at a time we increase power to "Static boost" i.e. the manifold

This view of TransValair's F-GDXP (c/n 32561) shows clearly the trailing edge of the wing with flaps retracted, plus the typical elevator and rudder locks used on a Dakota. These were often red or orange for high visibility. *(Don Hannah Collection)*

pressure is set to the air pressure of the day usually around 29 inches, this should produce an engine RPM of around 2500, anything less and we may have a problem. Also at this setting we can check the magnetos for their individual performance. We will see a little reduction in power output but it should not be more than 100 RPM and the difference between the two mags should not exceed 40 RPM. Hopefully all is well and good and we can now proceed with the pre-take-off checks and are now ready to commit aviation.

As part of our pre-flight discussions we will have gone through the take-off procedure in some detail and this will have been reviewed in our pre-take-off brief, so away we go. As we line up on the runway the first important thing to do is get the aircraft running straight before you engage the tail wheel lock. If we start the take-off roll heading for the grass there is a good chance that is where we will end up. If we have any crosswind remember we have a swept leading edge to the wing – just like a jet – so aileron into wind and hold it there throughout the take-off. Gently advance the throttles using a little differential power if necessary. A gentle forward pressure on the control column will allow the tail to lift at around 50 knots dependent on the aircraft loading. At this point we need to increase the forward pressure to stop the aircraft getting airborne before the safety speed of around 85 knots. By this time you will have your hands full with the controls so as the power passes 40 inches manifold pressure I will take the throttles from you and set full take-off power of 48 inches. This has the added benefit of avoiding any over-boost on the engines due to there being no automatic limiting of the power. Once safety speed is reached, a gentle backward pressure on the controls will allow the aircraft to lift off and we look to allow the speed to increase towards our normal climb at 110 knots. Now the two-crew part of the operation comes to the fore. You fly the aeroplane and ask me to do all the other jobs, retracting the undercarriage when safely climbing away, a two-handed job as the 1930s system has separate levers for the

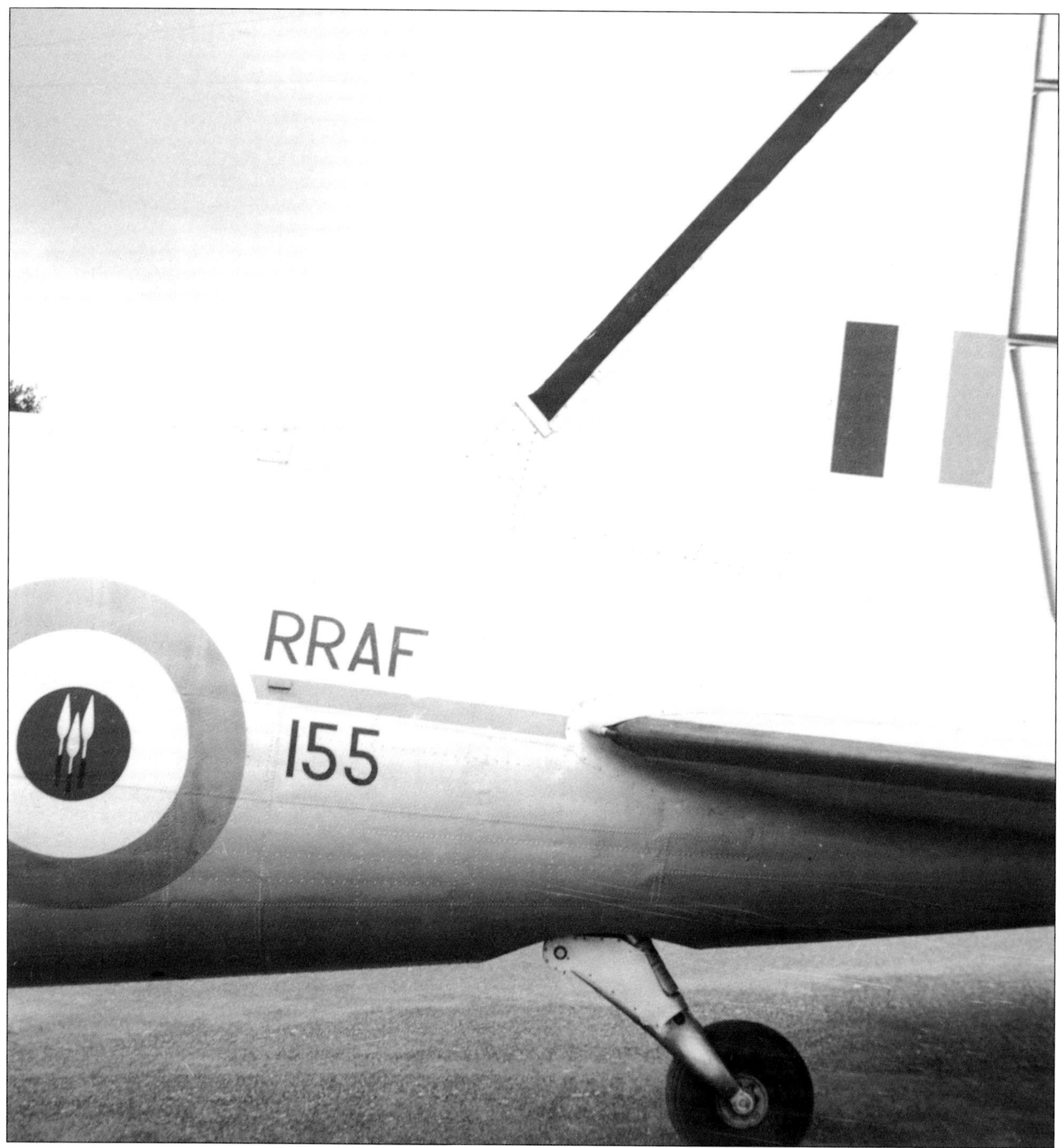

Close-up showing the non-retractable tailwheel of a Dakota. The aircraft is one of the Royal Rhodesian Air Force's fleet and the photo was taken at Nchanga, Northern Rhodesia circa 1956. *(R Sunderland)*

View of a Dakota showing its flaps in the extended position. The aircraft is N18255 (c/n 4583) of Bo-S-Aire. *(via Air-Britain)*

undercarriage latches and the hydraulic power supply and if moved in the wrong order not a lot will happen. Also as we increase speed and climb away, power can be reduced, firstly to the max continuous setting and then to normal climb power to reduce the strain on the engines. In order to maintain the balance of the gas loads inside the engine it is better if the throttles and propeller controls are brought back together so this is another two-handed job better done by the pilot not actually flying the aircraft. Finally at a safe height the 'after take-off' checks can be done.

On this take-off we did not experience any engine problems but if we had this is no great problem as long as it is handled correctly. Any problems before we leave the ground just entail closing the throttles and bringing the aircraft to a halt on the runway. Similarly if we were airborne but the undercarriage was still down we just chop the power and land straight ahead. If we are climbing away with the gear up and a problem occurs you continue to fly the aircraft, we identify the problem, close the engine down and feather the propeller. Then maintaining an accurate 91 knots we gently fly around the circuit and land straight away.

No dramas today, so we are climbing away and you can start to get a feel for the aircraft. It is surprisingly light in pitch, almost bordering on the unstable so you will find accurate trimming of the elevator a must. The rudder is heavy but effective. Ailerons are large, heavy and very ineffective. Any serious attempts at turns or higher angles of bank require careful co-ordination of rudder and aileron rather like a glider – hardly surprising with a 95 foot wingspan. Generally, however, whilst the balance of the controls is totally wrong according to the purists, it's a very pleasant machine to fly. During the climb due to the lack of automatic boost control you have to continually advance the throttles to maintain the climb power setting of 35 inches otherwise there is little to do but enjoy the ride.

Levelling off at the top of climb one sees the effectiveness of the large wing of the Dak – the wing area is the same as that of a Boeing 737 - and as the aircraft accelerates if the nose is not continually lowered you find yourself climbing at 400 or 500 feet per minute again. Once more, accurate elevator trimming is required. In the cruise you will find the machine is extremely stable and if left alone would most probably still be flying straight and level a couple of hours later if nothing had disturbed it. Therefore the fact that the original Sperry Gyro pilot has been removed from most Daks these days to make way for modern radio equipment is no great burden. Power has now been reduced to around 29 inches and 2050 RPM for the cruise equating to around 580 BHP per engine. The RPM is dictated by two vibration bands that exist above and below this figure so is fairly critical. Looking out the windows one can almost see the propeller blades passing by as the RPM is that of the engine not the prop which thanks to the 16 to 9 reduction gearing is nearer 1000. As the CHTs stabilise below 200 degrees the mixture can be brought to auto lean, saving around nine gallons an hour at a normal cruise altitude of eight or nine thousand feet. Finally the cowl gills can be closed, adding all of about two knots to the cruise speed.

General manoeuvring is not difficult once you become accustomed to the fairly heavy and uncoordinated controls and learn what your feet are for – something many modern aircraft pilots do not find natural. In steep turns above 45 degrees of bank there is a tendency for the aircraft to roll into the turn but this is easily controlled. Moving on to stalling manoeuvres, the aircraft is a great big pussycat in the clean configuration. Gently nodding away at the stall the only thing to watch is the fairly high rate of sink that can set in. Moving onto stalls in the approach or landing configurations life is somewhat different. With flap lowered and any amount of power on, the centre section certainly does not stall first as it does in the clean configuration. This leads to classic tip stall and with those elegant rounded wingtips when they let go they let go and a marked wing drop will occur. Adding to the excitement in this configuration is the almost total lack of any warning of the impending stall. In the clean configuration there is marked pre-stall buffet for some ten knots of speed reduction before the stall itself, again having flap down and a little power on removes this almost completely. However the fact that one is flying a twelve ton aeroplane at around 45 knots indicated with the nose some 20 degrees above the horizon should give some form of clue. The resulting stall when it occurs can easily lead to the machine going inverted or even entering a spin - not recommended close to the ground. However at altitude it is a very good training manoeuvre and something easily recovered from, provided the correct techniques are used.

Before long it is time to start our descent back to land. No real problems here, although a certain amount of descent pre-planning is required. Large radial engines do not take kindly to large power reductions as these can lead to shock cooling of the cylinders heads and in the worst case the propeller running the engine rather than the other way about, leading to reverse loading of the bearings and all sort of nastiness going on which will lead to engine failure in fairly short order. By far the best way to come down is from a long way out at cruise power. Unfortunately not all modern Air Traffic Controllers are aware of these limitations and think a Dak can go down and slow down all at the same time just like the jets.

As we approach the airfield we can carry out our descent checks followed by the prelanding checks. If, after levelling off from our descent from altitude the power is reduced gradually to around 25 inches, the speed will wash off to around 120 knots, which is ideal for flying the pattern. On base leg a power reduction to around 18 inches whilst lowering the gear and first stage of flap will set up a comfortable approach at 95 knots. 95 is the magic figure as it allows you to lower more flap, being below the limiting speed of 97, but would allow a climb away on one engine at 91 knots if this was required. On the approach the descent should be controlled by increasing the flap setting as required rather than changing the power for the sake of the engines. To avoid any reverse loading the manifold pressure should never be reduced below 15 inches until the final landing flare. Through all these procedures we again use the two crew concept with one pilot flying the aircraft and the other doing the checks, raising and lowering the gear and flaps etc.

The landing is always made on the main wheels first as three pointing the aircraft can be difficult or even impossible under certain loading conditions and if you get it wrong either a very heavy landing or swing off the runway will occur. In crosswind conditions remember the swept leading edge and land wing down into wind and hold those ailerons over as the aircraft slows. Once the mains are on the ground the non-handling pilot selects the flap up to reduce any tendency to bounce and also to allow the tail to be lowered at a higher speed whilst good rudder authority remains to keep the machine pointed in the direction we require. Only once all is under control do we take the tail wheel lock out so we can turn off the runway. In the event of a single engine approach being required all is very much the same, only of course requiring a slightly higher power setting from the good engine on the approach.

Once clear of the runway we taxi in, go through our checks and shut the engines down. After all is stopped we put in the undercarriage pins and the controls whilst waiting for the engines to cool. Once the temperatures are down we install the big wooden blanks over the front of the engines and close up the cowl gills, all in an attempt to keep the damp British climate out of the ignition system where it can easily play havoc.

Hopefully this gives some idea of flying the DC-3, a wonderful, wonderful aircraft which hopefully will grace our skies for many years to come. As I am sure you will have noticed, keeping the engines happy is a major part of operating this and all similar types and is an art that unfortunately the "jet jockeys" never learn. Their loss I think.

Using all the space . . . !

BOAC's G-AGFX (c/n 6223) demonstrates how to make maximum use of the landing area available at Croydon in the immediate post-war period. The flaps are extended and elevators raised slightly, with the Dakota touching down as close to the north-east boundary fence as possible. (via Jennifer Gradidge)

K-682 (c/n 20019) in the final camouflaged scheme carried during its last years of service with the Royal Danish Air Force. *(Brian Stainer/APN)*

Chapter 2 The Danish Dakota Friends DC-3 Operation

by Niels H Larsen

When the C-47 was withdrawn from use with the Royal Danish Air Force (RDAF) in July 1982, it was decided to save K-682 (c/n 20019) as a "museum object", but kept in airworthy condition. While K-681 and K-682 were Danish property, the other six MAP aircraft were officially returned to the United States Air Force. K-687 (c/n 19200) equipped with skis for operations in Greenland remained, however, in Denmark for static display.

In the first eight years K-682 (now registered OY-BPB) was on loan to the Bohnstedt-Petersen company, a Mercedes-Benz dealer. Unfortunately this company went bankrupt and the Danish Dakota Friends (DC-3 Vennerne) was formed in November 1991. At first there were some very enthusiastic people and a cigar box of cash and stamps and the hope of getting 250 to 300 members. Now, 18 years later, we have 3,200 members!

Foreningen for Flyvende Museumsfly (abbreviated to 3FM) – The Association of Flying Museum Aircraft – takes care of the operation and technical side, while DC-3 Vennerne (Danish Dakota Friends) looks after the members, arranges flights for the summer season, etc, but above all takes care of the financial side.

The operation is run on a non-profit making basis, the aircraft is restricted to 19 passengers plus a crew of three and flights are VFR only. The take-off weight is restricted to 1,000 pounds below the all-up weight. We fly in the summer season only (early May to the end of September); during the winter the aircraft is in the hangar (currently at Kastrup) for maintenance. Passengers must be a member of the Association in order to fly, and we are not allowed to pick up passengers outside Denmark. We fly around 50 hours a year, mostly within Denmark, but also undertake flights to the southern part of Sweden and Norway. The rocket museum at Peenemunde in northeastern Germany is also a popular destination. In addition, we have also carried out flights to Berlin (Tempelhof and Schoenefeld), Hamburg (Airbus Industrie) and Lelystad (Holland).

The five Nordic countries each have an airworthy DC-3, with Sweden having two. They are all operated on a non-commercial basis. The Danish DC-3 was originally operated on an "Experimental" certificate, but now operates on an annual "Permit to Fly". The Nordic Dakota associations meet annually. An umbrella organization, the "Nordic DC-3 Association", was inaugurated at the annual meeting in Helsinki in February 2009. At the annual meeting mostly operational and technical matters were discussed, but also matters concerning membership and magazines. We also coordinate our flying programmes, of course. Other matters concern the relationship with the local CAA and the EU (EU and JAR-OPS), flight permits, insurance, fuel prices, etc. Overall, the Nordic DC-3 associations have more than 11,300 members.

Hopefully, we will be able to keep our DC-3s airworthy for many years to come, although 2009 was disappointing as many flights had to be cancelled because of crew shortages, with some engine starting problems being experienced due to heavy rain while the aircraft was parked outside.

Niels Larsen is Editor of the magazine "DC-3 NYT" published by and for the Danish Dakota Friends.

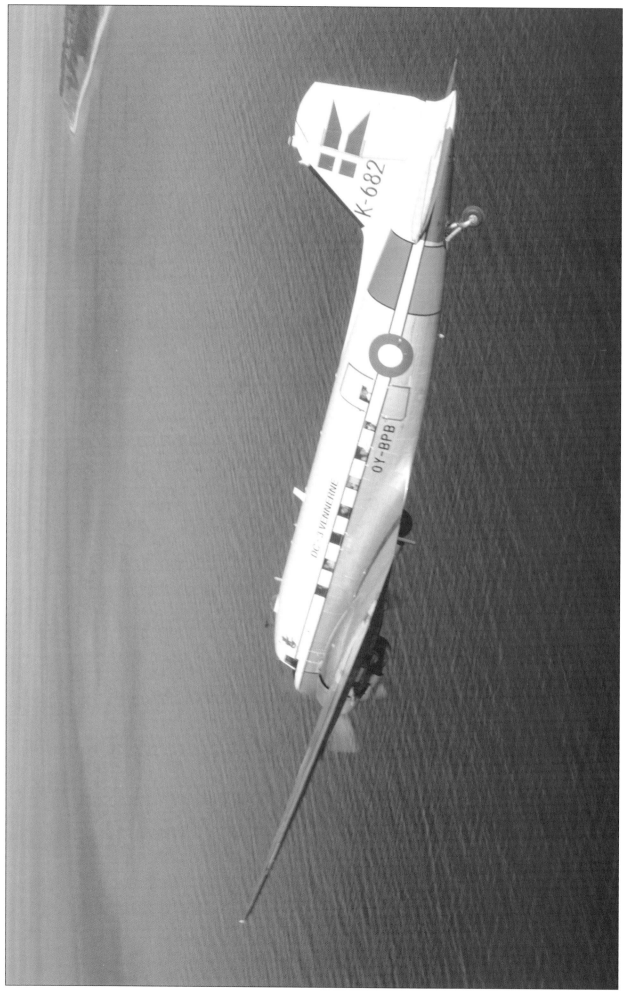

The DC-3 Vennerne (Danish Dakota Friends) C-47 OY-BPB/K-682 (c/n 20019) banks away from the camera on one of its pleasure flights. *(Niels Larsen)*

United States Marine Corps DC-2 (R2D-1) BuAer 9994 (c/n 1405), coded 2, shows the basic features of the predecessor of the DC-3. *(Jennifer Gradidge)*

Chapter 3
Douglas DC-2 Hybrids

by Jennifer M Gradidge

There has been considerable confusion over the various military DC-2/3 variants produced during the years just before the outbreak of the Pacific War in 1941. This was never completely clarified in 'The First Seventy Years' and as can be seen later, there remains some confusion which can only be cleared if one surviving aircraft is examined closely!

The original DC-2 was evaluated by the U S Army Air Corps as the XC-32 in September 1935. However, prior to this the US Navy bought its first DC-2 as the R2D-1 in November 1934. Unlike the Army, the Navy aircraft were standard commercial production models, similar to the DC-2 in every way, and only five were delivered.

The first USAAC deliveries were two YC-34s, later to become C-34, which were modified DC-2s with special interiors. The C-32A was a commercial aircraft impressed in 1942 from US airlines. Some went into service with the USAAF and others to the RAF or BOAC. Further DC-2s were bought as the C-33 which differed from the DC-2 in having a DC-3 vertical tail to compensate for an increase in engine power. They also had enlarged cargo doors, though smaller than the later C-39 and C-47. A C-33A was projected, but was redesignated C-38 in 1938. This was the first C-33 36-70, which became the aerodynamic prototype for the C-39. It had 975 h.p. Wright R-1820-45s. The C-39 had a DC-3 centre section and under-carriage and R-1820-55s of 975 h.p. Thirty-five C-39s were built, but the only one to survive is now in the USAF Museum at Dayton, Ohio. Seventeen were sold in S America, but six found their way to Australia with the USAAF, and three were briefly used commercially post-war. Two C-39s, 38-513 and 528 are reported by Francillon to have been brought up to C-42 standard (see later), but there is no mention of this in their service record.

Five DC-2s with Northeast Airlines were fitted with DC-3 wings, but on impressments they remained C-32As.

At this point there is some confusion over designations, and this relates to two aircraft, the C-41 and the C-41A that were ordered in 1938. The C-41 used what should have been a C-39 serial, 38-502, but it is designated DC-3-253 by Douglas and has DC-3 wings. It had 1,200 h.p. Pratt & Whitney R-1830-21s and was used as a personal transport by General Henry (Hap) Arnold in 1940. Post-war it saw commercial service with the CAA as N12. The CAA (later FAA) certifications A-618 and A-619 do not mention these aircraft, but in the FAA register for 1963 the C-41 is listed under code 302-14, whereas the DC-2 was the 302-13. In the 1975 register it remains a DC-3A.

The C-41A presents no problem as it was a standard DC-3A-253A bought by the USAAC for staff transport, fitted with swiveling seats and R-1830-21 engines. Amazingly, both the C-41 and the C-41A remain on the register and the C-41 visited Britain in 1994.

Although Fahey states that the C-41 and C-41A both had wing spans of 85' 0", he also states the C-41A is a DC-3, which had a span of 95'0". The writer's photo of the C-41 shows DC-3 wings with ailerons tapering at their distal end, as on the DC-3. Possibly the C-41 had DC-3 wings fitted at some time in its life. Unfortunately unless the fuselage is examined and its width measured, the exact nature of the C-41 will remain a mystery.

The final variant was the C-42, similar to the C-41, but with 1,000 h.p. Wright R-1820-53s. It was used as a staff transport. The two C-39s converted to C-42 had one cargo door permanently bolted closed.

A line-up of C-47s awaiting delivery to Russia in September 1944. The aircraft nearest the camera in full view is 348752 (c/n 26013). (McDonnell Douglas via Mike Hooks)

Chapter 4
Military Photo Gallery

Visionair International's fleet of nine C-47s and Dakotas assembled for the 1976 filming of "A Bridge Too Far". The aircraft carry a mixture of US civil registrations in the N998xQ series (eg N9983Q in the foreground and N9984Q the fourth aircraft) or fictitious USAF markings (eg the second aircraft carries "315317" and third "327185"). The aircraft were acquired from the Portuguese Air Force and civilian sources. (Aeroplane)

The last Royal Air Force serial to be allocated to a Dakota was ZD215 (c/n 27127) in 1980 for use on the delivery flight of former Royal Australian Air Force A65-69 from Australia to Berlin-Gatow for preservation. The aircraft is seen here arriving in Berlin with crowds assembled for the occasion.
(Pete J Bish)

Royal Air Force Dakota KP277 "Faith" (c/n 33579) was operated in Malaya between 1959 and 1961 with No.52 Squadron. Loudspeakers were fitted under the fuselage for psychological warfare use against the Malayan insurgents. Eventually it was sold as PI-C481 to Philippine Airlines.
(J Merryshaw a/sig, from Dakota KJ955 "Hope")

United States Air Force C-47A 42-23794 (c/n 9656) after making a forced landing on the Greenland ice-cap in December 1948, an incident from which the seven members of the crew survived. *(International News Photo via Aeroplane)*

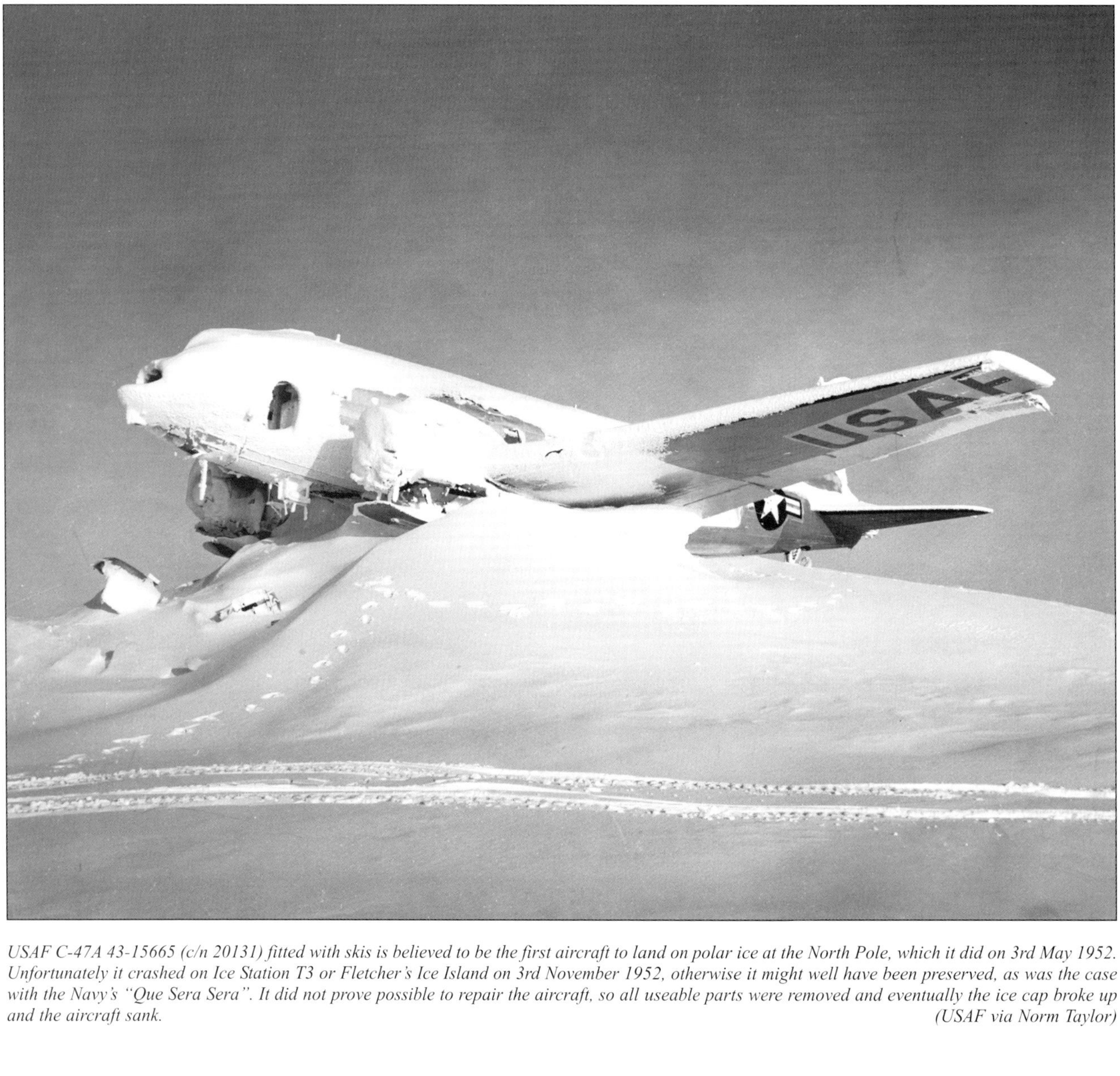

USAF C-47A 43-15665 (c/n 20131) fitted with skis is believed to be the first aircraft to land on polar ice at the North Pole, which it did on 3rd May 1952. Unfortunately it crashed on Ice Station T3 or Fletcher's Ice Island on 3rd November 1952, otherwise it might well have been preserved, as was the case with the Navy's "Que Sera Sera". It did not prove possible to repair the aircraft, so all useable parts were removed and eventually the ice cap broke up and the aircraft sank. *(USAF via Norm Taylor)*

Royal Air Force Dakota KJ947 (c/n 26239) stored at Little Rissington on 8th August 1952, prior to sale to the French Air Force. The airframe was still grey with coal dust, off the Berlin Air Lift. (Jennifer Gradidge)

C-47D serial 45-918 (c/n 34179) of the Cambodian Air Force. This photograph was probably taken at Kai Tak, Hong Kong, in the late 1950s. (via Jennifer Gradidge)

One of the many C-47s donated by France to the newly independent African republics was 48286/TL-KAD (c/n 25547) of the Air Force of the Central African Republic. *(MAP)*

French Air Force C-47 42-23941 (c/n 9803) taxying out at Paris-Le Bourget during preparations for the Salon, year unknown. Note the presentation of the serial number. This aircraft eventually went to the Air Force of Togo and its remains now reside in a mausoleum at Sara Kara in that country. *(Carson Seeley)*

Nepalese Royal Flight aircraft 9N-RF10 (c/n 9950) with a civil registration and the Royal Nepal Airlines emblem on the fin, but carrying the military roundel and titles of the Royal Nepalese Army. The photo was taken at Kathmandu circa 1970, with a Nepalese Il-14 visible on the right.
(via Mike Hooks)

Dakota HJ908 (c/n 11912) coded "Z" of the Indian Air Force at an unknown location. Details of the fate (and indeed identities) of most Indian Air Force Dakotas are unfortunately still unknown. *(Aeroplane)*

Royal Australian Air Force Dakota A65-81 (c/n 32673) of the Antarctic Research Flight being shipped by barge for use in the 1960-61 Antarctic spring. The aircraft was written off in May 1961. The titles A.N.A.R.E. denote the Australian National Antarctic Research Establishment. *(Aeroplane)*

An unusual presentation of the serial on United States Army C-47A 43-15760 (c/n 20226), taken at Love Field, Dallas, Texas in April 1965.
(EJ Bulban via Mike Hooks)

USAF 43-16229 (c/n 20695) "Nez Percé" was photographed at Nichole Field, Philippines on 21st June 1946. For reasons which are obscure, it was converted to a CG-17 glider and towed by Douglas C-54 to Tachikawa in Japan, where it was condemned as salvage on 5th May 1947. The cargo doors are open, so it is just possible a load was carried. *(USAAF via Doug Olson)*

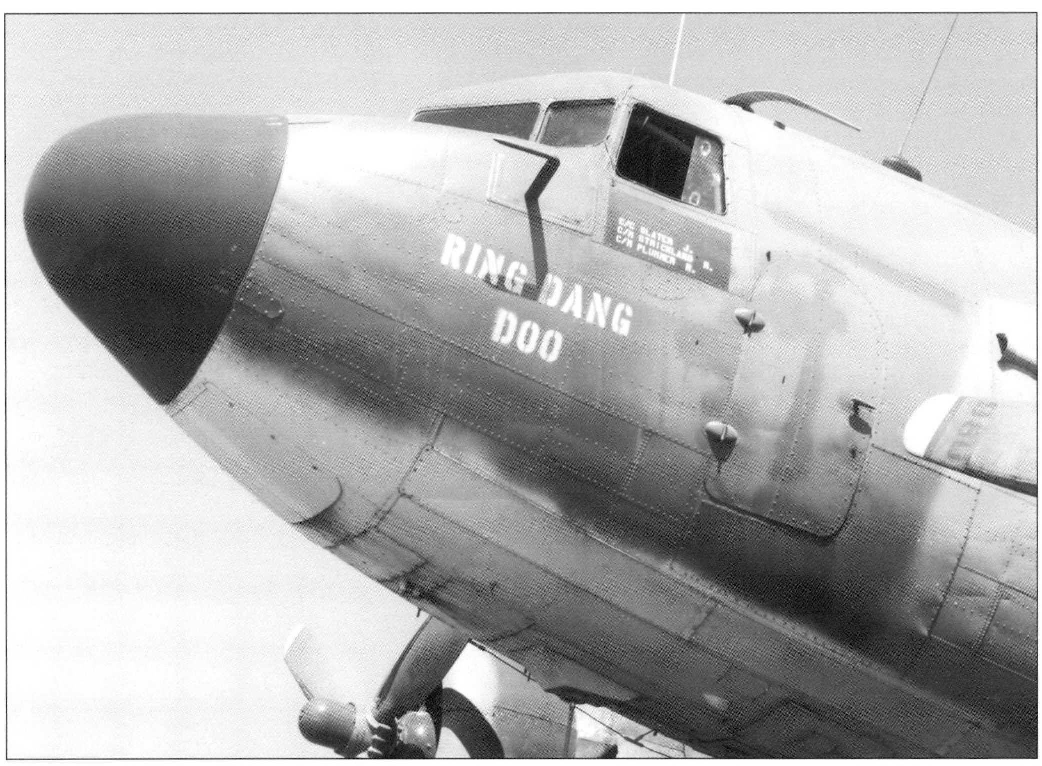

USAF serial 43-15980 was modified to EC-47N in 1967, and was serving with 361 TEWS at Pleiku in November 1967 when this photograph was taken. The aircraft was named "Ring Dang Doo" already (earlier than the date recorded on page 501 of Volume 2).
(Robert C Mikesh)

This photograph illustrates a Showa L2D2 (a DC-3 that was licence-built by the Japanese with Mitsubishi Kinsei 43 engines). It had large cargo doors for freight carriage, and was fitted with a 13mm machine-gun over the forward cabin. This aircraft, serial 501 and obviously derelict, is in the colours of the Chinese Nationalist Air Force. The photo was taken at West Field, Peiping (now Beijing), China on 30 November 1946. *(David Lucabaugh)*

This second photo of a Chinese Nationalist Air Force L2D2, serial 405, shows the more usual extended windows behind the cockpit of this version. The photo, which is of poor quality, was taken at Peiping (now Beijing), China on 18 November 1945. *(Peter M Bowers)*

Showa L2D2, serial 16, of the Japanese Air Force, shows well the extended windows behind the cockpit. This was a captured aircraft, hence the propellers have been removed. Note the unit markings on the rudder. *(Clay Jansson, via David Lucabaugh Collection)*

An Air Ministry photograph dated July 1943 shows Royal Air Force Dakota III FD903 (c/n 9625) in 24 Squadron service coded "NQ-I".
(Air Ministry via Mike Hooks)

KN589 (c/n 33224), an uncoded Dakota IV of 267 Squadron, showing the Pegasus (winged horse) emblem of that squadron on the nose. Note the South East Asia style roundel.
(Aeroplane)

Dakota III KJ900 (c/n 25931) is seen here without squadron markings, but unusually with the "last three" of the serial on the fin. *(Aeroplane)*

Dakota IV KN392 (c/n 32813) of 78 Squadron, Royal Air Force, seen at Almaza (Egypt) in 1945 coded "EY-G". *(PJ Marson Collection)*

Dakota III FD772 (c/n 6226) of the Royal Air Force, possibly of 25 Squadron, coded "Y-ZK" with the name "Windsor Castle" just visible on the nose. *(via Jennifer Gradidge)*

Dakota IV KN275 (c/n 27210) in the post-war silver scheme in service with 271 Squadron and coded "G-YS". *(via Jennifer Gradidge)*

An impressive scene at Airwork's rework base, taken in the immediate post-war period at Gatwick Airport and showing an assortment of Dakotas in various stages of conversion for civilian use. In the top centre of the photo is KN453 (c/n 32924), a Dakota IV still in 525 Squadron markings with code "WF-Z", while behind is an unidentified RAF aircraft showing the part code "7Z". Among the aircraft already converted for civilian use are two BEA examples (one is G-AHCW), and also one of the three aircraft (G-AHLX/HLY/HLZ) earmarked for the United Nations Relief & Rehabilitation Administration - UNRRA. The photo was probably taken in the autumn of 1946.

(Aeroplane)

Dakota III KG712 (c/n 13579) of 216 Squadron, Royal Air Force, with code "JW" on the nose. The photo was taken at Almaza in 1945.
(PJ Marson Collection)

A summer's day at a grass airfield in post-war Britain, but the exact location was not recorded. Royal Air Force Dakota IV KP251 (c/n 33553) carries the outlined code "NU-G" for No.240 OCU, 4 Group, which was formed on 5th January 1948 at RAF North Luffenham. *(via Barry Wheeler)*

No.53 Squadron at Netheravon flew Dakota IV KN632 (c/n 33289) between November 1946 and November 1948. The aircraft carries the squadron code "PU-W" with the vestiges of another code on the rudder which has been sprayed out. *(via Barry Wheeler)*

KK135 (c/n 26716) is a Dakota III coded "M" being collected by Field Aircraft Services in the mid-1950s for rework into a C-47 for the West German Air Force. (via Jennifer Gradidge)

The fuselage of former Royal Air Force Dakota KN346 (c/n 32663) arriving on a low loader at Croydon on 6th March 1948, still carrying the code "7Z-L" from its use with 1381 TCU. The Dakota had presumably been bought for spares use. (Mike Hooks)

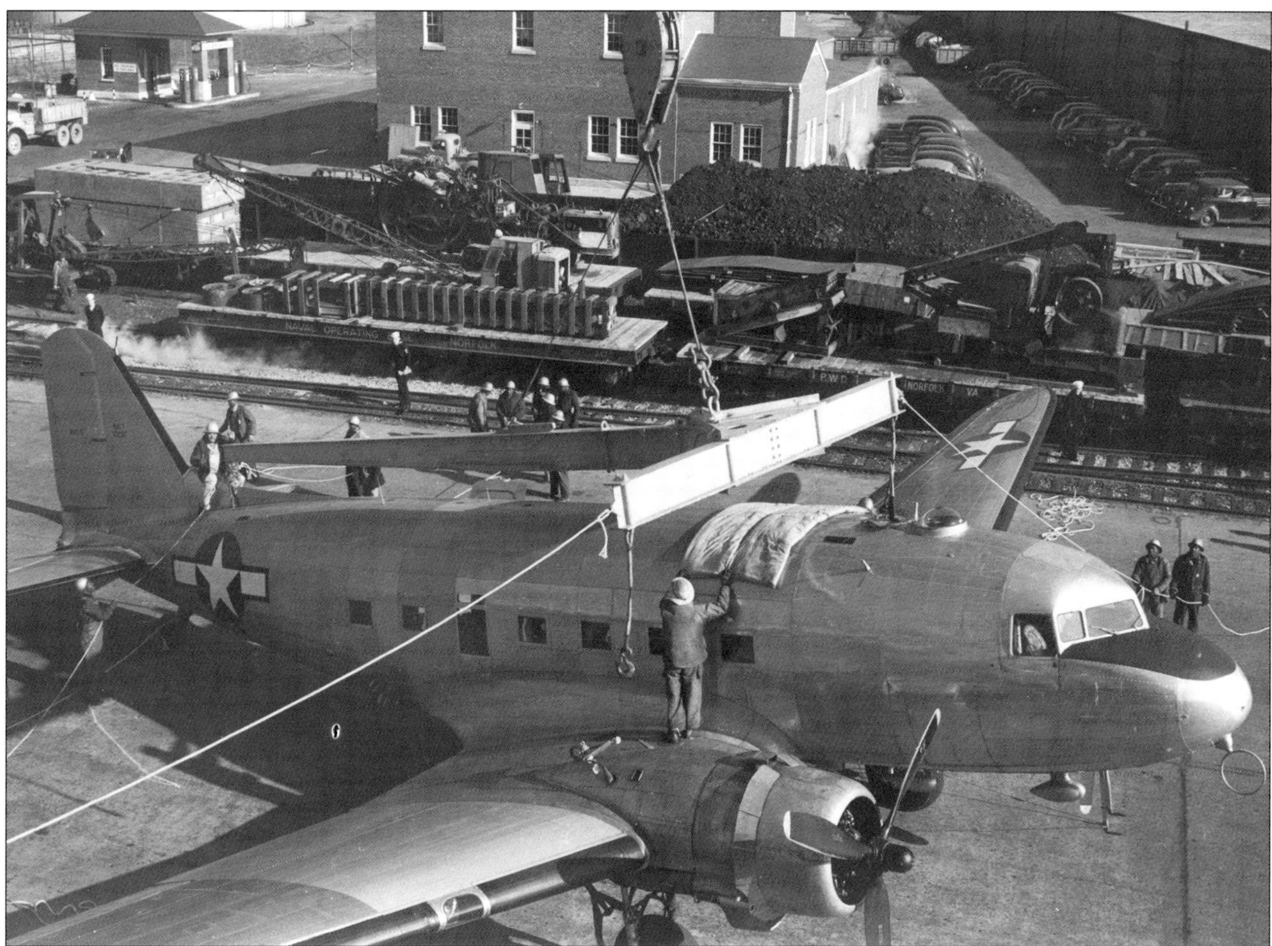

United States Navy R4D-5 BuAer 17237 (c/n 25316) being loaded from the dockside at Norfolk, Virginia in 1947 onto the aircraft carrier "USS Philippine Sea" for operations in Antarctica. *(US Navy Dept. 80-G-615134)*

Chapter 5
The DC-3 in the Antarctic

by Jennifer M Gradidge

Before 1914 aircraft were too flimsy to be of practical use in the Antarctic, though there has been a suggestion that a Vickers Monoplane did accompany one expedition. Remains of this were found in 2009. Post 1918 several expeditions were accompanied by various types of aircraft but no significant flights were achieved until Cdr Byrd (later Admiral Byrd) and crew flew their Ford Trimotor 4-AT '*Floyd Bennett*' over the South Pole on 28th-29th November 1929. This was the first time such a feat had been achieved.

Sir Hubert Wilkins, having successfully completed prolonged flights over the Arctic, ordered a second Lockheed Vega 1 X7439 to accompany his Antarctic expedition in 1928-29, for use charting unknown territory. This was accompanied by the first Vega X3903, both of which flew with floats during 1928-29. They were stored in the Antarctic and used in the second expedition in 1929-30 and were then given to the Argentine Government.

One DH 60 Gipsy Moth operated by the Royal Australian Air Force from RRS *Discovery II* in the Bay of Whales, was used to locate the missing Antarctic explorer Lincoln Ellsworth in January 1936, but again on floats. No doubt other aircraft were used in the Antarctic before 1939, but Byrd's was the only significant achievement and it remained for the U S Navy to use Douglas R4Ds with skis in January 1947, with Rear Admiral Richard E. Byrd on board.

Six ski-equipped Douglas R4Ds were chosen to take part in '*Operation High Jump*' operating from Little America, the US Navy Antarctic base. As it was thought that the R4Ds range was inadequate to fly from New Zealand, it was decided to launch them from the deck of the aircraft carrier '*Philippine Sea*' at the edge of the pack ice. The carrier sailed from Norfolk, Virginia with the R4Ds as deck cargo, already fitted with combined ski/wheel undercarriage which could be retracted. Take-off was assisted with four JATO bottles fitted in line with the wing

Six R4D-5s of the United States Navy (BuAer 12415, 17101, 17197, 17237, 17238 & 39092) aboard the aircraft carrier "USS Philippine Sea" making their way through the Panama Canal on 8th January 1947, en route to Antarctica. *(US Navy Dept. 80-G-615041)*

Close-up of two of the US Navy R4D-5s, with BuAer 17101 (c/n 11878) in the foreground, on board the aircraft carrier "USS Philippine Sea" en route to Antarctica in January 1947. *(US Navy 85-9238)*

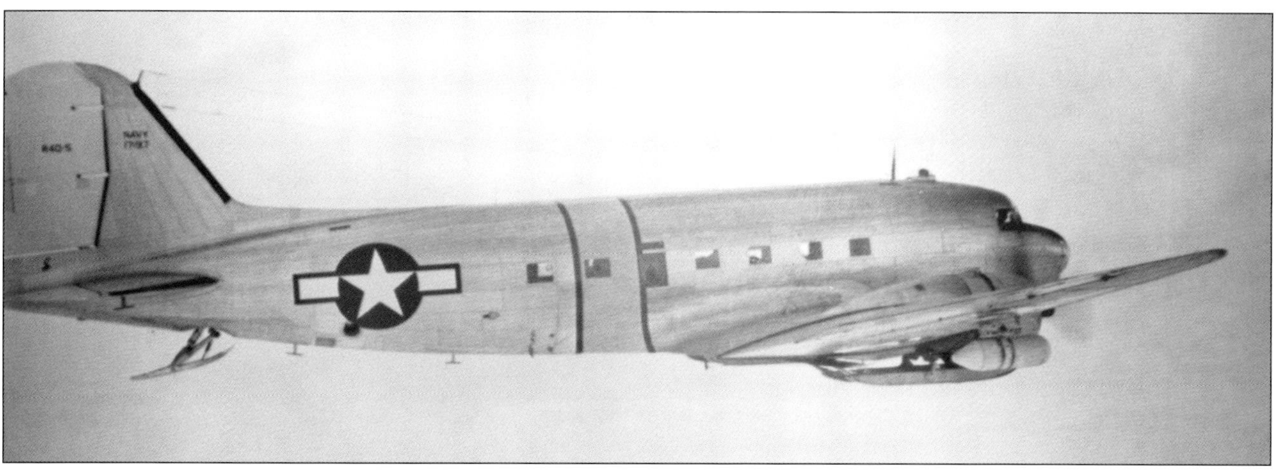

One of the original six R4D-5s, BuAer 17197 (c/n 13008), showing the skis fitted to the main undercarriage wheels, in the retracted position, and the tail-wheel. Note also the underwing supply canister. *(US Navy Dept. 80-G-614845)*

A fine air-to-air shot of US Navy R4D-5 BuAer 17246 (c/n 25444), modex XD-1, "Korora II" over typical Antarctic scenery. Note the retracted position of the skis over the wheeled undercarriage. *(via Arthur Pearcy)*

trailing edge. None of the pilots had ever flown an R4D off a carrier deck – and only two had any deck experience. Some pilots let the JATO off at the start of take-off, and others after covering a third of the deck, but all six took off successfully. The first two completed their 660-mile flight to Little America successfully, and only then did the other four R4Ds take-off. Once on the snow it was found that the wheels, which had three inches protruding through the skis, caused excessive drag, so they were later operated without wheels.

The R4Ds were used from 4th February to 21st February 1947 to explore and photograph the coast of the Ross Sea and parts of Marie Byrd Land. One, Bu 12415 carrying Admiral Byrd, flew over the South Pole. When the flying was completed, the aircraft had to stay at the base, because they could not be flown onto a carrier deck and no ship was large enough to carry them as deck cargo. They were secured to the snow by burying the skis and removing fragile parts. A year later they were still there, and the engines of one were run, but no more. A later visit in 1955 showed no signs of the aircraft at the Bay of Whales, as the ice had calved and about two thirds of 'Little America IV' including the airstrip and the aircraft had drifted away. The aircraft concerned were Bu serials 12415, 17101, 17197, 17238, 17237 and 39092, and all were lost in the Antarctic Ocean, on a date unknown.

Operation Deep Freeze

Deep Freeze was planned for the 1955-56 season as part of the International Geophysical Year. A special aviation unit was organized to support these operations and designated VX-6 Air Development Squadron Six, later to become VXE-6 or Antarctic Development Squadron Six. As ski-equipped aircraft were needed for operations from the polar plateau the R4D was again chosen. Two aircraft, R4D-5 Bu 12418 '*Que Sera Sera*' and R4D-6 Bu 17274 '*Charlene*' were allocated and modified so that the R4D-6 was similar to the R4D-5. Four 200-gallon tanks were fitted in the fuselage of each plane to allow sufficient range to fly from New Zealand to McMurdo Sound. They flew from Patuxent River, MD to Christchurch, New Zealand, arriving on 30th November and 2nd December 1955. They were to be accompanied by two P2V Neptunes, two R5Ds and two UF-1 Albatrosses, leaving New Zealand on 20th December.

Ships were strung out at 250 mile intervals along the route to provide navigational and meteorological assistance, and rescue services if needed. The Neptunes and R5Ds coped with head winds along the route, but the R4Ds were slowed down too much and had to return to New Zealand, with the Albatrosses. Neither type was used that season.

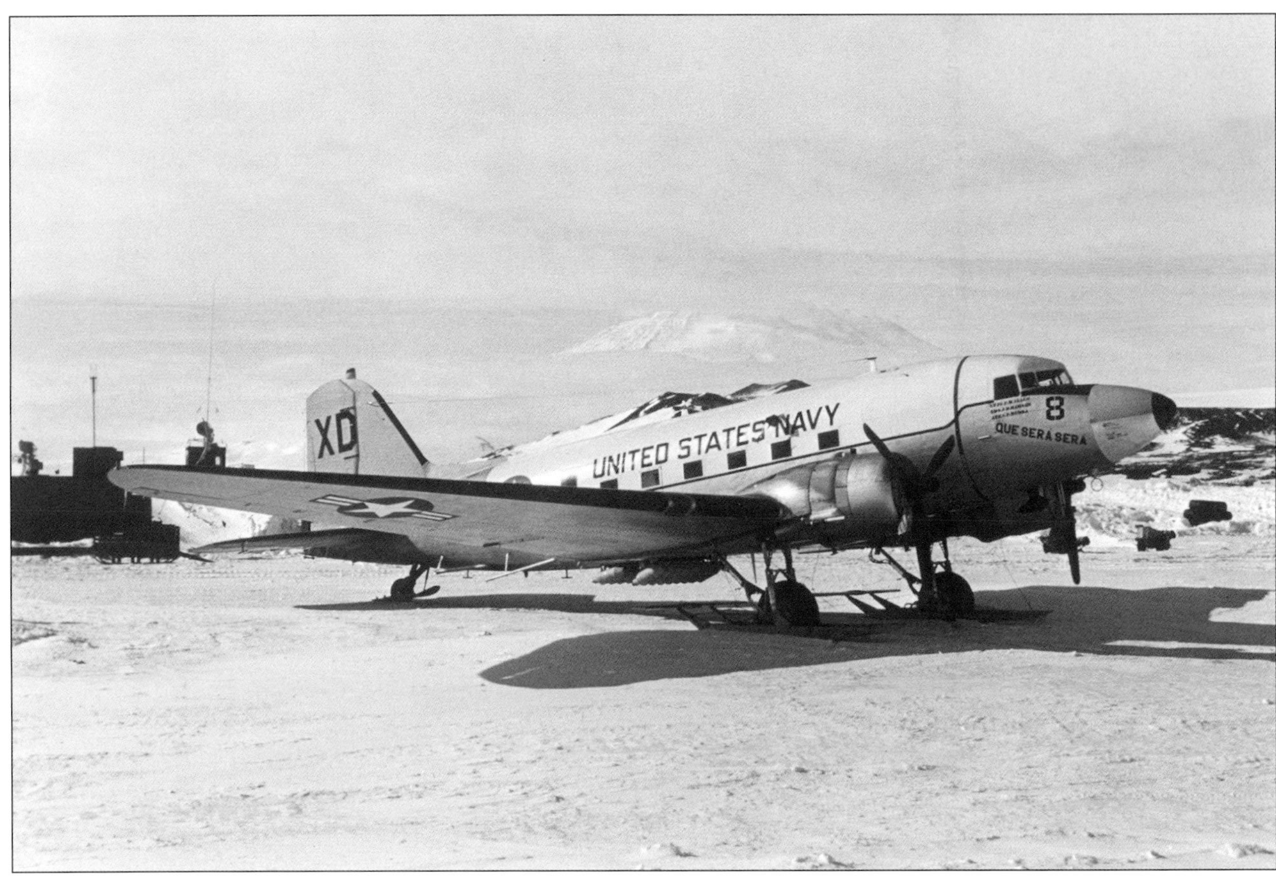

The US Navy R4D-5 "Que Sera Sera" BuAer 12418 (c/n 9358), modex XD-8, which made the first landing at the South Pole on 31st October 1956.
(McDonnell-Douglas via Mike Hooks)

US Navy R4D-6 BuAer 17274 (c/n 25777), modex XD-4, "Charlene", probably taken at Christchurch, New Zealand, prior to flying to Antarctica.
(Brian Stainer/APN)

Operation Deep Freeze II

Further stations had been built, Naval Air Facility McMurdo and Little America V were joined by Byrd Station on the coast and others inland to be supplied by larger aircraft. Both P2Vs were lost in accidents, so the four R4Ds that flew to McMurdo from New Zealand in October 1956 had a greater workload than originally planned. The aircraft were R4D-5s Bu 12418 '*Que Sera Sera*', Bu 17163 '*Takahe*', Bu 17246 '*Little Horrible*' and R4D-6 Bu 17274 '*Charlene*'. An auxiliary summer station was needed near the foot of the Beardmore Glacier to act as a refuelling stop for the flight to the South Pole, since McMurdo was further away than Little America (which had been lost). This base was set up on 28 October and designated Beardmore-Scott Auxiliary Air Base after a preliminary reconnaissance flight two days earlier. A C-124 Globemaster was able to drop further supplies on the 30th, followed on the 31st by the remaining four men making a complement of eight. That same day they had visitors, Admiral Dufek and the first party to stand on the Pole for 44 years. Dufek decided that a test landing was needed at the Pole, so he went along as part of the crew, made up of Capt Cordiner, CO of VX-6, Lt Cdr Shinn, Co-pilot Hawkes, Lt Swadener and Petty Officers Strider and Cumbie. They were accompanied by an R5D and a C-124, to provide help and to take photographs. However, the cameras all froze up and little was recorded. The R5D had to return to base with engine trouble, but after three low passes by the R4D Bu 12418, it landed at the Pole at 0834 GMT on 31 October 1956. The surface was very hard and it was very cold, at -58 degrees F. The engines were kept running, but when the time came to depart, the aircraft had become frozen to the ice! The first four JATO bottles had no effect, but the remaining 11 bottles made '*Que Sera Sera*' look as if it had blown up – but it started moving and got into the air, returning safely to Beardmore-Scott, to refuel and continue on to McMurdo.

The four R4Ds were used through the season to reconnoitre routes for proposed stations and to carry equipment and materials and to supply the trail parties on the snow. Heavy tractor trains were used to deliver building materials for the site at Byrd Station, but they were supported by DHC-3 Otter UC-1s, which lacked the range and load carrying ability available in the R4Ds.

Further flights to the South Pole were undertaken by R4Ds on 20th November 1956, so that a base could be established there. Although such flights were completed, they were not without problems. Three aircraft had polyethylene-coated skis but could not taxy under power on the high plateau. Only the aircraft with Teflon coated skis was able to do this. To gain capacity the fuselage tanks were eliminated, and a landing had to be made at Beardmore-Scott Station to refuel. On one flight an R4D developed an oil leak and had to land on the ice shelf, 260 miles south of McMurdo. Fortunately the mechanic on board was able to make a temporary repair to allow the flight to continue.

Hopes that the Neptunes could be used to do much of the carrying did not come off, as the ski equipment proved a problem and in the end the R4Ds had to do all the carrying. The summer temperatures melted the snow at McMurdo and the C-124s were

US Navy R4D-5 BuAer 17163 (c/n 12519), modex XD-7, "Takahe", probably taken at Christchurch, New Zealand in the late 1950s. This aircraft was written off in September 1959. (Brian Stainer/APN)

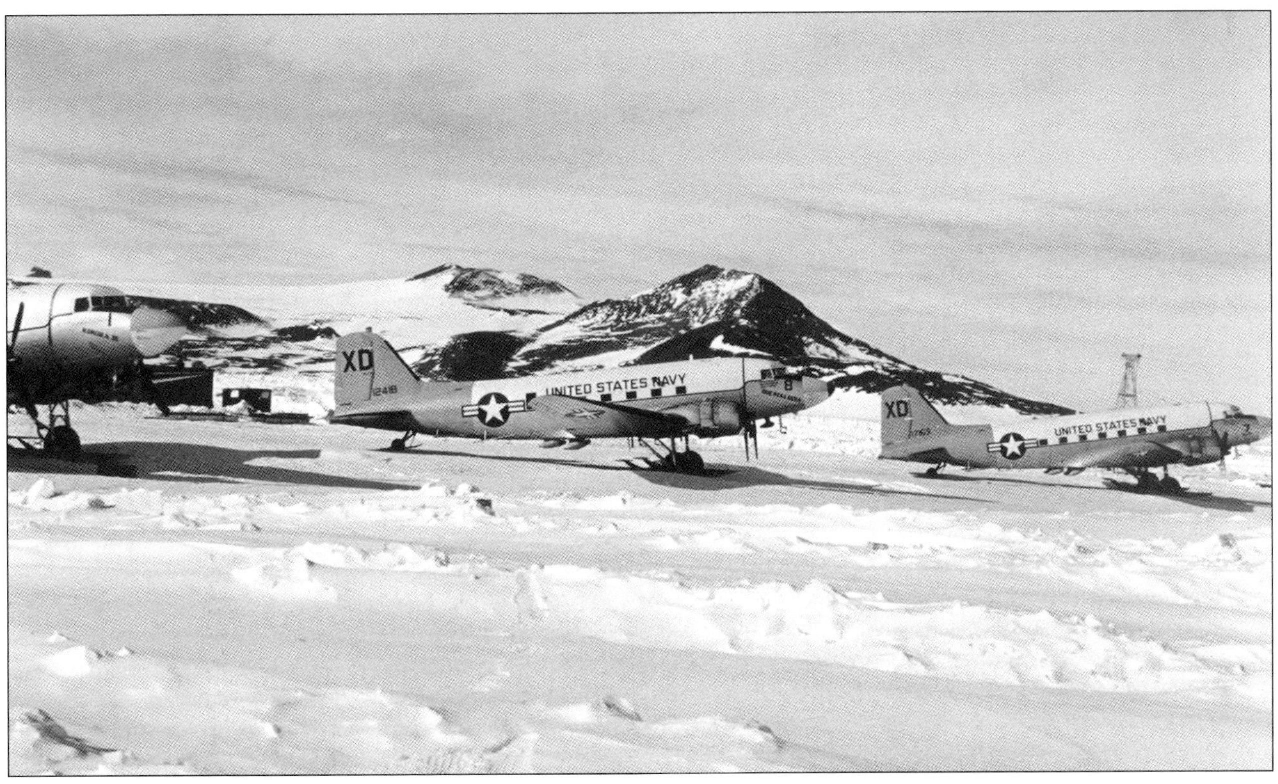

A line-up of three R4D-5s of VX-6 Squadron (BuAer 17163/XD-7, 12418/XD-8 & 17246/XD-1) at McMurdo Sound in Antarctica on 10th January 1957. (Douglas Santa Monica 230473)

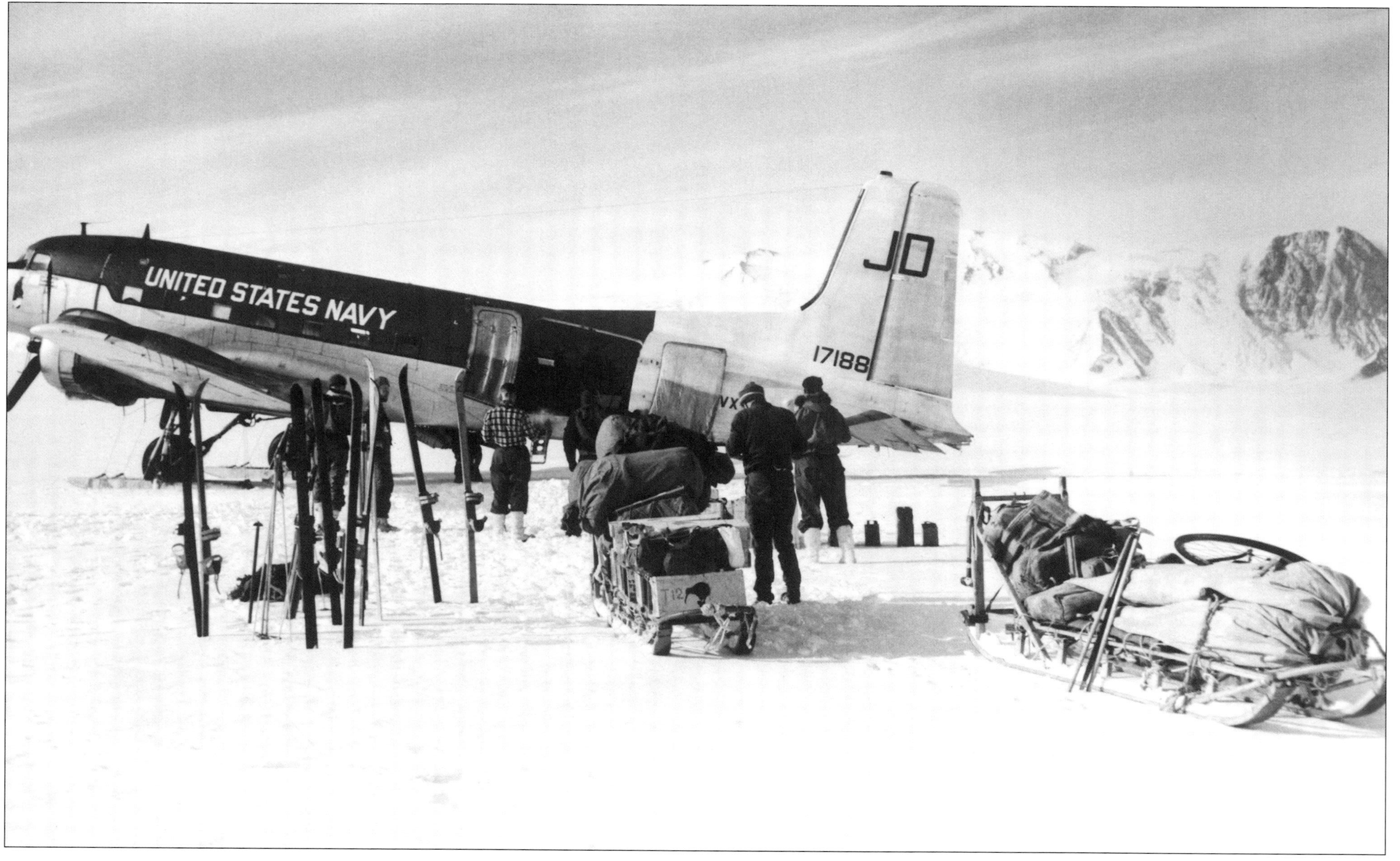

Four New Zealand scientists unload supplies from R4D-8L BuAer 17188 (c/n 43384), modex JD-7, at their camp site on Nimrod Glacier in Antarctica on 30th November 1960, in preparation for geological survey work. (US Navy)

too heavy so they were flown back to New Zealand. In the end out of 1662.8 hours flown, the R4Ds accounted for 906.4 hours on Deep Freeze II. Only one engine had to be changed through the whole season. The aircraft were flown until 12 April, when darkness prevented further operations, and the aircraft were stored in the open at Little America.

Deep Freeze III

When daylight returned in August 1957, the R4Ds were dug out of the snow at Little America and on 3 September two moved to McMurdo Station whence they supported the construction of a summer refueling and weather station on the Ross Ice Shelf near the Beardmore Glacier which was later named Liv Station. This was fully operational by the time the first of VX-6's long-range aircraft arrived on 1 October. Apart from a Neptune, there were two R4D-8 Super DC-3s. These were less reliable than the R4D-5s, and Bu 99853 '*Wilshie Duit*' had a ski stick at an angle of 70 degrees. When an engine caught fire it had to land before it had been lightened by burning off fuel and ground looped. It came to rest on the port gear and starboard wing tip. The fire was put out and no-one was hurt but the damage was not repaired until 8 February, due to lack of spares.

The second R4D-8, Bu 17219 '*Semper Shafters USMC*' arrived on 22nd November and remained based at McMurdo. It later had the port landing gear collapse on landing on the Hollick-Kenyon Plateau when an oil leak developed. It was rescued by an R4D-5 and duly repaired, and both aircraft were back at Little America within 20 hours. The four Neptunes proved to be more reliable than in the previous year, so the R4Ds were kept for fuel transport and support for various scientific traverses. One R4D was the first aircraft to land at Hallett Station which had been considered suitable only for emergency use.

By 25th January 1958 ice conditions had deteriorated and all aircraft except the R4D-5 and the R4D-6 were returned to the United States for overhaul. The R4D-8s needed work on their skis. The R4D-5s were again stored in the open.

During late 1957 the United States Air Force undertook tests with a new electronic positioning device (long before the days of GPS) using two C-47s 45-1134 and '59554' [obviously incorrect]. These flew to Ellsworth Station on the Filchner Ice Shelf, via South America. They stopped off at Robert Island in the South Shetlands which had a flat ice-cap. There the Chilean Navy had set up a cache of fuel. Bad weather caused a landing at Dolleman Island instead of Ellsworth but there was only sufficient fuel for one aircraft to get to Ellsworth, causing further delays. On completion of the work one C-47 was in poor condition so both were brought out by the Argentine Navy icebreaker '*General San Martin*'.

Deep Freeze IV

For the 1958-1959 season two R4D-8s were added to the fleet although one of these was nearly lost on the ferry flight from the US. It lost an engine 500 miles from Canton Island and flew for six hours on one, nearly running out of fuel before it finally landed. Another was forced to land at Hallett when McMurdo was closed by weather. Hallett had no landing aids, but four C-124s had to join the R4D-8 and the latter guided them in from the end of the runway. Operations during Deep Freeze IV followed the previous seasons. Four landings were made by R4Ds at the Pole and three by Neptunes. Bu 12418 was returned to the US in December 1958 for preservation with the NASM and loan to Pensacola, where it still resides.

Deep Freeze 60

Because there was to be a need to continue Antarctic research over many years, the support operations' designation was changed to a numerical one. The equipment available was now reviewed and the elderly R4D-5s were considered to be expendable. In fact, one was written off before the season started when its gear collapsed on landing at Hallett in a medical emergency flight. The patient survived, but the aircraft (Bu 17163) could not be recovered. Despite this feeling, the R4Ds made 78 flights during the season, mainly in support of field

US Navy R4D-8 Super-Dak BuAer 17154 (c/n 43373) showing the later modex code JD-(9) used by VX-6 squadron. The aircraft was named "Negatus Perspitus" and was used for only two Antarctic seasons (1958-59 and 1959-60) before being written off. *(via Arthur Pearcy)*

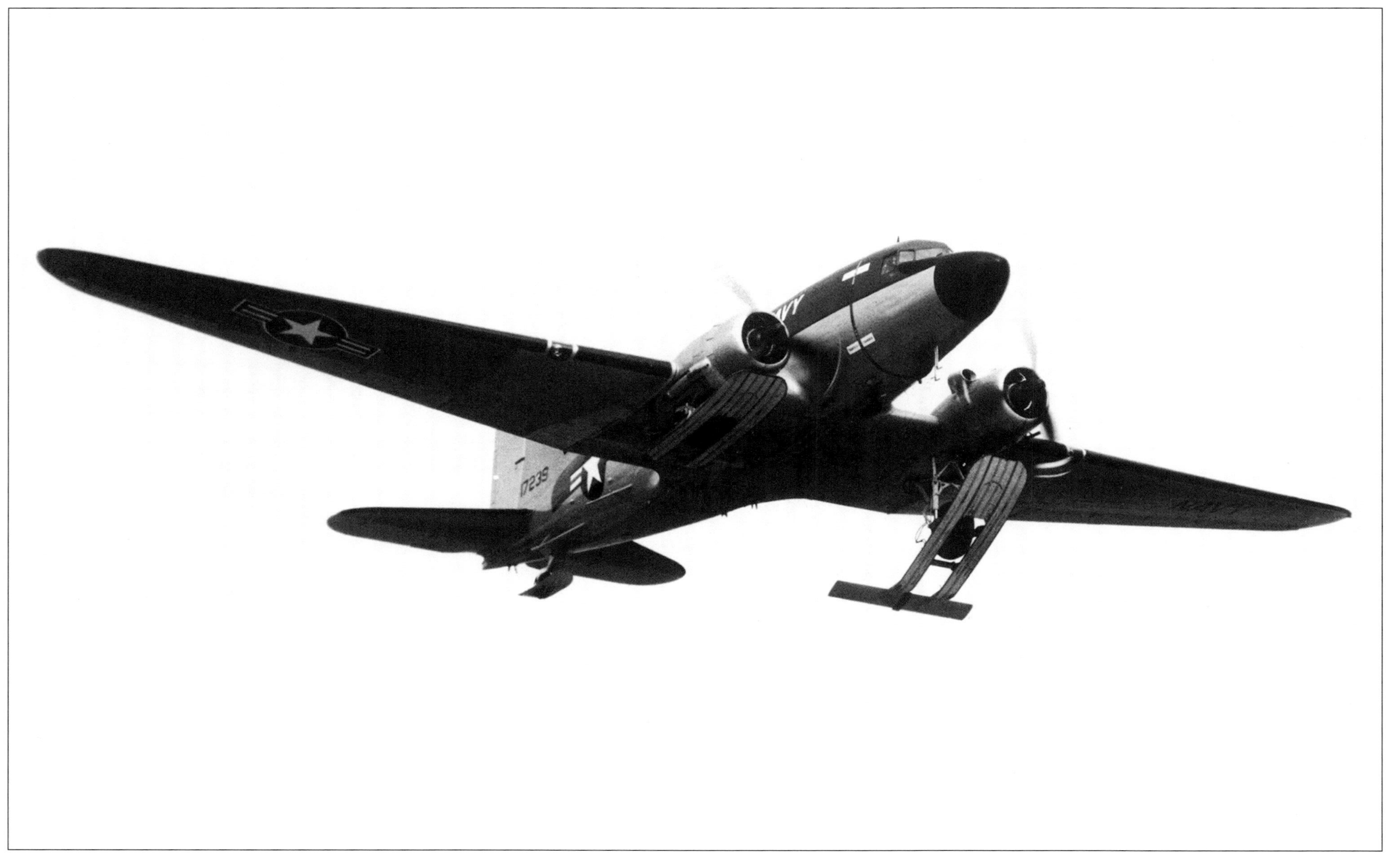

A Dakota with ski trouble! This interesting photograph of US Navy R4D-5 BuAer 17239 (c/n 25424) shows one ski retracted and one ski still extended on the main undercarriage. The incident occurred on a test acceptance flight from Dallas, Texas. The aircraft later flew with VX-6 Squadron in Antarctica. *(via Arthur Pearcy Collection)*

parties and inland stations. A further R4D-8 (Bu 17154) was lost on 6 January 1960, in a near-whiteout near Byrd Station, when conditions made it impossible to see the horizon and there were no shadows. The end of R4D operations was coming closer and the LC-130F Hercules was beginning to appear. Seven of the type were sent in late in the season to carry building material to the South Pole and Byrd.

Despite having the extra capacity of the LC-130s, it was now clear that R4Ds were going to be needed for years to come when landings on unprepared surfaces were required. There were no other aircraft that could meet those needs until turbine-powered helicopters became available.

Deep Freeze 61

For the 1960-61 programme four R4Ds were assigned, only one of which was an R4D-5. The bulk of the work was done by LC-130F Hercules and the R4Ds were kept for the support of field parties and carrying cargo to Hallett and the summer weather stations, and for search and rescue. On 10 December 1960, two Hercules flights took a University of Minnesota geological traverse party to Jones Mountain, some 1,400 miles from Byrd Station. An R4D-8 preceded the C-130s to select a suitable landing site and to supply weather information and to act as a navigational aid. The R4D-5 used was Bu 17246 and R4D-8s Bu 17188, 17219 and 99853. Bu 17246 was retired in May 1961, after five years on the Antarctic. R4D-8 17219 had a landing gear failure while making a rough snow landing in the Hollick Mountains on 25 November 1960 but it was patched up in the field and flew back, gear down, to Byrd and McMurdo. It was then shipped back to the US for overhaul. One R4D-8 remained at McMurdo over the winter, the other returning to the US for overhaul.

Deep Freeze 62

Although it had been recommended that the R4D fleet was standardized on the -5s, R4D-8s continued in use and the two returned from the US with R4D-5 Bu 17239. However, R4D-8 Bu 17219, which had only just returned from repairs in the USA, had a pin shear on its port landing gear. The damage was such that it could not be repaired on site and it had to be abandoned there – later serving as a storm shelter for a geological party. Later, on 1st February, Bu 99853's JATO bottles failed to ignite on take-off, after the gear had been retracted and it fell back onto its belly. Too late in the season, it was repaired the following summer.

At the end of the 1962-63 season, Commander Greenwell commented that:-

"The R4D had again proven herself a valuable friend and the 'Grand Old Lady' of Antarctic Operations. She is economical and durable, and her versatility in short range, open field ski operations remains undisputed. It is not difficult to see the day, perhaps in the near future, when an equally versatile, longer range, greater-payload, higher-flying turboprop replaces the old warrior, but until that day comes, treat her kindly, keep her warm, push the right JATO buttons, and navigate clear of all obstacles"

Despite this, VX-6 continued to use them until 1967.

Deep Freeze 63

By 1962 the R4D-5 and -6 had become the LC-47 and the R4D-8 became the LC-117D when the Navy adopted the USAF system. "L" indicated ski equipment. There were problems at the beginning of the 1963 season, as the damaged LC-117D still awaited repairs and Bu 17239 had been storm damaged and also awaited repairs. However, 1,319 hours were flown on 260 flights. Having said that, two aircraft were lost within three days of each other. LC-117D Bu 17188 crashed in the Sentinel Mountains on 22nd November 1962 and could not be repaired locally, so had to be abandoned. Then on 25th November LC-47 Bu 50777 crashed at Davis Glacier and was also written off. The damaged Bu 99853 had to be shipped back to New Zealand for repairs, so as replacements LC-47s Bu 17107 and 50778 were taken out of storage at Davis-Monthan.

Deep Freeze 64

In 1964 the LC-47 was very much in the majority, with only one LC-117D, the now-repaired Bu 99853. There were four LC-47Hs, Bu 12407, 17107, 17221 and 17239 and LC-47J Bu 50778. Two, 12407 and 17221 were newcomers to Deep Freeze, replacing damaged aircraft.

Deep Freeze 65

Because of a shortage of spares it was concluded that the Dakotas could only be operated in established areas. The Hercules was expected to do much more of the work hitherto carried out by Dakotas (as the Navy often called them). In this Antarctic year there were two losses. Bu 12407 crashed on 22nd October 1964 on Lillie Glacier, and on 11th January 1965 Bu 50778 crashed on Shackleton Glacier and both were written off.

Deep Freeze 66

The aircraft used this year were LC-117Ds Bu 12441 and 99853, LC-47H 17221 and 17239, and LC-47J 50832.

This was the worst year for Dakota accidents. LC-47H Bu 17239 crashed about two miles from Williams Field on 6th October 1965 and two months later Bu 17107 was lost on 5th December in the Horlick Mountains. The final LC-47J accident was to Bu 50832 which crashed on the Ross Ice Shelf on 2nd February 1966 killing all six of the aircrew, and the first fatal Dakota accident in eighteen years of Antarctic operations. LC-117Ds 12441 and 99853 were undamaged. However, because of these three accidents, it was decided to limit their use to prepared 'skiways' and open field areas where the snow was known to be good.

Deep Freeze 67

This was to be virtually the last season when Dakotas were to be used by the U S Navy in the Antarctic. Three LC-117Ds were on charge, one new to the area. This was Bu 17092 which arrived at Williams Field on 28th November 1966. Bu 99853 flew for the last time on 10th January 1967 and Bu 12441 a week later on the 17th . They were stored until shipped out in January 1968. Bu 17221 remained in New Zealand.

Deep Freeze 68

Bu 17092 made the last Dakota flight in Antarctica on 2nd December 1967 and was stored until its was prepared for shipment out in January 1968, along with Bu 12441 and 99853 in USNS '*Pvt. John R Towle*'. They had their wings removed, and were to be slung on board from the dock. Unfortunately Bu 99853 slipped out of its slings and fell back onto the dock and was damaged sufficiently to write it off. It was pushed off the ice, but could still be seen a year later, refusing to sink! LC-47H 17221 was only used in New Zealand for this season as it was in Deep Freeze 68. It was retired there on 18th April 1969 and presented to Ferrymead Museum, where it is displayed to this day.

Conclusion

Twenty-three Dakotas were used in the Antarctic and of these seventeen were written off for one reason or another. Two were given to Museums, and the remaining four were retired on return to the USA. There are continuing memorials to commemorate these brave aircraft, and the maps now show '*Dakota Pass*', '*R4D Nunatak*' and '*Skytrain Ice Rise*'.

SUMMARY OF AIRCRAFT USED

Bu	c/n	Designation	Assigned*	Lost	Fate	Name	Modex code
12407	9179	LC-47H	Oct63	Oct64	w/o		
12415	9305	R4D-5	Jan47	1948	Abandoned		none
12418	9358	R4D-5	Oct56		Preserved	Que Sera Sera!	XD-8
12441	43389	LC-117D	Dec64	Jan68		City of Invercargill	JD-11
17092	43381	LC-117D	Nov66	Jan68			
17101	11878	R4D-5	Jan47	1948	Abandoned		none
17107	11938	LC-47H	Nov62	Dec65	w/o	Ahab's Clyde	
17154	43373	R4D-8	Nov58	Jan60	w/o	Negatus Perspitus	JD-9 /JD-8
17163	12519	R4D-5	Jan57	Sep59	w/o	Takahe	XD-7
17188	43384	R4D-8L	Nov60	Nov62	w/o	Lou Byrd II	JD-7
17197	13008	R4D-5	Jan47	1948	Abandoned		none
17219	43323	R4D-8L	Nov57	Nov61	w/o	Semper Shafters USMC	JD-9
17221	13319	LC-47H	Feb67	Jan68	Preserved	Kool Kiwi	JD-14
17237	25316	R4D-5	Jan47	1948	Abandoned		none
17238	25324	R4D-5	Jan47	1948	Abandoned		none
17239	25424	LC-47H	Nov61	Oct65	w/o	Snafu	JD-8?
17246	25444	R4D-5	Oct56	May61	wfu	Little Horrible/Korora II	XD-1
17274	25777	R4D-6	Oct56	Jan59	w/o	Charlene	XD-4 /XD-8
39092	19063	R4D-5	Jan47	1948	Abandoned		none
50777	26378	LC-47J	Nov62	Nov62	w/o		
50778	26383	LC-47J	Nov62	Jan65	w/o	Gotcha	
50832	26983	LC-47J	Nov65	Feb66	w/o (note 1)		
99853	43339	R4D-8	Dec60	Jan68	w/o	Wilshie Duit	JD-10

** The date in the Assigned column is for the aircraft's arrival in Antarctica.*

Note 1: This was the only fatal accident

This is not quite the end of the story because a Basler BT-67, C-FMKB undertook survey work in Antarctica in 2008. It was damaged in a landing accident, but the rear fuselage was replaced by that of N23SA, and it made a full recovery, such was its value to science. Further BT-67s have been used by Kenn Borek Ltd for survey work These include C-FTGI c/n 26268, C-GAWI c/n 19227, C-GEAI c/n 33053 and C-GVKB c/n 12300.

Argentine DC-3 Operations

The Argentine Navy and Air Force have both operated the DC-3 in the Antarctic, starting in 1954. At that time the Air Force created the Antarctic Air Task Force which used Dakotas to fly weather reconnaissance sorties between Rio Gallegos Air Base in Southern Patagonia and the Antarctic.

In 1961-62 the Navy flew two DC-3s [CTA-12 and CTA-15] to the South Pole using a base camp on the Larsen Ice Shelf and Ellsworth Station. They landed at the Amundsen-Scott South Pole Station on 7 January 1962, supported by the U S Navy. The following year the Air Force attempted to repeat the feat, but the aircraft caught fire on take-off and was destroyed. They tried again in October 1965 and were successful. This DC-3 was fitted with R-2000 DC-4 engines and an auxiliary jet in the tail. The route was via Rio Gallegos to Teniente Matienzo, and to General Belgrano Station on the Filchner Ice Shelf, reaching the South Pole on 3 November 1965. The aircraft then completed the Antarctic crossing to McMurdo Station. It returned home via the Pole again, with support from the U S Navy.

The Air Force carried out various survey flights from Teniente Matienzo in 1967.

Russian Antarctic Operations

The Russians operated a number of Lisunov Li-2s in the Antarctic. In 1955-56 two aircraft were brought in by ship to Mirnyi Station. They were used initially for reconnaissance flights and then in support of a scientific party in the Bungers Hills. In July 1956 the two Li-2s, and Il-12 and an An-2 delivered cargo to Pionerskaya Station on the polar plateau. The Li-2s carried out seismic soundings of Drygalski Island and also landed scientists to make astrofixes. Some aircraft were used to ferry ashore passengers and cargo from ships unable to penetrate the pack ice.

From the initial pair used in 1955-1956, there were six in 1957 and seven in 1958. The number fell to four in 1959 and 1960, three in 1961 and only one in 1962, increasing to two in 1964 and at least one until 1967, when the report ends.

Aircraft known to have operated in the Antarctic include CCCP-N499, CCCP-N496, CCCP-N501, CCCP-N531, CCCP-N465, CCCP-N455, CCCP-N470, CCCP-N495, CCCP-N502, CCCP-N527, CCCP-N556, CCCP-04212. Others were used by Polar Aviation, but it is not certain if in the Antarctic. (see Vol II pp 682 to 693). Several were written off during this time.

References

Summary of R4D-Type Aircraft By Bureau Number Used by the United States Navy in Antarctica from Operation '*Highjump*' through '*Operation Deep Freeze*' and by the USAF Electronics Test Unit. Compiled in the History and Research Division, U.S. Naval Support Force, Antarctica, Washington D.C. by Captain Peter J Anderson, USAF 1972.

Dakotas in the Antarctic, A Study in Versatility. Monograph Number One in a series. History and Research Division, U.S. Navy Support Force, Antarctica. Washington, D.C., September 1970.

Antarctic Journal of the United States. Vol II, No 3, May-June 1967.

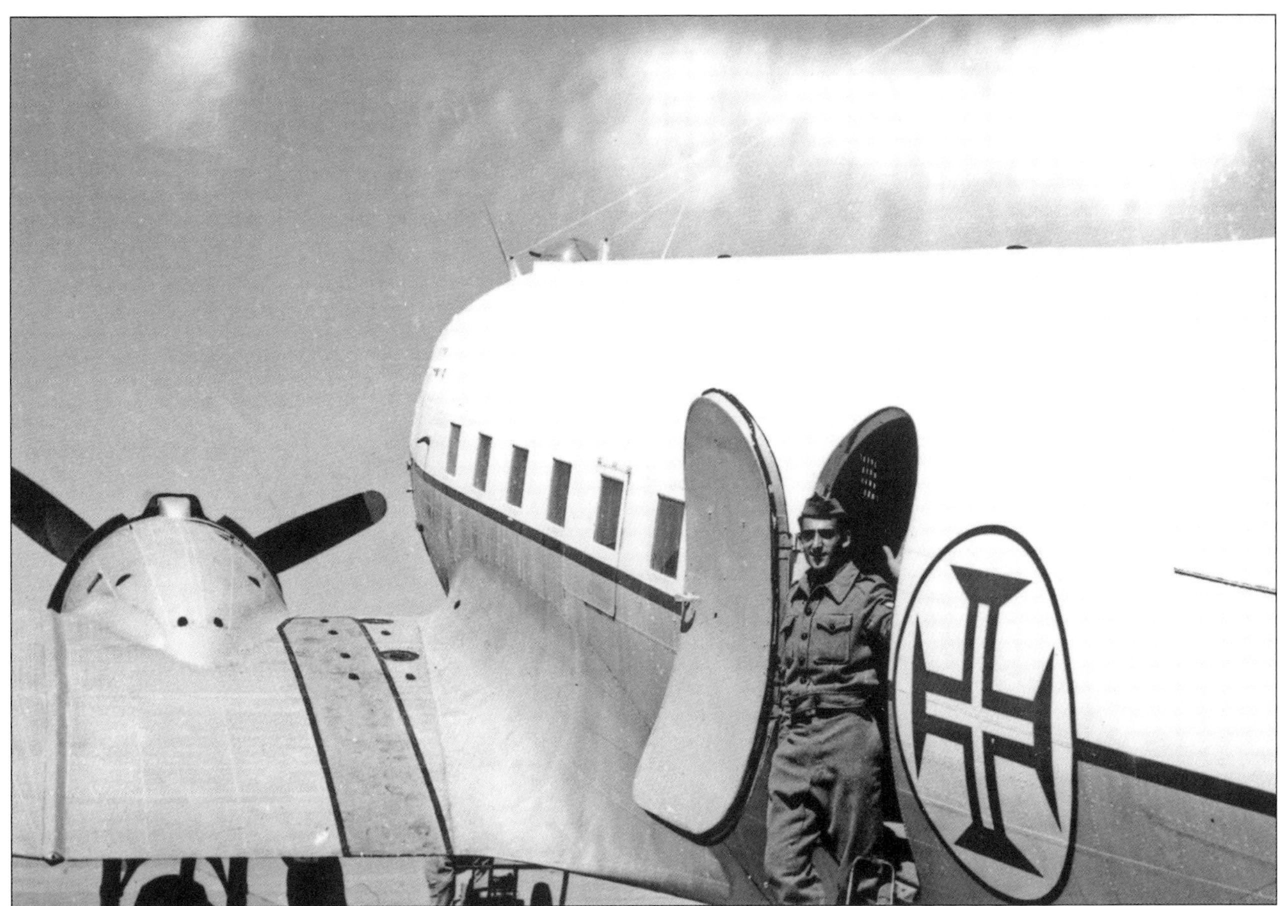

Close-up of a Força Aerea Portuguesa C-47A serial 6154 (c/n 10049) showing the Portuguese national emblem and the passenger door – the aircraft was formerly operated by the Portuguese airline Transportes Aéreos Portugueses - TAP as CS-TDH. *(BA7 via Luis Tavares)*

Chapter 6
The Douglas C-47 / Dakota in Portuguese Military Service

by Luis Tavares

Note that throughout the text the C-47 and Dakota designations are used as they appear in official documents.

This article was prepared with the use of data collected during the course of many years, but mainly during the author's service with the Portuguese Air Force Material Command from 1971 to 1973. In addition, much data was gleaned from pilots' log-books and from Air Base movements. A bibliography has been added at the end.

During WWII three C-47s force landed in Portugal. These were:-

USAAC 1st Troop Carrier Command C-47 **42-24171** was flying from St.Mawgan in Cornwall to Casablanca on 20th September 1943 and belly landed near Sagres. All the crew were unharmed.

USAAC C-47 **43-15307** landed on 12th April 1944 at Portela Airport, Lisbon.

USAAC 440th Troop Carrier Group C-47 **42-100930**, landed, probably on 17th July 1944.

To try to clarify the relationship between these C-47 aircraft and the first aircraft that entered Portuguese military service, and to establish the service entry dates and serial changes, details of flights collected from several log-books of Portuguese military pilots have been summarized below.

According to a letter from the Minister of War to the Secretariado da Aeronáutica Civil dated 28th October 1944, the Comando Geral da Aeronáutica Militar had three Dakota aircraft at their disposal on that date which could be used as commercial aircraft. This document also stated that the Dakota aircraft did not have spares, and that one aircraft was being repaired at OGMA, and only one had been adapted already for commercial service. By 1944/45 the "**Secção de Transportes**" in Portela Airport-Lisbon was formed with a Hudson, Liberators and Dakotas.

The first known reference to a C-47 flying with a Portuguese military serial was on 28th April 1944, when Captain Costa Macedo test flew Dakota D-1 from Sintra Air Base for 30 minutes, reaching a height of 200 metres. Some C-47 flights with Portuguese pilots were recorded at BA4 (Açores-Lajes) in aircraft with serials 6397 and 9750 at the beginning of 1947, but presumably these were American aircraft (matching serials 43-16397 and 43-49750, that were based by that time with the American forces at Lajes) and were probably used for training or familiarization flights.

Until 1952, a C-47 aircraft with serial 250 was based at Sintra, but it was not until July 1953 that this aircraft began to appear in pilots' log-books as belonging to the Comando de Instrução e Treino of Aeronáutica Militar based at Lisbon-Portela. From October 1953 their flights were recorded as for the "Subsecretariado de Estado da Aeronáutica", the Government body that controlled the newly-created Força Aérea Portuguesa – FAP (Portuguese Air Force).

From April 1954 the unit was called the "**Esquadrilha de Transportes**", and from August 1956 "**Esquadrilha de Transportes Militares**". By December 1958 the unit was renamed "**Esquadra 31**". The last known recorded flight of serial 250 was on 19th September 1956, and the first record of a flight with serial 6150 appeared on 1st October 1956 in Portela as a test flight.

On 12th May 1958 C-47 6150 left Portela for a mission that would take it to the Portuguese African colonies of Cabo Verde, Guiné, SaoTomé, Angola and Moçambique.

Força Aérea Portuguesa (Portuguese Air Force) C-47 serial D1 in a very early scheme taken at BA1 Sintra in the late 1940s.
(BA1 Sintra via Luis Tavares)

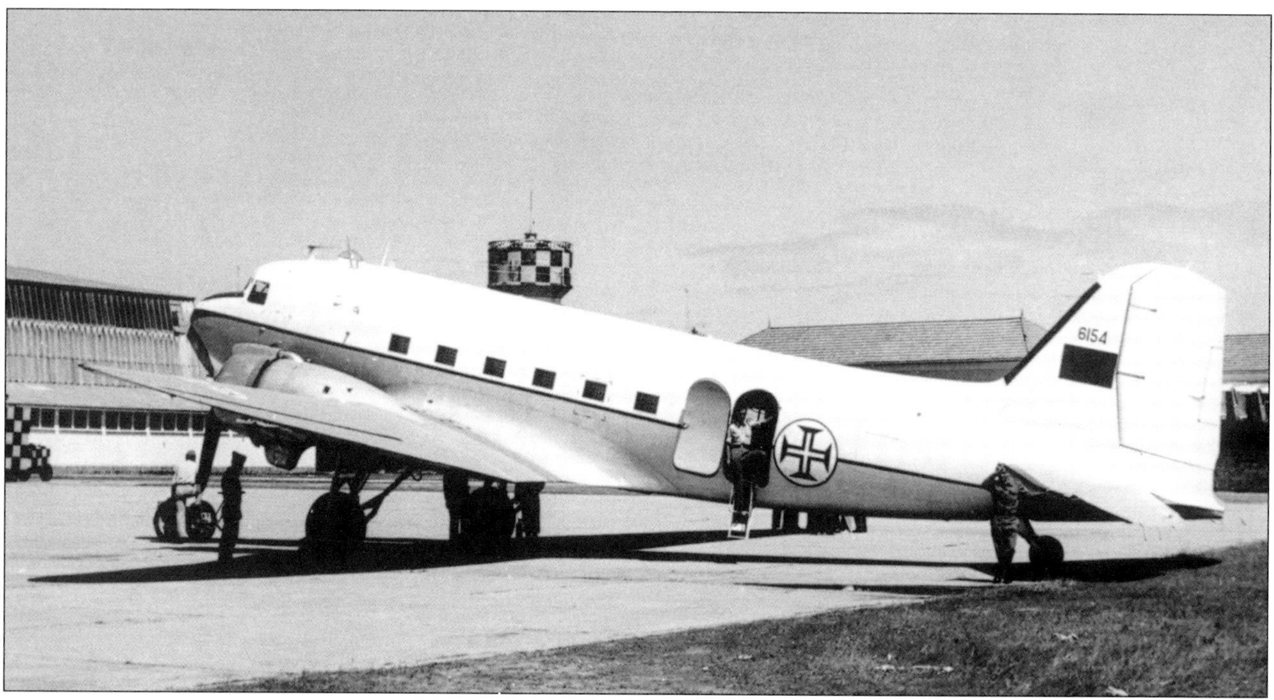

Força Aérea Portuguesa (Portuguese Air Force) C-47A serial 6154 (c/n 10049) on the ramp at an unknown location in the late 1950s.
(BA7 via Luis Tavares)

6151 was delivered to the FAP on 30th October 1958. This was formerly CS-TDC with the national airline, Transportes Aéreos Portugueses (TAP), and was cancelled from the civil register on 11th November 1958. Serial 6152 was taken on charge by the end of 1958, being also ex TAP (CS-TDD), and was cancelled from the civil register on 12th November 1958. From FAP records it is known that by December 1958, there were three C-47s in service, these being 6150, 6151 and 6152. At the beginning of 1959 (a flight was recorded on 11th March), 6153 was taken on charge, this aircraft also being ex TAP (CS-TDE), and was cancelled from the civil register on 14th February 1959. Finally, 6154 was received from TAP, where it had been CS-TDH, having been cancelled from the civil register on 14th February 1959.

Three C-47s (6150, 6153 and 6154) departed for Angola on 12th April 1959 for integration into '*Operation Himba*', a show of force of military aviation in that African colony. 6150, however, unfortunately crashed into the Tejo (ie Tagus) River after taking off, killing all crew and passengers. The two others made stops at Gando (Canary Islands), Sal, Bissau, Sao Tomé and Luanda, where the last aircraft to arrive was 6153 on 19th April 1959. In June 1959, there was no any longer mention of Esquadra 31, but all the C-47s were still recorded as being flown from Portela. By May 1960, besides the aircraft in Portela, there was at least one (6151) serving on Search and Rescue duties at BA4 in the Açores, where it was photographed in the Search and Rescue livery.

The next aircraft to be received were 6155 and 6156, both of which came from Israel. These two belonged to a group of eight ex-RAAF aircraft which had been put up for sale via Israel Aircraft Industries. 6156 left Israel in May 1961 and was integrated into **Esquadra 81** at Portela. According to FAP records the incorporation date was 25th May 1961.These two C-47s, together with 6151, were sent to Guiné where they continued flying until 1965. Meanwhile serial 6154, which had been detached to the Cape Verde Islands, had been lost there in an accident by October 1964. One interesting fact is that 6155 was converted into a bomber by OGMA in the summer of 1965, returning to Guiné in October 1965 where it was used on operational missions, carrying six 50 kilogram and two 200 kilogram bombs under the wings and twenty 15 kilogram fragmentation bombs and 50 magnesium grenades inside the fuselage. 6156 was also used in the same theatre for bombing missions.

To return to 1960, the **Esquadra de Instrução Complementar de Pilotagem de Aviões Pesados (EICPAC)** was formed at BA2-Ota, equipped with one C-54 and three C-47s (6151, 6153 and 6154). However, according to the history of BA2 the C-47s were not received until 1962, which seems to be proven by the flights of Captain Macedo in 6151 from Portela in 1961.The name of this Esquadra was changed to the **Esquadra de Instrução Complementar de Pilotagem e Navegação de Aviões Plurimotores" – EICPNAP** by Portaria (decree) nº 19686 of 6th February 1963. This Esquadra moved to BA4-Lajes in 1964.

Again in 1960, the new Chief of Staff for the FAP went to the USA and negotiated the sale to FAP of eight former USAF aircraft that received the serials 6157 to 6164 inclusive. According to FAP records they were taken on charge on 19th May 1961, except for 6161 (on 25th May), plus 6162 and 6164 (on 4th May). Of these, 6157 and 6160, which were passenger configurated, were earmarked for transportation and VIP duties based at Portela. 6163 was sent to Guiné, and 6159 plus 6161 to Moçambique.

On 5th February 1962, **Esquadra 101** was formed with C-47 aircraft at BA10-Beira in Moçambique. By 2nd September 1962 the first Noratlas had arrived at BA10, and together with the C-47s formed **Esquadra 102**. However, by 19th November 1962 the C-47s were transferred to AB8 at Lourenço Marques (nowadays called Maputo) where they formed the **Esquadra 801.** Next in the FAP list, C-47s 6165 and 6166 appeared, which were also bought from the USAF and came from USAF bases in Europe. It seems from some reports that 6165 suffered an accident on 10th May 1968 (a fire at Lourenço Marques in Moçambique), although the FAP record card from 1973 does not mention this. By the end of the sixties there was also a special unit, the **Esquadrilha de Ligação Treino e Socorro,** based at Portela and using one Douglas C-47, three C-45 Expeditors and three Max Holste Broussards. According to the operations manual of this unit, published on 9th July 1970, the C-47 was 6160, equipped with ten seats. In an emergency, however, it could also be used for paratrooping. A reference recently published states that the last C-47 in service in the American detachment at Lajes was transferred to the FAP on 16th June 1970. This would appear to correspond to aircraft 6171.

In July 1971, there were 18 operational C-47s in the FAP. These were 6151 - 6153, 6155 - 6164 and 6166 - 6170.

The remaining C-47s used by the FAP were obtained mainly from Angola or Moçambique, being ex-commercial aircraft, either from DTA or DETA, as mentioned in the specific files for each aircraft. The missions carried out by the FAP C-47s were many and varied, as in every country of the world, from carrying parachutists to general transport, through bombing missions as seen above, chemical defoliation missions, photo-survey, VIP transportation, and so on. With the end of war in Africa, many were left there, and by 1st July 1976 only four remained in service, including two, 6153 and 6157 which were used for photo missions at BA1-Sintra. This last one is now at BA1 and belongs to the Air Museum. Thus 1976 marked the retirement of the C-47 in FAP service.

Individual histories of FAP C-47s/DC-3s

The early aircraft

D1 or D-1 The first record of this aircraft was on 28th April 1944 and last record was in June 1945, when it was serving with the Comando Geral da Aeronáutica Militar (Army Air Force High Command). If it was one of the interned aircraft it could be only **42-24171** or **43-15307**, the two known to have landed in Portugal before that date. As the first one (according to the accident report) belly landed in soft ground, it could probably have been repaired by April of the following year. As **43-15307** landed intact at Portela, this could also be D1/D-1. However an article in the magazine MAIS ALTO states that 42-24171 took a long time to repair and was not delivered to TAP as CS-TDB until 19th December 1946. If this is true then D1 must be 43-15307**.** According to the same article, D1 made at least one flight to Cape Verde and was refurbished internally as a VIP aircraft.

D2 This aircraft was first recorded on 9th November 1944.The last record was on 21st November 1944. This aircraft became CS-TDA with TAP, being registered on 28th May 1945, after conversion to civilian standards by Scottish Aviation Limited between 30th May 1946 and 1st October 1946, and was delivered to TAP on 2nd October 1946. This seems to agree with a known photo of CS-TDA in an olive drab paint scheme, probably indicating that it was used as a training aircraft for TAP before conversion.

If, as mentioned above, 43-15307 became D1 and 42-24171 went to the repair shop, D2 could be only **42-100930** that later became CS-TDA. As CS-TDA was sold to DETA as CR-AGD, and was later passed to the FAP as 6175, it seems that 42-100930 served in two widely-separated periods with the FAP, first as D2 and then as 6175!

CS-EDA This was first recorded on 9th November 1944. E = Exercito (Army), D = Dakota. The last record was on 5th January 1945. In the Portuguese civil register this registration is said to have been taken up in 1944 and cancelled on 14th February 1946. According to a photo that has recently come to light, this registration was actually painted on the aircraft, at least during a flight to the Cape Verde islands from 10th to 15th January 1945.

CS-EDH The only record of this was on 1st October 1944 and was probably a clerical error, as there are no records known of CS-EDB to EDG.

D250 The only record of this is a photograph showing this serial on an aircraft at Lajes Field in 1946 or 1947.

250 The first record of this serial was on 2nd June 1946. It was recorded in 1947 and 1948 in service with the "Comando Geral da Aeronáutica Militar" (CGAM). It carried out several flights to the Açores including a flight Sintra-Lajes in 6 hours in July 1946 (with extra tanks fitted in the cabin). It was also one of the aircraft sabotaged at BA1-Sintra on 10 April 1947, but was apparently repaired. It was still recorded in 1951 with the CGAM, and also in 1952. In 1953 and 1954 it is recorded with the "Secretariado da Aeronáutica" (SA), the organization that replaced the CGAM, after the Portuguese Air Force was created in 1952. From March 1955 at least, it was based at Lisbon-Portela. In 1956 it was still at Lisbon and the last flight recorded for 250 was on 19th September 1956.

Acquisitions in the 1950s

6150 FAP records of 1973 do not mention this aircraft. According to MAIS ALTO, this aircraft was c/n 19773 USAF 43-15307 which makes it the second C-47 to be interned. The same reference also makes it as ex-D-1 and D250 and later 250. The first recorded use of 6150 was on 1st October 1956, based at Portela. It was also recorded as being at Portela in 1957, 1958 and the beginning of 1959. 6150 made a trip to Cape Verde, Guiné, Sao Tomé, Angola and Moçambique, departing Portela on 12th May 1958. Tragically, on the night of 11th – 12th April 1959, after taking off from Portela as the third Dakota of '*Operation Himba*' flying to Angola, it crashed into the Tagus Estuary, killing all on board. The pilot was Lt.Col.Brandão Calhau; very few parts of the aircraft were recovered from the river. This, together with the fact that there was no communication with the aircraft after take-off, meant that the reason for the crash was never determined.

6151 C-53D-DO c/n 11765 ex USAF 42-68838. This aircraft was delivered to the FAP on 30th October 1958. It had seen service with the Portuguese national airline TAP as CS-TDC and was cancelled from the Portuguese register on 11th November 1958. The first known record of a flight with the FAP was on 5th February 1959 at Portela, where other flights were recorded in October 1960 and April-May 1961. In May 1960 it was seen at BA4-Lajes with the Search and Rescue paint scheme, probably during a period in 1960 it served with Esquadra 41 (Search and Rescue) at BA4. Also during 1960, 6151 was assigned to the "Esquadra de Instrução Complementar de Pilotagem de Aviões Pesados" – EICPAP (Complementary Flight Instruction for Heavy Aircraft Squadron) at BA2-Ota, moving to BA4-Lajes in 1964. By April 1965, 6151 was flying at BA12-Bissau, making trips to Sal (Cape Verde) that took four hours. It was later modified as a bomber (as 6155 qv) and used for many night bombing raids. In June 1971 it was again at Portela. According to MAIS ALTO, however, it was left at Guiné-Bissau, where it could be seen in 1979 and also in 1983, until it was eventually used for spares.

6152 C/n 11668 ex USAF 42-68741 and CS-TDD of TAP, reportedly delivered on 25th November 1958. A flight was recorded on 21st April 1959, and it was also recorded at Portela in July and August 1959. This aircraft was detached to the Cape Verde islands in the summer of 1959, to replace the aircraft of the local airline TACV -Transportes Aéreos de Cabo Verde, while they were not operational. However, when landing on the island of Fogo on 25th November 1959, it crashed due to the short length of the airfield. The pilot, Captain Santos Gomes, survived but with severe burns.

6153 C/n 11675 ex USAF 42-68748 and CS-TDE of TAP. According to FAP records it was received on 12 May 1959, but as there is a flight recorded on 11th March 1959, the date of 12th November 1958 as reported in MAIS ALTO is more probable. This aircraft went to Africa on '*Operation Himba*' in April 1959. It was transferred again to Cape Verde and Guiné in January 1960, staying in Guiné until at least July 1960. Later it was placed with EICPAC at BA2. On 15th October 1968 it suffered an accident while landing at Flores Island in the Açores. Although it was still operational in 1976, it was sold on 16 July 1976 as N9984Q to be used in the filming of '*A Bridge Too Far*'.

6154 C/n 10049 ex USAF 42-24187, reportedly delivered on 19th February 1959. Its first recorded flight was on 21st June 1959. From October to December 1960, it made a long trip from Lisbon to Moçambique, where it was attached to Esquadra 81 at Lourenço Marques. By 9th December 1960 it had left Moçambique for Luanda (Angola), arriving on 12th February 1961. Later in February 1961, however, it was back in Lourenço Marques. While in use with BA9, it was completely destroyed when it stalled at Chitado (Angola) on 10th November 1961, killing all 18 crew and passengers. The pilot was Captain Francisco Fernandes de Carvalho, who had been 2nd Pilot of 6153 in '*Operation Himba*'.

Aircraft delivered in the 1960s

6155 C/n 15927/32675 ex USAF 44-76343 and RAAF A65-76. This aircraft was acquired via Israel Aircraft Industries and was delivered in 1961. There is a record of a flight in April 1961 at Portela. In October 1963 it was flying in Guiné and Cape Verde. In 1965 it received modifications at OGMA, enabling it to carry 650 kilograms of bombs under the wings, and launching tubes in the cabin for despatching illumination grenades. It returned to Guiné in October 1965 and carried out many night bombing missions thereafter. After the African War it was left in Guiné.

6156 C/n 16345/33093 ex USAF 44-76761 and RAAF A65-93. Sold to the FAP by Israel Aircraft Industries (as 6155) and delivered on 25th May 1961. In February 1964 it was based at Bissau. It was still operational at Bissau in 1973 and was abandoned there.

6157 C/n 19755 ex USAF 43-15289. As 0-315289, it was in use with the 7th Air Division at USAF Burtonwood during the late fifties. The FAP received the aircraft on 19th May 1961 and was used at Portela, where it was still assigned in 1976. Later it was recorded in use at BA1 as a photographic aircraft. Retired in 1976, it is currently preserved with the Museu do Ar at BA1.

6158 C/n 19818 ex USAF 43-15352. After being used by the USAF 7th Air Division as 0-315352 at Greenham Common, England during the fifties, it was received by the FAP on 19th May 1961. It was recorded at AB8 in 1970 with Esquadra 801. It was used during the war in Africa for defoliation by chemical spraying. According to Cardoso (see references at end), it was targeted during one of these missions in 1973 by fire from light weapons that killed the radio operator. It was later abandoned in Moçambique.

VIP-configured former VC-47A serial 6160 (c/n 20587) of the Força Aérea Portuguesa (Portuguese Air Force) taking off at Lisbon on 8th January 1968. (Luis Tavares)

6159 C/n 20111 ex USAF 43-15645. This aircraft was also used by the USAF 7th Air Division (as 0-315645) and was received by the FAP on 19th May 1961. The aircraft was used in Moçambique by Esquadra 801 and by 1970 it was equipped with loudspeakers for psychological warfare duties. Donated to Moçambique in 1975, it became FP-502 with the Moçambique Air Force, according to MAIS ALTO.

6160 C/n 20587 ex USAF 43-16121. This aircraft was formerly a VC-47A with the USAF 7th Air Division and was recorded with the abbreviated serial 0-3121. It was delivered to the FAP on 19th May 1961 and was based initially at BA2. It was later transferred to BA1, where it stayed during the remainder of its active life with the FAP as a VIP transport. The aircraft was abandoned at Guiné-Bissau.

6161 C/n 10076 ex USAF 42-24214. This aircraft, modified as a VC-47A, served with the USAF 7th Air Division as 0-24214, and later with the 3910th Air Base Group at Wiesbaden, Germany, where it was recorded on 25th June 1960. Delivered on 25th May 1961 to the FAP, it was assigned to Esquadra 801 at AB8 and used for VIP transportation. In 1975 it was donated to Moçambique. MAIS ALTO reports that it became 75-15 with the Moçambique Air Force.

6162 C/n 14134/25579 ex USAF 43-48318. Served with the USAF 7th Air Division as 0-38318 and later as 0-48318, and seen at Wiesbaden as such on 28th September 1959. Delivered on 4th May 1961 to the FAP, it was assigned to Esquadra 801 at AB8. The aircraft suffered an accident when taking off from Vila Cabral (now Lichinga) on 8th January 1974. and was damaged beyond repair. The remains were still there in October 2002.

6163 C/n 14699/26144 ex USAF 43-48883. Served with the USAF 7th Air Division as 0-348883 at Northolt, England, and later as 0-48883 at Greenham Common, England. With the FAP from 19th May 1961, it was assigned to BA12, and abandoned there in 1975. However, it was later seen at Bissau in 1979 and 1983 as CR-GBL (or GBO?). According to recently published information, including a photo, the aircraft was flown to Cape Verde and abandoned there.

6164 C/n 15023/26468 ex USAF 43-49207. This aircraft served as 0-49207 with the USAF 7th Air Division and was then transferred to Wiesbaden, where it was seen on 30th January 1960. Delivered on 4th May 1961 to the FAP, it operated in Angola, where it was abandoned in 1975.

6165 C/n 15522/26667 ex USAF 43-49406. As 0-49406 this aircraft served with the USAF 7th Air Division, and was seen at Frankfurt (Rhein-Main) on 24th January 1960. Delivered on 2nd June 1961 to the FAP, it was assigned to Esquadra 801 at AB8. It was destroyed by fire inside a hangar at AB8 on 10th May 1968.

6166 C/n 14077/25552 ex USAF 43-48261. Delivered to the FAP in 1961 (exact date unknown), a flight was recorded on 2nd May 1961.It was also recorded at BA12 in February and April 1961. By January 1969 the aircraft was at BA9. Later the aircraft was used in Moçambique as a defoliation aircraft, and was abandoned at Guiné-Bissau.

6167 C/n 13018 ex USAF 42-108917. After use as CR-AFR, it was delivered to the FAP on 31st December 1967 and assigned to Esquadra 801 at AB8. It was destroyed in an accident on 11th March 1968 at Mueda. A photo of the crashed aircraft has been published on the Portuguese website www.voaportugal.org.

6168 C/n 20173 ex USAF 43-15707. After use as CR-LCC, the aircraft was delivered to the FAP on an unknown date, and was seen at AB4 on 9th August 1968. It was assigned to Esquadra 403 at AB4, where it was seen again on 24th June 1970. The aircraft was abandoned in Angola in 1975.

6169 DC-3 c/n 42968, ex NC 34972. Delivered on 6th July 1967, and reportedly flown to Angola by mercenaries. Assigned to Esquadra 403 of AB4, it suffered an accident on 31st March 1973 at location 13°30'S and 19°03'E (Cuito Cuanavale area) while making an emergency landing after an engine failed. The aircraft was abandoned there as no means of removing it were available.

The final deliveries in the 1970s

6170 C-53D c/n 11698 ex USAF 42-68771. Originally delivered to DETA as CR-ABJ on 3rd July 1946, this aircraft reached the FAP on delivery in 1971. Assigned to Esquadra 801 at AB8, it was abandoned in Moçambique in 1975. Later it was reportedly used by the Força Aérea Popular de Libertação de Moçambique, still as 6170.

6171 C/n 16784/33532 ex USAF 44-77200. In service with MATS as 0-7200 at Lajes, it was delivered to the FAP on 16th June 1970. No details of FAP use have been found. The aircraft was sold on 6th July 1976 as N9983Q for use in the film '*A Bridge Too Far*', but was abandoned in Ethiopia in 1977 as ET-AHR.

6172 C/n 13140. A former TAP aircraft (CS-TDG from 5th February 1947) and later CR-AGC, the aircraft's delivery date and use with the FAP are not known. The remains were seen in April 2003 at Montepuez (Moçambique).

6173 C/n 11763 ex USAF 42-68836. Formerly used by DETA as CR-ABK, this aircraft was probably used by Esquadra 801 at AB8, but details of its exact use and fate have not yet been uncovered.

6174 C/n 12760 ex USAF 42-92907. Formerly used by DETA as CR-ABQ, this aircraft was reportedly delivered in 1972 to the FAP. It was transferred to Zaire on 8th April 1977.

6175 C/n 19393 ex USAF 42-100930. Probably first used by Aeronautica Militar as D2 (see above). Formerly registered CS-TDA with TAP and later CR-AGD with DETA, it was received in 1971 by the FAP and assigned to Esquadra 801. It was shot down by an SA-7 Grail missile on 6th May 1974. With one engine on fire and a heavily damaged wing, the aircraft made an emergency landing on the small airfield at Nacatari (near Mueda). There were no casualties. Details of the crash can be found on the Portuguese website www.voaportugal.org. The remains of the aircraft were still in situ in May 2003.

6176 C/n 9948. Formerly with DETA as CR-AHB, its delivery date to the FAP is not known, but the aircraft was used in Moçambique, probably by Esquadra 801, in the early 1970s. It was later abandoned in Moçambique.

6177 C/n 18977 ex USAF 42-100514. Received by the FAP in 1972, according to MAIS ALTO, but its use with the FAP is unknown.The aircraft was sold as N9984Q in 1976 for use in the film '*A Bridge Too Far*', then transferred to Zaire on 8th April 1977.

6178 C/n 12066 ex USAF 42-92283. Received from South Africa in April 1972 (it was ZS-DBP until December 1971). Donated to the FAP by the Pretoria Branch of the Southern Cross Fund and fitted with nine stretchers and eight seats to transport wounded soldiers. The aircraft was seen at Luanda Airport in May 1977.

The main sources used are listed below. In particular, the reader's attention is drawn to the Reader's Forum of www.voaportugal.org, a rich source of Portugal's aviation history.

1: Letter from the Minister of War to the Secretariado da Aeronáutica Civil dated 28th October 1944
2: "Bordo de Ataque" by José Krus Abecasis (FAP pilot) – Coimbra Editora-1985
3: Article in MAIS ALTO in December 1997 and January 1998 by M.C.Lopes
4: Base Aérea das Lajes- Contribuição para a sua história – Manuel Martins 2003
5: Data from pilots' log-books and Air Base movements
6: The Douglas DC-3 and its predecessors – by J M Gradidge, Air-Britain 1984
7: Letter from Peter-Michael Gerhardt, 23rd June 1983
8: E-mail from Matt Miller, 1st August 1998
9: "Aeronaves Militares Portuguesas no Sec.XX" by Adelino Cardoso - Lisbon 2000
10: www.aerotransport.org
11: www.voaportugal.org

C-47D serial 6163 (c/n 26144) of the Força Aérea Portuguesa (Portuguese Air Force) seen in the 1960s. The aircraft was formerly based in Europe with the 7th Air Division, United States Air Force. *(PJ Marson Collection)*

This photo and the following photos all show aircraft stored at Aero American's facility at Ryan Field, Arizona in 1976. 41-20088 (c/n 4858) is a former United States Air Force C-53. This aircraft was allocated the civil registration N87625. (MAP)

Chapter 7
Ryan Field C-47s

by Karl Hayes

A first visit to an exotic foreign destination tends to leave a lasting impression, particularly if the destination is Tucson, Arizona and one has a liking for 'round engined' aircraft, as the Americans refer to big pistons. A May 1974 trip to Tucson left many fond memories, but one place in particular stands out, Ryan Field. Now, 35 years later, time has at last been found to carry out some research, to find out what exactly was going on there.

Sonora Desert Location

Heading west out of Tucson, Route 86 runs between the Papago and San Xavier Indian Reservations. Not far from the Arizona Sonora Desert Museum, a museum of a different sort was encountered at Ryan Field, and although it was an active airfield, aircraft movements were few and far between. A remote, outback place, it was nevertheless most scenically located, against the backdrop of the Tucson Mountains and the many large saguaro cactus plants native to the region. It served as a general aviation airfield for Tucson, being only thirteen miles west of the city but the aircraft inhabitants were mostly of the elderly type, Cessna 195s, Luscombes, Fairchild 24s, a few Stinson Gull Wings. There was no control tower, no fences, no "security" and no terminal building, the lack of which only added to the remote ambience of the place.

All that could be observed driving in to the airfield were a few World War II vintage hangars. Not a person was to be seen in the midday heat of the desert. A tumbleweed blew across the deserted airfield, and the rudder of a derelict former Braniff DC-7C (N5906) creaked in the wind. Parked nearby was an abandoned Central Air Transport DC-4, N90405, which had also seen better days. And then, rounding the corner of one of the hangars, came into view the reason for visiting Ryan Field, its stored Douglas C-47s.

Here in May 1974 resided 36 former USAF C-47s, and a further five civilian registered examples. The owner of these machines was soon found, sheltering from the heat in one of the hangars. Work outside is only possible during the early morning and in the evening. Being of an amiable disposition, he gave permission to wander at will around his large collection of retired C-47s. It soon became clear however that, just like Davis-Monthan Air Force Base on the other side of Tucson, this was not entirely a 'boneyard' and that some of these C-47s were destined to fly again. The civilian registered examples were visiting for modification and overhaul, to take advantage of the DC-3/C-47 expertise that had been developed here.

Airfield History

World War II set the stage for the birth of Ryan Airfield. With the outbreak of war, there was a huge need for aircraft and trained pilots to fly them. Under US Army Air Force supervision, nine civilian flying schools were chosen to instruct military pilots for the war effort. One of these schools was the Ryan School of Aeronautics of San Diego, California. Fearing a possible coastal invasion, the Ryan School sought an inland training site and found it 13 miles west of Tucson. Arizona's clear blue skies were perfect for the purpose. On 13th June 1942 ground was broken and in three months a section of desert was transformed into the Tucson Primary Flying School, complete with paved runways, apron, hangars, classrooms and barracks. The San Diego operation was closed down and in one weekend aircraft, personnel and equipment were transferred to the new location.

The School even brought its own training aircraft, the Ryan PT-22 Recruit, a sturdy two-seat trainer of which more than a thousand had been produced. They stood up well to the heat, wind and dust storms of the Sonora Desert and proved exceptionally well suited. A full course of flight instruction normally required four months, but at Tucson this was compressed into just nine weeks. As well as the main airfield, four outlying auxiliary airfields were established, where the students could undertake touch-and-gos and full stop landings, so that the entire area around Ryan Field was a hive of activity. This continued until September 1944, more than two years and six thousand pilots after it first opened. At that stage the flying school was closed, but the name of Ryan Field was retained. The airfield was taken over by the City of Tucson as a general aviation airfield, and the four auxiliary airfields were reclaimed by the desert.

Davis-Monthan AFB

Across town, just to the south east of the city of Tucson, an air base which became known as Davis-Monthan AFB had been established. After World War II, when vast numbers of combat aircraft returned to the United States, they had been flown for the most part either to Ontario, California or Kingman, in northern Arizona for disposal. With the formation of the USAF it was recognised that a permanent storage facility was required and Davis-Monthan had been selected for this purpose. The US Navy chose Litchfield Park near Phoenix, Arizona as their aircraft storage facility.

The first Air Force aircraft arrived for storage at Davis-Monthan in 1946, comprising several hundred Boeing B-29 bombers, which were ultimately broken up, and a few hundred Douglas C-47s, which were refurbished and returned to service. During the 1950s, thousands more aircraft arrived for storage, most of which would never fly again. By 1958 disposal of reclaimed aircraft hulks became a serious problem, as the base itself could not cope with the huge number of aircraft being processed, a situation which would worsen when the Naval facility at Litchfield Park closed in 1965 and Naval aircraft were also stored at Davis-Monthan.

This situation led to outside civilian contractors being employed to smelt down the hulks of aircraft, which in time spawned the growth of the privately owned scrap yards and smelters around the perimeter of Davis-Monthan with which we are all so familiar today, many of which began trading in some types of aircraft which were declared surplus by the military. The countless thousands of aviation enthusiasts who have over the years made the pilgrimage to Tucson, Arizona will well recognise the names of Air Met (Kolar), Allied Aircraft Sales, Consolidated Aeronautics Corporation (Delcon), Desert Air Parts (Petrowskis), Dross Metals, Southwestern Alloys and Time Aviation, whose yards starting in the early 1960s immediately adjoined the perimeter fence of Davis-Monthan.

Visiting enthusiasts will have developed a certain familiarity with the dusty roadways around the base, such as Wilmot Road, Kolb Road, Drexel Avenue and Old Vail Drive, which over the years have been the scene of such a weight of aviation history; which have seen the destruction of countless thousands of aircraft, as well as the uplifting spectacle of many other aircraft escaping the breaker's axe to continue with their careers under civilian registration. Some transport types such as the C-124 Globemaster were deemed to have no commercial future and were scrapped. Others, such as the C-54, C-118, Convairs etc were very much in demand and large numbers were sold on to civilian operators, some actually taking off from improvised dirt strips outside the Davis-Monthan perimeter fence, to save the considerable cost of having to use the base runways.

Aero American Corp

One of the first of these civilian contractors to be established at Tucson, if not the first, was the Aero American Corporation, established around 1958, a subsidiary of the American Compressed Steel Company of Cincinnati, Ohio. Although its original task was to smelt down aircraft for their metal for the parent company, Aero American would quickly develop into a specialised overhaul, repair, refurbishment and modification centre. Associated companies were also established, Aero American Aircraft Parts Company, to deal in spare parts, and Acme Aircraft Company, to trade in aircraft. This group of companies was established at Tucson but instead of locating at the perimeter of Davis-Monthan, as the later companies did, Aero American established its base at Ryan Field, finding the near empty base ideal for its purposes.

Details of its early operations are somewhat scarce but it is known that it acquired a number of Boeing B-17s out of Davis-Monthan, one of which in 1961 was at Ryan Field, with another six in storage in Dallas, Texas. The manager of Aero American at Ryan Field was a colourful Australian character by the name of Gregory Board, who would go on to have a chequered career in aviation. In 1961 he was approached by the producers of the film "The War Lover", starring Steve McQueen, who were looking for B-17s for the movie. He sold them the aircraft at Ryan Field N9563Z and two of the B-17s stored in Dallas, N5229V and N5232V, both of which were flown back to Ryan Field where all three were prepared for the long ferry flight to the UK, where the film was made. A number of B-25s were also acquired, civilianised and sold on.

Mr Board's next publicised aviation involvement was in 1964 when he arranged for the supply of twenty Douglas B-26 Invaders to Portugal. He called this venture Aero Associates Inc. Large numbers of B-26s were available from storage in Davis-Monthan. He arranged for twenty B-26s to be overhauled at Hamilton Aviation, Tucson before being flown to Portugal. Seven of the B-26s had been delivered when the US Customs took an interest in the proceedings, as the aircraft had no export licence, and Mr Board fled the country before he was arrested, never to be heard of again.

In the meantime, on a less controversial note, Aero American Corporation had bought 52 USAF C-47s in 1961, which had been in storage at Davis-Monthan since their retirement from military service the previous year. These 52 were flown to Ryan Field and were registered to Aero American Corp in the sequence N87623 to N87674 inclusive, although only a handful ever carried these civilian registrations. Between 1962 and 1973, seventeen of these 52 were disposed of, one sold to Taiwan, one to Peru, one to Bolivia, one to Costa Rica, one scrapped for spare parts, two to Canada, two to New Zealand and the rest to buyers in the United States. That left 35 of the original 52 still in storage at Ryan Field. In addition, other C-47s which Aero American Corp dealt with during the 1960s and early 1970s were N47218 (c/n 4785) and N4795 (c/n 11772), both acquired from Venezuela and sold on; N86467 (c/n 20716) and N86410 (c/n 25707); and N72859 (c/n 26457) and N86441 (c/n 32734) both sold to the Spanish Air Force.

May 1974 Visit

In May 1974 the writer paid a first visit to Tucson. It was a particularly auspicious time to make the trip as by the end of 1973 American military involvement with the Vietnam War had come to an end, for the most part, and combined with the withdrawal of most piston-engined aircraft from the US military inventory, the storage compounds at Davis-Monthan had swollen to an all-time high of over six thousand aircraft. Although many of these were bombers and fighters, transport and piston-engined aircraft were present in "industrial strength".

Already it was too late for the Douglas C-133 Cargomasters, only one of which remained (a few had escaped elsewhere, but the rest had been scrapped). Present in the storage compounds in May 1974, in round numbers, were some 120 Douglas C-47s, 170 C-54s, 60 C-97s, 40 C-117s, 220 C-119 Packets, 180 C-121 Super Constellations, 110 C-124 Globemasters, 230 S-2 Trackers, 280 P-2 Neptunes, 90 U-6A Beavers and 150 Grumman Albatross, as well as thousands of bombers, fighters and helicopters. The era of the big piston with the US military was coming to an end, the only remaining types being T-29/C-131 Convairs, C-118s and KC-97Ls and it would not be too long before these were in storage as well. Trying to take a good look at and photograph even a representative selection of this vast number of aircraft in the huge storage compounds at Davis-Monthan proved quite a challenge.

It was therefore a much more pleasurable experience to arrive at the somewhat laid-back Ryan Field, with ample time to appreciate its C-47s. Thirty-five of the original fifty two ex-USAF C-47s purchased by Aero American were still present. Here was history "in the raw", aircraft in the markings they had carried during their service during the 1950s. The colours may have been somewhat faded after years of outside storage under the desert sun, but they were genuine. Many of the C-47s still carried dayglo nose and tail bands. All of course featured the "0" (for obsolete) prefix before the tail number, indicating an aircraft more than ten years in service. Some carried five digit serials but many still featured the earlier six digit serial presentation, for example, 0-316097. Many carried MATS titles, referring to the Military Air Transport Service, which had since been replaced by the Military Airlift Command. These aircraft had come from bases all over the United States and Europe, including four from Maxwell AFB, Alabama and two from Pepperell, Newfoundland. Three had come from Bolling AFB, Washington and featured Headquarters, White House Command markings.

Most of these former USAF C-47s were parked in the grass, but a few had been brought onto the main ramp in front of the hangar, where they were being dismantled for their spare parts. Also on this ramp were to be found the visiting DC-3s and C-47s which had come to Ryan Field for repair, overhaul or modification, which was an important part of Aero American's business, including N28U, N42V and N142A. N87644, one of the original ex-USAF C-47s, was being worked on for ultimate sale to Millardair in Canada. Also here was N18255 a former French Air Force C-47 which Aero American had acquired and CF-YED of Northway Air Surveys, which Aero American were modifying for the survey role. Being worked on was 0-16232 (c/n 20698), which was not one of the original 52 acquired from USAF stocks, but had been donated by the USAF to the Smithsonian Institute in September 1970. However, they did not want it, and had sold it to Aero American. It was being civilianised for sale to Falcon Airways of Texas to whom it was eventually delivered as N83FA.

Export C-47s

In the years that followed, Aero American were successful in rebuilding and exporting several of these C-47s to Canada, in addition to the two they had already sold to Canada prior to 1974, which were CF-TFV (ex N87637) to Reindeer Air Service and CF-AAL (ex N87661) to Austin Airways. Next to go, in September 1975, was C-GZOF (ex N87650) to Contact Airways of Fort McMurray, Alberta. Aero American also had a paint shop at Ryan Field and so could deliver the aircraft to the customer ready for service, in the customer's colour scheme. To see this aircraft ready for delivery in the most attractive yellow, black and white scheme of Contact Airways was to witness a remarkable

Former USAF C-47A 42-92075 (c/n 11835), with registration N87642 allocated. (MAP)

A former USAF SC-47D 43-48307 (c/n 25568). The registration N87653 was allocated to this aircraft. (MAP)

C-47D 43-49275 (c/n 26536), formerly of the USAF, was not part of Aero American's inventory, but was restored by them to fly for Jim Hankins Air Service in 1974. *(MAP)*

Former USAF C-47D 43-48398 (c/n 25659). This aircraft was registered N87654 and was restored to fly again (as C-GABH) later in 1976. *(MAP)*

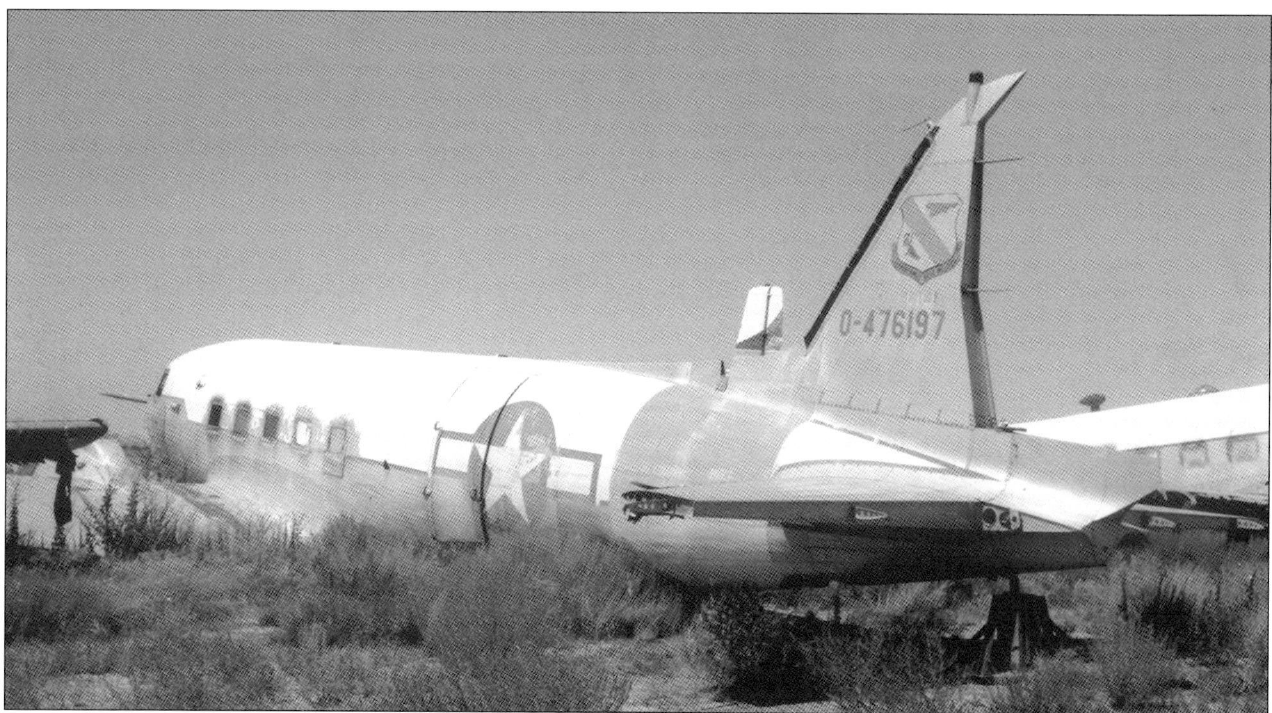

A former USAF VC-47D 44-76197 (c/n 32529). This aircraft was registered N87664 and was restored to fly again (as C-GGCS) later in 1976. *(MAP)*

Formerly stored as a fuselage at Ryan Field, Arizona, C-47D N87660 (c/n 26815) was restored by Aero American for Air Brazeau as C-GABI, one of three supplied to the Canadian operator. (MAP)

C-47D c/n 26817 was stored at Davis-Monthan prior to restoration by Aero American on behalf of the US Government and supplied to the Nicaraguan Air Force in 1976 as 418 under the Military Aid Programme. (MAP)

An HC-47D 44-76306 (c/n 32638) with registration N87667 allocated. (MAP)

transformation from the derelict hulk which had lain at Ryan Field for years. C-GZOF would return to Ryan Field for overhaul while operated by Contact Airways. This was followed by C-GGCS (ex N87664), delivered to Millardair in 1975, as well as C-GABG (ex N87645), C-GABH (ex N87654) and C-GABI (exN87660) to Air Brazeau of Quebec in early 1976.

In February 1976 Aero American received a contract to prepare two C-47s which were being supplied by the US Government to Nicaragua under the Military Aid Program. These two aircraft were not part of Aero American's own stock, but were still present in storage at Davis-Monthan. The two C-47s, 17181 (c/n 12780), a former US Army aircraft, and 0-49556 (c/n 26817), a former USAF aircraft, were flown the short distance to Ryan Field where they were overhauled, repainted in Fuerza Aerea de Nicaragua markings with serials 417 and 418 respectively, and delivered to Nicaragua during May 1976.

A second visit by the writer to Ryan Field during October 1976 revealed 27 of the original 52 ex-USAF C-47s still lying there, as well as N42V and N142A which had been present during the previous May 1974 visit. A new aircraft present was an early, 1939-vintage DC-3 N101MX (c/n 2102) which Aero American had just acquired and which was disposed of later that year. Also present was N502PA (c/n 26744) which was receiving a new wing prior to operation by Summit Airlines of Philadelphia. Aero American had of course many spare wings for use in such rebuilding projects.

Across town at Davis-Monthan, the storage compounds had been swollen by the arrival of hundreds of Convair T-29s, C-131s and Douglas C-118s, which the other scrapyards were busy processing, the C-118 in particular being much sought after as a civilian freighter. For some reason, apart from the two C-54s destined for Millardair as already mentioned, Aero American did not get involved with these other types of aircraft, but continued to work on their C-47s.

During 1977 many of the remaining C-47s in storage were scrapped at Ryan Field, and Aero American continued with its business of overhauling DC-3s and C-47s for customers and supplying spare parts. The last of its own aircraft to be rebuilt and sold was C-GNOA (ex N87644) which went to Millardair in November 1978. In the opposite direction, ex Millardair C-47 CF-WTU was noted at Ryan Field in February 1979 being worked on, prior to sale in the United States as N3146Z. Also noted on overhaul at Ryan Field during September/October 1979 were N8042X, for delivery to Audi Air in Fairbanks and N59314 of Frontier Flying Service, down from its base at Fairbanks. One of the last C-47s to be overhauled by Aero American, noted there in May 1981, was N37529, a former Spanish Air Force C-47 which had been registered G-BGCE prior to export to the United States. It was headed after overhaul to McAllen, Texas for freight work.

The End

By February 1982 only six of the original 52 ex-USAF C-47s acquired by Aero American remained at Ryan Field, all the others having been sold on or parted out. That month those six aircraft (N87626/627/643/649/665/666) were re-registered to associated company Acme Aircraft Company of Tucson. By May 1984 these too had been scrapped and having finally processed their extensive C-47 inventory, Aero American was closed down.

The writer's final visit to Ryan Field took place a year later, in May 1985, which sadly confirmed the demise of Aero American. Where once had stood this vibrant hub of C-47 activity, all was now desolate and deserted, every trace of Aero American and its activities having disappeared. For the record, of the 52 C-47s the company had acquired in 1961, 22 had been rebuilt and sold on, and 30 parted out and scrapped. In addition, over the years, many more DC-3s and C-47s had been traded, overhauled, modified and repaired at Ryan Field, which has certainly earned its place in DC-3 history.

C-47s REGISTERED TO AERO AMERICAN CORP

N Number	*Constructors Number*	*Disposal*
N87623	34195	B-241 Far Eastern Air Transport
N87624	9147	Parted out
N87625	4858	Parted out
N87626	9988	Parted out
N87627	13660	Parted out
N87628	19747	North Cay Airways
N87629	20749	North Cay Airways
N87630	25449	N395R Midwest Air Freighters
N87631	25678	N1346 Midwest Aviation
N87632	26783	Parted out
N87633	32546	CP-729 Aerolineas Abaroa
N87634	32678	Parted out
N87635	32762	Parted out
N87636	33612	TI-1042C A.Carillo Ltda
N87637	34295	CF-TFV Reindeer A/S
N87638	7390	N569R Island Creek Coal Co
N87639	9198	Parted out
N87640	9633	World Weather Service
N87641	10193	Parted out
N87642	11835	Parted out
N87643	13060	Parted out
N87644	19627	C-GNOA Millardair
N87645	19661	C-GABG Air Brazeau
N87646	19772	Parted out
N87647	20457	N169AP Pan Am UAR Oil Co
N87648	20563	Parted out
N87649	20627	Parted out
N87650	20833	C-GZOF Contact Airways
N87651	25521	Parted out
N87652	25534	Flightways Corp
N87653	25568	Parted out
N87654	25659	C-GABH Air Brazeau
N87655	26030	ZK-CQA James Aviation
N87656	26136	Parted out
N87657	26360	OB-PBO-676 Faucett
N87658	26602	Parted out
N87659	26631	Parted out
N87660	26815	C-GABI Air Brazeau
N87661	26828	CF-AAL Austin Airways
N87662	26917	Parted out
N87663	27141	Parted out
N87664	32529	C-GGCS Millardair
N87665	32572	Parted out
N87666	32589	Parted out
N87667	32638	Parted out
N87668	33028	Parted out
N87669	33126	Parted out
N87670	33176	Parted out
N87671	34340	Parted out
N87672	34360	ZK-CHV Airland NZ Ltd
N87673	34367	Parted out
N87674	34404	Parted out

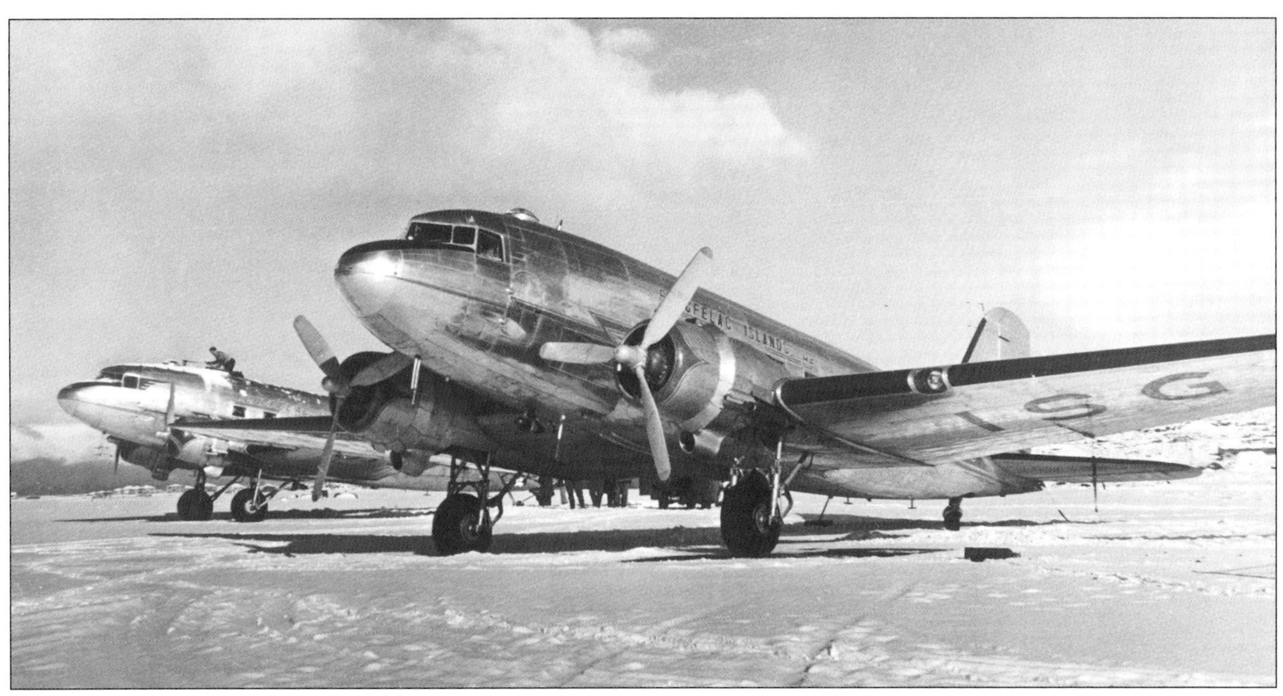

Several C-47s were converted by Scottish Aviation for Flugfelag Islands HF/Iceland Airways, two of which including TF-ISG (c/n 12482) are seen here in the immediate post-war scheme. *(via Arthur Pearcy)*

Chapter 8
Scottish Aviation Limited & the Douglas Dakota 1945-1955

With special emphasis on the work carried out on behalf of British European Airways

by Peter J Marson

Scottish Aviation Limited was founded in 1935 by Group Captain David F McIntyre and the Marquess of Douglas & Clydesdale, both pioneer aviators. Land was acquired at Monkton, near Prestwick, and hangars, a small control tower and offices were constructed. The company began pilot training for the Royal Air Force in 1936 with a fleet of DH.82A Tiger Moths (as No.12 EFTS), later expanding to include navigation training with Avro Anson Is (No.1 AONS). Repair and overhaul facilities were added during the late 1930s. During the war, RAF Prestwick became the trans-Atlantic terminal for deliveries and ferry services.

At the end of the war, Scottish Aviation Ltd became one of the first post-war companies in Britain to use its facilities for the conversion of military aircraft for commercial use and very soon became the official repair, overhaul and conversion centre for the Douglas Aircraft Corporation. Among military types converted for civil use were the Consolidated Liberator, Supermarine Walrus, Stinson Reliant, Fairchild Argus, Beech Expediter and the Consolidated Catalina. During the first decade after World War Two, however, the Douglas Dakota and C-47 made up a substantial proportion of the conversions or overhauls carried out, with a total of 353 different examples passing through the workshops of Scottish Aviation, out of a total of over 1,000 airframes.

Aer Lingus was the first foreign airline to place an order post-war with Scottish Aviation, with its first two Dakotas arriving on 2nd December 1945 (EI-ACG & EI-ACI) for conversion to civil use, following on from the three for Scottish Aviation's own airline offshoot Scottish Airlines, which had been stored since the autumn of 1945, with the first two (G-AGWS & G-AGZF) registered on 18th December, followed by the third (G-AGZG) two days later. Orders during the first six months of 1946 were for KLM - Royal Dutch Airlines (three in January/February 1946), Transcontinental & Western Air (one in February), DDL - Danish Air Lines (two examples in February & May), three further Dakotas for Aer Lingus in April, four for the Portuguese Government on behalf of TAP - Transportes Aereos Portugueses in May/June 1946), one for American Overseas Airlines, followed by two for Fred Olsen Air Transport in Norway and one for Swiss Air Lines in June.

A SECTION OF OUR NO. 3 FACTORY

We have 1,000,000 sq. ft. of Factory space devoted to the overhaul and conversion of aircraft.

The efficiency of an organisation materially depends upon the skill and ability of its personnel. We are staffed by men who have experience in the construction and overhaul of Aircraft since the earliest days of the Aviation Industry. Our factory, fully equipped with the most modern machinery, is capable of accommodating aircraft of all sizes. Let us quote you for repairs, overhauls, conversions, annual C. of A. and servicing. We are able to undertake overhaul of engines and all ancillary equipment.

WE ARE THE AUTHORISED DOUGLAS REPAIR, OVERHAUL AND CONVERSION CENTRE FOR GREAT BRITAIN

3

SCOTTISH AVIATION LTD • PRESTWICK AIRPORT

TELEPHONE : PRESTWICK 7272 9 LINES

MAY-JUNE, 1947 AERONAUTICS 23

A Scottish Aviation advertisement from Aeronautics (May-June 1947) announcing that they are the authorised Douglas conversion centre for Great Britain.

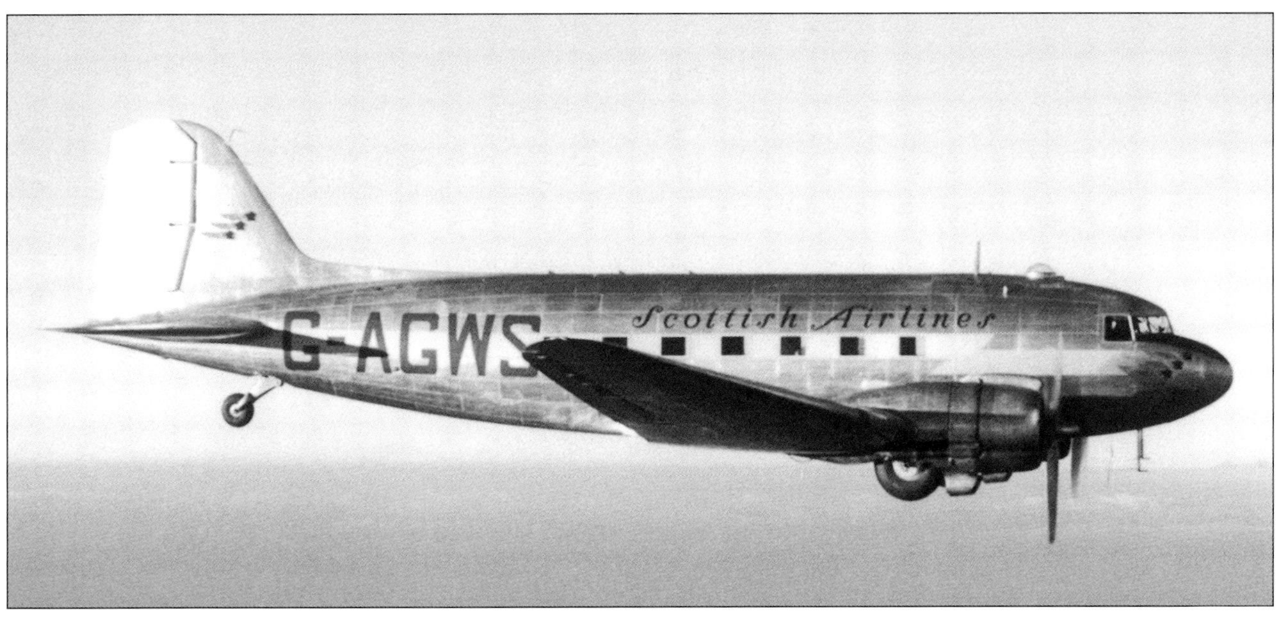

The first C-47 to arrive for civilian conversion for Scottish Airlines with sister company Scottish Aviation Limited was G-AGWS (c/n 6208) in September 1945. *(Don Hannah Collection)*

The only C-47 to be converted by Scottish Aviation Ltd for American Overseas Airlines was NC90908 (c/n 25228) in the spring of 1946. This photo shows the unusual presentation of the titles and the name "Flagship Nairobi" on the nose. *(Don Hannah Collection)*

Scottish Aviation converted a number of former military aircraft for Swiss Air Lines, the first of which, HB-IRF (c/n 26465), arrived in June 1946. *(Don Hannah Collection)*

Scottish Aviation converted many C-47s /Dakotas for use with British independent airlines, including several for Air Transport Charter (Channel Islands) Ltd. G-AJBG (c/n 25448) is illustrated here. *(via Jennifer Gradidge)*

Another British independent airline that took advantage of Scottish Aviation's expertise was Hornton Airways, whose Dakota G-AKLL (c/n 25450) arrived for civilian conversion in May 1947. *(via Jennifer Gradidge)*

Ethiopian Airlines was one of Scottish Aviation's customers in Africa, with ET-T-15 (c/n 13483) one of a batch of three aircraft for the airline that arrived at Prestwick for work in October 1946. *(via Jennifer Gradidge)*

2 Advertisements.  FLIGHT JUNE 5TH, 1947

Douglas C.47 becomes Luxury Air Liner

Scottish Aviation Douglas C.47 Conversions are operated with conspicuous success by leading Airline operators. We are the authorised Douglas Repair, Overhaul and Conversion Centre for Great Britain and can supply these aircraft in the following four categories:

(1) Freighters
(2) Standard 21-seater airliners
(3) De-luxe 21-seater airliners
(4) Executive models

Write for our illustrated brochure which gives full details of Douglas and other Conversions.

Scottish Aviation are fully equipped to undertake the overhaul of all aircraft, including airframes, engines and ancillary equipment. We have a fully approved Inspection Department and our manufacturing and servicing experience is at your disposal. We welcome any enquiry relating to aircraft conversions, repairs, annual C. of A. or any other servicing matter.

SCOTTISH AVIATION LIMITED

Telephone: Prestwick 7272 (9 lines) **Prestwick Airport** Telegrams: Aeronautics, Prestwick

I

A Scottish Aviation advertisement from Flight (5th June 1947) illustrating one of the more unexpected airlines for whom they had converted a Douglas C-47.

Construction, Conversions, Repairs and Overhauls

Scottish Aviation de luxe conversion of Douglas C-47

The capacity and unparalleled experience of Scottish Aviation are available to the airlines, the aircraft industry, and the private owner alike.

Aircraft converted and equipped by the Prestwick organisation are already flying for Aer Lingus, American Overseas Airlines, British Aircraft Services, D.D.L., K.L.M., Fred Olsen Aero Transport (Norway), Portuguese Airlines, Sabena, Scottish Airlines, Swissair, and T.W.A.

If you have a problem connected with the manufacture of components, or with conversions, overhauls, or aircraft repairs, it will probably pay you to refer it to us (telephone : Prestwick 7272).

SCOTTISH AVIATION

Scottish Aviation Ltd., founders of Prestwick Airport, are concerned solely with the development of aviation in its various branches

HEAD OFFICE : PRESTWICK, AYRSHIRE

Sole Conversion, Repair and Overhaul Centre in Great Britain for the Douglas Aircraft Co. Inc., Santa Monica, California

MARCH, 1947 AERONAUTICS 7

A Scottish Aviation advertisement from Aeronautics (March 1947) showing a "de-luxe" conversion of the Douglas C-47.

The first C-47 to be converted for the Royal Belgian Air Force was fitted out as a VIP aircraft for the King of the Belgians, seen here without a serial. It was listed in Scottish Aviation's records as "K.16357", and later became K-16 (c/n 20823) with the RBAF, having formerly been USAF 43-16357 which had arrived at Prestwick in March 1947. *(Scottish Aviation Ltd)*

A number of French independent airlines received Dakotas or C-47s from Scottish Aviation, one of which was Air Algerie's F-BCYO (c/n 12101), which was converted for civilian use in late 1947. *(Don Hannah Collection)*

One of the most interesting Dakota conversions undertaken by Scottish Aviation was that for Bharat Airways, which was fitted out with a pressurised capsule in the fuselage. The aircraft, G-AJLX (c/n 25483), which arrived at Prestwick in February 1947, was eventually delivered to India early in 1950! *(via Rod Simpson)*

As 1946 progressed, and no doubt encouraged by Scottish Aviation's standard of workmanship, airlines from other countries in Europe and even farther afield placed orders for the conversion of military Dakotas or C-47s to airline standards, with aircraft for Sabena – Belgian Airlines and Iceland Airways arriving in August and October respectively. Three for Ethiopian Airlines (at the time under Transcontinental & Western Air management) arrived in October of 1946 and one for Airways (India) in November. British airlines, both the newly formed state airline British European Airways (BEA) and several privately-owned British charter companies followed with orders for Dakota conversions in November and December. During the following years, airlines calling on Scottish Aviation's expertise to convert former military Dakotas to various airline configurations formed an impressive list, with airline companies from Africa, Asia and the Middle East, as well as further British independent companies, joining the queue for aircraft.

The first conversion work on former Royal Air Force Dakotas or United States Air Force C-47s for European air arms commenced in March 1947, when the first of fifteen aircraft arrived for the Belgian Air Ministry for use by the Royal Belgian Air Force. Similar work was undertaken for the French Government from 1947, for the Saudi Arabian Government from 1948, the United States Air Force in 1951, and for the Southern Rhodesian Air Force in 1954. During the Berlin air lift (1948-49) 72 Royal Air Force Dakotas were overhauled in Scottish Aviation's workshops. Conversions of military aircraft to private aircraft with a luxury interior were carried out for royalty, for example for the Belgian Royal Flight in 1947, the King of Greece (1950) and several Indian rulers (1947 and 1950). The aircraft for King Paul of Greece, for example, was fitted out as a luxurious 'flying palace' with plush chrome lounges, bed-sitting rooms, a refrigerated kitchen and every possible safety device. A complete list of customers who used Scottish Aviation Limited's workshops for Dakota conversion, overhaul or rework is appended to this article.

One of the most interesting conversions undertaken by Scottish Aviation must surely be what was the first ever "pressurised" Dakota. The Dakota in question was G-AJLX, which had originally arrived at Prestwick on 25th February 1947 for Bharat Airways. The aircraft was actually for the Indian Government which needed an aircraft with a special pressurised VIP compartment for the use of the Deputy Prime Minister (Sarder Patel) who suffered from severe health problems which meant that he was unable to fly above 1,000 feet. The pressurisation obviously caused a considerable headache for Scottish Aviation, as it was August 1949 – ie two and a half years later – before the aircraft was ready for testing.

Scottish Aviation's solution was to incorporate a pressure "sub-cabin" within the fuselage of the Dakota. This sub-cabin or "igloo" was situated in the rear half of the Dakota's cabin and had accommodation for the minister plus an attendant or secretary, including a divan bed and two adjustable seats. It was also fitted with a toilet compartment. The sub-cabin was elliptical in section and was fitted with an airlock or "trap" to permit entrance to and exit from the unit when under pressure. The entrance to the sub-cabin was at the aft end and there was a passage along the port-side exterior of the sub-cabin to allow movement between the front and rear of the main fuselage of the Dakota. The pressurised unit had four windows, and the windows in the Dakota's fuselage were modified to give a reasonable field of vision for the occupants of the sub-cabin.

Scottish Aviation contracted with Normalair Limited to produce the pressurisation equipment. When in use, the sub-cabin retained an atmospheric pressure of 1,000 feet up to an actual height of 8,000 feet. A rate of ascent up to 2,400 feet per minute was permitted, and rate of descent up to 2,999 feet per minute. A further problem that had to be solved was that of flying at such low altitudes and in rain. Attention also had to be paid to cooling the pressure cabin in the warm climate of India. The newly developed air intakes were so designed to prevent the blower system from delivering water instead of air into the pressure cabin. The aircraft was operated by Bharat Airways for the Indian Government after delivery, but was not registered in India until April 1950. The Dakota was used for less than two years before being sold in the United States in February 1952.

The largest customer for Dakota conversion work was doubtless the UK state-owned airline BEA, who not only used the skills of Scottish Aviation's workforce in the early years, with sixteen aircraft either converted by Scottish Aviation or purchased from them after conversion between November 1946 and July 1950, but also for the radical modification of 38 aircraft between November 1950 and January 1952 from a Dakota III to a standardized "Pionair" configuration. Modification work from a standard Viking to "Admiral" configuration followed on in the years 1952-53.

British European Airways' Dakota fleet was acquired from a variety of sources, beginning with the aircraft handed down from British Overseas Airways Corporation's European Division as part of BEA's initial fleet in 1946. The original fleet transferred from BOAC to BEA in July to October 1946 consisted of twenty-three aircraft (although three were immediately transferred on for use by the United Nations organization UNRRA). By April 1947, with 27 aircraft in the fleet (20 at Northolt, two on loan from BOAC at Northolt, one of which was used for spares, two in use with Scottish Airlines and three cannibalized at Speke), BEA's Dakota IIIs were of four distinct types: These were referred to by the airline as the "18" (18-seater aircraft originally with BOAC, with four crew, two pilots, navigator and a radio officer), the "21A" (a 21-seater converted by Airwork Limited, with three crew, ie two pilots and a Radio Officer), the "21S" (a 21-seater converted by Scottish Aviation Limited, and also with a crew of three), and the "F1" aircraft, used for freight-carrying only, having been converted by Airwork Limited with minimum modifications only. The two 21-seater passenger types differed in the position of one of the three cargo holds – Number 1 hold was situated in both types on the starboard side forward of the radio officer's compartment, Number 2 hold was situated in both types in the former navigator's compartment, Number 3 hold in the Airwork conversions was opposite the main passenger entrance and the door between the pantry and the toilet, while in the Scottish Aviation conversion it was located aft of the toilet in the tail of the aircraft. Both these 21-seater types had the false forward bulkhead of the passenger cabin deleted to make room for the additional row of seats (all passenger aircraft at the time were in a 2+1 seat configuration). Although nominally of four main types, the 27 aircraft consisted in fact of thirteen variants of the basic Douglas DC-3/C-47/Dakota!

During 1947, BEA purchased five more Dakotas (G-AJHY to G-AJIC inclusive) from Scottish Aviation after conversion from military aircraft, for which £12,000 each was paid, followed by two for subsidiary Cyprus Airways (G-AKIJ & G-AKIK), with further aircraft bought from Scottish Aviation in 1948 (G-ALLI) and 1949 (G-ALYF). BEA had seven of the 18-seater ex-BOAC aircraft converted to 21-seaters in the years 1948 to 1950 (see note 1). BEA subsequently (in August 1950) awarded Scottish Aviation Limited a contract valued at £150,000 to modifiy all the 28 Dakotas in its fleet at the time to a standard configuration. The prototype conversion was undertaken by Scottish Aviation on one of their own aircraft (G-ALYF) which had arrived originally for civilian conversion on 28th December 1948. In fact it had been used as a source of spares until an aircraft was required for Scottish Aviation's own "Super Dak" project, at which time (March 1950) it was registered to Scottish Aviation, converted in record time and later demonstrated to BEA at Northolt.The aircraft was further modified according to BEA's specifications and completed in preliminary form on 26th September 1950, with the first flight taking place three days later. Further modifications were, however, deemed necessary. The Dakota was sent back to Scottish Aviation to be brought up to a revised production standard. Delays were then caused by technical difficulties and also labour troubles at Scottish Aviation's works. G-ALYF, christened "RMA Pionair", was bought by BEA on 9th December 1950, but it was not until 23rd February 1951 that the first "Pionair" was eventually delivered and accepted by BEA. By 31st March of that year four Pionairs had been delivered to the airline for the start of the summer timetable (G-ALYF, G-AMGD, G-AGJV & G-AGJW).

The modification to "Pionair" configuration was substantial. The aircraft was operated by two crew only. By the addition of VHF radio transmitters, the radio officer's position could be deleted. The passenger cabin was improved in comfort and the seating capacity increased to 32 by using a 2+2 layout. The cockpit was re-equipped with British instruments (which was later to cause problems when BEA tried to sell its aircraft within the USA!), and the whole structure of the Dakota was rebuilt. The fuselage was reskinned, the floor was lightened, with plywood replacing the original metal, and integral airsteps were added to the passenger door. A small number of aircraft (ten) were modified to "Pionair Leopard" standard as convertible passenger-cargo aircraft, with the retention of the cargo-door. Folding seats were provided for an extra crew member in the cockpit and for a steward aft of the passenger entrance door. The Pionairs were fitted out with a red carpet, grey leather upholstered chairs, grey sidewalls and a white ceiling. Light catering equipment could be carried without modification, but if full catering equipment was needed, the rearmost double-seat chair on the port side had to be removed. Freight could be carried in the rear of the cockpit (26 cubic feet), and in the three freight holds (total 67 cubic feet), and a toilet was standard to the rear of the passenger entrance door. Baggage could be loaded through the small door to the rear of the passenger door (see drawing). The Pionair had a maximum take-off weight of 12,700 kilos and could carry a payload of 2,970 kilos up to 305 nautical miles, or 1,627 kilos up to 1,191 nautical miles. The block speed was 126 knots in the former configuration (with maximum payload), or 136 knots in the latter (with maximum fuel). This performance compared very favourably with the standard Douglas Dakota/C-47 (if there was such an aircraft!). BEA estimated that the annual savings from the Pionair conversion would be about £100,000 (in 1950 figures).

BEA delivered its fleet to Scottish Aviation at Prestwick for Pionair conversion between 5th November 1950 (G-AMGD & G-AGJV) and 10th April 1952 (G-AGZD). Eight additional aircraft were purchsed during this period for Pionair conversion (see note 2).

During the first half of the 1950s, Scottish Aviation Limited's work on aircraft other than Dakotas increased, but much work on the type was carried out nevertheless. In 1951-52, a large number of United States Air Force C-47s were sent to Prestwick at regular intervals for overhaul and rework by Scottish Aviation. The first of the nineteen aircraft – virtually all from various bases around Europe – arrived on 17th May 1951 (43-15346), followed by 44-76594 on 18th May. During the course of 1951, seven more USAF C-47s arrived, with this overhaul work continuing during 1952.

During 1952-53, Aden Airways' fleet of Dakotas was ferried to Prestwick at intervals for conversion from 32-seaters to 40-seaters. The decision to award the contract to Scottish Aviation for this work had been made in November 1951. The extra seating capacity was needed to be able to offer lower fares on services within the Aden Protectorate and to nearby African destinations such as Djibouti, Hargeisa, Berbera and Dire Dawa. The

The tasteful interior of the Dakota aircraft converted for British European Airways as "Pionairs" by Scottish Aviation Limited. The aircraft seated 32 passengers in a 2+2 configuration with storage racks for light baggage and a carpeted cabin floor. *(British Airways Archives)*

A USAF C-47 that was overhauled at Prestwick was 44-76594 (c/n 32926), which arrived in May 1951 and is seen here at an unknown location in the early 1960s. *(Brian Stainer/APN)*

During the early 1950s, Scottish Aviation gained a contract for the overhaul of USAF C-47s in Europe. Among the many aircraft overhauled were 44-76600 (c/n 32932) in June 1952, seen here at an airshow at a later date. *(PJ Marson Collection)*

Among the air forces for whom Scottish Aviation provided aircraft was the Royal Rhodesian Air Force, with eight aircraft supplied during 1954-55, the first few listed as for "Southern Rhodesia", with the later ones for the Royal Rhodesian Air Force. Aircraft 153 (c/n 33410) arrived at Prestwick in September 1954 for rework. *(via Jennifer Gradidge)*

modifications included moving the radios so that the radio officer could be dispensed with, thus enabling the forward bulkhead to be moved forward and the fitting of one extra row of four seats forward. At the rear of the aircraft the toilet was repositioned to enable a further full row of four seats to be installed. The first aircraft to arrive at Prestwick was VR-AAD on 14th February 1952, followed by VR-AAC (20th April), VR-AAA (5th June), VR-AAE (30th July), VR-AAF (23rd October) and VR-AAB (14th January 1953). Other conversion work on Dakotas (apart from the military work mentioned above) involved one aircraft from British West Indian Airways and an aircraft for Williamson's Diamonds in Tanganyika, both arriving in May 1953, plus a single Dakota for Arab Airways in September 1953. With Dakota work slowing down overall, Scottish Aviation received a major contract from Aer Lingus in 1955 for modification work on the whole of their Dakota fleet (with Viscounts taking over the bulk of the passenger work). EI-AFC was the first of the fleet to arrive on 5th February 1955, with two aircraft following in March, five in April and four in May, with the final one (EI-ACE) received at Scottish Aviation's facility at Prestwick on 3rd June 1955. Scottish Aviation was kept busy otherwise during the period 1953 to 1955 with such types as the Viking, York and even with the fitting of cabin equipment in Air India's Super Constellations.

Scottish Aviation Limited also produced aircraft of its own design, namely the Pioneer and Twin Pioneer in the 1950s and later, in the 1970s, bought the production rights to the Beagle Bulldog trainer and later the Handley-Page Jetstream light transport, in addition to their work in overhauling and reworking other aircraft types. Unfortunately the problems involved in the production and marketing of the former Handley-Page Jetstream resulted in Scottish Aviation going bankrupt in 1977 and then being merged into British Aerospace.

List of customers who contracted with Scottish Aviation Limited for work on Douglas Dakota/C-47 aircraft during the period 1945-1955 (in order of first aircraft arrival in each area)

The registrations and owners given are as at arrival at Scottish Aviation Ltd, Prestwick.

Date/registration of first aircraft		*Customer*	*Total aircraft for customer*
EUROPEAN AIRLINES			
02Dec45	EI-ACG	Aer Lingus	15
27Jan46	PH-TBR	KLM	4
12Mar46	OY-DDA	DDL	2
03May46	CS-TDF	TAP	4 (note 3)
24Jun46	LN-NAD	Fred Olsen Air Transport	2
29Jun46	HB-IRF	Swiss Air Lines	4
07Aug46	OO-CBK	SABENA	5
07Oct46	TF-ISG	Iceland Airways	5
18Oct46	SX-BBC	Hellenic Airlines	4
05Jan50	TF-RVM	Icelandic	2
			Total: 47
BRITISH AIRLINES			
Sep45	G-AGWS	Scottish Aviation Ltd	16 (note 4)
02Oct46	G-AIRG	British Aviation Services	4
30Nov46	G-AJIC	British European Airways	51
12Dec46	G-AJAZ	Westminster Airways	2
Jan47	G-AJBG	Air Transport Charter (CI)	4
28Mar47	G-AJVY	London Express Newspapers	1 (note 5)
09Apr47	G-AKNB	John Jamieson	1 (note 6)
16Apr47	G-AKSM	Sivewright Airways	3
28May47	G-AKLL	Hornton Airways	1
26Jun47	G-AKJN	Ciro's Aviation	1
06Aug47	G-AKNM	Fairey Aviation	1 (note 5)
06May48	G-AJZX	Field Aircraft Services	1 (note 7)
30Jul48	G-AGHN	Guinea Air Traders	1 (note 6)
21Dec48	G-AGNG	Blue Line Airways	1
29Jun54	G-AMZC	Manx Airlines	2
			Total: 90
REST of WORLD AIRLINES			
16Feb46	NC54548	Transcontinental & Western	2
Apr46	NC90908	American Overseas Airlines	1
21Oct46	ET-T-15	Ethiopian Airlines	5
20Nov46	G-AJBB	Airways (India)	1
25Jan47	F-BEFL	Soc Transatlantique	6
Feb47	NC74139	D W Conner	1 (note 8)
25Feb47	G-AJLX	Bharat Airways (India)	1 (see text)
15Apr47	G-AKII	Cyprus Airways	4
08Aug47	F-BCYO	Air Algérie	5
09Oct47	SR-AAD	Syrian Airways	2
26Nov47	F-BEFF	Aigle Azur	4
09Jan48	F-BEIH	Ste Anonyme Air Nolis	3
24Mar48	F-BEIQ	Air Maroc	1
28May48	G-AGHE	BOAC	5 (note 9)
26Sep48	G-AGFX	Westair Transport (Pty) Ltd	5 (note 10)
05Oct48	VT-AZU	Indian Overseas	2
Jan49	F-BEIZ	Alpes Provence	1
05Mar50	EP-AAJ	Iranian Airways	1 (note 11)
03Mar51	N94528	Mallard Air Services	4
18Aug51	SU-AHO	Fox & Sons	2
14Feb52	VR-AAD	Aden Airways	6 (see text)
25Sep52	N54333	Republic Aviation	1
01May53	VR-ABJ	British West Indian Airways	1 (note 12)
20Sep53	TJ-ABR	Arab Airways	1
			Total: 65
FOREIGN AIR ARMS & GOVERNMENTS			
12Mar47	"K-16357"	Belgian Government (RBAF)	15 (note 13)
20Mar47	KK107	French Government (FAF)	15
13Oct47	39109	United States Navy	1
20Nov47	G-AKJH	Maharaja of Baroda (India)	1
30Jul48	KN476	Royal Air Force	75 (note 14)
14Dec48	SA-T-10	Saudi Arabian Government	3
May49	KN672	Royal Hellenic Air Force	7
15Aug49	TS423	Ministry of Supply	1
22Jun50	VT-CMZ	The Newab of Bhopal	1
29Oct50	KN542	King of Greece	1
17May51	43-15346	United States Air Force	19 (note 15)
27Apr54	975	Royal Canadian Air Force	3
12Jul54	SR.25	Southern Rhodesian AF	3 (see below)
31May55	RRAF154	Royal Rhodesian Air Force	5 (see above)
			Total: 150
NON-CLASSIFIED			
19May53	VR-TBI	Williamson's Diamonds	1

Grand total: 353 aircraft (Sep45-31Dec55)

Notes:-

1 Work on the conversion of former BOAC 18-seater aircraft to 21-seaters for BEA involved G-AGZB, G-AGHS & G-AGHJ in February 1948, G-AGZC (February 1949) and G-AGJW & G-AGIZ (May 1950). G-ALCB, which also arrived in May 1950 for BEA, never in fact entered service and was scrapped in December of that year.

2 The eight aircraft purchased by BEA for Pionair conversion were G-AGHM, G-AIWD & G-AKJH (from Skyways), G-AKNB, G-ALPN & G-AMFV (from Field Aircraft Services), G-AMDZ from Airtech and G-AJDE from Astra Aircraft. The two Dart-powered Dakotas (G-ALXN & G-AMDB) were originally converted from the military by Scottish Aviation Ltd. G-ALXN (KJ934) arrived at Prestwick on 3rd February 1949, but was not delivered to BEA until 22nd September 1950, while G-AMDB (KJ993) arrived for conversion for BEA on 24th (or 27th) July 1950, with acquisition by BEA on 10th October 1950. The two aircraft were then converted to Dart power by Fields and flew with the turboprop engines from mid-1951 until August 1953, after which they were converted to standard Pionair Leopards with Pratt & Whitneys.

3 Owner listed as Portuguese Government.

4 Scottish Aviation Ltd aircraft were in most cases operated by subsidiary company Scottish Airlines. Scottish Airlines operated scheduled services on behalf of the following airlines during the period in question: British European Airways, KLM, Air France, COBETA (Belgium), Luxembourg Airlines and Hellenic Airlines. One aircraft (G-ALYF) which arrived originally on 28th December 1948 was later converted to the prototype "Pionair" for BEA (see text). The two aircraft that arrived in February 1950 (G-ALXO & KN660) were converted for Aer Lingus and the Greek Air Force respectively.

5 These aircraft were operated by Westminster Airways.

6 John Jamieson operated as Guinea Air Traders. The second aircraft arrived under the latter ownership. Neither aircraft was registered in New Guinea or Australia.

7 This aircraft was converted on behalf of British Nederland Airways.

8 February 1947 is actually the arrival date as G-AJLC.

9 Of the five aircraft, the first was converted/reworked for Malayan Airways, the next aircraft was in fact sold on to Scottish Aviation, who sold it on to North-West Airlines (Isle of Man), the third was for Hong Kong Airways and the last two were for East African Airways.

10 Westair Transport was a South African airline.

11 This aircraft had been converted earlier and came to SAL for overhaul.

12 This aircraft was modified for Aden Airways, but the owner on arrival was listed as BWIA, despite the Aden registration!

13 "357" is the 'last 3' of the USAF serial 43-16357, K-16 is the Belgian serial.

14 72 of these aircraft were during the Berlin Air Lift, the remainder September 1949 onwards.

15 The majority of the C-47s were allocated to AFE Burtonwood at the time, while others were with AFE Bovingdon, AFE Orly, Upper Heyford or HQO London.

Acknowledgements:
Original listing from Scottish Aviation Limited via David Reid & Jennifer Gradidge, with additions from Tom Macfadyen, British Airways Museum & Archives and "Red Sea Caravan" (Dacre Watson).

DC-2-112 NC13733 (c/n 1259) of General Air Lines. The photo is dated October 1934, the date of the aircraft's delivery! General Air Lines was formed by Eastern Air Transport in 1934, but taken over by Eastern Air Lines in December of the same year. This DC-2 ended up in Australia, where it was operated by the Air Force and later Australian National Airways. It eventually crashed with New Holland Airways in April 1947. (Douglas Aircraft Co)

Chapter 9
Civil Photo Gallery

When DC-3 flying was luxury travel! This photo shows part of the 12-passenger interior of a United Air Lines DC-3 in 1937.
(McDonnell Douglas via Harry Gann)

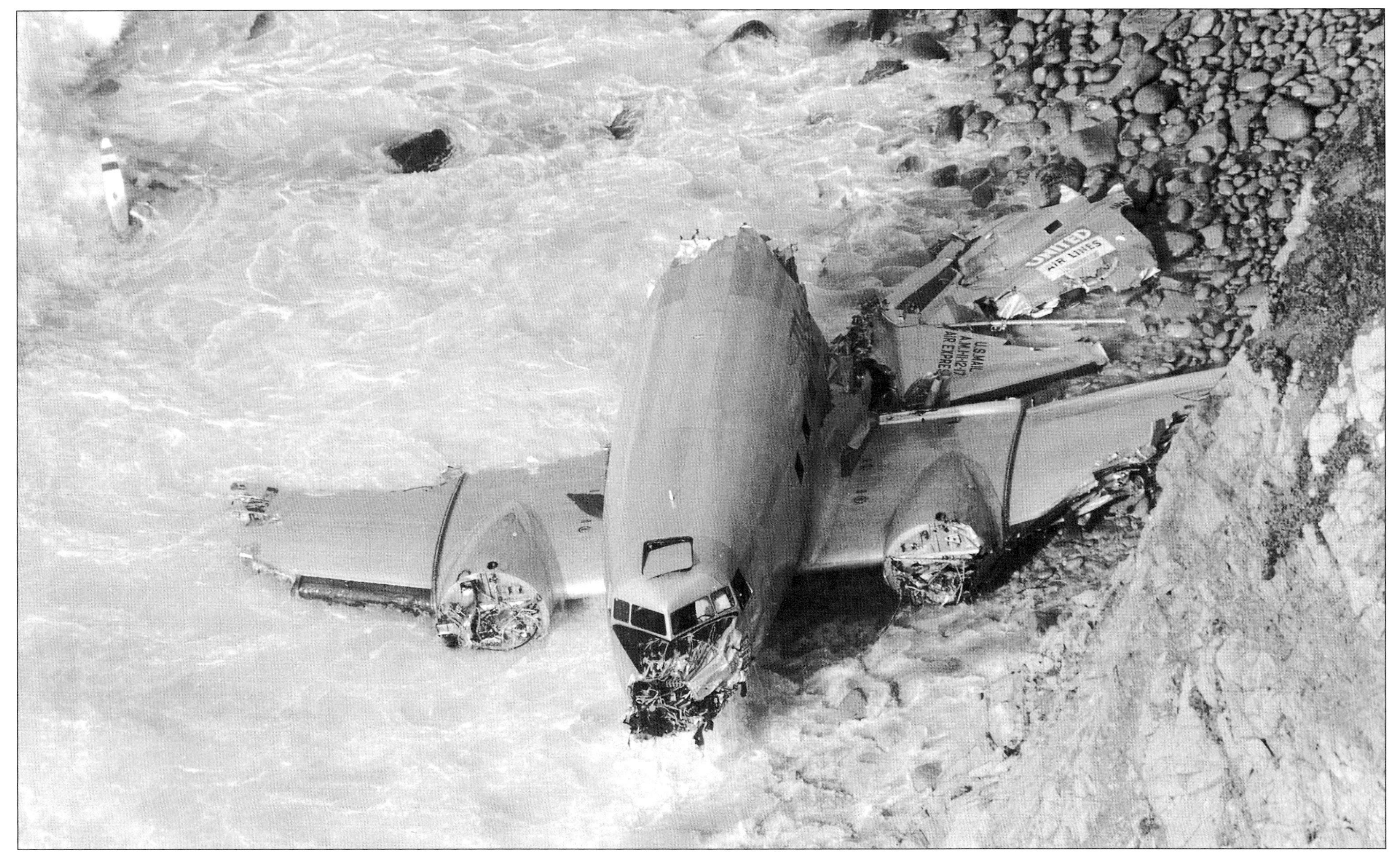

DC-3 NC16066 (c/n 1906) of United Air Lines was lost and ran short of fuel on 29th November 1938. Fortunately the aircraft was landed in the sea off the rugged coastlaine at Point Reyes, California without loss of life. (William T Larkins Collection)

A line-up of Ceskoslovenska Letecka Spolecnost - CLS DC-2s and DC-3s after they were taken over by Lufthansa in August 1939. The aircraft visible include D-AAIE to AAIH (DC-3s) and in the distance D-AAIB & AAID (DC-2s). *(Lufthansa via Don Hannah Collection)*

KLM's fleet of DC-2s and DC-3s in their high visibility scheme with the large "Holland" insignia taken in the autumn of 1939. *(Flight via Mike Hooks)*

Part of KLM's large fleet of Dakotas in the post-war period (probably circa 1947-48) with the aircraft in various stages of repainting. Aircraft visible include PH-TDU and PH-TAY in the new colour-scheme of the era, while in the earlier scheme are PH-TBM, TCW & TCK, some of the others are without KLM titling. In the centre background is an Aero Holland aircraft. (KLM via Mike Hooks)

A few former Linee Aeree Italiane - LAI Dakotas continued to fly for a few years with Alitalia after the take-over in October 1957, including I-LORO (c/n 4297) seen here. (Alitalia via Mike Hooks)

An early user of the C-47 for aerial survey work with a magnetometer was the Aero Service Corporation of Philadelphia, whose NC9032H (c/n 6353) is seen here flying over opencast mining activity in the late 1940s. *(Aeroplane)*

Seen at Kai Tak, Hong Kong in Far East Air Transport colours is B-257 (c/n 19950). The photo was probably taken in 1969 or 1970. The Dakota was destroyed by fire in a rocket attack on Phnom Penh in January 1975. *(FE Naylor)*

One of many DC-3s flown by oil companies over the years was this immaculate example used by CALTEX in Indonesia. PK-PAA (c/n 20832) has received the modified cowling and undercarriage door kit marketed by the Garrett Corporation in the 1960s. The photo was taken at Singapore-Paya Lebar in February 1967. *(RJ Hobbs)*

A close-up showing the cowling and undercarriage door modification introduced by the Garrett Corporation for the US market, looking very similar to the Air France "Maximiser" modification (see photo of F-BEIE on page 90). *(Garrett Corporation)*

Displaying its BOAC connections, VR-OAH (c/n 13384) is shown in service with Borneo Airways in 1963. After transfer to Malaysian Airways and later Malaysia-Singapore Airlines, the aircraft was destroyed in a rocket attack in February 1975 at Phnom Penh. *(Aeroplane)*

A highly modified Dakota, A2-ADL (c/n 33581) of Aerial Surveys Botswana. The aerial survey equipment, comprising nose and tail magnetometers as well as wing-tip housings, was fitted at Toronto in 1982 and removed on the aircraft's return to the USA. It was converted subsequently to a BT-67 in June 1992. *(MAP)*

Tunis Air F-BAXV (c/n 12380) was formerly an Air France aircraft. The photograph was taken in the early 1950s, prior to its re-registration in Tunisia. The Royal Air Force Shackleton in the background suggests that this photograph might have been taken in Malta. *(Bill Grundy)*

Formerly G-AGGA of BOAC, Air Outre Mer's F-OACA (c/n 6241) was photographed by Roger Caratini as the aircraft flew over the delta of the Red River at Tonkin, near Hanoi, in 1949/50. Roger sometimes co-piloted this Dakota, having formed the airline concerned. *(Roger Caratini)*

Formerly used by both BOAC and BEA, HR-LAG (c/n 12450) was flying for LANSA of Honduras in 1971. The aircraft had been withdrawn at La Ceiba by 1974. *(John M Davis)*

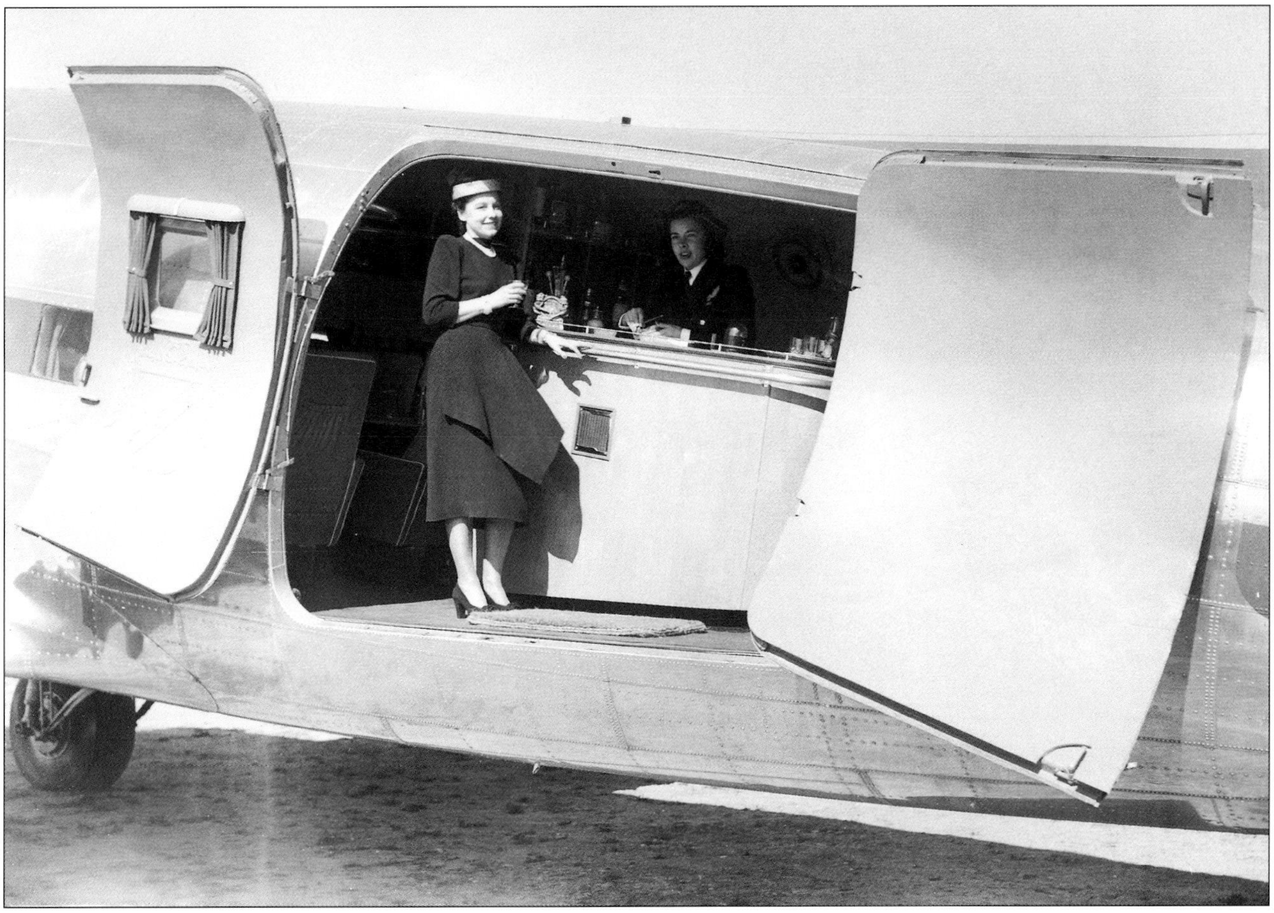

Post-war luxury in England is illustrated by the bar on board Ciro Aviation's G-AIJD in April 1948. *(Flight 21386s via PJ Marson)*

This former DST N67000 (c/n 1498) has been much modified, with panoramic windows, airstairs and undercarriage doors. It had a long life, ending up as ZS-DAK, although unfortunately is no longer flying. *(via Jennifer Gradidge)*

Super DC-3 N16012 (c/n 43193) "Capitaliner Cotton Queen". The photograph was taken in Pittsburgh, PA on 11th April 1953, a year after Capital Airlines sold the aircraft to the United States Steel Corporation. *(Ken Sumney)*

A large number of C-47s flew with Aeroflot during the post-war years alongside the Russian Li-2 version. Many carried the olive drab scheme prior to the introduction of the all-over silver scheme of the 1950s, including CCCP-L976. This photo was taken in Switzerland and the aircraft helpfully still has the former USAF serial 349071 on the fin. *(via Mike Hooks)*

A rare photo – the original is in colour – of a Czechoslovak Airlines DC-3, OK-XDH (c/n 19587) taken at Vienna-Schwechat in June 1955. *(David Lucabaugh Collection)*

Former C-47B 44-77107 (c/n 33439) after conversion to a TS-82, in service with Aeroflot as CCCP-L1201. The aircraft was used for Ash-82FN engine tests. Note the right-hand passenger door fitted to bring the US-built aircraft into line with Russian-built aircraft. *(via Nigel Eastaway, RART)*

Polar Aviation Li-2 CCCP-N496 pictured after it stalled on take-off from Mirny in Antarctica in February 1958. *(via Nigel Eastaway, RART)*

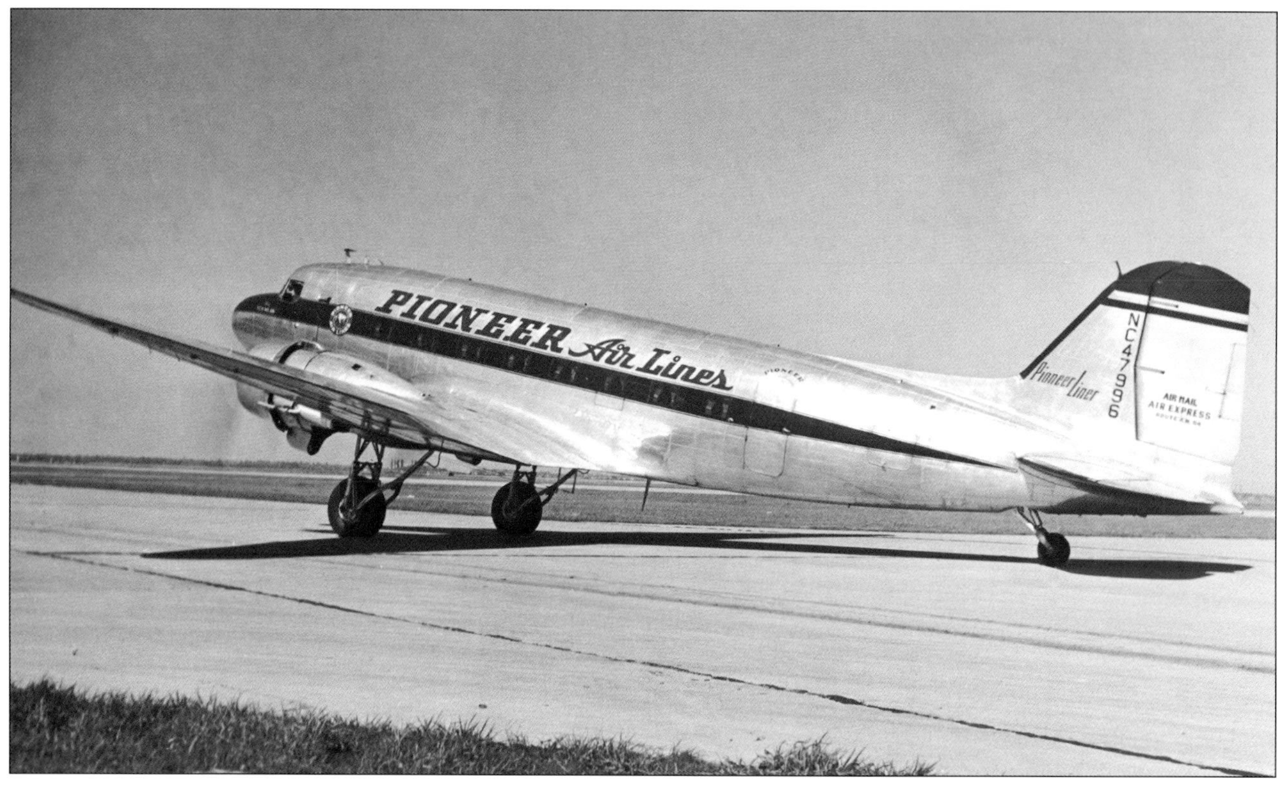

DC-3 "Pioneer Liner" NC47996 (c/n 4422) of Pioneer Air Lines, named "Ben Milam". The company operated DC-3s from Dallas, Texas in the immediate post-war period. This aircraft was returned to the United States Air Force as a C-117C. *(Douglas Aircraft Co)*

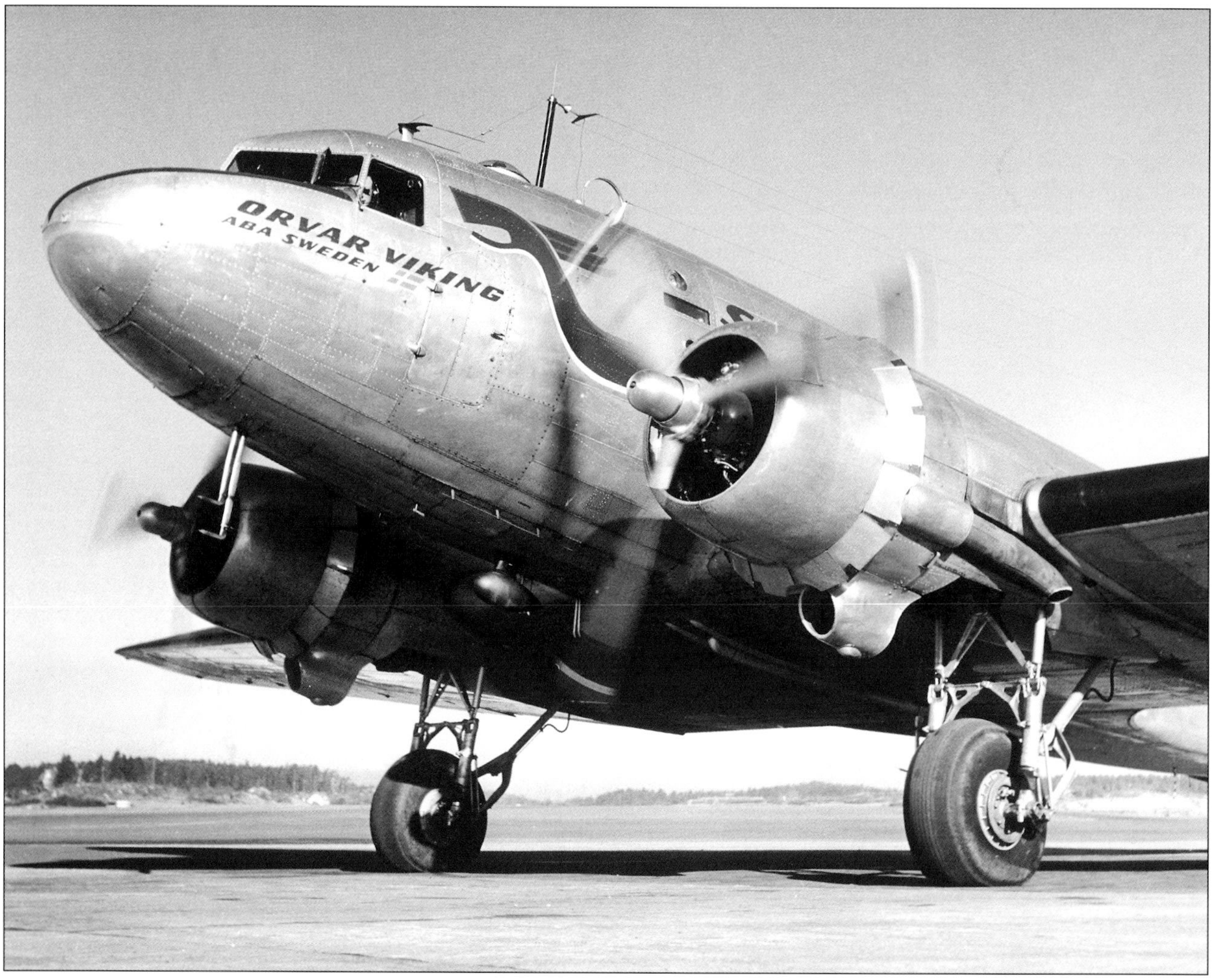

DC-3 SE-BBO (c/n 13637) in the early colours of the Scandinavian Airlines System, when the constituent company name was still carried on the aircraft – here Sweden's ABA, with the name "Orvar Viking". The photo was probably taken in 1948/49. *(SAS photo no.RA7)*

G-AGHK (c/n 9406) showing the camouflaged scheme used by BOAC with the civil registration in black and "speedbird" (also in black) on the nose. Note the BOAC Lodestar painted in a similar scheme in the background. *(via Jennifer Gradidge)*

Chapter 10 BOAC & its Dakotas

by Peter J Marson

This article relates the complete history of one stage of an individual aircraft's life and also illustrates the amount of information that is available today – if one knows where to look.

BOAC operated more Dakotas than any other type of aircraft during the whole of its existence. A total of 81 flew under the "Speedbird" insignia during the years 1943 to 1950, excluding the five pre-war built DC-3s leased from KLM during the early years of the second world war (from August 1940) and examples purchased on behalf of BOAC's Associated Companies in the 1950s.

The first Dakota to enter service was G-AGFX on 12th March 1943 on the route from Leuchars in Scotland across the North Sea to Stockholm in Sweden, followed by services to Lisbon and Gibraltar or Fez from Bristol-Whitchurch or Chivenor, and in the Middle East and Africa from Cairo. A vast network of services was built up with during the years 1943-1946, with the Dakotas replacing particularly Lockheed Lodestars and Armstrong Whitworth Ensigns on Middle Eastern and African routes radiating from Cairo to West Africa (Takoradi), Kenya (Nairobi) and British India (Karachi). In Europe, services were flown from Whitchurch to Portugal, Spain, Gibraltar and North Africa, and from Croydon (or at times from Whitchurch) to Rineanna (Shannon). With the end of the war, many BOAC long-haul services were first flown with Dakotas, initially from Hurn (Bournemouth) until 14th June 1946, and then from Northolt or the new London Airport (Heathrow) to the Middle East, Far East and Africa, until replaced by four-engined equipment. The peak of BOAC's Dakota use was recorded in June 1946, with 69 aircraft in service. At this time, the main Dakota routes were from London to Cairo, Accra, Lydda, Lisbon and Gibraltar, and from Cairo to Accra.

The disposal of BOAC's Dakotas began with the transfer of three aircraft to Railway Air Services on 27th July 1946 for use on British domestic routes, followed by twenty-one to the European Division, which became British European Airways during the period 1st August to 2nd October 1946. Other Dakotas were written off or sold abroad, but twenty-four were still on BOAC's books in March 1949, the number being halved by 14th October of that year. The last BOAC mainline Dakota service was flown from Cairo to London on 5th December 1946, while the last services operated under BOAC flight numbers and British registration were by the six aircraft used on local services radiating from Aden to Cairo, Nairobi and Addis Ababa in January 1950. Although these six aircraft were transferred to the new Aden register on 1st February 1950, they continued to use BOAC flight numbers until the late spring of 1950. The final aircraft of BOAC's wartime Dakota acquisitions was sold on 2nd June 1950, after which the only aircraft to fly with BOAC titles were the two aircraft acquired in January 1952 to fly on behalf of the Kuwait Oil Company/British International Airlines.

BOAC's Dakotas carried a variety of colour-schemes during their service with the airline. During the years 1943-45 the aircraft flew mainly in camouflage with the British registration underlined in red, white and blue, or overall silver with a "Speedbird" on the nose, large registration and very small BOAC titling (in full – see illustration). For a period during 1944-46 some aircraft carried four or five letter codes, roundels and their previous RAF serials as civilian aircraft were not allowed to overfly France. Variations of the overall silver scheme with "Speedbird" and airline titling remained in use until the last scheduled BOAC Dakota services in 1950. The later well-known white top and dark blue cheatline with two blue lines across a white fin appeared on the aircraft flown on behalf of the Kuwait Oil Company, and while the blue fin with two white lines scheme introduced in 1957 appeared on BOAC's Associated Companies' Dakotas, it is believed that no Dakota actually flew with BOAC titles in this scheme.

In order to give a flavour of BOAC's Dakota operations over the years, the history of one aircraft has been chosen that flew regularly for the company for over five years –namely G-AGHE which served from April 1943 until May 1948. G-AGHE, the former FD827 (c/n 9189) fitted with two Pratt & Whitney R1830-92 (C3G) engines and Hamilton Hydromatic 3-blade propellers was delivered from the USA to Prestwick on 28th April 1943, continuing to Whitchurch on 30th April, where pre-service modifications were carried out. (Most BOAC Dakotas were modified for service at Croydon, with a few examples being sent to Whitchurch). Pre-service modifications began on 1st May and G-AGHE was recorded as being serviceable for a "compass loopswing" on 18th May 1943, with a one-year Certificate of Airworthiness issued on the 19th. The Dakota entered service on 21st May at Whitchurch, with the BOAC Operations Chart number "7". (All aircraft in BOAC's fleet were recorded by Chart number, with regular cross-reference updates by aircraft name or registration. Dakotas were cross-referenced by registration, whereas the Lodestars, for example, were cross-referenced by name during this period). G-AGHE's first service was from Whitchurch to Lisbon and Gibraltar on BOAC flight 7M91. (All BOAC's services at the time were designated by a number or numbers plus letter, the latter denoting the geographical area, followed by a number beginning with '1' for the inaugural service and continuing until the routeing was changed. G-AGHE's first service was therefore the 91st service on route 7M). The Dakota was turned round and returned to Whitchurch, from where it flew service 13M2 on 2nd June to Lisbon, Gibraltar and Fez, arriving on the 3rd and returning the same day, with arrival back in the UK on 4th June. The following day 'GHE deputized for one of the leased KLM DC-3s on BOAC's flight 1L575 from Whitchurch to Lisbon, but did not return until 11th June. Another service to Lisbon and Gibraltar (flight 7M102) was then flown, outward on 12th June, and returning as 6M102 on the 15th.

The Dakota was then taken out of service until 19th June while auxiliary fuel-tanks were fitted. Service 13M14 to Lisbon and Fez via Lyneham and Chivenor was taken out on the same day, returning to the UK with service 14M14 on 21st–22nd June. G-AGHE next departed Whitchurch on 1st July with service 13M26. Calls were again made at Lyneham and Chivenor, and delays occurred en route, as Lisbon was not reached until 4th July. The Dakota was turned round on the same day and continued via Gibraltar back to England, arriving the following day. Further services on the same route were then flown: flight 13M30 on 6th July, arriving in Lisbon on the 7th and back to Whitchurch (7th–8th), followed by 13M34 on 9th July via Lyneham and Lisbon to Gibraltar which was reached on the 10th , then returning from Gibraltar direct to Whitchurch on 12th July as 14M34. Services 13M37 followed on 13th–14th July via Lyneham to Lisbon and Fez this time, returning on 15th–16th via Gibraltar and Bristol-Lulsgate to its base at Whitchurch. On the aircraft's return from the last-mentioned service, the auxiliary tanks and SBA (Standard Beam Approach) equipment were removed between the 17th and 21st, prior to the Dakota's delivery flight to its new base at Cairo via Lyneham, Lisbon, Gibraltar and one further stop (unspecified) as DM3 from 22nd to 25th July.

For nearly a month, G-AGHE appears to have sat on the ground at Cairo before making three supply flights Cairo-Khartoum-Asmara-Cairo with spare parts for the disabled Armstrong Whitworth Ensign "Everest" (G-AFZU). The Ensign had damaged its port elevator at Cairo (Almaza) on 19th August and had to await engineers and a new elevator. The three flights operated by 'GHE were designated 14E5AS (Cairo-Khartoum) on 21st August, return flight 8S + 9S the same day and 4R101S (Asmara-Cairo) on 22nd August. The "S" is each case presumably denoting "supplies" or "supplemental" flights , ie in addition to the normal scheduled services. The Dakota then started flying BOAC schedules from Cairo on 27th August with a service to Takoradi (West Africa) as 9T38, calling at Khartoum, El Geneina (night-stop – N/S) and Kano. After a further night-stop for aircraft and crew, 'GHE departed Takoradi on 29th August as 10T38 calling at Lagos (N/S), Maidugari (N/S), El Geneina and Khartoum (N/S), arriving back at Cairo on 1st September. (See timetable illustration). After a break of three days, the Dakota was in the air again on 5th September, flying a supplementary return schedule to Lydda (Palestine) as 3R102S and 4R102S. The Dakota then settled in to the more leisurely routine of flights 9T and 10T from Cairo outbound to Takoradi via Khartoum, El Geneina and Kano (normally over two days) and then four days return via Lagos, Maidugari, El Geneina and Khartoum. This schedule was flown ex-Cairo as 9T48 (28th October), and 10T48 (2nd November), followed by service 9T52 (11th November), returning with 10T52 ex-Takoradi on 13th November, 9T55 on 22nd November and 10T55 delayed to 27th November ex-Takoradi, and service 9T59 from Cairo on 6th December, returning with 10T5<u>8</u> from Takoradi on 8th December. A service to Khartoum and return via Asmara in each direction was then flown as flights 3R106AS and 4R106AS on the 15th of the month. After flying a further service to Takoradi, departing Cairo on 20th December as 9T63 and returning two days later as 10T63, the final service of the year for G-AGHE was an Adana schedule 1N91S, departing Cairo on 29th December and returning home to Cairo on 1st January 1944.

The year 1944

The new year started for Dakota G-AGHE with a final flight terminating at Takoradi, departing Cairo on 6th January as service 9T68, and returning as 10T68 on the 8th back to Cairo. The 9T/10T services were subsequently routed to Lagos or Accra, with one further flight carried out in January, departing Cairo on 20th January as 9T72 and returning from Lagos on the 25th as 10T72 (see timetable).

For the next four months, G-AGHE was used entirely on the services from Cairo to Accra or Lagos, which were also designated services 9T and 10T. The aircraft flew outbound via Wadi Halfa, Khartoum, El Geneina, Maidugari and Kano as service 9T, and departed Lagos in general three days later to Cairo as service 10T via the same intermediate points with the additional stop at El Fasher (between El Geneina and Khartoum). February's flights were 9T78 departing 10th February and 9T81 on the 22nd, followed by three in March. The first of these (9T84) departed Cairo on 5th March, but problems of over-revving on the engines after arrival from Accra at Lagos caused a delay in the return to Cairo from 7th March to 10th March. The aircraft arrived on flight 10T84 back at Cairo on 12th March. Service 9T88 went without problems on 16th March, arriving Accra two days later and continuing to Lagos, where the aircraft and crew had a break before returning with service 10T88 on 20th March with arrival back in Cairo on the 22nd. BOAC service 9T92 departed on the 30th of the month, this time via Lagos to Accra, with arrival on 1st April, returning to Lagos to night-stop until 3rd April when 'GHE took out service 10T92 back to Cairo, arriving two days later. The flights in April with G-AGHE continued in a

16/2/44

Dakota Timetable
Cairo/Takoradi

	G.M.T.		G.M.T.				G.M.T.		G.M.T.	
Monday	04.00	Thursday	04.00	dep	Cairo	arr	11.25			Wednesday
	07.45		07.15	arr	Wadi Halfa	dep	07.40			& Sunday
	08.15		08.15	dep	Wadi Halfa	arr	07.10			
	10.55		10.55	arr	Khartoum	dep	04.30			
	11.25		11.25	dep	Khartoum	arr	~~15.00~~	Tuesday	~~14.30~~	Saturday
	-		14.20	arr	El Fasher	dep	- 14.30		11.40 15.00	
	-		14.50	dep	El Fasher	arr	-		11.10	
	15.35		16.05	arr	El Geneina	dep	09.50		09.50	
			04.30	dep	El Geneina	arr	09.20		09.20	
			08.30	arr	Maidugari	dep	05.00		05.00	
Tuesday			09.00	dep	Maidugari	arr	14.35			Monday
Friday			11.00	arr	Kano	dep	12.15			Friday
			11.30	dep	Kano	arr	11.45	If terminated		
	If terminating		14.30	arr	Lagos	dep	08.00	Accra		
	at Accra		15.00	dep	Lagos	arr	10.30	08.30		Saturday
	16.30		-	arr	Accra	dep	-	07.00		Wednesday
			-	dep	Accra	arr	-			
			17.30	arr	Takoradi	dep	08.00			

Effective from 19/2/44

A sample timetable for the "Trans-Africa" service flown by BOAC Dakotas on services 9T/10T (Cairo-Accra or Takoradi) dated 19th February 1944. (BOAC file 6222)

similar vein , with the next departure from Cairo on 13th April (9T96) via Lagos to Accra and back to Lagos on the 15th. The return flight (10T96) departed on 17th April with only one night-stop (at El Geneina), and with arrival at Cairo on 18th April. A note on the Operations Chart gave the reason for this: overnight accommodation at El Geneina was very limited, so from 24th April all odd-numbered services were to operate 24 hours late to relieve the problem! Service 9T99 departed therefore on 25th April (instead of the originally planned 24th) to Lagos (N/S 26th–27th), then on to Accra (27th) and back to Lagos the same day. The planned departure on 29th April was, however, delayed with engine problems, resulting in night-stops both at El Geneina (29th–30th) and also at Wadi Halfa (30th–1st May), prior to arrival back at Cairo later on 1st May.

May's flights started with service 9T102, departing on 4th May and arriving at Lagos on 5th May for a night-stop before continuing via Accra on the 6th and back to Lagos. Departure was on 8th May from Lagos with arrival in Cairo on the 9th – a faster schedule being introduced from this flight at the request of Royal Air Force Transport Command. Dakota G-AGHE's next flight was 9T107 on 23rd May, arriving at Accra (direct – ie not via Lagos) on the 24th and continuing the same day to Lagos, where aircraft and crew stopped for three nights. The return flight (10T107) was further delayed at Khartoum, resulting in a further night-stop (28th–29th May), before returning to Cairo on the latter day. The final flight of this series departed Cairo as 9T112 on 8th June, with a night-stop at Khartoum (8th–9th) as no accommodation was available at El Geneina. A further (unscheduled) night-stop was made in Kano, before arriving in Accra on 10th June and continuing on to Lagos the same day. Departure from Lagos (as 10T112) was on 12th June, with the usual night-stop at El Geneina and arrival back at Cairo on 13th June. G-AGHE's CofA had actually expired on 18th May, but this was extended by one month to 18th June, so the aircraft was taken out of service after arrival at Cairo for overhaul, CofA renewal and other work, which lasted from 15th June until 23rd August 1944, with the CofA actually being renewed already on 30th June.

Dakota G-AGHE resumed BOAC services on 5th September with a service to Lagos (9T137) including a night-stop at El Geneina. Departure from Lagos for the return service (10T137) was on 9th September, again with one night-stop en route at El Geneina back to Cairo. For the next three months, the Dakota shuttled back and forth between Cairo and West Africa, with some flights going to Lagos and others to Accra. The next flights with 'GHE however, were not without problems: The service on 19th September from Cairo (Almaza) 9T141 went smoothly as far as the first stop at Wadi Halfa for the three crew and 15 passengers. The only item noticed was what appeared to be a small oil-leak on the top of the starboard engine nacelle. The crew experienced some difficulty restarting this engine at Wadi Halfa, but during run-up, everything seemed in order. About an hour after take-off, however, while en route to the next scheduled stop at Khartoum, the starboard engine started vibrating and running very rough. On checking the engine after landing, the sump filter was removed and found to contain quite a number of large flakes of white metal. The main filter was also checked and found to be choked with carbon and flakes of metal, and the filter itself had completely collapsed! This meant an engine change, so the passengers were off-loaded to wait for the subsequent flight to Accra. G-AGHE then departed Khartoum for Cairo as service 10T140R on 24th September. Then between Wadi Halfa and Cairo, a slight oil leak that had been noticed on the port engine seemed to be getting worse, with oil coming back over the mainplane and cowling. The Captain therefore decided to make a precautionary landing at Luxor at 09.15 (GMT). It was discovered on inspection that the exhaust push-rod cover of number 2 cylinder had cracked right across, the push-rod itself was bent and the whole engine covered in oil. As the Dakota was carrying a spare engine as cargo, RAF personnel at Luxor removed a push-rod cover and push-rod from the spare engine, fitted them in place of the broken items on 'GHE's port engine and cleaned and tested the engine, after which the crew and 15 passengers (who had spent most of the night at Luxor) continued on to Cairo at 04.45 on the morning of 25th September. It was assumed the damage had probably been caused originally by a large bird striking the aircraft during flight!

The Dakota next departed Cairo on 28th September (as 9T144), with night-stops at El Fasher and Kano to arrive in Accra on the last day of the month, then continuing on to Lagos, where the aircraft stayed for two nights before returning on 2nd October as 10T144 with again two night-stops (at Maidugari and Khartoum), reaching Cairo on the 4th . Four further flights to Lagos followed: Service 9T147 departed on 10th October and with a night-stop and quick engine change at El Geneina, reached Lagos on the 11th, the Lagos-Accra-Lagos sector being cancelled. G-AGHE returned to Cairo as 10T147 on the 14th, with two night-stops en route, at Maidugari and Khartoum, to arrive on 16th October. Flight 9T149 departed Cairo on the following day, and made two night-stops this time (El Geneina and Maidugari), with the Lagos-Accra-Lagos sector again being cancelled, and instead a further night-stop made at Kano before continuing to Lagos on the 20th. Departure on 10T149 was made from Lagos the following day, with a single night-stop this time (at El Geneina) en route to Cairo. Service 9T152 departing on 26th October made only one night-stop at El Geneina en route to Lagos, (with the extra sector to Accra being cancelled again, after yet another engine change), with the return flight to Cairo departing as 10T152 on 1st November with only the El Geneina night-stop prior to arrival in Cairo on the 2nd . The Dakota then rested for a week before departing with service 9T156 on 9th November, making the usual El Geneina night-stop en route to Lagos, where two further night-stops were made before returning from there on 12th November via El Geneina (N/S) back to Cairo. G-AGHE then operated two 9T schedules to Accra, the first as 9T159 via a night-stop at El Geneina 21st–22nd November, followed by a night-stop at Accra then returning as 10T159 on 23rd November via Lagos (two night-stops) and El Geneina to Cairo, with arrival back on the 26th. The same pattern was followed for service 9T163, outward Cairo-Accra (5th–6th December), followed by 10T163 with departure from Accra on 7th via Lagos (two nights), El Geneina (N/S) to Cairo on 10th December. There followed a further Lagos schedule (9T166), outbound 14th–15th (with the Lagos-Accra-Lagos sector cancelled), returning as 10T166 (18th–19th December), with one night-stop en route at El Geneina. 'GHE then operated a special flight from Cairo to Basra and return on 21st December, before making the final flight of 1944 with a further service to Lagos only, oubound as 9T169 (26th–27th December), inbound as 10T169 (30th–31st December), with a night-stop at El Geneina only in both directions.

The year 1945

1945 started for Dakota G-AGHE with a further flight to Lagos as 9T171, departing on 2nd January, and returning as 10T171 from Lagos on 6th January. The return flight, however, was delayed at Maidugari until the 7th, resulting in the arrival back in Cairo on 9th January. The Dakota's next service was unusually a BOAC 3N/4N schedule to Teheran, usually flown by BOAC's Lodestar fleet. Departure was on 10th January from Cairo on service 3N223, but already on the way outbound to Damascus there were unspecified problems, resulting in the Dakota returning to Lydda. The aircraft then continued to Damascus, where a night-stop was made, owing to the bad weather. The Dakota eventually reached Baghdad on the following day, although there were still problems with the weather, so that it was not until after a further night-stop that the flight could continue to Teheran, which was reached on 12th January. There the Dakota was grounded by the weather until 15th January, when the Dakota took off with the return schedule (4N223). By the time the aircraft reached Baghdad, however, it was suffering from unspecified mechanical problems, which resulted in an unscheduled night-stop being made, with the Dakota arriving back in Cairo later on the following day (16th January).

A variation on the usual BOAC camouflage scheme with a large Union Jack on the nose is seen on G-AGGB (c/n 6227) in this landing shot.
(Don Hannah Collection)

G-AGHF (c/n 9186) under overhaul at BOAC's maintenance base at Croydon showing the camouflaged scheme and black registration underlined with red, white and blue stripes. *(Brian Stainer/APN)*

A BOAC Dakota taken at Almaza in 1945 showing the military scheme used for a period, with RAF serial KJ928 (c/n 26099) and four-letter code "OFZQ", alias G-AGKI. *(FJ Hill via RC Jones)*

G-AGHE then returned to its normal West African routine until early May 1945. Service 9T176 to Lagos departed Cairo on 18th January, with delays en route at Khartoum and arrival in Lagos late on the 19th. The return flight operated as 10T176 on 22nd January with arrival back in Cairo on 23rd January as scheduled. The next flight for the Dakota was to Accra as 9T179 on 30th January, returning from Lagos as 10T179 on 3rd February. An extra flight was then operated, outward as 9T183X to Lagos on 15th February and returning as 10T183X from Lagos on the 18th back to Cairo. There followed the last series of Lagos flights for G-AGHE before the Dakota returned to the United Kingdom. These flights were 9T/10T187 outbound 27th–28th February, inbound 3rd–4th March, followed by 9T/10T191 outbound 13th–14th March & inbound 17th–18th March back to Cairo. There was a night-stop in each direction at El Geneina. Slightly different timings were introduced from this flight onwards to and from Lagos. The subsequent flights all went off without problems, namely 9T/10T195 outwards 24th–25th March, returning to Cairo 27th–28th March and 9T/10T201 outwards to Lagos 14th–15th April and returning 17th–18th to Cairo. On 'GHE's final schedule on the Cairo-Lagos route, however, there were some problems. Service 9T206 flew to schedule outbound on 3rd–4th May. After the usual night-stops, the return flight 10T206 departed Lagos on 6th May, but by Kano there were unspecified mechanical problems with the Dakota, resulting in an unscheduled night-stop. The problems were rectified and the flight continued on the usual routeing, with the El Geneina night-stop, and arrival back in Cairo on 8th May.

On 13th May, G-AGHE departed Cairo on the second through-service via West Africa to England. At this stage it used the usual "9T" designator as far as Lagos (9T209), and made the usual night-stop at El Geneina, arriving in Lagos on 14th May. After a further night-stop the Dakota continued from Lagos as service 22W98 to Accra, Takoradi with night-stop 15th–16th, Freetown, Bathurst (night-stop 16th–17th), Port Etienne, Rabat, Lisbon (night-stop 17th–18th) continuing on the 18th to Hurn and finally to Bristol (Whitchurch). The following day, G-AGHE flew to Croydon for modifications, which resulted in the Dakota being out of service for over six months, as the Croydon works was so busy.

During this period G-AGHE was allocated the military code ODZGK on 15th July 1945. These codes were allocated to commercial aircraft to enable them to overfly countries such as France that allowed only military aircraft in this era. Many Dakotas of BOAC were allocated such codes, as well as other types such as the Lancastrians and Hythes. As 'GHE had still not returned to service by the autumn, a new code ODZGW was

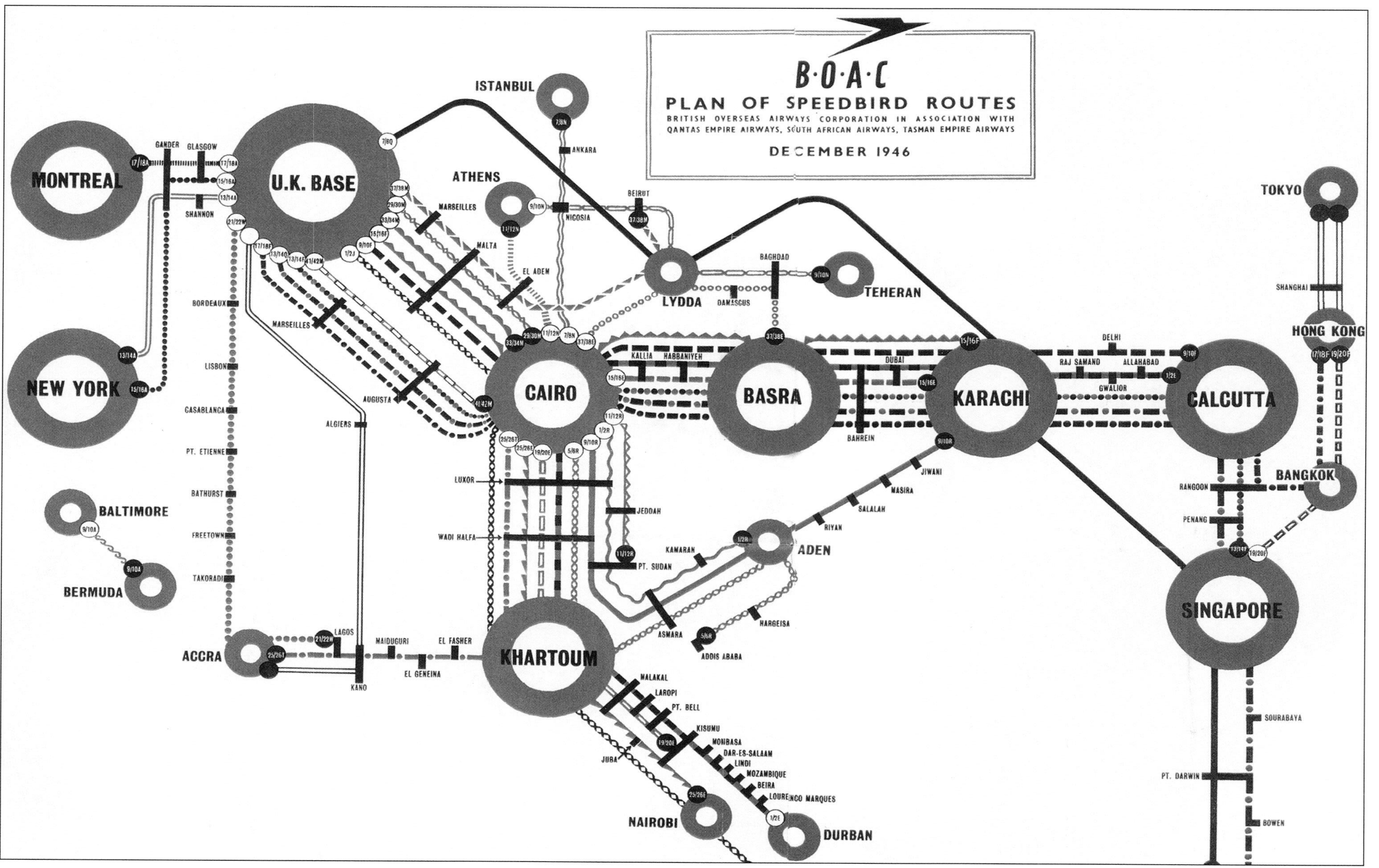

Detail from a diagram showing BOAC's routes flown and service designators as of December 1946. (BOAC Archives)

G-AGFY (c/n 6224) in the plain silver scheme with "speedbird" on the nose, but with registration underlined with red, white and blue stripes as in the camouflaged scheme. Note also the small fin titling showing "British Overseas Airways" only. This photo was taken at Croydon on 14th August 1945. (Mike Hooks)

284 **LONDON (HURN)—MALTA—CAIRO (Daily)**
BRITISH OVERSEAS AIRWAYS CORPORATION

Miles	Airports of	Service ...	29M					Airports of	Service ...	30M				
0	HURN	...dep	14 0	...	...	...	...	CAIRO	...dep	19 30	...	...	...	...
678	MARSEILLES	...arr	18 0	...	...	...	...	EL ADEM	...arr	22 40	...	...	...	...
	,, ...	...dep	19 0	...	...	...	...	,, ...	...dep	23 45	...	...	...	...
1396	MALTA	...arr	0 30	...	...	...	...	MALTA	...arr	3 15	...	...	...	...
	,, ...	...dep	1 30	...	...	...	...	,, ...	...dep	4 15	...	...	...	...
2006	EL ADEM	...arr	6 25	...	...	...	...	MARSEILLES ...	...arr	8 15	...	...	...	...
	,, ...	...dep	7 30	...	...	...	...	,, ...	...dep	9 15	...	...	...	...
2136	CAIRO	...arr	10 15	...	...	...	...	HURN	...arr	13 40	...	...	...	...

Free baggage allowance 20 Kgs.

A sample United Kingdom-Egypt timetable from Bradshaw's Air Guide May 1946.

allocated in November 1945 and 'GHE reverted to its former military serial FD827 when it re-entered service after CofA renewal on 5th December 1945 (although BOAC's records continued to refer to the Dakota by its British civil registration and chart number, log-books however generally recorded flights under the military serial). The Dakota then started on a long period of flights on the UK-Cairo route designated 29M outbound and 30M inbound, with 'GHE's first service after overhaul departing Hurn as 29M/809 (ie the 809th service on this route!) on 11th December 1945. At this stage, BOAC were operating up to two services daily on this route, although this was cut back to once daily early in 1946. A typical service would depart Hurn at 13.00 GMT and would route via Marseilles-Marignane (18.00-19.00 local), followed by a night flight over the Mediterranean to Malta-Luqa, which was transitted from 00.30 to 01.30. The flight then continued to North Africa, with a stop at El Adem (Libya) from 06.25 to 07.30, before reaching Cairo-Almaza at 10.15 local the day after departure. Passenger seating on this route was for sixteen only at this time, and the time in the air averaged fifteen and a half hours eastbound and seventeen and a quarter hours westbound. After resting for the rest of the day and night at Cairo, the return schedule 30M would typically depart Cairo at 19.30 and following the same route back to the UK call at El Adem (22.40 to 23.35), Malta (03.15 – 04.15) and Marseilles (08.15–09.15), with landing back at Hurn scheduled for 12.40. G-AGHE returned to the UK on its first service on 13th December, and subsequently operated the route at regular intervals for the next four months, with two further flights in December, 29M & 30M/824 departing 16th December and returning three days later, followed by 29M & 30M/849 from 27th to 30th December.

1946, the Cairo schedule continued

Dakota G-AGHE operated five further return flights during January on the same route, 29M & 30M/867 (7th–9th January), 29M & 30M/873 (11th–13th), 29M & 30M/879 (16th–20th), 29M & 30M/889 (24th–27th) and 29M & 30M/900 from 30th January. The Dakota experienced a broken hydraulic pressure pipe at Malta on service 30M/879, resulting in two night stops at Malta (18th–20th January), while a spare was flown in and the pipe replaced.

Five services were also operated in February, namely 29M & 30M/907 departing on 4th February, 29M & 30M/916 from 11th , 29M & 30M/924 from 16th , 29M & 30M/929 on 20th and 29M/939 departing on 27th February. The Dakota had problems with an oleo strut at Marseilles on the last-mentioned flight, resulting in three night-stops there before continuing to Cairo (2nd–3rd March). The Dakota returned from Cairo on 3rd–4th March as 30M/942. Similarly, five return services were operated in March, beginning with 29M & 30M/949 (6th–8th), when the service frequency was changed to ten flights weekly. This was followed by 29M & 30M/955 (10th–12th March), 29M/961 departed Hurn on 14th March, but the Dakota again suffered hydraulic problems, this time at Malta on the return 30M/961 service, which resulted in a stay there from 16th to 18th to fix the problem, with arrival back at Hurn on the 19th . 29M & 30M/976 went according to plan (25th–27th), as did the final flight for March (29M & 30M/982) from 29th to 31st March.

With the introduction of British Summer Time, the timings changed slightly, with departure from Hurn from 14th April at

14.00 and return arrival at 13.40 two days later. After 'GHE's 3rd April departure on service 29M & 30M/990 (returning on 5th April), the sequential series ran to service 999 and then restarted at '1'. Dakota G-AGHE's next flight which departed on 11th April from Hurn was therefore designated 29M/1, returning as 30M/1 (12th–13th April). The last UK-Cairo return flight carried out for a while was 29M & 30M/19, outward 28th–29th April and returning 29th–30th April from Cairo to Hurn.

For G-AGHE there was a slight change of scenery for its sole service in May, when the aircraft took out 31M/7 from Hurn to Lydda via Marignane, Luqa and El Adem on the 20th of the month, returning with 32M/7 (late!) on 21st May back to Hurn. For nearly two months, the Dakota then stood idle before a flurry of activity in July 1946. In the meantime, the military colours were removed and the Dakota reverted to an overall silver scheme (see photo) with "Speedbird" on the nose and the BOAC titling (in full) on the bottom of the fin. The aircraft's next departure was again on the Cairo route, but with a change of departure point from Hurn to the new London Airport or "LAP" as it was usually recorded (ie the present-day London-Heathrow). Service 29M/104 departed LAP on 11th July to Cairo, arriving back at London with 30M/104 on 13th July. The Dakota was then turned round to take out service 29M/110 on the 15th with the return schedule 30M/110 (16th–17th July), the flights operating ten times weekly in July (all with Dakotas). On 20th July 'GHE was allocated to a Special flight 1XP/12 to Cairo with a very quick turn-round to bring back service 30M/118X ('X' for extra) to the UK on 21st arriving back the following day. A further Special flight was operated by 'GHE designated 1XP/14 to Cairo on 25th July, with another quick turn-round to return with 30M/123X on 27th July, with arrival in London on the 28th.

After a number of hectic days' flying, Dakota G-AGHE remained on the ground at London for over a week before taking out a normal scheduled service to Cairo again (29M/142) on 9th August, returning with BOAC service 30M/142 on 10th August. After a further week on the ground, 'GHE was allocated to a training sortie on the 20th of the month to Castel Benito (Libya) and then on to Cairo, where the aircraft was used for a further incoming extra flight (30M/160X) on 26th August. After a couple of days on the ground, the Dakota was used to operate a further Special flight 1XP/22 to Cairo on the last day of August. The Dakota then remained in Egypt for a week before returning on 9th September with another extra flight (30M/181X) to the UK, arriving the following day. One further Special flight was undertaken during September as 1XP/26, flying eastbound to Cairo on the 18th and returning to the UK under the same flight prefix.

Only three more return flights were carried out in 1946 by G-AGHE, all on the Cairo route. The first was on 20th October on service 29M/208 from London Airport, returning on the 22nd as 30M/208, with arrival the 23rd, followed in quick succession by 29M/218 (25th October) and returning on 30M/218 to London on 26th–28th October. The reason for the delay on the return flight was an electrical fault in the junction box of the "Wander" cockpit lamp on take-off from Cairo on 26th October. An electrical short-circuit occurred, resulting in a return to the airfield while the problem was fixed. The last of the three BOAC services left London Airport on 3rd November as 29M/236, with return service 30M/236 departing Cairo on 4th November for the UK. After a couple of days on the ground, 'GHE made the short flight over to Croydon on 8th November for a thorough overhaul and CofA renewal.

Into 1947

Dakota G-AGHE remained at Croydon for four months, where, after a test flight, the CofA was renewed for a further year on 21st March 1947. With the Dakotas in BOAC's fleet gradually being replaced by four-engined airliners, the airline found itself with a surplus of Dakotas. Some were stored for long periods, while others in the fleet were used for training purposes. 'GHE was allocated for the latter use and the aircraft departed Croydon on 25th March to Aldermaston in Berkshire, BOAC's training base at the time. Local flights on the Aldermaston circuit were not recorded individually in BOAC's operational records, only route-

Work underway in BOAC's maintenance hangar at Croydon to strip off the camouflage (seen on the aircraft far left). G-AGKA and G-AGKH are already in the post-war all-silver scheme with the "speedbird" emblem. The photo was taken in October 1946. *(Tom Samson)*

G-AGHE (c/n 9189) in the plain silver scheme with small titling on the lower fin and BOAC's "speedbird" with light blue and white stripes on the nose. (BOAC)

training flights abroad. During the five months G-AGHE spent at Aldermaston, five such training flights were recorded. On 11th April the aircraft flew out to Gothenburg in Sweden and return on a training sortie, followed by two foreign sorties in May, both to Lisbon, the first on 21st May and the second on the 29th. In June a further two training flights were carried out, this time on Scandinavian routes, one to Stockholm on 15th June and the other to Copenhagen on 20th June. All these foreign training flights were on routes that had been allocated from BOAC's European Division to the newly formed British European Airways.

September 1947 saw a complete change in the use of Dakota G-AGHE when the aircraft was one of eight Dakotas allocated to what became known as the "Pakistan Airlift" or "Operation Pakistan". 'GHE was one of the second batch of BOAC Dakotas to leave London Airport at short notice for Karachi. On 2nd September G-AGFX, 'GFY, 'GGA, 'GHN and 'GMZ departed in a group of two and three aircraft respectively, followed by G-AGHE, 'GGB and 'GKN the following day. G-AGHE routed via Marseilles-Marignane, Malta, Cairo, Basra and Dhahran to Karachi, arriving on 5th September. "Operation Pakistan" had been arranged at short notice with over 20 aircraft to fly 7,000 Muslim Pakistani officials, ministerial staff and their families from Delhi to their jobs and new homes in the Pakistan capital Karachi. Train travel had proved impossible owing to the rioting in the Punjab areas. Air transport had been requested so that a high-speed evacuation could take place to enable the officials to begin their work with the newly formed Pakistani government as soon as possible. Each aircraft used was ferried out to India with a double crew so that a non-stop, seven days a week service could be carried out until the evacuation was completed. In addition to the Dakotas of BOAC, one BOAC Lancastrian and two Yorks were used, as well as a number of Dakotas which BOAC chartered from various UK-based private airline companies (namely Scottish Airlines, Silver City Airways and Westminster Airways). The aim was to move approximately 7,000 people a distance of 700 miles in a week and a half (11 days). The operation was under the direction of Air Commodore H G Brackley and the fleet of over 20 aircraft was based at Palam Airfield, Delhi, with BOAC maintenance personnel ferried out from the UK and Egypt to keep the aircraft flying day and night. The airlift was completed by midnight on 15th September after an intensive operation which passed without serious incident. G-AGHE returned home to London from Karachi on 16th September as an "Indian Special" flight. The extent of the operations on behalf of the Government of Pakistan had been greater than originally envisaged, with a grand total of 8,500 persons and over 110,000 pounds of food and medical supplies flown between Delhi and Karachi. Of the passenger total, 1,500 people had been flown in the reverse direction, ie from Karachi to Delhi. The Journey Logs of most aircraft have not survived, but that of BOAC's Dakota G-AGGB has, and is reproduced on the next page to give a flavour of the intense operations that were carried out.

After arrival back in London on 19th September, 'GHE appears to have been parked out of service for a month before departing on a similar operation starting in October 1947 to move 35,000 Indian government officials, their families and "destitutes" between India, Pakistan and Baluchistan. G-AGHE departed London Airport (with sistership G-AGHH) at 07.45 on 17th October on an Indian Special flight, routeing via Marseilles-Marignane, Malta-Luqa, El Adem, Cairo-Almaza and Wadi Halfa to Karachi, which was reached at 15.34 (local) on 20th October. The aircraft continued to Delhi the following day to complete the allocation of four aircraft to the "Indian Government Number 1 Charter". BOAC had four Dakotas and five crews for this charter, plus a further two Dakotas and three crews for the "Orient Airways Charter". BOAC records state the G-AGHE was fitted for the Indian charter with only six seats forward and five in the middle of the cabin (the normal seating at the time being either 21, or 15 if extra tanks were fitted). "Operation India" was

True extract from journey Log of Dakota G-AGGB.

Date	Capt.	Place of departure	Place of arrival.	Hours of flight.
2.9.47	Richards	Aldermaston	L.A.P.	.35
3.9.47	"	L.A.P	Marignane	3.49
	"	Marignane	Luqa	3.40
	"	Luqa	Cairo (Almaza)	5.44
4.9.47	"	Almaza	Basra	6.10
5.9.47	Arnot	Basra	Sharjah	3.41
	"	Sharjah	Karachi	4.18
6.9.47	"	Karachi	Delhi	4.32
	"	Delhi	Karachi	4.22
7.9.47	Richards	Karachi	Delhi	4.18
	"	Delhi	Karachi	4.10
8.9.47	Arnot	Karachi	Delhi	4.16
	"	Delhi	Karachi	4.25
9.9.47	Richards	Karachi	Karachi	1.00
		Karachi	Delhi	3.50
		Delhi	Karachi	4.35
10.9.47	Arnot	Karachi	Delhi	4.19
	"	Delhi	Karachi	4.15
11.9.47	Richards	Karachi	Delhi	4.27
	"	Delhi	Karachi	4.35
12.9.47	Arnot	Karachi	Delhi	4.53
	"	Delhi	Karachi	4.18
13.9.47	Richards	Karachi	Jodhpur	2.33
	"	Jodhpur	Delhi	2.02
	"	Delhi	Karachi	4.27
14.9.47	Arnot	Karachi	Delhi	04.25
	"	Delhi	Karachi	04.09
15.9.47	Richards	Karachi	Jodhpur	2.31

An extract from the journey-log of one of the BOAC Dakotas (G-AGGB) which flew on the "Pakistan Airlift".

somewhat more complicated than "Operation Pakistan" the previous month, owing to the far greater number of airfields the Dakotas were using on the airlift, which was again based at Palam airfield, Delhi. The Operations Notes for G-AGHE have survived for "Operation India" and give the following flights made between 23rd October and 16th November 1947:-

23/10	Delhi-Multan-Delhi
24/10	Delhi-Rawalpindi-Delhi
26/10	Delhi-Chaklala-Delhi
27/10	Delhi-Sargodha-Delhi
28/10	Delhi-Dabeji-Ambala-Delhi
29/10	Delhi-Sargodha-Ambala-Delhi
30/10	Delhi-Lahore-Peshawar-Ambala-Delhi
02/11	Delhi-Khan-Ambala-Delhi
06/11	Delhi-Lahore-Peshawar-Lahore-Ambala-Delhi
08/11	Delhi-Lahore-Risalpur-Lahore-Delhi
14/11	Delhi-Lahore-Lyallpur-Lahore-Delhi
16/11	Delhi-Dabeji-Amritsar-Delhi.

A minor incident occurred on 31st October on the aircraft's return to Delhi from the operations of the previous day. On departing Chaklala en route to Ambala at 08.58 (GMT) G-AGHE was taxying past sistership G-AGKN with a crew of four and 33 passengers when the captain misjudged the distance between the other Dakota to port and the duty-crew hut to starboard, with the result that the starboard wingtip of 'GHE hit the roof of the hut, causing a tear six inches long in the underside of the wingtip and 18 inches inboard of the skin of the wing trailing-edge. The Dakota was being marshalled for clear passage on both sides of the aircraft at the time! A temporary repair was made at Chaklala the following day by cutting away the skin and fitting a temporary 12 inches by 8 inches patch of 22G alloy secured by kalons and rivets with the note "top surface slightly distorted". The Dakota then continued on its evacuation duties on 2nd November (see above), with a permanent repair carried out when 'GHE was flown to Karachi for a Check III on 10th November. At Karachi, the skin on the wing was renewed top and bottom by 18 inch x 7 inch pieces of 24G Alclad secured with solid and pop rivets.

During November 1947, G-AGHE continued in use as one of six BOAC Dakotas (the others being G-AGGA, 'GGB, 'GHH, 'GKN

G-AGNF (c/n 26979) in the final scheme carried by BOAC Dakotas in the immediate 1946-1948 post-war period with the Union Jack on the fin plus "speedbird" emblem with light blue and white stripes on the nose and the small BOAC titling (in full) on the bottom of the fin. (Brian Stainer/APN)

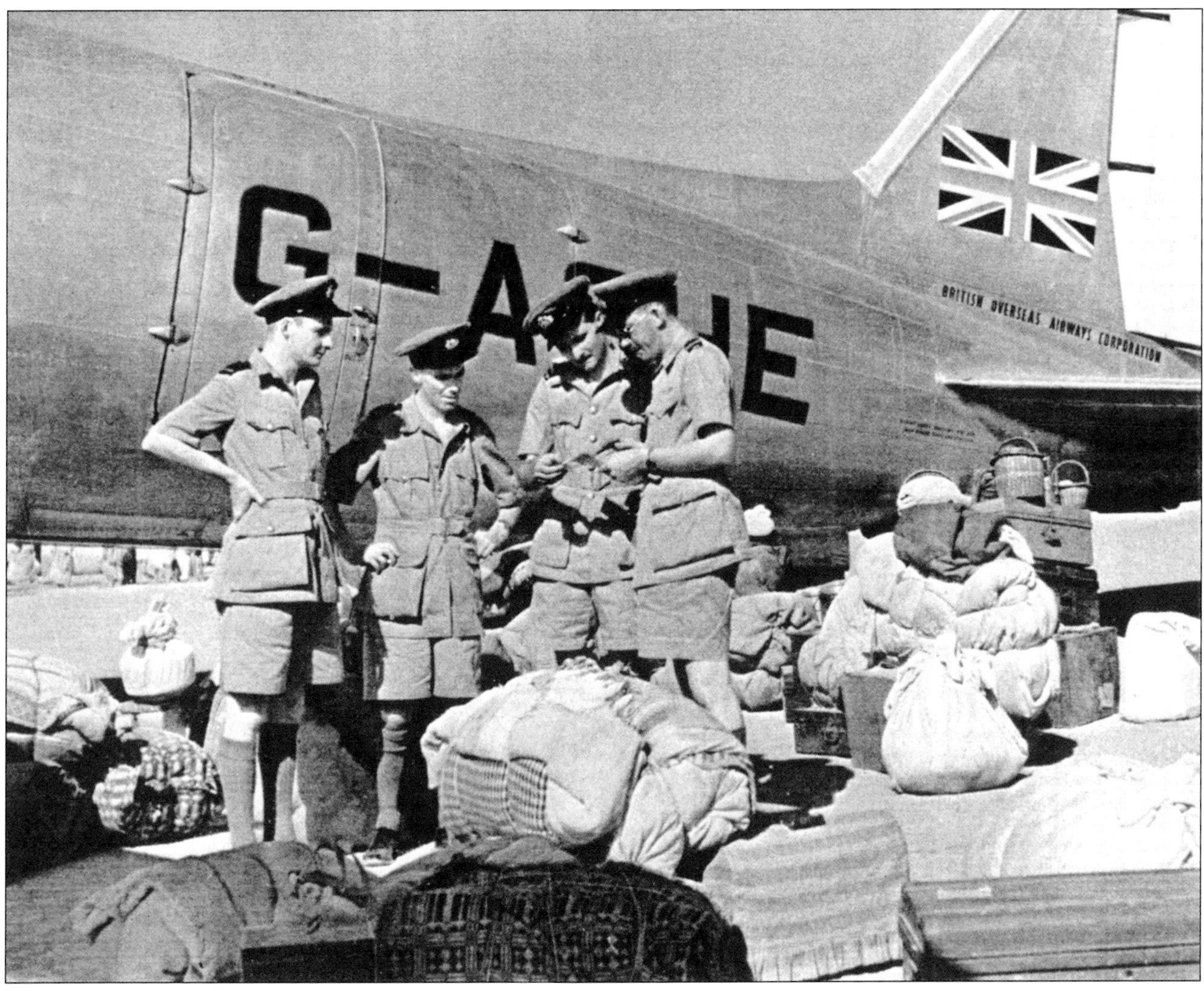

BOAC Dakota G-AGHE (c/n 9189) taken during "Operation India", showing well the position of the full BOAC titles on the fin. *(BOAC Archives)*

C. of A. Aircraft G-AGHE

	w/e 28th Feb.	w/e 6th Mar.	w/e 13th Mar.	w/e 20th Mar.	w/e 27th Mar.	Total.
Fitter/Riggers inc. Check 4 Eng.	209½	1078	1134	1046	322	3789½
Cleaning & Polishing	22	301½	227	110	61½	722
Electricians	21½	75	76	17	4	193½
Radio	15	226	88½	116	20¼	465¾
Carpenters, Painters, Fabric Wkrs.	4¾	124	220¼	100	56½	505½
Tinsmith		93½	79¼	47	3½	223¼
Hydraulic and Wheel Shop		91½	12½	-		104
Instruments		67	82	47¼	18½	214¾
Modifications		61½	122	143½		327
Flight Section					20¼	20¼
	272¾	2118	2041½	1626¾	506½	6565½

An illustration of the man-hours needed to overhaul a BOAC Dakota for the issue of a Certificate of Airworthiness. *(BOAC file 2039)*

and 'GZC) operating in India under the title of a "Detached Flight". Other BOAC Dakotas were used on charter to Orient Airways for regular airline services. These had their BOAC insignia removed and replaced by Orient Airways insignia and registration. By 18th November 1947, G-AGHE had been transferred to Orient Airways as a replacement for one of the original Dakotas. A formal request was made to the Ministry of Civil Aviation (MCA) in the UK for the operation of Dakotas for Orient Airways "with all chairs removed". Details of 'GHE's use with Orient Airways are not available, but G-AGHE continued in use with that company on charter until the end of November 1947. The Dakota was then handed back to BOAC and it returned to the UK between 2nd and 5th of December routeing via Karachi (2nd), Port Sudan, Cairo (night-stop 3rd–4th), Castel Benito and Marignane to London Airport, with G-AGHH following two days later and the Orient Airways charter continuing solely with G-AGGA and G-AGZC (until 17th and 18th December respectively).

After arrival back at LAP, G-AGHE continued the same day on to Aldermaston for use by Airways Training Limited (the training unit for both BOAC and BEA) until 4th January 1948. On 5th January, 'GHE was flown to Whitchurch (which was taking over the BOAC's Dakota overhauls from Croydon during the spring of 1948). The Dakota was parked at Whitchurch awaiting its turn in the CofA queue. Work for the renewal of its CofA took place between 28th February and 31st March at Whitchurch, with the CofA being renewed officially on 25th March 1948. An insight into the work involved in the CofA renewal of a BOAC Dakota at the time is given in correspondence concerning the length of time taken for 'GHE. In fact, G-AGHE did not re-enter service with BOAC after its CofA renewal, but instead was parked until 27th May 1948, when it flew to Prestwick for modifications to be carried out by Scottish Aviation Limited prior to delivery to Malayan Airways. G-AGHE was accepted by Scottish Aviation the following day and deleted from BOAC's books on 8th August 1948 on transfer to Malayan Airways as VR-SCR, at which time BOAC still had 31 Dakotas in its inventory.

Acknowledgements:

BOAC records, operations charts, aircraft cards and correspondence files for Dakota aircraft held in the British Airways Archives & Museum.

Files of the late Donald Hannah.

Log-books & timetables in the archives of the Croydon Airport Society.

A line-up of eleven BOAC Dakotas at London Airport awaiting sale in March 1949. Nearest the camera are G-AGKF, G-AGNF and G-AGKL. (Flight via Mike Hooks)

G-AIWC (c/n 13474) seen in the BOAC 1950s scheme with white cabin roof and two blue stripes across the fin. The photo, taken at Croydon, shows the aircraft wearing the full BOAC titling and the additional titles "on charter to Kuwait Oil Company". (via Jennifer Gradidge)

G-AMZD (c/n 32860) of Transair showing the "Dakmaster" undercarriage doors. This aircraft was one of the first batch in Transair's fleet to receive the modification. *(via Tony Merton Jones)*

Chapter 11
Transair and the Dakmaster

by Peter J Marson

In the mid 1950s, the long-standing British charter airline Transair operated a fleet of immaculate former RAF Dakotas on its passenger, newspaper and cargo flights from its base at Croydon Airport. The company, having noted the improvements the Douglas Aircraft Company had made with their "Super Dak" in the immediate post-war period, introduced several modifications to its own Dakota fleet during late 1955 to early 1956 to improve the aircraft's performance and payload, but without involving an extensive (and expensive) rebuild.

As a first step, the Pratt & Whitney R1830-92 engines were replaced by the R1830-94 engines, which gave an additional 100 BHP per engine and improved the cruising speed by 18 miles per hour (mph). The take-off and cruise performance was further enhanced by fitting a modified type of propeller which added an additional three mph to the cruising speed.

Further thought was then given to improving the take-off and climb performance, and, with this in mind, the hydraulic system was reworked to halve the time taken for the undercarriage to retract. The final modification undertaken by Transair aimed at reducing the drag created by the open wheel-wells of the Dakota's undercarriage doors, which caused a loss of up to 10 mph at cruising speed. Transair developed wheel-well doors which ensured a clean aerofoil area of the entire centre section without losing the useful feature of the slightly protruding main-wheels in the case of a "wheels-up" emergency landing. These newly designed wheel-well doors were made of fibreglass and fitted flush with the contour of the engine nacelles, and in addition completely sealed the main wheel-well area. After all the improvements had been incorporated, an increase of around 30 mph in the cruising speed was achieved.

The wheel-well doors were constructed by Thermo-Plastics from Dunstable in Bedfordshire, England. The strength of the doors was retained by adding metal plates and a thick layer of Hycar sandwiched between the fibreglass laminations. A nylon brush sealing strip was pop-riveted to the joint edges of the two hinged doors which thereby ensured a snug fit for the doors against the main wheels of the undercarriage. A third door was rigidly attached to the undercarriage diagonal member, which then sealed the rear of the wheel-well when the undercarriage legs were retracted.

Transair's own fleet of ten Dakotas had been modified by the beginning of July 1956, and henceforth were known as "Dakmasters" by the airline. The undercarriage door modification kits were advertised for sale to other Dakota operators, and a report dated 29th June 1956 suggested that 115 firm orders for the kits had been received in the first two months that they had been offered by Transair! The kits were marketed as "Transair DC-3

Close-up of the undercarriage, showing the side and and rear covers which fitted snugly around the tyre. *(via Tony Merton Jones)*

Close-up of the "Dakmaster" undercarriage door modification developed and marketed by Transair, seen from the rear. *(Transair via Mike Hooks)*

Close-up of the "Dakmaster" undercarriage door modification developed by Transair, seen here in a partially retracted montage.
(Transair via Mike Hooks)

undercarriage doors to improve the safety, speed and payload" of the type. By the end of 1956, the following airlines from all parts of the world had been supplied with the Transair undercarriage door kits for their Dakotas:-

Air Kruise, Airwork, BKS Air Transport, Hunting-Clan Air Transport; Braathens SAFE, SABENA; Africair (Rhodesia) Ltd, East African Airways Corporation, South African Air Force; Indian Airlines Corporation, and the L B Smith Aircraft Corporation in the USA.

Strangely, it was not until 1958 that the monthly British Civil Register published by the Air Registration Board acknowledged the full Transair modification by redesignating all the airline's Dakota Mk.4s as the "Dakota Mk.6". The official register showed the modified aircraft as Dakota Mk.6s in the following issues: June 1958 G-AMPZ, G-AMSV, G-AMZD, G-AMZF & G-AMZG; October 1958: G-AMYJ & G-ANTC; November 1958: G-AMRA & G-AOUD, and December 1958: G-ANTB. In addition to the fleet of ten Transair Dakotas, the full modifications to Dakota Mk.6 "Dakmaster" were incorporated in

An early (circa 1963) view of G-AKNB (c/n 9043) when in service with British United Airways after the fitting of a Transair "Dakmaster" door kit. *(MAP)*

Martin-Baker Aircraft's G-APML (officially in August 1958), followed by the two former Hunting-Clan examples returned from Iraq Petroleum Transport Co Ltd G-AMNL (May 1961) and G-AMSJ (August 1961), both for the newly-formed British United Airways. The final conversion was not reported officially until February 1964, after Jersey Airlines' G-ANEG was converted to a Mark 6. (Note 1)

Among the Dakotas that were modified with Transair's undercarriage door kits during the late 1950s and early 1960s were most of the British independent airlines' examples that were flying at the time. The following aircraft are confirmed as modified (in addition to those aircraft that were fully modified to Dakmasters, mentioned above):-

Air Kruise/Silver City: G-AKNB, G-ALPN, G-AMWV, G-AMYX & G-ANAE
Airwork (for Sudan Airways): ST-AAG & STAAH
BKS: G-AMSF, G-AMSH, G-AMVC & G-APPO
Cambrian Airways: G-AGHM, G-AGHS, G-AHCZ & G-ALCC
Dan-Air: G-AMPP, G-AMSU
Derby Airways: G-AGJV, G-AMSW, G-AMSX, G-ANTD, G-AOFZ, G-AOGZ & G-APBC
Hunting-Clan: G-AMHJ (+ Hunting Surveys: G-AMYW, G-ANAF & G-AVPW)
Starways: G-AMSN

Also modified were G-AMZH (operated by Transair for Niarchos) & Keegan's G-AJRY. Outside of Great Britain, airlines that used the kits (in addition to those already mentioned) were South African Airways, West African/Nigeria Airways, Ghana Airways, Rousseau Aviation's F-BNPT plus several privately-owned Canadian aircraft.

The French national airline, Air France, advertised a competing undercarriage door modification in 1961 under the name "Maximizer" and modified at least 28 aircraft of its own, including the CEPT Postale and SGACC fleets which it managed, plus those of some of its associated airlines in Africa. The Air France "Maximizer" modifications included fitting undercarriage doors to the main undercarriage (which, unlike the Transair kit, completely enclosed the main wheels), modifying the engine cowlings, installing a petrol-driven Janitrol heater and modernizing the radio installation. Aircraft were modified in this way during the years 1961 to 1966, with the first aircraft to be modified being F-BAXZ in March-April 1961.

Notes:

Note 1: G-ANEG had originally been Transair's Long-Range Freighter and was not converted to a Mark 6 with the rest of the fleet in 1956. It was fitted with a 200 Imperial Gallon long-range tank to the rear of the forward cabin bulkhead which extended the aircraft's range with a cargo load to over ten hours, for example El Adem (Libya) to Croydon. It was sold on to Don Everall Aviation (as a normal passenger aircraft) in March 1957.

Acknowledgements:

Transair, Captain Edward Hack (Transair & British United Airways), ARB records, Malcolm P Fillmore & "Flight" 29th June 1956.

Comparative views, showing (above) an unmodified Dakota – G-AKNB (c/n 9043) of Intra Jersey (Air-Britain), and (below) the later "Maximiser" undercarriage door modification introduced by Air France. In this modification, seen on F-BEIE (c/n 25848) , the wheels were enclosed completely within the doors when retracted. *(MAP)*

Florida Airmotive DC-3 N165LG (c/n 6314) in the company's smart scheme at its Lantana, Florida base in October 1979. *(Karl Hayes)*

Chapter 12
Florida Airmotive

by Karl Hayes

Compared to the "propliner" wasteland it later became, back in the 1970s and 1980s southern Florida positively teemed with large numbers of all the great aircraft – DC-3s, 4s, 6s, and 7s, Connies and Super Connies, C-46s, Martin 404s, Convairs etc. Apart from the "propliner" meccas of Miami International Airport, with its famed "Corrosion Corner", Opa Locka and Fort Lauderdale, even the smaller airfields such as Tamiami, Boca Raton, West Palm Beach etc would invariably host several items of 'round-engined' interest.

Lantana Airport

There was another small airfield, also well worth a visit, which was easy to miss and not too well known. Starting in Miami, the Interstate 95 highway (the I-95, as it is known) heads north, paralleling Florida's Atlantic coast, towards West Palm Beach, then continuing north all the way to Jacksonville and beyond. West Palm Beach has its own airport, known as West Palm Beach International Airport, a large and modern facility hosting scheduled services from the major airlines.

Six miles south of West Palm Beach, the highway passes the town of Lantana where, in the 1970s at least, a small and unprepossessing sign indicated the location of another airfield, the Lantana Airport, a mile or two off the highway. This was a much more humble facility which did not boast any scheduled services. It had three runways in a triangular pattern, each just under 3,500 feet in length, so there would be no passenger jetliners landing there. It was however the base of Florida Airmotive, with its superbly presented fleet of Beech 18s and DC-3s, and thus a place of much greater ambience than its "giant jetport" neighbour a few miles up the road.

Airport History

During the second World War, West Palm Beach already had a military airbase, called Morrison Field, which after the war became the West Palm Beach International Airport. Morrison Field was an important wartime airfield, used for C-47s and other aircraft ferrying to Europe using the southern route via South America and Africa. Despite the presence of such a large airfield only a few miles away, the US government built another airfield at Lantana, which opened in August 1941, to be used as an auxiliary airfield for Morrison. In December of that year the Civil Air Patrol (CAP) was formed and Lantana was one of three airfields chosen to host a CAP unit. The unit was transferred from Morrison Field to Lantana and flew from there for the duration of the War, patrolling for U-Boats operating off the Florida coast. The Lantana airfield also served as a US Navy auxiliary training field during the War

After the War, the airfield reverted to the local authority and became a civilian airfield. A local man, Owen Gassaway, is credited with making a success of Lantana Airport. He was the driving force behind the transformation of Lantana from an under-utilized, under-developed airfield to what would become one of the premier general aviation facilities on the US East Coast. He was based at Lantana from 1945, when it became a civilian field, and established Lantana Flying Service, which concentrated on charters to the Caribbean and Cuba and undertook aircraft maintenance at Lantana.

In 1948 he founded Florida Airmotive Inc as the Fixed Base Operator (FBO) at Lantana, which it still is to this day. During the 1950s, the airport became a popular destination for executive aircraft of the large corporations visiting Florida, which in those days were mostly converted former military types – B-17s, B-25s, B-26s etc. One evening over twenty DC-3s were counted on the ramp, along with 36 Beech 18s. The airfield was also a jumping-off point for the many aircraft flying to the Bahamas and other points in the Caribbean. Florida Airmotive was involved in the buying and selling of aircraft and during 1963/64 three DC-3s were registered to the company – N612F (c/n 1960), N28343 (c/n 2267) and N39393 (c/n 4943). These however were not operated by Florida Airmotive, just bought and sold.

Florida Airmotive

For the past sixty years, Florida Airmotive has essentially run and operated the county-owned Lantana Airport, as the sole FBO at the airfield. In 1972 the company decided to become involved in the aircraft charter business, and acquired four Beech 18s, N167LG and N169LG, both D18S models, N170LG a tri-gear H18S and N171LG an E18S. Florida Airmotive was also one of the largest Beechcraft agencies on the East Coast. Three DC-3s were added to the charter fleet starting in October 1975 with N168LG (c/n 4089), with N165LG (6314) and N166LG (4138) joining the fleet during 1978/79. With this fleet of Twin Beeches and DC-3s, all painted in Florida Airmotive's most attractive colour scheme but without titles, as well as many other general aviation types of aircraft, the company became the largest on-demand charter operator in Florida.

Operations continued throughout the 1980s, with most of the charter work being around the Caribbean, especially the Bahamas. There were also some charters within the United States and to Central America. The US Navy was a regular customer for the DC-3s, with flights between Jacksonville in northern Florida, a major Navy base, and Andros Island in the Bahamas where the Navy operated the AUTEC (Atlantic Undersea Test and Evaluation Center) test range. Based at West Palm Beach International Airport during this period was World Aviation Services/Imperial Aviation which operated DC-3 N61696 (c/n 25509) up to 1976 and Fairchild F-27/FH-227s thereafter, shuttling civilian contractor personnel to and from Andros Island. These flights were supplemented by the Florida Airmotive DC-3s flying on behalf of the Navy between Jacksonville and the Island. The DC-3s also undertook flying for Pompano Airways during the mid 1980s and three Britten Norman Trislanders were acquired which flew on behalf of another Florida-based carrier, Air South.

During 1989 however Florida Airmotive decided to discontinue the charter division and its Beech 18s and DC-3s were disposed of. DC-3 N165LG was sold in March 1989 and flew for a time in the Caribbean with Taino Air before being acquired in January 1993 by the Connecticut Aeronautical Historical Association, who run the New England Air Museum at Bradley Airfield, Windsor Locks, Connecticut. N165LG remains on display here in Florida Airmotive colour scheme but with Taino Air titles. N166LG was sold in February 1990, also operated for a time by Taino Air and last to go in June 1991 was N168LG, sold to Missionair Inc of Jacksonville and re-registered N79MA. As its name suggests, this was a company which undertook missionary work in Central and South America, supported by the DC-3.

Although it left the charter business, Florida Airmotive remained as the operator of the Lantana Airport, a role which continues to this day. The airfield is now known as the Palm Beach County Park Airport and is home to some 400 general aviation aircraft. As it has always done, it hosts many transient aircraft heading to or returning from the Caribbean. It is a thriving, modern facility although "propliner" enthusiasts will remember it more for its glorious past, when those superb DC-3s and the Beech 18 fleet of Florida Airmotive were active on a daily basis.

Florida Airmotive DC-3 N168LG (c/n 4089) was also photographed at Lantana, Florida in October 1979. *(Karl Hayes)*

Four of CNAC's DC-2s lined up at Lunghwa Airport, Shanghai in 1937 in front of the company's hangars. *(Ian Johnson Collection)*

Chapter 13
The DC-3 in China

by Martin S Best, China History Research Group

Introduction

This article describes the commercial operation of Douglas DC-2s and DC-3s in China and Taiwan. It is based on a series of articles on The Development of Commercial Aviation in China that is being published in Air-Britain's civil historical journal, *Archive*, over a period of at least six years. These articles record the current state of knowledge on Chinese airline fleets and indicate the many areas where further research is still required.

I - The Douglas DC-2 in China

China National Aviation Corporation

The Douglas DC-2 was first imported into China by China National Aviation Corporation (CNAC), in which Pan American Airways held a 45% shareholding in partnership with the Ministry of Communications (MOC) of the Nationalist Chinese government. In 1933 Pan American had acquired the interests of the Curtiss-Wright group, who had previously founded China Airways Federal, Inc. to operate three routes in China using Loening Air Yachts and Stinson SM-1F Detroiters. A new contract was signed between Pan American and the MOC that resulted in the formation of a second company called China National Aviation Corporation. (Later, in 1946, Pan American's shareholding was reduced to 20%, a second contract was signed and the third CNAC company was formed.)

By the time Pan American took over this shareholding, this equipment was obsolete and the airline was in dire need of fresh investment. Pan American provided this in the form of more modern equipment, such as Sikorsky S-38Bs, Douglas Dolphins, Sikorsky S-43s, Ford Tri-Motors and Consolidated Commodores as well as Douglas DC-2s and DC-3s. The use of amphibians was desirable considering the lack of suitable airfields in the early days. As well as supplying new equipment, Pan American also invested in the infrastructure required for commercial operations and a steady expansion of the route network.

As part of this fleet improvement, the first of eight DC-2s was imported in 1935. Initially these did not have conventional civil registrations but CNAC fleet numbers and aircraft names, as shown in the accompanying table. To make up the indicated fleet numbers, it seems likely that Chinese government DC-2s were probably used on lease. Civil registrations were only used on aircraft operating on international flights to Burma.

Incidents during the Sino-Japanese war

Captain Hugh Woods took off from Hong Kong's Kai Tak airport shortly after 8am on 24th August 1938, for Chungking in a DC-2 named *Kweilin*. He carried a full load of 14 passengers. A few minutes after crossing the boundary of the Colony, while climbing through 6,000 feet on a course of 297 degrees, Woods sighted eight aircraft ahead and above. Woods had run into similar flights of Japanese military aircraft on previous occasions, and he was not unduly concerned. CNAC was again a purely commercial company, and the Japanese seemed prepared to return to the status quo ante bellum and treat the airline as a non-belligerent. The DC-2 had an unmistakable silhouette; *Kweilin* had "CNAC" painted in large black letters on the upper and lower surfaces of the wings and the Chinese characters for mail on the fuselage.

Although Woods did not expect trouble, just to be safe he turned back toward the border of British territory. After the Japanese planes disappeared, Woods resumed his original course. As he reached the western end of the bay between the territory of Hong Kong and the Chinese mainland, north of Macao, five Nakajima pursuit planes swooped down on *Kweilin*. Woods put the DC-2 into a steep dive and headed for a small patch of clouds some 5,000 feet below and to the left. Unfortunately, the clouds covered the tops of several small mountains. After Woods had passed through the clouds, he turned to re-enter the clouds but heard machine-gun bullets striking the aircraft, so immediately started descending in a tight spiral. During this spiral, Woods could see the shadow of his plane and also the shadow of another plane directly to the rear. The terrain immediately underneath consisted of small rice paddy fields surrounded by dykes. He considered it too hazardous to attempt a landing on this land due to these dykes, so he headed for a river a short distance to his right. He shut off the engines, cut the motor switches, disconnected the battery, and glided into a landing on the water. During this time the plane was being struck by machine-gun bullets. The plane was landed safely near the right-hand side of the river. By the time the water cleared from the windshield, however, the current had caught the plane, and swept it into the middle of the current.

Woods found that none of the passengers had been injured. He raised the emergency hatch cover in front of the cockpit and looked skyward as Japanese aircraft came down to strafe the crippled *Kweilin*. Woods ordered the co-pilot and radio operator to get passengers into the water. Then he jumped into the river and began to swim toward a sampan, tied up on the shore opposite the aircraft.

Meanwhile, the DC-2 half-submerged, floated downstream. Japanese fighter planes continued their attack. Only two people survived besides Woods; the radio operator and an official of the Ministry of Finance. Fourteen died, including Wong Yu-mei of the Central Bank of China, Dr Liu Chung-chieh, former minister to Berlin, two women and two children. Nine of the bodies bore machine-gun bullet wounds.

CNAC had the dubious distinction of losing the first commercial airliner in the history of aviation to hostile aerial attack. Although later denied by the Japanese, there seems little doubt that the attack had been premeditated.

CNAC continued to face frightful difficulties in conducting aerial activities and had to pay a high price for maintaining services in war-torn China. An especially tragic loss came on 29th October 1940. Walter Kent was en route from Chungking to Kunming on that day. Kent's aircraft was the DC-2 *Kweilin*, which had been salvaged from the Pearl River following Wood's ill-fated encounter with Japanese fighters in August 1938. Ten passengers were on board in addition to four crew members. About 100 miles northeast of Kunming, Kent ran into a flight of five Japanese fighters and landed at a small emergency field near Changyi. The Japanese spotted the Douglas and began a series of strafing passes as the airliner taxied off the runway. On their first pass, Kent was hit in the back by a 20-mm shell and died instantly. The other crew members evacuated the passengers as the left wing of the aircraft caught fire. They were machine-gunned while crossing the field in search of shelter. Nine of the fourteen persons on board the DC-2 were killed, two suffered wounds, and three escaped unharmed. The Japanese government dismissed subsequent American diplomatic protests.

Other losses followed. Bernard Wong in a Ford tri-motor crashed in mountainous terrain near Kian in Kiangsi Province on 29th January 1941. The next month, Joy Thom in a DC-2 struck the top of a 7,000-foot mountain in southern Hunan. The crews perished in both instances; fortunately, neither aircraft were carrying passengers.

Two of CNAC's DC-2s were destroyed when the Japanese attacked Hong Kong on 8 December 1941, when many other aircraft were also destroyed.

China National Aviation Corporation (CNAC) received its first DC-2s in April 1935. *(Ian Johnson Collection)*

One of the CNAC DC-2s with fleet number 24 being loaded with the use of a home-made winch. *(Ian Johnson Collection)*

CNAC Douglas DC-2

f/n	*d/d*	*c/n*	*Model*	*p/i*	*Name*	*Fate*
24	01Apr35	1369	DC-2		Nanching (Nanking)	Destroyed by Japanese at Hong Kong, 08Dec41 [JMG, MC]
24	Aug35	1302?	DC-2-118B	NC14269		Cr at Nanking, 25Dec36 [IT, Davies]
-	-	1350	DC-2-118B	NC14290		To RAF as HK820 [Davies]
-	-	1351	DC-2-118B	NC14291		NTU, to Panair do Brasil as PP-PAY [IT, Davies]
26	01Oct35	1302	DC-2-118B	NC14269	Ch'engtu (Chengtu)	Destroyed by Japanese at Hong Kong, 08Dec41 [CF, JMG, MC]
28	28Jun36	1600?	DC-2-118A		Szechuen	Crashed at Chengtu, 25Dec36 [MC]
28?			DC-2		Szechuan	Crashed 6Jan37 (sic) [CF 17Mar2003, IJ 18Mar2003]
28	1936	1369	DC-2-118B	NC14297	Kueilin (Kweilin)	Force landed 24Aug38 & 29Oct40 [IT, Davies]
31	01Jul37	1567	DC-2		Chungshan	Cr at Kunming, 14Mar42 (13k) [JMG, MC]
31	18May37	1567	DC-2-221		Chungshan	Cr at Kunming, 14Mar42 [IT, Davies] (last DC-2 in fleet)
32	24Jun37	1568	DC-2-221		Kueilin (Kweilin)	Shot down (f/l) by Japanese nr Chungshan, 24Aug38 [JMG, MC], repaired as #39
32	30May37	1568	DC-2-221		Kweilin	Cr Kunming, 14Mar42 [IT, Davies] XT-OBF?
36	-	?	DC-2		Kwangtung	Belonging to Aviation Comm. [MC] (Lent to CNAC by CAF)
39	Jun39	1568	DC-2-221	(ex #32)	Ch'ungch'ing (Chungking)	Shot down by Japanese at Changyi, 27Oct40 [JMG, MC] or 29Oct40 [LA]
40	15May39	1586	DC-2-190	NC16048	K'angting (Kangting)	Crashed at Taohsien, 07Feb41 XT-DBF?
Candidates:						
36?	-	1560	DC-2-192			Nanking Govt. d/d 27Jun36
?	-	1598	DC-2-193			Canton Air Force d/d 28May36
28?	26Jun36	1600	DC-2-118A			Delivered unassembled.

[Sources: Moon Chin's fleet list [MC]; CNAC web site: www.cnac.org/aircraft04.htm; Gradidge, Vol.1, p.18, Vol.1, p.174, etc. [JMG]; Turner p.174; Pan Am p.44; CF 26Jan2006; IJ 07Jul2003; IT 25Sep2002; LA 23Mar2003; LA 24Mar2003; LA 26Mar2003; MM 25May2002; MM 24Mar2003; MM 26Mar2003]. See the end of this article for explanation of initials used in sources and abbreviations.

Pan Am. An Airline and its Aircraft, **by R E G Davies, (p.44) includes the following details for CNAC aircraft in its list of Pan American's DC-2 fleet:**

c/n	*N-no.*	*PAA d/d*	*f/n*	*Remarks*
1302	NC 14269	8Sep34	24	Crashed at Nanking on 25Dec36
1350	NC 14290	1935	-	To Royal Air Force, 1941
1351	NC 14291	Jan35	25	To Panair do Brasil. 29May41
1369	NC 14297	Mar35	28	*Kweilin*. Forced down and strafed by Japanese (14 killed) on 24Aug38. Salvaged but force landed and strafed again on 29Oct40 (9 killed)
1567	none	May37	31	Crashed at Kunming, 14Mar42 (10 killed)
1568	none	May37	32	Crashed at Kunming, 14Mar42 (10 killed)(*sic*)

The CNAC DC-2 "Kweilin" at Kai Tak, Hong Kong, after recovery from the Pearl River. *(Ian Johnson Collection)*

China National Aviation Corporation DC-2 fleet number 39 (c/n 1568) attracting the attention of the local populace. *(Ian Johnson Collection)*

Royal Netherlands Air Force Dakota coded "ZU-9" (c/n 33362) seen visiting the Paris Airshow at Le Bourget in 1957. (Mike Hooks)

Camouflaged Royal Hellenic Air Force Dakota KP255 (c/n 33557) seen at Rhodes in October 1970. (Mike Hooks)

Royal Belgian Air Force C-47 K-10, coded "OT-CWE" (c/n 25851) visiting the Paris Airshow at Le Bourget in 1969. (Mike Hooks)

Former Czech Air Force C-47 awaiting rework and resale at Paris-Le Bourget in 1961. This aircraft, formerly D-18 (c/n 25667) of the Czech Air Force and wearing OK-WZA while under Czech Ministry of Defence ownership, eventually made its way to the French Aeronautique Navale as serial 48406. (Mike Hooks)

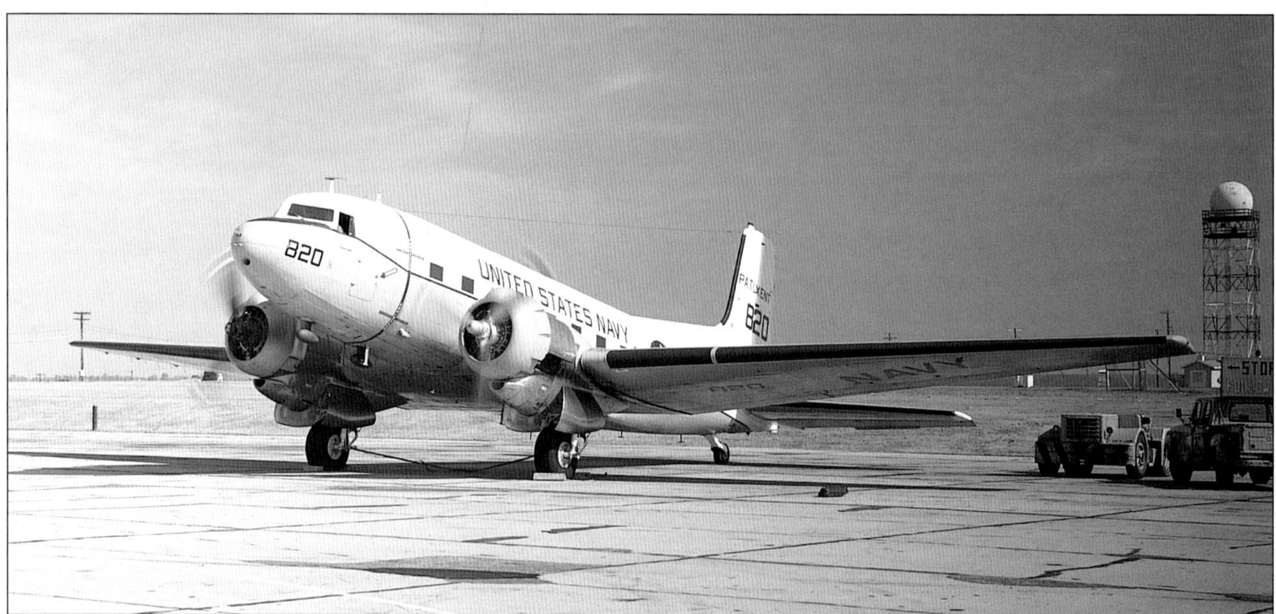

The prototype R4D-8/C-117D BuAer 138820 (c/n 43158) is seen running up engines at Patuxent River, Maryland in July 1966. (Stephen H Miller)

Mexican Navy DC-3 serial MT-203, with picture windows and undercarriage door modifications, is seen at Mexico City in September 1977. (Stephen Piercey Collection)

South African Air Force C-47 6877 (c/n 11925) of 25 Squadron, with target-towing equipment and high visibility colour-scheme, was photographed in October 1977. After conversion to turbo-prop power as a DC-3-TP65, this aircraft was withdrawn from use for preservation at AFB Ysterplaat.
(Stephen Piercey Collection)

Nicaraguan Air Force C-47 serial 416 was photographed in Arizona in July 1975 shortly after rework for Nicaragua. *(Stephen Piercey Collection)*

Royal Canadian Air Force Dakota 12933 (c/n 13383) was photographed while in use with 429 Squadron at CFB Winnipeg in June 1976. Note the under-fuselage radome which has been fitted. *(Stephen H Miller)*

French Air Force C-47 223480 (c/n 9342) in service with GTLA 2/60 Squadron in early 1969 with an unusual window configuration.
(Stephen Piercey Collection)

This camouflaged C-47 serial 3406 of the Dominican Air Force was photographed in June 1982. *(M O'Leary via Stephen Piercey Collection)*

A C-47 of the Honduran Air Force, serial 312, being serviced on 11th October 1974 at an unknown location. The national colours appear on the wingtips as well as on the rudder.
(Stephen Piercey Collection)

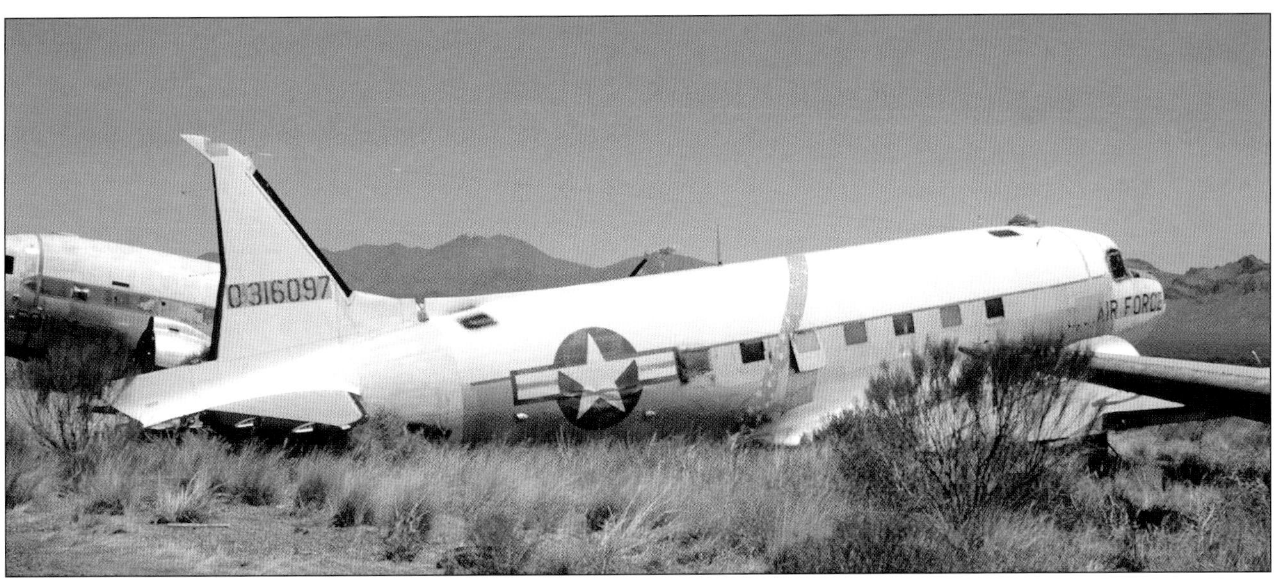

Stored with Aero American at Ryan Field, Arizona in May 1974 was C-47 0-316097 (c/n 20569), still showing a faded Strategic Air Command sash around the fuselage. *(Karl Hayes)*

Also stored at Ryan Field, Arizona in May 1974 were C-47s 0-32921 and 0-293717. Neither aircraft showed any signs of their allocated N876xx registrations. *(Karl Hayes)*

Three further former USAF C-47s stored in May 1974 were 0-224126 and two others still standing on their undercarriage legs. *(Karl Hayes)*

Newly overhauled at Ryan Field, Arizona in May 1974 was postwar DC-3D N42V (c/n 42974) *(Karl Hayes)*

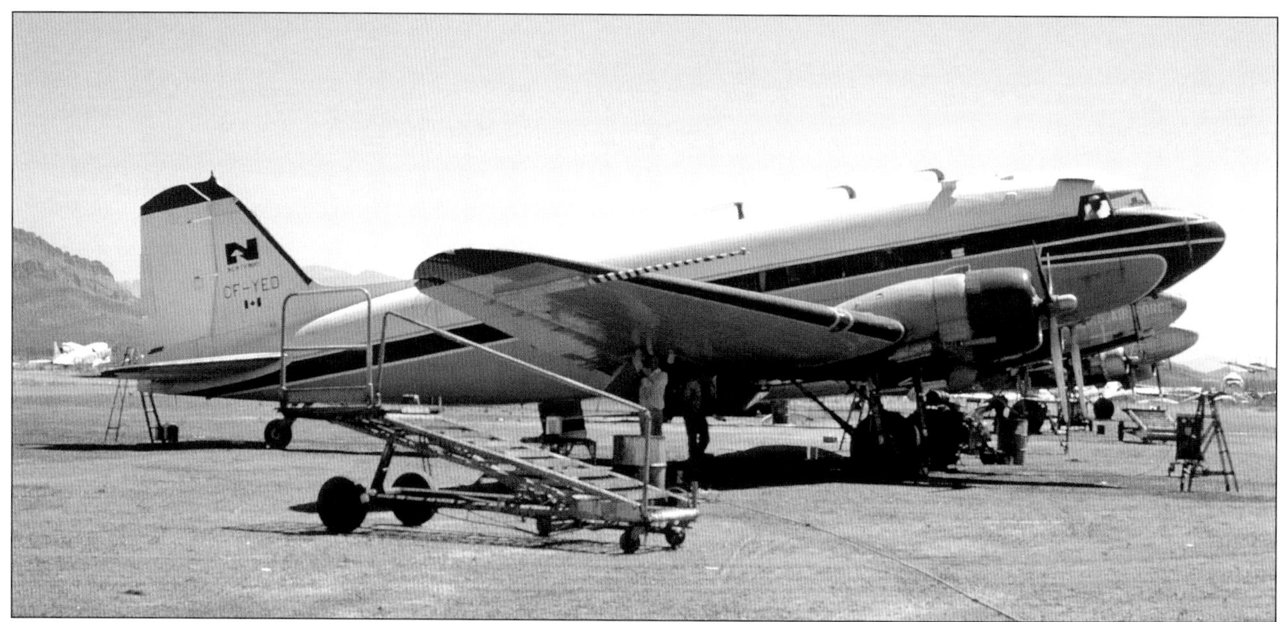

Overhauled and ready for delivery for survey work at Ryan Field in May 1974 was CF-YED (c/n 4433) of Northway Air Surveys. *(Karl Hayes)*

Seen during an October 1976 visit to Ryan Field, Arizona was the 1939-vintage DC-3 N101MX (c/n 2102) which had been purchased by Aero American for overhaul and resale. *(Karl Hayes)*

The US Army Missile Command operated a number of C-47s during the 1970s including NEC-47H serial 0-39103 (c/n 32818), which unusually – for military aircraft – had undercarriage door modifications. The photo was taken at San Francisco, California in May 1971. *(John P Stewart)*

In service with the Indonesian Army in November 1973, A-9038 was photographed at Jakarta with a second aircraft (A-9036) visible behind. *(Stephen Piercey Collection)*

The first Dakota in the Papua New Guinea Defence Force inventory was P65-001 (c/n 33109), a former Royal Australian Air Force aircraft, seen in this photograph dating from July 1976. *(Stephen Piercey Collection)*

A Royal Swedish Air Force C-47 photographed in the later camouflage scheme. Aircraft 79008 (c/n 33153) was operated by F13M Squadron and sported the later style 3-digit code "798". The photo was taken at Munich in July 1981. *(Reimar Wendt)*

A very smart C-47 of the Guatemalan Air Force, serial 580 , was photographed at Opa Locka in Florida at an unknown date. *(Stephen Piercey Collection)*

One of a number of C-117Ds operated by the United States Marines, in this case by MAW-3 Squadron at El Toro, BuAer 17182 (c/n 43375) was photographed in the transit aircraft park at Andrews AFB, Washington, DC in April 1972. *(Stephen H Miller)*

Florida Airmotive's smart DC-3 N168LG (c/n 4089) is seen being loaded at Lantana, Florida in October 1979, with an interesting mural on the inside of the cargo door. *(Karl Hayes)*

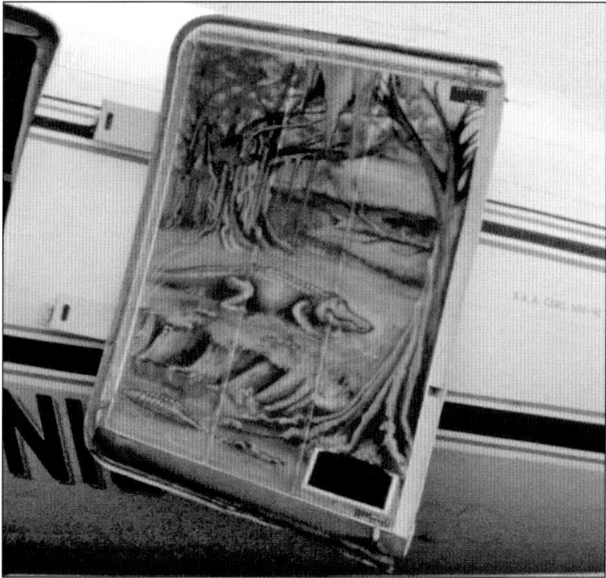

Close-ups of the Florida alligator mural on the inside of the cargo door of Florida Airmotive's DC-3 N168LG (c/n 4089) taken at the company's Lantana, Florida base in October 1979. *(Karl Hayes)*

Skyways of London Dakota G-AMWW (c/n 33010) taken at Beauvais in June 1959 while it was operating the regular Lympne-Beauvais coach-air service. *(Mike Hooks)*

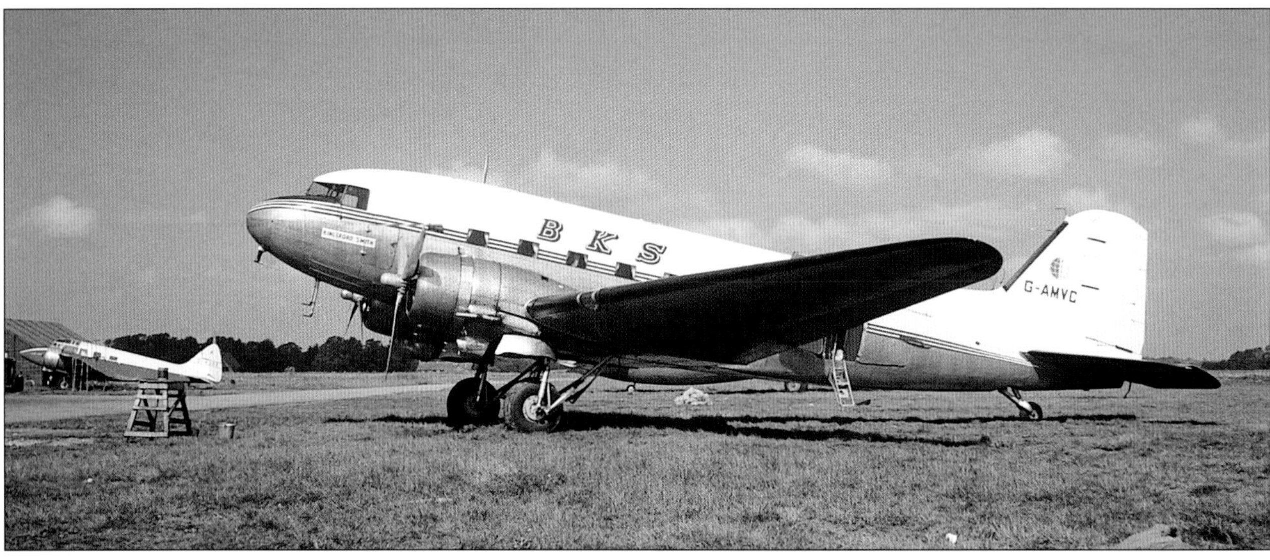

Dakota G-AMVC (c/n 33390) of BKS Air Transport seen resting between flights at Southend in May 1957, with an Airspeed Consul in the background. *(Mike Hooks)*

Dakota EI-ACH (c/n 12893) of Aer Lingus seen on approach to London Airport in the mid-1950s. This photo was taken prior to the introduction of the "green cabin top" scheme that came into use shortly after Aer Lingus started flying Viscounts. *(Mike Hooks)*

An interesting visitor to London Airport in September 1957 was Ariana's DC-3 YA-AAB (c/n 4275). Such exotic visitors – as in this case – were often en route to or returning from major overhaul with Field Aircraft Services at Tollerton or Wymeswold. *(Mike Hooks)*

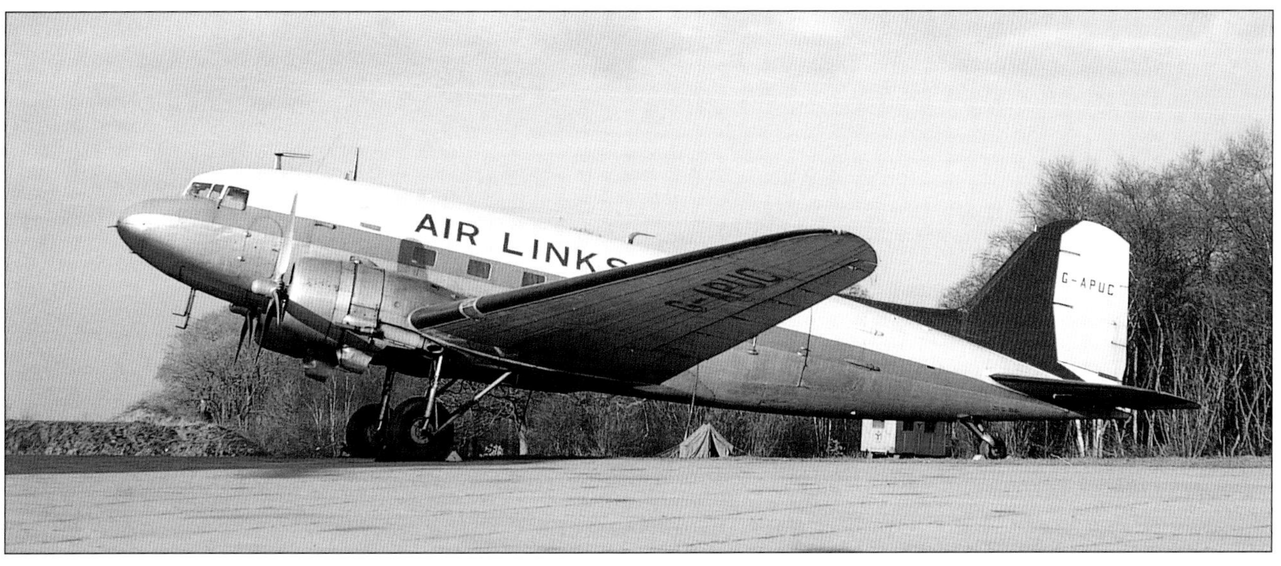

A short-lived colour-scheme was that seen here on Air Links Dakota G-APUC (c/n 12893) at Biggin Hill in 1960. The airline was later rebranded as Trans-Globe with the introduction of Britannias. *(Mike Hooks)*

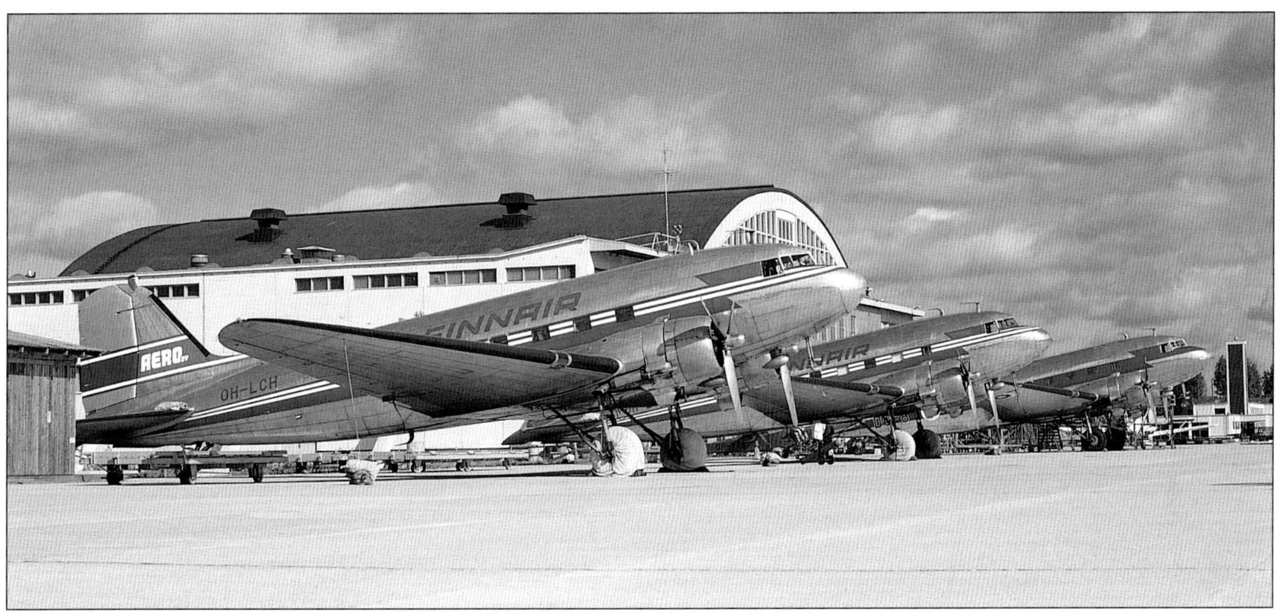

A striking line-up of Finnish Dakotas at Helsinki in June 1969, with two Aero O/Y Finnair machines plus one of the Finnish Air Force behind. The nearestt aircraft, OH-LCH (c/n 6346) has fortunately been preserved in flying condition. *(Mike Hooks)*

A former Linee Aeree Italiane Dakota, I-LENE (c/n 4325), was taken over in the LAI-Alitalia merger in October 1957 and is seen here, still in regular service in 1965, shortly before its sale in Ethiopia. *(Don Hannah Collection)*

One of a small fleet of Dakotas operated by Braathens SAFE Air Transport over the years was LN-SUK (c/n 4327). This photograph was taken around 1962, shortly before the aircraft's sale. *(Don Hannah Collection)*

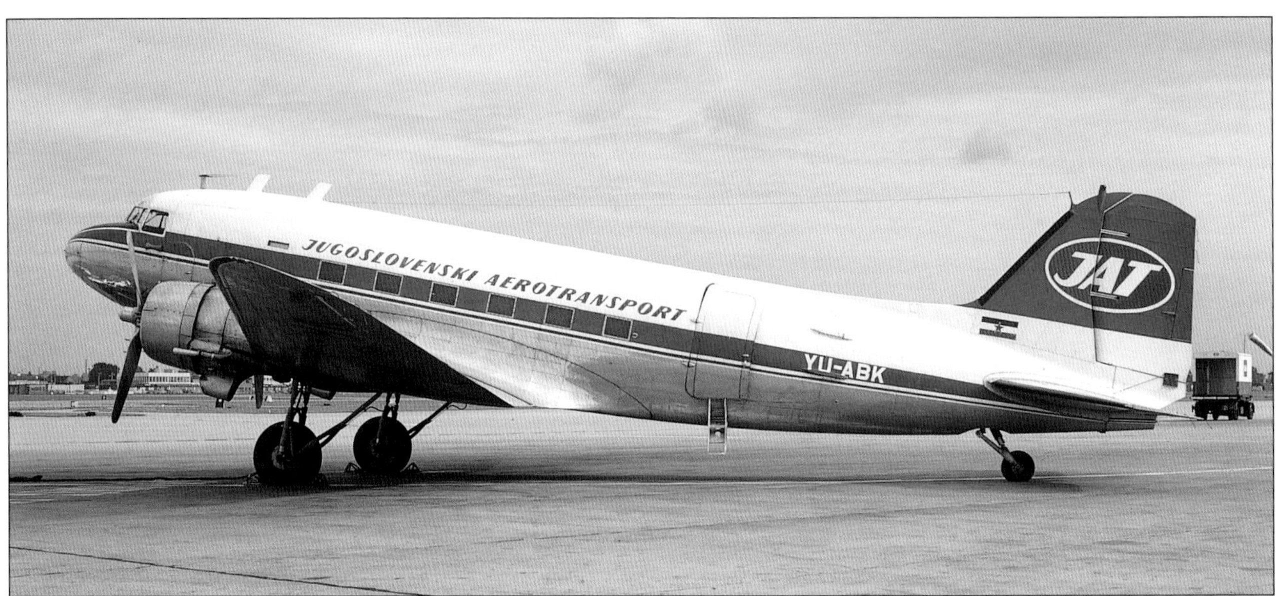

Dakotas of the Yugoslav national airline JAT were infrequent visitors to the UK, usually operating a cargo charter flight. YU-ABK (c/n 33277) is seen here in October 1977 in the later colour-scheme carried. *(Don Hannah Collection)*

After Swissair ceased flying its Dakotas on passenger and cargo schedules in 1964, three of the fleet were transferred to the Swissair training school SLS. One of these, HB-IRN (c/n 33393) is seen at Zurich-Kloten in April 1967 and has since been preserved at the national transport museum Verkehrshaus der Schweiz in Lucerne. *(Mike Hooks)*

Air France operated its DC-3s for many years in the post-war period, with a number continuing in service after withdrawal from the airline in the 1960s for pilot training or with the postal service. F-BAXP (c/n 19799), a former regular visitor to London Airport, is seen on an airfield in northern France in May 1957. *(Mike Hooks)*

CAAC Li-2 318 (c/n 18433809) was photographed at Xi'An (Sian) in November 1979, with a second example behind. *(Stephen Piercey Collection)*

Airnautic GECA DC-2 F-BJHR (c/n 1332) was the last of the type to see active airline service in Europe, from 1959 until 1961. The aircraft was photographed at its home base at Nice-Côte d'Azur. *(PJ Marson Collection)*

Dakota G-AMRA (c/n 26735): A long-serving British Dakota 1952-2010, and still going strong. A selection of the colour-schemes carried over the years is presented here over three pages.

After brief use by Starways, G-AMRA was transferred to Airwork in 1953 and later operated by Transair, in whose colours the aircraft is seen on a cargo charter to Amsterdam in 1959. (Air-Britain)

Transferred to the British United Airways group in 1960, G-AMRA was soon repainted in the colours of group member Morton Air Services, and is seen at its London-Gatwick base in August 1965. (PJ Marson)

When the Channel Islands division of British United Airways became independent of the parent company, G-AMRA was one of the few Dakotas to carry the short-lived colours of BUIA (British United Island Airways), with whom the aircraft served as a freighter. The photograph was taken at London-Gatwick in July 1969. (PJ Marson)

Shortly afterwards, the Channel Islands aircraft was rebranded as British Island Airways and received a colour-scheme which was completely different from British United. G-AMRA is seen departing from London-Gatwick in September 1971. *(PJ Marson)*

One of the subsequent operators of G-AMRA was the short-lived Humber Airways, in whose colours the aircraft is seen after withdrawal from service at Exeter in February 1976, with DH Dove G-AMZY on the right. *(Stephen Piercey Collection)*

G-AMRA was given a new lease of life by the Channel Islands based Intra Airways later in 1976. The smart colour-scheme carried with Intra is seen in this June 1978 photograph taken at Castle Donington (East Midlands). *(Stephen Piercey Collection)*

The Dakota G-AMRA was transferred subsequently to Eastern Airways, receiving yet another colour-scheme seen in this fine air-to-air shot in 1979. *(Stephen Piercey)*

In October 1981, G-AMRA was bought by Air Atlantique, with whom the Dakota still serves. Several colour-schemes have been carried over the years. This one was the second carried in Air Atlantique service, in June 1986. The photograph was taken at North Weald while the Dakota was operating pleasure flights. *(PJ Marson)*

During its later years of passenger flying, G-AMRA carried the same scheme as the company's Lockheed Electras and Douglas DC-6ACs, as seen here at the Coventry (Warwickshire, England) airshow in May 2003. *(PJ Marson)*

Nationalist Government of China

CoAA fleet list 1936

Type	*Number*	*Seats*	*Payload (kg)*	*Status*
DC-2	n/a	18	2800	ready

This DC-2 is one of the following:

"C/n 1560 DC-2-192 Nanking Govt., China 27Jun36. This aircraft is believed to have been converted into a luxury transport for Generalissimo Chiang Kai-shek and nicknamed the "Flying Palace". This has been reported to have been destroyed in a Japanese air raid on Chungking, possibly in May 1939." [JMG p.302]

"C/n 1598 DC-2-193 Canton AF (China) D28May36. It is uncertain if this or c/n 1560 was the aircraft used by the Ministry of Communications during 1937 and 1938 and probably used to check mercenary pilots hired in late 1937. Possibly crashed at Taohsien 07Feb41." [JMG p.303]

There should have been two other DC-2s in China by late 1936. The first is DC-2-192, serial number 1560, that was ordered by the Nanking Government (Dr H H Kung) and delivered on 27th June 1936. The second is DC-2-193, serial number 1598, ordered by the Kwangtung Government and delivered on 28th May 1936. According to reports, one was used by the Chinese Air Force and the other by Chiang Kai-shek. [MM 20Mar2003]

"When Canton was visited by British officers in January 1937 Lam Wai-shing was second in command. Among the aircraft observed at Shoukouling was the Douglas DC-2 that was purchased by Canton, which was then used by the 4th Route Army for liaison flights." [LA 22Mar2003]

"An American officer visited the CAF in June 1939 and flew in a CNAC DC-2 to Chungking (pilot Hugh L Woods). Three DC-2s were on the field. One of them belonged to the CAF, but was operated at all times by CNAC personnel and was used four days a week by the Commission on Aeronautical Affairs and three days by CNAC." [LA 24Mar2003]

"According to the memoir of Gen. I Fu-en, who was Chiang Kai-shek's personal pilot, the Abyssinia government had ordered a DC-2 but the aircraft later went to Kwangtung Government. That should be DC-2-193. After the Kwangtung air force merged into Central Air Force in Nanking in 1936, the DC-2 was borrowed by CNAC as No. 36 because no CNAF pilot could fly it. Later the DC-2 was back to the CNAF and flown by Mr. I. It was destroyed in a Japanese raid." [CF 21Mar2003] (Note: no evidence of an order from Ethiopia has been found; other members have questioned the lack of CNAF pilots.)

"More about the DC-2 #36 from General I's memoir. In the winter of 1939, he was the deputy commander of 9th Squadron, which flew SB-2 at the time. One day General Chou Chi-ro ordered him to go to Chungking to take back that DC-2 from CNAC. That plane was previously ordered by Abyssinia as King Sai La Si (Chinese transcription)'s (Haile Selassie) VIP plane. Because the country was defeated by Italy, the plane could not be delivered. It was then bought by the Kwangtung Province Governor Yu Han-mo. Kwangtung Air Force was ordered to take care of this plane. It later went to central government together with other defecting Kwangtung planes. No one in CNAF could fly or maintain that DC-2, so it was leased to CNAC.

In the early morning of 11th August 1941, the DC-2 was parked in Chengtu. Usually it stayed in remote airfields to escape Japanese air raids, but the big brass said there was no need because the weather was not good and the Japanese would not come. But four Zeros did appear and finished that poor #36." [CF 27Mar2003, 12Nov2006]

CNAC
中國航空公司
CHINA NATIONAL AVIATION CORP.
CHUNGKING, CHINA.

TIME TABLES
PASSENGER FARES, FREIGHT RATES
GENERAL INFORMATION

REGULAR SERVICES:-

HONGKONG TO:—

RANGOON	KWEILIN
LASHIO	HANOI
KUNMING	LUCHOW
CHUNGKING	SUIFU
CHENGTU	KIATING

BOOK YOUR PASSAGE THRU:

EFFECTIVE: FEBRUARY 15th, 1940.

The DC-2 featured in CNAC publicity in the late 1930s. (Ian Johnson Collection)

Given this evidence, there can now be little doubt DC-2-192 c/n 1560 was Chiang Kai-shek's VIP aircraft "*Chung Mei*", nicknamed the "Flying Palace", and DC-2-193 c/n 1598 was transferred from Kwangtung to the CAF in 1936 and then leased by the CoAA to CNAC as fleet number 36 "*Kwangtung*" before return to the CoAA. It was destroyed at Chengtu on 11th August 1941. It has been suggested that Chiang Kai-shek might have used c/n 1598 as a VIP aircraft after his c/n 1560 was lost and before he received a C-53. See VIP aircraft below, Andersson p.264.

Nationalist Government VIP flight

Make/Model	*ID*	*c/n*	*d/d*	*Notes*
Douglas DC-2-192	Flying Palace	1560	27Jun36	see above & below
Douglas DC-2-193	?	1598	Jul36	see above

A single Douglas DC-2-192 c/n 1560 was sold to the Nanking Government (Dr H H Kung) on 27th June 1936. It was fitted out with a luxury VIP interior and was intended for Chiang Kai-shek's growing fleet of VIP aircraft. It was called "The Flying Palace". [Andersson p.124] This DC-2 was named "*Chung Mei*". The interior was described as 'red plush', lined with a veneer of black wood and red floor carpet. It had upholstered chairs, two full-length lounges, a small radio, food box and an ornate writing desk. The exterior was natural silvery duralumin skin, unmarked except for Douglas logos. The Flying Palace was destroyed at Chungking as a result of a Japanese fire bomb. [MM 12Nov2006; RSA p.4]

Some photographs show four DC-2s at Shanghai. CNAC DC-2s #24, #26 and #28 had a narrow chord fin and were DC-2-118 models. An unmarked DC-2 had several distinguishing features: broader fin; two extra small circular windows in the rear fuselage; some kind of logo on the fin and on the nose. This may have been c/n 1560. Chiang Kai-shek's aircraft was a DC-2-192 and the one for Canton was a DC-2-193. It is very unlikely that the Canton aircraft would have been shipped to Shanghai, so we can assume that the unmarked aircraft is Chiang's c/n 1560. The caption of a photo of an unmarked DC-2 at Hankow in 1938 simply states probably s/n 1560. The small marks on the nose and fin of the unmarked DC-2 are the Douglas logo; an earth surrounded by words. [CF 25Mar2003; CF 26Mar2003; LA 26Mar2003; MM 26Mar2003] A photo of #31 shows that it has a broad fin but not the two extra windows in the rear right fuselage. [CF 26Mar2003]

"A large Douglas DC-2 15-passenger plane arrived in Hong Kong shortly before noon yesterday from Canton and is now in the hangar at Kai Tak. The plane is the property of Marshal Chiang Kai-shek and has been in Canton for the last six months undergoing repairs following an accident there, when a wing was damaged. Yesterday the plane was ordered by Nanking to proceed to Hong Kong and await instructions here." [SCMP 20Aug1937/ IDJ 27Mar2003]

"Chiang Kai-shek's plush DC-2 was finally destroyed, probably sometime previous to October 1938, at the island airport at Chungking. "The Flying Palace" took a direct hit, dead centre, from a Japanese fire bomb." [RSA p.10] See CoAA aircraft above.

II - The Douglas DC-3 in China

China National Aviation Corporation

Given the success of the DC-2 in China, CNAC was keen to introduce the bigger DC-3 to its fleet but these aircraft were difficult to obtain even before the start of the war in the Pacific.

CNAC went to great lengths and displayed incredible ingenuity to keep its dwindling supply of aircraft in service. For example, in May 1941 Japanese fighters intercepted Hugh Woods in one of CNAC's new DC-3s while en route from Chungking to Chengtu. He made a forced landing at Suifu as the Japanese dived to attack. Although crew and passengers escaped without injury, Japanese bombs blew the right wing off Wood's DC-3. The 24,000-pound aircraft had to be moved from the airfield as soon as possible in order to escape damage from a second strike. CNAC did not have a spare wing section in stock for a DC-3; however, a slightly smaller DC-2 wing was available in Hong Kong. No one really knew if a DC-3 could fly with a DC-2 wing, but it seemed worth a try. The spare wing section was lashed to the fuselage of a DC-2 for the 860-mile flight from Hong Kong to Suifu. While the aerodynamic effect of this strange configuration could not be predicted, CNAC's engineering staff believed that the aircraft could be controlled in flight – theoretically, at least. Harold Sweet, an expert pilot with more courage than sense, volunteered for the trip. Fortunately, the aircraft flew normally, except for a slight longitudinal instability and some buffeting.

While Sweet was en route to Suifu via a refuelling stop at Kweilin, a gang of coolies pushed the damaged DC-3 three miles down a highway and hid it in a clump of trees. Japanese bombers arrived over Suifu to complete their work just as Sweet approached the area. Sweet avoided the Japanese planes by landing at nearby Chautong. After the bewildered Japanese had left Suifu without locating the camouflaged DC-3, Sweet flew into the airfield with the spare wing. The new wing and damaged aircraft were mated, with only a little ingenuity and effort. The aircraft, renamed a "DC-2½", was then flown to Hong Kong for permanent repairs. The "DC-2½" performed well on the flight, the pilot reported; she needed no more than full aileron-tab setting for stability. [An article on CNAC's DC-2½, May 1941, Suifu and back to Hong Kong: "My story of the DC-2½" by Zygmund Soldinski, reproduced from Wings Over Asia, Volume II, 1972, is included on the CNAC web site at www.cnac.org/aircraft02.htm.]

Douglas DC-3

f/n	*d/d or date received*	*c/n*	*Model*	*p/i*	*Chinese reg.*	*Name*	*Fate*
41	09Aug39, 01Oct39 (rcd)	2135	DC-3-228B		XT-BTA/B	Chiating (Kiating)	*"Whistling Willie"* To XT-91; CATI as N8360C via XT-1xx
46	Nov40, Jan41	2148	DC-3-294A			O'Mei (Omei)	"DC-2½". Damaged by f/l in Yangtze River nr Chungking, 13Feb43
47	Jul41	2261	DC-3-268C	NC19971	XT-BTA/B		To XT-92; CATI as N8359C (Dec49) via XT-1xx
[Sources: Moon Chin's fleet list; CNAC web site: www.cnac.org/aircraft07.htm; Gradidge, Vol. p.174, etc.; IT 25Sep2002; MM 25May2002]							
XT- civil registrations may have been allocated for flights to Burma.							

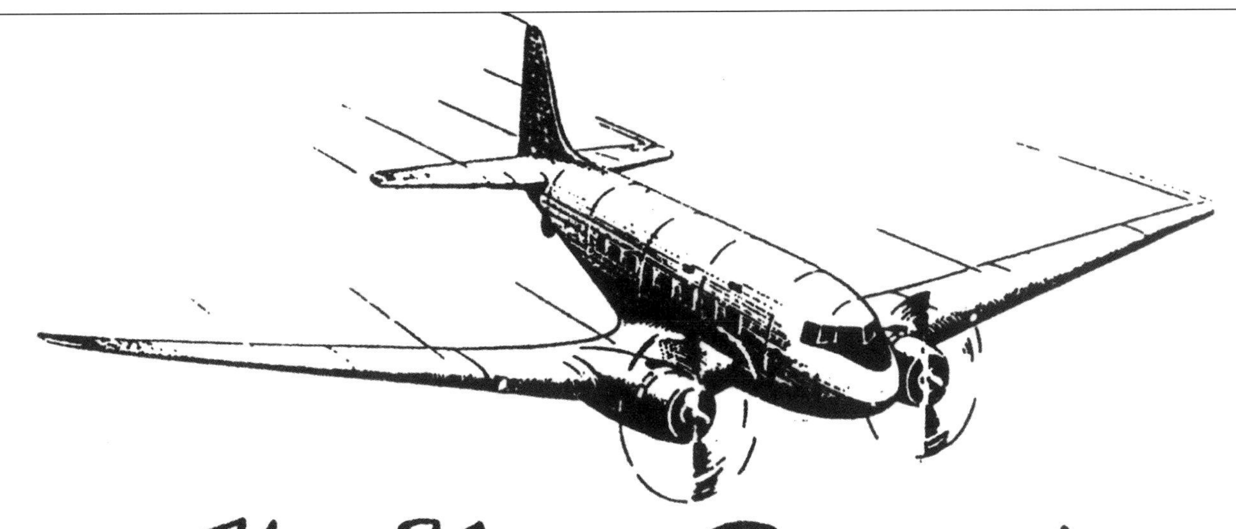

Hong Kong to Rangoon!
• VIA CHUNGKING, KUNMING AND LASHIO — WEEKLY SERVICE.
• LUXURIOUS, SOUNDPROOFED DOUGLAS AIRLINERS — EQUIPPED WITH TWO-WAY RADIO.
• FARES (EFFECTIVE JAN. 1ST) — £49 SINGLE, £98 RETURN.
• FOR SCHEDULE INFORMATION AND FURTHER PARTICULARS APPLY TO —
CHINA NATIONAL AVIATION CORPORATION
GENERAL TRAFFIC AGENTS FOR
PAN AMERICAN AIRWAYS SYSTEM

Above: An advertisement for CNAC's services from Hong Kong to Rangoon, Burma.
(Ian Johnson Collection)

Right: The famous "DC-2 & a half" created when the left wing of a DC-2 was attached to DC-3 c/n 2148 after it was damaged by Japanese bombing at Suifu. The aircraft is seen here at Kai Tak, Hong Kong, with CNAC Curtiss Condors in the background.
(Ian Johnson Collection)

Lend-Lease and The Hump

In March 1941 President Roosevelt declared that China was eligible to receive military aid through Lend-Lease. Allotments to China were continually being diverted, either at source or en route to China. Many of these C-53s, C-47s, C-47As and C-47Bs were allocated to CNAC for use on The Hump airlift over the Himalayan Mountains between India and China. A fleet list compiled by Captain Moon Chin gives details of many of these aircraft but not the C-47Bs, so it is then necessary to study Lend-Lease records. We assume that CNAC allocated fleet numbers when the aircraft arrived at Dum Dum airport, Calcutta but the order of arrival was not necessarily the same as the order of departure from Florida. There was a high rate of attrition during operations over The Hump, as shown in Table 1 (page 116).

Lend-lease DC-3s for China / CNAC

#	*s/n*	*c/n*	*Model*	*d/d*	*Fate, CNAC f/n*
1	41-20082	4852	C-53-DO	25Mar42C	CNAC #48 D26Feb42
2	41-20083	4853	C-53-DO	25Mar42C	CNAC #49 D26Feb42
3	41-20101*	4871	C-53-DO	12Apr42C	CNAC #50 D12Apr42; to XT-90, N8362C
4	41-20109*	4879	C-53-DO	12May42C	CNAC #51 D12May42
5	41-20111	4881	C-53-DO	09Jun42C	CNAC #56 D09Jun42
6	41-20113	4883	C-53-DO	12Jun42C	CNAC #57 D12Jun42
7	41-20132	4902	C-53-DO	19May42C	CNAC #52 D19May42
8	41-20134	4904	C-53-DO	28May42C	CNAC #53 D25May42
9	42-6475	4927	C-53-DO	26May42	CNAC #54 D28May42; to XT-45, N8361C
10	42-6477	4929	C-53-DO	05Jun42	CNAC #55 D04Jun42
11	42-6500	4952	C-53-DO	29Jun42C	COAA (not CNAC)
12	42-6501	4953	C-53-DO	15Jul42C	COAA (not CNAC)
13	42-15889	7406	C-53-DO	07Oct42C	CNAC #59 D07Oct42
14	42-15890	7407	C-53-DO	18Sep42C	CNAC #58 D18Sep42
15	41-18556	4681	C-47-DL	18Oct42C	CNAC #60 D18Oct42
16	41-38626	4729	C-47-DL	26Nov42C	CNAC #61 D26Nov42
17	41-38627	4730	C-47-DL	02Dec42C	CNAC #62 D02Dec42
18	41-38651	6034	C-47-DL	04Jan43	CNAC #63 D05Jan43
19	41-38652	6035	C-47-DL	06Jan43C	CNAC #64 D06Jan43
20	41-38654	6037	C-47-DL	10Jan43C	CNAC #65 D10Jan43
21	41-38655	6038	C-47-DL	20Dec42C	? (not CNAC)
22	41-38691*	6150	C-47-DL	10Feb43C	CNAC #66 D10Feb43
23	41-38692*	6151	C-47-DL	21Feb43C	CNAC #67 D21Feb43
24	41-38762	6221	C-47-DL	04Mar43C	CNAC #68 D04Mar43
25	41-38763	6222	C-47-DL	04Mar43C	CNAC #69 D04Mar43
26	41-18664	6025	C-47-DL	29Jun43C	? (14th AF) (not CNAC)
27	42-32787	9013	C-47-DL	10Apr43C	CNAC #71 D10Apr43
28	42-32788	9014	C-47-DL	30Mar43C	CNAC #70 D30Mar43
29	42-32883	9109	C-47-DL	13Apr43C	CNAC #73 D?
30	42-32884	9110	C-47-DL	17Apr43C	CNAC #72 D17Apr43
31	42-23429	9291	C-47A-20-DL	29May43C	CNAC #74 D25Jun43
32	42-23430	9292	C-47A-20-DL	06Jun43	COAA (not CNAC)
33	42-23554	9416	C-47A-25-DL	25Jun43C	CNAC #75 D25Jun43
34	42-23555	9417	C-47A-25-DL	04Jul43C	CNAC #76 D04Jul43
35	42-23734	9596	C-47A-30-DL	15Jul43C	CNAC #77 D15Jul43
36	42-23735	9597	C-47A-30-DL	15Jul43C	CNAC #78 D15Jul43
37	42-23898	9760	C-47A-35-DL	05Jul43C	CNAC #79 D12Aug43, to USAAF
38	42-23899*	9761	C-47A-35-DL	05Jul43C	CNAC #80 D13Aug43
39	42-24093	9955	C-47A-45-DL	03Aug43M	CNAC #81 D04Sep43
40	42-24094	9956	C-47A-45-DL	03Aug43M	CNAC #82 D05Sep43
41	42-24296	10158	C-47A-50-DL	12Sep43C	CNAC #84 D05Oct43
42	42-24297	10159	C-47A-50-DL	04Sep43M	CNAC #83 D03Oct43
43	42-100438	18901	C-47A-65-DL	06Nov43C	CNAC #86 D17Nov43; to XT-T86, N8358C
44	42-100439	18902	C-47A-65-DL	13Oct43M	CNAC #85 D10Nov43
45	42-100598	19061	C-47A-65-DL	13Dec43K	CNAC #88 D14Dec43
46	42-100599*	19062	C-47A-65-DL	05Dec43K	CNAC #87 D07Dec43; to XT-51, N8355C
47	42-100850	19313	C-47A-75-DL	06Mar44C	CNAC #89 D21Jan44; to XT-T48, N8348C
48	42-100851	19314	C-47A-75-DL	25Jan44C	CNAC #90 D10Feb44
49	42-100989	19452	C-47A-75-DL	06Mar44C	CNAC #91 D15Mar44; to XT-T54, N8352C
50	42-100990	19453	C-47A-75-DL	06Mar44	Crashed on delivery at Camaguey, Cuba 7Mar44
51	43-15154	19620	C-47A-80-DL	26Feb44C	CNAC #92 D12Apr44; to XT-85, N8349C
52	43-15155	19621	C-47A-80-DL	25Feb44C	CNAC #93 D14Apr44
53	43-15337	19803	C-47A-80-DL	04Apr44C	CNAC #94 D03May44
54	43-15338	19804	C-47A-80-DL	02Apr44C	CNAC #95 D05May44
55	43-15462	19928	C-47A-85-DL	24May44C	? (not CNAC)
x	43-15463	19929	C-47A-85-DL	14May44M	Crashed 5 miles N of Miami on del 14May44
56	43-15625*	20091	C-47A-85-DL	29May44C	CNAC #96 D13Jun44
57	43-15786	20252	C-47A-90-DL	18Jun44C	CNAC #98 D03Jul44

58	43-15787	20253	C-47A-90-DL	11Jun44C	CNAC #97
59	43-16233	20699	C-47B-1-DL	18Aug44C	CNAC ?105?
60	43-16234	20700	C-47B-1-DL	04Aug44C	CNAC ?99? D05Sep44
61	43-16235	20701	C-47B-1-DL	18Aug44C	CNAC ?106?
62	43-16236	20702	C-47B-1-DL	09Aug44C	CNAC ?100? D04Nov44
63	43-16337	20803	C-47B-1-DL	16Aug44C	CNAC* ?102?
64	43-16338	20804	C-47B-1-DL	13Aug44C	CNAC* ?101?
65	43-16339	20805	C-47B-1-DL	16Aug44C	CNAC* ?103?
66	43-16340	20806	C-47B-1-DL	16Aug44C	l/n 4193; CNAC* ?104?; to XT-20, N8350C
67	43-16401	20867	C-47B-1-DL	19Sep44C	CNAC* ?109?
68	43-16402	20868	C-47B-1-DL	24Sep44C	CNAC* ?110?
69	43-16403	20869	C-47B-1-DL	10Sep44C	?107?
70	43-16404	20870	C-47B-1-DL	16Sep44C	?108?
71	43-49044	26305	C-47B-10-DK	15Nov44C	CNAC* ?111?
72	43-49045	26306	C-47B-10-DK	15Nov44C	CNAC* ?112?
73	43-49046	26307	C-47B-10-DK	08Dec44C	?CNAF?
74	44-76195	32527	C-47B-25-DK	28Jan45C	CNAC ?136?; to XT-84
75	44-76198	32530	C-47B-25-DK	18Feb45K	CNAC ?137?; XT-58, XT-133, N8354C
76	44-76199	32531	C-47B-25-DK	18Feb45C	CNAC ?138?
77	44-76471	32803	C-47B-25-DK	16Mar45C	CNAC ?139?
78	44-76485	32817	C-47B-25-DK	22Mar45C	CNAC ?140?; XT-81, N8353C
79	44-76515	32847	C-47B-25-DK	29Mar45C	CNAC ?141?; XT-52, N8351C
80	44-76554	32886	C-47B-30-DK	30Mar45C	?145?
81	44-76583	32915	C-47B-30-DK	03Apr45C	?147? CNAF?
82	44-76615	32947	C-47B-30-DK	08Apr45C	?? CNAF?
[Butler & Hagedorn p.195; JMG2; Moon Chin fleet list; MM 11Mar2003]					
Notes:					
* s/n not listed as lend-lease by Butler & Hagedorn.					
d/d delivery date suffices: C – China; K – Karachi; M – Miami [JMG]; D- prefix: delivery to CNAC [MC]					
f/n 147 may be a C-46					
?? CNAC fleet numbers (to be determined) probably allocated on arrival at Calcutta or Kunming. These f/ns differ from those postulated in JMG2, because of the extra lend-lease aircraft listed above.					

Theatre transfers

#	*s/n*	*c/n*	*Model*	*d/d*	*Fate*
83	41-18481*	4573	C-47-DL	15May45?	XT-T56, N8356C
84	42-5657	6245	C-47-DL	10Sep45	ex FD781; CNAF
85	42-93348	13250	C-47A-25-DK	16Sep45	
86	42-93377	13282	C-47A-25-DK	16Sep45	
87	42-93489	13406	C-47A-25-DK	16Sep45	
88	42-93747	13693	C-47A-25-DK	16Sep45	
89	42-93748	13694	C-47A-25-DK	10Sep45	"42-93848"
90	42-93749	13695	C-47A-25-DK	16Sep45	
91	42-93763	13711	C-47A-25-DK	16Sep45	
92	42-108987	13718	C-47A-25-DK	16Sep45	
[Butler & Hagedorn p.195] Only c/n 4573 recorded with a CNAC connection.					

China National Aviation Corporation C-47 fleet number 87 in its original military scheme, prior to painting in airline colours.
(Ian Johnson Collection)

From about 1946, CNAC aircraft were allocated civil registrations in the XT-Txx alpha-numerical sequence. The following are extracts from a fleet list for CNAC on 27th February 1948, kindly provided by Liang-yen Wen:

Douglas DC-3	XT-45	54	passenger
	XT-48	89	passenger
	XT-51	87	passenger
	XT-54	91	passenger
	XT-55	55	passenger
	XT-56	136	passenger
	XT-82	62	passenger
	XT-84	107	passenger
	XT-85	92	passenger
	XT-86	86	passenger
	XT-87	67	passenger
	XT-88	68	passenger
	XT-90	50	passenger
	XT-91	41	passenger
	XT-92	47	passenger
Douglas C-47	XT-T-20	100	cargo
	XT-T-52	112	cargo
	XT-T-58	108	cargo
	XT-T-81	111	cargo
	XT-T-83	103	cargo
Douglas C-47	XT-T-60	?	training

These registrations were replaced by registrations in the XT-1xx sequence later in 1948.

CNAC DC-3 Fleet Composition (1949)

Item	*Model*	*Reg. No.*	*No. of Seats*	*Usage*
6	C-47A	XT-111	27	Passenger & Cargo
7	C-47A	XT-115	27	Passenger & Cargo
8	C-47B	XT-119	32	Air Bus
9	C-47B	XT-123	27	Passenger & Cargo
10	C-47A	XT-127	27	Passenger & Cargo
11	C-47B	XT-131	27#	Passenger & Cargo
12	C-47B	XT-133##	27	Passenger & Cargo
13	C-53-DC	XT-121	21	Passenger
14	C-47A-DC	XT-125	21	Passenger
15	C-47-DC	XT-129	21	Passenger
16	C-47-DC	XT-137	21	Passenger
17	C-47A-DC	XT-139	21	Passenger
18	C-53-DC	XT-141	21	Passenger
19	DC-3	XT-117+	32	Air Bus
[CF 01Jun2002, 04Nov2009, LYW 23Mar2003]				
Notes (as per original document): # Plane equipped with bucket seats & cushions (XT-131?) ## Plane under conversion (XT-133?) + Plane under repair at JAMCO (XT-117?)				

The following seven CNAC DC-3s were among the twelve Nationalist airliners that defected to Communist China on 9th November 1949: C-47: XT-115, XT-121, XT-123, XT-125, XT-129, XT-131, XT-139.

The following six CNAC C-47s were impounded at Kai Tak in November 1949 following suspension of their CofRs by the ROC CAA: XT-111, XT-117, XT-119, XT-127, XT-137, and XT-141. (XT-34 was reported as a C-47 but was probably a C-46.)

The Chinese Nationalist government sold CNAC (and CATC) to the Chennault and Willauer partnership on 12th December 1949 and these aircraft were registered in the USA on 19th December 1949, as listed in the section on Civil Air Transport, Inc. below.

The following 48 CNAC aircraft are listed in a Chinese document from the MOC for sale to Chennault and Willauer on 12th December 1949:

XT-101 (37-28), XT-102 (37-29), XT-103 (37-30), XT-105 (37-32), XT-106 (37-33), XT-111 (37-36), XT-114 (37-43), XT-115 (37-38), XT-116 (37-44), XT-117 (37-39), XT-118 (37-40), XT-119 (37-34), XT-120 (37-41), XT-121 (37-35), XT-122 (37-73), XT-123 (37-93), XT-125 (37-94), XT-127 (37-95), XT-129 (37-96), XT-130 (37-83), XT-131 (37-97), XT-136 (37-86), XT-139 (37-128), XT-140 (37-88), XT-141 (37-129), XT-142 (37-89), XT-144 (37-90), XT-147 (38-17), XT-148 (37-92), XT-154 (37-137), XT-160 (37-141), XT-162 (37-142), XT-164 (37-143), XT-166 (37-144), XT-168 (37-145), XT-170 (37-146), XT-172 (37-147), XT-401 (37-45), XT-402 (37-46), XT-403 (37-47), XT-404 (37-48), XT-405 (37-74), XT-406 (37-75), XT-407 (37-76), XT-408 (37-77), XT-409 (37-78), XT-410 (37-79), XT-411 (37-149). Numbers in brackets are Chinese Certificate of Airworthiness numbers. Prefix 37- is for 1948 and 38- is for 1949. Aircraft types were not included but DC-3s are proposed in the CNAC fleet lists given in Table 1.

Note: this list does not include the CNAC aircraft on Taiwan that were transferred to CAT in November 1949. Also, XT-137 is not included but was listed by the DCA at Hong Kong in November. [MSB 30Jun2007]

Central Air Transport Corporation

The Central Air Transport Corporation (CATC) traced its lineage back to Eurasia, the pre-war Sino-German airline. Eurasia had been taken over by the Chinese government on 1st August 1941, following the break in diplomatic relations between China and Germany. Eurasia was made bankrupt on 26th February 1943 and formally liquidated on 1st June 1943. [Andersson p.217; Leary TDW p.196])

When the Second World War came to an end in August 1945, CATC was able to secure a loan from a private banker to purchase twelve (The CA-number fleet list suggests that perhaps only 11 C-47s were acquired). Douglas C-47s from the USAAF in India. With these, it participated with CNAC in an airlift for the Nationalist Government to transfer government personnel and freight from the wartime capital in Chungking to the former capital, Nanking, and to the coastal cities, particularly Shanghai. [Davies p.362]

CATC had sufficient aircraft to establish a network of routes, mostly in northern China. At the end of 1947 the airline invested in five passenger-carrying DC-3s (not the military C-47 cargo- and troop-carrier) and was able to offer regular service over 27 routes, from Shanghai to Sinkiang in the far northwest. [Davies p.362]

The two CATC aircraft that defected to Communist China on 9th November 1949 were CV-240 XT-610 and C-47 XT-525. C-47 XT-501 had defected from Canton to Nanking on 25th August 1949 and C-47 XT-507 defected from Hong Kong to Canton on 27th October 1949. Neither of these two aircraft is included in the MOC sales list. [CF 01Apr2002] C-46 XT-512 and C-47 XT-533, included in the MOC sales list, are not accounted for on any list and may have remained on the mainland.

CNAC C-47 fleet number 68 (c/n 6221) photographed in December 1945 in full airline colour-scheme. The photo was possibly taken at Calcutta while operating the Peking-Calcutta passenger service. *(Peter M Bowers)*

A rare photo of a CNAC C-47 showing the XT-Txx style of registrations as used in the period 1946-48. Illustrated is XT-T58, fleet number 108, which was used for cargo only in 1948. *(Ian Johnson Collection)*

"Already on August 25 a CATC Chinese co-pilot, flying one of the airline's C-47s, had defected to mainland China. And on October 27 a CATC pilot deserted to the Communists, absconding with a CATC DC-3. On November 9, 12 commercial aircraft, two belonging to CATC and 10 to CNAC, defected to mainland China (11 arrived safely, one turned back to Hong Kong). Aboard the planes, all crewed by Chinese, were the managing directors of both airlines." [Wright p.304]

The Chinese Nationalist government sold CATC (and CNAC) to the Chennault and Willauer partnership on 12th December 1949 and these aircraft were registered in the USA on 19th December 1949, as listed in the section on Civil Air Transport, Inc. below.

According to the Chinese Ministry of Communications (MOC), the CATC fleet of 46 aircraft was due to be sold to Chennault & Willauer on 12th December 1949. The following 46 CATC aircraft are listed in the MOC document:

XT-502 (37-6), XT-503 (37-18), XT-505 (37-110), XT-508 (37-5), XT-509 (37-17), XT-510 (37-7), XT-511 (37-19), XT-512 (37-102), XT-513 (37-26), XT-514 (37-104), XT-515 (37-131), XT-516 (37-105), XT-517 (37-20), XT-518 (37-106), XT-521 (37-112), XT-522 (37-8), XT-523 (37-21), XT-524 (37-9), XT-525 (37-113), XT-526 (37-103), XT-527 (37-23), XT-528 (37-108), XT-529 (37-24), XT-530 (37-10), XT-531 (37-25), XT-532 (37-109), XT-533 (37-22), XT-534 (37-11), XT-535 (37-72), XT-536 (37-12), XT-537 (37-114), XT-539 (37-133), XT-540 (37-14), XT-541 (37-134), XT-542 (37-15), XT-543 (37-27), XT-544 (37-135), XT-600 (38-1), XT-602 (38-2), XT-604 (38-3), XT-606 (38-4), XT-608 (38-5), XT-610 (38-6), XT-701 (37-1), XT-702 (37-49), XT-703 (37-50). Numbers in brackets are Chinese Certificate of Airworthiness numbers. Prefix 37- is for 1948 and 38- is for 1949. Aircraft types were not included but DC-3s are postulated in the CATC fleet list given in Table 2. *Note: XT-543 was owned at this time by the Lutheran World Federation, so should not have been included in this sale.*

Thirty-nine 39 CATC aircraft, including 17 C-47s, were stationed at Kai Tak Airfield on 16th November 1949 and were detained there until September 1952:

C-47: XT-503, XT-505, XT-509, XT-511, XT-513, XT-515, XT-517, XT-521, XT-523, XT-527, XT-529, XT-531, XT-533, XT-537, XT-539, XT-541, XT-543 [HK DCA letter 16Nov49, CO537/5730 #208]

Great China Aviation Corporation

Great China Aviation Corporation (Dahua Hangkong Gongsi) was formed by Wu Shichang, Hu Shuchu and Lang Luxuen in Chongqing during the war with Japan. It was originally called Northwest Aviation Service Company. The name was officially changed to Dahua on 12th August 1945 by its accountant, Pan Lisheng, through his connections with the Guo Ming Dang (Kuomintang) Social Bureau. Dahua received notification on 13th September 1945 that its application for service was under review by the Transport Ministry. The Economy Ministry granted a business license Number 1788 on 19th October. At the same time Dahua ordered three C-47s from abroad. The owners claimed to have capitalisation of 100 million Yuan but in reality they had no assets.

With the exception of Hu Shuchu, the principals of Dahua had no experience of running an airline. Hu had studied aircraft manufacturing and business management in Germany and had spent several years working for Eurasia. As a result, Hu controlled both the technical and business management of the airline.

Secretary of State Song Zhiwen was against the approval of Great China since he was a strong advocate of China National Aviation Corporation (CNAC). He ordered the Social Bureau to withdraw the registration of Dahua, and the Economy Ministry to revoke the business license. Also, he issued an order preventing Dahua from using any airport in China, and prevented the Central Bank from issuing a loan of $200,000.

Despite the difficulties with the Department of State, who wanted Dahua to sell its planes to CNAC, they still received some support from other Government departments. In May 1946, Hu was introduced to Mr Kong of Central Air Transport Corporation (CATC). Dahua requested assistance from CATC for the purchase of their five C-47 airplanes from the US Army surplus commission. Each cost $20,000. Kong also provided $50,000 from CATC for airplane insurance and $20,000-$30,000 for office equipment and other supplies. Dahua set up headquarters in Shanghai, and its employees grew to more than 200.

In addition to the purchase of the five planes, Dahua also reached other agreements with CATC. One of the conditions for Dahua to begin business was that CATC would operate and maintain five planes. Dahua would pay CATC for these services, use CATC logo and tail numbers, and fly existing CATC routes. In the agreement, it stated that Dahua would have the right to hire flight crew, and market and run its own passenger and cargo business. This agreement was submitted to the Transportation Ministry for approval.

The five C-47s were assigned CATC fleet numbers CA32 to CA36 (see Table 2) but a photograph shows a GCAC C-47 marked "GCAC 101", suggesting that GCAC ignored the directive to operate in CATC logo. This also suggests that the GCAC fleet numbers may have been 101 to 105.

From 15th July 1946, Dahua officially flew Shanghai – Wuhan – Chongqing, and Shanghai – Guangzhou – Hong Kong. On average, Dahua flew one flight per day.

In addition, it was claimed that business connections were used to engage in smuggling flights.

During the cooperation with CATC, it was also claimed that Dahua took away some of CATC's cargo business illegally and also stole spare parts from CATC planes. For the above reasons and more, on 17th August the Transportation Ministry ordered CATC to buy Dahua's five airplanes immediately. CATC informed Dahua of the order and asked that it be done quickly. At the same time, CATC ordered a halt to the operation and maintenance of the five planes. On 24th August, the Transportation Ministry informed CATC that its agreement with Dahua would be withdrawn on 31st August. CATC was asked to complete the purchase of the five planes by 15th September.

On 2nd September, CATC announced that they had complied with the order to stop operating Dahua's planes, and were in the process of arranging their purchase. Dahua ignored these orders, however, and continued to fly between Shanghai, Wuhan, Chongqing and Xian. On 5th October, the Transportation Ministry and Air Force Headquarters ordered all their divisions and airports that as from 11th October Dahua's planes should not be allowed to take off from any airport. The planes should not be damaged in any way but should be detained. CATC asked its employees to monitor the situation carefully. They were requested to report if anything was found that ignored this order or any plane was damaged. As a consequence, Dahua were no longer able to operate.

Soon after, American pilots Willis P Hobbs and Weldon D Bigony left Dahua to join CNRRA Air Transport, which later became Civil Air Transport (CAT).

On 21st October 1946, CATC submitted a letter to the Transportation Ministry informing them that four of Dahua's planes were parked at Lunghwa Airport, Shanghai. Later on the fifth plane returned to Shanghai. In December 1946, a runaway CNAC C-47 collided with one of these planes on the ground. CNAC paid $20,000 in compensation. From a photograph, it is apparent that the Dahua plane was badly damaged and almost certainly was not repaired. Neither plane has been identified. The remaining four airplanes remained at the airport without adequate protection from the elements. In 1948, the Transportation Ministry advertised the four planes for sale in the local press. Due to internal disputes within the former Dahua management, however, none were sold.

After the Communist take-over, the local Shanghai Government submitted a report to the Central Government that the condition of the four planes was too poor to be able to fly and they were only good for spare parts. Ownership was transferred to the Chinese Government on 27th April 1951, since no one claimed them. [MM 02Nov2004]

Liang-yen Wen commented on the above as follows:

"To my knowledge, there are three 'Da-Hua' Airlines, namely: Japanese supported one in WWII, the GCAC we are talking about, and the one established in Taiwan. It is true, as stated by William Leary, GCAC was backed by San Min Chu I (three principles of the people) Youth Corp, the core of Kuomintang. But I doubt there was any direct connection with the Northwest Aviation.

"Mr Wu Shichang was the general manager, and the corporation was formed in Chongqing (Chungking) after two years of preparation from March 1943. It was said they had permission from Generalissimo Chiang, who even granted them two hundred thousand dollars for a start. In March 1945 GCAC was officially inaugurated. A notification of acceptance (this is not a permit) Number 13449 was granted by Ministry of Transportation on September 13, 1945 and later a license No. 1788 from Ministry of Economy on October 19. But on October 30, through Local Social Bureau (i.e. of Chungking City, not the Guo Ming Dang/Kuomintang, which was only a political body). It was said Secretary of State Song Zhiwen (actually he was the prime minister, Head of Executive Yuan, brother of Madame Chiang) gave a direct order to withdraw the license. This is another political trick; why should a central government administration give orders through local/city official? The Department of State (Executive Yuan, the supremacy that commanded five Ministries) also gave the order to Dahua to sell their five C-47 planes to CATC at a cost of $20,000 each.

"Dahua officially planned to fly:
Shanghai – Nanking – Hankow – Chungking – Chengtu;
Hankow – Canton – Hong Kong;
Hankow – Sian – Lanchow – Harmi – Dehwa;
Hankow – Peiping – Shenyan – Changtwen – Harbin
But I think this never worked out." [LYW 02Nov2004]

"The government, for example, was under great pressure to permit operations by the Great China Aviation Corporation, an organisation backed by a coalition of influential businessmen and politicians." [Leary PM p.11]

"Great China Aviation Corporation, on the verge of bankruptcy after several months of sporadic operations, provided former navy pilots Willis P Hobbs and Weldon D Bigony." [Leary PM p.25] "The CAF, which did not appreciate competition, earlier had used the same technique to crush the Great China Aviation Corporation, and now it seemed intent on undermining CAT." [Leary PM p.31]

"Great China had made contact with FLC concerning the purchase of transport aircraft, but nothing concrete developed by the time of the telegram" (from Col. James C Davis to General George C Marshall on 1st February 1946) [JMD 11Nov2004]

A photograph of a Great China Aviation Corporation C-47 shows the marking 'GCAC 101', suggesting that GCAC allocated their own codes. The photo also shows a flying goose logo. The company's name is written in full below the fuselage windows. [LYW]

When General Chennault was planning the formation of CNRRA Air Transport, he wanted John R Rossi to be Chief Pilot and Director of Flight Operations. Dick Rossi was a former AVG pilot who had spent the war flying the Hump. "Rossi had to tell the General that he had just been hired by Moon Chin, head of CATC, the second largest airline in China. Chennault said he was desperate, since it was essential to get someone responsible there to keep the operation moving. Dick was in sort of a bind. He was then Operations Officer and Chief Pilot for GCAC (Great China Aviation Corp), an airline started by a nephew of Chiang Kai-shek. He had arranged for the discharge from the U.S. Military of four pilots: from the U.S. Navy, Weldon Bigony and Bill Hobbs; and from the Marine Corps, Lew Burridge and Var Green. GCAC was having its own problems with airline certificate and landing rights, leading Rossi to resign in the face of an impossible situation." [Rosbert pp.15-16]

"Feeling responsible for the four pilots who would soon be in Shanghai and unemployed, he got the General's promise to hire them. He then arranged with Moon Chin to delay his employment with CATC until he could go to Honolulu and get the first flight of C-46s off to China, and make provision for the rest of them to follow." [Rosbert p.16]

Lutheran World Federation

XT-T72 "Saint Paul"

On Monday, 13th May 1946, Otto Hoefft and Max Springweiler drove to Kiangwan Airport, about 20 km west of Shanghai, with passes from the American military authorities giving access and permission to select an appropriate aircraft from amongst 1,200 surplus American military aircraft parked there and no longer required. They chose a Douglas C-47.

The C-47 was a transport aircraft with 27 passenger seats (all bucket seats) placed along both cabin walls that were not insulated. Springweiler says: "*we selected a C-47 on which the latest improvement specifications had already been introduced.*" (This suggests that the C-47 may have been a C-47B model.) Their C-47 was set up for a 3-man crew but they wanted to fly with only two men as Max Springweiler would combine the roles of co-pilot and radio operator. The radios were moved from the cabin to the cockpit, so that Max could use them simultaneously with his other tasks. [Springweiler p.148]

Otto and Max needed about four weeks to recondition the aircraft for their needs. Early every morning they went to Kiangwan Airport, where the guards checked their papers and allowed them to enter the airport and work on their C-47. One morning they discovered that a compass, a turn indicator, and the servo unit of the automatic pilot had been stolen during their absence. From that day they drove to the airport at 4 am, before the great majority of engineers and mechanics from other organisations arrived, and were able to replace their stolen instruments and gather sufficient spare parts, which were taken home for safe keeping.

After Dr Nelson had engaged the service of an USAAF pilot, their C-47 was ready for takeoff completely outfitted for its transfer from Kiangwan to the civilian airport at Lunghwa, Shanghai. It was registered in China as XT-T72. The first flight of "*Saint Paul*", as the C-47 was christened, took place on 4th July 1946. It flew from Shanghai to Haichow, a port 250 miles north of Shanghai and about two and a half hours away in Kiangsi Province, with a cargo of hospital and medical supplies. The same day the aircraft returned to Shanghai with good marks from both American pilots. [Springweiler p.149]

The LWF bought another surplus C-47 in 1947 to relieve any spare parts problems that might develop later (this preventative measure later proved wrong). In any event, they bought the aircraft to make spare parts available. [Springweiler p.150]

Crash of *Saint Paul* (1)

XT–T72 was damaged beyond repair at Kweiyang on 10th February 1949. There are accident reports by Bill Dudding and Max Springweiler in Appendices Nos.18 and 19 respectively of Springweiler's autobiography. [Springweiler pp.376-380]. The crew consisted of Captain William Dudding, co-pilot and radio operator Max Springweiler, and flight engineer Otto Hoefft.

Before take-off at Chungking, Dudding received the latest weather report for Kweiyang (KYG). The weather at that time was reported as: broken 10/10 2,500 ft; 7/10 1,500 ft, scattered; visibility 3 miles, lower in the west. This weather, although not good, was above minimum, so they took off as scheduled.

St Paul took off at 00:25 GMT and arrived over KYG at 02:05 GMT, flying at an altitude of 10,000 ft. They received the following weather report: light snowing 10/10; 1,500 ft; visibility one mile (below the minimum). The ground was not visible and a normal instrument let down was started at that time. The procedure used called for a spiral down over the city to 7,000 ft and then continue on a heading of 240 deg for 5 minutes, which should bring the aircraft directly over the airport. They could see the ground clearly at 6,500 ft over the city and all the way out on the final leg of the let down, although the visibility decreased as they flew to the west. At the end of the 5 minutes the airport was nowhere to be seen, although it should have been almost below the aircraft.

Although they tried two different letdowns, they could not locate the Ching-cheng field as it was obscured by low scattered clouds and haze. In order to wait for better weather at the Ching-cheng field, they landed on the city field. While landing they observed a wire across the field about 20 ft above the ground. In order to avoid this wire, they had to add power. Although they had the wheels on the ground immediately, the end of the field with mounts and ditches was approaching rapidly. Captain Dudding only partly succeeded in making a ground loop. They hit with the right gear the first mount and the aircraft came to a stop about 20 yards beyond the field. The damage done to the aircraft included: right gear and engine torn off, right wing and wing tip badly deformed, centre section damaged and the fuselage visibly twisted.

Springweiler stated: "... *this plane would be beyond repair even if it would not be at an inaccessible place like Kweiyang.*" It was insured with the International Insurance Corporation, who promptly paid for the damages.

In order to preserve what was still considered useable, they removed all removable instruments and radio equipment. For the first day, they engaged the police to watch the aircraft and also made an arrangement with the Yemen to have soldiers safeguard the wreck by day and night until further notice. [Springweiler pp.376-380]

XT-543 "Saint Paul II"

The LWF aircrew planned to fly to Manila as soon as possible to try to acquire a used C-47 from Philippine Air Lines (PAL). One problem was that Max Springweiler and Otto Hoefft still had German passports with swastikas in them and these could not be used. Nevertheless they received Chinese passports that carried the notation "nationality German". They booked tickets on PAL from Shanghai to Manila, where their passports were accepted without difficulty. After arriving at Manila they immediately set out for the main office of PAL, where they announced their desire to buy a well-maintained C-47. They were taken to the airport where the American director left them to choose an aircraft from among those parked there. The price would be US$24,000.

They inspected about a dozen of the aircraft offered for sale that were in more or less poor condition. They had been damaged by seawater while transporting fish among the many islands. The expense of preparing an aircraft for service was hardly calculable, and the repairs would take more time than was available. They wanted an aircraft immediately, for in addition to the evacuation flights from northeast China, requests for evacuation flights from Tibet had come in just before they left Shanghai. They could not decide to buy any of the C-47s they had inspected.

In the meantime another C-47 [PI-C54] had landed on the airfield, and they found it was the best maintained machine there. Perhaps it had never been used to haul fish. The damaging effects of seawater could not be found anywhere. The aircraft had probably been used to transport passengers. They decided immediately to take this aircraft for the price of US$24,000, but the American resisted. He did not want to sell this aircraft at that price because he too could tell it was in good repair. He wanted US$30,000 for it. So haggling began and finally they agreed that the price should not be more than US$25,000 but not less than US$24,000. The price was agreed by a toss of a coin, which Max lost, so they had to pay the higher price. Nevertheless, they were satisfied that they had obtained a good aircraft.

Otto and Max remained in Manila to take care of the formalities of purchasing the aircraft and also waited for Bill Dudding to come to Manila, so that they could fly the new *Saint Paul* back to Shanghai.

This was flown to Shanghai on 16th March 1949. Documentation included in Springweiler's book shows this as "type C-47A, Army serial no. 43-15466, factory serial number 15437" and this contradictory information has caused a lot of confusion. C-47B-20-DK c/n 15437/26882 was s/n 43-49621, whereas C-47A s/n 43-15466 was c/n 19932 (see below). In view of this confusion, as much detail as possible is included in this article.

A photograph on page 374 of Springweiler's book shows XT-543 in Central Air Transport colours. The caption refers to *St Paul II* but the "II" of this name was not painted on the aircraft. Although registered in the CATC XT-500 series, at no time was this aircraft owned by CATC.

On 16th March 1949, after they had flown their newly reconstituted C-47, the *St Paul II*, to Shanghai, they had to reconfigure the aircraft to meet their needs, get it registered, and obtain the necessary flight permits.

It was also necessary to reconnect with the heavy flight schedule of their good, departed *St. Paul*. A more or less general flight by Chiang Kai-shek's government to Formosa (Taiwan) began at that time. Foreign firms, including German ones, were moving to Taipei. For example, Gerhard Kuelps, a director of Siemssen [Siemens?], and his wife and children were among the passengers on their first flight to Taiwan on 11th December 1948. This was also Max's first visit to Taipei. [Springweiler pp.171-175]

What had happened was that the crews of about 12 aircraft belonging to the two Chinese airlines, CATC and CNAC, had decided overnight to leave Hong Kong and fly their aircraft to Communist China on 9th November 1949. LWF did not operate the *St. Paul* with their own flight permit but under charter as a CATC aircraft. The license and registration [XT-543] were painted on the tail and wings of the aircraft. XT-543 was one of the CATC registrations suspended by the Nationalist CAA on 13th November 1949. (Leary p.92.) XT-543 was also listed as one of the CATC aircraft to be sold to Chennault & Willauer on 12th December 1949. [Springweiler pp.183-185]

XT-811

At this point the LWF was obliged to dissolve their connection with CATC and seek out a contractual relationship with CAT that would allow them to continue their missionary flights. CAT agreed, so LWF was able to continue their work, as CAT aircraft registrations had not been suspended.

After the war in 1945, CNRRA Air Transport (CAT), the third Chinese airline, was established. American General Claire Lee Chennault was its founder. Chennault agreed to the re-registration of *St Paul*. This was the only way for LWF to maintain limited flights to Chinese cities still in Nationalist hands.

Beginning on 10th November 1949 they flew under a CAT registration [XT-811]. The quick change from CATC to CAT was possible because an old friend from Springweiler's days with Eurasia, Dai An-go, the Chinese Director of Civil Aviation, was coincidentally in Hong Kong and could immediately authorise a new registration. On 8th December 1949, LWF made their last flight to far away Chengtu.

A report on this flight by Margit S Grytting is included at Appendix No.20 of Springweiler's book [Springweiler pp.381-384]. A photograph of XT-811 "*St Paul*" in 'CAT' markings is shown on *Archive* page 2009/112. *Note: The date 10th November 1949 may be too early. Twelve CNAC and CATC aircraft defected from Hong Kong to mainland China on 9th November, but the fleets of these airlines, including XT-543, were not grounded until 16th November following suspension of their registrations by the Nationalist Government on 13th November.*

The LWF missionary flights were then over. The missionary leadership was appreciative and grateful. Otto Hoefft decided to return to Germany and was satisfied with a cash settlement. Bill Dudding and Max Springweiler were offered the *St Paul* as separation pay, and they both accepted it, thereby together becoming the *St Paul*'s new owners. It was now necessary to establish an aviation corporation so they could operate under a British flag, initially being content with charter flights. [Springweiler pp.185-186]

The Hong Kong DCA file for VR-HEX includes a letter from the Chinese CAA, dated 23rd January 1950, advising determination of the license for XT-811, in consequence of the termination of the agreement between CAT and LWF. The translation of the letter to CAT reads as follows:

> "Subject: Cancellation of Certificate of Registration of plane XT-811 on expiry of Agreement with L.W.F.
>
> Your application ref:3679 dated 11.1.50 noted.
>
> As the Agreement between Civil Air Transport and the Lutheran World Federation has expired, the Certificate of Registration No.38-18 and the Nationality and Registration Marks of plane XT-811 of the Civil Air Transport is hereby cancelled with effect from today's date. Besides making official announcement and reporting to the Ministry, you are informed to forward the Certificate for cancellation.
>
> Sd. C. C. Cho, Director
> Copy to: Lutheran World Federation."

During January 1950 and following the civil war in China, the Lutheran World Federation decided to terminate the operation of *St Paul* and the aircraft was donated to Captain William Dudding and Mr Max Springweiler in lieu of pay on 13th February 1950. The transfer of *St Paul* to Dudding and Springweiler is recorded in a letter from the Lutheran World Federation, China Office, dated 13th February 1950:

"This is to certify that ownership of the Lutheran Mission Plane – "St. Paul" has been transferred from the National Lutheran Council, National Committee of the Lutheran World Federation to Captain William Dudding and Mr Max Springweiler.

The one (1) airplane is more particularly described as follows:

Aircraft Type – C-47A
Army Serial No. – 43-15466
Factory Serial Number – 15437
Signed: Arthur S Olson, China Director,
Lutheran World Federation,
February 13, 1950."
[Springweiler, Appendix No.23, p.391]

Note that no civil registration is quoted in this letter. In fact, at this time, *St Paul* was on the US Civil Aircraft Register as N8399C.

N8399C

The FAA (CAA) aircraft record for N8399C includes the following Deed of Sale of an Aircraft:

"Know All Men by These Presents

"That the Lutheran World Federation, a Federation duly registered under the laws of Switzerland with head offices at Geneva and represented in this act by Mr John L Benson, President of the Board of Directors of the Lutheran World Federation for and in consideration of the sum of Twenty Nine Thousand Five Hundred U.S. Dollars ($29,500.00) paid and duly receipted for by these presents by the National Lutheran Council, U.S. National Committee of the Lutheran World Federation, said National Lutheran Council being duly registered under the laws of the State of New York, U.S.A. with headquarters at 231 Madison Avenue, New York City, New York, U.S.A. and represented in this act by Mr Arthur S Olson, duly appointed by the National Lutheran Council as China Director of the Lutheran World Federation, China Branch, does hereby sell, transfer, and convey by these presents to the said National Lutheran Council, its successor and assigns (1) one airplane, more particularly described as follows:

Aircraft Type	C-47A
Army Serial No.	43-15466
Factory Serial No.	15437
License No.	PI-C54

Of which it is the sole and absolute owner free and clear from liens and encumbrances whatsoever.

In witness whereof, the Lutheran World Federation has caused these presents to be signed by the President of its Board of Directors.

Lutheran World Federation (China Branch)

Signed by John L Benson, President, Board of Directors" (and witnessed).

The Application for Registration (Form ACA-500) in the name of National Lutheran Council, U.S. National Committee, Lutheran World Federation is dated 13th January 1950. The Certificate of Registration (Form ACA-500-1) has the same date. This registration was cancelled on 4-7-50 (i.e. 7th April 1950) as Exported to China.

The file also contains a Western Union telegram from Hong Kong to Administrator Civil Aeronautics Administration (date not visible):

"Please be advised that Aircraft C-47A factory serial no 15437 license no N8399C previously owned by National Luthern (sic) Council address New York has been sold in presence of American Consulate Hong Kong to International Air Transport Ltd British Company Registration Certificate was lost by Overhaul=
C-47A 15437 N8399C="

A hand-written note says: State Dept is dispatching cable today – per Mr Calaway – JR-500, *WM* 4-19-50" (i.e. 19th April 1950). (See below for similar information in the DCA file for VR-HEX.)

Although the N-number of LWF C-47A N8399C, registered on 13th January 1950, is sandwiched between a block of ex-CNAC aircraft acquired by Civil Air Transport, Inc. registered as N8343C to N8393C on 19th December 1949, and a block of ex-CAT aircraft of C.A.T., Inc. registered as N8400C to N8425C on 5th January 1950, there is no connection between N8399C and CATI, despite the potential for selling XT-543 with the CATC aircraft (N8300C to N8342C). This coincidence arises simply because these were the N-numbers allocated by the CAA at that time. (N8394C to N8399C were not CATI aircraft.)

International Air Transport Company Limited

Bill and Max faced the task of obtaining a Hong Kong registration for their aircraft. The first requirement was proof of airworthiness, not an altogether simple matter since the aircraft would have to go to a qualified and recognised aircraft maintenance facility in Hong Kong, and that cost money. The work was entrusted to the Pacific Air Maintenance and Supply Company (PAMAS).

Then a British aviation company had to be established. Their attorney said Max could not participate in the registration of this new enterprise since as a German he belonged to a hostile nation. He feared that Max could be threatened with the confiscation of his property, his share of the company. When war broke out in 1939 German property in Hong Kong had been confiscated, and in 1950 it still had not been returned. It was held by the "Custodian of Enemy Property". So officially Max was neither a participant nor co-founder of their company. However, he owned fifty percent of its shares. *Note: A share certificate at Appendix No.25 [Springweiler p.393] shows that the company had share capital of $1,000,000.00 divided into 100,000 shares of $10.00 each. Certificate No.8, dated 20th January 1954(!) is only for 30 shares, numbered 19,971 to 20,000. Presumably in 1950 Springweiler had another certificate for 50,000 shares.*

When they founded their company, Blair and Company was a big help taking care of all the paperwork for them. The boss and sole owner of this commercial firm was Mr Dalziel. Other leading men in the company, Mr van Helden and Mr Turvill, were also helpful, cooperative, and friendly. It seems that Blair & Co. Ltd. acted as agents of IAT in Hong Kong. Letters were signed by E C Van Helden, a director of Blair & Co., Ltd., and IAT's registered address at Windsor House was also the address for Blair & Co.

Their company also had to have a name so in the absence of anything more appropriate they decided on International Air Transport Company, Limited. (IAT) [Springweiler pp.228-229] [See Springweiler Appendices Nos.25 & 26]

The DCA wrote to IAT on 29th March 1950: "With reference to your application for registration of a C-47A aircraft please note that it is not possible to register an aircraft in Hong Kong which is registered in another state. You should therefore take steps to cancel the U.S.A. registration and then return the attached form to me with Item 7 duly amended. This aircraft has at one time been registered by the Chinese Civil Aeronautics Administration as XT-543. I shall therefore require evidence that this registration has been cancelled."

The American Consul General in Hong Kong, Karl L Rankin, cabled the US Secretary of State in Washington on 31st March 1950: "March 31 for CAA aircraft C-47 registered number 8399C National Lutheran Council now sold to International Air Transport Ltd Hongkong registered British company requests cancellation American registration to permit Hongkong registration telegraph confirmation." Subsequently the American Vice Consul certified that the following telegram was received from the Department of State, Washington, D.C. on 21st April 1950: "823 April 20 your 797 April 14 – CAA RPT CAA advises U.S. registry number 8399C assigned Douglas aircraft No.15437 cancelled April 7." (These documents are included in the DCA file for VR-HEX.)

Mr A G Daziel also signed letters as a director of International Air Transport Ltd. For example, a letter to the DCA dated 30th March 1950 says: "*We wish to notify you that Aircraft XT-811 is now the property of this Company, and all matters concerning this Aircraft should be referred to our office in Hongkong.*"

A Chinese employee of the Blair firm designed their letterhead and documents that in addition to the registered English name, also had to have a Chinese name because they wanted to present themselves to Chinese customers too. On inspecting the prepared letterhead Max noticed their company name in Chinese symbols. The word "Wan" (ten thousand) was placed before the word "Go" (land). There is no Chinese equivalent to the word "international". Instead any number may be placed before "Go", so in this case Wan Go, meant Ten Thousand Countries. Their Chinese name could be translated as the "Airline of Ten Thousand Countries", which always amused Max.

In the meantime PAMAS was working on their aircraft. One day Max was informed that the refurbishing was complete, and it was ready to be handed over to IAT. Max immediately went to Kai Tak Airport, inspected the aircraft, and was shocked and surprised to find seventeen rivets loose or altogether missing in the airframe and wing roots. He refused to accept the aircraft, and though three days later these difficulties had been resolved to his satisfaction, his trust in the quality of the PAMAS work had suffered a severe shock. On earlier jobs PAMAS had always performed well. [Springweiler p.229]

On 21st April 1950 the DCA wrote to International Air Transport Co. Ltd. and said: "With reference to the attached copy of a certificate from the American Consulate General stating that the U.S. registry of aircraft No.15437 has been cancelled will you please amend and sign paragraph 7 of your application for registration of this aircraft in Hong Kong, which is forwarded herewith. As pointed out in my letter of 29th March the aircraft in question appears to have been registered in China as XT-543. A Chinese document dated 23rd January which you have sent me purports to cancel the registration XT-811. I shall be grateful if you can show me any evidence that this is the same as XT-543."

On 2nd May 1950, the DCA wrote to International Air Transport Co. Ltd. to say that "Yesterday I inspected your aircraft and the only serial number I could find thereon was 43-15466. There was also an order number AC32725. I cannot trace the number 15437 which was used for the registration of this aircraft in the U.S.A. and an additional number given on the Chinese Certificate of Registration and I shall be grateful if you can elucidate this matter." (C-47A-85-DL 43-15466 was c/n 19932.)

VR-HEX

On 3rd May 1950, IAT received their Certificate of Airworthiness. They handed in the appropriate application, and a few days later Max was called to the office of the Director of Civil Aviation (DCA), where he was informed that nothing stood in the way of issuing a permit to operate their aircraft under the British flag. Their aircraft registration letters were VR-HEX. Max was asked of this rather odd name was agreeable to him, and after consulting Bill, Max agreed to it. (In German Hexe means "witch".) Now that they had a Hong Kong registration, they had cleared the first hurdle. [See Springweiler Appendix No.27]

After the first flight of their Ten Thousand Country Airline they successfully made many more charter flights. They carried ping pong players, football clubs, and perhaps a singing group to Singapore or Bangkok, but financial success kept them waiting, and Max's efforts to obtain loads for their charter flights were not exactly successful.

Because of the pressing work finding loads for their charters, Max no longer had time to fly, so they had to hire at least one man to take his place in the cockpit. If they hired a pilot then he could not handle the radio and if they hired a radioman, he did not know anything about flying. That was not good business because it cost them money to pay a salary and flying hours to keep their not especially lucrative business going.

Max's efforts to arrange charters concerned flights to and from Hong Kong, Bangkok, Singapore, and Taipei. General Chennault had used his influence and good connections with the Chinese government in Taiwan to prevent IAT from making flights between Hong Kong and Taipei. The basis for his protest was that CAT and Hong Kong Airways had enough capacity to handle any increase in traffic, and that a third airline was absolutely unnecessary. He could not object, however, to charter flights between the two countries. It was interesting for Max to learn that their airline was regarded as a rival considering that they had problems paying for the fuel for their modest charter flights. [Springweiler pp.229-230]

Memo from General C L Chennault to Director of Operations dated 1st May 1980:

"Dudding and Springweiler have registered the St Paul in Hongkong under the British flag. They are also trying to get entry into Taipeh. Please oppose their entrance on the grounds that Hongkong Airways and CAT have far greater capability than the business justifies at the present time and that a second British airline is not consistent with the reciprocity policy established by the Director of Civil Aviation, Hongkong." [Springweiler Appendix No.27, p.395]

The DCA file for VR-HEX contains a hand-written note to DDCA dated 17/8/50: "On 13th July we were advised by S.A.T. that VR-HEX was undergoing a conversion of its cabin and that an additional fuel tank was being fitted. We have not received any notification from them that this work has been completed but

VR-HEX (c/n 19932) of the International Air Transport Company on charter to Civil Air Transport in late 1950 at Kai Tak, Hong Kong. (Ian Johnson Collection)

won't it affect the CofA before another flight is made? We also want to know the date on which repairs were finished as the aircraft was put on reduced accommodation rates while they were being carried out."

The DCA wrote to IAT on 17th August 1950: "On 13th July you advised me that your aircraft VR-HEX was undergoing cabin and fuel tank modifications. I should be glad to know on what date this work was completed and to receive your application for amendment of the Certificate of Airworthiness, which would appear to be necessary. The modifications must be certified by an aircraft maintenance engineer holding a licence in Category B for Dakota aircraft. The Certificate of Airworthiness is at present not considered valid for passenger carrying flights."

Max Springweiler replied on the same day: "We refer to your letter of even date … and wish to inform you that the work on our Aircraft will be concluded today, the plane being now in JAMCO area for the check and for work on the undercarriage hydraulic and brakes. We shall approach you in the matter of "airworthiness" tomorrow."

On 10th October 1950 the DCA wrote to IAT asking them to "confirm that the nationality and registration marks affixed to your aircraft VR-HEX are in accordance with the provisions of the Colonial Air Navigation Order, 1949, and that the name of the registered owner is displayed." A copy of the ANO was then requested and sent to IAT on 31st October 1950.

In a reply dated 14th November 1950, IAT wrote:

"As far as we are able to determine the aircraft bears marks, which are in accordance with and which do not conflict with the order received from your office. The letters VR-HEX are clearly marked and we contend that this shows that it is a British Aircraft registered in a British possession. In accordance with the terms of the Charter under which this aircraft is at present employed, the letters CAT are also marked. These letters have substituted the name of International Air Transport Co., Ltd., and we point out that the letters CAT are very necessary for identification in Japan and Korea where the aircraft is, most of the time, at present employed. We hope that the marking of CAT does not, in your opinion, conflict with current regulations."

Photographic evidence shows VR-HEX in Korea with CAT in large letters on the cheat-line ahead of the tail-plane and "CIVIL AIR TRANSPORT" above the windows. This correspondence suggests that perhaps CAT chartered VR-HEX in October 1950 rather November - as stated by Springweiler.

Lease agreements with CAT

Everything changed on 1st November 1950 (*Note: Although evidence suggests that CAT actually chartered VR-HEX during October 1950*). Chennault needed IAT, especially their C-47 (and they needed him). They rented their aircraft to CAT, and a little later they sold it to CAT, Chennault's airline, since registration in the Republic of China (Formosa/Taiwan) made everything simpler. The sale price of a single US dollar may cause some question, but naturally at the same time a further contract was signed giving them the right to buy the aircraft back at anytime for one US dollar. [Springweiler pp.230-231] [See Springweiler Appendices Nos.28 & 29]

International Air Transport wrote to the DCA, Hong Kong on 21st November 1950 to report that aircraft VR-HEX, which was then in Japan, had been sold to Civil Air Transport Inc. In a reply dated 23rd November 1950, the DCA asked for the return of the Certificate of Registration, duly signed, so that the aircraft could be struck off the Hong Kong Register. This letter was acknowledged on 24th November with the assurance that the Certificate of Registration would be returned on receipt from Japan, but there had been a change of plan by 4th December 1950:

"There has been a certain change of plans and we are at present uncertain of the exact position. When the aircraft left here, it was understood by both this company and the Civil Air Transport Co., that the aircraft would be sold to Civil Air Transport Inc., on its arrival in Japan. Mr Springweiler accompanied the aircraft to Tokyo and on receipt of your letter dated 23rd November, we wrote requesting him to return the British Certificate of Registration. In reply he has indicated that many issues which we thought satisfactorily settled in Hongkong have been the subject of further protracted negotiations in Japan, and now not only is the aircraft not finally sold to the Civil Air Transport, it is quite possible that the sale will not, in fact, be effected. Pending clarification of the situation, we request that action to strike this aircraft off the Hongkong Register be postponed."

These complications (possibly regarding Bill Dudding's flying, see below) were finally resolved in December, as stated in a letter from the DCA dated 14th December 1950:

"This is to certify that documentary evidence has been produced before me to the effect that aircraft Dakota Type C-47A registered in Hong Kong as VR-HEX and formerly owned by the International Air Transport Co. Ltd. of Windsor House, Hong Kong has now been sold with effect from 18th November, 1950, to Civil Air Transport of No.11 Section 1 Chungking Road, Taipeh, Formosa. The British Registration of the above named aircraft has now been cancelled with effect from the 18th day of November, 1950, on it ceasing to be owned by British Nationals."

Now *St Paul* had a Chinese registration5 again. The contract with CAT was extremely good for IAT. They were mainly needed for flights between Japan and Korea. CAT referred to this effort as "Operation BOOKLIFT"; it consisted of carrying armaments, supplies and even personnel to the US Army in Korea. *Note: The Chinese registration at this point is not stated. By November 1951, this aircraft was registered as B-809. Some B- registration prefixes did not get applied until mid-1951, although probably assigned by ICAO in 1950. Evidence suggests that VR-HEX was probably re-registered as B-809 in December 1950 but with backdated paperwork.*

From Taipei they flew VR-HEX first to Okinawa, an island between Formosa and southern Japan. From Okinawa they flew on to Tachikawa, an American supply base practically at the foot of the picturesque and extremely beautiful Fujiyama (3,776 metres high). Their flights to Korea left from Tachikawa.

On 25th June 1950 the North Koreans attacked the South Koreans, so the Americans hurried to the rescue since all of Korea could not be allowed to come under Soviet Russian or Red Chinese influence. The Americans greatly underestimated this task. In victorious battles strongly supported by the Red Chinese, the Americans were driven back from the demarcation line between North and South Korea right to the tip of South Korea.

They landed in Pusan under the strictest of military conditions. To the best of Max's recollection they flew the *St Paul* to Pusan four times. When they landed in Tachikawa after the fourth trip CAT Operations Manager Joe Rosbert approached with a foreboding look on his face and gave them a chewing out that they could not ignore or forget.

After taking off from Tachikawa they flew a direct course to Fujiyama that had not erupted since 1707, so hardly represented a danger. They had flown over the mountain at low elevation, violating military regulations in the process, as it was a closed military zone. The Air Force protested and demanded a strong reprimand for the offending pilots. But that was not all.

As they had done so often, the Americans had put down steel matting at the Seoul Airfield to secure the surface of the taxiway and runway. Nevertheless the runway still had significant depressions causing aircraft to bounce along on taxi and take-off. The automatic pilot built into the cockpit had to be caged, in other words its gyroscope had to be held down by a button so it would not be damaged during taxiing and takeoff. Bill Dudding almost always operated the aircraft during takeoff and until it reached the intended altitude. Then he would put the aircraft on automatic pilot, but he forgot that the gyroscope was arrested. He was talking with the passengers through the connecting door to the cabin as the aircraft stalled and began to dive. He corrected the situation by quickly moving the elevator, throwing the passengers, some Air Force officers, against the cabin ceiling that was neither insulated nor padded. One of the officers received a bloody cut on the head. It was not serious, and it should not have happened, but there was more to come.

In Pusan on another flight Bill Dudding offered an Air Force officer the co-pilot's seat. Bill obviously wanted to do the man a favour. Max agreed and took a seat in the cabin. It was only a short flight across the strait to the Japanese town of Shimonoseki. The weather was good. It was a night flight, and they saw the lights of the Japanese cities and towns soon after takeoff. Bill wandered off course but corrected himself after a few moments. The flight lasted a little longer. He was slightly late landing at the Japanese military airfield. The Air Force officer complained that "he got lost". This little incident was built up, and a report was filed, but that was still not the end of it.

Bill Dudding was further reproached for having told an Air Force officer that the aircraft he was flying was his personal property. In addition he said that they were under contract with CAT, so besides their salary and flight pay they were receiving rent for the use of the aircraft. The officer, who perhaps risked his life daily flying against the enemy and whose reward was little more than primitive living conditions, was very upset. His report to CAT reflected his feelings.

That sealed Bill Dudding's fate. He was fired on the spot; he left Japan the next day and went to the Lebanon, where Middle East Airlines hired him immediately as a captain. Now Max was alone in Japan with his C-47 but without a qualified pilot.

One must bear in mind that during the years they worked together Bill and Max had developed their own style. The USAF's strict procedures controlling them in Japan were quite foreign to them. They had been their own bosses for too long. [Springweiler pp.231-232]

This story is also reported by Leary [*Perilous Missions*, pp.118-119]:

"In early October Rosbert worked out an arrangement with Monson W Shaver, operations manager of Trans-Asiatic Airways, to charter five C-47s, complete with crews. He made a similar agreement with Max A Springweiler and William A Dudding, owners and operators of International Air Transport, to lease their single C-47. Painted with CAT insignia, the six aircraft were flying BOOKLIFT missions by October 10."

"Unfortunately, charter operations lasted only a week. Following takeoff from Taegu, Korea, in marginal weather, Dudding immediately switched to autopilot, a questionable technique that was observed by a ranking Air Force officer who happened to be on board. When this officer's damning report reached Tokyo, FEAF cancelled CAT's authority to carry passengers, charging the airline with violation of several safety regulations. Willauer responded by terminating the C-47 charters on October 17." [Leary pp.118-119]

The termination of Max's brief stay in Japan and Korea was by no means a disadvantage for him. Soon he became Chief of Maintenance for CAT in Indochina and together with Felix Smith, opened the Hanoi – Saigon route with their aircraft. That was why Max was transferred on short notice to Hanoi. For many reasons he was happy to have turned his back on the Korean War but a bitter war was raging in Indochina. The war was not felt in Hanoi and Saigon at that time. [Springweiler pp.232-233]

Hong Kong

After a brief stay in Indochina, Max returned to Hong Kong where he was introduced to General Chennault, the founder of the American Volunteer Group (AVG) and CAT. Max was made Assistant Manager responsible for traffic and sales for Southeast Asia, including the cities of Hong Kong, Manila, Bangkok, Singapore and Taipei, with headquarters in Hong Kong. His direct supervisor was Don Donaldson.

In February 1951, their company, the Ten Thousand Country Airline, still existed, but with neither aircraft nor personnel. With CAT, their C-47 came under the care of Hugh L Grundy, CAT's Chief Engineer. Their aircraft was given a general overhaul and outfitted with comfortable seats. The aircraft was placed in regular service between Okinawa and the other Ryukyu Islands (Nansei Shoto), and the rent calculated on the number of hours flown was paid to Bill and Max. *Note: A short autobiography of Hugh L Grundy is included in the CNAC website at http://www.cnac.org/grundy01.htm.*

B-809

Their aircraft was still being rented under a so-called dry charter. Max Springweiler no longer had to be concerned with transport rights, country permits, maintenance of the aircraft, or spare parts. Everything was taken care of by CAT. All Bill and Max had to do was take the money. [Springweiler p.238]

On 11th January 1955, Max A Springweiler (also on behalf of William A Dudding) wrote to CAT Incorporated as follows:

"We hereby agree to sell, assign and transfer to you all of our right, title and interest of, in and to a certain C-47 type aircraft bearing Manufacturers Serial number 15437, and currently registered in your name by the Republic of China under the designation B-809. In consideration therefore you agree to pay us the sum of US$61,600.00 (United States Dollars Sixty-one Thousand Six Hundred). Pending the opportunity to properly document this agreement, we have no objection to your use of said aircraft at your risk. It will be appreciated if settlement may be made at your earliest convenience."

Identity of relevant aircraft

XT-T72 *St Paul* (1) is identified in Part 8B (*Archive* p.2009/107) as ex 43-16428, i.e. C-47B c/n 20894. This aircraft crashed at Kweiyang on 10th February 1949 and was damaged beyond economical repair. (See Gradidge p.516)

The identity of C-47 "*St Peter*" (used for spares) is currently unknown.

XT-543 / XT-811 / N8399C / VR-HEX / B-809 *St Paul* (2) is identified as "C-47A c/n 15437 ex 43-15466". These identities are incompatible, which has led to a lot of confusion and speculation. C/n 15437 (26882) was C-47B 43-49621, KK185, whereas 43-15466 was C-47A c/n 19932. The latter is believed to be the correct identity. (See Gradidge p.484) XT-543 had MOC CofA 37-27, which dates from 1948, whereas XT-543 was acquired in 1949! (See *Archive* p.2009/086) (The Chinese C of A was dated 7th May 1949.) The DCA file quotes a C of R of 38-18 (see above), which is consistent with 1949.

Ian Terry's records show Douglas C-47A-85-DL PI-C54 as registered on 13th May 1946 with c/n 19932. Brian Austria-Tomkins' Philippines register shows PI-C54 owned by Philippine Air Lines, Inc., Manila and cancelled on 31st March 1949. [IT 07Feb2006; PY 11Oct2009]

The FAA card for N8399C reportedly shows c/n 26882 but 15437 and 43-15466 are also written on it. [MM 11Oct2002] We cannot explain the origin of spurious s/n '15437'. This seems to have originated in China, not the Philippines.

The FAA file cancellation sheet for N8399C c/n "15437" gives "now 2900B", which had a previous identity of SU-AHO. This is thought to be the true c/n 15437/26882. (See Gradidge p.576) [MM 07Feb2006]

The DCA's correspondence log relating to aircraft XT-811/ VR-HEX includes the following (edited) hand-written notes:

"D.C.A.
The Hong Kong office of the Lutheran World Federation state that they received a telegram from The National Lutheran Council in the USA saying that aircraft no.15437 was registered by U.S.C.A.A. on 13th January 1950 as 8399C (presumably preceded by N). It is accepted that XT811 is the same aircraft, previously registered as XT543.

The Chinese registration XT811 was cancelled by #1 on 23rd January, i.e. 10 days after American registration and therefore the American registration was illegal; but this has now been cancelled by #6 on 7th April.

I am not sure we can accept #1 as it is from a department of a government not recognised by the UK since 6th January.

I have inspected C of A issued by the Chinese CAA on 7th May 1949. This shows that XT543 has Serial No.15437 (43-15466) i.e. the same as XT811.

Lutheran World Federation agreement with C.A.T.C. was terminated on 17th November 1949 (CATC letter 0058 of 21st November). This was replaced by agreement with C.A.T. for aircraft XT811 which terminated on 28th December 1949. (CAT letter of 2nd January 1950). Paragraph 4 of CATC agreement states that the registration number shall be withdrawn and cancelled on termination. Similar terms is (sic) said to be in a CAT agreement but then was not produced.

XT543 or 811 is not listed in the letter from C.A.T.C. stating that certain aircraft have been requisitioned by the Central Peoples Government. But XT543 is in the list of aircraft which we told CATC were prohibited from flying.

To sum up, the aircraft (a) is not registered in the U.S.A.; (b) is not registered in Nationalist China; (c) there is no evidence of registration by the Central People's Government.

Submitted for your decision and registration in Hong Kong.

Signed by M 24/4.

D.D.C.A. I think we have explored every avenue and can now grant registration. 26.4.50."

B-809 was finally bought outright by CAT Incorporated on 18th January 1955 (see Quitclaim Agreement at Appendix 4 of Part 9) and was transferred to Air America, Inc. before sale to Vietnamese Air Transport (VIAT) on 9th June 1961. It was shot down in Ninh Binh Province on 1st July 1961 without re-registration in South Vietnam. The remains of this aircraft were picked up by the Government of North Vietnam and the tail surface of B-809 is exhibited at the Air Defence Museum at Hanoi. [Leeker] (VIAT was formed by the Central Intelligence Agency for deniable operations into North Vietnam.) The ROC CAA report that C-47A B-809 c/n 15437 was registered to AACL (Asiatic Aeronautical Company Limited) on 24th February 1955. [CAA 02Jul2007]

There is photographic evidence of VR-HEX operating in Korea in full Civil Air Transport/CAT markings, which, in theory, should only have been possible between 1st and 18th November 1950. The DCA file shows that there were complications in the sale of VR-HEX, however, and the Change of Ownership document was not signed until 13th December 1950, although backdated to 18th November 1950. As a result, VR-HEX was cancelled by the

DCA on 14th December 1950 but also backdated to 18th November, so there was more time for VR-HEX to be photographed in CAT markings. Also, there is evidence to suggest that CAT chartered VR-HEX in October 1950, probably on or before 23rd October.

Previous authors have assumed connections between XT-809 and B-809, and between XT-811 and B-811 but there is clear documentary evidence that XT-811 became B-809 via N8399C and VR-HEX. This anomaly may have arisen when the ROC civil aircraft register was left behind in Nanking, so the CAA in Taiwan would not have reliable records of previous identities. The normal practice with CAT aircraft was to issue completely new XT- registrations in 1950 (after cancellation of N-numbers) with the prefix being changed to B- (with same number) in 1951. (C-47 XT-801/B-801 was an exception to this rule.)

There is often confusion between XT-811/B-809 and B-811. The latter was Douglas C-47A c/n 18947, which ditched in the Gulf of Thailand off Hau Hin on 20th October 1954 (see Gradidge p.456). An Equipment List for CAT in February 1954 is included at Appendix D of Leary's *Perilous Missions*. B-809 is listed as MSN 15437 but no MSN is given for B-811. Both of these C-47As are shown as leased aircraft. B-801 & B-809 are listed as having "plushed" seats ("ordinarily used as passenger plane").

CNRRA Air Transport / Civil Air Transport

CAT's contract with CNRRA called for the continuous operation of twelve aircraft. To maintain this level, Chennault decided to acquire five C-47s and fourteen C-46s for flight and three for spare parts. Suitable C-46s were located among surplus stocks in Honolulu, but some time would be needed before they could be flown to China. The five C-47s, however, were available immediately in the Philippines. In early November, while Willauer negotiated with Chinese bankers and working capital was at an absolute minimum, Chennault gave Burridge and Green a certified cheque for $500 and sent them to the Philippines with orders to get the C-47s to Shanghai as soon as possible.

The former marines found a depressing sight when they arrived at Clark Field. The aircraft had been in deep storage for over a year, and decay had taken a heavy toll. Preparing the rusting aircraft for flight seemed an impossible task. They hired two Filipino mechanics with a jeep. With everyone working long hours and with liberal "borrowing" of parts and equipment from sympathetic Army Air Force former comrades-in-arms, the men worked a minor miracle. By mid-January the first three C-47s were ready for flight. There was even enough money remaining to paint #404 with airline colours. *Note: "#404" is probably the "last three" of a USAAF serial number, such as 43-16404 c/n 20870, which saw use in China but reportedly with the CAF. See CAT fleet list later in the chapter.*

Meanwhile, CAT's staff at Shanghai accelerated preparations for arrival of the first aircraft. The new boy on the block of Chinese aviation, CAT had to settle for two shanty-like buildings on Hungjao airfield, the least desirable of Shanghai's three airports. As they picked up rocks and filled in potholes preparing the landing area for operations, CAT personnel could only look with envy at the superior facilities at Kiangwan, used by the Army Air Force, and at Lunghwa, CNAC's main base. Hungjao even lacked a windsock. But Merv Garrold, demonstrating the "CAT spirit", solved the problem by designing one himself, purchasing several yards of silk, and arranging with a Russian dressmaker to stitch together the most elegant landing aid in China.

The three C-47s, flown by Burridge, Green, Cockrell, Dew, Holden, and Hughes, left the Philippines on 24th January. Delayed at Canton because of low ceiling and poor visibility at Shanghai, the aircraft did not reach Lunghwa, the designated port of entry, until the afternoon of 27th January. But discomfort in the cold weather was forgotten when the C-47s taxied up the ramp. All eyes turned to #404. Painted in silver trimmed with blue, with C A T in bold red letters on the side of the fuselage and the company insignia on the nose, the transport produced an excitement and pride that would remain vivid through the years. Following customs formalities and picture-taking, the aircraft were flown to Hungjao. [Leary PM pp.26-27]

The "official" start of the airline came – almost – on 29th January, when #404 left Shanghai for Canton with General Chennault, twelve company and CNRRA employees, a jeep and office equipment. Seventy-five miles out of Shanghai, however, the aircraft ran into severe icing. Because #404 lacked de-icing boots, Captain Hughes had no choice but to return. With bad weather forecast (wrongly) for the next day, the flight was rescheduled for 31st January." [Leary PM p.27]

Willauer took special pride in CAT's safety record, pointing out that only two aircraft had gone down during the frantic three-month period. The first one happened on 8th November, when an engine had failed on C-47 XT-805 while en route from Mengtze to Haiphong with a cargo of tin concentrates. Captain Norman R Jones, who stayed with the aircraft until his crew had bailed out, died in the crash; hostile tribesman in the isolated border area beheaded radio operator K V Chin, leaving co-pilot M H Kung the lone survivor.

By December 1949, following the fall of most of mainland China to the Communist Chinese, CAT had a large fleet of about 29 aircraft but almost nowhere to fly to. This caused severe financial difficulties and led to a rapid downsizing of the airline. Many of the aircraft were "mothballed" in Taiwan. By early 1950 CAT's active fleet had been reduced to six C-46s and one C-47 (XT-801). Two developments rescued CAT from inevitable bankruptcy. Firstly the Central Intelligence Agency (CIA) invested in CAT to provide them with logistics and cover for operations in Asia. Secondly, the North Koreans invaded South Korea on 25th June 1950. By October 1950 CAT was desperatly short of aircraft for use in Operation BOOKLIFT in support of the military airlift between Japan and Korea.

Nationalist Government of China

Douglas DC-3 (C-47 & C-53)

In March 1941, China's non-military aviation requirements up to June 1942 were placed at 18 DC-3s, three for passenger service and 15 for cargo operations. First priority was for three passenger aircraft, one for use by Chiang Kai-shek and two for CNAC. [Leary TDW p.136] It therefore seems likely that Chiang Kai-shek would have received one of the first lend-lease C-53s delivered to China. Two lend-lease Douglas C-53 were delivered to the CoAA in 1942: 42-6500 c/n 4952 and 42-6501 c/n 4953 (see *Archive* p.2008/185) and perhaps Chiang Kai-shek received one of these. [MM 11Mar2003]

Shortly after C-53 26500 arrived, it was piloted by Moon Chin, not a CNAF pilot, to test the Shingkiang-India line. He had taught General I to fly the DC-2 and General I flew it until it was destroyed. [CF 23Mar2003]

After five lend-lease C-47s reached China in mid-July 1943, Chiang Kai-shek notified CNAC on 2nd August that the Aviation Commission (CoAA) would operate the aircraft. Four of the Commission's lend-lease aircraft crashed during the next six months. [Leary TDW p.184] Looking at Part 6, Table 13, *Archive* page 2008/185 and above, it is hard to identify these five aircraft, as most lend-lease C-47s were delivered to CNAC. The CoAA's DC-3s appear to be C-53 c/ns 4952 & 4953; C-47 c/ns 6025 & 6038, and C-47A c/n 9292.

Madame Chiang's personal transport was C-47B 43-48806 c/n 26067, s/n C-51219 ('219') '*Meiling*', later renumbered s/n 7219, which was delivered on 26th January 1945. This is now on display in the RoCAF Museum at Kangshan, Taiwan. [CF 2Jan2005; LA 24Nov2003; MM 25Nov2003]

People's Aviation Corporation of China - SKAOGA

In 1950 the People's Aviation Corporation of China (SKAOGA) was formed to take over and expand the services within China that had been performed by CATC and CNAC. Hamiata, the joint Sino-Soviet company operating between Hami and Alma Ata, was also absorbed. The Russian airline, Aeroflot, helped in the formation of the company and provided the first fleet of aircraft, Li-2s.

The first network of services, in addition to linking Peking with Hankow, Kunming and Canton, also paralleled those of Aeroflot to Chita, Irkutsk, and Alma Ata. In 1953 a route was opened from Urumchi on the Peking-Alma Ata route, to Ksahgar, in the westernmost province of the Republic, Sinkiang. In 1954 the Chinese government took over complete control, and the airline then became known as the Civil Aviation Administration of China (CAAC) or Minhaiduy.

From November 1949, the People's Republic of China had the aircraft and personnel of CATC and CNAC that had defected from Hong Kong on 9th November and on previous occasions. These included C-46s, C-47s, one CV240 and a Catalina. The DC-3s were as follows:

Ex CATC: XT-501, XT-507, XT-525 + possibly XT-533 (4)

Ex CNAC: XT-111, XT-117, XT-123, XT-125, XT-129, XT-131 & XT-139 (7)

It is thought that the DC-3s were numbered 101 to 110 but tie-ups with previous identities are unknown.

Douglas DC-3 / C-47

f/n	*Name*	*Date*	*c/n*	*Fate*
101	?		?	
102	?		?	
103	?		?	
104	?		?	
105	?		?	
106	?		?	
107	?		?	
108	?		?	
109	China Youth	May51	?	
110	National Day	Aug51	?	
[MM 15Dec2003, 18Apr2005]				
Note: A photo of '109' shows a plane with a left-hand small passenger door, so possibly a DC-3 model. [MM]. For details of the Li-2s, see the Li-2 article in this volume.				

N8421C (c/n 20681) of Civil Air Transport photographed in the early 1950s at Kai Tak, Hong Kong. *(Ian Johnson Collection)*

Civil Air Transport, Inc.

The Chennault and Willauer partnership, registered in Delaware, USA, bought CATC and CNAC from the Nationalist government of China on 12th December 1949 and sold the aircraft on to Civil Air Transport, Inc. (CATI), a new company incorporated in Delaware, USA, on 19th December 1949, when the aircraft were registered in the sequence N8300C to N8393C. N8300C to N8342C were ex CATC aircraft and N8343C to N8393C were ex CNAC aircraft. Many of these aircraft were impounded at Kai Tak Airport, Hong Kong in November 1949 following the defection of 12 aircraft to Communist China on 9th November. The ownership of these aircraft was disputed and eventually resolved by the Privy Council in London (CATC) and the Supreme Court in Hong Kong (CNAC) in 1952, which allowed the detained aircraft to be shipped to the USA for resale, as shown below.

As of 10th July 1959, Civil Air Transport, Inc. had its assets absorbed under the new corporate identity of Air America, Inc., which officially had been formed four months earlier. [*Shadow War* p.29]

Acknowledgements

The author would like to thank the following for their help in the preparation of this article: Carl Modder, Clarence Fu, Felix Smith, Ian Johnson, Ian Terry, Dr Joe F Leeker, John M Davis, Liang-yen Wen, Matt Miller, Moon Chin (via John Wegg), Paul Howard, Stephen Darke, William M Leary, Jr.

Civil Air Transport, Inc. fleet list

N-reg.	*Type*	*c/n*	*s/n*	*p/i*	*Cancelled*	*Fate (s/i)*
Ex CATC aircraft:				registered 19Dec49		
N8324C	C-47A-90-DL	20388	43-15922	XT-5..	12Aug53	N1795B
N8325C	C-47A-25-DK	13186	42-93291	XT-5..	07Oct65	To PRC?
N8326C	C-47A-25-DK	13296	42-93390	XT-5..	12Aug53	N4660V
N8327C	C-47A-90-DL	20346	43-15880	XT-5..	22Jul53	N1796B
N8328C	C-47A-90-DL	20160	43-15694	XT-5..	12Aug53	N1797B
N8329C	C-47B-25-DK	32588	44-76256	XT-5..	22Jul53	N4663V
N8330C	C-47B-15-DK	26704	43-49443	XT-5..	22Jul53	N4661V
N8331C	C-47B-25-DK	32578	44-76246	XT-5..	22Jul53	N1799B
N8332C	C-47B-20-DK	26906	43-49645	XT-5..	12Aug53	N4662V
N8333C	C-47B-1-DL	20891	43-16425	XT-5..	07Oct65	To PRC?
N8334C	C-47B-1-DL	20817	43-16351	XT-5..	22Jul53	N1798B
N8335C	C-47B-5-DK	25888	43-48627	XT-5..	22Jul53	N68780
N8336C	C-53-DO	7313	42-47371	XT-5..	22Jul53	N1794B
N8337C	C-53-DO	4859	41-20089	XT-5..	12Aug53	N1793B
N8338C	DC-3A-269B	2183	n/a	XT-5..	22Jul53	N1791B
N8339C	DC-3A-269B	2184	n/a	XT-5..	22Jul53	N1792B
N8340C	DC-3A-269	2130	n/a	XT-5..	22Jul53	N1789B
N8341C	DC-3A-269B	2185	n/a	XT-5..	22Jul53	N1790B
N8342C	DST-A-207	1954	n/a	XT-5..	12Aug53	N1788B
Ex CNAC aircraft:				registered 19Dec49		
N8348C	C-47A-75-DL	19313	42-100850	XT-1..	26Feb53	N4884V
N8349C	C-47A-80-DL	19620	43-15154	XT-1..	07Oct65	To PRC?
N8350C	C-47B-1-DL	20806	43-16340	XT-1..	27Jan53	N?
N8351C	C-47B-25-DK	32847	44-76515	XT-1..	07Oct65	To PRC?
N8352C	C-47A-75-DL	19452	42-100989	XT-1..	26Feb53	N4883V
N8353C	C-47B-25-DK	32817	44-76485	XT-1..	07Oct65	To PRC?
N8354C	C-47B-25-DK	32530	44-76198	XT-133	07Oct65	VR-HEP
N8355C	C-47A-65-DL	19062	42-100599	XT-1..	07Oct65	To PRC?
N8356C	C-47-DL	4573	41-18481	XT-1..	07Oct65	To PRC?
N8357C	C-47-DL	6151	41-38692	XT-1..	26Jan53	N75097
N8358C	C-47A-65-DL	18901	42-100438	XT-1..	07Oct65	To PRC?
N8359C	DC-3-268C	2261	n/a	XT-1..	26Mar53	BU HK
N8360C	DC-3-228B	2135	n/a	XT-1..	26Mar53	BU HK
N8361C	C-53-DO	4927	42-6475	XT-1..	07Oct65	To PRC?
N8362C	C-53-DO	4871	41-20101	XT-1..	27Jan53	N26H
C.A.T., Inc. (Ex CAT aircraft):				registered 5Jan50		
N8421C	C-47B-1-DL	20681	43-16215	XT-801	07Mar50	B-801
[*Archive*; FAA files; MSB 29Jul2004; production lists; SMD 22Mar2005; USCAR 01Jan1964]						

List of References

A History of Chinese Aviation. Encyclopedia of aircraft and aviation in China until 1949, Lennart Andersson, AHS of ROC, 2008, ISBN 978-957-28533-3-7

Air Arsenal North America - aircraft for the Allies 1938-1956, purchases and Lend-Lease, Phil Butler and Dan Hagedorn, Midland Publishing, 2004 ISBN 1 85780 163 6

Aircraft and Anti-Communists: CAT in Action, 1949-52, William M Leary Jr, The China Quarterly, Volume 52, 1972, pages 654-669 [CAT]

Airlines of Asia since 1920, R E G Davies, Putnam Aeronautical Books, 1997, ISBN 0 85177 855 0

China Pilot; Flying for Chennault during the Cold War, Felix Smith, Smithsonian Institution Press, 1995, ISBN 1-56098-398-1

CNAC website, Tom Moore: http://www.cnac.org/

FAA aircraft registry: http://registry.faa.gov/aircraftinquiry/

Flying the Hump: memories of an air war, Otha C Spencer, Texas A&M University Press, 1992, ISBN 0-89096-513-7

Pan Am. An airline and its aircraft, R E G Davies, Orion Books, 1987, ISBN 0-517-56639-7 [PanAm]

Perilous Missions; Civil Air Transport and CIA covert operations in Asia, William M Leary, Smithsonian Institution Press, 2002, ISBN 1-58834-028-7 [PM]

Pioneer Aviator in China, Max Springweiler, translated by Larry D Sall, CAT Association & Air America Association, 1998, ISBN 0-9666-630-0-4

Planes for the Marshals of China, Richard S Allen, pp.2-10 (HKHAA files via IDJ, probably from Skyways magazine) [RSA]

Saga of CNAC #53, Fletcher Hanks, AuthorHouse, ISBN 1-4184-3174-5

South-east Asia Civil Aircraft Registers, Ian P Burnett, Air-Britain (Historians) Ltd., 1979, ISBN 0 85130 067 7

The Aircraft of Air America (4th edition), Dr J F Leeker: http://www.utdallas.edu/library/collections/speccoll/Leeker/index3.html [JFL]

The CIA's Airlines: logistics air support of the war in Laos 1954 to 1975, M S Best, Air-Britain Digest, Spring 2002, pages 17 to 25; *The CIA's Airlines in Laos, Update 1,* Air-Britain Digest, Winter 2002; http://www.vietnam.ttu.edu/airamerica/best/index.htm

The Douglas DC-1/DC-2/DC-3: The First Seventy Years (two

volumes), Jennifer M Gradidge, Air-Britain (Historians) Ltd., 2008, ISBN 0 85130 332 3 [JMG2]

The Dragon's Wings. The China National Aviation Corporation and the development of commercial aviation in China, William M Leary, Jr., The University of Georgia Press, 1976, ISBN 0-8203-0366-6 [TDW]

The History of Air America (2nd edition), Dr Joe F Leeker, 1 June 2009: http://www.utdallas.edu/library/collections/speccoll/Leeker/history/index.html [JFL]

Wings for an Embattled China, W Langhorne Bond, edited by James E Ellis, Associated University Presses, Inc., 2001, ISBN 0-934223-65-3

Wings over Hong Kong: a tribute to Kai Tak: an aviation history 1891-1998, Hong Kong Historical Aircraft Association, Pacific Century Publishers, 1998, ISBN 962-217-542-2 [WOHK]

World directory of Airliner Crashes, Terry Denham, Patrick Stephens Limited, 1996, ISBN 1 85260 554 5 [WDAC]

III - The Douglas DC-3 in China – Stop Press

The history of the Douglas C-47s used by Civil Air Transport (CAT) in China has been described above. Since the article was written, new information has been uploaded by Dr J F Leeker to his e-books "*The History of Air America*" and "*The Aircraft of Air America*" on the University of Texas at Dallas (UTD) website on 23rd August 2010.

A problem faced in these earlier articles was that five C-47s were acquired by CAT in January 1947, but apparently not registered until 1948. During this interim period other aircraft in China were registered in the XT-Txx sequence, but it was known that one Stinson L-5 was registered as XT-T519. Dr Leeker has demonstrated that three of the five CAT C-47s were also registered in this sequence, but these Chinese registrations were probably not applied until October 1947. Initially the five CAT C-47s were identified only by the "last three" digits of their USAAF serial numbers and during this time two of these C-47s were withdrawn from use in order to provide spares for the remaining fleet.

Of the three surviving C-47Bs, Dr Leeker suggests that the Chinese identities previously assumed for two aircraft have been reversed. This suggestion is based on the names given to the aircraft by CAT. Dr Leeker agrees with the usual nomination for these five C-47Bs and goes some way to explain why William Leary reported on the delivery of "404", which was not one of the five aircraft bought by CAT in the Philippines. According to Dr Leeker, the history of the five C-47Bs is as follows:-

43-16215 c/n 20681, acquired by CAT on 04Jan47 & delivered as "316215", abbreviated as "215", named "*Tientsin*", registered as XT-T501 & later re-registered as XT-801, N8421C, XT-801, B-801 & 9N-AAC.

43-16239 c/n 20705, acquired by CAT on 04Jan47 & probably delivered as "316239", abbreviated to "239", named "*Taiyuan*", registered as XT-T502 & later re-registered as XT-805, but crashed 08Nov49.

43-48572 c/n 25833, acquired by CAT on 04Jan47 & delivered as "348572", abbreviated to "572". Destroyed in a ground accident at West Field, Peiping on 11Apr47 & subsequently used for spares.

43-49571 c/n 26832, acquired by CAT on 04Jan47 & delivered as "349571", abbreviated as "571". Possibly broken up for spares in late March 1947, but misreported as "404".

43-49906 c/n 27167, acquired by CAT on 01Jan47 & probably delivered as "349906", abbreviated to "906", named "*Peiping*", later registered as XT-T503 & scrapped on 25Oct48.

It was decided to name all CAT aircraft after Chinese cities in August 1947, so "571" and "572" were probably not named, as they were no longer in use at that time. The reason why the c/ns of XT-803 and XT-805 have been reversed by Dr Leeker can be summarised as follows:

Photographs show that XT-801 (formerly "215") was named "*Tientsin*", "239" was named "*Taiyuan*" and "906" was named "*Peiping*". It is known that "*Peiping*" ("906") later became XT-803 and, by a process of elimination, "*Taiyuan*" ("239") must have become XT-805, because it is known that "*Tientsin*" became XT-801. A photograph of "906" ("*Peiping*") appears to show XT-T503 under the wing. This conclusion is a bit surprising, as the CAT C-46s were all numbered sequentially in the numerical order of their c/ns. The significant evidence cited by Dr Leeker is the CAT Maintenance Manual of 24Apr50, which was found in the Princeton University Library. Aircraft names are visible in photographs.

Given that c/ns 25833 & 26832 did not aspire to XT- registrations, we are left wondering what aircraft, if any, carried the registrations XT-807 and XT-809. Dr Leeker maintains (in his 'Japan' PDF file) that the four C-47s leased from Trans-Asiatic Airlines (TAA) were XT-811 (2)/B-811 c/n 18947, XT-813/B-813 possibly c/n 26816, XT-815/B-815 c/n 19258 and XT-817/B-817 c/n 19256, noting that XT-811 was re-used after "*St.Paul*" (c/n 19932) was re-registered as B-809. The fifth chartered aircraft, HS-TAD (c/n unknown) of TAAS was probably not registered in China.

References: "*The early days I – CAT operations in China 1946-48*", PDF file ('China 1') and "*Air America Japan – since the days of CAT*" PDF file ('Japan'), both by Dr Joe F Leeker, 23Aug10, within "*The History of Air America*" at http:/www.utdallas.edu/library/collections/speccoll/Leeker/history/index.html.

Abbreviations

AACL	Asiatic Aeronautical Company Limited
CAA	Civil Aeronautics Administration
CAT	Civil Air Transport; CNRRA Air Transport
CATC	Central Air Transport Corporation
CIA	Central Intelligence Agency
c/n	construction number
CNAC	China National Aviation Corporation
CNAF	Chinese Nationalist Air Force
CNRRA	Chinese National Relief and Rehabilitation Administration
C of A	Certificate of Airworthiness
CoAA	Commission on Aeronautical Affairs
C of R	Certificate of Registration
DCA	Director of Civil Aviation
d/d	delivery date
DBR	Damaged Beyond Repairs
FEAT	Far Eastern Air Transport
f/n	fleet number
IAT	International Air Transport Company Limited
JAMCO	Jardine Aircraft Maintenance Company
KNA	Korean National Airlines
l/n	line number
LWF	Lutheran World Federation
MOC	Ministry of Communications
PAMAS	Pacific Air Maintenance and Supply Company Limited
p/i	previous identity
PRC	People's Republic of China
ROC	Republic of China
SCMP	South China Morning Post
SKAOGA	Sovietsko-Kitaysko Aktsioneren Obschestvo Grazhdanskoi Aviatsii
s/n	serial number
TAA	Trans-Asiatic Airlines
TBC	To Be Confirmed
UNRRA	United Nations Relief and Rehabilitation Administration
W/O	Written Off (crashed)

Table 1: CNAC Douglas DC-3 / C-47 / C-53

CNAC fleet list by fleet number:

XT-reg.	*f/n*	*d/d*	*c/n*	*model*	*p/i*	*fate*
XT-T91	41	09Aug39	2135	DC-3-228B	-	XT-BTA/B; Passenger DC-3; XT-1..? Sold to C&W as N8360C (12Dec49)
	46	Jan41	2148	DC-3-294A	-	Damaged during forced landing at Yangtze River 13Feb46 [MC], repaired? Crashed at Chungking 13Feb43 [TDW] Totalled [Hanks]
XT-T92	47	Jul41	2261	DC-3-268C	NC19971	Passenger DC-3; XT-1..? Sold to C&W as N8359C (12Dec49)
	48	26Feb42	4852	C-53	41-20082	Missing during Dinjan-Kunming flight 11Aug43, crashed at Fort Hertz (3 killed) [ASN, Hanks, MC, TDW]
	49	26Feb42	4853	C-53	41-20083	Missing during Kunming-Dinjan flight 13Mar43 (3 killed) [ASN, Hanks, MC, TDW]
XT-90	50	12Apr42	4871	C-53	41-20101	Passenger DC-3; XT-1..? Sold to C&W as N8362C (12Dec49)
	51	12May42	4879	C-53	41-20109	Crashed near Chengtu 24Mar44, totalled [ASN, Hanks, MC] or 23Mar44 [TDW]
	52	19May42	4902	C-53	41-20132	Crashed & burned at Dinjan during practice flight 10Oct42 [MC] or Crashed on landing at Balijan during training flight 10Oct42 [TDW] Totalled [Hanks]
	53	25May42	4904	C-53	41-20134	Missing during Kunming-Dinjan flight 11Mar43, crashed near Luishui (3 killed) [ASN, Hanks, MC, TDW]
XT-45	54	28May42	4927	C-53	42-6475	Passenger; XT-1..? Sold to C&W as N8361C (12Dec49)
XT-T55	55	04Jun42	4929	C-53	42-6477	Passenger DC-3; Destroyed May45
	56	09Jun42	4881	C-53	41-20111	Crashed on side of Digboi Mountain, Naga Hills 30Nov44 (3 killed) [ASN] or Lost on Hump 12Dec44 [Hanks, TDW]
	57	12Jun42	4883	C-53	41-20113	Crashed on landing at Dinjan 18Feb44 [MC] or Crashed on take-off at Dinjan [TDW] or 17Feb44, totalled [ASN, Hanks]
	58	18Sep42	7407	C-53	42-15890	Missing during Dinjan-Kunming flight 7Apr43 (1 killed) [Hanks, MC], crashed into side of mountain near Minzong [ASN, TDW]
	59	07Oct42	7406	C-53	42-15889	Crashed & burned at Kunming when landing 19Nov43 (2 killed) [ASN, Hanks, MC, TDW]
	60	18Oct42	4681	C-47	41-18556	Missing during Kunming-Dinjan flight 17Nov42 (3 killed) [ASN, Hanks, MC, TDW]
	61	26Nov42	4729	C-47	41-38626	Crashed near Dinjan 23Oct43, totalled [Hanks, MC, TDW]
XT-62	62	02Dec42	4730	C-47	41-38627	Passenger DC-3; fate unknown
	63	05Jan43	6034	C-47	41-38651	Burned near Kunming 19Nov43 (3 killed) [ASN, Hanks, MC, TDW]
	64	06Jan43	6035	C-47	41-38652	?, 10 AF Karachi, Tata 21Dec45
	65	10Jan43	6037	C-47	41-38654	Returned to US Army on 19Jan43
	66	10Feb43	6150	C-47	41-38691	?, Tata 21Dec45
XT-87	67	21Feb43	6151	C-47	41-38692	Passenger DC-3; Crashed into a GCAC C-47 Dec46 but repaired. XT-1..? Sold to C&W as N8357C (12Dec49)
XT-88	68	04Mar43	6221	C-47	41-38762	Passenger DC-3; fate unknown
	69	04Mar43	6222	C-47	41-38763	Burned at Kunming after taking off 6Oct43, totalled [ASN, Hanks, MC, TDW]
	70	30Mar43	9014	C-47	42-32788	Crashed on Burma-China border 14Jan45 (4 killed) [ASN, Hanks], rice dropping mission at Ledo Road [TDW]
	71	10Apr43	9013	C-47	42-32787	Missing Kunming-Chungking 16Jun44 [MC] or One passenger killed Kunming-Chungking 23Jun44 [TDW] or Crashed at Chungking; or near Kweilin 18Jun44 (1 killed) [ASN, Hanks]
	72	17Apr43	9110	C-47	42-32884	Missing Dinjan-Kunming flight; chased by Japanese pursuit plane 13Oct43 (3 killed) [ASN, Hanks, MC]
	73	13Apr43	9109	C-47	42-32883	'883' Crashed 1Jul44 [MC] or Crashed 1Aug44 Baldy Mountain (3 killed) [ASN, CNAC, Hanks, JMG] or Crashed on take-off Kunming 1Aug44 [TDW]

	74	25Jun43	9291	C-47A	42-23429	Missing on a flight from China to Dinjan [*MM-Q*] Crashed 6Jan45 in Patkai Mountains (3 killed) [ASN, Hanks] or Drifted north of course in severe crosswinds Hump, 1Jan45 [TDW]
	75	25Jun43	9416	C-47A	42-23554	Missing Dinjan-Kunming 20Feb44 (2 killed) [ASN, Hanks, TDW]
	76	04Jul43	9417	C-47A	42-23555	Fate unknown
	77	15Jul43	9596	C-47A	42-23734	Crashed 6Jan45 near Dinjan, Kunming to Dinjan (4 killed) [ASN, Hanks, TDW]
	78	15Jul43	9597	C-47A	42-23735	Crashed during landing Dinjan 27Oct43 [MC] or Crashed on landing at Calcutta 26Oct43, repaired [Hanks, TDW]
	79	12Aug43	9760	C-47A	42-23898	Crashed during Dinjan-Suifu flight 18Dec43 [Hanks, MC]
	80	13Aug43	9761	C-47A	42-23899	Crashed near Dinjan 4Nov44, totalled [ASN, Hanks] or Crashed landing at Dinjan 13Nov44 [TDW]
	81	04Sep43	9955	C-47A	42-24093	Crashed between Yunnanyi & Suifu 15Jun45 (3 killed) [ASN] or Missing on flight from Xi Chang to Kunming, hit Lou Zi Mountain 30 km from Xi Chang, Sichuan, in bad weather 20Sep46, pilot A W Longbotham (31 killed), not found until 9Oct46 [MM]
	82	05Sep43	9956	C-47A	42-24094	Missing Calcutta-Dinjan 26May44 (12 killed) [ASN, Hanks, MC]
	83	03Oct43	10159	C-47A	42-24297	Crashed during Dinjan-Suifu flight 18Dec43 (3 killed) [ASN, Hanks, MC, TDW]
	84	05Oct43	10158	C-47A	42-24296	Burned at Kunming while taking off 17Oct43 [MC, TDW] or 16Oct43 [ASN, Hanks]
	85	10Nov43	18902	C-47A	42-100439	Burned in mid-air over Kunming 8Jun44 [Hanks, MC, TDW] or Crashed at Dinjan (6 killed) [ASN]
XT-T86	86	17Nov43	18901	C-47A	42-100438	Lost and out of fuel on Hump 11Mar44, rebuilt [Hanks, TDW] Passenger DC-3; XT-1..? Sold to C&W as N8358C (12Dec49)
XT-51	87	07Dec43	19062	C-47A	42-100599	Crashed on runway at Dinjan Jun45 [TDW] or 20May44, repaired [Hanks] Passenger DC-3; XT-1..? Sold to C&W as N8355C (12Dec49)
	88	14Dec43	19061	C-47A	42-100598	Gear collapsed on landing at Suifu 10Jan44, repaired [Hanks, TDW] and Crashed 9Apr45 between Sichang & Kunming (3 killed) [ASN, Hanks, TDW]
XT-T48	89	21Jan44	19313	C-47A	42-100850	Passenger DC-3; XT-111. Sold to C&W as N8348C (12Dec49)
	90	10Feb44	19314	C-47A	42-100851	Missing Dinjan-Kunming 15May44 (3 killed) [ASN, Hanks, MC] Crashed on descent into Kunming [IT] or 16May44 [TDW]
XT-T54	91	15Mar44	19452	C-47A	42-100989	Crashed 7Mar44 (2 killed) (or XT-T91?) [ASN]. Passenger DC-3; XT-127. Sold to C&W as N8352C (12Dec49)
XT-85	92	12Apr44	19620	C-47A	43-15154	Accident at Dinjan 18May44, brake locked on landing, ground looped into General Old's B-25. [ASN, IT, TDW], totalled [Hanks]; Passenger DC-3; XT-1..? Sold to C&W as N8349C (12Dec49)
	93	14Apr44	19621	C-47A	43-15155	Lost over the Hump 16Jan45 Chungking to Kunming, crashed near Kunming (3 killed) [ASN, Hanks, TDW]
	94	03May44	19803	C-47A	43-15337	Crashed at Dinjan 9May45 (2 killed) [ASN, Hanks]
	95	05May44	19804	C-47A	43-15338	Fate unknown
	96	13Jun44	20091	C-47A	43-15625	Power failure on take-off Kunming 24May44 [TDW] Undercarriage collapsed 18Mar45 at Kunming, repaired [Hanks] (*c/n from interpolation*) Missing on flight from Kunming to Tinjiang, 30Nov45, pilot Y G Wong [MM]
	97	21Jun44	20253	C-47A	43-15787	Crashed 31Aug44 over Huhuang Valley near Shimbuwang (2 killed) [ASN, Hanks, TDW]
	98	03Jul44	20252	C-47A	43-15786	Crashed 16Nov44 takeoff from Yunnanyi, undercarriage retracted prematurely, repaired [Hanks, TDW]
	99	1944	?	C-47*B*		Fate unknown

XT-T20	100	1944	?	C-47*B*		Cargo
	101	1944	?	C-47*B*		Crashed 7Oct44 over Sadiya (3 killed) [ASN, Hanks], wing torn off by severe turbulence [TDW]
	102	1944	?	C-47*B*		Crashed 7Jan45 above the city of Tali by Tali Lake (3 killed) [ASN, Hanks]
XT-T83	103	1944	?	C-47*B*		Cargo
	104	1944	?	C-47*B*		Hit high ground at Sui Chang, Zhejiang on flight from Shanghai to Hong Kong, 20Oct45, pilot F L Higgs [MM]
	105	1944	?	C-47*B*		Crew bailed out over the Hump, crashed 16Feb45 over Hukawng Valley, totalled [ASN, Hanks, TDW]
	106	1944	?	C-47*B*		Crew bailed out over the Hump, crashed 24Nov44 near Kunming, totalled [ASN, Hanks] or 25Nov44 [TDW]
XT-84	107	1944	?	C-47*B*		Passenger; Still active in early 1947
XT-T58	108	1944	?	C-47B		Cargo [IT; MM]
	109	1944	?	C-47*B*		Fate unknown
	110	1944	?	C-47*B*		Fate unknown
XT-T81	111	1944	?	C-47*B*		Cargo
XT-81?	?	22Mar45	32817	C-47B	44-76485	XT-1..? Sold to C&W as N8353C (12Dec49)
XT-T52	112	1944	?	C-47*B*		Cargo
XT-56	136		?	DC-3		Passenger
	137			?		Nothing known
	138		?	C-47		Hit high ground in Sichuan on flight from Guangzhou to Chongqing, 25Jan47, pilot J M Blackmore (19 killed) [MM] Crashed 120 miles S of Chongqing 25Jan47 (19k)[ASN]
	139		?	?		Missing on flight from Chungking to Shanghai, crashed near Enshi , Hubei, 19Mar46, pilot H C McCracken (30 killed) [MM], type unknown
	140		?	C-47		Crashed in fog at Shanghai-Lunghwa, 25Dec46, pilot J M Greenwood (19 killed) [ASN, MM 29Sep2002, Leary PM pp.22-23]
	141		?	C-47		Engine failed on takeoff at Shanghai-Lunghwa, overshot when attempted to abort takeoff, 25Apr47, pilot A P Moore, 3 farmers killed on ground [*Archive* p.93/26, ASN, MM]
	145		?	C-47		Crashed due to engine fire at Zhou Jia Wan, Tian Men County, SE of Wuhan, Hubei, 28Jan47, pilot J S Papajik (25 killed) [MM]
?	?		4573	C-47	41-18481	XT-1..? Sold to C&W as N8356C (12Dec49) – possibly XT-T56
XT-T60	?		?	C-47		Training
	?	4Dec45	20309	C-47A	43-15843	Fate unknown
?	?		?	DC-3		Crashed 16Dec46 Shanghai-Lunghwa (5 killed) (crashed into 3 parked a/c) [ASN] - possibly f/n 67 – see *Archive* p.2009/113
?	'89'		?	DC-3		Crashed 27Oct47 nr Yulin (2 killed)[ASN] Shot down by PLA on approach to Yulin during flight from Xian, pilot Chao Chi-tan [MM], believed to be XT-T89

CNAC fleet list by XT-1.. registration:

XT- reg.	*CofA*	*c/n*	*Model*	*p/i*	*Fate*
XT-34	?	?	(C-46?)		At Hong Kong, 16Nov49 [DCA] (sic) (C-46)
XT-111	37-36	19313	C-47A	42-100850	At Hong Kong, 16Nov49, sold to C&W as N8348C (12Dec49)
XT-113	?	?	C-47		Hit mountain on approach to Taipei, 32 km NE of Dan Bei, 12Dec48 [MM] Crashed on landing at Taipei, Taiwan 12Dec48. The 2 crew members lost their lives but all 8 passengers survived. [ASN; www.cnac.org/accident 074.htm]
XT-115	37-38	?	C-47A		Defected to China from Hong Kong on 9Nov49. Preserved at Chinese AF Museum, Datang Shan (N83..C)
XT-117	37-39	?	DC-3		At Hong Kong, 16Nov49, sold to C&W as N83..C (12Dec49)
XT-119	37-34	?	C-47B		At Hong Kong, 16Nov49, sold to C&W as N8350C (12Dec49)
XT-121	37-35	4927	C-53	42-6475	Defected to China from Hong Kong on 9Nov49 (N8361C)
XT-123	37-93	?	C-47B		Defected to China from Hong Kong on 9Nov49 (N83..C)
XT-125	37-94	?	C-47A		Defected to China from Hong Kong on 9Nov49 (N83..C)
XT-127	37-95	19452	C-47A		At Hong Kong, 16Nov49, sold to C&W as N8352C (12Dec49)
XT-129	37-96	4573	C-47		Defected to China from Hong Kong on 9Nov49 (N8356C)

XT-131	37-97	?	C-47B		Defected to China from Hong Kong on 9Nov49 (N83..C)
XT-133	?	32530	C-47B	44-76198	To Air Hoe as VR-HEP (Jul49), crashed in Thailand on 13Jan51. (N8354C)
XT-135	?	?	?		Nothing known
XT-137	?	6151	C-47		At Hong Kong, 16Nov49, sold to C&W as N8357C (12Dec49)
XT-139	37-128	?	C-47A		Defected to China from Hong Kong on 9Nov49 (N83..C)
XT-141	37-129	4871	C-53	41-20101	At Hong Kong, 16Nov49, sold to C&W as N8362C (12Dec49).
XT-143	?	?	?		Nothing known
XT-145	?	?	?		Nothing known

Table 2: CATC Douglas DC-3 / C-47 / C-53

f/n	*Model*	*c/n*	*p/i*	*Fate*
CA-1	C-47	4483	41-18421	to XT-T23
CA-2	C-47	4781	41-18620	damaged 3Mar46 Jinan, Shandong. Engine failed, no casualties
CA-3	C-47A	20388	43-15922	to XT-T24
CA-4	C-53	7313	42-47371	to XT-T21
CA-5	C-47A	13410	42-93492	destroyed 26Jan46 Wuhan, Hubei. Lost control in bad weather (3 killed)
CA-6	C-47A	13236	42-93336	destroyed 31Mar46 over Hunan en route Shanghai to Kunming. Engine failed, couldn't maintain altitude, crew bailed out.
CA-7	C-47A	10229	42-24367	"not use demolition"
CA-8	C-47A	13186	42-93291	to XT-T10
CA-9	C-47	6133	41-19490	"not use the grounding"
CA-10	C-47	4246	41-7759	"not use the grounding"
CA-11	C-47	4214	41-7738	W/O 14Dec46 missing over Chang Xing, Zhejiang en route Beijing to Shanghai
CA-29	C-47B	32588	44-76256	to XT-T22
CA-31	C-47B	32574	44-76242	destroyed 14Dec46 Changxing County, Zhejiang. Missing on flight from Beijing to Shanghai; lost due to bad weather (6 killed)
CA-32	C-47	?		GCAC, fate unknown
CA-33	C-47	?		GCAC, fate unknown
CA-34	C-47	?		GCAC, fate unknown
CA-35	C-47	?		GCAC, fate unknown
CA-36	C-47	?		GCAC, fate unknown
CA-38	C-47B	32769	44-76437	"borrowing has been returned"
CA-39	C-47A	13296	42-93390	to XT-T31
CA-41	C-47B	20894	43-16428	LWF, to XT-T72
CA-42	C-47B	26704	43-49443	to XT-T32
CA-43	C-47B	32578	44-76246	to XT-T33
CA-47	C-47A	20387	43-15921	to XT-T34
CA-48	C-47B	32986	44-76654	destroyed 25Dec46, crashed in fog on approach to Kiangwan, Shanghai (11 or 12 killed)
CA-50	C-47A	10160	43-15694	To XT-T36
CA-54	C-47B	26906	43-49645	to XT-T37
CA-56	C-47B	20891	43-16425	to XT-T67
CA-57	C-47B	20817	43-16351	to XT-T68
CA-59	C-47B	25888	43-48627	to XT-T70
CA-62	C-53	4859	41-20089	to XT-T74

Reg.	*Model*	*c/n*	*p/i*	*Fate*
XT-T10	C-47A	13186	CA8	> XT-5.., to N8325C (19Dec49), N4660V
XT-T21	C-53	7313	CA4	> XT-5.., to N8336C (19Dec49), N1794B
XT-T22	C-47B	32588	CA29	> XT-5.., to N8329C (19Dec49), N4663V
XT-T23	C-47	4483	CA1	fate unknown
XT-T24	C-47A	20388	CA3	> XT-5.., to N8324C (19Dec49), N1795B
XT-T31	C-47A	13296	CA39	Crashed due to pilot error Jinan, Shandong 13Dec47, repaired, > XT-5.., to N8326C (19Dec49), N4660V
XT-T32	C-47B	26704	CA42	> XT-5.., to N8330C (19Dec49), N4661V
XT-T33	C-47B	32578	CA43	> XT-5.., to N8331C (19Dec49), N1799B
XT-T34	C-47A	20387	CA47	fate unknown
XT-T36	C-47A	20160	CA50	> XT-5.., to N8328C (19Dec49), N1797B
XT-T37	C-47B	26906	CA54	> XT-5.., to N8332C (19Dec49), N4662V

XT-T67	C-47B	20891	CA56	> XT-5.., to N8333C (19Dec49), cancelled
XT-T68	C-47B	20817	CA57	> XT-5.., to N8334C (19Dec49), N1789B
XT-T70	C-47B	25888	CA59	> XT-5.., to N8335C (19Dec49), N68780
XT-T74	C-53	4859	CA62	> XT-5.., to N8337C (19Dec49), N1793B
?	C-47A	20346	43-15880	> XT-5.., to N8327C (19Dec49), N1796V
?	C-47B	26704	43-49443	> XT-5.., to N8330C (19Dec49), N4661V
?	C-47	?	?	W/O 15Dec46 near Changsing, China

Ex Northwest Airlines Douglas DC-3s:

N-#	*Model*	*c/n*	*Date*	*XT-#*	*Fate*
NC21715	DC-3A-269	2130	canx 20May48, 30Aug48 [JMD]; Apr48 [JMG]	XT-5..?	N8340C
NC25608	DC-3A-269B	2183	Apr48 [JMG]	XT-5..?	N8338C
NC25609	DC-3A-269B	2184	canx 8Apr49; 1948 [JMG]	XT-5..?	N8339C
NC25610	DC-3A-269B	2185	no canx; 1948 [JMG]	XT-5..?	N8341C
NC33324	DST-A-207	1954	canx 19Dec49; Jul48 [JMG]	XT-5..?	N8342C
None of these aircraft had US Export Certificates of Airworthiness. [JMD 20Aug2007]					

Reg.	*Model*	*c/n*	*CofA*	*p/i*	*Fate*
XT-501	C-47	?	?	?	defected from Canton (Guangzhou) to Nanking, 25Aug49
XT-503	C-47A	?	37-18	?	impounded at Hong Kong, Nov49
XT-505	C-53	?	37-110	?	Tire burst on landing at Yi Xiu Airport, Fuzhou, Fijian, 3Dec48, swerved off runway into ditch; impounded at Hong Kong, Nov49
XT-507	DC-3	?	?	?	defected from Hong Kong to Canton, 27Oct49
XT-509	C-47D	?	37-17	?	impounded at Hong Kong, Nov49
XT-511	C-47A	?	37-19	?	impounded at Hong Kong, Nov49
XT-513	C-47A	?	37-26	?	impounded at Hong Kong, Nov49
XT-515	C-47B	?	37-131	?	impounded at Hong Kong, Nov49
XT-517	C-47D	?	37-20	?	Landed long at Sanhupa Airport, Chongqing, 23Nov48, undercarriage collapsed, damaged; impounded at Hong Kong, Nov49
XT-519	?	?	?	?	nothing known (see note 10)
XT-521	C-47A	?	37-112	?	impounded at Hong Kong, Nov49
XT-523	C-47B	?	37-21	?	impounded at Hong Kong, Nov49
XT-525	C-47B	?	37-113	?	defected from Hong Kong to PRC, 9Nov49
XT-527	C-47B	?	37-23	?	impounded at Hong Kong, Nov49
XT-529	C-47B	?	37-24	?	impounded at Hong Kong, Nov49
XT-531	C-47/DC-3	?	37-25	?	impounded at Hong Kong, Nov49
XT-533	C-47/DC-3	?	37-22	?	impounded at Hong Kong, Nov49
XT-535	C-47/DC-3	?	37-72	?	fate unknown
XT-537	C-47/DC-3	?	37-114	?	impounded at Hong Kong, Nov49
XT-539	C-47/DC-3	?	37-133	?	impounded at Hong Kong, Nov49
XT-541	C-47/DC-3	?	37-134	?	impounded at Hong Kong, Nov49
XT-543	C-47A	19932	37-27	?	impounded at Hong Kong, Nov49, to N8399C, VR-HEX
XT-5..	C-47A	20388		XT-T24	To N8324C (19Dec49), N1795B
XT-5..	C-47A	13186		XT-T10	To (N8325C) (19Dec49), cancelled 7Oct65
XT-5..	C-47A	13296		XT-T31	To N8226C (19Dec49), N4660V
XT-5..	C-47A	20346		?	To N8327C (19Dec49), N1796B
XT-5…	C-47A	20160		XT-T36	To N8328C (19Dec49), N1797B
XT-5..	C-47B	32588		XT-T22	To N8329C (19Dec49), N4663V
XT-5..	C-47B	26704		XT-T32	To N8330C (19Dec49), N4661V
XT-5..	C-47B	32578		XT-T33	To N8331C (19Dec49), N1799B
XT-5..	C-47B	26906		XT-T37	To N8332C (19Dec49), N4662V
XT-5..	C-47B	20891		XT-T67	To (N8333C) (19Dec49), cancelled 7Oct65
XT-5..	C-47B	20817		XT-T68	To N8334C (19Dec49), N1798B
XT-5..	C-47B	25888		XT-T70	To N8335C (19Dec49), N68780
XT-5..	C-53	7313		XT-T21	To N8336C (19Dec49), N1794B
XT-5..	C-53	4859		XT-T74	To N8337C (19Dec49), N1793B
XT-5..	DC-3A-269B	2183		NC25608	To N8338C (19Dec49), N1791B
XT-5..	DC-3A-269B	2184		NC25609	To N8339C (19Dec49), N1792B
XT-5..	DC-3A-269	2130		NC21715	To N8340C (19Dec49), N1789B
XT-5..	DC-3A-269B	2185		NC25610	To N8341C (19Dec49), N1790B
XT-5..	DST-A-207	1954		NC33324	To N8342C (19Dec49), N1788B
[Andersson p.179; ASN; CF 01Apr2002; JFL/Japan; Springweiler p.367; WDAC]					

Table 3: Civil Air Transport (CAT) Douglas C-47 Dakota

Reg.	*Model*	*c/n*	*p/i*	*Fate*	*Notes*
'215'?	C-47	20681	43-16215	> XT-801 (q.v.)	Photo of '316215'
'239'	C-47	20705	43-16239	> XT-803	"Taiyuan"
'404'	C-47	20870?	43-16404?	To CNAF as '16404'	[Leary *Perilous Missions* pp.26, 27] TBC
'906'	C-47	27167	43-49906	> XT-805 (q.v.)	(photo) [Rosbert p.24] "Peiping"
348572	C-47B	25833	43-48572	> XT-807?	(photo) [Rosbert p.25] TBC
349571	C-47B	26832	43-49571	> XT-809?	TBC
XT-801	C-47B	20681	43-16215	To N8421C, B-801, 9N-AAC	Manila - CNRRA (04Jan47)(photo) [Rosbert p.90] "Tientsin" to AACL (R24Feb55)
XT-803	C-47B	20705	43-16239	Cancelled	Manila - CNRRA (04Jan47); B-803 = KB 47G-2
XT-805	C-47B	27167	43-49906	Crashed in Southern Yunnan 8Nov49 (1k)	Manila - CNRRA (01Jan47)
XT-807	C-47	25833?	43-48572?	Fate unknown	Manila - UNRRA (04Jan47) TBC
XT-809	C-47	26832?	43-49571?	Fate unknown	Manila - UNRRA (04Jan47) TBC; B-809 = c/n 19932
XT-811	C-47A	19932	43-15466, PI-C54, XT-543	To N8399C, VR-HEX, B-809	(photo)(leased from IAT) "St Paul", c/n '15437', w/o as B-809
XT-813?	C-47A	18947	42-100484, PI-C181	r/r B-811, w/o 20Oct54	(leased from TAA)
XT-815?	C-47B	26816	43-49555, PI-C182	r/r B-813, w/o 29Nov52	(leased from TAA)
XT-817?	C-47A	19258	42-100795, PI-C183	r/r B-815 (R16Jan51), w/o 27Dec63	(leased from TAA) to AACL
XT-819?	C-47A	19256	42-100793, PI-C???	r/r B-817 (R16Jan51) (acquired Jan52), XU-AAE	(leased from TAA) to AACL
XT-819	C-47	?	?	Fate unknown.	(leased from TAA) B-819 = Catalina (R24Feb55)
XT-821	C-47	?	?	Fate unknown	(leased)
XT-823	C-47A	13399	42-93482	r/r B-823, N6634C, CF-MCC, N14636	(leased)
XT-825	C-47	11921?	42-92152, VR-HDP?	Fate unknown	B-825 = Catalina (R01Sep52)
XT-827?	C-47A	13784	42-24413	r/r B-827	To AACL (R14Aug54)
XT-829?	C-47B	34298	45-1030	r/r B-829, XW-TFB	To AACL (R05May58)
[ACRO; Andersson p.179; *Archive* p.96/112; ASN; CLT 31Aug2002, 10Oct2003; JFL 12Mar2010; JMG2 p.175; Leary PM pp.218-219; MM 11Nov2003, 06Mar2005; MSB 07Mar2005; PCI; ROC CAA; WDAC]					

PI-reg	*Model*	*c/n*	*p/i*	*HS-reg*	*XT-reg.*	*Fate*
PI-C180	C-47A	20583	43-16117	HS-TA180	-	DBR at Mingaladon, Burma 17Nov49 (stbd wing used to repair VR-HDB)
PI-C181	C-47A	18947	42-100484	-	XT-811?	B-811
PI-C182	C-47B	26816	43-49555	?	?	unknown
PI-C183	C-47A	19258	42-100795	-	XT-815?	B-815, AAM
PI-C184	C-47A	19252?	42-100789?	?	?	Crashed Rangoon 18Jan50, F-OAMU
'0789'	C-47A	19252?	42-100789?			To PI-C184 (q.v.)
?	C-47A	?		HS-TA190	?	
?	C-47A	?		HS-TA191	?	
[*Archive* pp.2002/152-154; ATDB; IT 31Oct2004; JMG2 pp.207-208, 216; MSB 30Oct2004; PY 30Apr2006; SMD]						

CAT's first C-47s, January 1947.
(Courtesy RE Rousselot)

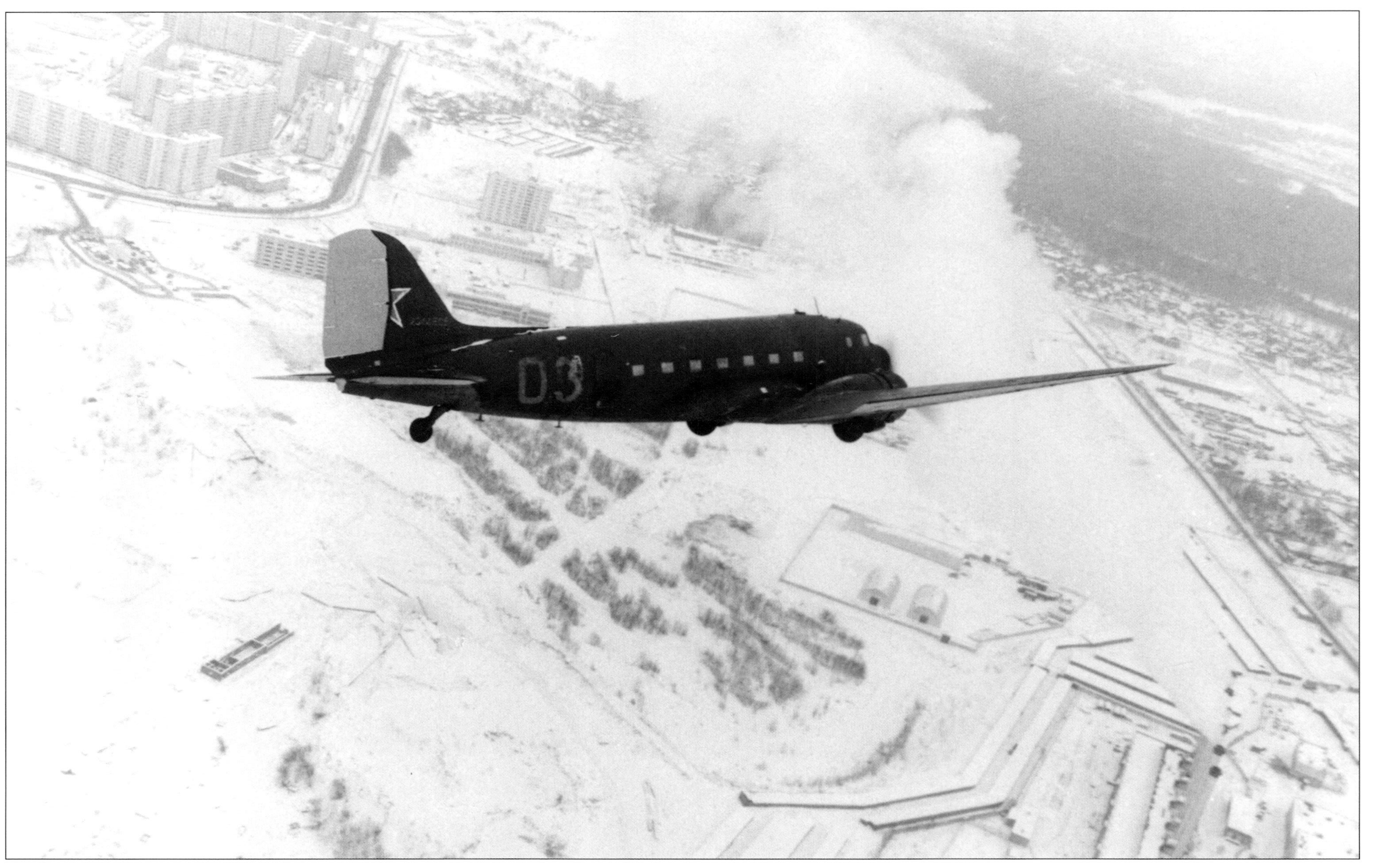

Russian Air Force Li-2, possibly 2344685, coded "03", flying over a snowy landscape. *(Aeroplane)*

Most of the photographs in this section have kindly been provided by the Russian Aviation Research Trust – RART. One of the early DC-3s delivered to Russia photographed in service with Aeroflot. *(Vladimir Kotelnikov via RART)*

Chapter 14 The Lisunov Li-2 in worldwide service

by Robert J Ruffle (Russian Aviation Research Group)

Licence Production

Adaption of the Douglas DC-3 for Soviet production was undertaken by a team headed by Vladimir M Myasishchev. Re-working the drawings from imperial to metric was an enormous task, the complexity of this work testified to by the fact that both the Mitsubishi and Fokker companies, which had also purchased similar licences in the USA, did not succeed in re-working the technical drawings and subsequently had to assemble the aircraft from imported parts.

Boris Lisunov was one of those charged with the establishment of production of the DC-3, as the PS-84 (based on the initial letters for Passenger Aircraft at Factory number 84) in Khimki in the northern suburbs of Moscow, but his name only came to prominence after Myasishchev was arrested and imprisoned in 1938. With the approaching German forces and the evacuation of GAZ 84 to Tashkent in October 1941, Lisunov was a main force in the re-establishment of production there with the first PS-84 being completed in early January 1942. In recognition of his work in Tashkent, and with Myasishchev otherwise detained, and with the introduction of the revised Soviet aircraft designation system, the PS-84 became the Li-2. This was announced first by the Red Army Air Force on 9th September 1942, and then on 17th September by the Commander of the Civil Air Fleet, but it would be a full year before documentation reflected the designation change.

As part of the agreement giving licence rights to the Soviet Union to build the DC-3, a number of American-built DC-3s were purchased through Amtorg, the Soviet Government body for trade with America. According to Soviet sources, 18 DC-3s were purchased, but more recent research has revealed that the number was actually 21. Aircraft were shipped from the USA to Cherbourg, France where they were assembled and flown to Russia. The licence production agreement was signed on 15th July 1936, with the first DC-3 delivered to Cherbourg on 30th November 1936 (other sources say 1st December 1936). To disguise the destination of the purchases Amtorg set up three fictitious companies, Excello, Mongolian Transport Company (MTC) and Northeast.

Type	*c/n*	*Soviet company*	*Delivery to Cherbourg*	*Comments*
DC-3-196	1589	Excello	30 November 1936 (or 01 December 1936)	to URSS-M132?
DC-3-227	1974	MTC	26 August 1937	Ferry regn F-2, to URSS M135?
DC-3-227	1987	MTC	20 September 1937	Ferry regn F-2
DC-3-227	1988	MTC	20 September 1937	Ferry regn F-2
DC-3-196A	2031	Northeast	19 May 1938	Ferry regn F-2, to URSS-M136, to URSS-M
DC-3-196A	2032	Northeast	21 May 1938	Ferry regn F-2
DC-3-196A	2033	Northeast	25 May 1938	Ferry regn F-2
DC-3-196A	2034		August 1938	Knocked down kit to GAZ-84
DC-3-196A	2035		August 1938	Knocked down kit to GAZ-84
DC-3-196A	2042	Northeast	June 1938?	Ferry regn F-2
DC-3-196A	2043	Northeast	03 June 1938	Ferry regn F-2, to URSS-M137, to URSS-N
DC-3-196A	2044	Northeast	18 July 1938	Ferry regn F-2
DC-3-196A	2045	Northeast	20 July 1938	Ferry regn F-2
DC-3-196A	2046	Northeast	25 August 1938	Ferry regn F-2
DC-3-196A	2047	Northeast	30 August 1938	Ferry regn F-2
DC-3-196B	2112	Northeast	01 March 1939	Ferry regn F-6
DC-3-196B	2113	Northeast	24 March 1939	Ferry regn F-6
DC-3-196B	2114	Northeast	26 March 1939	Ferry regn F-6
DC-3-196B	2115	Northeast	28 March 1939	Ferry regn F-6
DC-3-196B	2116	Northeast	29 March 1939	Ferry regn F-6
DC-3-196B	2117	Northeast	07 April 1939	Ferry regn F-6

DC-2 URSS-M25 (c/n 1413), which was purchased initially for evaluation and later used on the Moscow-Berlin and Moscow-Prague routes of Aeroflot. (Vladimir Kotelnikov via RART)

One of a batch of six DC-3s delivered in March/April 1939, all under the ferry registration "F-6", visible on the fin. This aircraft is depicted in Mongolia in 1939, flying in support of the Soviet-Mongolian Army fighting against Japanese troops at Khalkhin-Gol. (Vladimir Kotelnikov via RART)

VVS DC-3 "F-6", one of a batch of six aircraft delivered to the Soviet Union in March/April 1939, all of which carried the ferry registration "F-6", which is still retained on the fin in this photo.
(Vladimir Kotelnikov via RART)

Descriptions of the various PS-84 and Li-2 variants are given in this listing, with details of their roles

PS-84	Official designation PS-84 2M-621R
PS-84-K	With underside fuselage bomb-racks
PS-84-I Medevac	
PS-84 1941 model	Two beam-mounted machine guns. From 15 September 1942 fitted with dorsal gun turret. Earlier aircraft progressively upgraded. At front, machine guns and even a 20mm cannon mounted to fire from the cabin windows fitted to many aircraft
Li-2 Night bomber	Spring 1942. Some frontal adaptations made previously
Li-2 Night bomber with internal bomb carriage	Aircraft 5408 c/n 1845408 evaluated in February 1943, but failed trials
Li-2VP Night bomber with internal bomb carriage	September 1944. Second trial using aircraft 1846605 until March 1945, but considered no significant advantage
Li-2NB Night bomber	Batch 108 onwards. This featured windows added to the forward fuselage door. Aircraft 18411906 was submitted for State Acceptance Trials in December 1944
Li-2	Several aircraft upgraded with, reportedly M-88 engines, although some sources suspect these may have been M-82s
Li-2 Glider tug	
Li-2 Special Mission VIP aircraft	
Li-2 Extended Range Transport 1943.	Ten aircraft built
Li-2 Fuel Carrier	1943. Five aircraft converted into tankers to take fuel to the front-line for bomber units of Long-Range Aviation.
Li-2 with Caterpillar Undercarriage	This configuration tested in 1942/43
Li-2 Cannon-armed Attack version	Early 1945. Armed with two 45mm wing-mounted cannon. Trials successful, but with the end of the war in sight, no further interest
Li-2P Passenger version	Produced from May 1945 until April 1953
Li-2T Transport/cargo version	Produced from May 1945 until 1953
Li-2T Staff Transport (VIP) version/ Li-2 'Salon'	
Li-2 Mailplane/passenger	ASh-82FN engines. Reportedly "better than a DC-3"
Li-2 Glider Tug	For Yak-14 and Ts-25 transport gliders. Various trials, but underpowered for task
UchShLi-2 (UshLi-2/Li-2Ush)	Multi-purpose Training version
Li-2R Radar Operator Trainer	
Li-2 Gunner/Radio Operator Trainer	
Li-2Gr	Cargo/Passenger version
Li-2F Photographic version	Camera ports below fuselage, observation ports aft of cockpit
Li-2FG Photogrammetry aircraft	
Li-2SKh Crop Duster	Designated Li-2R in Poland
Li-2 Polar Aviation version	Fitted with skis as required
Li-2V	For Polar operations with turbo supercharger, 4-bladed propellers. Prototype c/n 18422804
Li-2D	Additional fuel tanks, used on routes to the High North, Far East and Polar regions. (This designation used in Czechoslovakia for Paratroop version)
Li-2LP (Li-2PPL)	Forestry Patrol aircraft. Observation blisters on sides, equipped to drop fire fighters from the air
Li-2PR Fishery Recce aircraft	Extended glazed nose (eg CCCP-63052)
Li-2 ELINT & ECM versions	
Li-2 TV-relay version	
Li-2 Meteo Weather Research	Modified by Minsk Aircraft Repair Plant No.407. Aircraft so modified were CCCP-L4890, CCCP-54909, CCCP-83962 (1) and CCCP-84713
Li-2LL	Generic designation for test-flying aircraft

A test PS-84 fitted with ski undercarriage for evaluation during 1939. *(Vladimir Kotelnikov via RART)*

A close-up detail of a PS-84 cockpit. *(Vladimir Kotelnikov via RART)*

PS-84 c/n 1843603, the unserialled prototype of the bomber version on NII VVS trials in the summer of 1942. *(Vladimir Kotelnikov via RART)*

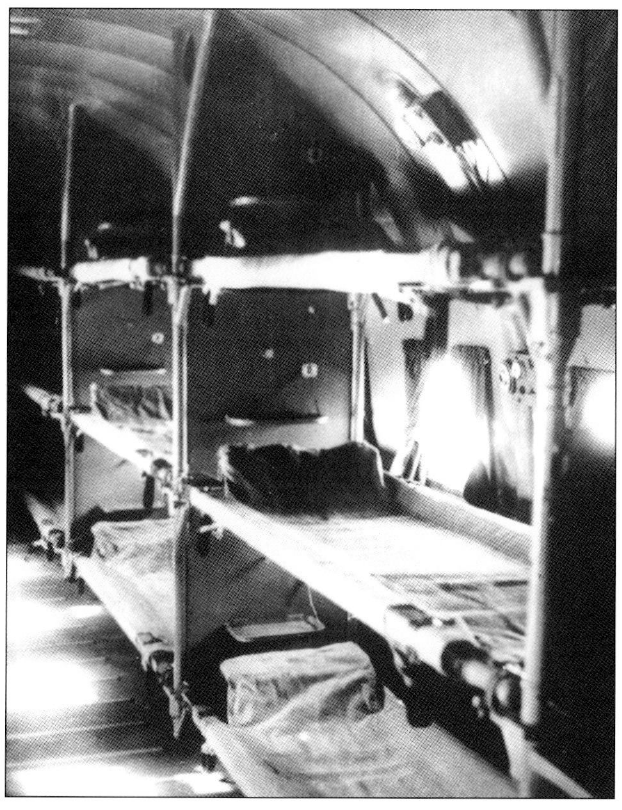

Above: The interior of a PS-84-I medevac version, depicting three tiers of stretchers fitted to each side of the fuselage cabin. *(Vladimir Kotelnikov via RART)*

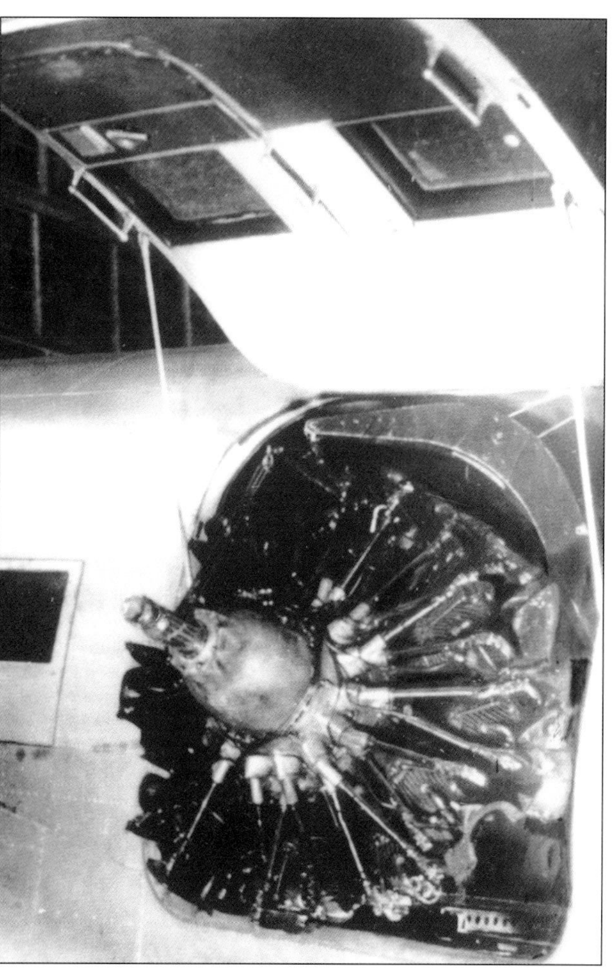

Right: A close-up of an M-62I engine being loaded into the fuselage of a PS-84-K by its cargo-door crane. *(Vladimir Kotelnikov via RART)*

A poor but nevertheless very rare photo illustrating an Li-2 re-engined with the M-88 engines in the immediate post-war period. The photograph was discovered at a small museum in Ulaangom in northwest Mongolia near the Russian border. *(Robert J Ruffle Archives)*

The Li-2 in Soviet Military Service

By the end of World War II (known to Russians as the Great Patriotic War) 2362 Li-2s had been built, almost all of which had seen military service at some point. For the most part, detail of Li-2 operations with the Soviet Air Force and Navy are still under wraps in Military Archives in Russia and alone would probably account for an entire book.

Of the 49 aircraft in use at 1st June 1941, eleven PS-84 aircraft were with front-line units, three with training institutions and five with the Navy. The type was also in use with NKVD units. One first-line unit had eleven DC-3s on strength plus a DC-2 from unknown origin; this was not URSS-M25 purchased from the USA because this had crashed on 6th August 1937 at Bistrita, Romania.

From the first days of the Great Patriotic War, following Hitler's invasion, Aeroflot changed from its administrational status and became subordinated to the People's Commissariat of Defence, forming six Special Mission Aviation Groups (AGON). At this point the Moscow Group (MAGON) had 50 PS-84s with the Kiev Group only four. During the 900-day siege of Leningrad, beginning in September 1941, 30 MAGON aircraft were used to deliver cargoes and for evacuation duties, with some aircraft from the Special Northern Civil Aviation group (OSAG) drafted to supplement MAGON operations.

Soviet units known to have operated the PS-84/Li-2 during the Great Patriotic War include the 1st GVF Air Transport Division of Long-Range Aviation, 62nd Guards Regiment of the GVF (Civil Air Fleet) on the Central Front, 8th Independent Air Regiment of the GVF in the Voronezh area, and the 13th and 14th Independent Air Regiment of the GVF during the celebrated Kursk battle. The 3rd Independent Communications Air Division of the GVF and the 1st GVF Air Transport Division had 74 aircraft on charge in November 1942, and by July 1943 had 200 aircraft on charge, at the end of 1943 had 266 aircraft on charge and on 1st July 1944 had 412 aircraft. This Transport Division was transformed into Regiments, each with three Squadrons of 30 aircraft.

The 2nd Special Mission Air Division was formed in autumn 1942 and operated Li-2s. Earlier, in April 1942, the first unit to operate Li-2s fitted out as bombers was the Long-Range Aviation 1st Air Transport Division, comprising the 101st and 102nd Air Transport Regiments. Each Regiment with two Squadrons had five Flights each with three aircraft per Flight. The 103rd Air Transport Regiment was formed during the summer of 1943 with 30 Li-2s. On the night of 26th August 1942, crews of the 1st Air Transport Division destroyed German bridges over the Don River. The following year they were tasked with airlifting troops and material on the Kursk Bulge.

In March 1945 the 1st and 299th Airlift Regiments re-equipped with 60 Li-2s. At the end of the Great Patriotic War the 2nd and 4th Special Mission Air Divisions had a total of 160-165 Li-2s on charge. In 1946 Airborne Troops had 43 dedicated Li-2s.

The 7th Guards Long-Range Aviation Regiment landed troops at Bookry on the River Dnepr, and in 1944 they were incorporated into the 4th Guards Air Corps. The 334th Bomber Regiment received the title "Berlinsky", awarded for their part in the taking of Berlin. By early 1944 Long-Range Aviation (ADD) units with Li-2s included the 5th, 6th and 7th Air Corps (see table below):

Li-2 units in the Long-Range Aviation Corps (ADD)

Corps	*Division*	*Regiment*
5th Air Corps	53rd Air Division	1st Guard Air Regiment 325th Air Regiment
	54th Air Division	7th Air Regiment 23rd Guards Air Regiment
6th Air Corps	9th Guards Air Division	4th Guard Air Regiment 11th Guards Air Regiment
7th Air Corps	1st Air Division	101st Air Regiment 102nd Air Regiment
	12th Guards Air Division	12th Guards Air Regiment 10th Air Regiment

GVF units with the Li-2 included the 6th Independent Air Regiment (later 69th Independent Air Regiment), the 19th Independent Air Regiment and the 10th Guards Transport Air Division.

PS-84 serial 4026 on a Second World War supply mission, with a ZIS-6 starter truck. Note the weathered, distinctly temporary winter paint scheme. (Vladimir Kotelnikov via RART)

VVS PS-84s in service at a front-line airfield during World War II. *(Vladimir Kotelnikov via RART)*

During a Finnish attack on Gorskaya airfield (Leningrad) on 9th - 10th March 1944 one Li-2 of the 110th Air Regiment was damaged and two Li-2s of the 23rd Guards Air Regiment were destroyed.

In the Far East operations against Japan included the following Li-2 units: 21st Guards Air Division, 54th Air Division, 281st Airlift Regiment and 344th Airlift Regiment.

The following Li-2s are confirmed as having operated with the Soviet Air Force.

1841107	490 white	18424702	
1841314		18426105	
1842001		18427804	
1842606		18430005	
1843603		18433205	05 red
1845408	5408	18435201	
1845701	4026 black	23440603	
1846102	4027 black	23440706	
1846310		23441201	05 red
1846602		23441605	07 yellow
1848703	6 red	23442505	
1849606	17 white	23443408	08 yellow
18411906		33443804	03
18412004		23444007	001
18414808		33444101	02 yellow
18416602		33444205	09 red
18418809		23444209	07
18421001		33444309	56 blue

A known Soviet Navy example was
23443108 14

At the end of the Great Patriotic War, the following Soviet Air Force divisions and regiments were operating the Li-2:-

1st Guards Long-Range Air Division:
31st GvAP DD, 32nd GvAP DD, 334th AP DD

12th Long-Range Air Division:
12th GvAP DD, 33rd GvAP DD, 338th AP DD

21st Guards Long-Range Air Division:
49th GvAP DD, 50th GvAP DD, 51st AP DD

22nd Guards Long-Range Air Division:
11th GvAP DD, 220th GvAP DD, 339th AP DD

53rd Long-Range Air Division:
1st GvAP DD, 239th GvAP DD, 336th AP DD

54th Long-Range Air Division:
7th GvAP DD, 29th GvAP DD, 340th AP DD

From 1946 the Li-2 relinquished its bombing role and formed into new transport units, such as the 331st Independent Transport Air Regiment (OTrAP). The 6th Guards Attack Air Division in the Kiev Military District became a training unit. In April 1945 transport units formed the Military Transport Aviation (VTA), with their prime role being to support Airborne Troops.

The 353rd Air Regiment, who had achieved best results in combat training, regularly took part in the annual Aviation Day display at Tushino airfield in Moscow. During 1945/46 the GVF resumed normal scheduled services as Aeroflot, administered by the Ministry of Civil Aviation. Many aircraft retained the olive drab military colour-scheme, however, well into the early 1960s.

In 1948 the 408th Training Air Regiment was equipped with the Li-2 which remained on strength until 1960. The Li-2 also served with the MVD, some aircraft bearing this inscription below the cockpit windows.

Several Li-2s were transferred to North Korea and in late 1947 North Korean military transports flew scheduled services from Pyongyang to Vladivostok and Khabarovsk, and to Harbin, China, with mixed Soviet/Korean crews, the routes mostly carrying diplomatic mail and specialist personnel. When the Korean war broke out the aircraft of the 51st Guards Airlift Regiment at Komsomolsk-on-Amur flew Soviet personnel and material to the war zone.

In 1956 the Chernovtsy-based division supported Soviet and WarPac forces in suppression of the Hungarian uprising.

In the late 1950s an Li-2 regiment based at Fergana in Uzbekistan, plus one from Zaporozhye, Ukraine – 36 aircraft in total – were posted to Vietnam, re-locating at Haiphong to supply Soviet Air Force crews in Vietnam.

The Li-2 remained on strength until 1964 when it was withdrawn from service. Some aircraft went to the paramilitary sport organisation DOSAAF, while others went to Aeroflot or were broken up.

The following table lists the number of Li-2s and air regiments in Soviet military transport aviation use for various years between 1940 and 1964 (totals include both the Li-2 and the C-47):-

1940	80
1943	355
1945	1046
1946	200 (10 regiments)
1949	230 (10 regiments)
1955	292 (16 regiments)
1956	576 (13 regiments)
1958	384 (9 regiments)
1959	288 (7 regiments)
1960	234 (4 regiments)
1962	142 (4 regiments)
1964	withdrawn from service

As in many air forces when a type of aircraft is officially withdrawn from service, isolated examples soldier on. One such example was 01 red, c/n 18438606, which flew with the 226 OSAP from the Soviet base at Oranienburg, in East Germany, until the mid-1970s.

Aeroflot and the Li-2

The PS-84/Li-2 and, to a much lesser extent the C-47, was the mainstay of airline services in the Union of Soviet Socialist Republics (USSR) from the later stages of the second world war until the early 1950s, when the Ilyushin Il-12 and Il-14 took over the longer and busier routes.

Aeroflot received twenty-eight PS-84s in 1940 for use by the Moscow, Georgian and Far East Directorates, and by the Moscow-Irkutsk route Directorate, followed in 1941 by the Moscow-Tiflis route. Special Air Groups were formed by Aeroflot in mid-1941 for military liaison and transport duties, and PS-84s were allocated to the Kiev, Northern, Karelia and Black Sea groups by April 1942.

The first international service to be opened by Aeroflot with Li-2s was from Moscow to Teheran via Baku late in 1942. This service was followed by Moscow to Sofia (Bulgaria) via Kiev,

Soviet Air Force Li-2 serial 01 red (c/n 18438606) was photographed at Oranienburg in the former East Germany in 1972. The aircraft was operated by 226 OSAP. *(via Nigel Eastaway, RART)*

An Aeroflot Li-2, believed to be CCCP-L413, taxying out at Moscow's Vnukovo Airport. *(Robert J Ruffle Archives)*

Li-2T CCCP-L4268 in use with Aeroflot for cargo work, conveniently showing the c/n 18422708 clearly on the fin. *(via Nigel Eastaway, RART)*

Odessa and Bucharest on 5th November 1944. In 1945, services from Moscow to Berlin via Königsberg, and Moscow to Vienna via Kiev, Lvov and Budapest were opened. At the end of 1945, flights to Warsaw started and the following year to Belgrade, and then Helsinki via Leningrad (from 25th November), with flights from Moscow to Tirana (Albania) following in 1947. In 1948 a service to Ulan-Bator (in Mongolia) was started.

By the summer of 1949, there were reportedly 679 weekly Li-2 departures from Moscow to points throughout the USSR, the longest routes operated by the type (normally in a 15-seat configuration) being:-

Moscow to Ulan-Bator – 5,135 kms,

Moscow to Chita (Manchuria) – 5,060 kms,

Sochi to Irkutsk – 5,280 kms,

Sochi to Alma Ata – 3,955 kms,

Simferopol to Alma Ata – 4,130 kms, and

Simferopol to Tashkent – 3,415 kms.

Despite the large increase in the use of Il-12s and Il-14s, the Li-2s, by this time normally modified to carry 21 to 24 passengers, continued to serve longer routes in the following directorates in the summer of 1967:- Azerbaijan (main base Baku), Kazakh (Alma Ata), Moldavian (Kishinev), North (Leningrad), Turkmen (Ashkhabad) and Ukrainian (Kiev).

In addition, local passenger services were flown by the Li-2s within the following directorates:- Eastern Siberia (Irkutsk), Estonian (Tallinn), Far East (Khabarovsk), Komi (Syktyvkar), Krasnoyarsk (Krasnoyarsk), Latvian (Riga), Lithuanian (Vilnius), Moscow (Bykovo), Tadjikistan (Dushanbe), Ural (Sverdlovsk), Uzbek (Tashkent), Volga (Kuybyshev), Western Siberia (Novosibirsk), White Russia (Minsk) and Yakut (Yakutsk).

By the mid-1960s, Li-2s were converted increasingly for all-cargo work, particularly in the following directorates:- North (Leningrad), Northern Caucasia (Rostov) and Volga (Kuybyshev). The largest number of cargo flights were operated to the highly industrialized area bordered by Gorkiy, Kazan, Sverdlovsk, Chelyabinsk, Ufa and Kuybyshev, with up to twelve all-cargo Li-2 flights a day from Moscow alone. Bykovo handled most of the cargo flights originating in or arriving in the Moscow area, with the Li-2s sharing the cargo work with Il-12s and Il-14s, prior to the introduction of the Antonov An-24 in 1965.

Despite the introduction of more modern types during the 1960s, the Li-2s continued not only to give sterling service on Aeroflot's passenger services, but also to open up new routes with the airline, some examples being:-

1964: Moscow-Kursk-Sumy; Voronezh-Volgograd and Moscow-Kotlas-Arkhangelsk

1965: Uzen-Zhetybai-Astrakhan; Uzen-Zhetybai-Makhachkala; Moscow-Kargopol-Arkhangelsk and Druskininkai-Kaunai-Riga-Leningrad

1967: Ivanovo-Cherepovets-Leningrad

1968: Guriev-Makhachkala; Guriev-Uralsk-Orenburg; Kursk-Kharkov-Rostov; Kursk-Tamlov-Gorkiy; Tula-Lipetsk-Rostov-Min'Vody; Tula-Lipetsk-Voronezh-Kharkov and Uzen-Shevchenko-Baku

1969: Kursk-Voronezh-Volgograd and Uzen-Zhetybai-Baku

In the 1970s, the Li-2 had largely been replaced by Il-14s or the later Antonov An-24, but were nevertheless still used on passenger services in the North directorate (Leningrad) in 1972, and on all-cargo services in a number of directorates (Central Regions/Arctic, Eastern Siberia, Far East, North, Ukraine, Ural and Yakut). The type was finally withdrawn from regular Aeroflot service in the mid-1970s.

For a list of PS-84s and Li-2s that are known to have served with Aeroflot, see the "DC-1/2/3 – The First Seventy Years" Volume 2, pages 682 to 693, and the updates in this volume.

АЭРОФЛОТ

АЛМА-АТА—КУЛЬДЖА—УРУМЧИ

(время местное)

МХД-204 Ли-2	АФЛ-204 Ли-2	4 Аэропорты	АФЛ-203 Ли-2	МХД-203 Ли-2
(3)	(5)		(6)	(2)
8.30	8.30	о Алма-Ата . . . . п	12.40	12.40
9.00	9.00	п Кульджа . . . . о	10.05	10.05
9.45	9.45	о Кульджа . . . . п	9.20	9.20
12.55	12.55	п Урумчи . . . . . о	8.00	8.00

Из Пекина пассажирские самолеты регулярно летают в Ханой (Вьетнам), Рангун (Бирма), Кантон, Нанкин, Харбин, Чунцин, Шанхай и другие города Китайской Народной Республики

РАСПИСАНИЕ ДВИЖЕНИЯ САМОЛЕТОВ

МЕЖДУНАРОДНЫЕ ЛИНИИ

№ 2 ЯНВАРЬ—АПРЕЛЬ 1957

МОСКВА—ХАРЬКОВ—СТАЛИНО—ДНЕПРОПЕТРОВСК—ЗАПОРОЖЬЕ—СИМФЕРОПОЛЬ

(время местное)

АФЛ-289 Ли-2	АФЛ-291 Ли-2	АФЛ-303 Ли-2	АФЛ-273 Ил-14	40 Аэропорты	АФЛ-274 Ил-14	АФЛ-304 Ли-2	АФЛ-292 Ли-2	АФЛ-290 Ли-2
#	#	#	#		#	#	#	#
15.30	14.00	11.20	8.25	о Москва . . . . . п	20.05	13.55	12.20	13.05
18.10	16.40	14.00	10.30	п Харьков . . . . . о	18.00	11.15	9.40	10.25
18.50	17.25	14.45	11.10	о Харьков . . . . . п	17.20	10.10	8.55	9.45
19.55				п Сталино . . . . . о				8.40
—	18.15			п Днепропетровск . о			8.05	—
—	—	16.00		п Запорожье . . . о		1.25	—	—
—	—	—	13.05	п Симферополь . . о	15.25	—		

Excerpts from a January-April 1957 Aeroflot mainline timetable illustrating two routes flown by Li-2s:- Timetable 4 shows the twice-weekly Alma Ata-Kulozha (now Yining)-Urumchi services flown by Li-2s of Aeroflot and the Chinese airline Minhanduy. The footnote states that at Peking the flight connects with services to Hanoi (Vietnam), Rangoon (Burma), Canton, Nankin, Harbin, Chumtsin & Shanghai. Timetable 40 shows that three of the four daily services are flown by Li-2s, the fourth by IL-14s. The route is from Moscow to Kharkov, Stalino (now Donetsk), Dnepropetrovsk, Zaporozhye (& Simferopol), annotated 'Service to Ukraine'.

Ski-equipped Li-2T of Polar Aviation, probably CCCP-04219, seen taxying at Wrangel Island, north of Siberia. *(via Nigel Eastaway, RART)*

Li-2 CCCP-04244 of Aeroflot, seen after an accident on the ice in the Canadian Arctic on 3rd May 1973. *(via Nigel Eastaway, RART)*

Li-2 CCCP-13325 (c/n 18438906) of Aeroflot, seen here in the olive drab finish. This aircraft survived into the mid-1970s. *(via Nigel Eastaway, RART)*

Former Aeroflot Li-2T CCCP-93914 was photographed at the Central Russian Air Force Museum at Monino in 1989. *(Robert J Ruffle archives)*

LZ-TUM, an Li-2P of Bulgarian Air Transport – TABSO – was photographed on a rare visit to Britain in the early 1950s. *(Don Hannah Collection)*

Li-2 OPERATORS OUTSIDE THE SOVIET UNION

There follows an alphabetical list by country of the Li-2 operators outside the Soviet Union

ALBANIA

Contrary to suggestions in some publications, the Li-2 was never operated by the Albanian Air Force.

BULGARIA

The first Li-2 deliveries to Bulgaria were for government use with LZ-LIA arriving in September 1946 and a second aircraft in October 1946. LZ-LIO was later reported in service with TABSO, but is likely to have been originally part of the government fleet. Although details are not available, the Bulgarian Air Force (BVVS) had twelve aircraft in service in 1969 with a few still in use in 1972. One was coded '41'.

TABSO – Bulgarian Air Transport (Bulgarian-Soviet Air Transport Company)

Li-2P	LZ-TUA	c/n 23443507	del 1953
	LZ-TUB	18432302	
	LZ-TUC	18431808	
	LZ-TUD		
	LZ-TUE	18432303	crashed 22 November 1952 Veghen
	LZ-TUF	18431803	
	LZ-TUG		
	LZ-TUH		
	LZ-TUM		
	LZ-TUO		
	LZ-TUQ		
	LZ-LIO	23443501	del 1953

CHINA

The first Li-2T was delivered to China on 13th September 1949, followed by another in October 1949. Six UchShLi-2 arrived in 1950 and four more Li-2T/Li-2P in 1951.

The PLAAF (People's Liberation Army Air Force) had taken delivery of 100 Li-2s before 1965, with 30 still in service in 1997. Recorded aircraft include:

3018, 3019 c/n 18439903, 3028, 3029, 3048, 3049 c/n 18440204, 4766, 5011, 5021, 5031, 5070 Li-2T c/n 18440106 and 8205 Li-2T c/n 18439709, 38043 and 38046

The PLANAF (People's Liberation Army Naval Air Force) had taken delivery of Li-2s before 1960, with nine in service in 1997.

Civil Li-2s first operated with SKOGA (Sino-Soviet Civil Aviation Society), which merged with CNAC (China National Airways Corp) in March 1954 to form CAAC (Civil Aviation Administration of China). CAAC operated 29 Li-2s:-

Serial	*c/n*	*Period operated*	*Operator*
301	18433601	1949-1982	CAAC Shanghai
		1982-1986	CAAC IASC, survey acft
		1986-	CAAC NCAA Tianjin instructional airframe
302	18433806	1949-1982	CAAC Xian. Broken up Xian 1984
303	18433602	1949-1982	CAAC Xian
		1982-1985	CAAC IASC. Broken up Lanzhou 1989
304	18433804	1949-1982	CAAC Xian
305	18440206	1952-1982	CAAC Shanghai
		1982-1986	CAAC IASC, survey acft
		1986-Oct 1997	CAAC NCAA Tianjin instructional airframe. Broken up December 1997
306	18433803	1949-1982	CAAC Xian
307	18439602	1951-1982	CAAC Shenyang. Broken up Shenyang
308	18433808	1949-1982	CAAC Guangzhou
309	18433606	1949-1982	CAAC Xian. Broken up Chengdu
310	18439704	1952-1982	CAAC Chengdu
311	18433707	1949-1982	CAAC 1st Fleet
		1982-1986	CAAC 2nd Fleet. Broken up Taiyuan 1987
312	18433510	1949-1982	CAAC Shenyang
		1982-1986	CAAC IASC
313	18433608	1949-1982	CAAC Shenyang
314	18436305	1950-1982	CAAC Shenyang
315	18433101	1949-1982	CAAC 1st Fleet
		1982-Oct 1987	CAAC IASC
316	18436304	1950-1982	CAAC Shenyang
		1982-1986	CAAC IASC. Broken up Shenyang 1988
317			CAAC Government
318	18433809	1949-1982	CAAC Xian
319			CAAC Government
320	18433904	1949-1982	CAAC Chengdu. Broken up Chengdu
321			CAAC Government
322	18439608	1952-	CAAC Chengdu. Broken up Chengdu
323	18439603	1951-1982	CAAC 1st Fleet
		1982-Aug 1988	CAAC IASC. Broken up Taiyuan 1990
324		-1981	CAAC Government Broken up Taiyuan1984
325	18440508	1952-1982	CAAC 1st Fleet
		1982-1987	CAAC IASC. Broken up Taiyuan 1988
326			CAAC Government
327	18440509	1952-1982	CAAC 1st Fleet
		1982-1987	CAAC IASC. Broken up Taiyuan
328			CAAC Government
329	18440205	1952-	CAAC Chengdu. Broken up Chengdu

CAAC IASC = Industrial Aviation Services Company
CAAC NCAA = North China Aviation Administration
CAAC 1st Fleet = Chinese National Carrier, International operations
CAAC 2nd Fleet = Chinese National Carrier, General Aviation Division
CAAC Government = Aircraft available for Government use, separated from airline and military operations, but flown by military crews.

CUBA

Six aircraft were delivered to Cubana, but no details are available.

CZECHOSLOVAKIA

CSA Czechoslovak Airlines took delivery of eight Li-2P in 1952 which remained in service until 1956 and were transferred to the Czechoslovak Air Force (CVL) in early 1957.

OK-GAA	23442105	leased Oct 1952	ex CVL D-29, to OK-BYO in 1953
OK-GAB	23441801	del 29 May 1952	WFU in 1956, to CVL as 1801
OK-GAC	23442305	del 02 August 1952	WFU in 1956, to CVL as 2305
OK-GAD	23442209	del 25 October 1952	to CVL as 2209 in 1957
OK-GAE	23442210	del 23 August 1952	WFU 29 Jan 1956, to CVL as 2210
OK-GAF	23442501	del 25 August 1952	to CVL as 2501 in 1957
OK-GAG	23442804	del 11 August 1952	to CVL as 2804 in Aug 1954
OK-GAH	23443002	del 21 October 1952	WFU in 1957, to CVL as D-38 (2)

The Czechoslovak Air Force (CVL) also took delivery of the Li-2 in 1952, reportedly receiving 19 aircraft in total:-

D-29	Li-2P	23442105	del 05 August 1952	Leased to CSA as OK-GAA Oct 52
D-30	Li-2T	23442106	del 03 January 1952?	To 2106
D-31	Li-2T	23442703	del 13 March 1952	To 2703
D-32	Li-2T	23442708	in svce 3 June 1952	To 2708
D-33	Li-2T	23442107	del 01 December 1952?	To 2107
D-34	Li-2T	23442109	del 20 February 1952?	To 2109 29 January 1957
D-35	Li-2D	23442801	del 24 April 1952	Cvtd to Li-2F 1956, to 2891
D-36	Li-2D	23442901	del 12 February 1952	To 2901
D-37	Li-2T	23442108	in svce 01 December 1952	To OK-BYP June 1955
D-38 (1)	Li-2	23442304	del 18 August 1952	To 2304
D-38 (2)	Li-2F(P)	23443002	del 14 June 1957	Cvtd to Li-2F 1957, to 3002

In mid-1957 a revised identification system was introduced comprising a four-number serial based on the last four of the constructor's number. (This system was applied to all types operated by the CVL and continued in use until the break-up of Czechoslovakia).

The second CVL serials are listed with the designation sub-types where known. Sub-types appearing in brackets denote the original variant. Li-2F is a Czechoslovak modification for photo/survey work. Details of the unit and base are given, where known.

1801	Li-2F(P)	23441801	del 1957 ex OK-GAB. Cvtd to Li-2F. WFU September 1963, used as bar near the old Prague Airport terminal. Marked OK-1962. Burned by Airport Fire Service 27 March 1972.
2105	Li-2P	23442105	ex OK-BYO. To VLU Kosice 1960. WFU 08 August 1966. Preserved at Banska Bystrica in VVS markings.
2106	Li-2T	23442106	ex D-30. Rvt Kosice 1960. Believed to be the aircraft preserved in VVS markings at Dukla, Slovakia.
2107	Li-2T	23442107	ex D-33. Rvt Kosice. Believed to be the aircraft preserved at Swidnik, Slovakia.
2108	Li-2 Salon	23442108	ex OK-BYP (originally Li-2T). PVOS Brno. WFU April 1966, to Zlutava.
2109	Li-2T	23442109	ex D-34. LO Kbely. WFU (after accident?) August 1957.
2209	Li-2F(P)	23442209	del 1957 ex OK-GAD. Cvtd to Li-2F & to FLS Hradcany. WFU August 1966.
2210	Li-2P	23442210	del 29 January 1957, ex OK-GAE. FLS Hradcany. WFU 1963 after accident.
2301	Li-2P	23442301	ex OK-BYA.
2304	Li-2F	23442304	ex D-38 (1). Cvtd to Li-2F in 1956 & to FLS Hradcany. WFU October 1966.
2305	Li-2P	23442305	ex OK-GAC. PVOS Zvolen. WFU July 1965.
2309	Li-2F(T)	23442309	ex OK-BYQ. Cvtd to Li-2F in 1956 & to FLS Hradcany. Used as bar at Novo Dubnica, Slovakia.
2407	Li-2	23442407	Instructional airframe at Prostejov.
2501	Li-2P	23442501	del 1957, ex OK-GAF. FLS Hradcany. WFU April 1968.
2703	Li-2T	23442703	ex D-31. Rvt Kosice. WFU July 1967. To Zilina Technical University, Slovakia.
2708	Li-2F	23442708	ex D-32. Rvt Kosice. WFU October 1966.
2710	Li-2D	23442710	del 30 May 1957. PVOS Zatec. WFU September 1967. To Prague-Kbely museum.
2804	Li-2F(P)	23442804	del 04 August 1954, ex OK-GAG. FLS Hradcany. WFU April 1968.
2891	Li-2F(D)	23442801	ex D-35. LO Kbely. Serial number 2891 probably painted in error. WFU June 1967.
2901	Li-2D	23442901	ex D-36. LO Kbely.
3002	Li-2P	23443002	ex D-38 (2). FLS Hradcany. WFU July 1967. Preserved at Prague-Kbely.

Czech Air Force Li-2F, serial unknown, was photographed at a Praha-Kbely airshow in the late 1960s or early 1970s. *(via Nigel Eastaway, RART)*

All CVL Li-2s were withdrawn from use by the mid-late 1960s.

The Czechoslovak Government Flight (LOMV) operated four Li-2s as follows:-

OK-BYA Li-2	23442301	del 27 August 1952. To CVL as 2301.
OK-BYO Li-2P Salon	23442105	del 1953, ex OK-GAA. To CVL as 2105 on 30 May 1957.
OK-BYP Li-2T	23442108	ex CVL D-37. Returned to CVL as 2108.
OK-BYQ Li-2 Salon	23442309	del 17 August 1952. To CVL as 2309.

HUNGARY

The Hungarian airline Maszovlet (Hungarian-Soviet Air Transport Society) was formed in 1946, taking delivery of eleven Li-2s, comprising five virtually new aircraft bought from TARS Romanian airline and six directly from the Moscow-Khimki production line.

Maszovlet started domestic Li-2 services on 15th October 1946, followed by the first international flight, to Prague, on 19th June 1947.

Below: A 1957 scene at Budapest Airport, showing three Li-2Ps of Hungarian Air Transport – Malev, HA-LIG/LID/LIO. *(via Mike Hooks)*

Li-2P HA-LIB (c/n 18423506) of MASZOVLET, the predecessor of MALEV, photographed in the early 1950s. (via Nigel Eastaway, RART)

A further photo from a visit to Budapest in 1957, showing Li-2P HA-LIP of Hungarian Air Transport – Malev. (via Mike Hooks)

HA-LIA "Aladar"	Li-2P	18423503	ex YR-TAC? WFU 31 December 1961.
HA-LIB "Bela"	Li-2P	18423506	ex YR-TAE? WFU April 1959.
HA-LIC "Cecil"	Li-2P	18423507	ex YR-TAH? WFU 31 December 1961.
HA-LID "Denes"	Li-2P	18423508	ex YR-TAJ? WFU 31 December 1961. Destroyed 1962.
HA-LIE "Elemer"	Li-2P	18423510	ex YR-TAO? WFU 1960.
HA-LIF "Ferenc"	Li-2P	18425604	Belly-landed near Polna 23 December 1954, due to de-icing problem.
HA-LIG "Geza"	Li-2T	18426601	To Hungarian Defence Association 24 January 1958.
HA-LIH "Helen"	Li-2P	18427005	WFU 31 December 1959. Broken up Budaörs.
HA-LII "Ilona"	Li-2P	18427006	Belly-landed near Brno 23 December 1954 due to de-icing problem. NB: Second acft with the same problem on the same day!
HA-LIK	Li-2P	18427501	Crashed 19 September 1949. Flew into Mecsek mountain due to ATC error.
HA-LIL	Li-2P	18428003	Crashed 02 October 1952. Ran into building on landing at Nyiregyhaza.
HA-LIM "Maria"	Li-2P	23441007	del 27 March 1952, ex Hungarian AF 007. Crashed 09 June 1957 on landing Budapest with engine problem, ran into bomb crater.

Maszovlet was wound up in 1954 with the newly-formed all Hungarian airline Malev (Hungarian Air Transport Company) taking over all its assets on 1st October 1954. In 1956 Malev increased its Li-2 fleet with the arrival of thirteen aircraft from the Hungarian Air Force. This transfer was dictated by Soviet authorities following the failed 1956 uprising.

HA-LIN "Nandor"	Li-2P	23442803	ex 803, del 04 March 1957. WFU 30 January 1963.
HA-LIO "Olga"	Li-2P	18439505	ex 505, del 29 March 1957. WFU November 1963, stored.
HA-LIP "Peter"	Li-2P	18439504	ex 504, del 01 July 1957. WFU April 1964, towed to Szolnok.
HA-LIQ	Li-2T	23441206	ex 206, del 20 March 1957. Returned to 206 on 20 May 1964.
HA-LIR "Robert"	Li-2T	23441303	ex 303, del 20 March 1957. WFU 17 March 1964, preserved Budapest until March 1967.
HA-LIS "Sandor"	Li-2T	23441301	ex 301, del 15 April 1957. WFU 20 March 1964, to Vidampark, Pecs.
HA-LIT "Tamas"	Li-2T	18435901	ex 901, del 12 March 1957. WFU 02 March 1964, preserved Szombathely until broken up in 1972.
HA-LIU "Ubul"	Li-2T	18439306	ex 306 (2), del 26 April 1957. Returned to 306 (2) on 20 May 1964.
HA-LIV "Vilmos"	Li-2T	18439310	ex 310, del 20 April 1957. Cvtd to the aerial mapping role 15 March 1962.
HA-LIW "Waldemar"	Li-2T	18439307	ex 307, del 30 July 1957. To Hungarian Defence Association 1959.
HA-LIX	Li-2T	18433209	ex 209 (1), del 24 March 1957. Returned to 209 (1) on 30 April 1964.
HA-LIY	Li-2T	18433203	ex 203, del 17 April 1957. To Hungarian Defence Association 26 August 1964.
HA-LIZ "Zoltan"	Li-2T	23441209	ex 209 (2), del 20 November 1957. To Hungarian AF 20 May 1964, but not used. Preserved at Mate Zalka Military Institute, Budapest. Destroyed some years later.

Between 1958 and 1961 Malev operated HA-TSA C-47A-90DL (TS-62) c/n 20492 with Russian Ash-621R engines replacing the original Pratt & Whitneys.

The Hungarian Air Force (MHRC) operated nineteen aircraft, made up of fourteen Li-2T and five VIP Li-2s, with aircraft delivered from September 1949. The fleet was depleted by thirteen aircraft by order of the Soviet Union following the failed uprising in October 1956, when strict limits on the amounts of military hardware were imposed. The thirteen Li-2s were transferred to Malev.

S101 109	Li-2T Li-2P	18433109	del 10 September 1949. Allocated code never applied. Cvtd to Li-2P 29 July 1950/1951 & used for government flights. re-regd 1952. To RKK Kecskemét 1957, to 86th Composite Sq Kecskemét 1958, to 86th Helicopter Regiment, Kecskemét/Szentkirályseabadja 1968, to 87th Transport Helicopter Regiment, Szentkirályseabadja 1971. WFU 1974, donated to Pioneers' children organization.
S102 201	Li-2T	18433201	del 09 September 1949. Allocated code never applied. re-regd 1952. Cvtd for aerial mapping. To RKK Kecskemét 1957, to 86th Composite Sq, Kecskemét 1958, renamed 86th Composite Detachment 1961. WFU 1963, stored at Szolnok.
S103 203	Li-2T	18433203	del 09 September 1949. Allocated code never applied. Cvtd to navigation trainer in 1950. re-regd 1952. To HA-LIY 17 April 1957.
206	Li-2T	23441206	del 27 March 1952. To HA-LIQ 20 March 1957. Returned to Hungarian AF 20 May 1964. To 86th Composite Sq, Kecskemét, to 86th Helicopter Regiment, Kecskemét/ Szentkirályszabadja 1968, to 87th Transport Helicopter Regiment, Szentkirályszabadja 1971. WFU 1974, stored at Budaörs until 1980.
S104 209 (1)	Li-2T	18433209	del 09 April 1949. Allocated code never applied. re-regd 1952. To HA-LIX 24 March 1957. Returned to Hungarian AF 30 November 1964. To 86th Helicopter Regiment, Kecskemét/Szentkirályszabadja, to 87th Transport Helicopter Regiment Szentkirályszabadja 1971. Last flight 11 January 1974. Preserved at Szolnok c 1992-October 1997.
209 (2)	Li-2T	23441209	del 27 March 1952. To HA-LIZ 20 November 1957. Returned to Hungarian AF 20 May 1964, but not used. Preserved at Mate Zalka Military Institute, Budapest. Destroyed some years later.
210	Li-2T	23441210	del 27 March 1952. To 37th Test Sq, Kiskunlachaza. Crashed 22 August 1952 near Apajpuszta during single-engined night flying.
301	Li-2T	23441301	del 27 March 1952. To HA-LIS 15 April 1957.
303	Li-2T	23441303	del 27 March 1952. To HA-LIR 20 March 1957.
306 (1)	Li-2P	18436306	del 19 September 1950. Damaged beyond repair while landing in cross-wind at Kunmadaras 12 December 1952. Used as instructional airframe Vasvar.
306 (2)	Li-2T	18439306	del 10 October 1951. Allocated code not applied until 1952. To HA-LIU 26 April 1957. Returned to Hungarian AF 20 May 1964. WFU 1964. Towed to Szentendre Military Institute.
307	Li-2T	18439307	del 10 October 1951. Allocated code not applied until 1952. To HA-LIW 30 July 1957.
310	Li-2T	18439310	del 10 October 1951. Allocated code not applied until 1952. To HA-LIV 20 April 1957.
503	Li-2P	18439503	del 24 October 1951. Allocated code not applied until 1952. To RKK Kecskemét 1957, to 86th Composite Sq, Kecskemét 1958, renamed 86th Composite Detachment 1961, to 86th Helicopter Regiment, Kecskemét/Szentkirályszabadja 1968, to 87th Transport Helicopter Regiment, Szentkirályszabadja 1971. WFU 1974
504	Li-2P	18439504	del 24 October 1951. Allocated code not applied until 1952. To HA-LIP 01 July 1957. Returned to Hungarian AF 20 May 1964. WFU 1972. Preserved at Szolnok-Szandaszölös.
505	Li-2P	18439505	del 24 October 1951. Allocated code not applied until 1952. VIP aircraft for Hungarian Government 1952. To HA-LIO 29 March 1957.
803	Li-2P	23442803	del 01 July 1952. Operated for Hungarian Government. To HA-LIN 04 March 1957.
901	Li-2T	18435901	del 08 September 1950. Allocated code not applied until 1952. To HA-LIT 12 March 1957.
902	Li-2T	18435902	del 16 August 1950. Allocated code not applied until 1952. To RKK Kecskemét 1957, to 86th Composite Sq, Kecskemét 1958, renamed 86th Composite Detachment 1961. WFU 02 March 1964 and scrapped.

The Hungarian Police received ex-Hungarian Air Force Li-2T serial 201 from storage in 1983, but it was never flown. It was used for anti-terrorist training at Budakesi and scrapped in 1993.

The Hungarian Defence Association (a para-military body akin to the Soviet DOSAAF) took five Li-2s on charge:-

HA-LIG	wef 24 January 1958. WFU 1962.
HA-LIW	wef 1959. WFU 1963. Used as a 'coffee house' to replace the earlier HA-LIA, destroyed 1973.
HA-LIV	wef 01 June 1964. WFU 18 August 1966. Preserved at Dunaujvaros. Scrapped 1975.
HA-LIY	wef 26 August 1964. Converted for aerial photography. WFU 31 October 1971. Stored at Tiszaliget. Scrapped 1997.
HA-LIO	wef 28 August 1964. Damaged by fire whilst defuelling at Szolnok 24 April 1968, broken up.

The Airport Fire Service at Budapest/Ferihegy received HA-LIB and HA-LIC, both of which were burnt for fire-rescue practice during 1962, followed by HA-LIE in 1963.

Li-2P c/n 23441007, delivered to the Hungarian Air Force on 15th January 1952, was planned to become serial 007, but the aircraft never carried the code and never entered military service. It was transferred to Maszovlet on 27th March 1952 as HA-LIM.

c/n 18433109 marked as "1975" was displayed at Zanka until scrapped in 1991.

HA-LIA from circa 1961 became the "Little Pilot Coffee House" in Budapest until destroyed by fire on 8th July 1968.

HA-LIG was preserved at Tatabanya Lido from 1962 until destroyed in 1968.

HA-LIN was displayed at Hüvösvölgy in Budapest on 10th April 1964, but burnt out in 1968.

HA-LIQ was displayed from circa June 1990 at Budaörs, ex-Farkashegy Technical College. From circa 1994 it has been preserved at Budapest/Ferihegy as part of the Malev Aircraft Collection.

HA-LIU was preserved at Szeged from 1969. It was damaged by fire in 1999, and scrapped on 3rd December 2006. The nose section was preserved at Budaörs in August 2008.

Hungarian Air Force 301 has been displayed at the Szolnok Museum since October 2006, marked as "HA-LIU". It is reportedly a composite airframe made up from c/n 23441301/301/HA-LIS and c/n 18439306/306/HA-LIU.

HA-LIX c/n 18433209 has been beautifully refurbished to flying condition by the Gold Timer Foundation. This machine was displayed at the Szolnok Museum prior to October 1997.

HA-LIP c/n 18439504 was at Szandaszölös for some years, and was moved circa November 2000 to Kukla Garage on Route 54, Bócsa.

LAOS

The Li-2 was operated by the Laos Air Force, but the only reported identity was serial/code 02 in December 1961.

MONGOLIA

Contrary to suggestions in some publications, the Li-2 was never operated by the Mongolian Air Force.

NORTH KOREA

The North Korean Air Force operated an unknown number of Li-2s, including 501, 504, 520 and 532. Some aircraft were modified for survey work. The fleet was operated in part for the North Korean airline Chosonminhang/Air Koryo, some aircraft being painted in a white/silver scheme with the North Korean flag across the fin and rudder, while others were olive drab with the air force insignia.

POLAND

Three Li-2s arrived in Poland in August 1944, immediately after the liberation of Poland from German troops. These were operated on behalf of the Poles by the Soviet 2nd Independent Staff Squadron, and manned by Soviet airmen. In early March 1945 the Polish Air Force (PWL) started its own Li-2 units, the 6th Independent Special Mission Air Transport Squadron based at Okeçie, operating domestic and international flights for the Provisional Polish Government and Polish military VIPs. It comprised five Li-2s and five C-47s. Co-located at Okeçie, the 7th Independent Air Transport Squadron was established in April 1945, operating nine Li-2s on domestic communications flights. It was disbanded in December 1945 when its aircraft were transferred to LOT Polish Airlines on its re-establishment. This left the PWL with four Li-2s.

In 1947 an Officer Flying School was established at Deblin.

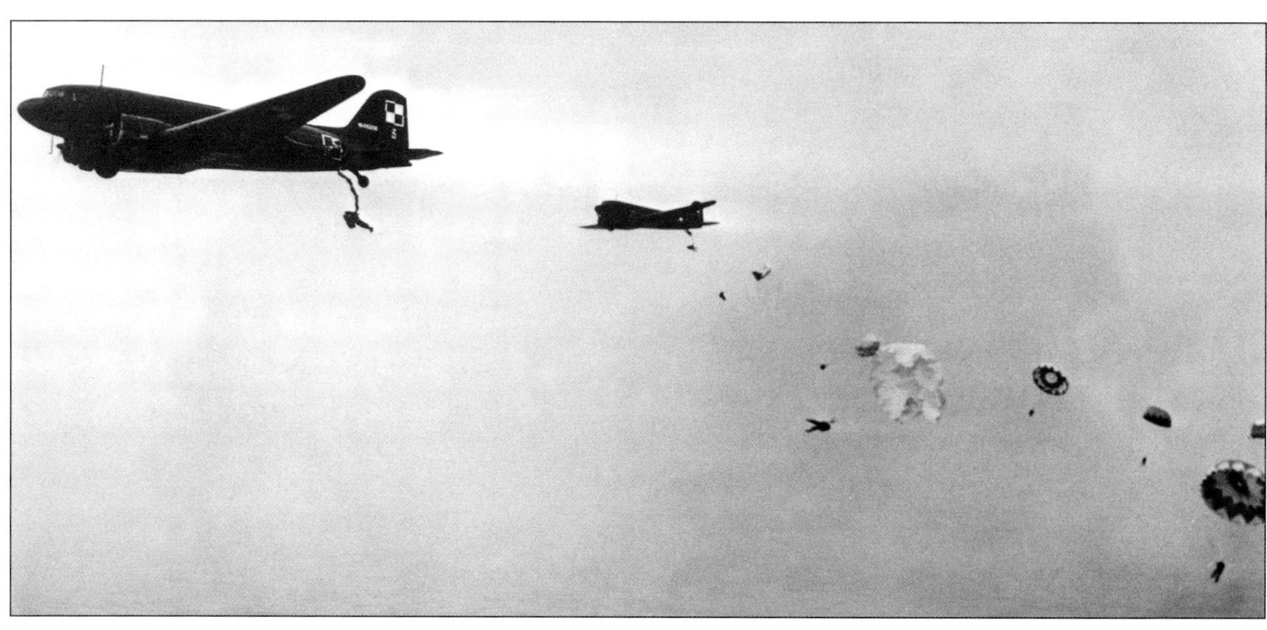

Polish Air Force Li-2T 18416208 coded "3" undertaking a demonstration parachute drop over Warsaw on Polish Air Force Day 30th August 1955. (Planet News via Mike Hooks)

The Polish embarked on several local modifications to the basic airframe, resulting in the Li-2 Bomber Training in March 1947, when three Li-2NB were converted, c/n 18416110 code 4 (white), 18416204 code 12 (white) and 18416208 code 3 (white). Li-2 VIP interior was for Staff Transport. In 1963, SP-LKE c/n 23442002 was converted to a Calibration aircraft for aeronautical navigation aids checks.

The Polish Air Force (PWL) listing may be subject to omissions and the codes applied have changed frequently as those cited are from observations, not from official records.

Some delivery dates cited in Polish publications differ from what is now considered accurate information, and these are given in brackets.

Polish Air Force Li-2F serial 39 (c/n 18436204), formerly 02, photographed at the Krakow Museum, but unfortunately destroyed by fire in the late 1970s. (via Nigel Eastaway, RART)

18416110	Li-2T (SB)	4	In service 29 January 1947 to 03 September 1960.
		11	Leased to LOT 12 February 1959, no civil markings
18416201	Li-2T		
18416204	Li-2T (SB)	12	In service (14 September 1946) 29 January 1947 to 1954. Canx 20 December 1955. To Zamoszcz Technical School.
18416207	Li-2T	15	In service 29 January 1947-June 1947.
18416208	Li-2T (SB)	3	In service from (May 1945) 21 July 1947
		14	Leased to LOT 12 February 1959, no civil markings
		03	
18419704	Li-2T		del September 1957, ex SP-LBJ
18419802	Li-2T		del October 1957, ex SP-LBB
18422610	Li-2P	63	del 01 September 1960, ex SP-LAM, canx 01 September 1963. Still in service 01 April 1964.
18423206	Li-2P	64	del 01 September 1960, ex SP-LAU, canx 01 September 1963. Still in service 01 April 1964.
18436203	Li-2	01	del 23 September 1950. Still in service 01October 1964.
18436204	Li-2F	02	del 23 September 1950. Photo-survey aircraft.
		39	Preserved Krakow Museum. Destroyed by arson in late 1970s.
18436205	Li-2T	03	del (1949) 23 September 1950.
18436206	Li-2	04	del 06 September 1950
		1	
		44	
18438102	Li-2	27	del 1951
18439101	Li-2T	04	del 04 August 1951.
		41	Still in service 01 October 1964.
18439102	Li-2T	05	del (1950) 04 August 1951. To SP-LDA 29 April 1965.
		027	Returned to PWL 08 June 1965. WFU 03 January 1971. Still in service 1974! To Krakow Museum.
18439103	Li-2T	06	del 04 August 1951. Still in service 01 October 1964.
23442609	Li-2P	07	del 29 October 1952.
		42	Still in service 01 October 1964.
23442610	Li-2T	08	del 21 October 1952.
		028	Still in service 28 March 1970.
23442701	Li-2T	09	In service (1951) 29 October 1952 to 1972.
		029	
		02	
		2	
23442702	Li-2T	10	In service (1951) 29 October 1952 to 1970.
		026	
		010	
23442704	Li-2T	03	del 21 October 1952.
		40	Still in service 01 October 1964
23442707	Li-2P	012	del 21 October 1952.
		43	
33444905	Li-2T	06	In service 1953 to 1973.
		1	
		014	
		01	
		06	Seen 01 January 1962 & 19 February 1970
		05	Displayed at Polska Wies 1987. Broken up?

LOT Polish Airlines operated over forty Li-2P and Li-2T, thirty of which were delivered between 1945 and 1947. The Li-2 was finally withdrawn from service in 1969. The Polish Aviation Authority operated SP-LKE after modification for Flight Navigation Aid Calibration from 08 July 1963 until 10 November 1970. It was then preserved at Krakow, but was destroyed by fire in the 1990s.

SP-LAA "Alina"	Li-2P	18422702	Regd 27 December 1945. Used as crop duster 1952/54. Canx 31 October 1964.
SP-LAB "Baska"	Li-2P	18422703	Regd 12 December 1945. Used for photo-survey work from 1953. Canx 30 November 1961
SP-LAC "Celina"	Li-2P	18422704	Regd 04 January 1946. Canx 31 October 1964
SP-LAD "Duska"	Li-2P	18422705	Regd 04 January 1946. Used as crop duster 1952/54. Canx 31 October 1964.
SP-LAE "Elka"	Li-2P	18424001	Regd 11 January 1946. Crashed near Katowice & W/O 14 April 1955.
SP-LAF "Fela"	Li-2P	18424004	Regd 08 February 1946. Canx 30 November 1961.
SP-LAG "Gabrysia"	Li-2P	18423202	Regd 08 January 1946. Canx 30 November 1961.
SP-LAH "Hela"	Li-2P	18423201	Regd 15 February 1946. Crashed near Limanova 19 March 1954.
SP-LAJ "Jasiek"	Li-2P	18424005	Regd 01 March 1946. Canx 30 November 1961.
SP-LAK "Krysia"	Li-2P	18424002	Regd 28 February 1946. Canx 30 November 1961.
SP-LAL "Lucynka"	Li-2P	18424008	Regd 23 March 1946, ex Soviet Air Force. Crashed Ugnowa, nr Tczew 25 (15) August 1960.
SP-LAM "Maciek"	Li-2P	18422610	Regd 11 January 1946. Used as crop duster 1952/54. To PWL '63' 01 September 1960.
SP-LAN "Nelli"	Li-2P	18424006	Regd 23 March 1946. Canx 30 November 1961.
SP-LAO "Olenka"	Li-2P	18424007	Regd 23 March 1946. Crashed 07 October 1952.
SP-LAP "Piotrus"	Li-2P	18423204	Regd 20 April 1946. Canx 30 November 1961.
SP-LAR "Rena"	Li-2P	18424003	Regd 14 April 1946. Canx 01 September 1960.
SP-LAS "Stasiek"	Li-2P	18423203	Regd 14 June 1946. Canx 30 November 1961 due wing fatigue. To Tourist Centre Sobieszów 1963. To Drzonów, Lubuskie Museum, Wojskowe 08 September 1989.
SP-LAT "Tomek"	Li-2P	18423205	Regd 10 July 1946. Canx 10 April 1961.
SP-LAU "Urszulka"	Li-2P	18423206	Regd 14 June 1946. To PWL '64' on 01 September 1960.
SP-LAW "Wójciech"	Li-2P	18424009	Regd 14 June 1946. Canx 24 November 1960.
SP-LBA "Antos"	Li-2T	18422009	Regd 10 July 1946. Crashed 29 March 1950.
SP-LBB	Li-2T	18419802	Regd 28 September 1946. Canx 24 October 1957 to PWL.
SP-LBC	Li-2T	18419010	Regd 26 October 1946. Crashed near Popowie 26 May 1948.
SP-LBD	Li-2T	18419804	Regd 21 August 1946. Crashed near Sowina 19 May 1952, canx 02 June 1952.
SP-LBE "Ewa"	Li-2T	18420203	Regd 21 August 1946. Canx 29 November 1951 as not repairable.
SP-LBF	Li-2T	18420205	Regd 08 January 1947. Canx 08 January 1964.
SP-LBG	Li-2T	18418308	Regd 09 January 1947. DBR Warsaw 16 December 1963, canx 30 December 1963.
SP-LBH	Li-2T	18419602	Regd 13 May 1947. Canx 31 October 1964.
SP-LBJ	Li-2T	18419704	Regd 13 June 1947. Canx 24 September 1957 to PWL.
SP-LBK	Li-2		Cannibalised circa 1947.
SP-LDA	Li-2T	18439102	Ex PWL '05'. Leased from PWL 29 April 1965 to 08 June 1965. Returned to PWL as '027'.
SP-LGL	Li-2		Seen Leipzig/Mockau 23 August 1956.
SP-LKA	Li-2P	18438505	Regd 30 July 1951. Crashed Lodz 15 November 1951.
SP-LKB	Li-2P	18438504	Regd 28 July 1951. Canx 10 November 1969.
SP-LKC	Li-2P	23441010	Regd 31 May 1952. DBR, location unknown & canx 22 September 1964.
SP-LKD	Li-2P	23441501	Regd 16 June 1952. Canx 24 March 1966.
SP-LKE	Li-2P	23442002	Regd 16 July 1952. Modified for Flight Navigation Aid Calibration, to ZRLiLK.
SP-LKF	Li-2P	23444510	Regd 21 May 1953. Canx 10 November 1969.
SP-LKG	Li-2P	23444801	Regd 05 June 1953. Canx 15 December 1967.
SP-LKH	Li-2P	23444507	Regd 18 June 1953. Canx 04 November 1968.
SP-LKI	Li-2P	23444804	Regd 01 July 1953. Canx 04 November 1968. Preserved Wieruszów.
11	Li-2T(SB)	18416110	Leased from PWL in military markings 12 February 1959.
14	Li-2T(SB)	18416208	Leased from PWL in military markings 12 February 1959.

Li-2P SP-LKI (c/n 33444804) of Polskie Linie Lotnicze-LOT. This aircraft was the last to be delivered to the Polish airline (in 1953) and has been preserved as a monument in the town of Wieruszów. *(via Nigel Eastaway, RART)*

Li-2P SP-LKE (c/n 23442002), formerly operated by LOT-Polish Airlines, was photographed in service with ZRLiLK as a flight navigation aid calibration aircraft. *(via Nigel Eastaway, RART)*

Li-2P YR-TAB (c/n 18423208) of TAROM – Romanian Air Transport, photographed at an unknown location during the 1960s. *(via Nigel Eastaway, RART)*

Romanian Air Force Li-2 206 seen at an unknown location. *(via Mike Hooks)*

ROMANIA

A joint Romanian-Soviet airline TARS was established in 1946 and operated until 1954 when the airline reformed as TAROM (Romanian Air Transport). Initial aircraft were Li-2s, with deliveries from January 1946.

YR-TAA	Li-2P	18423501	Regd 07 January 1946. Crashed Fagaras mountains 15 November 1950.
YR-TAB	Li-2T	18423208	Regd 08 January 1946. Canx 13 August 1970. Reportedly broken up, but also in use as café circa 1975.
YR-TAC	Li-2P	18423503	Regd 08 January 1946? To HA-LIA 01 August 1946
YR-TAD	Li-2P	18423504	Regd 08 January 1946. Canx 02 July 1969. Broken up.
YR-TAE (1)	Li-2P	18423506	Regd 07 March 1946. To HA-LIB 04 August 1946.
YR-TAE (2)	Li-2P	23441905	del 1952. Canx 11 March 1967. To Romanian AF as 905.
YR-TAF	Li-2P	18423505	Regd 18 June 1946. Canx 31 December 1968. Used as café at Herastrau Park, Bucharest.
YR-TAG	Li-2P	18428002	Regd 20 March 1948. Canx 11 March 1967.
YR-TAH	Li-2P	18423507	Regd 18 June 1946? To HA-LIC August 1946.
YR-TAI	Li-2P	18423509	Regd 03 January 1946. Crashed Phouznicie 21 November 1947.
YR-TAJ	Li-2P	18423508	Regd 18 April 1946? To HA-LID 21 August 1946.
YR-TAK	Li-2P	18428004	Regd 18 March 1948. Canx 31 December 1966. To Romanian AF as 004.
YR-TAL	Li-2P	18427502	Regd 05 February 1948. Canx 12 January 1960. To Romanian AF as 502.
YR-TAM	Li-2P	18423207	Regd 15 March 1947. Modified for Geo-Survey in 1963. Canx 13 August 1970, reportedly broken up, but in use as café circa 1975.
YR-TAN	Li-2P	18428005	Regd 19 March 1948. Crashed Lotriora Valley 11 August 1966.
YR-TAO (1)	Li-2P	18423510	del 1946. To HA-LIE 21 August 1946.
YR-TAO (2)	Li-2P	23441802	Regd 20 June 1952. Canx 20 March 1968. To Romanian AF as 802.
YR-TAP	Li-2P	18427505	Regd 23 January 1948. Canx 12 January 1960. To Romanian AF as 505.
YR-TAR	Li-2P	18423502	Regd 07 June 1946. Canx 10 July 1969, broken up.
YR-TAS	Li-2P	18424010	Regd 24 May 1946. To Agricultural High School in 1968. Canx 01 February 1972, broken up.
YR-TAT	Li-2P	18432802	Regd 24 July 1948. Canx 22 December 1970.
YR-TAV	Li-2	18423801	Regd 19 July 1946. Crashed Bucharest 13 August 1947.
YR-TAW	Li-2P	23444506	Regd 10 June 1953. Canx 20 November 1966. To Romanian AF as 4506.
YR-TAX	Li-2	18423803	Regd 24 July 1946. Crashed Mironeasa-Iassy 08 October 1960.
YR-TAZ	Li-2	18423804	Regd 24 July 1946. Canx 13 March 1966. To Romanian AF as 804.

The two final deliveries were from an unknown source.

YR-DAB	Li-2P	23444803	Regd 27 May 1953. Canx 23 August 1968. To Romanian AF.
YR-DAC	Li-2P	23441507	Regd 07 July 1952. Crashed Paragina Hill 13 June 1964.

The Romanian Government operated Li-2P aircraft from time to time between 1952 and 1976:-

YR-PCB	Li-2P	18439807	Regd 17 May 1952. To Romanian AF 807 in 1954.
YR-PCD	Li-2P	18439805	Regd 17 May 1952. To Romanian AF 805 in 1954.
YR-MIG	Li-2P	33444802	Regd 01 June 1960. Canx 17 November 1976.
YR-MIR	Li-2P	33444505	Regd 02 June 1970. Canx 17 November 1976.

The Romanian Air Force operated their first Li-2 in 1952, but little documentation is available. At least the following aircraft saw service.

008	Li-2P	23441008	del 1952.
102	Li-2		
206	Li-2		
209?	Li-2		Preserved near Faget
502	Li-2P	18427502	del 12 January 1960, ex YR-TAL.
505	Li-2P	18427505	del 12 January 1960, ex YR-TAP
607	Li-2		
702	Li-2T	23444702	
802	Li-2P	23441802	del 20 March 1968, ex YR-TAO
804	Li-2P	18423804	del 16 March 1966, ex YR-TAZ. Canx 10 October 1968 as broken up.
805	Li-2P	18439805	del 1954, ex YR-PCD.
807	Li-2P	18439807	del 1954, ex YR-PCB
905	Li-2P	23441905	del 11 March 1967, ex YR-TAE.
1001	Li-2P	23441001?	
1002	Li-2	23441002?	Noted Bucharest/Otopeni 06 May 1970.
1003	Li-2	23441003?	Noted Budapest/Ferihegy 1957.
1004	Li-2P	23441004	Noted Prague/Ruzyne 1965. WFU Timisoara LRTR. Towed to Busias & preserved as Night Club.
4506	Li-2P	23444506	del 22 November 1965, ex YR-TAW. Scrapped
4803/803?	Li-2P	23444803	del 23 August 1968, ex YR-DAB.
8002	Li-2P	18428002	del 11 March 1967, ex YR-TAG. As instructional airframe Buzau 13 February 1995 to 09 July 1996.
(8)004	Li-2P	18428004	del 20 November 1966, ex YR-TAK. To Baneasa Technical School circa June 1991 as "004".

Romanian Air Force Li-2 serial 102 showing the starboard side entry door and Ash-62 engines in a nacelle of similar dimensions to the Pratt & Whitney R-1820 engines. *(via Peter Hillman)*

VIETNAM (NORTH)

The North Vietnamese Air Force operated an unknown number of Li-2s. These included the two aircraft noted below:-

19	del 26 January 1956, ex CAAC. In 1959 with 919th Air Transport Regiment, Gia Lam.
198	ex CAAC.

YUGOSLAVIA

A joint Yugoslav-Soviet airline JUSTA took delivery of ten Li-2P aircraft in 1947. As with other Eastern Bloc airlines, the airline was reformed in the early 1950s under total Yugoslav ownership as JAT Yugoslav Air Transport.

YU-BAA	18425606	del July 1947. Retd to Soviet Union 10 September 1949.
YU-BAB	18427003	del 1947. Retd to Soviet Union as CCCP-L1268 on 10 September 1949.
YU-BAC	18427004	del 1947. Retd to Soviet Union 10 September 1949.
YU-BAD/13	18427009?	del 1947. Crashed Rumija 27 November 1947.
YU-BAE/16	18427010	del 1947. Retd to Soviet Union 10 September 1949.
YU-BAF/27	18427007	del 1947. Retd to Soviet Union 10 September 1949.
YU-BAG	18427509	del 1947. Retd to Soviet Union 10 September 1949.
YU-BAH	18427503	del 1947. Retd to Soviet Union 10 September 1949.
YU-BAI	18427008	del 1947. Retd to Soviet Union 10 September 1949.
YU-BAJ	18427510	del 1947. Retd to Soviet Union 10 September 1949.

Two Li-2T were also delivered in 1947:-

YU-BAP	18426603	del 1947. Retd to Soviet Union 11 September 1949.
YU-BAR	18426604	del 1947. Retd to Soviet Union 11 September 1949.

All the JAT Li-2s returned to the Soviet Union in September 1949 were returned via Hungary and ferried by Hungarian crews.

The Yugoslav Air Force (JRV) operated an unknown number of Li-2s and those recorded are listed below. Initially the JRV used a four-number identification system, but later on the Li-2s were re-numbered to conform with the five-number system employed throughout the air force.

In order to prolong the service life of the Li-2, the JRV retrofitted the Pratt & Whitney R-1830 engines and American propellers from their C-47 fleet, locally re-designating the type the Li-3.

Li-2	7001?	
Li-2	7002?	
Li-2	7003?	
Li-3	7004	111 PPA
Li-3	7005	111 PPA
Li-2	7006?	
Li-3	7007	111 PPA
Li-3	7008	111 PPA
Li-2?	7009	

Li-3	7010	111 PPA
Li-3	7011	18422308 To Belgrade Museum.
Li-2	7103	
Li-3	71101?	
Li-3	71102?	
Li-3	71103	Preserved near Bosanski Petrovak (Bosnia). Destroyed mid-1990s.
Li-3	71104?	
Li-3	71105?	

Preserved Li-3 of the Yugoslav Air Force (JRV) 7011 resident at the Muzej Ratnog Vazduhoplovstra (Yugoslav Aeronautical Museum) in Belgrade.
(via Mike Hooks)

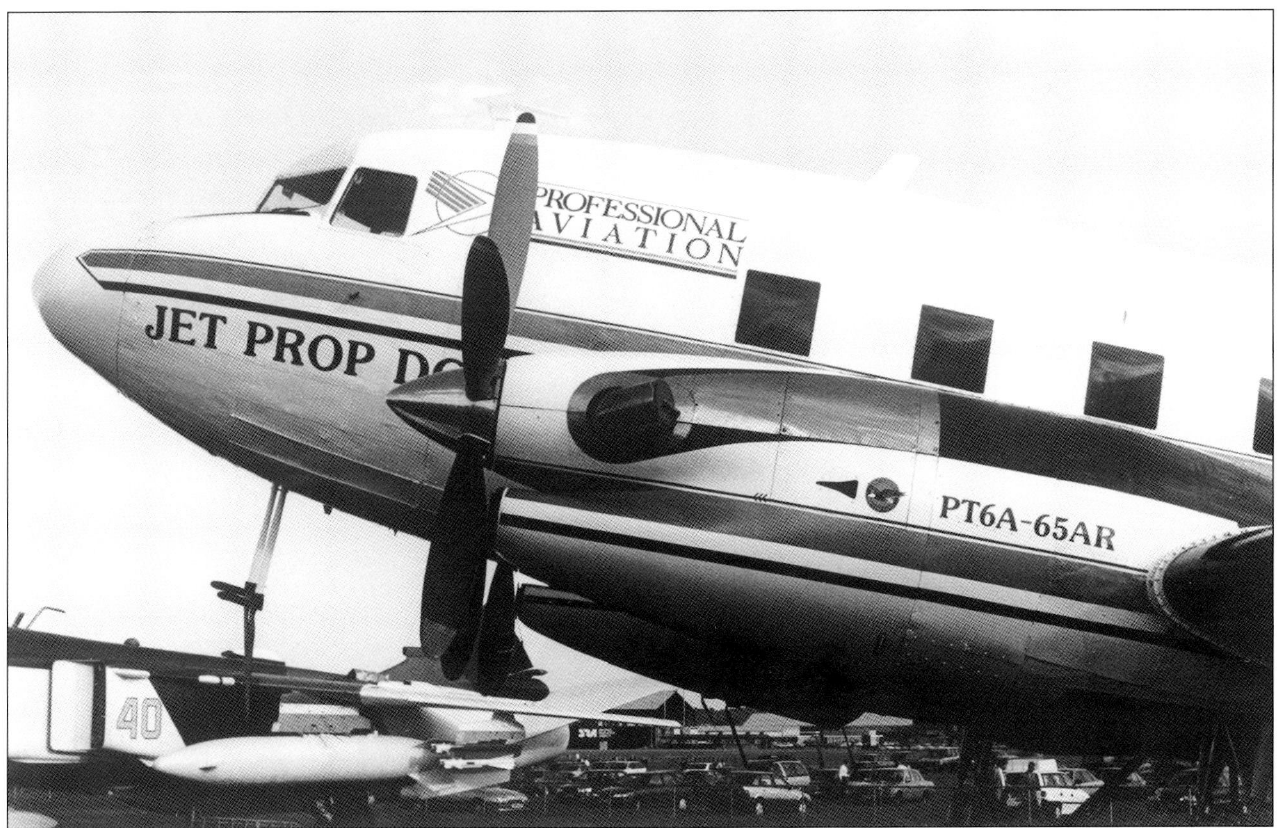

A close-up of the PT6A-65AR installation on the original South African AMI TurboDak conversion. ZS-LYW (c/n 25802) was photographed at Farnborough in September 1992. *(Jennifer Gradidge)*

Chapter 15
The Dodson TurboDak

by M D N Fisher

With the changes that occurred in South Africa in the late 1990s it was decided that some of the South African Air Force Dakotas converted to turbine configuration, or being converted, would be offered for sale through ARMSCOR (Armaments Corporation of South Africa Ltd., the government body responsible for procurement and disposals) and the Dodson organization, based in Ottawa, Kansas, were the highest bidders on 19 of the aircraft being sold.

There are two, closely related Dodson companies, Dodson Aviation Inc., the president of which is Robert Lee Dodson Senior. usually known as Bob Dodson and Dodson International Parts Inc., whose part base is at Rantoul, where Robert Lee Dodson Junior, usually known as JR Dodson is president and for financial reasons the package was split between father and son, although there was no expectation that the aircraft put on the books of Dodson International Parts Inc., would be dismantled for spares. The matter became more confusing when Bob Dodson started operating in South Africa, as Dodson International Parts (SA) P/L. A further change occurred in summer 2007, when Bob announced that he was preparing to retire and aircraft registered with the FAA to Dodson Aviation Inc., were re-registered to Dodson International Parts Inc. whilst marketing is being undertaken by AIL Corp. whose president is also JR Dodson.

Of the aircraft purchased, seven were still under conversion and two of those had not yet received the 40" fuselage extension which forms part of the turbine conversion. Consequently the unfinished fuselages have been placed in long term storage, away from the facility at Wonderboom, whilst the other aircraft are prepared for sale. The remaining 11 aircraft were initially flown to Kansas, although some have since returned to South Africa. These remaining aircraft fall into two groups, those re-registered in the ZS-OJI – M range forming a quasi hire fleet within Africa, whilst those remaining on the US register were intended for re-sale elsewhere. The exception being N194RD, the former SAAF 6868 which briefly became a demonstrator as ZS-OIR carrying the name " Lady Pam " (Pam being Mrs. Bob Dodson) before reverting to N194RD. That aircraft was sold on preferential terms to the Billy Graham organization and was registered to Samaritan's Purse of North Carolina. Now registered N467SP, it undertakes missionary work out of Nairobi and its operation is still supported by the Dodson family.

All aircraft are in the process of being converted to full Dodson TurboDak standard, which although similar to a Basler conversion, because both were developed from the original AMI conversion programme, are significantly different, not only in appearance and price but also in the alterations that have been

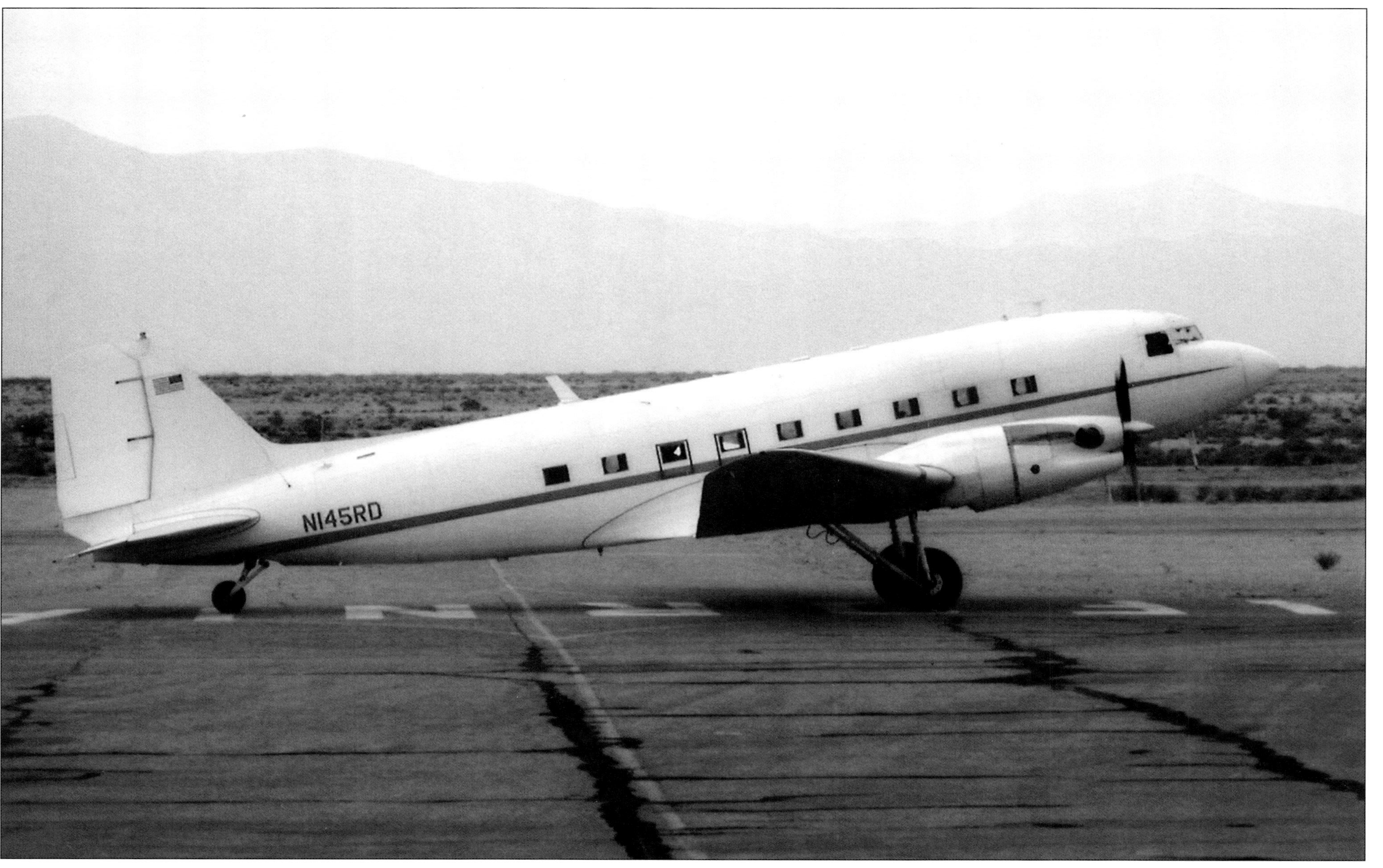

Dodson TurboDak N145RD (c/n 20175) taxying out at California City, California on 25th October 2002. *(M Doyle)*

undertaken. Whereas Basler take a standard Dakota and remanufacture it to their customers' requirements, all the aircraft purchased by Dodsons, except two, had already had many of the significant modifications undertaken. In particular a full airframe IRAN had been performed and factory new P&W PT6-65AR engines with Hartzell propellers installed. The engines selected for the South African conversions, although developing the same power as the -67's selected by Basler exhaust at each side of the engine cowling, rather than over the wing and are also used on other turbine aircraft, resulting in spares being more readily obtainable and lower overhaul costs.

The cost of undertaking that work was not fully reflected in the bids accepted by ARMSCOR and that, combined with the Dodson policy of direct dealing, rather than working through intermediaries, helps to account for the price differential between a Dodson and Basler aircraft. Unfortunately, although demonstrated to Colombia for two years it was found that the local purchasing system preferred the involvement of a local intermediary.

Bob Dodson saw the work that had been performed for the South African Air Force as only the first step towards producing a Superior Dakota and the conversions had been undertaken on military aircraft, with no associated civil approval. It was therefore necessary to design, and obtain FAA and South African DCA approval for a wide range of alterations, some already embodied and some required in order to produce what is now marketed as the Dodson TurboDak.

The Dodson TurboDak has a 40 inch fuselage extension, coupled with cabin floor and flight control extensions. The upper and lower wing centre-sections have been reinforced to allow for up to 29,200 lbs gross weight. Wing tips have also been modified. The TurboDak is fitted with the PT6-65AR engines as standard. These develop 1,646 eshp each and have a TBO of 2,000 hours. The –65AR engines are more economical than the –67R and there is a larger supply of engines and parts as this version of the PT6 is common to the Shorts SD 360 and Beech 1900C-65B. The engines are fitted with five-blade Hartzell propellers with electric de-icer boots. The engines are enclosed in a streamlined cowling of composite construction, each of which has a 118 US gallon fuel-tank in the unused wing nacelle.

Aircraft used in the conversion are all low-time quality airframes and have had their basic structure stripped, restored and corrosion-proofed. The wheels and axles are replaced and the standard C-47/DC-3 brakes replaced by heavy duty disk brakes. The tailwheel assembly is completely new. The aircraft's hydraulic system has an engine-driven variable pump on each engine, with a back-up handpump for the landing gear and flaps. The fuel system has an engine-driven pump on each engine and a header tank which feeds 118 gallons of fuel into the engine.

The cockpit is all new and modern with a crew galley. jump-seats and new engine and flight instruments. The electrical management panel has an FAR-25 approved electrical system with all new switches, circuit-breakers, avionics, etc. Aircraft are fitted with modern Garmin avionics and GPS systems, with the aim to obtain approval for a complete Garmin glass cockpit.

Other standard features of the Dodson TurboDak are long-range (1,030 US gallon) fuel tanks, storm-warning radar, an insulated crew area and cargo door. The cargo floor is of the heavy duty type with tracks, and the aircraft can easily be converted from cargo to passenger use. Both 29-seat and 32-seat interiors are offered and the passenger interior can be removed completely within 30 minutes when required as a freighter. There is a power receptacle for a winch (for the loading of cargo), the winch itself being optional. Other optional extras offered include outer-wing 780 US gallon tanks, wing de-icer boots, an electric windshield and a fuel-dump system.

Among the advantages of the Dodson TurboDak over the Basler conversion (apart from the lower cost) is the new fuel system. This includes individual fuel-pumps in each tank, connected in such a way that a pump can be utilized to draw fuel from any tank, together with additional fuel capacity between the original fire-wall and the engine, an option not available on the Basler conversion because the exhausts eject over the wing.

The Dodson TurboDak is advertized as having the edge over other turbo Dakota conversions in being able to "land shorter, climb faster, cruise faster and with more payload, and be less expensive on engine maintenance." The safety of the type is enhanced by the following features: the triple redundant fuel-system, an automatic power reserve, heavy duty disk brakes, and the lack of an exhaust inside the engine cowling near fuel or fuel-lines. Their advertizing slogan is:-

The only replacement for a DC-3 is a better DC-3: the Dodson TurboDak

Comparative statistics and performance figures are contained in the table below for the Dodson TurboDak, the AMI 65TP, the Basler BT-67 and a typical C-47/DC-3:

Feature	*Dodson*	*AMI*	*Basler*	*C-47/DC-3*
Basic weight (lbs)	15,800	15,800	15,827	18,000
Zero fuel weight	26,200	26,000	26,200	25,500
Max.take-off wt	29,200	26,900	28,750	28,000
Max landing wt	28,750	25,900	28,750	26,900
Max fuel range(mls)	7,408	6,955	5,042	4,800
Max payload (lbs)	10,400	10,200	10,373	7,500
Take-off (ISA) feet	4,500	3,680	4,550	2,600
Landing (ISA) feet	3,200	2,200	3,400	2,150

The main differences between the DC-3-65TP and the Basler BT-67 appear to be small at first sight. The wings on the AMI version are basically DC-3, though Dodson have installed some strengthening at the centre section outer wing junction, while the Basler model had this done much earlier, when it was realised that different vibration frequencies from the PT-6s were causing fatigue cracking.

The Basler BT-67 has remodelled wingtips and a more angular tailplane. The first BT-67 had rounded windows for some years, when it was used for cargo work. These were, however, replaced by rectangular windows when it was used for passenger work, and this is now standard for BT-67s used for passenger-carrying. The BT-67 engine nacelle is fitted with exhausts over the top of the wing to make it less vulnerable to heat-seeking missiles. The DC-3-65TP has the exhausts just behind the propellers, as on most PT-6As. This has been the cause of confusion to observers, but overall the DC-3-65TP has dirtier nacelles, while on the BT-67 they are clean!

DODSON TURBODAKs

(in Douglas c/n order) with last report:

9766 ex SAAF 6879. To ZS-MRR, 6879, N147RD, N200MF (3) Missionary Flights & Services. (Haiti March 2010)

12115 ex SAAF 6820. To N192RD (Stored Mena, AR September 2006)

12166 ex SAAF 6886. To N8194Z. Stored Wonderboom, unconverted as "F-1" until l/n Jan07, moved to Freeway airstrip by 18Feb10

12582 ex SAAF 6876. To N81949. Stored Wonderboom, unconverted as "F-7" until l/n Jan07, moved to Freeway airstrip by 18Feb10

12590 ex SAAF 6834. To ZS-OSO, N834TP Substantial damage Mojave, CA 4 Feb09. Trucked to Ottawa, KS & stored dismantled, fuselage on trailer for repair & corrosion check (November 2009)

20175 ex SAAF 6835 (2). To N145RD Stored Mena, AR. To Baja Air, California City, CA (July 2009)

25546 ex SAAF 6880 (2). To N330RD, ZS-OJL (1), 9U-BHL, ZS-OJM, N330RD, ZS-OJM. In use with ICRC in Afghanistan (June 2009)

25610 ex SAAF 6844. To ZS-OJK. Used by ICRC 2005. At Wonderboom (l/n 20Jun09)

26439 ex SAAF 6892. To N195RD, ZS-OJI, N9562N (never applied to acft). To YV2119 (in svce Oct09)

27199 ex SAAF 6853. To N148RD. Stored Wonderboom, unconverted as "F-2" 2006, moved to Freeway airstrip by 18Feb10

32644 ex SAAF 6882. To ZS-MAP National Test Pilot School. To N882TP as replacement for c/n 12590. In service in California (October 2009)

32825 ex SAAF 6874 (2). To N81952. Stored Wonderboom, unconverted as "F-6" 2006, moved to Freeway airstrip by 18Feb10

32897 ex SAAF 6858 (2). To N146RD, N8241T (ntu), N146RD. Stored Mena/AR, later Ottawa, KS. Sold to Lee County District Mosquito Control, fitted with spray equipment delivered January 2010

32948 ex SAAF 6868. To N194RD, ZS-OIR, N194RD, N467SP. In use with R Cloud, Livermore, CA (2006). In use on missionary work, Kenya September 2009.

32961 ex SAAF 6855 (2). To N8194Q, ZS-OJJ. Stored Ottawa, KS (see the "microburst" story below). In bean field 1.5 miles southeast of Ottawa Airport, KS (November 2009)

33024 ex SAAF 6891. To N198RD. Stored Mena, AR by 2006 (August 2009)

33134 ex SAAF 6846 (2). To N8241T. Stored Wonderboom, unconverted as "F-3" 2006, moved to Freeway airstrip by Feb10

33211 ex SAAF 6870 (2). To N332RD. Stored Mena, AR by 2006 (August 2009)

33313 ex SAAF 6883 (2). To N81907, ZS-OJL (2). Stored Wonderboom, under active conversion Sep10

33375 ex SAAF 6857. To N193RD. Stored Mena, AR by 2006 (August 2009)

33478 ex SAAF 6865 (2). To N8190X. Stored Wonderboom, unconverted as "F-4" 2006, moved to Freeway airstrip by Feb10

33552 ex SAAF 6890. To N149RD. Stored Wonderboom, unconverted as "F-5" 2006, moved to Freeway airstrip by Feb10

Notes:

The Freeway airstrip is approximately 20 kms north of Wonderboom.

c/n 32961. This aircraft appears to have a charmed life. It survived a SAM-7 missile while in service with the South African Air Force on 1 May 1986. The aircraft was standing at Ottawa/KS, after the PT-6A-65 engines and propellers had been removed as part of the rebuilding process and was tied down off the hard-standing. On 8 July 2009 a microburst or straight-line wind hit Ottawa Airport, destroying or damaging all the buildings as well as a number of aircraft. The wind struck the tied-down ZS-OJJ and all the moorings were torn out of the ground and the Turbo-Dak started moving backwards. It went over the adjacent road, over a drainage ditch, through a number of fences and over more drainage ditches, missing some hay bales and a row of trees. It ceased moving one and a half miles from its original position. The aircraft was not visible from the airfield, Mr Dodson found it by following the wheel tracks across country, which were continuous, indicating that the aircraft had never become airborne! The following damage was found: Starboard elevator damaged beyond repair, the port elevator had minor damage, a surface gouge about ten feet from the port wingtip (probably caused by a fence-post) and small lower fuselage nicks and scratches. The aircraft is expected to be repaired as soon as hangar space is available.

Sources used:-

Dodson Aviation Inc, Chris Chatfield, John M Davis, Gordon Reid & AB-IX reports.

The seven fuselages, marked "F-1" to "F-7", mentioned in the text above are seen here awaiting conversion to Dodson TurboDaks at the Freeway airstrip in South Africa in 2010. *(AB-IX contributor, via Airliners.net)*

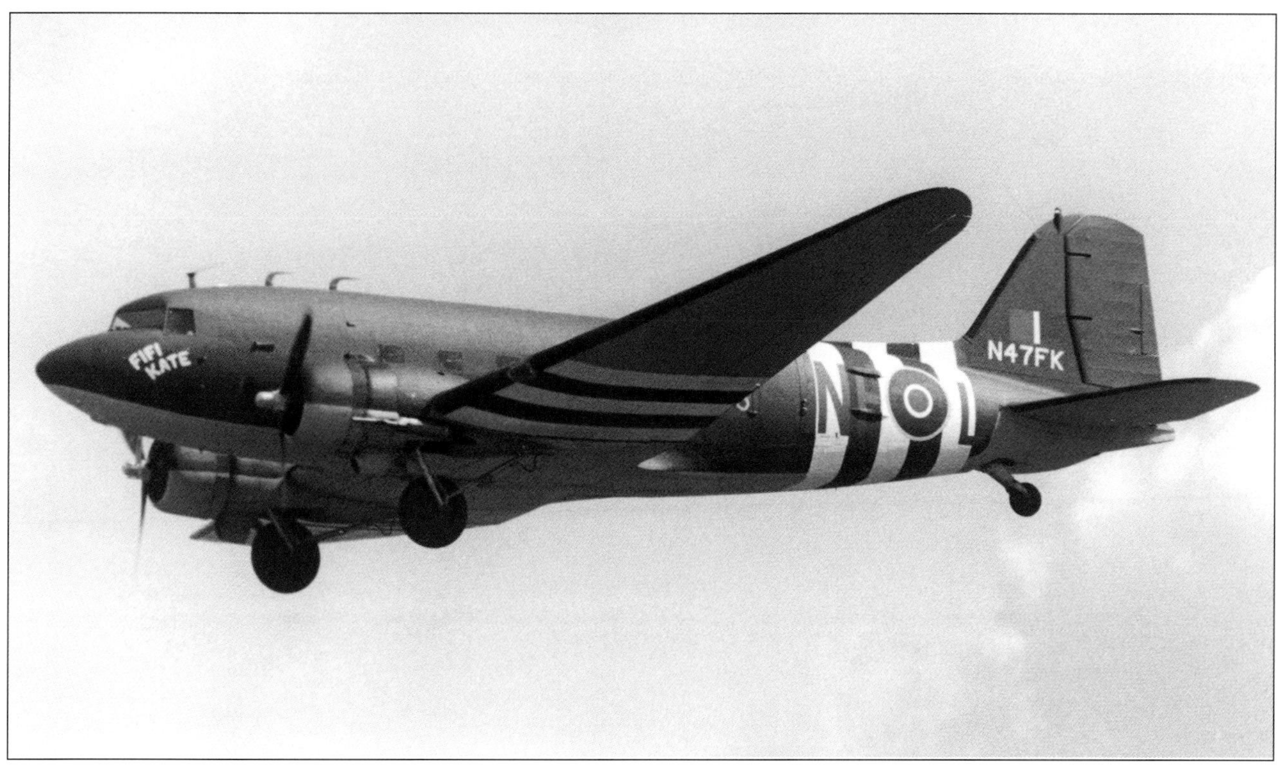

C/n 9700 C-47A N47FK "Fifi Kate" taking off from Fairford, Glos on 19 July 2004. *(Jennifer Gradidge)*

Chapter 16 Updated Information & Corrections to Volumes I & II of 'The Douglas DC-1 / 2 / 3, The First Seventy Years'

Part I – Military Operators: Volume I, Chapter 3

Documents acquired from the Public Records Office, London, reveal various reports, including some from British Air Attachés. The Google Earth photos are by satellite during 2006, and are none too sharp! However, they do identify a number of DC-3 airframes of which we know little or nothing.

p.49 BOLIVIA

Three C-47s were bought via AAXICO in early October 1949. There were seven C-47s in service at El Alto in December 1955.

p.49 BRAZIL

C-47 2068 Crashed 15Jun67 nr Coari, Amazonas, Brazil [NE/FP].

p.50 BURMA

Rangoon. A Google Earth 2006 photo shows one C-47, apparently intact.

p.54 CZECHOSLOVAKIA

D-21 listed as c/n 26455 and as c/n 19474. One apparently incorrect. D-28 and D-43 also reported.

p.55 ETHIOPIA

The Google Earth photo of Addis Ababa in 2006 shows three reasonably intact C-47s, one engineless and tailless and another apparently preserved, c/n 9628?

p.59 GREECE

Thanks to Themis Vranas who has supplied some useful information on Royal Hellenic Air Force C-47s we can add:-

49-2632 c/n unknown, crashed in Korea on 27Dec52. The aircraft painted 92532 is a corruption of 43-49532 c/n 26793 which is preserved at Tripoli with the 124 Basic Training Wing. It has been there since at least 1999

KJ960 c/n 26252 preserved at Tatoi Nov 2007

KN475 c/n 32952 on dump at Sedes Nov 2007

KN542 c/n 33146 preserved at Sedes Nov 2007

KN575 c/n 33199 preserved at Sedes Nov 2007

KN691 c/n 33404 was sold as scrap to a scrapyard in Thessaloniki in 1991

KK169 c/n 26860 was stored for the HAF Museum at Tatoi, as of Nov 2007

KP255 c/n 33557 was stored at Thessaloniki Nov 2007

43-49111 c/n 26372 on dump at Tatoi Nov 2007

49-2612 crashed on 26May51 6 mls south east of Taejon, S Korea.

49-2613 still with aero club at Mikra Nov 2007

49-2615 c/n 12843 was at Sedes, Thessaloniki in May 1994, when the c/n plate was checked

49-2616 collided with F-80C 49-722 (USAF 36 FBS) at K-13, Suwon, S Korea on 22Dec52

49-2617 had a landing accident at K-38 Wonju, S Korea on 04Jan51

49-2619 c/n 4749 was at Sedes in May 1994, when the c/n plate was checked

49-2620 had no c/n plate when checked at Sedes in 1994

49-2622 c/n 20474 active at Thessaloniki 06Nov07. This is the last survivor of the Korean War and may become part of an Aviation Heritage Flight, with KK156. It went to Korea in August 1951 with 13th Hellenic Flight

49-2623 could not be inspected at Sedes in 1994 due to nearby scrap metal!

49-2627 c/n 4658 was at Sedes on dump from 1994 to Nov 2007

49-2629 had no c/n plate when inspected at Sedes in 1994

49-2632 Crashed 1.5 ml S of K-10 Chinhae, Korea on take-off 26Dec52

49-2635 on dump at Sedes Nov 2007

49-2634 c/n 13836 was at Sedes from 1994, when c/n plate checked, to Nov 2007

49-2638 c/n 9720 was at Sedes in 1994 when the c/n plate was checked. Remained there Nov 2007

49-2639 crashed 08Dec54 on Elusina A/fld 10 mls W of Athens during parachute training

49-2641 continued to be displayed on a café roof at Katahas Nov 2007

Unknown – crashed near Villia on slopes of Mt Kithairon, 45 mls W of Athens 12Jan70

The block 49-2612 to 49-2641 was for 30 aircraft supplied to Greece in 1949. However, we listed 33 aircraft in Vol II. Of these c/n 4409 was believed incorrect. There was doubt about c/n 10246 (10240?), 10047 and 10128, or one too many serials.

p.62 INDONESIA

In January 1954 there were 25 C-47s with 2 Skadron at Halim Perdanakusama and 5 Skadron at Huseinstratenegara. In December 1956 2 Skadron had 14 C-47s and there were 15 with DAUM at Abdulrachman Saleh, plus six C-47s apparently unallocated – 35 aircraft in all. T-489 has been reported on display at a military establishment at Jakarta in Mar10.

p.65 LIBYA

A Google Earth 2006 shot of Tripoli Airport, shows one C-47 in a poor state, with no tailplane, engines or ailerons etc.

p.65 MALI

A Google Earth 2006 shot of Bamako shows two Basler BT-67 on the ground, presumably TZ-390 and 391.

p.66 MAURITANIA

A Google Earth 2006 photo of Nouakchott shows one BT-67 parked.

p.66 MEXICO

C-47 TED-6022, which has not been reported hitherto, was noted at a military camp Heroico Colegio Militar, near Cuenavaca, south of Mexico City. No c/n has been reported.

p.68 NICARAGUA

C-47 412 of Fuerza Aerea de Nicaragua crashed into the Pacific Ocean on 03Aug75 nr Amapala, Valle, Honduras about 1000ft offshore, some 150miles S of San Salvador.

p.69 PARAGUAY

A Google Earth 2006 photo of Asuncion shows three C-47s parked, only one with engines.

p.70 PHILIPPINE REPUBLIC

Thanks to the late Brian Austria-Tomkins, we can add - 1000 '*Lily Marlene*' which crashed on 18 May 1947 on Mt Makaturing, Lanao, Mindanao, and 1001. These were delivered in late 1945 to Fernando AB, Lipa City, Luzon, were the only aircraft in this serial number sequence, and are of unknown c/n.

p.72 SOUTH YEMEN

A Google Earth 2006 shot shows three C-47s at Sana'a, one engineless and two reasonably intact.

p.73 SRI LANKA

A Google Earth 2006 photo of Colombo Airport has one camouflaged DC-3, either CR-821 or 822.

p.74 TCHAD

A Google Earth photo of N'Djamena shows two C-47s, without ailerons, and two DC-4s nearby. The C-47s are TT-LAC and TT-LAJ.

p.75 TURKEY

A British Air Attaché report in January 1952 indicates 23 C-47s with 221, 222 and 223 Filo and 12 with 225 Filo at Kayseri. By 1956 there were 10 with 221 Filo, 10 with 222 Filo and 11 each with 223 and 224 Filo. There were ten in reserve. An unknown C-47 was lost in an accident between January and October 1956.

SOUTH VIETNAM – see VIETNAM (SOUTH)

p.88 UNITED STATES OF AMERICA

Allocations of C-47s to various Troop Carrier Squadrons have come to light, mostly from accident reports. They add to the rosters given on pp 97 to 102, and are as follows, in numerical order of TCS:-

1 TCS 41-19496, 41-38677,42-23368, 23619, 42-92971, 92978, 92979, 93372, 93585, 93598, 100619, 43-15053, 15367, 16211, 48635, 44-77138.

2 TCS 41-19471, 42-23607, 93355, 100694, 43-15560.

3 TCS 41-18462, 18466, 42-5672, 23312, 43-15183.

4 TCS 41-18382, 42-92118, 92982, 100943, 43-15575.

5 TCS 41-18385, 18478, 38650, 38727, 42-32809, 43-15534.

7 TCS 41-38654, 42-100955.

8 TCS 42-24388, 43-49788.

9 TCS 41-18482, 42-100790.

10 TCS 44-76234.

11 TCS 42-23368, 92686, 93382, 43-15367, 49406.

12 TCS 42-24207, 93727, 93802, 43-15494.

14 TCS 41-18393, 18430, 42-5695, 32833, 32913, 93731, 43-15142, 15647, 16046

15 TCS 41-18363, 18521, 18561, 42-32808.

16 TCS 41-7862, 42-24378, 108901.

17 TCS 42-23516

18 TCS 42-24194, 92054, 43-47988.

20 TCS 43-15942, 48003.

21 TCS 42-24227, 43-48481, 48482, 49750, 45-890, 949, 1126.

23 TCS 42-24291, 43-30692, 48069.

24 TCS 42-56099, 43-15962.

25 TCS 42-15551, 46609, 56636, 43-15560, 15870.

26 TCS 42-24019, 56089, 56101, 56610, 43-16366.

27 TCS 42-5679, 23357, 43-48622

28 TCS 41-7799.

29 TCS 41-18562, 20131.

31 TCS 42-56626, 56628, 45-1089.

32 TCS 41-20055, 38723, 42-23342, 93070, 108890, 43-15091, 15647.

33 TCS 42-100470.

34 TCS 42-68749, 43-48893.

35 TCS 42-100947, 100956, 43-15360, 49418.

37 TCS 41-18349, 42-23772, 24112, 100999, 43-48071, 48075.

38 TCS 41-20116, 42-15562 , 15566, 68747, 68800. [This unit remained in the USA for training only]

39 TCS 43-16213.

42 TCS 41-20048, 38638, 42-6495, 24274.

43 TCS 41-18608, 42-23480, 24176, 43-15251.

44 TCS 42-23886.

46 TCS 43-16120.

47 TCS 43-15120, 15197, 48562.

48 TCS 42-32929, 93725, 43-48933.

50 TCS 42-23396, 32850, 43-48935,

51 TCS 43-49191.

52 TCS 41-38689, 42-15539, 15874, 23365.

53 TCS 41-18416, 42-23635.

54 TCS 43-15738, 44-77252, 45-1037, 1048.

55 TCS 42-15550.

56 TCS 41-18407.

58 TCS 41-18637, 42-15561.

59 TCS 41-38594, 42-5698, 43-15312

60 TCS 41-18562, 20131.

61 TCS 41-18476, 42-5675, 5700, 15534.

62 TCS 42-68709.

64 TCS 41-38606, 42-23512, 68714.

65 TCS 41-19484, 20135.

66 TCS 41-18634.

67 TCS 41-18383.

68 TCS 42-23367.

69 TCS 42-68717.

71 TCS 42-23397, 24034, 68770, 100520, 43-16027.

72 TCS 42-15547, 68727, 68789, 43-16030, 48197.

73 TCS 42-24039, 24042, 24051, 92024, 100507, 43-15675.

74 TCS 42-24056, 24061, 24064, 43-16029,

75 TCS 42-23784, 68731, 100744, 43-15286, 56069, 48096, 48357, 48520.

76 TCS 42-23652, 24116, 43-48715, 48719, 48911, 48914, 48959.

77 TCS 42-24110, 24199, 43-15516.

78 TCS 42-68737, 100675, 43-15264, 30730,

79 TCS 42-93607.

80 TCS 42-24104, 24119, 100545, 100665, 100787.

81 TCS 42-24054, 100545.

82 TCS 42-68811.

84 TCS 42-100630, 43-48244.

85 TCS 42-92093, 100633.

86 TCS 42-93007, 100656, 100658.

87 TCS 42-100745, 43-15320, 49026.

88 TCS 42-100757, 100760.

90 TCS 42-68841.

91 TCS 42-100644, 43-15075, 15351.

92 TCS 42-92913, 100641, 43-15211.

94 TCS 42-100640, 43-15294, 15323, 15650.

95 TCS 43-15167.

96 TCS 42-68695.

98 TCS 43-48805.

99 TCS 42-68843, 43-48918, 48943.

100 TCS 42-23309, 24096, 32833, 32870, 92681, 92850, 43-15035.

301 TCS 42-23781, 24055, 93810, 43-15318, 15604, 30689.

302 TCS 42-23795, 24100.

303 TCS 42-92414, 92457, 92730, 92777, 108838, 43-15090, 48392, 48702.

304 TCS 42-92424, 92436, 93717, 100960, 43-15202, 15676.

305 TCS 42-92414, 108838, 43-49535.

306 TCS 42-100804, 43-15353.

307 TCS 41-18454, 18468.

308 TCS 42-68778, 43-30690.

309 TCS 42-68812, 101000.

310 TCS 42-23776, 68762, 68851, 92733, 92753, 92890, 92902, 93702, 93811, 108906, 108960, 43-15622.

313 TCS 43-30663.

314 TCS 42-93542, 43-30665.

315 TCS 41-18441, 42-24057, 100607, 100610, 100707, 100707, 108984, 43-15054, 30644, 48623, 44-76237.

316 TCS 42-32926, 43-48812, 49554.

317 TCS 42-23778, 23783.

318 TCS 42-100998.

319 TCS 42-100450, 43-15443, 16178, 16351, 48730.

320 TCS 43-16071.

321 TCS 42-93070, 43-16025 [Part of 9 AF].

322 TCS 42-93367, 43-40576 [This was part of 14 AF].

323 TCS 42-93721, 43-48262 [Part of AFE Italy, no doubt formed from earlier unit]

324 TCS 42-92056, 100471, 100554, 43-15050, 15104. [part of 516TCG based at Bovingdon, Herts]

328 TCS 43-15874, 49646 [ex 3 CCS].

330 TCS 44-77251

332 TCS 44-76247 [ex 11 CCS]

1 CCS 42-24124, 93161, 93178, 43-15563, 15811.

2 CCS 43-15552, 15561, 15906.

3 CCS 43-15858, 15907. [See 328 TCS]

4 CCS 42-24115. 93163, 93192, 43-15850.

6 CCS 42-93167.

7 CCS 42-93193, 108923 [New]

8 CCS 42-24120, 43-15682. [New]

9 CCS 42-93344, 93345, 93360.

10 CCS 43-16353, 48631, 48638.

11 CCS 42-93353, 93361, 93358, 93363, 93381, 93738, 93757, 93769, 100442, 43-16354, 16363, 44-76247, 76251. [See 332 TCS]

12 CCS 42-93383, 93392, 93758, 100686, 100702, 43-15052, 15767, 15791, 15793, 15796, 48631

13 CCS 43-16059 [4 CCG]

14 CCS 42-100492, 43-15767. [4 CCG]

16 CCS 42-23355, 93347, 43-15401, 48911 [4 CCG]

India China Wing Air Transport Command

Additional information has been researched by Matt Miller which expands considerably the details published in Volume I:

1 Ferry Group (1 FyG) was constituted on 03 March 1942, leaving by sea for India on 17 March 1942. This comprised 3 FyS, 6 FyS and 13 FyS. Deliveries in early 1942 were, in March – 2, May – 28, July – 1, August – 11, and September – 3. These included two C-39s and seven C-48Bs, C-47 and C-53s.

Ferry Command was redesignated Air Transport Command on 20 June 1942, under General Order #8. HQ & HQ Sq, India China Wing (ICW), ATC was activated on 01 December 1942 at Chabua.

3 FyS part of 1 FyG, based Chabua, India, was formed on 07 March 1942 at Pope Field, NC and assigned to 1 FyG. It was shipped overseas on 17 March 1942 under the authority of 10 AF until 01 December 1942 when ICW, ATC was established. 3 FyS became part of 3 TptS, 1 TptG based at Chabua, India.

6 FyS part of 1 FyG, based at Mohanbari, India, was formed in the same way as 3 FyS, and became 6 TptS part of 1 TptG based at Chabua, India.

13 FyS part of 1 FyG, was based at Sookerating, India and formed on the same dates etc, as 3 FyS. It became 13 TptS, part of 1 TptG, based at Chabua, India.

77 FyS part of 22 FyG was based at Chabua, India, under General Order (GO) #1, on 22 February 1943. It moved to Tezpur, India.

78 FyS part of 22 FyG was based at Chabua, India, under GO #1, on 22 February 1943. It moved to Jorhat. India on 09 April 1943. This became 78 TptS, part of 22 TptG based at Jorhat, India, renamed per Technical Order (TO) #1-657 25 May 1943, effective 01 July 1943.

HQ & HQ Sq, 22 FG based Chabua, India under GO #1 22 February 1943. To Jorhat 09 April 1943, and renamed 22 TptG as per TO #1-657 of 25 May 1943.

88 FyS, 22 FyG was formed 10 May 1943 and moved to Karachi on 30 October 1943.

96, 97, 98 TptS and HQ & HQ Sq, 28 TptG were formed at Tezpur, India under GO #4 on 21 June 1943. 96 TptS moved to Gaya, India on 30 October 1943.

99, 100, 301 TptS and HQ & HQ Sq, 29 TptG were formed at Sookerating, India under GO #4 on 21 June 1943.

302, 303 and 304 TptS, 30 TptG were formed on 10 December 1942 at Mohanbari, India under GO #4 on 21 June 1943.

The Assam-China Sector and India Sectors were formed at midnight on 15/16 September 1943. On 04 October 1943, Wing HQ moved from Chabua to Delhi and on 15 April 1944 from Delhi to Calcutta. On 12 October 1943 India Sector was renamed Western Sector and Assam-China Sector became Eastern Sector.

Under GO #27, dated 10 December 1943, Transport Groups and Squadrons were replaced by Stations, and these were dissolved and replaced by Base Units under AAF Base Units General Order, dated 01 August 1944. On that date India China Division, Assam Wing and India Wing were established.

Station	*Location*
1 Wing HQ	New Delhi, India
2 Eastern Sector ICW	Chabua, India Dissolved 18Apr44
3 Western Sector ICW	Calcutta, India Dissolved 18Apr44
4	Jorhat, India
5	Tezpur, India. Later 1327 BU
6	Chabua, India. Later 1333 BU
7	Sookerating, India. Later 1337 BU
8	New Delhi, India. To 1307 BU
9	Mohanbari, India. Later 1332 BU
10	Lalmanirhat, India. To 1326 BU
11	Misamari, India. To 1328 BU
12	Yunnanyi, China. To 1338 BU
13	Kunming, China. To 1340 BU
14	Yangkai, China. To 1341 BU
15	Chungking, China. To 1339 BU
16	Karachi, India. To 1306 BU
17	Agra, India. To 1303 BU
18	Ondal, India. To 1312 BU
19	Calcutta, India. To 1305 BU (Dum Dum)
20	Gaya, India. To 1311 BU
21	Moran, India
22	Dergaon, India. To 1329 BU
23	Golaghat, India
24	Kweilin, China
25	Ranchi, India
26	Fort Hertz, Burma
27	Bangalore, India. Activated 18Apr44. Later 1309 BU
28	Bombay, India. Activated 01May44. Later 1308 BU
29	Colombo, Ceylon. Activated 29Apr44. To 1310 BU
30	Chanyi, China. Activated 16Apr44. To 1342 BU
1302 Base Unit	New Delhi, India
1304 BU	Barrackpore, India
1325 BU	Chabua, India (HQ Assam Wing)
1343 BU	Luliang, China
1344 BU	Chengtu, China. Activated 01Oct44
1345 BU	Tezgaon, India. Activated 01Oct44
1347 BU	Shamshernagar, India. Activated 01Dec44
1348 BU	Myitkyina, Burma. Activated 10Oct44
1349 BU	Jiwani, India. Activated 05Oct44
1350 BU	Kunming, China. Activated 01Dec44 (China Wing, HQ)
1351 BU	Kurmitola, India. Activated 02Jan45

p.126 VENEZUELA

A British Air Attaché report in February 1957 shows 17 C-47s with T.1 Squadron at Boca del Rio. In May 1958 and July 1959 there were 15 C-47s with this unit. Nine were in the USA for major overhaul.

p.126 VIETNAM (SOUTH)

From the air force records a number of accidents have come to light. Some of these are identified only as three digit serials, which it is concluded must be the USAF three digit serials used in the final years of service, as they all fit known aircraft. The crash locations are given, but some are what can only be concluded as being map references. This data comes via Sid Nanson and is given in the Production List update.

p.129 ZAIRE/DEMOCRATIC REPUBLIC OF CONGO

This country had, according to an Attaché report, nine C-47s in May 1972. Three C-47s were lost between April 1971 and April 1972. One was lost at Kamina in August 1972. A Google Earth 2006 photo of N'Dolo airport, Kinshasa shows three C-47s, all engineless, one with no port wing.

Part II – Commercial operators: Volume I, Chapter 4

p.156 ANGOLA

DTA was Direccao de Transportes Aereos de Angola – it became TAAG in Oct73. Angola became independent on 11 November 1975.

CR-LOK and CR-LOI were offered by the Congo Brazzaville government to the MPLA in 1974 – they were noted at Luanda, all white. They were never with CTA.

CTA was Consorcio Tecnico de Aeronautica SRL.

p.157 AUSTRALIA

Classic Wings was declared bankrupt on 08 January 2007 and went into receivership on 21 February 2007. No news of fleet disposal.

p.181 ECUADOR

ANDES - Aerolineas Nacionales del Ecuador unidentified DC-3 HC-ATG was recorded as the previous identity of OB-T-1043, making it c/n 12876, registered in Peru 20Nov74.

p.186 GUINÉ-BISSAU

Lineas Aereas da Guiné Bissau was previously Transportes Aereos da Guiné Portuguesa; all DC-3s had been withdrawn by 1991.

p.187 HONG KONG

Several charter operators used DC-3s in Hong Kong, but were omitted from Vol I for lack of details. The following has now come to light:-

Air Asia Ltd was a charter operator with the same directors as Eastern Air Associates. The company also overhauled aircraft for resale, and operated VR-HEP between May 1952 and May 1953.

Air Carriers Ltd operated charter flights between August 1949 and November 1951. One of the directors, Aw Hoe was killed when VR-HEP crashed in January 1951. VR-HES and VR-HET were also used.

Tradeastern Ltd carried out charter work in Burma, Thailand and Singapore between June 1951 and April 1954, using VR-HET.

p.195 KOREA

Korean Airlines website quotes HL-03 as a Stinson L-5, not a DC-3. HL-05 and HL-06 were leased from CAT in 1951 and purchased in 1953. HL-07 was delivered in April 1956. HL-06, which was hi-jacked, was replaced by another aircraft with the same registration (HL-06) bought in the USA in April 1959. HL-101 is quoted as another DC-3.

p.197 LEEWARD ISLANDS

A DC-3 can be seen derelict on St Christophers Island, nr Basseterre, on a Google Earth 2006 photo.

p.207 PHILIPPINE REPUBLIC

The following aircraft reported to be DC-3s are now known to be other types:- RP-C124 was an Enstrom F-28C c/n 359; RP-C472 was an Aero Commander 500U c/n 1780-55; RP-C538 was a Beech M-35 c/n D-6925; RP-C549 was a Cessna 441 c/n 0115; RP-C563 was not a DC-3, but type unknown; RP-C782 is an error for RP-C82; RP-C868 was Islander c/n 725; PI-C72 was an L-4J Cub.

p.209 PORTUGAL

Four TAP DC-3s went to the Air Force and two to Mozambique. See also Chapter 6, page 39, in this volume.

p.215 SYRIA

YK-AAF actually crashed on 21 December 1952, not 1953, while searching for Catalina P-211 of the Dutch Navy which crashed in the mountains on the Syria-Lebanon border on 19 December 1952.

p.222 UNITED STATES

Nevada Airlines (p.233) – This airline ceased operating following an accident to Martin 404 N40438 and an FAA grounding of the airline.

P. 260 – Add to index:

CTA – Consorcio Tecnico de Aeronautica SRL
DTA – Direccao de Transportes Aereos de Angola

Turboprop Conversions: Volume II, Chapter 6

p.676 Turbo Express Conversions (paragraph 2)

When Jennifer Gradidge interviewed Warren Basler in 1982, he told her that he was working with USAC at Van Nuys on the Turbo Express. When they ran out of cash, Baslers took the project over and so the aircraft (N300TX) was to be seen at Oshkosh. It was not likely to have been traded in, as Baslers already had an interest.

p.677 The Basler Story (paragraph 2)

To say that it has been claimed that Baslers owned 80 different C-47s suggests there is some doubt as to this fact. The writer asked Mrs Pat Basler if she could help with the details, but there were so many that it proved impossible. Contrary to the suggestion that work on conversions only started at Oshkosh in 1990 after the new production facility was opened, the writer photographed several DC-3s under conversion in the old Basler facility near the airport terminal in August 1989. The original prototype Turbo Express N300TX was re-worked with round windows and many other modifications and re-registered N300BF to be used for certification; the Supplemental Type Certificate was issued in 1990.

p.678 (Column 2, line 8)

Contrary to what is said, the Tri-Turbo-Three N23SA never had three Darts. Three Pratt & Whitney PT-6A-45s were used (see p.675)

For further details of Turbine-powered DC-3s, see Chapter 15, page 147, in this volume.

Civil registration-constructor's number cross-reference: Volume II, Chapter 11

p.706 BOLIVIA

John Davis points out that CB-33 was ex-Panagra on 20May47. Two possibilities are given. C/n 4415 C-47 ex NC86564 or c/n 11774 C-53 ex NC30091. The former is more likely. CB-33 was destroyed in the civil war on 29Aug49 at Santa Cruz.

CB-77 was a C-47A delivered to Jorge Eulert F, circa Sep51. It crashed.

Part III – The PS-84/Lisunov Li-2: Volume II, Chapter 7

The PS-84 was redesignated the Lisunov Li-2 on 17th September 1942 in honour of B P Lisunov, who supervised the original production of the Russian version of the C-47/DC-3.

The PS-84/Li-2 was in production from 1939 until May 1953. The original production line was at Factory No.84 in Moscow (moved to Tashkent in 1941). 2,419 aircraft had been produced by December 1945, with production continuing until May 1953, latterly with the Li-2P. In addition, Factory No.124 built ten aircraft during 1940-1941, and Factory No.126 built 353 Li-2Ts during the years 1947 to 1950. A total of over 4,800 PS-84s/Li-2s was built.

Abbreviations are explained on page 162.

PS-84/Li-2 production

c/n unknown first aircraft from sub-assemblies built in the USA completed 1938 for VVS

c/n 841 (from sub-assemblies built in the USA) URSS-M138 regd 08May39, possibly to Hamiata, ret Moscow GVF 31st otryad Dec39-Jan40 (Finnish campaign), canx 20Jun40

c/n 1	CCCP-L3400	GVF (Aeroflot) regd 11May39, 31st otryad Dec39 (Finnish campaign), canx 1941
2	CCCP-L3401	GVF (Aeroflot) regd 28Jun39, 31st otryad Dec39 (Finnish campaign)
3	CCCP-L3404	GVF (Aeroflot) regd 04Sep39, still i/s Jul41
4	CCCP-L3405	GVF (Aeroflot) regd 09Mar40, canx 03Apr41
5	to VVS	
6	to VVS	
7	CCCP-L3406	GVF (Aeroflot) regd 25Feb40, still i/s Apr42
02 46	CCCP-L3409	GVF regd 29Apr40, canx 20Sep40
02 56	CCCP-L3408	GVF regd 29Apr40, lost Jul41 due enemy action
03 16	CCCP-L3945	GVF regd 15Aug41
03 26	CCCP-L3412	GVF regd 22May40, canx 20Sep41 (dbf under war conditions)
03 36	CCCP-L3943	GVF regd 11Aug41
03 46	CCCP-L3413	GVF regd 05Jul40, destroyed Jan42 due enemy action
03 56	CCCP-L3410	GVF regd 05Jun40, canx 20Sep41 (w/o under war conditions)
04 16	CCCP-L3411	GVF regd 11Jun40, canx 08Aug41
04 26	CCCP-L3414	GVF regd 11Jun40
04 36	CCCP-L3415	GVF regd 28Jun40, destroyed Jan42 by enemy action
04 76	CCCP-L3416	GVF regd 10Jul40, destroyed Feb42 by enemy action
04 86	CCCP-L3417	GVF regd 12Jul40, still i/s Jul41, canx 1941
04 96	CCCP-L3418	GVF regd 09 Sep 40, still i/s Apr 42
65 01	CCCP-L3419	GVF regd 07Sep40, still i/s Jul41
65 02	CCCP-L3420	GVF regd 12Sep40, still i/s Jul41
65 03	CCCP-L3421	GVF regd 12Sep40, still i/s Jul41, canx 1941
65 04	CCCP-L3422	GVF regd 04Nov40, still i/s Apr42
65 05	CCCP-L3423	GVF regd 05Oct40, crashed 18Jun42
65 06	CCCP-L3424	GVF regd 10Oct40, still i/s Apr42
65 07	CCCP-L3425	GVF regd 04Nov40, destroyed Feb42 due enemy action
65 10	CCCP-L3426	GVF regd 04Nov40, still i/s Jan41
65 11	CCCP-L3427	GVF regd 20Nov40, still i/s Apr41
65 12	CCCP-L3428	GVF regd 27Nov40, still i/s Apr42
65 13	CCCP-L3429	GVF regd 06Dec40, still i/s Jul41
65 16	CCCP-L3430	GVF regd 11Dec40, still i/s Apr42
65 18	CCCP-L3431	GVF regd 23Dec40, still i/s Jul41
65 20	CCCP-L3432	GVF regd 23Jan41, still i/s Jul41
75 01	CCCP-N310	GUSMP (Polyarnaya aviatsiya) regd 11Jan41
75 03	CCCP-N311	GUSMP (Polyarnaya aviatsiya) regd 11Jan41, still i/s Mar43
75 04	CCCP-L3433	GVF regd 30Dec40, canx 12Aug41
75 06	CCCP-L3434	GVF regd 27Jan41, still i/s Apr42
75 09	CCCP-L3435	GVF regd 14Jan41, still i/s Apr42
75 11	CCCP-L3436	GVF regd 11Jan41, still i/s Apr42
75 13	CCCP-L3437	GVF regd 23Jan41, with Moskovskaya agon 1942 (flew supplies to Sevastopol 29Jun-01Jul42)
75 15	CCCP-L3438	GVF regd 28Jan41, still i/s Jul41
75 17	CCCP-L3439	GVF regd 17Feb41
75 19	CCCP-L3440	GVF regd 13Feb41, still i/s Apr42
75 21	CCCP-L3441	GVF regd 10Mar41, still i/s Apr42
75 23	CCCP-L3442	GVF regd 22Feb41, still i/s Apr42
75 25	CCCP-L3443	GVF regd 27Feb 41, still i/s Apr41
75 26	CCCP-L3944(2)	GVF regd 14Aug41
75 27	CCCP-L3444	GVF regd 27Feb41, still i/s Jul41
75 29	CCCP-L3452	GVF regd 17Jul41, still i/s Apr42
85 01	CCCP-J335	regd 01Mar41 to Factory No.466
85 02	CCCP-L3445	GVF regd 12Mar41, with Moskovskaya agon 1942 (flew supplies to Sevastopol 22Jun-01Jul42), with 1ap 1 atd GVF Vnukovo 1943, damaged on take-off from Molotov (Perm) 04Jun43 when hit CCCP-L3962 (c/n 184 17 08)
85 03	CCCP-L3446	GVF regd 04Apr41, still i/s Apr42
85 04	CCCP-L3447	GVF regd 19Mar41, still i/s Apr42
85 05	CCCP-L3448	GVF regd 14Mar41, still i/s Jun42
85 06	CCCP-L3449	GVF regd 20Mar41, still i/s Jul41
85 07	CCCP-L3450	GVF regd 04Apr41
85 08	CCCP-L3459	GVF regd 21Mar41, canx 1941
85 09	CCCP-L3460	GVF regd 28Mar41, canx 1941
85 10	CCCP-L3461	GVF regd 05Apr41, still i/s Jul41
85 11	CCCP-L3462	GVF regd 29Mar41, still i/s Jul41
85 12	CCCP-L3463	GVF regd 07Apr41, still i/s Apr42
85 13	CCCP-L3464	GVF regd 03Apr41, dbf & canx 12Aug41
85 14	CCCP-L3465	GVF regd 07Apr41, with Moskovskaya agon 1942 (flew supplies to Sevastopol Jun-Jul42)

85 15	CCCP-L3466	GVF regd 07Apr41
85 16	CCCP-L3467	GVF regd 05Apr41
85 17	CCCP-L3468	GVF regd 09Apr41, to Aeroflot Georgia, canx 20Sep41 (dbf on special mission)
85 18	CCCP-L3469	GVF regd 17Apr41, canx 1941
85 19	CCCP-L3470	GVF regd 07Apr41, canx 12Aug41
85 20	CCCP-L3471	GVF regd 17May41
85 21	CCCP-L3472	GVF regd 16May41, still i/s Jun41
85 22	CCCP-L3473	GVF regd 10Apr41
85 23	CCCP-J339	regd 04Apr41, probably to Factory No.125
85 24	CCCP-L3474	GVF regd 10Apr41, still i/s Apr42
85 25	CCCP-L3475	GVF regd 17Apr41, with Moskovskaya agon 1942 (flew supplies to Sevastopol Jun-Jul42)
85 26	CCCP-L3476	GVF regd 17Apr41, destroyed Jan42 due enemy action
85 27	CCCP-L3477	GVF regd 17Apr41, still i/s Jul41
85 29	CCCP-L3478	GVF regd 05May41, still i/s Apr42

124 22	CCCP-J485	regd 29Jan43 to Factory No.22

The following aircraft were probably built by Factory No.124

401	CCCP-L3938	GVF regd 23Sep40, reregd CCCP-L3900, to Directorate, Moscow-Irkutsk route 20Sep41, destroyed by enemy action Jan42
402	CCCP-N313	regd 15Jan41, to GUSMP (Polyarnaya aviatsiya) Jan41
405	CCCP-L3939	GVF regd 02Jan41, canx 12Aug41
501	CCCP-L3902	GVF regd 12Feb41, still i/s Apr42
503	CCCP-N314	regd 15Jan41, to GUSMP (Polyarnaya aviatsiya) Jan41
505	CCCP-L3903	GVF regd 11Mar41, still i/s Apr42

184 09 01	CCCP-L3479	GVF regd 06May41, still i/s Jul41
184 09 03	CCCP-L3480	GVF regd 09May41, still i/s Apr42
184 09 04	CCCP-L3481	GVF regd 09May41, still i/s Apr42
184 09 05	CCCP-L3482	GVF regd 20May41, still i/s Apr42
184 09 08	CCCP-J340	regd 02Jun41, to Factory No.452
184 09 09	CCCP-J344	regd 19Jun41, to Factory No.84

184 10 12	CCCP-L3483 regd 30Jul41
184 10 13	CCCP-L3484 regd 30Jul41, still i/s Apr42
184 10 14	CCCP-L3485 regd 30Jul41, destroyed Jan42 by enemy action
184 10 15	CCCP-L3486 regd 25Jul41, lost 06Aug41 due to enemy action, canx 20Sep41
184 10 16	CCCP-L3487 regd 30Jul41, destroyed Jan42 by enemy action
184 10 27	CCCP-L3493 regd 03Aug41, del 20Sep41 to GVF Kharkovskaya agon, to Moskovskaya agon 1942 (flew supplies to Sevastopol Jun-Jul42)
184 10 30	CCCP-L3497 regd 04Aug41, to GVF Kharkovskaya agon 20Sep41

184 11 01	CCCP-L3494 regd 04Aug41, to GVF Kharkovskaya agon 20Sep41
184 11 02	CCCP-L3498 regd 18Jul41, to GVF Kharkovskaya agon 20Sep41
184 11 03	CCCP-L3499 regd 04Aug41, to GVF Kharkovskaya agon 20Sep41, still i/s Apr42
184 11 04	CCCP-L3495 regd 18Jul41, to GVF Kharkovskaya agon 20Sep41
184 11 05	CCCP-L3488 regd 19Aug41, to GVF Kharkovskaya agon 20Sep41
184 11 06	CCCP-L3489 regd 19Aug41, to GVF Kharkovskaya agon 20Sep41
184 11 07	CCCP-L3490 regd 04Aug41, to GVF Kharkovskaya agon 20Sep41 as 490 in Soviet AF c/s, to Moskovskaya agon 1942 (flew supplies to Sevastopol Jun42)
184 11 08	CCCP-L3491 regd 06Aug41, to GVF Kharkovskaya agon 20Sep41
184 11 09	CCCP-L3492 regd 04Aug41, to GVF Kharkovskaya agon 20Sep41
184 11 10	CCCP-L3496 regd 18Jul41, to GVF Kharkovskaya agon 20Sep41
184 11 11	CCCP-L3905 regd 22Jul41, destroyed Jan42 due enemy action
184 11 12	CCCP-L3906 regd 22Jul41
184 11 13	CCCP-L3907 regd 22Jul41, to GVF Kharkovskaya agon 20Sep41
184 11 14	CCCP-L3908 regd 07Aug41
184 11 15	CCCP-L3909 regd 24Jul41, to GVF Kharkovskaya agon 20Sep41, to Moskovskaya agon 1942, operated by 3 ae Moskovskoi agon 1942 (flew supplies to Sevastopol Jun-Jul42)

184 12 01	CCCP-L3910 regd 24Jul41, to GVF Kharkovskaya agon 20Sep41, Aeroflot Yakutsk 12Jun45, operated by 14 TO YaAG. Crashed 27Dec51 90 kms from Yakutsk
184 12 03	CCCP-L3912 regd 06Aug41, to GVF Kharkovskaya agon 20Sep41, operated by 3 ae Moskovskaya agon 1942 (flew supplies to Sevastopol Jun-Jul42)
184 12 04	CCCP-L3913 regd 28Jul41
184 12 05	CCCP-L3914 regd 07Aug41
184 12 06	CCCP-L3915 regd 07Aug41
184 12 07	CCCP-L3916 regd 28Jul41 to GVF, w/o under war conditions & canx 20Sep41
184 12 08	CCCP-L3917 regd 31Jul41
184 12 09	CCCP-L3918 regd 31Jul41
184 12 10	CCCP-L3919 regd 13Aug41
184 12 11	CCCP-L3920 regd 13Aug41
184 12 12	CCCP-L3921 regd 05Aug41
184 12 13	CCCP-J355 regd 03Sep41 to Factory No.84
184 12 14	CCCP-L3923 regd 08Aug41, still i/s Nov41

184 13 01	CCCP-L3924 regd 11Aug41, still i/s Apr42
184 13 04	CCCP-L3925 regd 16Aug41
184 13 05	CCCP-L3926 regd 16Aug41
184 13 09	CCCP-L3927 regd 19Aug41
184 13 10	CCCP-L3928 regd 19Aug41
184 13 11	CCCP-L3929 regd 19Aug41, still i/s Apr42
184 13 12	CCCP-J356 regd 03Sep41 to Factory No.84
184 13 15	CCCP-L3930 regd 23Aug41

184 14 01	CCCP-L3931 regd 26Aug41, still i/s Apr42
184 14 03	CCCP-L3946 regd 11Oct41, still i/s Apr42
184 14 04	CCCP-L3947 GVF regd 11Oct41, still i/s Apr42, to Moskovskaya agon (flew supplies to Sevastopol Jun-Jul42)

184 14 05 CCCP-L3911 GVF regd 26Aug41, to Chemomorski oao

184 14 10 CCCP-L3933 regd 29Aug41, reregd CCCP-L3932 to GVF. With 5 oap, w/o 03Jun43 on flight from Chklavoski to Belomorsk

184 14 15 CCCP-L3935 regd 03Sep41, reregd CCCP-L3933, still i/s Apr42

184 15 06 CCCP-J441 regd 16Jul42 to Factory No.1

184 15 07 CCCP-J357 regd 05Sep41 to Factory No.18

184 15 08 CCCP-L3934 regd 05Sep41, destroyed by enemy action Jan42

184 15 09 CCCP-L3935 regd 07Sep41, still i/s May42

184 15 10 CCCP-L3936 regd 08Sep41

184 16 02 CCCP-L3940 regd 18Dec42

184 16 04 CCCP-L3936, reregd CCCP-L3937 09Sep41, still i/s Nov41

184 16 05 CCCP-L3951 regd 12Sep41

184 16 06 CCCP-L3952 regd 13Sep41, still i/s Apr42

184 16 10 CCCP-L3953 regd 13Sep41, still i/s Apr42

184 17 02 CCCP-L3964 regd 23Sep41

184 17 03 CCCP-L3965 regd 20Sep41 to GVF, with Moskovskaya agon 1942 (flew supplies to Sevastopol Jun-Jul42)

184 17 04 CCCP-L3954 regd 20Sep41 to GVF, with Moskovskaya agon 1942 (flew supplies to Sevastopol Jun-Jul42)

184 17 05 CCCP-L3955 regd 20Sep41

184 17 06 CCCP-L3956 regd 20Sep41, still i/s Jul42

184 17 07 CCCP-L3961 regd 20Sep41, still i/s Apr42

184 17 08 CCCP-L3962 regd 22Sep41, damaged 04Jun43 Molotov (Perm) – see entry to c/n 85 02

184 17 09 CCCP-L3958 regd 22Sep41

184 17 10 CCCP-L3957 regd 23Sep41

184 18 01 CCCP-L3959 regd 23Sep41 to GVF, with Moskovskaya agon 1942 (flew supplies to Sevastopol Jun-Jul42)

184 18 02 CCCP-L3960 regd 23Sep41, destroyed Jan42 by enemy action

184 18 03 CCCP-L3966 regd 23Sep41 to GVF, with Moskovskaya agon 1942 (flew supplies to Sevastopol Jun-Jul42)

184 18 04 CCCP-J456 regd 30Jan43 to NKAP Air Unit

184 18 06 CCCP-L3969 regd 23Sep41, still i/s Apr42

184 18 09 CCCP-L3972 regd 27Sep41, still i/s Apr42

184 19 03 CCCP-L3976 regd 16Aug43(?), with GVF Moskovskaya agon 1942, i/s Apr42 (& flew supplies to Sevastopol Jun-Jul42)

184 19 05 CCCP-L3978 regd 06Oct41

184 19 06 CCCP-L3979 regd 29Sep41

184 21 06 CCCP-J406 regd 19Oct42 to Factory No.84

184 21 07 CCCP-L3988 regd 21Oct41 to GVF, with Moskovskaya agon 1942 (flew supplies to Sevastopol Jun-Jul42)

184 21 09 CCCP-L3990 regd 18Oct41 to GVF, with Moskovskaya agon 1942 (flew supplies to Sevastopol Jun-Jul42)

184 21 10 CCCP-L3991 regd 20Oct41 to GVF, with Moskovskaya agon 1942 (flew supplies to Sevastopol Jun42)

184 22 03 CCCP-J405 regd 19Oct42 to Factory No.84

184 22 04 CCCP-J371 (2) regd 16Apr43 to Factory No.153

184 22 05 CCCP-J414 regd 17Jun42 to Factory No.24, reregd CCCP-J373 (2)

184 22 08 CCCP-J376 (2) regd 12Jan43 to Factory No.292

184 22 10 CCCP-L3993 regd 20Oct41, to VVS KA, reregd CCCP-J486 29Jan43 to Factory No.22

184 23 08 CCCP-J495 regd 10Mar43 to Factory No.26

184 23 10 CCCP-J450 regd 15Oct42 to NKAP Air Unit

184 24 03 CCCP-J403 regd 19Oct42 to Factory No.84

184 24 04 CCCP-J408 regd 19Oct42 to Factory No.84

184 24 05 CCCP-J409 regd 19Nov42 to Factory No.29

184 24 07 CCCP-J415 regd 17Jun42 to Factory No.24

184 24 08 CCCP-J378 regd 04Jun42 to Factory No.39

184 24 09 CCCP-J379 regd 16Apr43 to Factory No.153

184 24 10 CCCP-J400 regd 20May42 to Factory No.16

184 25 01 CCCP-J442 regd 16Jul42 to Factory No.1

184 25 02 CCCP-J401 regd 10Mar43 to Factory No.26

184 25 03 CCCP-J402 regd 04Mar43 to Factory No.30

184 25 04 CCCP-L3996 regd 20Jan43(?), with GVF Moskovskaya agon 1942 (flew supplies to Sevastopol Jun-Jul42)

184 25 06 CCCP-J544 regd 21Aug43 to Factory No.31

184 25 08 CCCP-L3998 regd 20Jan43(?) with GVF Moskovskaya agon 1942 (flew supplies to Sevastopol Jun-Jul42)

184 29 06 CCCP-J521 regd 09Jun43 to Factory No.21

184 30 01 CCCP-J407 regd 31Aug42 to Factory No.166

184 31 06 CCCP-J601 regd 14Feb44 to Factory No.456

184 33 10 CCCP-L4002 regd 12Aug43

184 34 06 CCCP-L4003 regd 22May43

184 34 10 CCCP-L4004 regd 06Jan43

184 35 01 CCCP-L4005 regd 12Aug43

184 35 02 CCCP-L4006 regd 15May43

184 35 04 CCCP-L4008 regd 20Jan43

184 35 05 CCCP-L4009 regd 26Mar43

184 35 06 CCCP-L4010 regd 20Jan43

184 35 07 CCCP-L4011 regd 12Aug43

184 35 08 CCCP-L4012 (1) regd 20Jan43, regd CCCP-L4012 (2) 16Aug43

184 35 09 CCCP-L4013 (1) regd 20Jan43, regd CCCP-L4013 (2) 16Aug43

184 45 05 CCCP-J455 regd 16Nov42 to Factory No.126

184 50 09 CCCP-L4015 regd 11Nov42

184 50 10 CCCP-L4016 regd 11Nov42

184 50 14 CCCP-J661 regd 30Apr44 to LII

184 52 01 CCCP-L3949 regd 24Feb43

184 53 06 CCCP-L4017 regd 11Nov42

184 56 01 CCCP-L4021 regd 16Aug43

184 56 09 CCCP-L4018 regd 16Aug43

184 57 01 CCCP-L4026 (1) regd 20Jan43, regd CCCP-L4026 (2) 16Aug43
184 57 07 CCCP-J540 regd 05Aug43 to Factory No.84

184 58 02 CCCP-L4020 regd 12Aug43
184 58 03 CCCP-L3941 regd 06Mar43
184 58 09 CCCP-L4030 regd 15May43

184 59 09 CCCP-L4022 regd 16Aug43
184 59 10 CCCP-L4023 regd 20May43

184 60 01 CCCP-L4024 regd 20Jan43
184 60 02 CCCP-L4025 regd 16Aug43

184 61 02 CCCP-L4027 regd 20Jan43
184 61 05 CCCP-L4028 regd 02Feb43

184 62 01 CCCP-L4029 regd 12Aug43

184 63 02 CCCP-L4031 regd 06Mar43
184 63 05 CCCP-L4032 regd 06Mar43
184 63 07 CCCP-L4033 regd 06Mar43

185 65 06 CCCP-L4034 regd 15May43
184 65 07 CCCP-L4105 regd 24Apr44
184 65 10 CCCP-L4035 regd 15May43 to GVF. DBR 14Jun43 30kms SE of Maksatikh, USSR, on flight from Moscow to Leningrad.

184 66 02 CCCP-L4036 regd 15May43
184 66 04 CCCP-L4037 regd 12Aug43
184 66 05 CCCP-L4038 regd 26Mar43
184 66 09 CCCP-J515 regd 02Jun43 to Factory No.466

184 67 02 CCCP-L3987 regd 11Feb44
184 67 05 CCCP-L4039 regd 31Mar43

184 69 03 CCCP-L4040 regd 15May43
184 69 04 CCCP-KH360 regd 18Mar43 to Tankoprom, reregd CCCP-L3942, reregd CCCP-L4100
184 69 08 CCCP-L4041 regd 15May43

184 70 01 CCCP-KH362 regd 18Mar43 to Tankoprom, reregd CCCP-L4101

184 74 07 CCCP-L4104 regd 04Jun43

184 77 01 CCCP-L4102 regd 26Apr43
184 77 02 CCCP-J516 regd 04Jun43 to NKAP Air Unit
184 77 04 CCCP-J504 regd 28Apr43 to NKAP Air Unit
184 77 05 CCCP-J501 regd 22Apr43 to NKAP Air Unit
184 77 06 CCCP-J502 regd 22Apr43 to NKAP Air Unit
184 77 10 CCCP-J530 regd 17Jun43 to Factory No.36

184 78 09 CCCP-L4103 regd 26Apr43

184 80 01 CCCP-J531 regd 21Jun43 to LII

184 85 08 CCCP-J517 regd 07Jun43 to NKAP Air Unit

184 88 10 CCCP-L4042 regd 31Aug43

184 91 01 CCCP-J608 regd 11Dec43 to NKAP Air Unit

184 94 01 CCCP-J535 regd 24Jul43 to Factory No.19
184 94 05 CCCP-J536 regd 26Jul43 to Factory No.29

184 99 03 CCCP-J545 regd 31Aug43 to LII

184 100 07 CCCP-L4043 regd 06Sep43
184 100 08 CCCP-L4044 regd 06Sep43
184 100 10 CCCP-L4045 regd 06Sep43

184 103 08 CCCP-ZH62 regd 23Sep43, with NKVD railway building section Sep44
184 103 09 CCCP-ZH63 regd 23Sep43, with NKVD railway building section Sep44

184 104 07 CCCP-L4046 regd 24Sep43
184 104 08 CCCP-L4047 regd 24Sep43
184 104 10 CCCP-L4048 regd 24Sep43

184 105 01 CCCP-L4049 regd 24Sep43
184 105 02 CCCP-L4050 regd 24Sep43
184 105 03 CCCP-L4051 regd 24Sep43
184 105 04 CCCP-L4052 regd 24Sep43
184 105 05 CCCP-L4053 regd 28Sep43
184 105 07 CCCP-L4054 regd 28Sep43
184 105 08 CCCP-L4055 regd 24Sep43
184 105 10 CCCP-L4056 regd 28Sep43

184 106 02 CCCP-L4060 regd 21Oct43
184 106 03 CCCP-L4057 regd 28Sep43
184 106 04 CCCP-L4058 regd 21Oct43
184 106 06 CCCP-L4059 regd 21Oct43

184 108 08 CCCP-L4061 regd 21Oct43
184 108 09 CCCP-L4062 regd 21Oct43
184 108 10 CCCP-L4063 regd 21Oct43

184 109 01 CCCP-L4064 regd 21Oct43

184 110 06 CCCP-L3989 regd 03Dec43
184 110 09 CCCP-J642 regd 23Mar44 to Factory No.29

184 112 06 CCCP-J596 regd 24Nov43 to Factory No.18

184 114 01 CCCP-L4065 regd 17Feb44
184 114 02 CCCP-L4066 regd 09Dec43
184 114 03 CCCP-L4067 regd 06Dec43
184 114 05 CCCP-L4068 regd 17Feb44
184 114 06 CCCP-L4069 regd 17Feb44
184 114 10 CCCP-L4072 regd 09Dec43

184 115 01 CCCP-J612 regd 29Dec43 to Factory No.292
184 115 05 CCCP-L4074 regd 11Feb44
184 115 06 CCCP-L4070 regd 25Dec43

184 117 02 CCCP-L4075 regd 25Dec43
184 117 03 CCCP-J614 regd 11Jan44 to Factory No.31
184 117 06 CCCP-J616 regd 15Jan44 to Factory No.23

184 121 01 CCCP-L4077 regd 17Feb44
184 121 03 CCCP-L4078 regd 17Feb44
184 121 04 CCCP-L4079 regd 16Feb44
184 121 06 CCCP-L4082 regd 17Feb44
184 121 07 CCCP-L4083 regd 05Apr44
184 121 08 CCCP-L4084 regd 17Feb44
184 121 10 CCCP-L4080 regd 07Mar44

184 122 01 CCCP-L4085 regd 14Mar44
184 122 03 CCCP-J636 regd 11Feb44 to Factory No.447
184 123 10 CCCP-L4081 regd 07Mar44
184 124 06 CCCP-L4086 regd 26Feb44
184 125 01 CCCP-L4087 regd 25Feb44
184 131 09 CCCP-KH386 regd 05May44 to Tankoprom
184 132 04 CCCP-L4088 regd 09May44
184 136 01 CCCP-L4089 regd 09May44
184 136 02 CCCP-L4093 regd 09May44
184 137 03 CCCP-L4090 regd 09May44
184 137 10 CCCP-L4095 regd 23May44
184 138 03 CCCP-L4096 regd 23May44
184 138 09 CCCP-L4091 regd 09May44
184 139 07 CCCP-L4092 regd 09May44
184 140 07 CCCP-L4094 regd 09May44 (L4094 formerly allocated 184 137 10 – qv)
184 143 02 CCCP-J675 regd 22Jun44
184 143 05 CCCP-L4098 regd 23May44
184 143 07 CCCP-L4097 regd 09May44
184 145 01 CCCP-L4099 regd 23May44
184 145 09 CCCP-L4111 regd 23May44
184 150 06 CCCP-L4113 regd 10Jun44
184 258 02 Soviet AF '08'
184 272 02 CCCP-N458 Aeroflot i/s 1958/59 – reregd CCCP-04238.
184 281 07 CCCP-04204 Aeroflot i/s 21May59.
184 282 02 CCCP-04226 Aeroflot i/s Jan60 to Jun61 – w/o May62 – sank in Antarctic.
184 307 03 CCCP-N499 Aeroflot - CCCP-04208 Aeroflot i/s Oct59 – Sank in Antarctic 1959.
184 307 05 CCCP-N502 Aeroflot – taxied off ice shelf at Mirny Ice Station 16Feb58 [tail wheel locked!]
184 307 10 CCCP-04228 Aeroflot – i/s 21Sep59 – Landing accident 14Feb64 – Repaired by Mar65.
184 343 06 CCCP-N531 Aeroflot i/s 28May58.
184 346 06 CCCP-N53? Aeroflot i/s 1954.
184 346 10 CCCP-04213 Aeroflot i/s 21Sep59 – w/o 11Apr67.
184 357 08 CCCP-04214 Aeroflot i/s 14Oct59 – damaged Dec68 and destroyed by storm.
184 359 04 CCCP-04215 Aeroflot i/s 21Sep59.
184 359 09 Del. by Air Force to Aeroflot as CCCP-63916 on 25Aug64.
184 366 06 CCCP-04121 Aeroflot i/s 21May59.
184 375 03 Del. by Air Force to Aeroflot as CCCP-63918 on 25Aug64.
184 398 02 CCCP-04217 Aeroflot i/s 24Sep62 to Mar65.
184 398 04 CCCP-N578 Aeroflot i/s May58.
184 401 02 CCCP-04220 Aeroflot i/s 03Sep59.
234 415 08 CCCP-L4938 Aeroflot Yakutsk-YKS 1954 – with 139 tao.
334 439 09 Del. by Air Force to Aeroflot as CCCP-63917 25Aug64.
334 444 08 CCCP-N602 Aeroflot i/s 1958-59.
126 50 10 Del. by Air Force to Aeroflot as CCCP-04368 03Mar61.
126 51 09 Del. by Air Force to Aeroflot as CCCP-04369 03Mar61.
126 56 01 Del. by Air Force to Aeroflot as CCCP-04367 03Mar61.
126 56 05 Del. by Air Force to Aeroflot as CCCP-04370 03Mar61. Cr 13Oct64 nr River Anabar, Tiksi Region.
126 57 08 Del. by Air Force to Aeroflot as CCCP-04371 03Mar61.
126 57 10 Del. by Air Force to Aeroflot as CCCP-04372 03Mar61.

The following Li-2s are known only by registration mark, and were in the Aeroflot fleet on the dates given:-

CCCP-N393 Polyarnaya Aviatsiya – photo in 1950.
CCCP-N458 29May58
CCCP-N503 29May58
CCCP-N534 09Mar58
CCCP-N555 22Jan58
CCCP-N560 10Jan58
CCCP-N580 Polyarnaya Aviatsiya DSK 26Jul52.
CCCP-N581 Forced landing Jan58.

CCCP-L4658 Aeroflot, E Siberia – W/o 12Oct48 forced landing in Siberian forest.

CCCP-04205 20Jul62
CCCP-04218 25Apr60 until Mar65
CCCP-04219 12Mar60 until 14Mar66
CCCP-04221 12Mar60 – sank through ice between Mirny Station and Oasis Station 08May65 after forced landing.
CCCP-04229 Crashed 12Nov59 3km short of Ust/Tareya [BW]
CCCP-04240 W/o 02Dec62 gear failure.
CCCP-04241 25Dec65
CCCP-04246 Jan64
CCCP-16158 Aeroflot – Yakutsk-Butagai Directorate – W/o when landed beside runway at Moma 20Feb61.
CCCP-54795 Aeroflot Yakutsk – with 139 ATO – Crashed 10Aug59 nr Kovrik river (150kms SE of Toko, Yakutiya, on supply flight for geologists.)
CCCP-63919 Sank at SP Station, Arctic 08May65
CCCP-69919 08May66

'CCCP-76959' Preserved at Baikonur, Kazakstan autumn 2007.

Since the completion of the main text for this volume, further details have emerged on Aeroflot and other Li-2 aircraft.

184 216 01 CCCP-L4228 Aeroflot/Yakutiya w/o 27Dec51 on a flight from Yakutsk to Vilyuisk
184 226 07 CCCP- ?? Aeroflot. W/o 22Mar46 on a flight from Anadyr to Uelkal. Aircraft crashed into a mountain between the slopes of the Zolotoi Khrebet ridge and the Ushkanyi Gory Range, 85kms from Anadyr.

C/ns unknown:-

CCCP-L4138 Aeroflot. W/o 21Jun47 on a flight over the Black Sea when an engine failed. The aircraft landed in the waters of Karkitinski Zaliv Bay and sank after 15 minutes.

CCCP-L4145 Aeroflot/Privolzhsk. W/o 09Nov46 on a flight from Kuibyshev to Sverdlovsk.

CCCP-L4150 Aeroflot/Ukraine. W/o 14Jan46 on a flight from Kharkiv to Moscow-Vnukovo.

CCCP-L4181 Aeroflot/Turkmenistan. W/o 05Nov46 on a flight from Ashkhabad to Moscow-Vnukovo via Voronezh-Chertovitskoye.

CCCP-L4207 Aeroflot/Lithuania. DBR 05Nov46 on a flight from Vilnius to Moscow-Vnukovo.

CCCP-L4214 Aeroflot/Moscow. W/o 30Dec47 on a flight from Chelyabinsk to Moscow.

CCCP-L4228 Aeroflot/Yakutiya. W/o 27Dec51 on a flight from Yakutsk to Vilyuisk.

CCCP-L4275 Aeroflot. W/o 18Nov48 on a cargo flight from Stalinabad to Leninabad. The aircraft encountered bad weather and crashed into the western slope of the Khrebet Mogol-Tau ridge, near Leninabad.

CCCP-L4460 Aeroflot. W/o 24Apr48 on a flight from Kirensk to Bodaibo, after it encountered adverse weather and crashed near Mamakan, 15kms west of Bodaibo, landing on the ice of the Vitim river.

CCCP-L4463 Aeroflot. W/o 22Nov48 on a flight from Zyryanka to Srednekolymsk after losing radio contact. The aircraft attempted to land on a small strip on the banks of the River Kolyma, but stalled and crashed through the ice of the river 400metres from the airstrip.

CCCP-L4498 Aeroflot. W/o on 04Sep48 after the pilot became disoriented after take-off from Moscow-Bykovo. The aircraft touched the ground with the port propeller, continuing until the port wing hit a fence & telegraph pole before finally crashing into a garden & burning out.

CCCP-L4500 Aeroflot. W/o 25Oct48 on a flight from Klukhori to Sukhumi, when the crew encountered bad weather and strayed from the prescribed flight path, crashing into the Caucasus mountains.

CCCP-L4591 Aeroflot/Belarus. Cancelled Sep63 & preserved in the Gorki Park at Minsk.

CCCP-L4658 Aeroflot. W/o 12Oct48 on a cargo flight from Kirensk to Bodaibo when both engines stopped due to fuel starvation after one hour and 13 minutes. The fuel filters & pipes were clogged with ice as the fuel loaded at Kirensk contained too much water. The aircraft crashed 25kms from Parshino in the Kirensk District of the Irkutsk Region and caught fire.

CCCP-51186 Soviet Air Force. Ferried 13-18Jan61 from Zaporizihye to Hanoi. Operated in Vietnam and Laos from 21Jan61 and donated to the Vietnam Air Force in Jun61.

CCCP-51190 Soviet Air Force. Ferried 13-18Jan61 from Zaporizihye to Hanoi. Operated in Vietnam and Laos from 21Jan61. W/o at Xam Nua, Laos on 23Jan61.

CCCP-51191 Soviet Air Force. Ferried 13-18Jan61 from Zaporizihye to Hanoi. Operated in Vietnam and Laos from 21Jan61 and donated to the Vietnam Air Force in Jun61.

CCCP- ?? Soviet Air Force. A fourth aircraft was ferried at the same time as the above three aircraft to Hanoi for use in Vietnam and Laos.

CCCP-71162 To Aeroflot/Moscow MagSPiVS 01Mar60.

CCCP-71163 To Aeroflot/Moscow MagSPiVS 01Mar60.

CCCP-71164 To Aeroflot/Moscow MagSPiVS 01Mar60. Transferred to Aeroflot/Privolzhsk. Noted at Samara-Bezymyanka 08Feb64.

CCCP-71165 To Aeroflot/Moscow MagSPiVS 01Mar60.

CCCP-71166 To Aeroflot/Moscow MagSPiVS 01Mar60.

CCCP-71167 To Aeroflot/Moscow MagSPiVS 01Mar60. Transferred to Aeroflot/Urals. Noted at Yekaterinburg-Koltsovo 26Sep62.

CCCP-71168 To Aeroflot/Moscow MagSPiVS 01Mar60

Russian abbreviations

ADD	aviatsii dalnego deistviya	Long-range aviation
Aeon	aviaeskadrilya osobogo naznacheniya	Special operations squadron
Agon	aviagruppa osobogo naznacheniya	Special operations aviation group
Apdd	aviapolk dalnego deistviya	Long-range aviation regiment
Ato	aviatransportny otryad upravieniya	Transport aviation squadron
GUSMP	glavnoe upravlenie Severnogo morskogo puti	Chief administration of the Northern Sea route
GVF	grazhdanskii vozdushnyi flot	Civil Air Fleet
Gv.Korpus	gvardii korpus	"Guards" corps
Korpus ADD		Guards Corps of Long-range Aviation
LII	letno-issledovatel'skii institute	Flight Research Institute
NKAP	narodnyi komissariat aviatsionnoi promyshlennosti	People's commissariat for aviation industry
NKVD	narodnyi komissariat vnutrennykh del	People's commissariat for internal affairs
Otap	otdelny transportny aviapolk	Independent transport aviation regiment
Otryad		Squadron
Pad	peregonochnoi aviadivizii	Ferry aviation division
Pap	peregonochny aviapolk	Ferry aviation regiment
Parm	polevaya aviaremontnaya masterskaya	Field aircraft repair workshop
Tankoprom		Tank industry
Tap	transportny aviapolk	Transport aviation regiment
TO	transportny otryad	Transport squadron
VVS	voenno vozdushnye sily	Military Air Forces (Soviet Air Force)
VZLU	vyzkumny a zkusebni letecky ustav	Aeronautical Research & Test Institute

C/n 1368 DC-2 N4867V was operated for many years by Johnson Flying Service, until sold to the Donald Douglas Museum in 1974. This aircraft now flies as N1934D with the Museum of Flight, Seattle. The photo was taken at Missoula, Montana. (Clay Jannson)

Part IV – Production List: Volume II, Chapter 5

Abbreviations are explained on page 247.

Douglas DC-2

1239, **1249**, **1310**, **1311**, **1312**, and **1367** were all acquired by the UK government for BOAC to be operated by Atlantic Airways Ltd, Miami, FL. c/o Pan American Airways, Washington, DC as of 11Jun41. They were delivered to West Africa as US8, US9, US2, US3, US1 and US10 respectively, of Procurement Division, Treasury Dept, US Government with flight approval issued on 23Jul41. The British registration marks were not used and the aircraft were handed over to the RAF and USAAF serials were issued on paper only.

1251 DG476 served in French Equatorial Africa where it had a forced-landing following engine failure. It was later flown out. In Iraq it was damaged when strafed on the ground, and had 200 bullet holes. After repair it was used for cargo near the Libyan Frontier in the Western Desert. It was later SOC in India.

1286 'PH-AJU' was removed temporarily from display on poles at Albury, NSW, but by Nov08 it had returned to display. It was available for sale or 'give away' by Albury Council, as it is not the real 'Uiver'. DISPLAY [Despite the caption on page I of the colour section in Volume I, this was never used by Marshalls of Cambridge and never left Australia]

1288 'PH-AJU' [another] is stored at Lelystad, but it is probably too corroded to be restored. STORED

1292 A30-9 was with the Moorabbin Air Museum, Melbourne, Vic. It was disassembled in Jan08. STORED

1304 was delivered to Pan American Aviation Supply on 20Sep34 and to Pan American Airways on 20Dec34. It went to Mexicana as XA-BJI on 20May37. The US marks were cancelled on 26May37.

1311 Phil Butler has questioned the use of HK867 for this aircraft, suggesting that the serial was allocated after the aircraft crashed in September 1941. After consulting Jim Halley's RAF Aircraft HA100 to HZ999, it seems that there was no logic in the allocation of the aircraft at this time. The origin of the original report is now 'lost in the mists of time'

1313 NC14280 was bought by the US Treasury, Procurement Division for the War Department and leased to PAA for use in Africa by 12Sep41. Then to RAF.

1331 PH-AKF was ntu. X-1331 was demonstrated at Croydon, UK on 22May35.

1351 NC14291 to Pan American Aviation Supply Corp 21Jan35 and to PAA 10Apr35. Quoted as to Panair do Brasil 05Jul40 and regd in Brasil 23Jul40. However, PP-PAY was registered on 29May39.

1354 Finnish AF DO-1 remains stored at Tikkakoski, Finland, awaiting restoration. STORED

1363 After seizure by RAF at Flensburg this DC-2 was allotted VP102 on 02Feb46 to BAFO Comms Sq. It was at Luneburg in Dec45, but the RAF serial appears not to have been used.

1368 N4867V A J Levin's address was N Hollywood, CA.- N1934D Museum of Flight Foundation f/f 07Jun07 after restoration in TWA colours. Delivered to Seattle on that day. Flying Oshkosh 2010. N13711 reserved 24Feb11. ACTIVE

1371 NC14950 to Pan American Aviation Supply Corp. on 14Nov35 and to PAA on 23Dec35. To Mexicana on 23Sep40 and NC number canx 08Nov40. Delete S A Panini as this does not agree with RAF use.

1376 Restoration of VH-CDZ resumed in 2002 at Bankstown, after a chequered history, but there is no recent news. STORED

1378 DC-2-115F YR-GAD DBF at Boteni following enemy action, [German or Russian?] probably late Aug44.

1404 N39165/'PH-AJU' was under repair at Schiphol, following damage in July 2005, and flew again on 29May07. ACTIVE

1406 history as for c/n 1313. Bought by US Treasury.

1408 NC14978 to PAA on 25May37. Regn Canx 09Oct39 for use as XA-BKQ.

1413 URSS-M25 for Dereluft read Deruluft. This has also been reported w/o on 06Aug38.

1415 36-345 Crashed 03Jan43 MacDill Fld, FL.

1505 36-72 2 TS was at Olmstead – based at Brookley and crashed on 13Jan42 at Craig Fld, AL.

1506 36-73 Luke was 23BS and is noted as crashing at John Rogers Apt, HI on 16Jun42.

1508 36-75 crashed at Patterson AAF, OH.

1511 36-78 unit was 6 ABS, crash date 07Dec40.

1512 36-79 crashed at Winterset, IA on 23Dec41 due to engine failure.

1513 36-80 had a landing accident on 27Oct41 while with 7TS, 62 TCS. Another accident on 04Dec41 was with 8 TS. It was back with 7 TS at time of final crash.

1517 36-84 crashed 22Mar42 at McClellan AAF, CA. It was based at Mines Fld.

1519 36-86 crashed at Lake Charles AAF, LA on 25Apr42.

1562 The fuselage of DO-3 remains stored at Vantaa Airport, Helsinki, but restoration looks doubtful. STORED

1564 OK-AIZ – It has been suggested that this was shipped to Spain by sea, and that the boat was sunk by the Nationalists in 1937. OK-AIZ was registered on 05Oct37 and canx 11Dec37.

1586 CAA file gives:- NC16048 Douglas Acft Co R07Aug36 – Mfg 29Jul36 – Capt G Whittell was president of Nevada Exploration Corp so that name may be deleted. Nevada bought the aircraft on 06Aug36. They sold it to China National Avn Corp. and NC16048 canx 25Apr39, but delivery probably much earlier. CNAC no 40, named "Kangting". Believed to carry XT-DBF for flights to Burma. W/o 12Feb41 when crashed at Taohsien.

1599 transfer to Mexicana as XA-BKV and NC number cancelled on 02May40.

2059 38-501 – A crash is noted at Gowen AAF, ID. No date.

2067 38-510 crashed 04Apr44 Alligator Pond Beach, Jamaica [FP]

2072 38-515 remains on display in the USAF Museum, Dayton, OH. [2009] DISPLAYED

2073 38-516 crashed 29Nov42 at Danbury, CT, due to bad weather and pilot fatigue.

2081 38-524 insert Crashed and BF on 01Oct42, 15mls NW of Caomo, en route Losey Fld to San Juan, PR.

2082 38-525 crashed on 05Mar42 in St Louis River, Point Sewall, FL.

2057 is now quoted as becoming Agentine Navy 0104 [not 0105 – see later].

2063 was suggested as going to the Argentine Navy and a web site indicates it became 0105.

2084 38-527 had an accident on 15Nov43 in California – probably leading to relegation to Class 26 Instructional airframe.

2085 38-528 18 TS, 64 TG, crashed 14Feb42 on take-off Swan Island Apt, Portland, OR, into Colombia River. Little damage! Later in its life, it is now reported to have become Argentine Navy 0108.

2092 Mexican registration was probably XA-DOO as this was delivered to Mexico City on 16Nov44. It made a wheels-up landing on 25Nov44 and was canx as wfu.

Douglas DC-3

1494 42-43619 crashed on 15Oct42 while with 24 TCS. This, the prototype DC-3, was reported crashed on 15Oct42 at Knobmaster, MO, but the accident report indicates that it crashed on that date 2.5 m SW of Chicago Mun. Apt., IL when it hit a tree following a missed approach [PE/BW].

1495 As John Davis points out, there is some variation in the dates quoted in files. An example is for NC16001. The Bill of Sale [BoS] for Douglas to American was 01Jun36. It went to Defense Supplies Corp., Washington, DC for Air Service Command, Army Air Forces 27May42, but BoS was 25Aug42. It went to War Department on 23Mar43. NC16001 was canx on 22May43 as being operated under Army insignia! For obvious reasons this will not be repeated for other aircraft.

1496 NC16002 – comments as for 1495. See also c/n 1497, 1498, 1499, 1500, 1549, 1976, 2216 and 2217.

1497 NC16003 bought by American Airlines again on 07Oct44. To Max Walen & Jay Simmons, Dallas, TX on 29Apr49. To Desmond A Barry, Dallas, TX on 03May49. To RAMSA on same date and US regn canx 08Jul49.

1499 42-56092 was operated by American Airlines when it had an accident on 29Jun43.

N133D was reported derelict at Griffin, GA in May07 with Academy titles. Restored as NC16005 American Airlines 'Flagship Orange County' at Orange County, CA in Aug09 at Lyon Air Museum, John Wayne Apt, CA. DISPLAYED.

1545 This aircraft had reverted to its correct registration, PP-ANU, by 2006 and is displayed in Museo do VARIG, Porto Alegre. DISPLAYED

1549 NC16007 L.B.C. Aircraft Corp, Camp Hill, PA – To HC-SMB on 19Aug49.

1555 NC16017 had a collision with B-34 41-38116.

1904 NC16064 hit tree on approach to Patterson Fld 18Nov42. [PE]

1910 N16070 Regd to Michael King Smith Foundation, McMinnville, OR 15Feb07. Although reported in the book as 'stripped' in 2004, that does not mean any more than being prepared for a repaint. ACTIVE

1911 EI-AYO remains as such in the Science Museum collection at Wroughton, Wilts in 2010. PRESERVED

1915 NC16094 from Eastern to DSC for War Dept, and leased to Pan American for use in Africa by 12Sep41.

1917 N17331 remains noted with Tradewinds Aircraft Supply, San Antonio, TX in Aug09. DERELICT

1919 N17333 Howell to O'Vestor Cash, Lafayette, CA 23Jun50 – Sky Coach Agency of California Inc, Burbank, CA 13Oct50 – Air International Inc, Burbank, CA – L Figueredo (USA) Corp, New York, NY 16Feb51. PSA probably leased this from Air International.

1920 XB-HED returned to US as NC4843N prior to 18Jun48. N17334 is now in period American Airlines c/s and was based at Kansas City, MO by May 2005 – 'Flagship Detroit' (Oshkosh 2009). ACTIVE

1923 NC17313 to US Treasury Dept for War Dept and leased to PAA for use in Africa by 12Sep41.

1931 NC17316 to NX17316 14Dec40 and back to NC17136 16Dec40! Although with DSC from 18Aug42 this was only taken on War Dept charge from 23Mar43 – which does not relate to dates given in book! Returned to PAA 08Aug44 – To DC-3A 18Oct44 – From Western Div to Pacific Alaska Div Jul46 – Leased to Mexicana XA-GUF 10Feb48 – Bought 03Nov51 [Then to Aeronaves?].

1944 VH-ANR was taken by road to the Queensland Air Museum, Caloundra, and remained there in 2009 in Airlines of NSW c/s. PRESERVED

1948 42-56614 crash site was 30 m NW of Del Valle AAB, Austin, TX.

1949 NC16082 Eastern to DFC and lsd to PAA for use in Africa 12Sep41 – and to RAF.

1952 42-56611 landing accident at Omaha Mun. Apt., NE on 28Jun44 while based with Hq Sq, Bolling. NC18104 was with WAA which leased it to United Airlines, not DPC.

1954 NC18106 to DSC 21Sep42 and to War Dept 23Mar43. NC33324 canx as exported 19Dec49 to XT-… C.L.Chennault & W Willauer – Civil Air Transport as N8342C 19Dec49 – N1788B CAT 1953 – To TEMCO Aircraft Co. 09Dec53 – Later became N490.

1955 NC18107 – For DPC read WAA.

1957 NC18109 to DSC 03Aug42 – 42-56090 sold to PAA, Brownsville, TX in crashed condition 08Aug44 and rebuilt as DC-3A NC18109 25Jan45 – To Avianca 03Mar49 and US regn canx 30Mar49, therefore must have been HK-142 as the change from C- to HK- was on 01Jan49.

1958 42-56099 unit 24 TCS – Taxying accident 09Feb43 Del Valle AAB, Austin, TX leading to survey.

1959 42-56609 was with 25 TCS at Sedalia in Mar43.

1969 N17323 TWA to Union Steel & Wrecking and IJ Cohen & Co Inc., St Louis, MO B15Jan53 – Witbeck Acft Corp, Gainesville, TX 16Jun53 – USAF, Wright Patterson AFB 18Jun53 – Govt of Ecuador/FAE 13Aug53. As HK-3350, the fuselage remained at Villavicencio, Bogota in Jul08 and Feb10. STORED

1973 OK-AIH del to CSA 08Sep37.

1975 OH-VKB is currently displayed in the Helsinki Air Museum (Suomen Ilmailmuseo). DISPLAYED

1976 42-56093 is also quoted as crashing at Florence AAF, SC on 01Jul42. Premier, WV is the most recently quoted on Form 14.

1977 42-56101 was with 26 TCS, Bergstrom in Mar43.

1983 N18111 – On the death of David Tallichet in 2007 this DC-3, which had been displayed outside one of his Air Transport Command Restaurants at New Castle, DE, was bought by the Massey Aerodrome Museum at Massey, MD. They are restoring it for static display, but there is too much corrosion for it to be made airworthy. William Doucherty has kindly provided details from the FAA records and as this is comprehensive, it is given in full here:-

NC18111 United Air Lines Transport Corp, B02Sep37 R13Oct37 – United Air Lines R01May44 – Reed Pigman (American Flyers) B18May54 – Charter Air Center, Gainesville, FL B07Sep73 – Shawnee A/l, Orlando, FL B17Oct73 – Transecutive Avn Inc, Pittsburgh, PA B02May77 – Ernest & George Stern, Pittsburgh, PA B31Jul80 – Harvest Fields Missionary & Evangelistic Assoc, Sacramento, CA B05Sep80 – NASCO Leasing Co, Incline Village, NV B22Sep80 – Mercantile National Bank of Dallas Rep. 07Jan81 – Regn Canx 05Nov84 and sold to Specialty Restaurant Corp (never regd) – Dismantled

C/n 1973 DC-3 OK-AIH of Ceskoslovenska Letecka Spolecnost – CLS awaiting delivery from the USA. The photo is dated 20 August 1937, a couple of weeks prior to the official delivery date. This aircraft later became D-AAIH and crashed in 1940. *(Douglas Aircraft via Mike Hooks)*

and trucked to New Castle, DE between 1985 and 1990 [See book entry] – Gate guard to Air Transport Command Restaurant, New Castle, DE until 29Mar06, when restaurant closed. PRESERVED

1984 ZS-PAA (C9-ATG) noted at Rand Apt Jan07 and again in Apr09, devoid of wings or engines. STORED

1986 YR-PAF LARES to TARS – Transfer to Directorate of Civil Aviation 25Apr53 – TAROM op. by Aurel Vlaicu Flying School for Public Transport ca 1956 – wfu 07May59 fatigue – Canx 30Nov64 scrapped.

1989 NC18113 PAA to C-102 Avianca 06Jun40 – NC18113 PAA 23Jul40 – XA-BLN Mexicana 03Feb41 – C-105 Avianca 23Mar43 and PP-BHF.

1991 NC18115 Douglas to PAA 04Oct37 – Avianca 24Jun40 and US regn canx – probably as C-101 (unconfirmed.)

1992 NC18116 PAA to XA-BLW Mexicana 06May41 – C-104 Avianca prior to 25Jan44. PP-ANN remained in a children's playground at Sao Bernard do Campo. No recent news.

1993 NC18117 PAA to XA-BLO Mexicana 20Mar41 – NC18117 not cancelled but to DSC 17Jul41 – Lsd to PAA Air Ferries Inc by 12Sep41 for use in Africa. Crashed 19Apr42.

1995 is displayed as OK-XDM at Prague-Ruzyne airport. DISPLAYED

1997 N18121 was restored in Eastern A/l c/s in 1995, and remains with the Olympia Flight Museum, Vancouver, WA. ACTIVE

1998 CP-1128 – Restoration had been halted by Mar06. Remained at Cochabamba in Mar10, less many parts. STORED

1999 42-56632 forced landing 28Jul44 [EF], while with 4121 BU Kelly. See c/n 2246.

2000 N18124 continues to be displayed at the Smithsonian NASM in downtown Washington, DC. DISPLAYED

2008 ZS-KEX was in store, dismantled, with Springbok Flying Safaris at Rand Apt 2006-Sep 2010. STORED

2012 NC18937 actually went to C-100 with Avianca on 24Jun40.

2015 NC18951 crashed at Linden, MO.

2022 G-AGBE was regd to KLM at its London address on 01Aug40 – Canx 05Feb46 – Skyways Ltd R16Aug46 – Crashed 18Nov46.

2029 VH-ABR remains airworthy in ANA colours at Tullamarine, VIC. ACTIVE

2031 URSS-M Aeroflot still in service Apr42.

2032 URSS-B Aeroflot, op by 1 magon GVF 19Jul41.

2033 URSS-N Aeroflot crashed 06Jun43 in desert between Tihwa and Hami (China).

2053 N41HQ was flying as 38-0502 from Sausalito, CA in 2010. [See chapter on hybrid DC-2s] ACTIVE

2054 N134D of Cryder Networks is believed airworthy since 2005. ACTIVE

2096 MT-16 became URSS-L3403 R 29Jun39 and then URSS-D which was op. by 1 magon GVF on 19Jul41.

2102 N101MX fuselage has been separated into three parts, the nose and tail going to a local church for display!

2103 N294R was canx in 1975 and again on 24Jul09 as withdrawn.

2105 NC28340 was mounted on a pole at Augusta Richmond County Museum, Augusta, GA, but sold to Valiant Air Command to be used for spares to repair N3239T.

2108 N4565L fuselage was on display at AeroVenture, Doncaster, Yorkshire in Jul08. STORED

2110 Correct spelling of name as PH-ASR with KLM was "Roek".

2118 N14931 was named 'Northliner Michigan' with NCA. XA-KTB in store with Aero JBR at Laredo, TX Aug09. STORED

2119 ZS-JMP regd to T Robbertse & C J Muller was canx on 05Jul06.

2128 NC21717 sold by Douglas to Pan American Aviation Supply Corp, New York, 09Jun39 and to Pan American Airways on 20Jun39. Operated by UMCA, Cristobal, CZ – To Mexicana 20May41 (as XA-CAB). NC21717 canx 12Jul41.

2130 NC21715 was canx 20May48 on export to China. To C.L. Chennault & W Willauer to Civil Air Transport as N8340C 19Dec49 – Canx 22Jul53 – To N1789B C.A.T. SA 1953 – To TEMCO Acft Corp. 09Dec53 – Canx 19Mar68.

2134 NC21718 sold by Douglas to Pan American Aviation Supply Corp 19Jun39 and to PANAGRA 23Jun39 – Pan American Airways 23Jan47 – NC21718 canx 17Apr47 as to PP-PCP Panair do Brasil.

2135 Export CofA issued to Pan American Aviation Supply Corp 12Jul39 for use in China – To XT-91 – C.L.Chennault & W Willauer to Civil Air Transport as N8360C 19Dec49 – Scrapped in Hong Kong – Canx 26Mar53.

2137 Not suitable for BT-67 conversion. XA-RPE was removed to Tulsa, OK on 05Sep08, to be restored as N18141 in American colours and made airworthy. Regd to Tulsa Air & Space Museum 08Dec08. DISPLAYED

2141 carries dual marks C-GDAK and KN458 and was airworthy in Aug08. ACTIVE

2144 NC21728 continues to be displayed at the Henry Ford Museum, Dearborn, MI but in 2010 was painted in a period Northwest Airlines scheme (formerly in North Central colours). DISPLAYED

2145 N341A Legend Airways was last reported in Mar03 at Morrison, CO. ACTIVE

2148 was bought by Air France but not delivered – Sold to CNAC in Nov40 – Del Dec40 and i/s Jan41

2165 NC21752 Regd to Douglas Aircraft 06Jun39. Regd N900 to Owens-Illinois Glass – Ohio State University, Columbus, OH R27Dec62 and Reregd N110SU 08Jan63. N139D was withdrawn at Sonora Valley Apt, CA in Oct06, and removed to Schellville, CA for preservation. PRESERVED

2167 was still in store at Oshkosh in Jun10, as XA-RPN. It is being used for spares as the airframe is not suitable for BT-67 conversion. Officially regd N22357. STORED

C/n 2213 DC-3-277B N25673 is still airworthy and is flown in Continental Airlines colours. The aircraft was formerly kept at the Lone Star Flight Museum in Galveston, Texas, but is now at Houston. This photograph was taken when it flew to Oshkosh in July 1990. (Jennifer Gradidge)

2168 '39-2168' ground accident on 07May43 when it collided with 43-1963 at Washington, DC. It eventually crashed on 21May43 2m NW Robins, FL [nr border with GA]. Not used by PCA after this date.

2169 N26MA was airworthy at Lake Elsinore, CA in Nov07. At Hemet Valley, CA Aug09. ACTIVE

2170 N21782 shows no fate. It made a forced landing near Belle Glade, FL on 13Jul79. The airframe was 'turned over' to Frank Hill who salvaged the engines and removed the wings. The latter were run over by a vehicle from a nearby sod farm [whether intentionally is not specified!] and the fuselage was left at the crash site, but is no longer there. How this ties in with M J Supply at Aurora, CA is not known. [See c/n 2246]

2172 See also c/n 2246

2182 had no USAAF serial when it had an accident on 18Jun43 at Brownsville, TX while with 18 TTTD.

2183 NC25608 M 08Jan40, R21Aug40 to NWA – To Central Air Transport Corp, Shanghai B15Jan48 – N8338C to Chennault & Willauer – Civil Air Transport Inc, Dover, DE B19Dec49 - Canx 22Jul53 – N1791B C.A.T. SA 1953 – To TEMCO Acft Corp. 09Dec53 – Allied Aircraft Co B22Feb55 – Canx 30Apr56 [to Paraguay]

2184 NC25609 Northwest D13Jan40 – Canx 08Apr49 to China – C L Chennault & W Willauer – To Civil Air Transport Inc as N8339C 19Dec49 – Canx 22Jul53 – N1792B C.A.T. SA 1953 – TEMCO Acft Corp. 09Dec53 – Beldex Corp, St Louis, MO 03Mar55 – N41F Rr 15Mar55 – N1000A Rr 09Jun55 – Air Reduction Co 16Jun55 – Gordon Acft Inc., Union, NJ 26Feb63 – Premier Lsg 13Apr63 – R.R.Schubert 08Oct65 – Peter B Wise 12Jul78 – Estate of P B Wise – Jimmie H Falls, McAllen, TX 23Aug85. Destroyed in Mexico shortly thereafter (smuggling?) – Canx 10Jun02 [Delete ref to scr. Ft Lauderdale].

2185 N25610 M Jan40, R Feb40 to NWA to XT-... 01Feb50 Chennault & Willauer – N8341C Civil Air Transport 19Dec49-19Dec53 – N1790B C.A.T. SA 1953 – TEMCO Aircraft Corp 09Dec53 (after return by Communists?) – Then N491 etc.

2187 was '39-2187' when it was destroyed in mid-air collision on 05May44. It crashed off-shore 6m SW of Lake Worth, FL.

2193 N600RC was in use as an advert for 'Fantasy of Flight' at Polk City, FL in Oct05. STORED

2198 CF-PWH still on display in the Canadian Museum of Flight & Transportation, Langley, BC Jul09 - DISPLAYED

2201 YV-440C was noted at Ocumare Tuy Dec07, i/s with Aeroejecutivos. ACTIVE

2202 N21798 was in American Airlines colours at C R Smith Museum, Fort Worth, TX in Nov06. ACTIVE

2203 42-65581 was at Rosecrans Fld, MO by 22Nov43.

2204 N922CA of Champlain Air was at Plattsburgh, NY in Nov08 being prepared for delivery to Swiss Constellation Flyers Assoc. At Opa Locka, named 'Priscilla' 06Dec08. Registered to Dakota Air Services LLC, Miami, FL on 14Jan09. By April 2009 HB-IRJ had been applied and was regd to Francisco Agullo, Geneva on 14Apr09. It was delivered to Switzerland on 19May09. ACTIVE

2213 N25673 was in Texas Hall of Fame in Nov06. It was flown to Houston, TX to escape hurricane damage, and was present in Sep08. ACTIVE

2216 N61981 was noted at Oshkosh in 2008 and Jun10, for eventual conversion to BT-67. STORED

2217 RP-C368 was derelict at Manila, Philippines between Dec07 and Mar10. DERELICT

2223 42-38324 crashed 06Dec42 Presque Isle AAF, ME.

2224 NC25649 Eastern f/n should read 501.

2234 N25646 regd to Rich's Flying Service Inc, Newport, OR on 07Mar06, and is believed active. ACTIVE

2235 NC25647 was involved in a mid-air collision with A-26C 41-35553 in bad weather. Crashed 7 m SW of Burlington, SC on 12Jul45.

2236 N20TW was stored at Lake Elsinore in Jan08. At Hemet Valley, CA in Aug09. STORED

2239 N28AA had 'Poly-Fiber' titles from Jul00 to Jul09. ACTIVE

2241 N25668 remains noted near San Antonio Apt with Tradewinds Aircraft Supply in Aug09. STORED

2245 continues on display at Museum of Flight Foundation, Seattle as of Jul10, painted as NC91008. DISPLAYED

2246 NC15595 was operated by Eastern for the USAAF as 42-2246. It collided with B-18 37-566 at 36th Street Airport, Miami on 22Sep42. The DC-3 was on the runway, taxying towards the B-18 which was taking off. Both were destroyed. It therefore seems likely that 42-56632 was never used, so c/n 1999 is correct. It can never have returned to Eastern in Dec44. Apart from this C-49, two others, c/ns 2170 and 2172 were given pseudo USAAF serials – and neither ever received proper serials. 42-56619, 56622 and 56624 were not taken up (see p.120, Vols 1 & 2), so may have had some connection.

2247 N408D 'Lady Luck' was reported stored at Chicago in Jul08, but noted in poor condition at Ottawa, IL in 2009. STORED

2248 NC15592 was badly damaged on 10Mar41 nr Cincinnati, OH, but repaired.

PT-BFU is believed to remain on display at Fortaleza, Brazil, where it has been since 1993. DISPLAYED

2250 N72B after 29May53 insert People's Research & Mfg Co, Columbus, OH (1956).

2253 N28323 was reported derelict at San Juan in 1970 and was cancelled on 21Jul09 as wfu!

2255 42-56628 crashed 28Feb43 6m NE of Austin, TX with 31 TCS [FP].

2257 N102AP L A Puertorriquena, Carolina, PR. Canx 31Mar09 – probably w/o following forced landing in the Dominican Republic on 07Jun91.

2261 EI-ACB Douglas to Aer Lingus 18Oct40 ntu – Pacific Alaska A/ws 18Oct40 – NC19971 R02Nov40 – PAA 05May41 – Canx 19Jun41 – CNAC 29May41 – XT-92... Chennault & Willauer – N8359C Civil Air Transport 19Dec49 – Scrapped Hong Kong – Canx 26Mar53.

2263 The second N15583 was only issued on 06Oct50 while Island Air Ferries bought it a year earlier, and there is some doubt as to whether they actually used it under these marks, before its sale to Hercules Powder.

2266 NC25693 was with Braniff by May44.

2270 N496 of EAS Inc has been retired permanently at Houma, LA. Canx 23May07.

3250 NC28394 Eastern f/n 504.

3251 NC28395 Eastern f/n 505 [index has NC28393].

3260 XA-FUW Aeronaves de Mexico – Aerolineas Mexicana SA Apr56 – Aeronaves de Mexico 20Sep60.

3261 XA-FUV ownership as for c/n 3260. Apparently sank in Lake Casa Blanca, TX, but was recovered and is now displayed at the lakeside.

3263 42-38325 crashed on 19Jun43 at Whitehorse, YT, Canada.

3264 CF-VQV was reported displayed with Arctic Outposts Camps titles in Sep08. DISPLAYED

3265 42-56610 was with 26 TCS when it crashed 23Mar43 at Austin Municipal Apt, TX. The survey may refer to an earlier incident.

3269 N760 was at Hawthorne Science Centre until 2001. Displayed at Flight Path Museum, Los Angeles Apt in Jun08. DISPLAYED

3270, **3272** and **3282** are listed as 41-7685, 7687 and 7690 going to ATC Amberley (in Australia) in Feb42. It has been suggested that as the directive assigning them to the 5th AF in Australia was dated 03Jul42, they did not go to Australia before this. However, it may be that with ATC they did visit Amberley earlier on TDY. There was, surely, a need for transport in that theatre?

3275 DC-3A was PK-WWL until cancelled in 1981, when it disappeared! A DC-3A is on display as RI-001 in a museum in Jakarta as of Apr10, and may be this aircraft. DISPLAYED

3276 NC25623 NWA to DSC and leased to Pan American for use in Africa by 12Sep41.

3278 N28341 continues to fly in Delta A/l pre-war colours. ACTIVE.

3283 ETM-6045 Mexican AF is believed no longer in service.

3285 42-68860 was operated by Chicago & Southern for ATC when it crashed on 06Nov42 due to bad weather.

3289 41-7702 was damaged in an accident at Mullins, SC on 01Nov42 and assigned to Columbia, SC on 15Nov42 – and to Class 26 on 20Jan43 – instructional airframe. It appears that 'VHCDH' is an error, possibly for 41-7732.

3291 N600NA M C Flyers was reported at Daytona Beach, FL in Mar01, but is now at New Smyrna Beach, FL.

3294 NC1945 was under restoration in early TWA c/s with Save-A-Connie up to 2005 – On display in TWA museum hangar, Kansas City Jul09. PRESERVED

3297 41-7694 – a similar problem to c/n 3270 etc has been posed. However, here it would appear that the aircraft did not leave for Australia until 04Sep42 (not Jul42).

4082 N107B should be owned by Lehigh University. N200MX to Bobby L Willis, Kirtland, NM, R13Mar07. ACTIVE

4084 41-7696 after Chicago 01Aug43 should read 'Scott 11Jul44' and then RFC 23Jan45 [mix-up over date style!].

4085 N33639 was derelict at Dekalb Peachtree, GA, but may well have been removed by now.

4089 N79MA regd to Robert Lee Truelove, Durham, NC on 29Jun06. To WWII Airborne Demonstration Team Foundation, Frederick, OK 21Feb07 – Painted as '414089 A/8C 'Boop B Doop' in Jul09. ACTIVE

4093 YV-426C was derelict at Caracas in 2001, but no report since.

4110 N340EL was destroyed in film-making in 1973.

4112 N10CR National Cash Register add Dayton, OH (1956).

4113 42-56089 served with 26 TCS in Apr43.

4116 NC33653 American to DSC and lsd to PAA for use in Africa 12Sep41. See also details for c/n 4118 in Vol.2.

4120 VH-ANH was on display in Ansett-ANA c/s in Sep05 at Melbourne. DISPLAYED

4123 N33644 airworthy in Western A/l c/s in Apr04 to 2010. ACTIVE

4125 42-72087 crashed 06Feb43 5 mls WNW of Watson Lake, AK. The 1947 date seems doubtful.

4126 N129H is reported to have 'located' a new engine after six years grounded at Tullahoma, TN. ACTIVE

4128 N137PB was last reported in store at Fremont, OH in Sep04. STORED

4129 42-56636, accident 21Mar43 while with 25 TCS.

N715F del by road to Proud Bird Restaurant, east of Los Angeles Apt, 01Aug07 and was on display in Feb08. Tail removed by Aug09. DISPLAYED

4130 NC33674 Penn Central to DSC and lsd to Pan American for use in Africa by 12Sep41. Dates for these aircraft are almost certainly on paper only.

4132 42-56626 accident 30Mar43 while with 31 TCS.

4134 N1559K was finally canx on 09Oct09 (in FAA clearout). Last reported dumped at Bridgewater, VA.

4136 41-7701 was DBR at Bowman Fld, KY on 14Sep42 and condemned 16Sep42.

4138 N33632 was named 'Northliner North Dakota' with NCA. N166LG was reported active in Sep01, but by Dec08 it was reported dumped at Rialto airfield, CA in poor condition. DERELICT

4142 & **4143** – the fates for these two aircraft have been reversed according to the USAAF Form 14s. 41-7717 had a mid-air collision near Waller Fld, Trinidad on 01May43. 41-7718 crashed when it hit a mountain nr Palo Seca, Canal Zone on 16Jan43.

4144 41-7719 was with 204 BU Peterson 2AF, when it had a ground accident on 22Mar45 – probably resulting in its transfer to RFC Bush.

4174 AN-AWT was last reported wfu at Tegucigalpa in Nov07. STORED

4176 42-38336 had a take-off accident on 13Nov43 at Masira Island, Arabia. It is unlikely to have been salvaged as quoted.

4179 N49FN was last reported on the dump at Madrid, Colombia in Sep97. No recent report.

4201 17723 was still on display at Pima Museum, AZ in Feb08. DISPLAYED

4202 41-7724 was with 2527 BU South Plains on 14Nov44, then to 2539 BU, Foster CFTC in Mar45.

4203 41-7725 was del by 12 FRG in Jun43 and was with 12 TCS when it crashed on 24Feb44.

4211 41-7732 while with San Bernardino 4126 BU, CA this belly-landed at Santa Maria AAF, CA on 23Feb45, and so to instructional airframe and eventual sale as NC74654.

4215 41-7736 was with 6 FRS when it made a forced landing on 12Mar43.

4217 41-7738 Hq, 12 FrG, landing accident at El Fasher, Sudan Aug43. Possible cause of Cond.

4218 NC88771 Lsd by Lester R Daniels Jr, Sacramento, op. by Pacific A/l to Jun47 and name changed to Pacific A/ws Sep47.

Recently XA-CIL was reported stored at Nogales in Mar08. STORED

4219 N783T was last reported i/s in Feb10 at San Juan. ACTIVE

4221 MM61825 Italian AF continued to sit on the dump at Pratica di Mare in May08. DERELICT

4223 NC95433 was canx on 14Oct52 on sale to Jordan.

4236 MM61893 Italian AF was on the dump at Pratica di Mare in May08, but was restored as 'Gate Guard' there later in the year as MM61775. PRESERVED

4238 41-7751 to Central African ATC by 30Aug44.

4243 41-7756 6 FRS, 10 AF Mar43 and India-China ATC until at least 17Aug44.

4248 41-7761 Hq 6 AF Allbrook, CZ, landing accident at Rey Isle AF, Panama Aug46, from which it was not repaired.

4249 41-7762 was with ATC at time of accident.

4257 41-7770 6 AF, overran while landing on wet runway and hit house on19Aug42 San Jose, Costa Rica, but was repaired. [Runway drops 60ft between ends] – As given on p.323 this a/c crashed on 26Apr46 La Sabana Fld, San Jose, Costa Rica, and was w/o.

4259 41-7772 Oran (Stn 11), 12 AF, Algeria, landing accident 16Jan44. After repair it crashed 75mls ESE of Castel Bonito, Tunisia on 11Nov44.

4260 MM61800 was at Ditellandia Air Park, Italy, where it was last reported in Jan01. (Collection dispersed)

4261 41-7774 accident at Aldermaston, Berks on 16Sep42 – indicating arrival in UK.

4262 41-7775 5 FyG, Palm Springs, CA in Jun45.

4265 41-7778 taxying accident at Naha AB, Okinawa 16Jan46, leading to salvage.

4266 41-7779 crashed 15Oct42 Aldermaston, Berks. As there was no crew, this was probably parked. See c/n 4375.

4274 41-7787 India-China 3 FRS - Crashed on take-off Chabua 06Jan43.

4275 41-7788 13 FRS, 12 FrG, ATC 17May43 - Jun45 to 1345 BU, Kurmitola A/fld, India.

4279 41-7792 503 BU Washington Nat. Apt - take-off accident La Guardia 24Jul44, repaired.

4280 TC-27 continues to be displayed at Museo Aeroposta Gral Pecheco, Argentina. DISPLAYED

4281 NC21902 PAA bought from FLC (Italy) on 11Oct46 – The FAA file does not mention Westland – Avianca 28Jan47 but sold to Mexicana as XA-GEU Feb47 – US Regn Canx 13Feb47.

4282 'MT-203' has been on display at Museo Tecnologico de la CFE, Mexico City since Feb99, and was noted there in September 2009 in Mexican Navy colours. DISPLAYED

4291 41-7799 5 TCS Apr43.

4306 N781T was last reported wfu at San Juan, PR in Dec05 – Used as Restaurant Los Aviones, Barranquitas, Puerto Rico. DISPLAYED

4307 N50037 was only canx on 01Mar50 (oversight?).

HK-1315 was airworthy with VIARCO at Villavicencio in 2001. It was transferred to SADELCA and was in full c/s in Oct08. By May09 it had gone to ALIANSA and was in service at Villavicencio. ACTIVE.

4311 41-7812 TDY Hq 382 ASG, 10 AF, crashed at Mingaladon, Burma on 29May45 [EF]. The condemned date quoted on p.324 does not agree with the later fate, but the 1945 date seems more likely.

4314 FLC (Italy) to Pan American as NC21942 on 11Oct46 – Avianca 28Jan47 – US Regn Canx 17Feb47.

4315 41-7816 327 FRS, 12 AF 02Jul44, at time of accident.

4319 41-7820 1266 BU, Abadan, Iran ATC Aug45.

The FAA file for N53F gives:- W F Remmert/Beldex B24Dec55 ex Turkey – Beldex Corp R20Dec56 – Norman B Woolworth R24 Dec57 – Pauline E Woolworth R31Aug62 – Jack Richards Acft Sales Corp R29Nov62 – Peter Hand Brewery Co R17Dec64 – Houston Air Center Inc 07Jul65 – Rich-Air Co 03Feb67 – N2111M reserved. 03Jul67 for Wm B Blackmore – One-Eleven Aviation Corp R14Jul67 – Great Planes Sales Inc, 16Feb72 – Air Charter Inc R16Feb72 – Great Planes Sales Inc ret.02Apr76 – Florida General Aviation Corp R04Jun76 – R H Deskins R25Oct76 – Florida General R06Apr77 – Air Martinique LMay78 – Opa Locka Flight Center R26Jun78 – Titan Investments Phase I Inc R29Nov79 – Anglers Club LDec79 – Oslek Inc R18Jan80 – Seized at Cerro la Teta, Colombia 23Nov80 [Drug smuggling?] – HK-3994 Soc Aereo del Caqueta Ltda (Sadelca) R10Feb95 – restored at Villavicencio in Sep97 – Rr HK-4189 to SADELCA i/s Oct01. ACTIVE

4322 41-7823 811 BU, Lawson Fld, GA, take-off accident 27Nov44 Lawson Fld. Then instruction airframe.

4323 41-7824 crashed 11Jul43 during Operation Husky. [day/month inverted!].

4331 41-7832 accident on 08Sep45, leading possibly to its sale unrepaired?

4333 41-7834 is reported to have crashed 12 mls NW Casper, WY on 13Nov44, with 7 FyS Gore Fld. This conflicts with the book. Another report suggests a crash on 30Nov43! Form 14 gives date as 24Aug43['44?] Problems here! We prefer the latest date, with the Olmstead accident repaired.

4338 41-7839 Tinker Fld, ATSC Jun45.

4347 PT-KUC remained on display in Parque Jaime Duque, nr Bogota, Colombia in Mar08. DISPLAYED

4349 FLC (Italy) to Pan American as NC22428 and to Avianca on 28Jan47 as C-124.

HK-124 of LACOL remained in store at El Dorado, Bogota in Mar08. STORED

4358 41-7859 mid-air collision with B-26G 44-67970 13Dec44 Marrakech AB, French Morocco.

4359 41-7860 516 BU Rosecrans Sep44.

As N728G this was in service in May05 with K W Plastics Inc. Flying at Oshkosh 2009. ACTIVE

4363 ZS-MRU canx 14Jan08 as exported. To TF-AVN (ntu?) It was still stored at Dunsfold, Surrey in Jan08 and Aug09 as ZS-MRU. STORED

4369 N190BB reported sold by Hess Marketing to Efrain Stern et al 08May09. However this was sold as TG-ASA in 1979 and then as XA-KIK in 1980, becoming derelict in 1996.

4370 41-7862 16 TCS, 12 AF Jul44 – FLC (Italy) to NC21904 Pan American A/ws 11Oct46 – Turin to Brownsville DNov46 – Avianca D28Jan47 – US Regn Canx 17Feb47.

4374 41-7866 Burma on TDY with 18 TCS and suffered a landing accident at Myitkyina, Burma on 23May44. This may be cause of condemning.

4375 41-18337 Crashed 15Oct42 Aldermaston, Berks. A further accident was reported at Whitchurch, Bristol on 06Apr43 when it collided with c/n 4266.

4380 MM61826 Italian AF remains on display at Museo dell'Aviazione, Cerbaiola in 2005. DISPLAYED

4382 N782T Tol-Air ditched 1.5kms offshore St Thomas, US Virgin Islands 19Jul06 [EF].

4383 XA-GUX Aeronaves to Aerolineas Mexicanas SA Apr56 – Aeronaves 20Sep60.

4384 41-18346 15 AF, mid-air collision 30May44 with 41-18356 over Bari Apt., Italy.

4387 41-18349 37 TCS Catania 24Nov43.

4392 41-18354 51 TCS, 12 AF 14Apr44 and 23Jan45 in Italy.

4394 41-18356 – mid-air collision with 41-18346 30May44 – see above.

4395 41-18357 18 TCS 08Feb45 when it had a minor mid-air collision.

4401 41-18363 15 TCS Lawson, Feb43 – Accident on 26Jul43 at Muskogee County Apt, GA. – probably cause of loss to inventory?

4402 41-18364 Bergstrom Oct44.

4404 NC18648 Universal ex RFC 07Feb46 - Stuart Robertson, New York, NY 13Jun47 [after Universal's bankruptcy] – Universal Equities Inc, New York 14Jun47 – Chesapeake A/ws Inc, Salisbury, MD 04Jan48 – LANSA Airlines DMar49.

4405 41-18367 35 TCS, 12 AF 29Oct44, when it was bogged down. It was hit by A-20K 44-350 at Cherbourg.

4406 41-18368 fate is given as taxying accident at Rome, Ciampino, so maybe forced landing after the mid-air.

4408 41-18370 crashed at Le Khroub AB, Libya.

4409 49-2625 Greek AF stored at Athens-Ellinikon Nov00. STORED

4412 41-18374 18 TCS moved on TDY to Burma with 18 TCS and ground-looped on 20May44 at Myitkyina, Burma. This was a write-off.

4414 FLC (Italy) to NC2241 Pan American A/ws 11Oct46 – to Brownsville, TX DNov46 – Avianca 28Jan47 – US Regn Canx 17Feb47.

HK-122 ALIANSA was stored at Villavicencio in Jul08. STORED

4415 NC86564 was allotted to RFC initially but first regd to Panagra. This may have become CB-33.

4417 41-18379 with 15 TCS when crashed 16Sep42 at Pope Fld, Ft Bragg, NC [PE]

4420 41-18382 4 TCS, 62 TCG, 15 AF, crashed 30Jun44 at Ponte Olivo, Sicily [EF]

4421 41-18383 67 TCS, mid-air collision with 42-23367 at Sedalia AAF, MO and crashed, 16Apr43.

4423 41-18385 5 TCS in Apr43, and 813 BU Sedalia in Jun44. As VR-HDB this remains on display in the Hong Kong Museum of Science and Technology as of May09. DISPLAYED

4431 41-18393 14 TCS Mar43 - Hit trees on approach and crashed 16Dec44 George Fld, Lawrenceville, IL [PE/BW]. This disagrees with earlier report, but was from accident report.

4433 The file for C-FYED shows no reference to PT-LGO and the aircraft was operated as C-FYED throughout 1985 and 1986. N193DP remained stored at California City, CA in July 2009, and had not flown for three years. STORED

4437 Bu 01981 VMJ-253, hit mountain on take-off 09Oct42 1ml from Tontouta, New Caledonia

4438 N220GB was noted at Shell Creek Airpark, FL in Mar07, in operational condition. Sold to Flightstar Group Inc, 29Nov07, R02Jun08 – Madken LLC, Lewes, DE – i/s at Ft Lauderdale Dec08 – Stored at Shell Creek in Feb10. STORED

4439 WAA to Oliver W Hiester, Elizabeth, NJ as NC15587 – Bruning Avn., Springfield, MA 16Dec46 – Babb Co Inc, New York, NY 15Jul49 – USAF 23Aug49. [No ref. to Regina Cargo on file – so possibly leased]. This was one of 30 C-47s sold by Babb to the USAF and converted to C-47 by Aviation Maintenance Corp, Van Nuys, CA for Greece under MAP. No papers were filed for the transaction. A USAF serial 49-29xx would have been used.

4442 41-18395 807 BU Bergstrom, taxying accident Bergstrom Fld, TX 12Aug44.

4443 41-18396 crashed 2.5mls from Grenada AAF, MS 13Feb44 [PE]. Although the date nearly agrees with the earlier report, the place is not the same. Grenada seems more likely. 307 TCS moved there on 28Jan44.

4451 41-38570 12 FyG, ATC 05May43.

4453 41-38572 Hq 12 FyG Mar43.

4455 41-38574 6 FyS 23Apr43.

4457 41-38576 1306 BU, Karachi Feb45.

4459 41-38578 6 FyS, take-off accident 23Apr43, Chabua, when lost.

4462 41-18400 1105 BU Miami ATC May45 – Accident Miami in Oct45, from which it was possibly never repaired.

4463 N150D Ozark Airlines Museum, St Louis, MO. Preserved Oct03. ACTIVE

4466 NC14937 Air Cargo Transport Co. R10Oct45 – International Airlines Inc. Chicago, IL R21Jun46 – to Cuba as CU-P-144 prior to 08Jul47.

4469 41-18407 56 TCS May43.

C/n 4414 C-47-DL HK-122 was operated by SELVA Colombia, where this photo was taken at Villavicencio in November 1980. The aircraft was operated by the same airline until 1994. *(Rob Hemelrijk)*

4473 41-18411 15 AF, France by 24Oct44.

4474 41-18412 ground accident at BAD.2 Warton, 8 AF on 15Apr44. As there is no further data, this could have been a write-off.

4478 41-18416 53 TCS Pope Fld, Mar43.

4479 EC-EJB, after storage at Son Bonet, Majorca since 1993, this was placed on a pylon as a gate guard at Son Bonet on 11Dec07. Some components are still missing. DISPLAYED

4481 49-2620 Greek AF stored at Sedes in 1996. Current state unknown. STORED

4489 41-18427 313 TpS, 31 ATG, 9 AF, Chartres (A-40), France Nov44.

4490 41-18428 314 FyS, 9 AF May44.

4492 41-18430 14 TCS 10Feb43. Crashed on that date.

4500 U-603 Indonesian Navy is believed still stored at Surabaya, Java. STORED

4501 NC67826 Cal Aero was based at Glendale, CA (not Burbank).

4502 41-18440 DBR in ground collision with C-47 41-18591 at Maxton AAB on 23Jan43. Laurinburg and Maxton were merged.

4503 41-18441 315 TCS Dec42 – 86 TpS, 8 AF on 10Aug43.

4508 41-18446 the accident report gives Gaudo, not Gando, neither of which can be found on a map of Italy.

4510 41-18448 9 AF by the time of its accident on 15Sep44.

4511 41-18449 4 TCS – Crashed 23Aug42 Patterson Fld, OH, [brakes failed to hold due to wet runway and a/c hit fence [PE]]

4513 41-18451 2528 BU Midland, TX – Crashed 20Apr45 3.5mls S of Sweetwater, TX [BW/SF]

4516 41-18454 307 TCS, Grenada AAF, MS Feb44 – NC86565 was at first allotted to RFC but registered to Panagra – Sold to Argentine AF in 1947.

4519 NC67825 Cal Aero was based at Glendale, not Burbank, CA.

AN-ASP LANICA remained on the dump at Tegucigalpa in Mar09. DERELICT

4523 41-18461 86 ATS, Heston, 8 AF 27Sep44.

4524 41-18462 3 TCS Mar43. Scottsbluff is in NE not NB.

4526 41-18464 15 AF, at Bari, Italy, had a take-off accident at Kerman, Iran on 15Mar45. Delete 22Dec44.

4527 41-18465 813 BU Sedalia May44.

4528 41-38579 12 AF, Sicily Jun44.

4530 41-38581 12 FyG, ATC Hq, when it crashed on 16Feb43, nr Takoradi, Gold Coast [now Ghana]

4531 41-38582 12 FyG - crashed 22Apr43 Cape Palma, Liberia [SF].

4532 41-38583 del by 12 FyG 30Jun43.

4533 41-38584 12 FyG Hq, Jul43.

4537 41-38588 in Dec44 Lubbock was 2527 BU South Plains.

4538 NC17884 was lsd to United Air Lines by WAA (not DPC).

N91314 McCollough Holdings LLC, Parker, CO R06Jul06 – Lsd to Cascade – Airworthy in Sep08. ACTIVE

4539 41-38590 by Dec43 this was based at Grenada.

4541 RX-87 was re-registered effective 15Nov51.

4542 41-38593 was based at Grenada in Nov43.

4544 41-38595 2527 BU South Plains in Jan45.

4545 41-38596 813 BU Sedalia, crashed 05Jun44 3mls SE of Fayette, MO. Although fatal, the a/c seems to have been repaired. A fatal accident could mean ground crew walking into a propeller, but this accident involved a survey, so there must be some reason why there appears to be a seven year gap in the history.

N44V with Carolinas Historic Avn 2010. ACTIVE

4546 41-38597 97 FyS, ATC15Sep43.

4547 41-38598 9 TCS, 813 BU Sedalia May44.

4549 41-38600 43 TCS, 315 TCG 8 AF 21Jan43.

4550 N51D probably still derelict at El Mirage, CA – last noted Oct07. DERELICT

4558 41-18466 3 TCS at time of accident 27Jun43.

4560 41-18468 307 TCS, Grenada, when it crashed on 03Mar44 [EF]. Delete 'USA 10Mar44' as crash date prior to this.

4563 NC50474 owner's name changed to Pacific Airways Sep47. Bankrupt later in year.

CF-IAE remained preserved Province of Alberta Museum, Wetaskiwin in Sep08. PRESERVED

4564 N57626 Nord Aviation was noted in service at Montgomery, AL in Jun07. ACTIVE

4565 41-18473 807 BU, Bergstrom Dec44.

4567 41-18475 Hq 12 FyG Jun43.

4568 41-18476 61 TC, 807 BU, Bergstrom May44.

4570 41-18478 had an accident at Auburn-Opelika Apt, AL. Another reported accident was 2mls NE of Pope AAF, NC. With 5 TCS in May43. No date for either accident, but obviously repaired.

4571 41-18479 – Bases in Nov42 are confused. It had an accident at Santa Monica on 09Nov42, based at Lawson. In May44 it was with 805 BU at Alliance.

4572 41-18480 15 AF, Hq Italy, May45.

4573 N8356C canx 07Oct65 – Fate unknown but probably remained in China, with communists.

4574 41-18482 9 TCS, Jun43 and 807 BU Bergstrom on 19Nov44.

N99 FAA to US Forest Service 09Mar77 – Canx 29May02 – Stored in Alaska Historical and Transportation Museum, Wasilla, in FAA colours Jul10. STORED

4575 41-18483 13 FyS – Crashed 0Jun43 Sookerating, India. DBF.

4576 41-18484 landing accident 04Apr45 La Senia, Algeria.

4577 41-18485 unit 43 TCS at time of accident, nr top of Kittatinny Ridge, 5mls west of Blairstown, NJ [PE/BW]

4579 41-18487 preserved at Ste. Mère l'Eglise – Dismantled and moved to Lorient-Lann-Bihoué 07May10 as gate guardian. PRESERVED

4583 Although this is reported to have crashed in Feb85 as N28BA at Charlotte, NC, it is now reported to have been rebuilt as HR-ALU with SETCO in 1988 (c/n hitherto unknown). WFU at Tegucigalpa in 1992, it has been restored to Aerovias Centroamericanos (Aviac), named 'La Pinta', flying again on 13Nov09 from Tegucigalpa, after 20 years inactivity. ACTIVE

4584 NC18639 European Div., ATC, War Dept. Canx 03Jan46 at War Dept's request. Broken up?

4593 41-18501 2527 BU South Plains Jan45.

4596 41-18504 2527 BU South Plains.

4597 41-18505 base 568, ATC, Iceland - Crash-landed 05Aug45 30mls SE Des, Iceland.

4598 41-18506 805 BU Alliance May44.

4599 41-18507 Form 14 gives date as 22Aug43 not 1944.

4600 41-18508 Aden ATC – Crash 15Jul44 in Aden,

4602 41-18510 take-off accident 23Aug44, Idalou Aux. Fld, South Plains (2527 BU), TX [EF] – 2539 BU Foster, accident 31Mar45.

4605 41-18513 airstrip A-25C was in France at Bolleville.

4606 41-18514 33 FS, 342 CG. Accident was a ground loop.

4607 NC67827 Cal Aero was based at Glendale, CA, not Burbank.

4610 41-18518 3 FRS, Apr43 – With 6 TpS when it went missing.

4612 41-18520 18 TCS, 30Jul44.

4613 41-18521 15 TCS, mid-air collision with 42-32871. Repaired. In Jan45 it was still attached to 805 BU George.

4620 41-18528 was based at S.19 at time of accident.

4622 41-18530 crashed 24Apr46 10m from Tarawa Atoll, Gilbert Island, SW Pacific [EF]

4627 FAEC 203, crashed 27Aug47 (or 27Aug48 according to Lloyds List) while on test flight with Aerovias Cubanas Internacionales at Havana. Whether this had a civil registration is unknown.

4632 41-38604 813 BU Sedalia, crashed 21Jul44 Grandview Apt, MO.

4634 41-38606 64 TCS, Pope, May43 – 811 BU, Lawson, 1 TCC, Dec44.

4636 41-38608 37 TCS 05Nov43, when it had a landing accident at El Aouina, Tunisia while being ferried by 313 FyS to 12 AF, not 9 AF. It was repaired and went via 313 FRS to 9 AF in Jul44. It crashed subsequently on 22Dec44 on Nadens-Dawstore Farm, England (county?), while with 363 TrG.

4640 41-38612 cause of accident PE/BW.

4641 41-38613 crashed 18Apr44 2 mls S of Chowdhurani, India.

4646 41-38618 was with 6 Ferry Div, ATC when it crashed on 26Aug42 [SF –elevator detached].

4654 C-FYQG remained stored at Red Deer, Alta, in Sep08. STORED

4658 49-2617 Greek AF still on dump at Sedes Nov07. DERELICT

4662 41-18537 caught fire during test flight on 06Oct42. Forced landing at Buena Park, CA. Nose section damaged, but repaired and test flying with Douglas continued.

4664 0296 CTA-15 Argentine Navy, first flight from the Americas to Antarctica and back, preserved at Buenos Aires-Ezeiza. PRESERVED

4666 41-18541 45 TCS, 9 AF, accident at Folkingham, Lincs on 05Apr44.

Was displayed at Whitehorse, YT as CF-CPY with Yukon Transportation Museum. Removed from pole as serious corrosion had set in and future was uncertain. After restoration, placed on a new pole.

4667 HB-ISB continued to be stored at Mollis in Aug08, for sale. PRESERVED

4668 41-18543 6 TpS, ATC, 10 AF, crashed on 25Aug43.

4670 41-18545 was with 13 FyS when lost.

4672 41-18547 crashed 10Nov44 11mls from Yunnanyi.

4678 41-18553 cause of accident was engine failure, leading to forced landing.

4679 41-18554 crash date was 03Mar45.

4682 41-18557 Sedalia Oct44.

4684 RFC to NC18775 Pacific Coast A/l 05Jan46 – Pacific Finance Loans (California), Los Angeles, CA prior to 25Oct48 – Kirk Kerkorian, Los Angeles 17Dec48 – K Kerkorian and Rose Pechuls t/a Los Angeles Air Service, Los Angeles 20Feb50 – K Kerkorian, t/a LAAS 05May50 – Canx 05May50 to Brasil [Op as Pacific A/l, ceased ops Jun47, to Pacific A/ws Sep47].

4686 41-18561 15 TCS, Mar43, in USA.

4687 41-18562 60 TCS, crashed 15May43 on Gingercake Mt, NC.

4688 FLC (Italy) sold to Pan American as NC22410 and on to Avianca on 28Jan47 – C-122 was an error because c/n 4414 was already C-122, and C-101 was used.

4693 41-18568 40 TCS, 17Jul43.

4704 41-18579 5 FyG, Love ATC Aug45.

4705 41-18580 805 BU George Mar45. YV-C-AKE believed preserved in Museo Aeronautico de la F A Venezolana, Maracay. PRESERVED

4707 41-18582 crashed 13Mar45 35mls W of George, McMillan, TX [BW].

4711 41-18586 2527 BU South Plains, Nov44 and Jan45.

4715 N86553 Antillian Puerto Rico Inc, San Juan, PR R24Jul06 – to Linea Aerea Puertoriquena Inc, Carolina, PR R15Mar07 – Thirsty 13th LLC, New York, NY R21Jan10 – At Vintage Flying Museum, Meacham Fld, Ft Worth, TX. ACTIVE

4726 41-18601 1537 BU Harmon, ATC had a taxying accident at Harmon Fld, Guam on 09Apr46. It had a take-off accident on Guam on 05Jul46, which may have caused w/o.

4727 N734H Good Avn LLC, Grand Rapids, NE was i/s Jul01 and on maintenance at Oshkosh Jun10. ACTIVE

4728 41-18603 was with 35 TCS at time of crash, 3mls SW of Montieri.

4733 N1XP was painted 'Duggy' in Apr05. To Duggy Foundation, Page, ND R28Aug07. Preserved at Page, ND Jul08-2010. ACTIVE

4735 41-38632 805 BU George, 1 TCC had an accident at Chicago in Dec44.

4737 41-38634 574 BU Winslow, AZ, landing accident 9Aug45 Winslow, AZ. DBR.

4738 41-38635 – Crash location was south shore of Lake Iliamna, but another report gives Lake Wiamann, AK. Wreckage not found until 19Aug43 [probably BW]

4739 41-38636 2527BU South Plains, Jan45.

4740 41-38637 had an accident on 05Aug45 in Mississippi, possibly the cause of its move to RFC Bush – which it failed to survive.

4741 41-38638 42 TCS 02Jun43. Based at 807 BU, Bergstrom Dec44.

4743 41-38640 crashed 22Jan44 at Granada, MS but was repaired. It was based at 2517 BU Ellington with CFTC in Feb45 when it had a minor accident.

4747 N19906 was leased to Majestic A/l from Apr91 to Jan96. Stored at Anchorage, AK in Jun08 and Jul10, engineless in basic Reeve Aleutian colours. To be donated to local museum. STORED

4751 41-38648 Courtland was 2115 BU.

4752 41-38649 813 BU Sedalia, MO when it crashed.

4753 41-38650 5 TCS Feb44. George was 805 BU in Dec44.

4765 41-18604 transfer to Hamiata as URSS-R R26Aug43.

4766 41-18605 Hq 12 Tpg at time of crash.

4769 41-18608 had a landing accident at Burtonwood 8 AF on 14Apr43. Possibly a w/o?

4771 became first C-47 on Soviet register as CCCP-X361 op. by Daltroi NKVD.

4772 41-18611 805 BU George, crashed 05Jan45 8mls NW of Sumner, IL.

4773 41-18612 560 BU Palm Springs, taxying accident there, leading to its sale.

4774 41-18614 crashed 10Nov42 6mls NW of Lockhart, SC. [broke up in turbulence]

4777 41-18616 unit at time of accident was 6 TCS. Place was Gioia de Colle.

4778 41-18617 India-China Wg, taxying accident 14Jun45 at Wellingdon AD, New Delhi. W/o.

4781 41-18620 1346 BU, Tezgaon AB, India in Oct45.

4782 41-18621 807 BU Bergstrom when it crashed on 16Apr44.

4784 N7119 of Aero Service crashed on 17Jun73 at Tamanrasset, Algeria.

4785 41-18624 805 BU George in Dec44. C-FFAY Buffalo, fuselage remains stored at Red Deer, Alta in Sep08. STORED

4787 41-18626 crash date was 26Aug43.

4790 '434790' was stored, derelict, at W Palm Beach, FL in Mar04. As Speciality Restaurants ceased trading, this may have been moved.

4795 41-18634 with 66 TCS in Jun43.

4798 41-18637 58 TCS, Baer, Mar43 – 9 TCS Oct43.

4799 regd 24Sep43 to Aeroflot as CCCP-L829.

4805 operated by American as 41-7711 from 28Jun44 – NC15577 American R23Aug44 – B07Oct44.

4806 PI-C718 David M Reyes, CofA quoted in 1968 register as expired.

4810 41-20045 was delivered to Hawaii on 17Dec41 (not '42). N90A was reregd N711T on 04Jun62.

N1030D remained derelict at Hawkins Fld, MS in Jul08. DERELICT

4814 41-7715 was reported DBR on 23Jul44 at Isla del Rey, Panama and condemned 27Jul44. It was rebuilt by Pan Am so the subsequent history is not incompatible.

4817 41-20047 42 TCS – Crashed 19Oct42 near Fort Randall, Cold Bay, AK [BW]

4818 41-20048 42 TCS - Crashed 05Jul42, Bering Sea, 25mls NE of Ft Randall, Cold Bay, AK.

4819 41-20049 805 BU Alliance 'hit the ground' 07Jun44 at Alliance, but was repaired.

4823 PI-C149 Philippine Airlines to Ladnor M Moore, c/o Indonesian A/ws, Rangoon, Burma 07Feb50 – N4630V LM Moore Arcadia, CA 30Jun51 – Aircraft Sales Ltd, Los Angeles, 17Aug51 – Wardell Hatch 21Aug51 – Cruzeiro 21Nov51 – etc.

4824 670 F A Colombiana believed preserved at Madrid, Bogota Jun08. PRESERVED

4825 41-20055 32 TCS Feb43.

4826 41-20056 TDY 6 FyS – Crash location was Hkashanga, Myitkyina Hills in northern Burma.

4827 N122CA fuselage derelict at Plattsburgh-Clinton City Jul02. No further news.

4828 'HB-IRN' preserved at Munich-FJS since 1993. PRESERVED

4830 OB-R-581 was preserved at Lima, Peru in Nov01. Current? PRESERVED

4836 41-20066 which crash-landed at Vansittart Bay, WA (Australia) on 25Feb42, was visited by retired Qantas pilot Toby Gursansky on 17Jun08. The wreck has become an attraction for tour ships, and apart from removal of engines and control surfaces, is relatively intact 66 years after it landed. Part of the fuselage has been removed, possibly to build a shelter. DERELICT

4839 41-20069 - the accident date was 16Jun42 according to official sources.

4844 41-20074 2527 BU Lubbock, take-off accident 03Aug44 Idalon Aux. Fld, South Plains, TX.

4846 41-20076 13 FyS, 10 AF, when it crashed on 26May43.

4848 41-20078 returned to Homestead in 1944, not 1945.

4849 41-20079 returned to Homestead in 1944, not 1945.

4850 41-20080 Bocca di Falso is at Palermo, Sicily.

4852 CNAC 48 was ferried from Miami on 16Feb42 and was i/s 01Mar42.

4853 CNAC 49 was ferried from Miami with #48 on 17Feb42 and entered service on 05Mar42.

4854 41-20084 41 FyS 14Apr43 [del W Africa to Washington].

4856 41-20086 10 AF, accident at Agra, India on 22Feb45.

4857 41-20087 missing 03Jan43 on flight from Kunming to Chabua. No sign of wreckage by Aug44.

4858 N87625 Aero American Acft Parts Co, dismantled ca 1977.

4859 XT-... Chennault & Willauer to Civil Air Transport as N8337C 19Dec49 – N1793B C.A.T. SA – To TEMCO Acft Corp 09Dec53 – Canx 30Jun71.

4860 41-20090 48 TPS, 14 TPG Jul43.

4861 41-20091 PAA, Miami in Jun43.

4862 N2647 was stored at San Juan-Isla Grande in Oct00. No recent news.

4863 41-20093 reported stored on south base at Edwards AFB, CA in Mar09. This served with the US Navy until 1946, so must be suspect. STORED

4865 41-20095 12 AF, damaged May44 Casablanca. '41-20095' pres. at USAF Museum, Wright Patterson, OH. PRESERVED

4866 41-20096 ran off end of runway at New Delhi on 23Jun44. Although not seriously damaged, was not repaired

4867 41-20097 operated by Northwest during WWII – DPC via RFC to NC15583 05May45 and leased to Panagra 16May45; B02Jul45, f/n P-54 – CB-35 LAB B02Jan48, R22Apr48. [22Aug45 incorrect].

4868 41-20098 missing on 20Dec42 between Yunnayi and Chabua. Wreckage found in Assam, Himalayas in Aug77. Named 'Lady Luck'.

4869 N19919 now reported sold to Ernest Stern 12May09. It was canx in 1982 as wfu at Sarasota, FL.

4870 41-20100 6 TpS Jul43. It actually crashed into the River Ganges nr Bhagalpur (1303 BU), India, while engaged in low flying on 06Dec44 [PE]

4871 XT-90 - Chennault & Willauer to Civil Air Transport Inc N8362C R19Dec49 – N26H Halliburton Oil Well Cementing R26May53 – P & M Leasing R13Oct67 – First National Bank R 18Mar69 – Oklahoma State Univ. 01Apr71 – William E Harrison t/a Bixby Acft Sales 19Feb74 – Midwest Ltd, Lenexa, KS 14Mar74 – Richard B Bergstrasser 03Apr75 – Mace Aviation, Globe, AZ 10Dec?? – La Mesa Lsg 11Sep80? – N39DT Rr15Nov80 – DBR 28Jul87.

4873 41-20103 is quoted as DBF on 03Jan43 at Kano, Nigeria [EF]. This presents a problem. Does DBF mean 'damaged by fire' in this case?

4874 41-20104 10 AF, ground accident 09Jun45 at Ondal, India.

4875 41-20105 12 TpG ATC, minor mid-air collision on 30Sep43 – Nth Africa Wg ATC 24Mar44

4877 N242SM was still mounted on plinth at Santa Monica Apt in Oct09. This was officially re-regd N242SM on 31Jul09, although painted as such since Dec05! 'Spirit of Santa Monica' PRESERVED

4886 41-20116 38 TCS, at Sedalia in Feb43. In-flight collision with NC18951 on 04Nov42, losing 12ft of starboard wing. Landed safely. See c/n 2015 in Vol 2.

4889 41-20119 31 TCS, take-off accident at Bergstrom AAF, 11Oct43 [PE]. Sold to Pan American for repair.

NC19949 sold by Flying Tiger to TACA late 1948.

4890 ZS-OJD was last reported in Aug01 at Lubumbashi, DRC. Current status unknown.

4892 NC45398 was leased to United by WAA, not RFC.

4894 N763A was displayed at Bloomington in Jul08 in Ozark A/l colours, as part of Prairie Avn. Museum. To Antique Aircraft Restoration, Marathon, FL R28Apr09 and then to Thomas F Kirby, Marathon, FL 04May09. Ferried to Marathon on 23Apr09. There Jan10. ACTIVE

4897 41-20127 43 TCS 8 AF had landing accident at Boxted on 24Jun43, leading to write-off.

4898 41-20128 13 FyS missing 26Jan43 between Yunnayi and Sookerating. No signs by Aug44.

4899 41-20129 44 TCS, 12 AF at time of crash. Crash site given as Bo Rizzo, Sicily.

4900 N56V in Piedmont A/l colours was displayed at Durham Museum of Life & Science at Durham, NC from Jan02. PRESERVED

4901 41-20131 60 TCS crashed 17Apr43 Wiley Post Apt, OK [EF].

4903 N23SA remains dumped at Basler's hangar, Oshkosh 2009. Rear fuselage used to repair accident to BT-67 in Antarctic. Remains of aircraft still in field at Oshkosh Jul10. DERELICT

4904 CNAC #53 – the crash site, on Kao 1 Kung Ridge S of Hpimaw Pass, was visited in Oct96 and the airframe was subsequently moved to Pimaw, China. The right wing was then moved to Kunming to become part of a memorial in honour of the crews who flew the 'hump'.

4905 41-20135 65 TCS Alliance Feb43.

4906 41-20136 had an accident in Germany on 27Feb45, but this may be too early to account for exclusion in Feb47.

C/n 4932 XC-53A serial 42-6480 was tested with full-span flaps in 1943/44 and went to the USAF Museum in 1945, but was reclaimed in 1949. It was sold and converted to DC-3 standard and is now registered N603MC. The photograph was taken as the XC-53A in 1946. (Harold Martin)

4910 42-6458 41 FyS ATC Jan43.

4913 42-6461 9 AF 31 ATG, 325 FyS crashed on 13Mar45 1ml NE of Vitra, NW St Dizier, France [EF]. Or Vitre, E of Rennes.

4915 42-6463 was with 15 TCS at Pope on 15Aug42. The pilot became lost in bad weather and hit high ground. There was no radio operator on board [PE/BW]

4918 XB-EMX was to become part of Technological Museum of Space, Toluca, but remained on dump in Nov07. STORED

4923 42-6471 India-China ATC 22 TpG/88 TpS when it crashed 0.75ml N of Dum Dum, Calcutta.

4924 42-6472 landing accident at Chabua AB on 22Apr44 due to EF. This might have been the cause of exclusion a year later.

4926 42-6474 was at South Plains by 26Apr44.

N22RB To Dodson International Parts Inc – Canx 24Feb06, probably dismantled.

4927 XT-... Chennault & Willauer to Civil Air Transport as N8361C 19Dec49 – Canx 07Oct65 as WFU – probably remained in China and date is a tidying up exercise.

4928 42-6476 807 BU Bergstrom Jun44 – NC19932 was actually leased by WAA to United – not DPC.

4932 N603MC Odegaard Avn Inc, Fargo, ND. Preserved at Fargo Jul08 - 2010. ACTIVE

4935 N86584 Skydive Arizona, Eloy, AZ was active in Oct08 and Aug09. ACTIVE

4936 N90U reregd N9012 on 14Jun67.

4938 42-6486 with 381 SrS, 7 PRG, 8 AF, crashed 27Nov44 at Bas Wareton, Belgium.

4939 N169RB was officially canx on 01Jul09 as WFU. This is part of an FAA catching-up exercise!

4941 N15563 although canx in 1982, this is now given as canx, WFU 30Jun09

4944 42-6492 N Africa ATC 47 FyS 05Jul43.

4945 42-6493 lost in take-off accident.

4947 42-6495 42 TCS 08Dec42.

4955 WAA to Great Continental A/l, Miami, FL as NC18491 24Sep46 – To Venezuela 02Apr48.

4966 43-2020 9 AF, 44 TCS by 29Feb44.

4968 PP-CBT was preserved in Cruzeiro c/s in park at Manaus, Amazonas in 1996. DISPLAYED?

4975 NC86596 was leased to United by WAA not by RFC.
This airframe was reported derelict at Bayamon, PR in Nov01.

4978 10 TCG, Alliance Mar44. N32MS Regd to Delaware Warbirds LLC 03Mar06 – On display at Best museum, Netherlands, as '290321' Jun07 – Regd to Robert Reid, Mesa, AZ 29Mar10 – presumably still DISPLAYED

4979 NC19934 was leased to United by WAA not by DPC.

With Musée Européen de l'Aviation de Chasse in Apr02. DISPLAYED

4980 43-2024 Sedalia Apr44.

4983 N12978 was named 'Northliner Masali' with NCA.

4984 N207U listed as canx 1970, has now been canx by FAA on 13Jul09.

4988 43-1963 1105 BU, Miami AAF, 08Mar45.

4990 43-1965 with 7 Ferry, Gore, this crashed on take-off at Gore, MT 07Dec44 [Crossed controls]. Probably to RFC as was and used for spares.

4991 43-1966 with American Airlines while based at La Guardia in May43.

4992 XA-JOI was impounded at Oaxaca for non-payment of landing fees in 1987, and was still there in 1992. No further news.

4995 43-1971 crashed 19Aug43 at Boston, MA. Also reported crashed Hampstead, NH but no date.

4996 N12954 owner R L Kreloff, Eugene, OK was last reported in Oct99.

4999 NC17109 was leased to United by WAA not DPC. Cvtd to DC-3A by United 10Dec45.

5000 43-1982 crashed on 02Jan44 at Mines Fld, Los Angeles, CA.

6000 regd 10Nov43 to Aeroflot as CCCP-L809.

6001 regd 24Sep43 to Aeroflot as CCCP-L810.

6002 regd 24Sep43 to Aeroflot as CCCP-L811.

6004 41-18643 transfer to Hamiata as URSS-P R06Aug43.

6005 regd 04Oct43 to Aeroflot as CCCP-L830.

6007 'VH-EWE' on display at Karoonda, SA in Jun00. DISPLAYED

6009 41-18648, the wreckage is still on site at Mondo, QLD where it crashed on 21Nov43.

6011 MM61895 Italian AF. Fuselage stored at Roma-Guidonia Apr01.

6015 Photo shows this to be painted PT-FBR in Nov74, but PP-FBR in 1971 register, so possibly a mispaint.

6018 41-18657 468 FS, 508 FG, 20 AF. Hit by P-47D 42-75320 at Mokuleia, HI 21Aug45.

6021 VH-AES airworthy in Trans Australia colours, operated by Qantas from Tullamarine Oct93 to Nov08 – Painted in KLM-Royal Dutch Airlines c/s, race number 44 to celebrate the 75th anniversary of the 1934 race to Melbourne in October 2009. ACTIVE

6024 VH-AEQ – the dismantled remains were sold by Alvin Petersen who sold his property near Bendigo, VIC to David Hamilton. He sold the DC-3 to Jason Burgess on 13May06. It was to be moved to a farm near Swan Hill, VIC as VH-QLD. DERELICT

6030 41-18669 2527 BU South Plains Dec44.

6037 41-38654 1 TCS 10Nov43, DBR 13Mar45, landing accident at Schwebo, Burma.

6039 41-38656 was operated by 6 FrS at time of crash.

6043 41-38660 5 OUT, Palm Springs, CA Jul45.

6051 VH-DAS Heritage Homestead Museum, wreck stored since Apr84 at Kurunda, QLD. STORED

6054 N784T MBD Corp, lsd to Tol Air, stored Dec05 San Juan, PR. STORED

6055 N4550J noted parked at Shelbyville, TN in Oct07. Believed i/s. ACTIVE?

6061 YS-53C noted at Ilopango Nov07. ACTIVE?

6062 N737H Airborne Imaging Inc, i/s in Aug02 and 2010. ACTIVE

6064 N30088 was again canx as WFU on 27Jul09. Paper work catching up?

6068 WAA to Argonaut A/ws Corp, Miami, FL as NC18649 19Sep46 – Frank J O'Connor, Miami, FL 06Jun49 [Sheriff's sale] – American Airmotive 26Jul49 – Avianca B02Jun50. HR-AJY wfu at Tegucigalpa in Mar02. This was being worked on early in 2009, together with HR-ALU - STORED

6072 41-38677 1 TCS on 19Feb43 when it was involved in a mid-air collision with 41-19496. Both survived.

C/n 6024 C-47-DL VH-AEQ of Trans-Australian Airlines at Melbourne-Essendon, Victoria at an unknown date. The aircraft is currently derelict on a farm in Victoria as VH-QLD. *(Ed Coates)*

6080 41-18674 39 TCS actually crashed 12Dec42.

6085 N8061A J Hawkins, WFU at Hawkins Fld, MS Jul08. STORED

6093 41-18687 take-off accident in China-Burma-India theatre on 24Feb45 – probably cause of salvage.

6094 41-18688 landing accident on 11Jan44 at Chabua Station. No later report, so probably w/o.

6095 from FAA file:- N51F Wm F Remmert/Beldex R20Dec56 – General Mills Inc B18May57 – Robert J Pond R02Jun70 – Concare Acft Lsg Corp R15Apr71 – CF-NWU Northwest Territorial R06Jul71 – Canx 30Oct71 – N62BA Berne Aviation B06Nov91 – Destroyed by tornado (in Florida?) 13Mar93.

6097 N1010S Regn Canx 18Sep09 as permanently retired. It had been WFU for about thirty years.

6098 N145A used by G T Baker Aviation School as instruction airframe from 1990. STORED

6099 41-18693 was with 6 FyS on 18May43 with 10 AF. A take-off accident on 05Feb44 at Karachi was probably not a write-off, as it was with India-China ATC on 30Aug44 when it had a landing accident at Barrackpore, India. This conflicts with the book. Delete salvage 20Jan44.

6100 41-18694 crashed on 25Mar45 15 mls N of Taza, French Morocco.

6102 HR-ATH operator Aerovias Centroamericanos i/s Tegucigalpa Nov07 & Oct09. ACTIVE

6114 41-19471 2 TCS Apr43.

6116 41-19473 ditched nr Lacedonia, Italy on 28Apr44.

6117 41-19474 landing accident on 22Feb45, so must have been repaired after strafing.

6120 41-19477 landing accident at 805 BU, Alliance Mun. Apt, NE on 21Jun44. Did this lead to the survey?

6122 VH-SBI was reported derelict in 1975 at Lae City Apt. Almost certainly no longer there?

6124 41-19481 had a landing accident on 02Aug45 at Labe, Fr Guiana (Guyane Française).

6125 41-19482 10 AF 1 ACG Hq, landing accident at Mingaladon, Burma 25Jul45.

6127 41-19484 65 TCS accident Grand Rapids, NE in Feb43.

6129 41-19486 accident on 21Dec44 in California.

6131 41-19488 with 4 FyS collided with 41-38726 on the ground, at Chabua.

6135 YV-500C re-registered YV1854, still with Aeroejecutivos, by Oct02. At Opa Locka Oct08 and Nov10. STORED

6136 41-19493 was with 6 FyS, 1 FyG, 10 AF at time of crash.

6139 41-19496 10 AF, 1 TCS. Mid-air collision with 41-18677 on 19Feb43

6144 FLC (Italy) to Pan American Airways 11Oct46 – NC22434 R14Oct46 – Lsd to COPA as RX-86 10Feb47 – US Regn Canx 04Mar47 – COPA B10Dec49 – Rr HP-46 15Nov51. HK-3286 to Aerovanguardia by Dec06. I/s Jul08 and Feb10 Villavicencio, Colombia. ACTIVE

6148 41-38689 61 TCS in Apr43 and 52 TCS in Jun43.

N87T Tolair, in 2005, no titles. By March 2010 it was stored at San Juan, PR. STORED

6151 XT-87 Chennault & Willauer to Civil Air Transport as N8357C 19Dec49 – Canx 27Feb53 – CAT, SA to Witbeck 14May53 – N79097 Canx 07Oct53.

6160 FLC (Italy) to Pan American Airways as NC25389 – Avianca 28Jan47.

6162 41-38703 crashed at 805 BU, George AAF, IL on 07Jul45. Probably not repaired, but to RFC.

6164 41-38705 7 FyG, ATC Great Falls Jul45.

N2028 canx 14Feb85 and reportedly to Panama. However a 2009 report states it has been derelict at Mayaguana, Bahamas since the 1980s. Drug-runner.

6165 41-38706 was with India-China ATC when it crashed.

6167 41-38708 2 TCS, 1 FyG Mar43.

6170 WAA to Harry Cefalo as NC17091 04Jun46 – Trans Luxury A/l 27Aug46 – Repossessed by WAA prior to 20Feb48 – Canx 19Jan50 as 'no record of ownership'.

6174 41-38715 1325 BU Chabua AF, ATC, India Sep45.

6176 41-38717 21 FyG Palm Springs Jan45. RFC to Air Cargo Transport 10Oct45.

6177 NC54374 Universal Equities to Chesapeake A/ws, Salisbury, MD 04Jan48.

6178 41-38719 6 FyG Long Beach ATC Jul45.

6179 C-FQBI preserved at Harbor Grace Apt. Oct94. PRESERVED?

6180 41-38721 crashed 10Apr44 Burma [SF] but probably repaired.

6181 41-38722 805 BU George Apr45.

6182 41-38723 32 TCS Sedalia 12Feb43.

6183 41-38724 1250 BU ATC, N Africa Jan45.

6184 41-38725 had a taxying accident at Maison Blanche, Algeria on 10Nov44 when it hit Dakota FZ570.

6185 41-38726 had a taxying accident with 41-19488 at Chabua on 03Jun43.

6186 41-38727 was with 5 TCS when it had an accident at Grenada, MS.

6187 NC67136 Charles H Babb Co, Glendale, CA was first owner.

6188 41-38729 805 BU Alliance – Forced landing 6mls N of Alliance, NE 25May44 [EF].

6190 CC-CBO was WFU engineless at Puerto Montt, Chile in Dec99. No recent news.

6193 41-38734 2 TCS, 10 AF 11Aug43 and in May44.

6203 41-38744 had an accident at its base 813 BU, Sedalia, MO on 09Jun44. An earlier accident was reported as 30Nov43, but not DBR.

6204 BT-67 119 Fuerza Aerea Salvadorena became FAES 119. It ran into a tree on landing at Chilangi-Los Comandos Apt, El Salvador on 19Nov00, but it is not known whether the aircraft was repaired.

6205 41-38746 1330 BU when it crashed on 05Jun45.

6207 41-38748 8 ADG when it had an accident on 23Jul43.

6208 N305SF to Majestic Air Leasing Inc 19Feb88 – Lsd to Majestic Airlines Inc Feb88 to Jan96 when trading ceased – Lsd to Galaxy Air Cargo Inc, Anchorage, AK Jul97 to Jan2001 when trading ceased – Ret to lessor and regd to Tammy Maxwell, Spring Creek, NV Aug02 – Stored 2001 to Jul10 Palmer, AK. STORED

6215 YN-BVK was WFU at Los Brasilias Apt in Aug00, but no further news.

6216 9N-AAH R24Feb61 according to Nepalese register.

6218 41-38759 Hq, 14 FyG, Oran Sep43.

6219 41-38760 77 FyS when it crashed at Jorhat, and never got to India-China ATC.

6223 N473DK painted as '4X-AES' stored at Eilat-J Hozman Apt Apr04. STORED

6228 regd 26Mar43 to Aeroflot as CCCP-L800.

6229 regd 07Apr43 to Aeroflot as CCCP-L801.

6230 regd 24Sep43 to Aeroflot as CCCP-L817.

6231 regd 01Jun44 to Aeroflot as CCCP-L908.

6232 [42-5644] Soviet AF, 8 tap – Crashed 28Aug43 on northern side of Ushkanyi Khrebet range, 50km from Egvekinot [PE]

6233 regd 14Apr43 to Aeroflot as CCCP-L802.

6234 regd 25Feb44 to Aeroflot as CCCP-L806.

6235 regd 24Sep43 to Aeroflot as CCCP-L818.

6236 regd 24Sep43 to Aeroflot as CCCP-L826.

6237 regd 27Apr44 to Aeroflot as CCCP-L807.

6259 43-1983 operated by American Airlines on 02Jun44.

6261 C-FTDJ Canadian Avn Museum. Was preserved at Rockcliffe prior to Feb84. PRESERVED

6263 43-1980 crash date was 05Sep43, place St Joseph, MO, unit 68 TCS. On KS/MO border [BW].

6264 N30079 Fleetways Inc to F A del Paraguay as T-21 Jan53 – No trace of N79 in records, probably just a shortened reference to N30079.

6314 N165LG was on display at New England Air Museum, Bradley Locks, CT in Jun05. DISPLAYED

6315 N87745 in store at Gainesville-Municipal, TX painted "0-50972" with "Southern Cross" titles, May08-Jul10. Now carries "41-6315" (port) & "41-6531" (starboard). ACTIVE

6316 43-1976 while with 3 Ferry Romulus it had a take-off accident at Memphis Mun. Apt, TN on 17Dec44 due to EF. W/o.

6317 43-1977 Hq Sq, Memphis Jul44.

6318 NC19930 was leased to United by WAA (not DPC) and converted to DC-3A 10Aug45.

6321 CU-T102 to NC12923 WAA 09Sep47 – Sold by WAA 12Feb48 (to whom is unknown) – Canx 09Aug48 as to Venezuela (probably YV-C-AVF).

6325 N486C to E&L Leasing, Vichy, MO R07Dec05. DBR 05Jan08. Parked in poor condition at Rolla National [aka Vichy] Aug09. STORED

6328 43-2003 55 AES Love Sep44.

6329 43-2004 Hq ATC – Crashed 06Feb43 Ft Nelson, BC, Canada. Delete cond. 02Mar45.

6334 43-2009 Pan American – Crashed 20Jun43, Biscayne Bay, Miami, FL. Cause uncertain.

6337 'NC91008' fuselage stored at Paine Fld, Seattle, WA Jun01. Serious corrosion & poor condition Jul10. STORED

6338 223835 remains on display at EAA Oshkosh in Jul09. DISPLAYED

6342 43-1986 was with Colonial by 01May43.

6343 N37FL Caribkist Intl Corp stored Bell Buckle, TN 2001. Current status unknown.

6344 43-1989 was operated by Continental A/l on 23Feb43. when it crashed 5mls W of Husted, CO.

6346 OH-LCH Airveteran Ry, airworthy at Helsinki May87. ACTIVE

6347 43-2034 crashed at RAF Valley, Wales 1407 BU on 02Sep44. It was Class 26 at Prestwick.

6354 initally regd C-71X and then C-71.

HK-140 ALICOL, WFU at Villavicencio Jan96. STORED?

6355 N226 preserved at Ragged Isle, Bahamas. PRESERVED

7313 N8336C was canx 22Jul53 when Rr N1794B to CAT SA – TEMCO Aircraft Corp 09Dec53 – Rr N67K 13Sep55 – Executive Aircraft Services Inc 14Nov55 – Rr N47L Union Chemical 15Nov55.

N943DJ to Turbo DC-3 MA Inc (Jul06) – Don Jones, Oshkosh – JM Air LLC, Phoeniz, AZ R03Jun09. ACTIVE

7315 42-47373 41 FyS at time of crash.

7316 42-47374 12 FrG at time of accident at Half Assani, Gold Coast on 27May43.

7320 N213MA Mid America Air Museum, stored at Chino, CA Sep01, dismantled.

7321 42-47379 crashed at Blythe AAB, CA on 16Dec42.

7326 42-15531 Hq, 12 AF landing accident at Malignano, Italy on 27Jan45.

7327 42-15532 12 AF when it made a wheels-up landing at Casablanca on 16Jan44. Was reported destroyed on 09Jul43, but appears to have been recovered.

7329 42-15534 5 TCS at time of accident in May43.

7332 42-15537 accident was due to bad weather while towing CG-4A 42-46327. Crew bailed out.

7334 42-15539 52 TCS when it crashed on 07Feb43, 25mls N of Harpers Lake, GA, but was repaired.

7336 42-15541 2527 BU South Plains/Lubbock in May44 and Jul44.

7338 9N-AAI crashed 30Dec62.

7339 XA-GEV – this is given as operated by Rutas Aerea Costenas at the time of the accident, but Archive for Spring 2007 suggests it was on the inaugural service by Aerovias Rojas to Mexico City from Agua Scalientes, when it hit Mt Transfiguracion, nr Villa del Carbon on 10Apr68.

7340 NC49541 was leased by WAA (not DPC) to United. W Canada Avn. Museum derelict May05 Winnipeg, MAN. DERELICT

7342 42-15547 72 TCS in May43.

7344 42-15549 14 PRS, 9 AF when it crashed on take-off at Sandweiler A/fld (A-97), Luxembourg on 28Dec44.

7345 42-15550 55 TCS Sedalia Feb43.

7346 42-15551 25 TCS Del Valle Feb43.

7347 N19915 was stored at Lake Elsinore in Jan08, on display Proud Bird Restaurant Jun08. PRESERVED

7348 42-15553 513 FS, 406 FG Jun45, Nordholz (R-56), Germany, 9 AF.

7351 42- 15556 was back at Sedalia AAF by 19Oct44.

7353 42-15558 813 BU Sedalia Jun44.

7354 42-15559 805 BU Alliance May44.

7355 42-15560 25 TCS Feb44.

7356 42-15561 58 TCS Sedalia Feb43.

7357 42-15562 38 TCS Mar43.

7361 42-15566 38 TCS May43. 2527 BU South Plains, take-off accident on 11Jul44. It was rebuilt by Pan American.

7363 NC17890 was leased by WAA (not DPC) to United.

7364 42-15569 forced landing on Greenland Ice Cap on 05Nov42 at 61.30N x 42.00W. In radio contact, but no further messages. Weather good.

7366 42-5672 5 TCS Alliance Mar44, and 805 BU Alliance May44.

7369 42-5675 61 TCS, 314 TCG at Lawson in Mar43, and with 805 BU George in Jan45, and Mar45.

7373 42-5679 27 TCS Jun43 and 2525 BU Liberal in Aug45. It crash-landed 18Jul45 20mls SW Gage, KS [EF] but was repaired and crashed again 8mls S of San Antonio, TX on 03Aug45.

7377 was stripped of controls, hydraulics and all removable items and was in use as a home at Mobile, AL. It was rebuilt by Beldex being bought from NAVCO, St Louis, MO as N5874V 04Sep51. Sold to Secretaria de Hacienda on 26Dec51. Canx 16Jan52 as sold to Mexico. Regd as XC-ABF to Secretaria de Hacienda y Credito Publico in 1954.

7382 N81B was broken up in Dec04. Canx 16Jun08.

7386 YV-222C WFU by Feb01. No recent news.

7387 42-15870 25 TCS when it crashed on 23Apr43 at Austin Mun. Apt, TX. It was rebuilt by Pan Am.

7389 41-15872 cause of accident on 16Sep42 pilot error, unit 34 TCS.

7390 41-15873 damaged at RAF Hendon 22Jan43. Unit was 34 TCS, 315 TCG, 8 AF. No other record of it visiting UK, but there is a six-year gap in the history.

7391 42-14874 had a landing accident 24mls N of Harpers Lake, CA on 30Apr43 while with 52 TCS. There was a take-off accident on 03Jul44 at Idalon Auxiliary Field, South Plains while based at 2527 BU South Plains. This was rebuilt by Pan Am as NC33321.

7392 N90079 canx 31Jan05 as destroyed by storm.

7402 42-15885 314 ATS, 9 AF 03May44 [EF].

7403 N872A – No news since 1994.

C/n 7403 C-53-DO N872A operated by American Flyers Inc. The photo was taken at Opa Locka, Florida in June 1978. *(Dennis Goodwin)*

C/n 9059 C-47-DL N25641 of Legend Airways Inc, Nashua, New Hampshire visited Oshkosh, Wisconsin in July 1994, when this photo was taken. (Jennifer Gradidge)

7410 42-15893 operated by 328 FyS at time of take-off accident 11Sep44 at El Aouina AAB, Tunisia.

9001 R Swedish AF 79001, which was shot down on 13Jun52 by a Russian fighter, crashing in the Baltic, was salvaged from the seabed on 01Mar04 and was being cleaned for display in Swedish AF museum, Linkoping when visited on 13May09. DISPLAYED

9002 42-5695 14 TCS when it crashed.

9005 42-5698 59 TCS Mar43.

9007 42-5700 61 TCS, 9 AF was based at Mourmelon (B-44), France when it had the accident on 15May45.

9016 regd 12Apr43 to NKAP Air Unit as CCCP-J500.

9017 regd 26Jan44 to Aeroflot as CCCP-L814.

9019 regd 12Oct43 to Aeroflot as CCCP-L815.

9020 regd 24Sep43 to Aeroflot as CCCP-L819.

9021 regd 05Nov43 to Aeroflot as CCCP-L816.

9022 regd 24Sep43 to Aeroflot as CCCP-L821.

9024 regd 13Nov43 to Polyarnaya aviatsiya (GUSMP) as CCCP-N329.

9025 42-32799 was being delivered by 1 FyS in Feb43, before handover to Russia.

9028 42-32802 805 BU Alliance Aug44. 805 BU was also George? By Jul45 it was with 1010 BU Redistribution Centre. N92578 Airborne Imaging Inc, Wilmington R29Jan04. ACTIVE

9030 42-32804 6 AF, Puerto Rico in Jan45. NC50041 was canx 08Mar48 on sale to TAM.

9033 42-32807 14 TCS from 07Jun43. It was DBR at Constantine, Tunisia (not Italy) on 06Jul43.

9034 42-32808 15 TCS Mar43.

9035 42-32809 5 TCS, Alliance Mar44, and 805 BU George in Nov44 and Feb45 – Ops Rome AAF, ATSC, Jul45.

9036 Despite a report that TT-LAC was shipped to France and broken up, it was still in store at N'djamena in Aug08 with Tchad AF. STORED (See also c/n 26122 in Vol 2).

9038 42-32812 landing accident at Magenta AAB, SW Pacific on 21Aug45. Mechanical failure.

9040 N84KB was airworthy with T W Hunt at Corvallis, OR in Apr04. ACTIVE

9041 C-FFST is preserved with Frontiers Antique & Military Aviation Museum, St Chrystome, PQ. PRESERVED

9043 N59NA regd to BGA-Viation Inc, Bennettsville, SC 30Nov07, i/s 2010. ACTIVE

9049 XA-REP AeroLibertad was reported at San Antonio, TX in Apr98 and again in Aug09 in poor condition. STORED

9053 N47FJ Baron Air Services to E & L Leasing, Vichy, MO R07Dec85. Reported stored at Vichy Mar99. Derelict there by 11Apr99, and in Jul09. DERELICT

9058 N5106X last reported i/s with Pleasant Avn LLC, Mt Pleasant, TX in Jul01 and 2010. ACTIVE

9059 42-32833 14 TCS Pope Fld, Mar43 and then 9 AF, 100 TCS based at Dreux, France on 01Jan45.

As N25641 this was airworthy with Legend A/ws in Sep00 at Morrison, CO and 2010. ACTIVE

9060 42-32834 take-off accident at Hunter Fld, GA on 09Jul45, after return from ATC Europe.

9061 YV-C-LBO made emergency landing after losing a prop 19May65. Derelict in Canaima National Park, S Venezuela, 05.88.3N x 62.28.3W. DERELICT

9062 42-32836 base S.7, had a take-off accident on 27May45 at Willingdon, New Delhi, India.

9064 42-32838 was based at 813 BU Sedalia in Jul44.

9067 42-32841 was with 1332 BU Mohanbari on 12May45, when it had a ground accident at Willingdon AS, New Delhi. It was w/o in a landing accident at Dinjin, India on 25May45.

9069 42-32843 was with 10 AF, 6 TpS in Aug43. In Jun45 was with 1305 BU Dum Dum A/fld, ATC. It was with India-China Wg Aug45.

9070 42-32844 6 FyS Apr43.

9071 42-32845 taxying accident 09Dec43 at Chabua Station, India. It was with ATC by then.

9072 42-32846 1328 BU Misamari, India Apr45, and 1345 BU Kurmitola A/fld, India on 05Oct45.

9087 42-32861 crashed 15May43 with 77 FyS, TSP.

9089 C-FJWP was still unrestored at Reynolds Aviation Museum in Sep08 – Fuselage and centre section moved to Red Deer, Alta by Jun09. DERELICT

9092 42-32866 take-off accident at Chabua AB, India 11Apr43, was with 6 FyS in May43.

9094 42-32868 1 FyG in Oct43.

9095 42-32869 14 AF in Apr44.

9096 42-32870 9 AF in Apr44, and 100 TCS by Dec44.

9097 42-32871 15 TCS when it crashed.

9099 42-32873 take-off accident due to icing.

9100 580 Fuerza Aerea Guatemalteca – Accident was on 17Apr03 at Santa Elena and props, engines and main gear were damaged. Status uncertain.

9102 42-32876 was del. to 55 TCS Sedalia in Mar43.

9103 79002 R Swedish AF, preserved at Skoklosters Motor Museum from 1983. Sold to Fallskarmsjagarskolans Veteranklubb, Karlsberg. Dismantled 09May09 and moved by barge to Karlsberg 13May09. STORED

9106 42-32880 50 TCS, Mourmelon (B-44), France by 06Apr45.

9108 1676 F A Colombiana was derelict at Gomez AB in Feb97.

9115 regd 16Oct43 to Aeroflot as CCCP-L832.

9116 regd 24Sep43 to Aeroflot as CCCP-L820.

9118 42-32892 to Soviet AF 1 pad. R11Nov43 to Polyarnaya aviatsiya (GUSMP) as CCCP-N328, Arctic Aviation [used for ice reconnaissance] – Chukotskaya aviagruppa 1945 – hulk existed in 2007 on Taimyr peninsula. DERELICT

9119 regd 30Jan44 to Aeroflot as CCCP-L843.

9137 YV-822C WFU at Ciudad Guayana, Venezuela Feb07 in Avensa colours. STORED

9139 42-32913 12 AF, 14 TCS had a minor accident on 29Jun43 in N Africa.

9147 N87624 Aero American Corp dismantled during 1977.

9152 42-32926 316 TCS, Camp Mackall 14Aug44 – To Carib Defense Command. Crashed 16May47 Mariscal Sucre Apt, Quito, Ecuador [EF].

9155 42-32929 48 TCS Mar43.

9157 42-32931 9 AF, 59 TCS by 14Apr44.

9159 42-3293 15 TCS, 9 AF, base B-92, crashed 27Mar45 Neuville, nr Lyons, France.

9161 42-32935 9 AF, 18 WRX? – landing accident at Orly (A-47), France on 19Sep45.

9164 42-23302 crashed 22Jan44 Central Apt, Richmond, VA. [Conflict]

9168 42-23306 9 AF 59 TCS taxying accident at Barkston Heath (483), UK on 02Jun44. Reported to be with 813 BU Sedalia in May45.

9171 42-23309 100 TCS Pope Fld Feb44.

9172 42-23310 accident in Germany on 31Oct45, which probably led to its sale after repair by SAL.

In Nov06 it was painted F-BBBE on starboard side in Air France colours, and PH-PBA KLM on port side. Painted as F-BEFD in Aigle Azur colours Sep06 to celebrate that company's 60th anniversary. #5141406 is the part number for 'fuselage assembly complete' in C-47 parts book. This has also been reported in Belgian AF colours as K-24 'CW-X'. Legal regn is F-AZTE. ACTIVE

9174 42-23312 3 TCS Sedalia Mar44. In Mar45 was with 554 BU Memphis.

9175 42-23313 813 BU Sedalia, 1 TCC Nov44.

9176 42-23314 with 807 BU Bergstrom Nov44.

9186 N46877 sold to Puma Air Leases in Sep84. HK-3293 Air Colombia i/s at Villavicencio in Jul08 and Feb10. ACTIVE

9196 42-23334 collided with 43-15097 on 28Jul44, at Broadwater.

9198 N87639 Aero American Corp, dismantled by 1977.

9204 42-23342 9 AF 32 TCS, landing accident 29Jan45 RAF Harlaston, Grantham, Lincs.

9210 42-23348 1 TCC, TP-1 813 BU Sedalia by Nov44.

9212 42-23350 5 Prov., Pope May45

9213 42-23351 May44 quoted as 805 BU Alliance. [Same as George?].

9214 NC57850 owner was Edward Ware Tabor, Capay, CA; t/a Trans-Luxury A/l, Teterboro, NJ.

9215 42-23353 taxying accident Pope 16Dec44. To 13 AF, 570 ASG, 40 AES – Crash-landed Yontan Fld, Okinawa 14Oct45.

9217 42-23355 16 CCS, Syracuse, 11Aug44.

9219 42-23357 27 TCS Dunnellon Jun43 – 805 BU with George – DBR 04Mar44 at Rockport, IN when hit by C-60A 42-55962 [also reported 05Mar45]

9221 42-23359 accident was 3.5mls NE of Gaddo Gap, AR.

9222 42-23360 813 BU Sedalia, hit Reeser's Summit, 8mls W of Olmsted Fld, Harrisburg, PA 25Dec44 [BW]. Also given as 3.5mls NW of New Cumberland, PA. The two are probably the same. No part can have been used in rebuild of c/n 34373.

9223 42-23361 – NC20756 Pan American R14Oct46 – Canx 02Oct47 as to Brazil – [Probably used for spares in Europe as no ferry flight was ever authorised]

9225 42-23363 50 TCS Mormelon (B-44), France, 9 AF Feb44 - Crashed 06Apr45 20mls NW Limburg, Germany. (Book error).

9226 42-23364 283 BU Galveston, 2 AF Jun45.

9227 42-23365 52 TCS Apr43.

9229 42-23367 68 TCS, mid-air collision with 41-18383 over Sedalia AF on 16Apr43 and was DBR.

9230 42-23368 11 TCS, AFE, crashed 22Apr47 Karlovy Vary (Karlsbad), Czechoslovakia – abandoned after becoming lost on training flight [not on del. to Czechoslovakia].

9247 42-23385 807 BU Bergstrom Jan45. N23AJ still as such at Glendale, CA Jun05. N243DC noted at Buckeye, AZ with Hans Laurisden collection in Aug09. STORED

9251 42-23389 813 BU Sedalia 1 TCC, Jan45.

9252 ETM-6011, although on overhaul in 1993, this is almost certainly out of service by now.

9253 42-23391 83 TCS in Oct43.

9255 42-23393 9 AF, 50 TCS, base Mourmelon (B-44), France – Crashed 06Apr45 12mls NW Malmedy, Belgium.

9257 Polish AF '11' canx 27Apr55. Fate unknown.

9258 42-23396 9 AF, 50 TCS base Mourmelon (B-44), France, landing accident at Erding (R-91), Germany on 19Jun45.

9259 42-23397 To 71 TCS in Mar43.

9267 42-23405 crashed on 21Jun44 in Albania.

9270 42-23408 1107 BU, Waller ATC Aug45.

9271 42-23409 Forced landing 20May43 [EF] 60mls W of Zandery Fld, Dutch Guiana (Surinam).

9273 42-23411 11 TCS Jun44.

9276 Reported to have been EATM-6041 in 1994 when Ernesto Zedillo, son of the president, had it restored for his own use. It flew as 'XA-CMA' at this time and later as 'FAM-UNO'. XB-UNO regd Apr04 and then reregd XB-JSJ which was noted at Ft Lauderdale, FL in May07. To N8WJ World Jet of Delaware Inc, Wilmington, DE R06Aug07. At Fort Lauderdale Executive, FL Nov10. ACTIVE

9282 42-23420 "Pushy Cat" broke up in a storm over the Carnavon Gorge, 60 mls S of Springsure, QLD. Part of the wreckage serves to this day as a memorial nearby.

9286 VH-CWS Classic Wings was airworthy in Oct08 but was withdrawn by Jan09 and parked at Perth-Jandakot for sale. It was regd to Westpac Banking Corp, Concord West, NSW on 12Jan09. Slattery Auctions Australia Pty, Ltd., Hexham, NSW, R17May10 – VH-CES JNP Enterprises Pty, Ltd., Broome, WA R24Jun10, op by Peter Christoudias. ACTIVE

9290 883/46153 R Thai AF BT-67 Jun98, i/s Dec08. ACTIVE

9295 42-23433 Russian AF, 8 tap - Crashed 09Jun43 shortly after take-off from Magadan, nr River Dukcha [Technical problem]

9327 42-23465 12 TCS hit by B-24H 42-52099 at Brindisi, Italy on 16Sep44. Candidate cause of write-off?

9328 42-23466, Hq, Orly (A-47), France, 9 AF, take-off accident at Eschborn (Y-74), Germany on 18Sep45.

9335 42-23473 12 AF when lost.

9336 42-23474 8 AF, 314 TpS, 31 TpG in Aug45. Station 343.

9342 42-23480 with 43 TCS, but 8 AF, on 31Oct43.

9347 42-23485 based at Amberley, QLD, when it had an accident on 15May45. It had a taxying accident at an airfield 5mls SE of Brisbane on 18Sep45.

9352 42-23490 2527 BU South Plains Jan45.

9357 Bu 12417 – skis collapsed on rough ice, 82.34N x 145.20W on op. 'Ski Jump' 27Mar52 and abandoned.

Found by Russians near Pole of Relative Inaccessibility in May54 – Repaired using parts of Soviet C-47 with 'zero hours' and regd CCCP-H417 – Used for resupply flights to polar ice station in Oct54 – DBR late 1954 when landing at SP-3 – fuselage used as sauna and eventually sank.

9358 Bu 12418 'Que Sera Sera' was still on external display at Pensacola in Dec02. DISPLAYED

9365 42-23503 124 FS, Des Moines, IA, crashed 4mls NW Manitou Springs, CO, on 14Oct47. Written-off.

9369 42-23507 12 AF, 45 TCS (08Jan44) Sicily – then to 8 AF. 9U-BRZ remained in store at Bujumbura, Burundi, in Jan07. STORED

9371 C-GWIR Buffalo Airways was in service in Sep08. ACTIVE

9373 42-23511 with 8 TCS until 12Nov44 at least.

9374 42-23512 64 TCS at time of crash.

9377 42-23515 crashed 1.5ml E of Isle of Vis, Yugoslavia.

9378 42-23516 12 AF, 17 TCS on 11Aug44.

9380 N53ST was in a sandy camouflage c/s in 1980, when first registered, and remains flying in 2010. ACTIVE

9382 42-23520 Crash-landed 23May43, ATC 59 FyS Lungi, Sierra Leone.

9389 42-23527 mid-air collision was with 42-92982 and 41-18446.

9394 42-23532 204 BU Biggs 2 AF Aug45.

9395 FLC 02Nov46 but only regd as N1534V in 1951 (not NC).

9400 42-23538 crashed 18May48 [EF] 3.5 mls N of Dillon, CO.

9407 9G-AAF cause of accident was engine failure.

9410 C9-ATH abandoned at Mbuji-Mayi, Dem. Rep. of Congo in Jul04 – With Air Link, Goma Jul07. STORED?

9414 223552 R Thai Army as HS-TDF in Dec66 – Displayed at National Science Centre for Education, Sukhumvit, in R Thai AF colours Aug02. Returned to Don Muang by Nov09. DISPLAYED

9415 N400BF Basler Turbo Conversions LLC. ACTIVE [reported to R Thai AF, but unconfirmed]

9424 42-23562 Soviet AF TO Upr – DBR while landing at Yakutsk 06Jan44. Hit Polikarpov P-5 CCCP-N65.

9425 regd 16Oct43 to Aeroflot as CCCP-L831 – Reported to CCCP-L3831? GVF – '831' Soviet AF 101 apdd.

9426 regd 10May44 to Aeroflot as CCCP-L891.

9427 regd 29Oct43 to Aeroflot as CCCP-L835.

9431 regd 04Dec43 to Aeroflot as CCCP-L838.

9436 regd 24Sep43 to Aeroflot as CCCP-L825.

9440 regd 24Sep43 to Aeroflot as CCCP-L822.

9441 regd 24Sep43 to Aeroflot as CCCP-L823.

9452 9Q-CTR was in use with Air Kasai, Kinshasa in Dec03. It was noted at Kinshasa-N'dolo airport in September 2009, looking very complete, but with Russian engines and four-blade propellers from An-2 biplanes. Whether it had flown with these is unknown. STORED

9457 42-23595 destroyed at Funafuti Tarawa Atoll, Ellice Is, 17Nov43.

9459 42-23597 16 HqSq, 15 SRG, 6 AF Panama Jun45.

9466 42-23604 unit is quoted as 86 TpS.

9469 42-23607 10 AF, 2 TCS in Apr44.

9470 42-23608 93 ADG, Elmendorf on 25Jan46 when it had a landing accident at Iliamna, AK.

9479 42-23617 crashed 12Apr54 on take-off Elmendorf, AK.

9481 42-23619 1551 BU Henderson Fld, Dutch Guinea 10Aug45, when it belly-landed. It was missing in the Philippines on 05Feb46, while with 1 TCS.

9497 42-23635 53 TCS at time of landing accident.

9501 ET-AGH – the wing went to ET-AGI.

9512 42-23650 561 BU Rosecrans, ATC Jun45.

9514 42-23652 76 TCS crashed 25May43 45mls S Nashville, TN after bird strike – presumably repaired because crashed 03Aug44 3mls W of Naper, NE when based with FPTS Bruning AAF, 2 AF [BW/SF].

9522 42-23660 was also named 'The Stud Duck' while with 67 TCS.

9525 'VR-HDA' is preserved in Cathay Pacific colours at Cathay Pacific maintenance base, Hong Kong Intl Apt, Chep Lap Kok since 2006 – Visited Nov09. DISPLAYED

9530 N60480/0-23668 remained on display at Chino, CA in Apr08. Regd to Charles F. Nichols, Baldwin Park, CA 07Jan08. At Chino, CA with Yanks Air Museum Aug09. DISPLAYED

9531 N103NA was being restored to airworthiness at Rubidoux/Flabob Apt, CA in Nov07, with EAA Chapter One. It was i/s at Flabob, CA by Dec08 & active 2010. ACTIVE [see also c/n 33569]

9535 42-23673 was being del by 9 Ferry on 18May43, hence its late delivery to RAF.

9551 PK-VDM preserved Indonesian Army Staff College at Jakarta-Saryanto as T-459 to Jun00. DISPLAYED

9555 42-23693 Alliance by 26Apr44, and 805 BU George in Mar45.

9561 42-23699 Spokane 4134 BU, ground collision Jun45 at Spokane AAF, WA.

9563 42-23701 while with HQ Hanara AB, Japan this crashed at Haneda AAB, Japan on 13Aug47. W/o unlikely.

9568 42-23706 814 BU Stout 9 TC in Nov45 and at San Bernardino in Jan46.

9577 42-23715 805 BU George, forced landing Attlebury, IN 05Mar45 [BW].

9578 '5-T-22' Argentine Navy preserved Ushuaia, Tierra del Fuego Feb06. DISPLAYED

9581 42-23719 was delivered on 22May43. Ferried by 6FyG Long Beach Apr45.

Airworthy as ZS-GPL with Springbok Flying Safaris Sep08. It had Indigo Air titles by Mar09 and was due for delivery as 5H-DAK on 06Mar09, R24Apr09. ZS-GPL Canx 17Apr09. Noted 13Jul09 at Dar-es-Salaam, named 'Wave Dancer'. ACTIVE

9587 42-23725 belly-landed at Finschafen, New Guinea, 1552 BU, on 13May45, probably leading to write-off.

9593 VH-MMA Hardy Aviation, Parap, NT in service Jul01. ACTIVE

9598 42-23736 – Soviet AF - ATO Upr – VTKU 07Jan44. Regd 22Jun44 to Aeroflot as CCCP-L914.

9601 Regd 06Sep43 to Aeroflot as CCCP-L827.

9602 42-23740 – Soviet AF – TO Upr – VTKU 05Aug43 – Became ATO Upr. VTKU 07Jan44.

9603 42-23741 Soviet AF – ATO Upr – VTKU 07Jan44.

9604 Regd 06Dec43 to Aeroflot as CCCP-L839.

9605 42-23743 Soviet AF – TO Upr – VTKU 05Aug43 – To ATO Upr. VTKU 07Jan44 – Damaged 31Jul45 in forced landing.

9612 Regd 24Sep43 to Aeroflot as CCCP-L824.

9614 42-23752 Soviet AF – TO Upr – VTKU 05Aug43 - To Aeroflot 14 TO, Yakutsk 1946.

9615 Regd 20Nov43 to Aeroflot as CCCP-L837.

9619 Bu 12436 displayed at Camp Blanding, FL 2000. DISPLAYED

9622 FD922 collided with US Navy PB4Y-1 63943 of VPB-114.

9623 5B-CBD removed from roundabout when that was remodelled, post 2006. Possibly scrapped.

9624 G-AJIB was sold to EAFS/Channel in 1960, not 1950.

9628 'ET-T-1' preserved at Addis Ababa in Dec03. PRESERVED

9631 42-23769 813 BU Sedalia Jul44.

9634 42-23772 37 TCS, 812 BU, 1 TCC, Pope Aug45.

9638 42-23776 310 TCS hit ground while low flying [PE].

9639 42-23777 813 BU by Sep44.

9640 42-23778 317 TCS Dunellon AAB, crashed 27Jul44 Peterson Fld, Colorado Springs, CO [Mid-air collision].

9643 42-23781 301 TCS Camp Mackall, NC Feb43 [EF].

9645 42-23783 crashed 5mls W of Camp Mackall, NC on 24Sep44. Unit was 317 TCS.

9646 42-23784 was with 75 TCS at time of accident.

9648 42-23786 collided with 42-68785 on 10Jul43.

9654 42-23792 Bergstrom 807 BU by 05Nov44.

NC79044 operated by Pacific A/L and Pacific A/ws in Sep47, leased by Lester R Daniels, Jr.

9656 42-23794 ATC 1 AS&RS Feb45. This crashed in southern Greenland on 09Dec48 and was not repaired.

9657 42-23795 302 TCS at time of accident.

9659 42-23797 2 Prov.Tra., Pope, NC 12Apr45.

9661 42-23799 807 BU Bergstrom from Nov44.

9664 42-23802 805 BU, Alliance Jun44. and 805 BU George in Dec44. K-681 WFU 16Dec80 – Stored Vaerlose – to Kastrup in DDL colours as 'OY-DDA' 16Aug86 and to Billund 16Aug86 – Helsingor Museum now closed.

9666 42-23804 for Higgs (03Jan45) read 'Biggs'. Biggs was 204 BU, 2 AF in Apr45.

9668 42-23806 813 BU Sedalia, 1 TCC, Dec44.

CP-583 stored engineless by F A Boliviano at Trinidad, Bolivia, May09. DERELICT

9670 N840MB BT-67 # 45 to US Dept of State, R13Sep06, but operated as PNC-0257 by Colombian Police in 2008 and Mar09. ACTIVE

9696 42-23834 was under contract to American Airlines when it had a ground collision at La Guardia.

9699 42-23837 – the B-24D involved in the ground collision at Shemya was 41-23884.

9700 N47FK Martin Aviation, Santa Ana, CA in service May06 at Orange County, CA in Aug09 with Lyon Air Museum – To HK-4700X, del 02-11May10 to LASER, Colombia. R08Jul10 to Combustibles y Transportes Hernandez y Cia Ltda as HK-4700. ACTIVE

9701 42-23839 805 BU Alliance May44.

9704 42-23842 – the B-24D was 41-23884. [see c/n 9699]

9707 42-23845 repaired after 11May44 landing accident. Suffered a mid-air collision on 31Oct44 with 42-23608 and 42-23846 (which survived), 13mls N of Elmendorf, AK.

9708 42-23846 with 54 TCS until at least Oct44.

9717 42-32855 is quoted as having an accident, but this went to the RAF, so this was probably 42-23855 for which we have no data after Oct43 in Alaska. So, after Elmendorf 06Oct43 insert 3701 BU Amarillo, and then had a mid-air collision 5mls NW of Glendale, CA on 22Apr45.

9720 42-23858 247 BU Smoky Hill by 15Feb45. 49-2638 Greek AF on dump at Sedes 1994 to Nov 2007. DERELICT

9728 42-23866 314 TCS, Alliance Feb44, and with 312 TCS, Pope, when it suffered engine failure on 11May44.

9744 42-23882 was actually named 'Heradnaw II'.

9746 42-23884 accident in the Philippines 23Jul46 led to salvage and sale.

9750 42-23888 ATC Washington, DC Mar44. N11461 no news since 1996. Finally canx 25Jun09.

9752 42-23890 take-off accident 12Jul44.

9753 42-23891 ATC Manila in Feb45.

9766 DC-3-65TP N200MF Missionary Flights & Services, was operating in Haiti (after the earthquake) in March 2010, carrying supplies into an airstrip too small for larger aircraft. ACTIVE

9771 42-23909 crashed in Missouri on 13Oct43, leading to survey.

9776 42-23914 to Philippine AF, Nichols AB 20May63.

9777 42-23915 accident 10Sep43 when based at Warrensburg, OH.

9783 42-23921 in Jan46, still with 4108 BU, AOATSC, Newark.

9786 42-23924 3502 BU Chanute ETTC Apr45.

PI-C647 in 1968 register, owner given as ADECOR, Manila.

9787 42-23925 crashed 06May44 3mls SSE of Pope Fld, NC [not NB]

9794 42-23932 90 TCS, 9 AF by Apr44.

9797 42-23935 45 TCS, 12 AF 17Nov43.

9798 G-DAKK CofA exp. 23May03 – Delivered on ferry permit ca 24Sep06 via Lee-on-Solent, North Weald and to Aviodrome, Lelystad, Holland. Stored Lelystad Sep06. STORED

9802 TT-LAJ although reported sold to France, remained stored at N'Djamena, Tchad in Nov08. STORED

9813 C-FCQT Points North Air Service Inc, was i/s in Apr98. No recent news.

9825 42-23963 accident in Alaska on 27Mar45 probably led to commercial sale.

9828 42-23966 325 FyS, 1 TpG, 9 AF, Creil (A-81), France, 21Apr45.

9829 42-23967 86 ATS, 27 ATG, 8 AF by 23Aug43, when it had an accident at Langford Lodge, UK. It crashed in France on 20Sep52.

9831 HC-BOT was stored at Guayaquil in Apr03. STORED

9832 N21BF Basler A/l was seen at Oshkosh in Jul08-Jun10. STORED

9836 'PH-TCB' ex G-BVOL remains on display at the Aviodrome, Lelystad. DISPLAYED

9838 42-23976 – Soviet AF ATO Upr. VTKU 07Jan44 – 4 pap 1 pad Yakutsk – Hit car on landing Yakutsk 30Sep44. Status unknown.

9839 42-23977 – Soviet AF TO Upr. VTKU 05Aug43 – ATO Upr. VTKU 07Jan44.

9848 42-23986 8 tap Soviet AF – crashed Ushkanyi Mts 26Nov43, W of Uelkal [FIRE]

9852 Regd 13Nov43 to Aeroflot as CCCP-L836.

9854 42-23992 – Soviet AF – ATO Upr. VKTU 07Jan44. Regd 15May44 to Aeroflot as CCCP-L892.

9860 TF-ISB was noted out of hangar storage in June 2007. Moved to Keflavik Apt 14Oct07 for restoration by Thristavinafelagid (Friends of DC-3). STORED

9868 42-24006 Hq 2 ACG, 10 AF, taxying accident at Barrackpore, India on 20Feb45.

9871 42-24009 R Thai AF del 19Aug46 – Transport Sq 1 L2-1/90 [presumed lost by 01Jun51 – see also c/n 13546]

9874 is listed as with 4 FyG on delivery at Bahamas on 19Jul43. Of course this was also FD953, so when was it taken on RAF charge? Noted at Lagos in wrecked condition as 5N-AAQ in May70.

9881 42-24019 26 TCS Bergstrom Mar44.

9882 42-24020 815 BU Malden Jan45.

9883 42-24021 crashed 07Jan44 2mls NE of Magnolia, NC. Conflict.

9889 42-24027 312 FyS, Villacoublay (A-42), France when it crashed at Nice.

9890 42-24028 9 AF Nov43.

9891 42-24029 813 BU Sedalia June 1944.

N9891A was regd to Three Inc, Rifle, CO in Jan98 – J W Duff, Denver, CO R01Dec08. ACTIVE

9892 42-24030 9 AF Nov43.

9894 42-24032 82 TCS, Melun (A-55), France in Apr45 – NC19997 Pan American R14Oct47 - Sold to Air France as F-BCYS – As YV-610C with Servivensa was on overhaul in Feb01. No recent news.

9896 42-24034 71 TCS, 9 AF, 28Nov43.

9897 42-24035 had an accident in Greece on 14Apr55, but was repaired.

9898 42-24036 operated by Polish AF 6 ESP as tactical no. 7.

9899 42-24037 Wilmington, 2 FyG May45. It seems likely that 2-Gt-19 was the anonymous aircraft which crashed on 08Jul48 nr Coronel Pringles.

9901 42-24039 73 TCS, Fulbeck by 21Feb44.

9902 42-24040 73 TCS, Gotha North R-4, until Apr45 and to 4 FrG Memphis by Dec45.

9903 42-24041 79 TCS, Melun (A-55), France, accident on 10Apr45. Repaired. To SP-LCC LOT – Crashed 28Mar50 in Poland.

9904 42-24042 73 TCS Dec43.

9905 42-24043 46 DRS, 45 ADG, 9 AF in Jan46 and when it had a take-off accident at Capodichino AAF, Italy on 06Nov46.

9909 42-24047 73 TCS 14May44.

9910 MM61777 Italian AF. Fuselage stored at Rome-Guidonia in Apr01.

9911 42-24049 was still displayed at Hotel Roslagen, Norrtalje, Sweden in SAS c/s in 2006. DISPLAYED

9913 42-24051 crashed at Aldermaston, Berks on 04Jan45.

9914 T-3-28/G-BHUA was preserved at Salamanca-Matapan in Mar01. DISPLAYED

9916 42-24054 81 TCS base Melun (A-55), France, had a landing accident at Kassel (Y-96), Germany on 09Apr45. It also reportedly had a further accident on 12Aug46 while with 1 FG, 27 FS, while taxying at March Fld, CA. This must be an error if the 12Apr44 condemning is to be believed. Possibly repaired after original condemning.

9917 42-24055 301 TCS Camp Mackall, NC in Feb44 - By Feb45 it was with 810 BU at Laurinburg-Maxton.

9918 42-24056 reportedly had a taxying accident at Le Havre, (Y-30) on 10May45 with 74 TCS (base A-80 Mourmelon). This conflicts with book.

9919 42-24057 315 TCS Camp Mackall, NC May44.

9923 42-24061 74 TCS Aldermaston, 9AF Oct44.

9926 42-24064 to 74 TCS, Mourmelon (A-80), France, 9 AF by Apr45. N74589 Dixie Jet Services Inc, Newnam, GA, B13Jun08 – Preserved New Covington, GA Jun08 – Wells Fargo Bank Northwest, Trustee Regd 03Jun10 – Retd to flying condition Jul10 – At Waterbury Oxford, CT Sep10. ACTIVE

9929 42-24067 hit a 7296ft peak, Mt Cimbeils in E. Pyrenees, France on 26Sep53.

9933 42-24071 813 BU Sedalia 23Nov44.

9937 42-24075 813 BU Sedalia Jul44.

9949 VT-DDW remains stored at Delhi, Palam. STORED

9950 9N-AAQ R17Jul64. Royal Nepal A/l give c/n 9948 which seems unlikely, but they give delivery date as Aug43, whereas 9950 was delivered in Jul43. 9948 was derelict at Maputo in 1993 as C9-AHB.

9958 42-24096 100 TCS Grenada AAF, MS. Feb44. It actually crashed on 04Mar54 on Pointe des Trois Hommes, near St Etienne-de-Tinee, Alpes Maritimes, France, when it hit a mountain at 8,000 ft. It disintegrated and burnt, so 'Broken up' is unlikely!

9959 42-24097 813 BU Sedalia Dec44.

9961 42-24099 78 TCS 28Apr44.

9962 42-24100 302 TCS, 9 ASC, Hanau Y-91 Sep45.

9963 42-24101 repaired after 28Aug43 crash (not 1944), when it was based at Sedalia. Crashed 04Mar45 after mid-air collision with C-47 43-16144 3mls N Lawrenceville, IL.

9965 42-24013 6 FyG, Long Beach Jun45.

9966 42-24104 81 TCS, Melun (A-55), France, 9 AF on 20Apr45.

9967 N138FS to GD Aircraft LLC, Atherton, CA 17Jan06. – Leased to Four Stars, Atherton, GA – i/s Mar08. ACTIVE

9969 42-24107 accident at Bowman Fld was on 17Nov43. It had a landing accident at Lawton Mun. Apt, OK on 26May44 when it was based at 813 BU Sedalia.

9970 42-24108 6 FyG, Long Beach Oct45.

9971 42-24109 4112 BU Olmsted, when it had an accident on 21Feb46 at Andrews AFB, MD. [not a w/o but card was missing].

9972 42-24110 9 AF, 77 TCS, landing accident at Woodley, Berks on 17Oct44.

9974 42-24112 37 TCS, Pope, crash-landed 2mls N of Ft Bragg, NC on 16Jan46.

9976 42-24114 79 TCS Melun (A-55), France, 9 AF, Apr45.

9977 42-24115 4 CCS, Bowman 05May44.

9978 42-24116 76 TCS, 9 AF 06Jul44. 8P-AAA was derelict at Grantley-Adams, Barbados in Aug01.

9980 42-24118 WAA to Pacific National A/l., San Francisco, CA as NC18664 09Aug46 – Atlantic Aircraft Distributors Inc, Baltimore, MD 05Oct48 – Buenaventura Foreign Trade Corp., New York, NY prior to 23Sep49 – Canx 28Sep49 – Exported to HC-SGG on 01Dec48.

9981 42-24119 80 TCS Melun (A-55) France, when it crashed on take-off at Helmstedt on 08May45.

9982 42-24120 8 CCS, Syracuse, forced landing 23Jun44 1ml W of Pulaski, Lake Ontario, NY [EF].

9984 42-24122 DBR when 42-100633 landed on top of it.

9985 42-24123 813 BU Sedalia May44 and 23Dec44.

9986 42-24124 1 CCS, Bowman Jun44.

9988 N87626 Aero American Parts Corp to Acme Acft Feb82 but already stripped to fuselage. Broken up by 1984.

9990 42-24128 10 TCG, Alliance Mar44.

9993 42-24131 was with 807BU Bergstrom, 1 TCC in Dec44.

9995 HB-ISC Verein der Freunde der Swissair, Dübendorf, i/s Jan01. Airworthy but stored. STORED

10004 42-24142 Soviet AF – ATO Upr. VTKU 07Jan44 – 2 pap 1 pad, Uelkal.

10007 Regd 24Sep43 to Aeroflot as CCCP-L828.

10011 42-24149 Soviet AF to Aeroflot, 14TO, Yakutsk 1946

10013 42-24151 Soviet AF to Aeroflot, 14 TO, Yakutsk 1946.

10028 CU-T1192 stored at Key West, FL in May05. Donated to Houston-Hobby Airport for Air Terminal Museum. Still at Avon Park, FL in 2010. STORED

10033 42-24171 with 1 TCC, 8 AF when forced landing at Sagres, Portugal on flight from St Mawgan, UK to Casablanca, Morocco on 20Jun43. After repair this became CS-TDB with TAP D19Dec46.

10035 N12BA to Southwind at McAllen, TX Nov06 – Harbock Inc, Wilmington, DE R22Feb07 – Yesterday's Wings Inc, Wilmington, DE R01Feb08 – Noted Punta Gorda-Shell Creek, FL 06Dec08 and Opa Locka, FL Nov10. ACTIVE

10038 42-24176 crashed on 12Aug44 at Boothby-Graffoe, S of Waddington, Lincs, England.

10043 42-24181 crashed on take-off 07Apr52 3mls SE of Beirut, Lebanon.

10049 6154 FA Portuguesa – Lisbon to Mozambique Oct60 and to Lourenco Marques Esq 81 – Luanda 12Feb61 – BA9 – Crashed 10Nov61 Chitado, Angola [1964 date is incorrect].

10050 42-24188 crash on 19Sep43 was in Greenland.

10056 42-24194 to 18 TCS by Feb45.

10061 42-24199 77 TCS, Welford Jan45.

10069 42-24207 12 TCS, 12 AF, Feb45.

10071 42-24209 7 TCS, 62 TCG, 12AF, landing accident 20mls W of Cairo, Egypt on 09Jul45.

10075 42-24213 crash site was at Tarquinia, N of Civitavecchia.

10076 6161 FA Portuguesa to Esq 801 at AB8 Mozambique, VIP use. To Mozambique AF 1975.

10088 42-24226 204 BU Fairfax Field, 2 AF Jan46.

10089 42-24227 5 AF, 21 TCS, ground accident at Garbutt Fld, Australia on 01Dec43.

10106 5B-CAW was still derelict at Dhahran in Jun06. No recent news. DERELICT

10130 42-24268 61 TCS, Mourmelon (B-44), France, 9 AF, landing accident at Rheims (A-62), France on 03Jul45.

10132 HvHO-035 Turkish AF – preserved in aviation department of Erciyer Universitesi, the Sivil Havacilik Yukekokulu Fohmi Osihan on road 38-33 in Mar09. PRESERVED

10133 42-24271 ATC, not 10 AF, in Nov43.

10136 42-24274 42 TCS, 11 AF, Dec43.

10138 42-24276 42 TCS, 11 AF, landing accident at Amchitka, AK on 07Jan44,

10153 42-24291 23 TCS, Pope, 4149 BU, Jan45 – Crash-landed 23Jun47 Hamlin RCAF Station, Sask. DBR.

10156 PP-VBF VARIG colours, was on display at Rio de Janeiro-Galeão in Nov01.

10157 42-24295 was based at Maxton when first delivered on 15Sep43.

10160 42-24298 807 BU Bergstrom Jun44.

10161 42-24299 1000 BU Bowman Sep45.

10164 42-24302 1 TTC Stout Nov44 - 136 AACS, 766 BU Harmon Fld, Newfoundland Oct45.

10166 42-24304 cause of accident was [EF]. Wreckage remained at crash site in March 2007.

10168 42-24306 810 BU Maxton Apr45.

10171 C-503 SAM regd May47. C- changed to HK- 01Jan49.

10178 VT-CTV canx 11Apr92. Derelict at Delhi-Palam in 2008. DERELICT

10179 42-24317 813 BU Sedalia, mid-air collision 14Sep44 with 42-24321 nr Sedalia.

10180 42-24318 813 BU Sedalia 1 TCC, Dec44

10182 42-24320 813 BU Sedalia Apr44 – accident there on 09Jun44, leading to grading as Inst Airframe.

10183 42-24321 813 BU Sedalia, mid-air collision with 42-24317 nr Sedalia.

10184 42-24322 15 TCS, Abbeville (B-92), France, 9 AF, landing accident on 09Apr45 at Sissonne, nr Laon, France.

10187 NC20956 Pan American B02Oct46/R14Oct46 – Panair do Brasil SA 29Sep47 – US Regn Canx 02Oct47 – No Brazilian regn known. Spares?

10192 42-24330 landing accident 02Sep44 Valance (Y-23), France. [Correction]

10193 N87641 Aero American Corp, broken up by 1977.

10195 42-24333 4 TCS moved to Italy by 12Apr45 – Landing accident 19Sep45 at Elizabethville, Belgian Congo with ATC, and may well have been sold unrepaired to DTA.

10199 N64767 Environmental Air Services Inc, active at Houma, LA in Aug02. [see also c/n 13303 in Vol 2]. ACTIVE

10200 ZA947 active with Battle of Britain Memorial Flight, UK from Jul93 to date. ACTIVE

10201 HK-2666 to YV-201T AeroEjecutivos mid-2006 – AECA titles, airworthy Sep07 – Believed returned to HK-2663 with LLANERAS, at Villavicencio in Mar08 and Feb10. [See also c/n 11775]. ACTIVE

10216 42-24354 – R Thai AF Transport Sq 1 – L2-5/90 – i/s 1960 and 1964 – SOC 11Mar65.

10221 42-24359 accident was on 31May44. Some doubt about year.

10225 42-24363 crashed 26Sep43 at Parnamirim Fld, Natal, Brazil, while on delivery to India-China ATC – hence the discrepancy in the book.

10228 42-24366 1352 BU on 19Apr45. It was on a routine search, but the crash site is unknown.

10230 42-24368 landing accident at Hsain H+1, China on 13Dec43. It was with India-China Wg on 03Aug44; delete European Wg ATC.

10232 42-24370 10 AF taxying accident on 21Jan44 at Ft Hertz, Burma (Stn 29).

10233 42-24371 India-China – Landing accident at Chabua, Stn 6, India on 27Mar44, and another on 11Feb45.

10239 N2270M to Jesada Technik Museum, Nakhon Chaisi, Thailand by 2006 and displayed 2009. DISPLAYED

10240 42-24378 4 TCS, 12 AF, went to 16 TCS by Dec44 – NC50039 Harry A Cefalo, Staten Island, NY, op by Trans-Luxury A/l Inc, by Aug46 – Canx 22Aug49 – R Hellenic AF.

10241 42-24379 14 TCS by 29Dec43.

10245 42-24383 51 TCS, 12 AF, crash 09Nov45 nr Boccadi, Sicily, Italy [BW].

10250 42-24388 8 TCS, 62 TCG, crash 21Nov44 NNW of Bastia, Corsica on 21Nov44 [SF].

10253 As F-BEIG this was delivered to Air France on 28Mar46 and transferred to SGAC on 01Aug49.

LX-DKT was stored at Ostend in Jan02, until roaded to Melsbroek barracks, Brussels 08Mar11 for restoration. PRESERVED

10255 42-24393 had an accident on 26Oct43 which may have led to salvage in Apr44.

10258 42-24396 ran out of fuel 08Apr44.

10267 N136FS Four Star Aviation Inc, in service Dec05. DBF at San Juan, PR 26Apr09.

11622 42-68695 96 TCS, 440 TCG crashed at Jarne strip A-94, France 06May45.

11625 N115NA stored with Basler's at Oshkosh Jul05. In Jun10 only the fuselage remained. DERELICT

11626 42-69699 9 AF, 99 TCS crashed 12Sep45, [EF].

11628 42-68701 97 TCS, Orleans (A-50), France, 9 AF in Jul45.

11629 NC45399 was leased by WAA to United A/l, not by RFC.

11630 42-68703 315 FyS, 9 AF, crash cause PE/BW.

11636 42-68709 was del to 62 TCS Lawson in Apr43 - In Jul44 it was at 807 BU Bergstrom.

11637 N85SA stored at Fremont, OH from Nov97 to Sep04. STORED

11639 N101KC was regd to Boeing Co, Seattle on 11Jul07. Believed airworthy. ACTIVE

11640 42-68713 100 FW Hq, 9 AF, landing accident at Westhampnett (352), Sussex on 24Nov44.

11641 42-68714 del initially to 64 TCS in Mar43.

11644 42-68717 69 TCS in Jun43.

11645 CU-T1059 Aerotaxi, Havana, stored Feb02. Preserved Havanas Air Park in Cubana c/s as CU-T1559 Apr09. PRESERVED.

11648 NC19428 was leased by WAA to United A/l, not by DPC.

11651 42-68724 813 BU Sedalia May44.

11654 42-68727 del to 72 TCS in Jun43 - in Jun44 it was with 805 BU at Alliance.

11658 42-68731 del to 75 TCS Bowman in May43.

11662 42-68735 805 BU George Sep44.

11664 42-68737 78 TCS, 9 AF on 25Jan44 – NC86594 was leased by WAA to United Air Lines, not by RFC.

N784V designated as Southwest Florida Veterans War Memorial, Ft Myers, FL Sep92. DISPLAYED

11665 N353MM Daniel D Merritt, Oakville, WA R16Nov06. This was ferried to Puyallup-Thun Field in August 2009. Re-regd N43XX 12Jul10. ACTIVE

11668 6152 FA Portuguesa detached to Cape Verde Islands summer 1959. Landing accident Island of Fogo 25Nov59 [PE]

11670 42-68743 Laurinburg-Maxton AAB on 23Sep43.

11672 NC49543 was leased by WAA to United, not by RFC.

N4003 remained engineless at Petal, MS in Dec02 – Noted in town centre of Petal Jul08. DISPLAYED

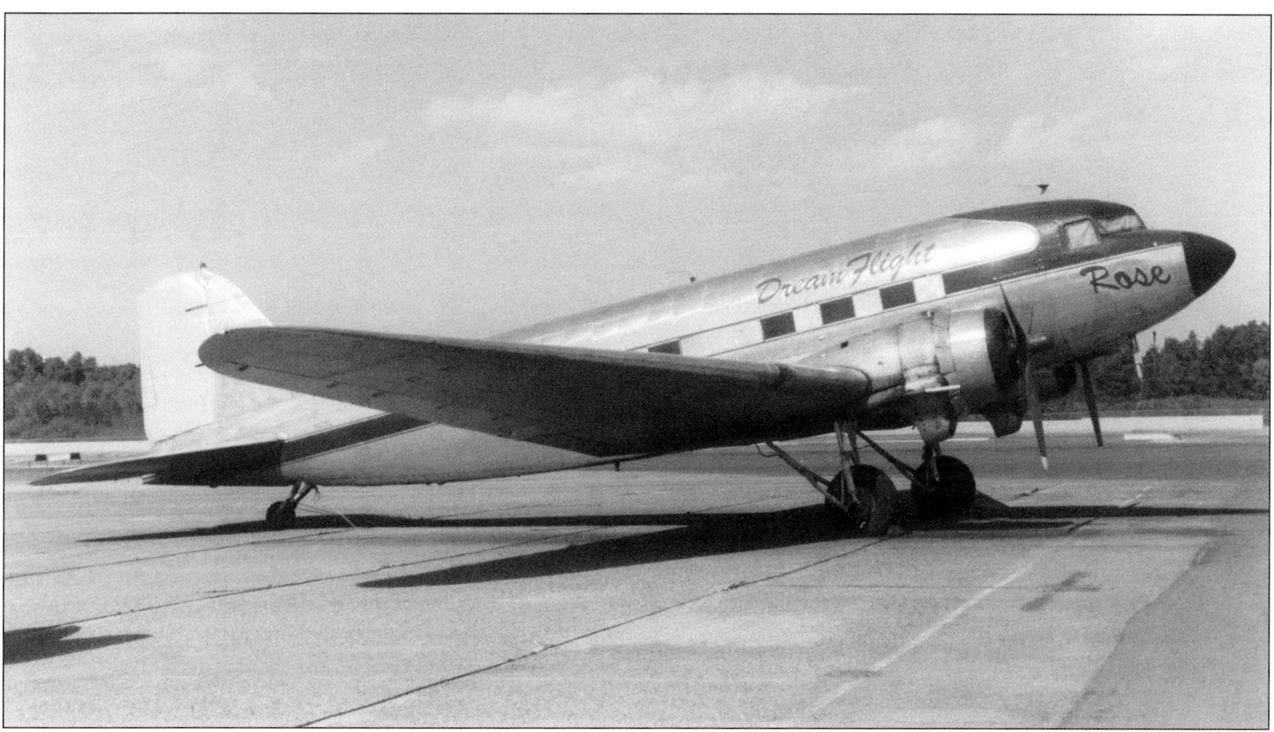

C/n 11639 C-53-DO N101KC "Dream Flight" was photographed at Corona, California in October 2000. *(Eric Wagner)*

11673 42-68746 crashed 11mls SW Garland, NC. No date. (Dec44?)

11674 42-68747 38 TCS Maxton, Mar44.

11675 6153 FA Portuguesa to Africa in Apr59 and to Cape Verde and Guiné in Jan60. To EICPAC at BA2 – Sold 1976.

11676 42-68749 9 AF, 34 TCS, landing accident 16Apr45 at Amiens (B-48), France.

11684 RFC to DPC, Washington, DC as NC18646 13Jan45 – Pan American A/w Inc 26May45 – Lsd Cia Nacional de Aviacion Nicaragua, Managua 29Jun45 – Pan American Sep45 – CU-T266 Cubana 25Oct48 – Reregd CU-P266 08Nov48. Ref to Western is incorrect. (See c/n 18662 Vol 2).

11689 42-68762 310TCS Spanhoe, 9 AF Nov44.

11692 42-68765 based at Voisins (A-58), France in May45.

11693 N7500A was badly damaged 24Oct05 by a hurricane at Opa Locka, FL, nose and tail fin crushed. Noted Shell Creek, FL in Apr08. Fuselage only noted Feb10. DERELICT

11696 NC86593 was leased by WAA to United, not by RFC.

11697 42-68770 del to 71 TC Jun43.

11698 CR-ABJ to 6170 F A Portuguesa – Esq 801 at AB8 – Abandoned in Mozambique 1975 – Probably used by Forca Aerea Popular de Libertacao de Mocambique as 6170 – WFU at Maputo by Dec85.

11700 HH-CNE was reported stored at Santo Domingo-Herrara, Dominican Republic in Mar03 – In Jun09 it was reported dumped at Herrara, Dominican Republic. STORED

11701 N902 became N503 on 19Oct66 – Dates refer to sale to Falstaff.

11705 42-68778 308 TCS, Granada Feb44 – to 813 BU Sedalia, Jun44

11706 NC44991 was leased by WAA to United, not by RFC.

11707 42-68780 crash site was 20mls SW Knollwood, NC.

11709 42-68782 del ATC Jun43, then 79 TCS, Melun (A-55), France, 9 AF.

11710 42-68783 crash site to read Hope Mills, NC.

11716 42-68789 72 TCS, Jun43.

As N19912 this was used by Pan American in Europe in about May/June 1963 between Stuttgart and Frankfurt while work was done on the runway at Stuttgart. On conclusion of this work it went on lease to Treasure Cay. This was the last Pan Am DC-3 operated in Europe, passing through Prestwick on 02Jul63.

11717 42-68790 at Sedalia Apr44.

11719 NC44995 was leased by WAA to United, not by RFC.

XA-IUI was reported for sale in damaged state at Guadalajara in 2001.

11722 42-68795 at Sedalia Apr44.

As F-BFGX this was displayed at Technikmuseum Speyer, Germany in Apr08. DISPLAYED

11726 ZS-NZC last reported in 1998.

11727 42-68800 was with 38 TCS at time of accident.

11729 'EM-3' lsd ex China A/l as B-1531 Apr73 – Crashed 29Dec73 Dalat/Cam-Ly, S Vietnam – Salvage Jan74.

11731 N134D wreck still at Hattiesburg, MS Oct06. DERELICT

11737 N49AG was still at La Ferte Alais in Jun07 – operational in Marine c/s. ACTIVE

11738 42-68811 82 TCS, 9 AF in May45, based at Melun (A-55), France – NC44992 was leased by WAA to United, not by RFC.

11739 42-68812 309 TCS, 9 AF landing accident 04Oct44, Brussels/Evere (B-56), Belgium.

11741 HK-1514 WFU at Guatemala City as 'TG-CHP', a drug runner, Sep03. STORED.

11746 Yugoslav AF 71237 operated by 111 ppa in 1975 – YU-ABW O.C.Z.S = Obrazovni Centar Zracnog Saobracaja [Civil Training Center].

DC-3-65TP SAAF 6875 stored for SAAF Museum at Ysterplaat Sep08-Sep10. STORED

11747 'CA-747' displayed at Museo de la Base Aerea Latacunga, Cotopaxi, Ecuador in Nov01. DISPLAYED

11749 42-68822 315 ATS, 9 AF, Creil (A-81), France had a landing accident at Cambrai (A-74), France, on 01Nov44.

11750 LN-WND is kept airworthy by Steiftelsen Dakota Norway. Visited Duxford, UK in Jul08. ACTIVE

11751 N90SA was reregd N906A on 14Jun47, so delete 'ntu'

11757 N45366 was operational with Inland Empire Wing of Commemorative Air Force at Riverside Municipal Airport, CA in Nov07, in WWII c/s as 268830 'M2/R' "D-Day Doll". I/s May09. ACTIVE

11758 42-68831 315 ATS, 1 ATG, 9 AF, crashed 01Oct44 Toul-Croix de Metz (A-90), France.

11759 NC19453 was leased by WAA to United, not by RFC.

HK-3462 was bought by TARI on 13Aug91. W/o when damaged by fire following an emergency landing at Miraflores, Colombia on 06Jun05.

11761 N130Q was operated as a floatplane by Folsom's Air Service, Greenville, ME in 2004. Current status unknown. ACTIVE?

11762 N19924 painted as '268835' displayed at McClellan AFB, CA in Oct96. Canx by FAA 09Jul09. DISPLAYED

11765 6151 FA Portuguesa operated from BA4 Lajes, probably with Esq 41 (Search and Rescue), ca 1960. In that year it served with EICPAP (Esq. de Instr. Complementar de Pilotagem de Avioes Pesados) at BA2 Ota. To BA4 Lajes 1964 – Based at BA12 Bissau in Apr65 – Mod as bomber but back at Portela-Lisbon in Jun71 – Guiné-Bissau by 1974 where it was abandoned and seen in 1979 and 1983.

11768 42-68841 90 TCS, 438 TCW at the time of its accident [SF/PE]

11770 42-68843 99 TCS, 9 AF Dreux (A-41), France, landing accident 18May45 Le Bourget (A-54), France.

11772 NC17397 was leased by WAA to United, not by RFC.

11775 Despite being reported derelict in 2001 this airframe was registered HK-3348P and test flown on 23Dec04. To YV-1179C and then YV-201T with Aeroejecutivos at Caracas in Jun06. YV-201T noted at Caracas Nov07. ACTIVE [There is confusion here over YV-201T which has also been reported as c/n 10201. The latter was also given as derelict at one time]

11778 42-68851 310 TCS, 9 AF Spanhoe in Nov44.

N45338 regn. canx May09. Scrapped at Ft Lauderdale, FL by 1993.

11779 42-92024 was reported in collision 08May43 at Tinker, according to Form 14.

11780 42-92025 ATC, SW Pacific on 17Apr45.

C-FGHX, or parts of, are preserved at North Atlantic Aviation Museum, Gander.

11797 42-92041 132 FS, 101 FG, Dow, landing accident 3.25 mls NW Limestone, ME on 20Oct50.

11800 42-92043 450BU, Hammer Field, Fresno, 4 AF, Nov45.

11808 Bu 17094 – with VMR-243 by 24Jul43.

11809 42-92051 was actually named 'Green Banana II'.

11810 42-92052 to 9 AF by Feb44.

11812 42-92054 18 TCS, 12 AF on 05Aug44.

11814 42-92056 324 TCS – Accident report shows crashed on take-off Bovingdon, Herts 18Apr46 (fatal) – delete other accident data. Aircraft cartwheeled, so may well have been broken up.

11815 42-92057 315 TCS in May44.

11825 HK-3349 VIARCO noted 'derelict' at Villavicencio in Jul08 and Feb10. DERELICT

11830 42-92070 807 BU Bergstrom Nov44.

11835 N87642 Aero American Corp, broken up by 1977.

11836 42-92076 crashed into river at Portland, ME on 26Jun49 [PE]. It was salvaged and scrapped.

11837 PT-KYZ was preserved at Madrid AFB, Colombia in Feb95. PRESERVED

11839 42-92078 crashed nr South Park, 15 mls S of Pittsburgh, PA, [Pennsylvania ANG]

11842 42-92081 116 FS – Crashed 01Jun48 2.5 mls N of Omara, VA

11846 42-92085 556 BU Long Beach in Mar45 and to MAT, 6 FyG Long Beach on 17Apr45.

11852 42-92090 Wright-Patterson, 4000 BU from 14Aug45 to 02Jan46.

11853 N91016 was canx 27Jun65 after accident on 29May65. The fuselage on landing gear, with wings alongside, can still be found at Nikolski A/fld, Umnak Island, Alaska. DERELICT

11855 42-92093 85 TCS Voisin (A-58), France, 9 AF May45.

11863 42-92100 4100 BU Wright-Patterson, where it had a minor accident, from which it may not have been repaired.

11865 42-92102 61W, 1 TTC Sedalia in Nov44 – To 6 FyG Long Beach, Apr45.

11867 42-92104 to F A Salvadorena 106 (1970?) – i/s Ilopango Nov07. ACTIVE

11870 42-92106 63 TCG Sedalia in Mar44, and 813 BU Sedalia 1 TCC in Dec44.

11871 42-92107 crashed Laurinburg-Maxton AAF, NC in Nov43 – 807 BU Bergstrom in Aug44.

Sold to Pan American, Brownsville to be used in the repair of c/n 1957, but was not so used.

11872 42-92108 was with 813 BU Sedalia in Mar45. Based at 313BU Greenville, it had a landing accident at Lowry Fld, on 07Nov46.

11879 Regd 10May44 to Aeroflot as CCCP-L888.

11883 42-92118 4 TCS, 1 TCC Pope, crashed Mt Vernon, IL in Apr44. There was a further accident in Michigan on 13Feb49 which probably led to salvage and sale – N4868V canx 27Nov53 on sale to Chile.

11885 Regd 28Oct43 to Aeroflot as CCCP-L834.

11887 Regd 20Dec43 to Aeroflot as CCCP-L841.

11889 Regd 16Oct43 to Aeroflot as CCCP-L833.

11891 Regd 07Mar44 to Aeroflot as CCCP-L851.

11892 42-92126 Soviet AF to Aeroflot 14TO, Yakutsk 1946.

11893 Regd 11Dec43 to Aeroflot as CCCP-L840.

11895 Regd 22Dec43 to Aeroflot as CCCP-L842.

11899 Regd 08Apr44 to Aeroflot as CCCP-L875.

11901 Regd 31May44 to Aeroflot as CCCP-L907.

11903 '315156' was no longer displayed at the 84th Aero Squadron Restaurant near Miami Intl. in Jul07 and it is suggested it may have been scrapped.

11906 CF-TES was due to go on display at Greenwood, NS in Apr02. DISPLAYED

11925 6877 SAAF C-47-65TP i/s Sep08, noted at Ysterplaat, Sep10. ACTIVE

11926 ZS-NTE stored with Springbok Flying Safaris at Rand Apt since about 2002. Overhauled and test flown 10Sep09. In Springbok Classic Air c/s at Rand 20Sep10. ACTIVE

11928 42-108808 was on display at Dyess AFB in Sep01 [owner USAF museum]. DISPLAYED

11935 Regd 18Mar44 to Aeroflot as CCCP-L860.

11939 Regd 09Feb44 to Aeroflot as CCCP-L846.

11941 Regd 07Mar44 to Aeroflot as CCCP-L852.

11944 Regd 08Apr44 to Aeroflot as CCCP-L868.

11947 42-92176 Soviet AF to Aeroflot 14 TO, Yakutsk 1946.

11950 Regd 27Mar44 to Aeroflot as CCCP-L864.

11952 Regd 11Feb44 to Aeroflot as CCCP-L848.

11955 Regd 23May44 to Aeroflot as CCCP-L899.

11957 42-92185 Soviet AF to Aeroflot 14 TO, Yakutsk 1946.

11959 42-92186 Soviet AF to Aeroflot 14 TO, Yakutsk 1946,

11960 42-92187 Soviet AF staff aircraft of Gen. E F Loginov, CO of 2 gv, korpus.

11961 42-92188 Soviet AF to Aeroflot 14 TO, Yakutsk 1946.

11962 Regd 14Mar44 to Aeroflot as CCCP-L856.

11964 42-92191 Soviet AF to Aeroflot 14 TO, Yakutsk 1946.

11969 Regd 08Apr44 to Aeroflot as CCCP-L874.

11973 N2-23 R Australian Navy preserved at W Wyalong, NSW in 1996. PRESERVED

11986 C-47-65TP 6811 SAAF stored Snake Valley Feb04 to Jul06 for sale. STORED

11989 Z-WRJ Ormonds Air last reported 1993.

11990 C-47-65TP 6814 SAAF i/s Feb08. Stored Cape Town, noted 24Sep10. STORED

11991 ZS-DIW i/s Phoebus Apollo Sep08. At Rand Apt Apr09-Sep10. ACTIVE

12004 N123DZ was noted at Opa Locka in Nov06, WFU, with no wings or engines, but is not derelict and could fly again if there was a demand. STORED

12026 ZS-DRJ WFU Mar06, but i/s with C J Mueller, Rand, Mar08 – To Turbine Versions (Pty) Ltd B19Nov09 – Rest to airworthiness 30Jan10 and flown Rand-Wonderboom – Noted in Africa Charter Airlines c/s at Wonderboom 22Sep10. ACTIVE

12030 Regd 14Mar44 to Aeroflot as CCCP-L858.

12054 is claimed to be CS-TAI, R01Sep61 and canx 06Aug71 as exported to EL-AAB. This does not account for 9G-AAE being canx 09Nov70, though there may have been a paperwork lapse in Ghana! The only photographic evidence seen of 9G-AAE was taken in Sep60 by Roger Caratini. Another photo, of EL-AAB, was taken in Aug60. There have been two EL-AABs, but the first was canx in 1953. Thus, the second EL-AAB cannot have been ex CS-TAI as there is an eleven year discrepancy.

12056 VH-SBL Discovery Airways airworthy at Sydney-Bankstown Mar10. ACTIVE

12060 CS-TAI Lsd from Atlantico Interplano – Op. by SATA – N751A to WWII Airborne Demonstration Team Foundation, Frederick, OK R15Aug07. ACTIVE

12064 C-47-65TP 6884 SAAF Stored Bokrivier AFB Jul08. STORED

12073 ZS-DAK and 5Y-DAK ntu. ZS-MFY ICRC titles, DC-3-65TP – Stored Lanseria Jan07 engineless – To New Order Vehicle Sales CC, i/s Sep09 – Wonderair, noted 22Sep10 at Wonderboom. ACTIVE

12075 G-AGIZ actually crashed at Guernsey Airport on the date given, having hit the boundary hedge on approach, ending up on her nose. She was rebuilt.

12090 SAAF 6866 reported stored at Snake Valley Sep96, fuselage only. Presumably ex ZS-DCA.

12100 42-92313/FZ565 – the accident report for the former gives date as 06Dec43, so never handed over to RAF.

12105 FZ570 was hit on ground by C-47 41-38725 at Maison Blanche, Algeria on 10Nov44 (correction). The latter was salvaged.

12106 N4991E W C Dause, Lodi, CA, i/s Oct03. ACTIVE?

12107 ZS-BXF SAA Museum, Rand Apt i/s Nov06. ACTIVE

12111 FZ576 – according to a memorial at Port Hardy, BC, crash date was 19Apr44

12115 N192RD stored engineless at Mesa, AR Sep06. Regd to Dodson International Parts Inc, Rantoul, KS 11Aug07. STORED

12117 Regd 10May44 to Aeroflot as CCCP-L889.

12119 42-92330 Soviet AF. CCCP-L857 R14Mar44 to Aeroflot. Soviet AF 10 gatd GVF [also 40430] – also GC3 Normandie-Niemen 1944.

12123 Regd 09Feb44 to Aeroflot as CCCP-L845.

12127 42-92338 – Soviet AF '026' R10May44 to Aeroflot as CCCP-L890.

12129 Regd 10Apr44 to Aeroflot as CCCP-L877.

12131 42-92341 - Soviet AF to Aeroflot 14 TO, Yakutsk, 1946.

12133 Regd 10Feb44 to Aeroflot as CCCP-L847.

12136 Regd 25Mar44 to Aeroflot as CCCP-L862.

12150 HS-SAF Siamese A/ws – W/o 20Aug51 Hua Hin – fuselage used for parachute ground trainer at Hua Hin Apt, PARU base, from before 1995 to 2007. STORED

12160 C-47-65TP 6825 SAAF i/s Sep08, noted Ysterplaat Sep10. ACTIVE

12164 was originally given as going direct from FZ609 to Spanish AF. However new research shows it was regd EC-EAC before T3.1, not as given on page 213 of Vol 1.

12166 N8194Z still at Wonderboom and marked c/n 6886 by Jan07 – Regd to Dodson International Parts Inc, 11Aug07 – Freeway airstrip by 18Feb10. STORED

12172 N3BA Jim Hankins, WFU Jul08 at Hawkins Fld, MS. STORED

12187 VH-BPA ex N5590C 'Bush Pilots' display at Cairns, QLD 2001. Broken up at Cairns Feb09 because of salt corrosion. Cockpit to Mareeba.

12192 XA-UDY California-Pacifico R Dec05 ex XA-RNF [or XA-RZF?]. ACTIVE?

12196 510 F A Guatemalteca in very poor condition at Guatemala City Feb06 and Nov07. DERELICT

12205 C9-STF displayed at Ratanga Jct, Cape Town in Sep08. DISPLAYED

12212 42-92415 9 AF, 303 TCS in Jun44 and then to 305 TCS – Forced landing Gravesend, Kent after damage by friendly fire 15Mar45.

12217 FZ658 also carries CAF serial 12963. Remains present at Trenton in Jun05. DERELICT

12221 42-92422 crashed 06Apr45 at Hesse (B-24), Germany

12223 42-92424 9 AF, 304 TCS, crash-landed 19Jan45 St Andre-de-l'Eure (B-24), France.

12224 Regd 08Apr44 to Aeroflot as CCCP-L876.

12225 Regd 07Mar44 to Aeroflot, Moscow as CCCP-L854. Operated by 15 ATO. W/o 31Jan46 on a positioning flight from Bykovo to Vnukovo after the port engine failed 15 minutes into the flight & the propeller could not be feathered. The crew decided to make an emergency landing at Sukovo (now the Solntsevo district of Moscow), but had to go around as the undercarriage was not locked down. Climbing out, the starboard engine overheated and failed, the aircraft entered a spin and crashed into a forest, killing 3 of the 5 crew.

12228 42-108838 9 AF, 303 TCS was damaged at Weston Zoyland on 21Jun44 and with 305 TCS had a landing accident at Wiesbaden (Y-80), Germany on 09Aug45. The latter may have caused demise.

12230 Regd 03Feb44 to Aeroflot as CCCP-L844.

12231 Regd 27Mar44 to Aeroflot as CCCP-L863.

12237 Regd 06Mar44 to Aeroflot as CCCP-L849.

12241 42-92440 Soviet AF to Aeroflot 14 TO, Yakutsk 1946.

12243 Regd 08Apr44 to Aeroflot as CCCP-L871.

12248 '212248' R Thai AF toc 22Oct53 – 61 Sq Nov53 – Thai A/w L06Feb61 – HS-TDI R03Mar61 – 212248 RTAF 61 Sq 15Nov61 – FTS 18Dec61 – 21 Sq 30Oct64 – 23 Sq 10Sep65 – TAC 10Aug67 – SOC 23Apr91 – Tango Sq – by Jan94 for static display Chiang Mai and still there Mar09. DISPLAYED

12251 '2100558' continues in D-day c/s at Musée de l'Air, Le Bourget, Paris Mar08. DISPLAYED

12253 C-FDTD preserved Quebec Air & Space Museum, St Hubert, QC 1996. Stored Montreal, QC by Aug10. DISPLAYED

12254 'G-AMZZ' preserved Al Mahata Museum, Sharjah, UAE Nov08, in Gulf Airways c/s. DISPLAYED

12256 FZ671 CAF, preserved Comox CFB, BC Aug01. PRESERVED

12259 42-92456 was based at St André-de-l'Eure (B-24), France at time of accident.

12260 42-92457 303 TCS, 442 TCG, AFE in Apr46.

12261 N224GB remained in storage at LeHigh Acres, FL as of Feb07, engineless. Broken up by Dec08.

12262 42-92459 was based at St André-de-l'Eure (B-24), France at time of accident.

12267 N983DC 'Air North' i/s Nov05 & Jul10. ACTIVE

12269 N489F finally canx by FAA 27Jul09.

12287 XA-ROM S A Ejecutivos, Guadalajara, stored 2001 to Nov09. STORED

12295 C-GRSB Govt of Canada, i/s 2001. ACTIVE

12297 NC67796 Moebus & Wells was regd as an R4D-5 so must be Bu 17139 c/n 12297 NOT 34406. Transfer history to 12297.

12300 N907Z was noted at Oshkosh in Jun06 with MVA titles. In Jul07 it had lost engines and titles. Stored Jul08 at Oshkosh. In Jul09 this was BT-67 conv. number 54 – Oiland LLC, Grand Rapids, MI, R23Sep09 – C-GVKB Kenn Borek Air Ltd, R 22Oct09. [Fitted with skis for Antarctic operations]. ACTIVE

12303 PP-YPU Coop. Colon. Preserved 1996 Canarana, Matto Grosso, Brazil. DISPLAYED

12317 N47TF Chino Warbirds Inc, was noted at Chino, again, in Oct03 – To Air Museum Inc, Chino, CA 30Jan09 – In Pacific Southwest c/s at Chino Aug09. ACTIVE

12318 still marked as OO-AWM at Lagos-Ikeja 16May70 – No Nigerian AF titles – Semi-derelict.

12327 C-GWZS Buffalo Airways, i/s Sep08. ACTIVE

DC-2 and DC-3 publicity through the ages

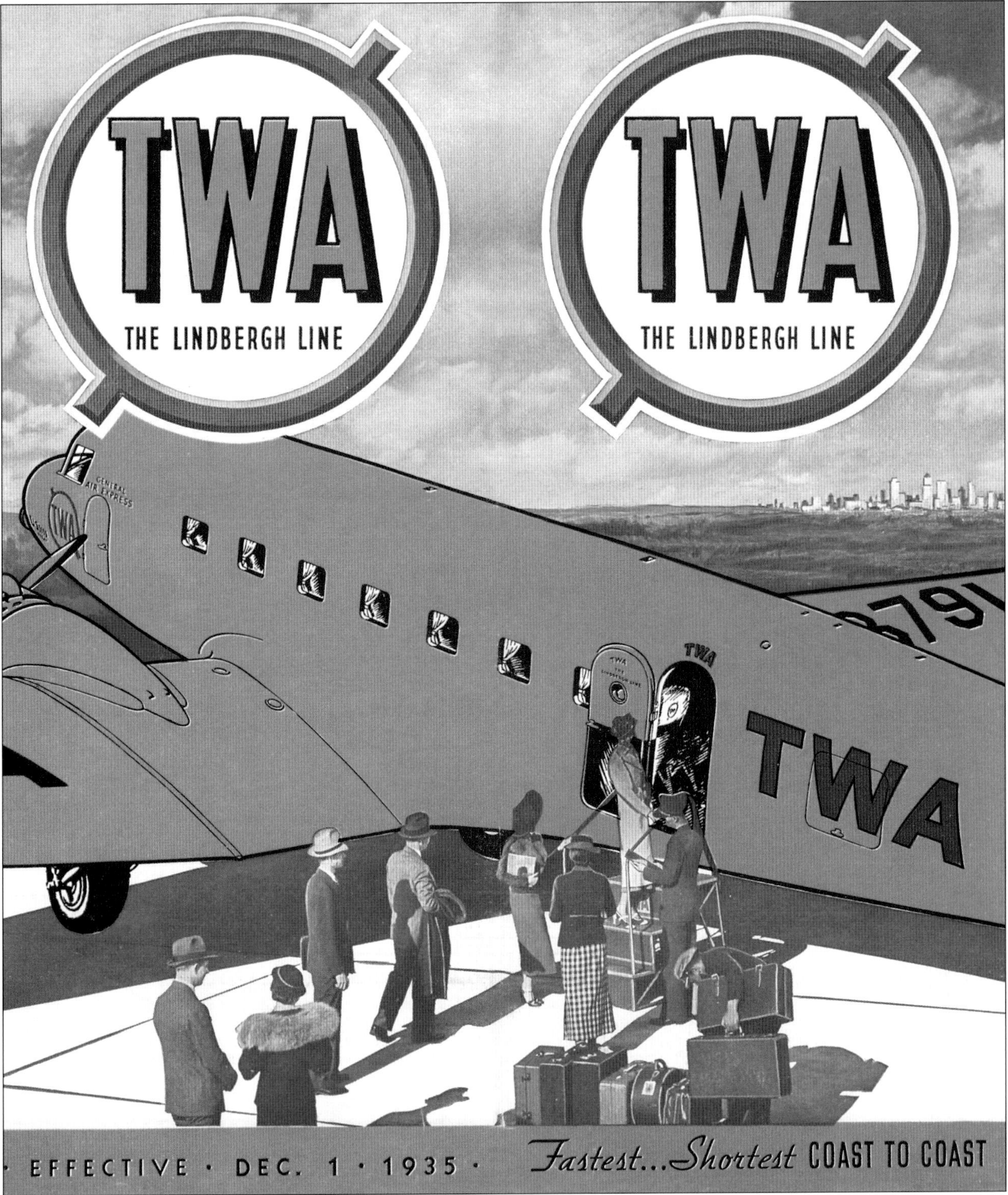

The cover of Transcontinental & Western Air's timetable effective from 1st December 1935 with DC-2 "NC13791" and passengers boarding. The fleet was referred to as "TWA's luxurious Douglas twin-engined Skyliners". The coast-to-coast (New York-Los Angeles) schedules even have the footnote "over Grand Canyon & Boulder Dam".

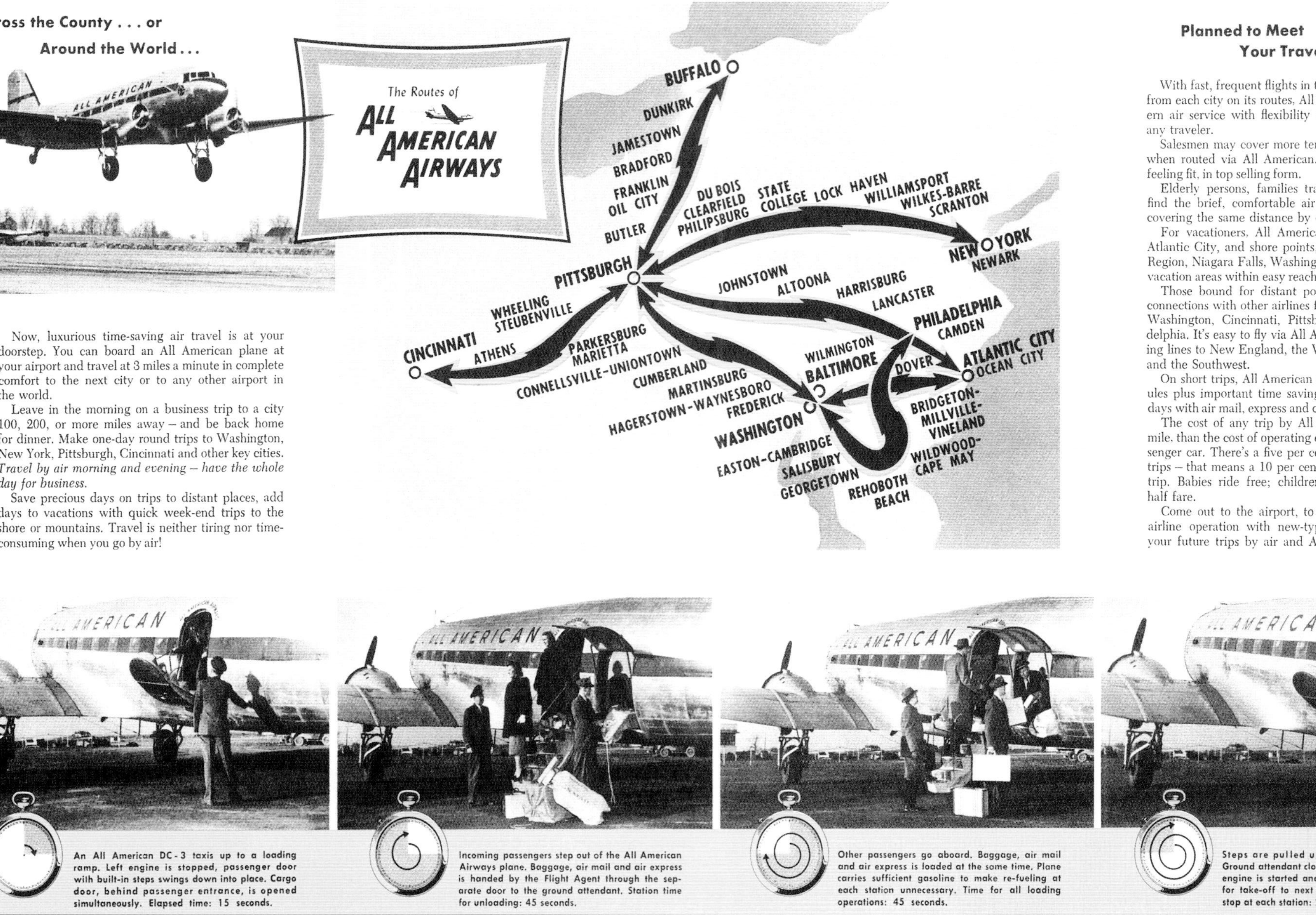

Across the County . . . or Around the World . . .

Now, luxurious time-saving air travel is at your doorstep. You can board an All American plane at your airport and travel at 3 miles a minute in complete comfort to the next city or to any other airport in the world.

Leave in the morning on a business trip to a city 100, 200, or more miles away – and be back home for dinner. Make one-day round trips to Washington, New York, Pittsburgh, Cincinnati and other key cities. *Travel by air morning and evening – have the whole day for business.*

Save precious days on trips to distant places, add days to vacations with quick week-end trips to the shore or mountains. Travel is neither tiring nor time-consuming when you go by air!

Planned to Meet Your Travel Needs . . .

With fast, frequent flights in two or more directions from each city on its routes, All American offers modern air service with flexibility to meet the needs of any traveler.

Salesmen may cover more territory, cover it faster, when routed via All American. They arrive fresher, feeling fit, in top selling form.

Elderly persons, families traveling with children find the brief, comfortable air ride less tiring than covering the same distance by car, bus, or train.

For vacationers, All American brings New York, Atlantic City, and shore points, the Chesapeake Bay Region, Niagara Falls, Washington and other favorite vacation areas within easy reach.

Those bound for distant points make convenient connections with other airlines flying from New York, Washington, Cincinnati, Pittsburgh, Buffalo, Philadelphia. It's easy to fly via All American and connecting lines to New England, the West Coast, to Florida and the Southwest.

On short trips, All American offers frequent schedules plus important time saving. Business firms save days with air mail, express and cargo.

The cost of any trip by All American is less, per mile, than the cost of operating even a low-priced passenger car. There's a five per cent discount on round trips – that means a 10 per cent saving on the return trip. Babies ride free; children two to twelve pay half fare.

Come out to the airport, to see this new type of airline operation with new-type planes. And plan your future trips by air and All American Airways.

An All American DC-3 taxis up to a loading ramp. Left engine is stopped, passenger door with built-in steps swings down into place. Cargo door, behind passenger entrance, is opened simultaneously. Elapsed time: 15 seconds.

Incoming passengers step out of the All American Airways plane. Baggage, air mail and air express is handed by the Flight Agent through the separate door to the ground attendant. Station time for unloading: 45 seconds.

Other passengers go aboard. Baggage, air mail and air express is loaded at the same time. Plane carries sufficient gasoline to make re-fueling at each station unnecessary. Time for all loading operations: 45 seconds.

Steps are pulled up, passenger door closed. Ground attendant closes baggage door. Left-hand engine is started and plane taxis out on runway for take-off to next city. Total elapsed time for stop at each station: 2 minutes.

All-American Airways' brochure introducing a "more useful kind of air service" circa 1950-51 and illustrating the short turn-rounds at intermediate stops – total elapsed time: two minutes, contrasting dramatically with today's airport experiences.

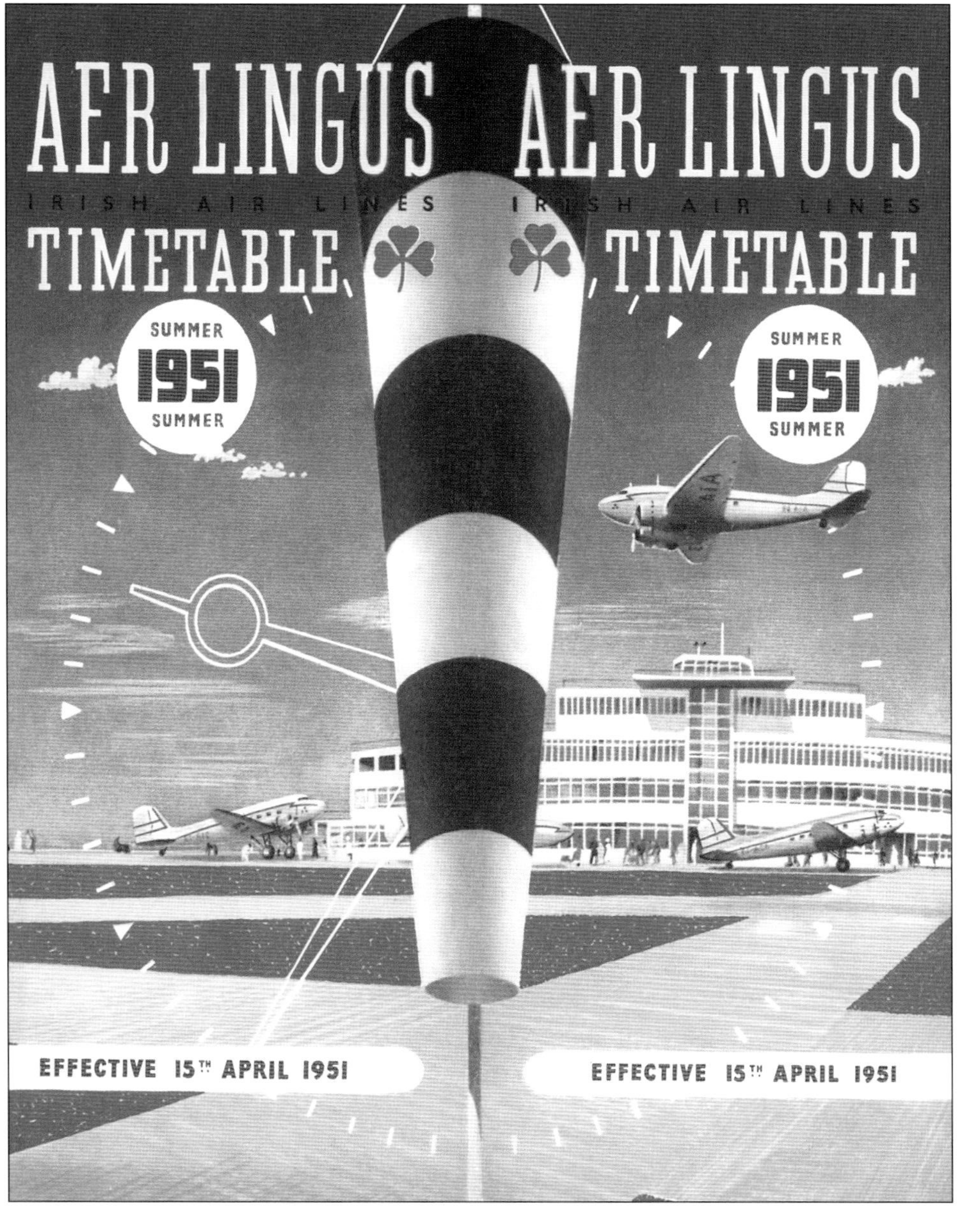

In Europe, DC-3s and Dakotas formed the mainstay of air travel into the 1950s, as illustrated by the cover of this Aer Lingus timetable of the airline's summer 1951 schedules. The back cover advertises BP's aviation gasoline and includes a fine painting of EI-AFC "St.Enda" with the correct name and "last two" of the registration on the nose.

PRESENTATION DE L'AVION
Il n'est pas lent, il est paisible.
Il n'est pas démodé mais très confortable.
Il n'est pas cher mais... c'est une qualité !!

CARACTERISTIQUES

Equipage : 2 pilotes et une hôtesse
Altitude de croisière : 3 à 4000 m
Autonomie : 1500 kilomètres sans escale
Piste accessibles : 800 m en herbe
Aménagements : galley - possibilité de repas chauds, catering à la demande.
Versions :
. mixte - fret et passagers -
. passagers : 34 maximum
. fret : 3,5 tonnes maximum

SON EMPLOI AU SEIN D'UNI AIR
Le DC 3 est avant tout un avion robuste et pratique dont les qualités de sécurité ne sont plus à démontrer. Il «s'habille» pour vous en fonction de vos besoins. Il sait être «exécutive» et transportera confortablement votre équipe de cadres. Il sait se transformer en version «mixte» (passagers et matériel). Il peut prendre des allures d'avion de «ligne» ou devenir, sur votre demande, un transporteur de fret.

European charter companies utilized DC-3s throughout the 1960s and into the 1970s, as illustrated by this Uni-air brochure from the early 1970s. Two former Air France maximiser-modified DC-3s head the brochure, while the smart interior is illustrated below. The aircraft was available for 34 passengers, 3.5 tonnes of freight or mixed cargo-pax interior. One of the aircraft illustrated is F-BCYT.

DOUGLAS DC3 DAKOTA
F–GEOM

IN *"CLASSIC AIRWAYS"* LIVERY

Delivered Long Beach Californian to USAF in 1942, eventually to be re–registered in France, to French Air Force, and finally to Transvalair ACE, before being re–registered to **Classic Airways** as **G–OFON** this May 1993 on UK register.

We'll fly you as far as your imagination...

Air Atlantique

FLY TO THE AIRSHOW

IN THE DAKOTA!

Nostalgic flights in Dakotas continued in Europe and the USA throughout the 1990s and into the 21st century, as shown by these advertising flyers from Classic Airways and Air Atlantique in the mid-1990s, the former using a genuine photographic print! G-OFON was not taken up, but the aircraft flew for many years in the illustrated colour-scheme as G-DAKK for South Coast Airways.

Survivors

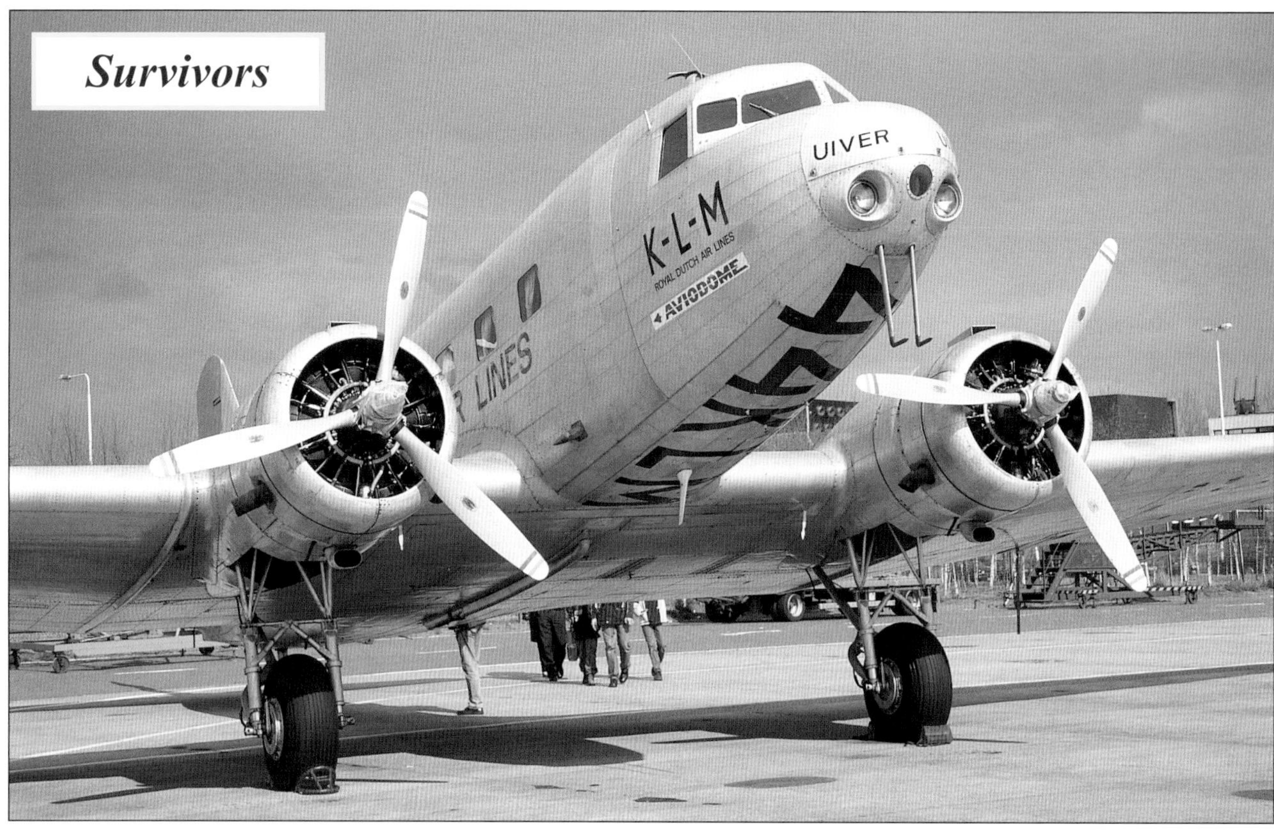

C/n 1404 DC-2-142 N39165 painted as 'PH-AJU' to commemorate the England-Australia race in 1934. This is the only airworthy DC-2 in Europe and is kept at Amsterdam-Schiphol. The photo was taken in March 2000. *(Michael Prophet)*

C/n 1911 DC-3A EI-AYO is a former American Airlines aircraft, now preserved in the Science Museum Collection at Wroughton, near Swindon in south-west England. *(Stephen Piercey)*

C/n 1920 DC-3 NC17334 painted in its original American Airlines colours. After four other registration marks, the aircraft's original marks were reclaimed in 1995. The current owner is the Flagship Detroit Foundation. The aircraft was photographed at Oshkosh, Wisconsin in July 2009. *(Al Hansen)*

C/n 2053 DC-3/C-41 NC41HQ painted as '38-502' (the serial the aircraft carried with the USAAC). This aircraft served originally with 1st Staff Squadron at Wright Field, remaining with the Air Force until 1945. Photographed at "The Last Time Douglas DC-3 & C-47 Reunion" at Rock Falls, Illinois on 25th July 2010. (Ralph M Pettersen)

C/n 2072 DC-2/C-39 serial 38-515 modified with DC-3 tail and freight door. This hybrid aircraft is preserved at the Museum of the United States Air Force at Dayton, Ohio, where this photograph was taken. (Charles N Trask)

C/n 1997 N18121 in Eastern Air Lines 1950s colour-scheme is seen taking off from "The Last Time Douglas DC-3 & C-47 Reunion" at Rock Falls, Illinois on 26th July 2010, en route for Oshkosh, Wisconsin. (Ralph M Pettersen)

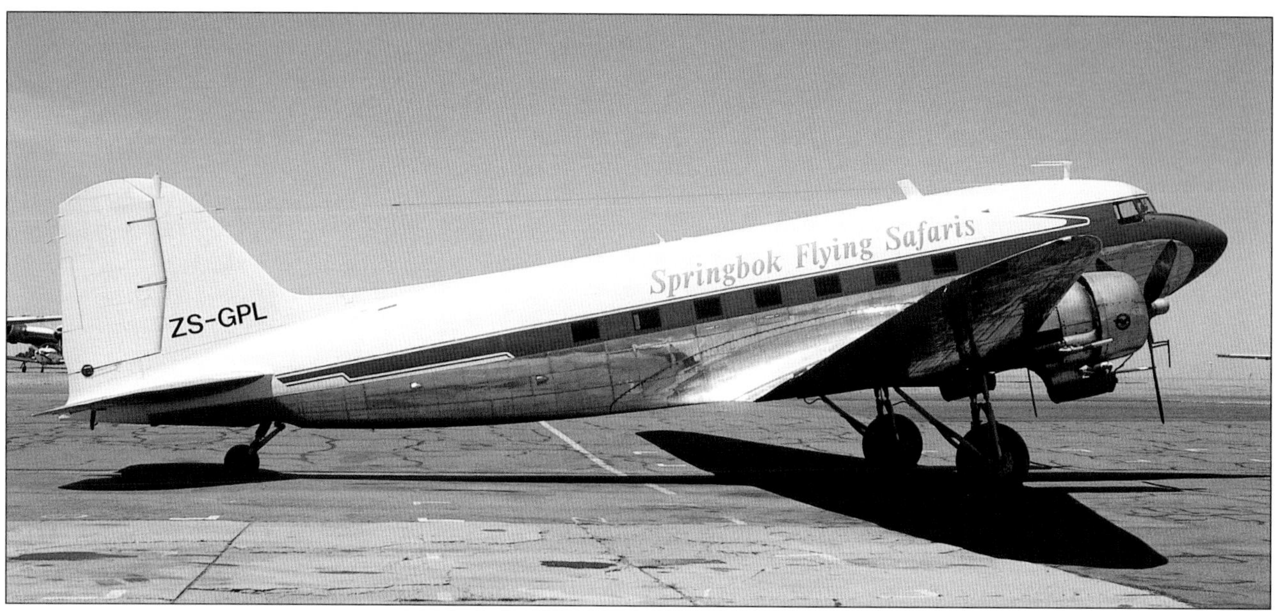

C/n 9581 ZS-GPL owned by Springbok Flying Safaris, based at Johannesburg-Rand where it was photographed in October 2003. *(Andy Heape)*

C/n 11750 LN-WND of 'Dakota Norway' and currently operated by the Stiftelsen Dakota Norway. The aircraft was photographed at Duxford in July 2003. *(Jennifer Gradidge)*

C/n 2054 N143D in "Herpa Wings" colours, complete with 75th Anniversary logo, at "The Last Time Douglas DC-3 & C-47 Reunion" at Rock Falls, Illinois on 24th July 2010. *(Ralph M Pettersen)*

C/n 13296 CC-CLDT in LAN-Chile colours at the Museo Nacional Aeronautica y del Espacio at Los Cerillos, Santiago. *(PJ Marson Collection)*

C/n 13331 ZS-CRV in Rovos Air colours and named "Delaney", taken at Lanseria in February 2008. The aircraft was taken over by Namibia Commercial Aviation for safari work later in 2008. *(Andy Heape)*

C/n 13448 CF-BZI preserved in the colours of Northwest Territorial Airways at the Calgary Air & Space Museum in Alberta, where it was photographed on 20th July 2001. Note the additional ski undercarriage. *(PJ Marson)*

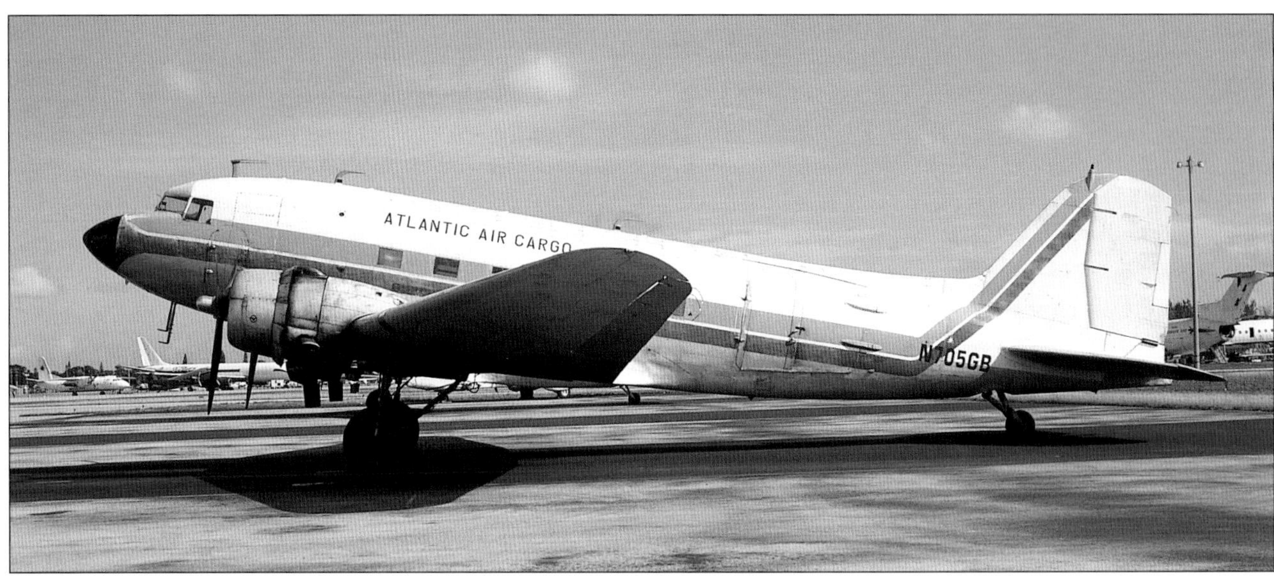

C/n 13854 N705GB of Atlantic Air Cargo, taken at Opa Locka, Florida in May 2002. This aircraft continues to operate to the Caribbean islands on cargo charters. (Joe Handelman)

C/n 13861 TF-NPK was painted in the colours of Icelandair (Flugfelag Islands HF) to celebrate the 50th anniversary of the company's first international flight in July 1945. The aircraft visited the Flying Legends air show at Duxford, England, where this photo was taken on 9th July 1995, and is still airworthy in Iceland. (Jennifer Gradidge)

C/n 13877 YSL-52 of the Turkish Air Force was photographed at the Havacilik Müzesi (Air Force Museum) at Istanbul-Yesilkoy, and is one of the two Dakotas preserved there. (PJ Marson Collection)

C/n 13883 SE-CFP of the Stiftelsen Flygande Veteraner, based at Stockholm, has been painted in an early Scandinavian Airlines System colour-scheme and was photographed visiting a European airshow. *(Mike Hooks)*

C/n 18923 ZK-CAW, formerly used by Fieldair in the agricultural role, has been given a new lease of life as a tourist attraction at the McDonalds' restaurant in Taupo, South Island, New Zealand, where it was photographed on 21st March 2007. *(PJ Marson)*

C/n 19661 HK-3292 of Air Colombia is one of a number of DC-3s still seeing regular use in Colombia. The photo was taken at Villavicencio on 28th February 2005. *(Karl Krämer)*

C/n 25634 N777YA in the colours of Woods Air Service. This aircraft, now used by Bush Air Cargo, is still active in Alaska. It was photographed at its Palmer base in August 2000. (Al Hansen)

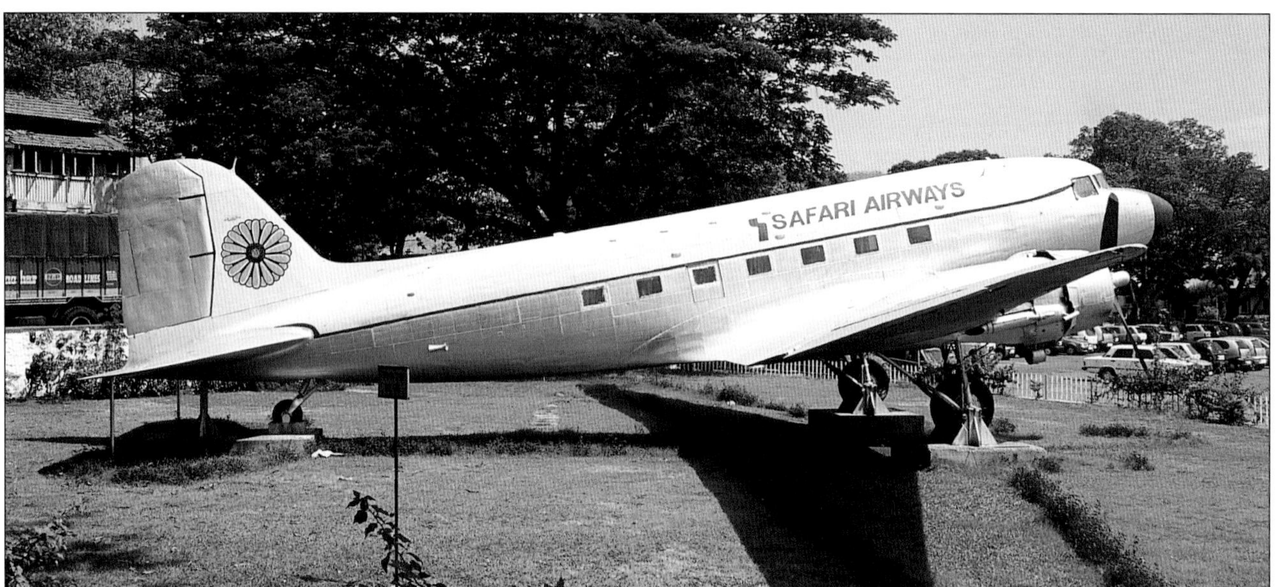

C/n 26491 VT-CEB, formerly of the Raymond Woollen Mills, is one of a number of Dakotas that are preserved in India. This example is displayed in the colours of Safari Airways at Mumbai (formerly Bombay). (Jimmy Wadia)

C/n 26569 G-AMPY of Air Atlantique in the colours of Royal Air Force Transport Command as 'KK116' at Coventry-Baginton in March 2008, when the type was still permitted to carry out passenger flying in the UK. Hopefully regulations will allow the Dakota to return to its passenger flying role in the not too distant future. (Jennifer Gradidge)

C/n 33048 44-76716, a TC-47B officially registered as N8704, in typical USAF 1960s colour-scheme, and owned by the Yankee Air Museum, is seen taking off from "The Last Time Douglas DC-3 & C-47 Reunion" at Rock Falls, Illinois on 26th July 2010, en route to Oshkosh, Wisconsin. (Ralph M Pettersen)

C/n 27098 serial 2032 of the Paraguayan Air Force in storage at Asuncion. (PJ Marson Collection)

C/n 32884 VH-TMQ in immaculate condition at Melbourne-Essendon on 23rd October 2003, in use with Air Nostalgia Pty Ltd. The aircraft is fitted with TV monitors at every seat. (PJ Marson)

C/n 33419 KP208 photographed in a dismantled state at North Weald, England, in June 2009, prior to moving to its new location at Chelmsford in eastern England for further preservation. The photo shows well how the airframe can be dismantled for transport. The centre section is behind the nose and the wings can be seen behind the fuselage. Unfortunately this aircraft would in fact never have carried D-day stripes, as it was not delivered to the Royal Air Force until June 1945. (Jennifer Gradidge)

C/n 33436 G-ANAF of Atlantic Air Transport at Coventry-Baginton in March 2009. The Dakota is leased to Thales Avionics and used to test radar – note the radome under the nose. An APU is fitted on the starboard side, behind the wing, to power the radar equipment. (Jennifer Gradidge)

C/n 34370 N814CL owned by Clay Lacey and painted in 1940s style United Air Lines colours as "Mainliner O'Connor". The aircraft was photographed at Van Nuys, California in July 2001. (Al Hansen)

C/n 42961 N3006. One of the postwar production of DC-3Ds, this aircraft is unusual in having been delivered directly into corporate use in 1946. The aircraft is owned by DC-3 Entertainment LLP and was photographed in July 2006. *(C Waldenman via Lionel Paul)*

C/n 43301 N32TN in the colours of the Super DC-3 prototype and operated by TMF Aircraft Incorporated, Opa Locka, Florida, where this photo was taken in October 2007. The aircraft was previously operated by Trans Northern, hence the "TN" suffix to the registration. *(PJ Marson)*

C/n 43312 N587MB, in contrast to N32TN, is operated by TMF Aircraft Incorporated in a plain overall bare metal scheme from Opa Locka, Florida. The Super DC-3 was photographed at Miami International in December 2003. *(Joe Handelman)*

C/n unknown, serial IJ817, of the Indian Air Force, is preserved at the IAF Museum at Palam, New Delhi where it was photographed in July 1994. (Eric Wagner)

C/n 34378 N1944H in the lovely Era Classic Airlines scheme taxies by at "The Last Time Douglas DC-3 & C-47 Reunion" at Rock Falls, Illinois on 25th July 2010. Note the picture windows fore and aft. (Ralph M Pettersen)

C/n 32961 ZS-OJJ Dodson TurboDak in Air Services markings taken at Bathurst, NSW, Australia on 24th March 2009. The aircraft had been operating in Australia since at least 2007. (Keith Palmer)

12331 N9382 Pro Freight, stored Opa Locka, FL Jul05 – Aeromarine Airways Inc., Miami, FL R23Jul10 – was stored at Richards Field, FL. STORED

12352 HK-2666 was stored at Villavicencio in 2005, but there has been no recent news, so probably broken up.

12363 N59314 has been stored at Palmer, AK since owner Abbe Air Cargo ceased trading in 2004. Still stored there Jul10. STORED

12369 N583V WFU at Fort Worth Sycamore Strip, TX Sep07 – Regd to Sun Coast 25Feb05 – Regd to James P A Thompson, Longwood, FL 03Jan08 – Stored at Sycamore Strip. STORED

12374 HC-SBR f/n 18 "Star of Altar" was almost certainly del ex Canadair on 29Jan47 as it entered service with Shell on 07Feb47.

12377 CF-ILQ, which crashed near Rupert River, QC remains at crash site as of June 2009.

12381 YU-ABE JAT – Caught fire in flight, then forced landing 08Jun51 – DBF.

12386 '1840' noted at Maracay Museum, Venezuela Dec07. DISPLAYED

12390 42-92574 – Soviet AF. R06Mar44 to Aeroflot as CCCP-L850. – GVF 101 apdd – fitted with dorsal turret – GVF '2574E'

12393 42-92577 C-47C 11 AF, 7 FG Alaska, landing accident 22Sep44.

12394 Regd 08Apr44 to Aeroflot as CCCP-L873.

12398 Regd 03Apr44 to Aeroflot as CCCP-L865.

12399 Regd 07Mar44 to Aeroflot as CCCP-L855.

12400 Regd 18Mar44 to Aeroflot as CCCP-L861.

12402 Regd 04Apr44 to Aeroflot as CCCP-L867.

12405 Regd 08Apr44 to Aeroflot as CCCP-L872.

12407 Regd 19Apr44 to Aeroflot as CCCP-L879.

12409 42-92591 Soviet AF to Aeroflot 14TO, Yakutsk 1946.

12410 Regd 07Mar44 to Aeroflot as CCCP-L853.

12413 ZS-BXJ SAA Historic Flight, i/s 2008. ACTIVE

12415 C-47-65TP 6828 SAAF i/s Ysterplaat Sep08. ACTIVE

12425 N99FS 'KG395' Brooks Avn Inc, Douglas, GA i/s Jul08-2010. ACTIVE

12438 N700CA Champlain Air, believed airworthy. ACTIVE?

12445 CR-LDK was with ARTOP in 1961 and to Consorcio Tecnico de Aeronautica SRL in 1965 – To D2-FDK in Nov75 – TAAG (1979). Quoted as CU-T1558 with Aerotaxi at Havana May06 wfu. [Not CU-T1058, see c/n 32664]. STORED

12446 1120 F A Colombiana – wreck on dump at Madrid, Jun08. DERELICT

12449 BJ764 Indian AF – Preserved Bangalore to Feb08. PRESERVED

12471 '71' Aéronautique Navale, Musée de l'Air, Dugny store, Le Bourget, noted Mar08 and Sep09. STORED

12472 PH-MAG was noted at Lagos still as such on 05Mar74 with 'Dakota Airlines' titles, probably connected with Scorpio Films ownership.

12478 6832 SAAF, preserved SAAF Museum, Ysterplaat Sep10. DISPLAYED

12486 4X-FNL/04 IDF/AF Museum, Hatzerim, Israel, preserved Dec08. PRESERVED

12487 L2-33/13 R Thai AF 62 Sq toc 07Jul72 – Std Takhli Sep76 – SOC 14Aug81 and broken up.

12490 KG455 CAF Airborne Museum, Petawawa CFB, ON - Preserved 1996. DISPLAYED

12494 BJ496 Indian AF preserved Bangalore Feb08. PRESERVED

12498 2108865 R Thai AF, '865' toc 16Feb71 – 62 Sq 20May71 – to AC-47 – 42 Sq 25May77 – rn 402 Sq 01Oct77 – 603 Sq 21Nov83 – wfu by Feb84 – to Lopburi for display Nov88 – on display since approx May89 – Mar09. DISPLAYED

12506 42-92679 36 TCS, 9 AF had mid-air collision with C-47 42-108877 12May44, nr Berwick, E Sussex. [Correction].

12508 '0-28866' was no longer at Pate Museum, TX, on 18Nov06.

12509 42-92681 100 TCS, 9 AF crash-landed at Dreux (A-41), France on 10May45.

12514 42-92686 11 TCS, 12 AF, in Jun44.

12524 N837M noted airworthy at LeHigh Acres, FL in Feb07, but by Dec08/Feb10 it was engineless. STORED

12528 42-108868 was still listed as a C-47C with the 11 AF on 15Apr45.

12530 42-92700 the mountain crash site was near St Chamond, St Etienne, France.

12531 42-92701 operated by Polish AF as tactical no 5 SPL.

12534 42-92704 was based at Melun (A-55), France in Apr45.

12536 42-92706 crash-landed 13Nov45 3mls S of San Bernardino, CA, 126 BU.

12537 42-92707, unit at time of crash was 9 TCP [not 9 TCS], 15 AF.

12538 42-108869 crashed 08May55 15 mls ESE Barnesville, OH.

12539 XW-PFT leased to Air America 24Jun69 for one flight. Returned to CASI Jun69.

12540 VH-MMF was moved to Bankstown on 21Jun02 for restoration to airworthiness for Geoff Leach. ACTIVE

12542 N2-43 HMAS Albatross, R Australian Navy, Nowra. Preserved Nowra 2001. PRESERVED

12543 5T-MAH returned from Basler's to Mauretania on 13Sep06 after overhaul. ACTIVE

12547 42-92716 90 TCS, 9 AF landing accident 17May45 Le Bourget (A-54), France.

12550 VQ-TAF WFU at Port au Prince, Haiti in Oct01.

12557 2030 F A Paraguaya, WFU as instructional airframe at Asuncion, Oct03. STORED

12561 42-92728 was named 'Eightball Charlie' in April 1945.

12563 42-92730 303 TCS, 9 AF, Metz (Y-34), France in Jul45.

12564 42-92731 99 TCS by 26Apr44.

12566 42-92733 310 TCS, 9 AF from Oct44, was hit by 42-23474 on ground at Biggin Hill, Kent on 22Aug45, but not written off, as with 325 TCS, 9 ASC it had a taxying accident on 30Jan46 at Ansbach, Germany. This was the probable cause of salvage.

12568 42-108872 23 FS, 26 FG, 9 AF, R-12 Germany had a landing accident at RAF Penshurst, Kent, 10Jul45.

12570 LAB's records for CB-34 give date of purchase from Panagra as 27Aug47 (not Aug45).

CP-607 was still derelict at Cochabamba in Mar06, but by Jul08 it was with TAVIC [Cochabamba parachute club] awaiting certification on 13Dec08. ACTIVE

12578 42-108873 collision was with C-47 43-15341 on 08Jul44.

12580 6864 SAAF was stored at Boksrivier Military Training Facility in Sep08, for survival training. STORED

12582 N81949 stored at Wonderboom Jan07, marked c/n 6876. To Dodson International Parts Inc, Rantoul, KS R15Aug07 – To Freeway airstrip by 18Feb10. STORED

12586 6859 SAAF, SAAF Museum, Swartkop, noted Sep10. DISPLAYED

12590 N834TP National Test Pilots School, Mojave, CA [DC-3-65TP] – l/s Mar03 – DBR 04Feb09 Mojave. Fuselage noted on trailer at Ottawa, KS in Jul09 – For repair Nov09. STORED

12591 C-FDTH Buffalo Airways – Stored Sep08 Red Deer, Alta. STORED

12596 C-47-65TP 6885 SAAF – Stored Cape Town Sep08 and Sep10. STORED

12597 C-FDTB Buffalo Airways – Stored Red Deer, Alta Sep08. STORED

12599 42-92762 – Soviet AF '10' – Canx 13Sep51.

12600 Regd 08Apr44 to Aeroflot as CCCP-L869.

12601 Regd 04Apr44 to Aeroflot as CCCP-L866.

12602 Regd 03May44 to Aeroflot as CCCP-L883. To 'URSS883' Jun45, '883' Sep45.

12611 42-92773 1107 BU Waller in Aug45 – Czech AF 1946 – OK-WCT 1947.

12615 42-92777 landing accident with 303 TCS, AFE in Jun46.

12617 D-19 Czech AF visited Ringway, Manchester in Aug47 and again on 09May51.

12618 42-108877 mid-air collision was at Berwick, E Sussex.

12619 42-92780 814BU Stout, crashed 3mls N of Spirit Lake, LA 29Oct45 [EF].

12622 42-92783 was del by 11 FyS in Mar44.

12647 ETM-6046 F A Mexicana – preserved at Base Aerea 1, 2000. PRESERVED

12652 PK-IBA was in use for fire drill at Surabaya in Oct08 – stored at Surabaya Dec09. STORED

12655 42-92813 landed with unlocked gear at Nichols Fld, Manila on 07Jun46 and never flew again – hence salvage.

12666 42-92823 5 AF, 63 ASrG accident on 28Apr46 at Johnson AAB, Japan. Probably repaired?

12667 R Thai AF L2-14/96 to Transport Sq 1 Nov53 – Crashed 31Mar56.

12675 42-92831 was still with 54 TCS in Mar45.

12679 N242AG preserved Museo dell'Aviazione, Cerbaiola, Italy Aug01. PRESERVED

12680 42-92835 at ATC, 36th St Apt, Miami in Aug45 - NC49952 Edward W Tabor lived at Capay, CA, but Trans-Luxury was based at Teterboro, NJ.

C/n 12679 R4D-5 N242AG of Aerojet General taken at Oshkosh in 1957. Note the JATO bottle behind the centre section – this was one of the many aircraft types tested by the company with Jet Assisted Take-Off. The R4D is now preserved in the Museo dell'Aviazione at Cerbaiola in Italy. (Art Krieger)

12682 42-92837 crashed 26Nov44 into Leith Hill, nr Coldharbour, Surrey, in formation with 43-47975 and 42-93754.

12683 '892953' preserved at Oklahoma State Fairground, Oklahoma City, in Sep09. PRESERVED [This has also been reported as c/n 12733, but that was sold in 1964 with no further history, whereas c/n 12683 has no gaps.]

12686 42-92841 was for sale at Phillips A/fld on 23Aug78. It had been used for trials at Aberdeen Proving Ground, MD and was in poor condition. To USAF Museum, Dover AFB, DE 2001 to 2009. PRESERVED

12693 N88874 reported to be airworthy with Randsberg Corp of WI, R26Sep03, then with Champlain Air Museum, Mesa Falcon Field, AZ in Apr07. Regd to Basler Turbo Conversions, Oshkosh, WI 03Dec08. Stored at Oshkosh by Jul09-Jun10 in USAF c/s as '42-847/EN'. STORED

12695 42-92849 43 TCS by Aug44.

12696 42-92850 100 TCS, 9 AF, Eschborn (Y-74), Germany landing accident at Bremen (R-40), Germany on 25Sep45.

12703 Regd 03May44 to Aeroflot as CCCP-L884.

12704 42-92857 – Soviet AF – Polish AF 04 19Jul44 – SP-LCB – 71241 Yugoslav AF 1972 op by 111 ppa (1974/75) – YU-ABU and then as in book. C-47-65TP 6887 SAAF on display at Ysterplaat Nov03 to Sep08. DISPLAYED

12706 42-92859 apparently damaged at Ladd AFB, 11 AF, in Mar44.

12707 Regd 08Apr44 to Aeroflot as CCCP-L870.

12709 42-92861 HqSq, 86 FBG, Neubiberg AB (R-85), Germany had a landing accident there on 26May50.

12711 42-92863 remained with 83 TCS on 27Dec44.

12712 N37906 wreck was still at Hattiesburg, MS in Oct06 and Jul08. DERELICT

12714 42-92866 was del by 19 FyS.

12715 N75T Colegio de la Salle, Bogota preserved Apr08. This is not c/n 12726, as photos of data plate show, which WAS reclaimed in 1970. PRESERVED

12719 T-474 Indonesian AF – Preserved Museo Akademi Angkatan, Jawa Tengah. PRESERVED

12729 42-92879 303 TCS, 9 AF, crashed 02Feb46 24km E of Pie des Mouches, France,

12739 42-92888 crash date was 28Jul44.

12741 42-92890 with 310 TCS in Oct44.

12742 42-92891 312 FyS, 8 AF had a take-off accident at Stn 180, Europe on 29Jul45.

12744 42-92893 accident in Germany on 25Feb46 which may have led to reclamation.

12748 42-108890 32 TCS, 9 AF, crash-landed 2.5mls of Poix (B-44), France on 05Mar45.

12754 42-92902 310 TCS Spanhoe Mar45.

12757 Turkish AF 42-6059 is one of six C-47s stored behind 222 filo hangar at Kayseri Erkilet in Mar09. STORED

12758 42-108891 97 TCS from (Jul44).

12766 42-92913 92 TCS, 9 AF, Chateaudun (A-39), France, crashed at Geisen (Y-84), Germany on 18Apr45.

12770 42-92916 DBF at Bien Hoa, Vietnam on 06Sep65 while involved in 'Operation Red Chief'.

12772 42-92918 306 TCS, Metz (Y-34), France to Jun45.

12774 42-92920 operated by Polish AF as tactical no. 6.

12781 42-92926 82 AES, 6 ASG, 13 AF in Jun46. when it had a taxying accident at NAB Samar. Presumably this is in the Philippines.

12784 42-92929 20 AF on 16Oct45.

12785 NC88783 was used by 20th Century Fox for a tour of USA and S America from Sep to Nov47. It was named 'The Geek'.

12786 42-92931 7 AACS, Hickam Fld, HI in Jan45.

12789 'N142A' - forward fuselage "space shuttle café" was seen at Camarillo, CA in Aug07.

12790 is quoted as B-301, but Martin Best gives B-308 which was unknown hitherto. This is quoted as regd 15Aug67, whereas B-301 would be earlier.

12792 42-92936 ATC Hickam Fld, HI in Feb46.

Preserved as TC-34 Campo Ernesto Colombo, Argentina 2004. PRESERVED

12795 42-92939 1452 BU Edmonton ATC in Jun45. Crashed 11Oct57 nr Adrian, MO.

12797 Regd 17Apr44 to Aeroflot as CCCP-L878.

12801 42-92944 91 FyS when it crashed at Buckley Fld, Denver, CO.

12802 Regd 25Apr44 to Aeroflot as CCCP-L880.

12819 MA965 (quoted in D Gero) as M1965 (RIAF), crashed on 31Oct47 nr Srinagar, Jammu and Kashmir, India.

12830 TC-ALI preserved in Rahmi M Koc Museum, Golden Horn, Istanbul 2001. PRESERVED

12831 42-92971 1 TCS, 10 AF on 17Sep44, and in Nov44 was attached to 84 ADG Hq - Crash site in Mar45 was Shingwiyang, Burma.

12832 XV-NIA escaped from Saigon to U-Tapao 29Apr75 – moved to Bangphra late 80s/90s and painted as HS-ISS. PRESERVED

12835 42-92975 report states Monglong, in Burma. Delete China.

12839 42-92978 1 TCS, 10 AF, take-off accident at Myitkyina, Burma on 15Sep44.

12840 42-92979 with 1 TCS 02Feb45, Sookerating, India. Then to India-China, 63 AACSG Hq Sep45.

12841 42-92980 27 TCS, 14 AF when it crashed, [BW].

12843 42-92982 mid-air collision on 14May44 while with 4 TCS over Gaudo(?).

49-2615 Greek AF on dump at Sedes May94. Scrapped about 1996.

12844 N54705 was noted in Oct59 at Idlewild (JFK) with 'Instrument Laboratory' titles and the latest 'meatball' PAWA colour scheme. It was used for pilot instrument training. Within a year it was delivered to Spantax. EC-AQB was reported derelict at Alicante, Spain until Nov01.

12846 42-92985 was storm damaged on 24Jun45 in the Caribbean.

12848 42-108900 1348 BU Myitkyina, Burma Apr45.

12849 42-92987 ATC had a landing accident at Atkinson Fld, British Guiana on 05Aug45.

12851 42-92989 1346 BU, Tezagaon AD, India by Jan45.

12852 N16602 To Jimmy Doolittle Air & Space Museum Education Foundation, Vacaville, CA R24Apr06. ACTIVE

12857 N44587 Desert Air was operational at Anchorage in May 2007. It was parked at Anchorage in Sep08, engineless, but otherwise intact. To Desert Air Transport Inc, R16Jun10. Flying again Jul10. ACTIVE

12858 42-108901 16 TCS, 12 AF (Jul44 & Nov44).

12860 42-92997 crashed on take-off at Parnamirim Fld., Brazil.

12863 42-93000 was still with 54 TCS on 20Feb45, so delete Div.

12866 42-93003 Hq, 9 Air Dis G, Kellineen (R-94), Germany, had a taxying accident at Hanau (Y-91), Germany 30Sep45.

12871 42-93007 86 TCS, Ramsbury by 31Dec44.

12872 R Thai AF L2-13/96 Transport Squadron 01Nov53 – VIP Conv Jun67 – 603 Sq Jan69

12873 VH-BPL owner John Darcey – Canx 17Aug86. Not flown since. Stored at Outback Museum, Longreach, QLD Mar05. STORED

12874 VH-EDC WFU and stored at Camden Apt 2001. Badly corroded. DERELICT

12876 OB-T-1043 regd 20Nov74 to ALPA, canx 17Aug76. Peruvian records show this as ex HC-ATG previously unidentified.

12883 Regd 17May44 to Aeroflot as CCCP-L896.

12884 Probably regd 30Apr44 to Aeroflot as CCCP-L882. (listed as ex-2930019)

12890 Regd 25May44 to Aeroflot as CCCP-L901.

12891 42-93025 had an accident in Alabama on 23Oct45 which led to RFC and sale.

XA-HUE was named "Eusebio Quino" with Trans Mar. When the latter ceased operations the aircraft went to F A de Mexicana in 1962 or '63.

12893 G-APUC was regd on 03Jun59 to Barry Engineering Services – and to Air Links in 1961.

12898 42-108905 ETO, 58 ACS, Forced landing Regensburg (R-66), Germany on 20Jul45.

12899 42-93032 45 RpS, 45 ADG, 9 AF had a taxying accident on 11Jul45 at Hanau (Y-91), Germany.

12905 42-93038 hit cliff in flight, West Freugh, Wigtown, 27Jul44.

12906 42-93039 Hq 86 FG, 9 AF, crashed 24Dec45 at Kengersfeld (R-25), Germany.

12907 N941AT was in store at Gainesville, TX in Oct07, painted as 42-93040 – To R F Diver, Crossroads, TX May08 – At Gainesville Aug09, fuselage on gear. STORED

12908 42-108906 310 TCS, 9 AF by Oct44. It must have gone to RFC Bush in Sep45.

12909 42-93041 30 ADG, 30 DRS, 9 AF crashed 01Nov45 Bembach, nr Herrenalb, Germany [BW/PE].

12931 42-93061 309 TCS landing accident on 12Dec44, RAF Kemble, Glos.

12932 42-93062 484 BU Topeka in Sep45.

12937 961 F A de Chile – Museo Nacional de Aeronautica, Los Cerillos, Santiago, Oct03. PRESERVED

12941 42-93070 32 TCS, 9 AF, Eschborn (Y-74), Germany crashed 1ml NW Ettringen, nr Karlsruhe, Germany 10Nov45 [BW].

12943 42-93072 82 TCS, Melun (A-55), France in May45.

12944 42-93073 9 GTF, Hq, base R-25 Germany, 9 AF, taxying accident at RAF Biggin Hill on 19Jul45.

12945 42-93074 441 TCG at Frankfurt, Eschborn, AFE in Jan46. – Crashed 07Nov59 after take-off Tainan, Taiwan.

12947 42-93076 crashed at Fairfax, KS in Apr44, so probably not cause of salvage.

12949 12-42 Turkish AF stored Erkilet Apr94. STORED?

12950 42-6033 preserved Cigli Air Hava Kuvvetleri Ust Kolleksion Apr00. PRESERVED

12956 42-93084 was again with 97 TCS in Jun45.

12959 42-93086 add 8 ARS Peterson Fld, CO – Crashed 15Dec62 17mls S of Thule AFB, Greenland.

12961 42-93088 50 TCS, 9 AF, B-44 – Crashed 06Apr45 12mls NW Malmedy, Belgium.

12962 304 – F A Hondurena WFU at Tegucigalpa, Guatemala Nov07. Serial removed. STORED

12963 42-93090 crashed on 13Jan66 on Mt Helmos, Peloponnese, Greece.

12966 42-93093 305 TCS, 9 TCC at St André-de-L'Eure (B-24), France Jan45.

12967 42-93094 is unlikely to have gone to Chile after accident on 14May44.

12970 42-93096, N58NA is now preserved in National World War II Museum at New Orleans Lakefront Airport, LA del 30Aug06. PRESERVED

12975 '315623' preserved Fort Bragg Airborne Forces Museum, Fayetteville, NC 1977-Nov04. PRESERVED

12982 42-93107 8 AF forced landing following explosion over Naples, Italy 28Mar45.

12983 C-FCUE Buffalo Airways i/s Sep08. ACTIVE

12986 42-93111 813 BU, 1 TCC Sedalia in Nov44.

C/n 12937 C-47A-DK serial 963 of the Fuerza Aerea de Chile taken at El Bosque. This aircraft is preserved at the Museo Nacional do Aeronautica de Chile and was originally reported as 961, but now appears to have been repainted in 1974. *(Michael Magnusson)*

12990 42-93114 1258 BU Casablanca AD, 12 AF in Jan45.

XA-JEL was named "Junipero Sierra" with Trans Mar. To F A Mexicana on its demise, 1962/63.

12991 42-93115 destroyed in take-off accident 30May44 at Myitkyina, Burma.

12994 Regd 06May44 to Aeroflot as CCCP-L885.

12996 42-93120 – Soviet AF. Regd 27Apr44 to Aeroflot as CCCP-L881. 'CCCP-L3881' GVF – Mod with gun turret. '881'.

12997 Regd 08May44 to Aeroflot as CCCP-L886.

12998 Regd 19May44 to Aeroflot as CCCP-L897.

13000 Regd 08May44 to Aeroflot as CCCP-L887.

13001 Regd 25May44 to Aeroflot as CCCP-L902. To '902' 30Nov44.

13002 Regd 23May44 to Aeroflot as CCCP-L898.

13004 '42-93149' preserved Ellsworth AFB Air & Space Museum, Ellsworth, SD Sep01. DISPLAYED

13009 121 Chilean Navy, preserved Torquemada, Chile Mar04. PRESERVED

13018 CR-AFR to 6167 F A Portuguesa, Esq 801, AB8 31Dec67 – Probably destroyed as 6167.

13019 VT-CYG was at Bombay, Santa Cruz in Safari titles in Sep74. N47AZ Sofair was canx 22Feb06 as exported to UK, but had been in Kenya since 1997 and at Nairobi in May06, where it remained in Aug07 – Shipped in 40ft container to USA in Jan09 – Reported broken up, but more likely for spares or rebuild due to cost.

13028 C-FROD Buffalo Airways – '12927' CAF Alberta Aviation Museum Sep08. DISPLAYED

13040 42-93159 crashed 14Dec45 nr Villieau, France [FP].

13041 N341W remains stored at LeHigh Acres, FL in May08, engineless – In police training area Feb10. STORED

13042 42-93161 1 CCS, Bowman, in Jun44 – It was with Hq CAF, Peterson, 2 AF in Jul45.

13043 42-93162 313 TCS, Pope, 1 AF landing accident on 20Nov44 at Auburn Apt, AL 2143 BU. Probably a write-off.

13044 42-93163 was with 805 BU George in May45 - 320 TCS, 509 CpG Roswell SAC – Ground accident 06Jul46, Chicago Mun Apt.

13045 42-93164 2 Prov. TC, landing accident 30Mar45, Knolwood Aux Fld, NC. W/o.

13048 42-108920 was with 4136 BU Tinker, ATSC, in Jul45.

13049 42-93167 2 CCG, 6 CCS, Syracuse – Landing accident 05Aug44 (in USA).

13050 N90830/293168 remained at Kalamazoo Museum, MI Jun06-Jul10. DISPLAYED

13051 42-93169 crashed 24Oct53 ½ ml N of Calham, CO.

13053 42-93171 33 FW – Take-off accident 13Jun49 Harrisburg Apt, PA.

13054 42-93172 805 BU George – Crashed Emison Aux Fld, IL 27Apr45.

13056 NC88726 Panagra – Sold to F A Argentina 1947.

13057 42-93175 813 BU Sedalia in Sep45.

13058 42-108921 ground collision with C-46 44-77989 on 24May45 at Sedalia, MO, 813 BU.

13060 N87643 Aero American to Acme Acft, though the aircraft was already reduced to fuselage. This was scrapped by May 1984.

13061 42-93178 1 CCS, Bowman in Jun44.

13066 42-93183 Crashed 13Apr58 McChord AFB, WA.

13070 N844TH Fly One LLC, i/s Mesa Falcon Fld, AZ Nov05. ACTIVE

13073 42-93189 based at 813 BU Sedalia in Dec44 and Aug45.

'OE-LBC' 1st Austrian DC-3 Club, Salzburg, display from 2006. DISPLAYED

13074 YV-670C noted at Valencia, Venezuela Dec07. DERELICT

13075 42-93191 815 BU Malden, crashed 16Jan45 2mls W of Brownfield, IL.

13076 42-93192 4 CCS, crashed 15Jun44 7mls NW of North Vernon, IN.

13077 42-93193 was with 7 CCS Syracuse in Jul44 – Crashed 22Feb52 Millinocket, ME.

13078 42-108923 7 CCS, Syracuse where it had engine failure on 21Jul44.

13084 'VH-EWE' Central Australian Avn Museum, Alice Springs, NT Oct95. DISPLAYED

13087 N47FL Distressed Area Missions, McMinnville, TN i/s Jan00. ACTIVE

13089 Regd 26May44 to Aeroflot as CCCP-L903.

13090 Regd 26May44 to Aeroflot as CCCP-L904.

13091 Regd 26May44 to Aeroflot as CCCP-L905.

13093 Regd 16Jun44 to Aeroflot as CCCP-L911.

13094 Regd 01Jun44 to Aeroflot as CCCP-L906.

13096 Regd 15May44 to Aeroflot as CCCP-L893. To 'USSR 893' 06Nov44.

13097 Regd 15May44 to Aeroflot as CCCP-L894. Later CCCP-L3894.

13103 Bu 17203 was on rebuild in Dec68/Jan69 to replace N91260 c/n 25372 on mapping mission in Ethiopia. It then went to Iran for Topographic Training Team. No further report.

13110 PNC-212 crash site was Oscana-Aguas Claras, Colombia.

13112 '40223' R Thai AF L2-36/14 – 42 Sq 25May77 – rn 402 Sq 01Oct77 – 603 Sq 21Nov83 – wfu by Feb84 – Dumped at Lopburi by May89 and to Phuket 2008 - Sunk as diving attraction about 1 km off Bang Tao Beach, Chemg Talay, Phuket Nov08 – coded 'D3'.

13113 42-93225 814 BU Stout, CAF Sep45.

13114 42-93226 815 BU Malden in Jan45.

13139 N9838A regn canx May09. USCAR states exported to UK in Jul82.

13140 6172 F A Portuguesa – Derelict Montepuez, Mozambique Apr03.

13142 F-BLOZ now painted as 313142 at La Ferte Alais in USAAF D-Day c/s. DISPLAYED

13144 Polish AF '8' – Canx 21May55.

13145 42-93254 8 TCS, 12 AF, crashed on take-off 7mls S of Rome, Italy. Delete 9 AF.

13146 42-93255 operated by Polish AF as tactical no. 9.

13149 CAF 12928 was painted as C-GNTK for delivery to Northwest Territorial on 20Jul76 from Saskatoon to Yellowknife. It was sold to Buffalo Airways and towed across the frozen Great Slave Lake to Hay River, where it was seen in May95. It was broken up for spares.

13155 C-FLFR Buffalo Airways i/s Sep08. ACTIVE

13174 42-93280 54 TCS, 11 AF. N650K was in Sahakol titles at Seletar on 14Sep74.

13177 42-93283 4149 BU Olmsted, take-off accident at RCAF Rockcliffe on 05Mar47. Probably sold on site.

OB-1756 stored at Villavicencio Mar02 – HK-4292 Aerovanguardia Feb10. ACTIVE

13178 42-108933 1305 BU Calcutta A/fld in Jun45.

13187 42-93292 India-China until 06Apr45 – Taxying accident 06Apr45 in India.

13190 42-93294 1305 BU, Calcutta-Dum Dum in Nov45.

13191 42-93295 at Dum Dum ATC, crash was 1ml NW Lalmanirhat, India.

13193 42-93297 Hollandia, New Guinea with SW Pacific ATC in Apr45.

13194 42-93298 1562 BU Sorido A/fld, Biak ATC, Sep45.

13196 42-93300 ground accident 09Oct44 Jackson AD, New Guinea, later at 1562 BU, Biak Island AD Apr45.

13199 42-93302 crashed in Australia on 14Apr45. This might be the accident reported.

13203 42-93306 taxying accident 16Sep44 Nadzab #1, SW Pacific. W/o? Not Sep45.

13206 42-93309 ATC – Accident 17Apr45 Sentani Strip, Hollandia, New Guinea.

13208 42-108936 1562 BU Biak A/fld, New Guinea Apr45.

13215 42-93317 to Soviet AF '3' – magon GVF. Regd 15May44 to Aeroflot as CCCP-L895. In Yugoslavia 1944/45.

13216 Regd 14Jun44 to Aeroflot as CCCP-L910.

13217 42-93319 to Soviet AF - Polish AF '10' 25Jul44 – active 01Jul52.

13227 N64605 F E Weisbrod Aircraft Museum, Pueblo, CO – Preserved Oct02. PRESERVED

13228 N843MB State of Florida Agriculture & Consumer Service i/s 2003 – Basler Turbo Conversions, Oshkosh, WI R15May09 – Stored at Oshkosh Jun10. STORED

13229 42-93329 9 CCS, 10 AF Jan45.

13230 42-93330 9 CCS, 10 AF Nov44 when w/o.

13231 VT-AUI remains stored intact at Kolkatta Jan09, in bushes. DERELICT

13233 42-93333 9 CCS, 10 AF (to 05Aug44).

13235 42-93335 9 CCS, 10 AF.

13237 42-93337 9 CCS, 10 AF Feb45.

13238 42-108939 6 AF, HQ – take-off accident 29May44 at Aden [EF] on delivery flight.

13239 42-93338 9 CCS, 10 AF May45.

13240 42-93339 1304 BU, crash-landed 29Jan46 Barrackpore, India.

13245 42-93344 9 CCS, 10 AF May45.

13246 42-93345 9 CCS, 10 AF Jul44, then 62 AACS at time of accident.

13249 42-93347 16 CCS, 10 AF Ledo in Sep45.

13257 42-93355 2 TCS, 10 AF 07Jul44 and 11 CCS on 13Jul44.

13258 42-108941 9 CCS, 10 AF and crashed 4mls from Lashio.

13260 42-93357 9 CCS, 10 AF Feb45.

13261 42-93358 11 CCS, 10 AF – Landing accident 03Aug44 Myitkyina, Burma.[not 1945]

13262 42-93359 10 CCS, 10 AF Feb45.

13263 42-93360 9CCS, 10 AF - DBR landing at Warazup, Burma on 01Mar45 – so repaired after being shot down.

13264 42-93361 11 CCS, 10 AF 07Jul44 - 10 CCS (May45).

13265 42-93362 11 CCS in Jun44.

13266 42-93363 11 CCS, 10 AF – Landing accident 13Apr45, India.[w/o?]

13269 42-93365 11 CCS (29Jul44), 9 CCS (Dec44), 10 AF.

13271 42-93367 322 TCS, 14 AF crashed 28Apr45 Barrackpore, India. Conflict with book.

13276 42-93372 1 TCS, 10 AF 15Jun44.

13286 42-93381 11 CCS, 14 AF - Take-off accident Luliang, China 08Jul45.

13288 42-108944 - Crashed 19Aug55 Ryan Canyon, in Gillis mountain range nr Hawthorne, NV.

13289 42-93383 12 CCS, 10 AF Oct44.

13291 42-93385 was probably repaired after Apr44 accident as it had another accident on 28Jun44 with 10 AF.

13296 N8326C canx 12Aug53 – CAT SA to Civil Air Transport Inc, Sun Valley, CA 24Sep53 – Rr N4660V 29Sep53 – Allied Aircraft Co., N Hollywood, CA R22Sep53 – Aviation Mart Co, Alexandria, VA 16Feb54 – To Linea Aerea Nacional as CC-CBJ 16Feb54. CC-CBX preserved in LAN c/s Museu Nacional Aeron. & Espace Nov00. Currently painted CC-CLDT. DISPLAYED

13297 42-13193 crash site quoted as Makum, India, presumably based at Chabua.

13298 42-108945 10 AF in Sep44.

13299 42-93392 12 CCS, 10 AF had a landing accident at Myitkyina, Burma. on 26Jul44.

13304 remained as 5N-AAP in wrecked condition at Lagos-Ikeja in 1970.

13310 RCAF KG587 went to NWAC Whitehorse in Dec50 according to station diaries.

N115SA to James T Hunt, La Habra Heights, CA, R23Feb07 – Classic Aircraft Aviation Museum, Hillboro, OR DOct09 – i/s 2010. ACTIVE

13319 Bu 17221 US Navy – Preserved Ferrymead Aeronautical Society, Harewood, Christchurch Apr69. DISPLAYED

13331 ZS-CRV Rovos Air – i/s Namibia Commercial Aviation Oct08. ACTIVE

13333 C-GPNR Buffalo Airways – i/s Sep08. ACTIVE

13334 JZ-PDF was delivered to Garuda on 31Dec62 and canx 09Feb63.

AF-4776 Satuan Udara FASI, i/s Sep03. ACTIVE?

13342 C-FOOW Triumph A/ws, Oshawa, i/s Jun05. Sold to ALCI-Antarctic Logistics Center Intl Sep10. ACTIVE

13346 Regd 19Jun44 to Aeroflot as CCCP-L913.

13348 42-108950 – Soviet AF. Regd 08Jun44 to Aeroflot as CCCP-L909. To Polish AF '3' – personal acft of Marshal Rola-Zymierski.

13349 42-93437 – Soviet AF – Polish AF '2' SPL – Canx 07Jan56.

13350 Regd 03Jul44 to Aeroflot as CCCP-L915.

13353 Regd 19Jun44 to Aeroflot as CCCP-L912.

13357 42-93445 accident at 1562 BU Hollandia A/fld, New Guinea 02May45.

13358 42-108951 accident in New Guinea on 15Dec44. W/o uncertain.

13360 42-93447 Hq 7 ASC – Crashed 12Jan46 Nichols Fld, Philippines.

13361 42-93448 ATC – Ditched in Pacific 06Jun44.

13368 ZS-NZE ex Armée de l'Air Malgache – WFU Apr01 Tananarive-Ivato.

13370 KG611 – fuselage remained at Standard Telephone's factory in Southgate, London until after April 1968.

13373 T-104 F A Argentina, preserved Estancia Santa Romano Collection, Villa Reynolds Nov05. PRESERVED

13375 T.3-67 believed sold as N8041C but missing after take-off from Cuatro Vientos in 1980 with ferry regn ECT-025. Crashed in sea?

13378 is listed as going from KG619 to Spanish AF T3-2. However new information suggests that it was regd EC-EAB for delivery [See p.213 of Vol 1]. See also c/n 12164.

XA-ION Aerovias Oaxaquena, impounded Base Aerea 1, Santa Lucia, derelict Feb02. DERELICT

13383 TZ-391 was overhauled by Basler's at Oshkosh Jan07, and regd to Basler Turbo Conversions LLC as N167BT 13Jun07 – C-GJKB Kenn Borek D15Oct08 – ALCI Aviation Oshkosh Oct08. ACTIVE

13392 CF-QHF fuselage at Hay River, NWT in Jul95. Removed by Sep08 – Regn Canx 31Mar10.

13399 42-93482 was sold to W R Brucker who sold it to Civil Air Transport on 05Jul55 (the Bill of sale date), and R18Aug55. It was certainly B-823 but may not have been XT-823 as that would have been with CAT in 1950/51, when it was not disposed of by the USAF until Jul55.

N14636 preserved City of Brownsville, TX Apr05. PRESERVED

13406 42-93489 India-China ATC in Feb45.

13407 42-93490 crash date 01Mar45

13427 42-93508 9 AF - Crashed 23Nov44, Warton, Lancs – probably repaired, as with 325 FyS when it crash-landed 22Dec44, Ramsbury (469), England.

13429 42-93509 of TUSAFG had take-off accident at Etimesgut AB, Ankara, Turkey on 06Jan50 [EF].

13436 Turkish AF 6039 stored at Etimesgut in Mar09. STORED

13439 N36AP was bought by Basler Turbo Conversions LLC on 28Apr06. By Jul07 the engines had been removed. Still stored at Oshkosh Jul09 & Jun10. STORED

13443 42-93522 crashed 08Jul48 in Germany.

13444 6095 Turkish AF. This was believed sold to Iran, but is now reported to be stored at Kayseri-Erkilet AB as of Mar09.

13445 N50CM Barton M Tierman should read Tiernan. Stored Palmer, AK Sep07-Jul10. STORED

13448 42-108960 310 TCS Spanhoe 9 AF, Feb45.

CF-BZI Calgary Aviation & Space Museum, Calgary, AB, preserved Aug02. PRESERVED

13455 42-93533 reported crashed in Austria 28Nov47, possibly after SAL overhaul?

13458 for Zandeney read Zanderij.

13459 VH-MIN Discovery A/ws, stored Sydney-Bankstown Jul07, awaiting engines for restoration to airworthiness – Moved by road Bankstown to Molong 10Dec09. STORED

13460 9U-BRY Burundi A F was in store at Bujumbura in Jan07 and Oct09. STORED

13464 42-93541 8 AF, crashed on take-off from Burtonwood, Lancs 30Jun44.

13465 42-93542 314 TCS, 9 AF - Crash-landed 08Nov45, Villeneuve-le-Comte, France.

13467 F-BEFM was sold by Air France to CNET [Centre Nationale d'Etude Telephonic] as 'F-SEBE'. It was flown with the serial '20423' which was something of a mystery, but research shows this to be the C de N or Certificat de Navigabilité [C of A]. Nothing is known of its fate.

13468 G-AMHJ Assault Glider Association preserved Shawbury, Shropshire, Dec03-Dec10. PRESERVED

13485 N472AF noted stored at Gainesville Municipal, TX Oct07 – To R F Diver, Gainesville, stored May08 – Noted at Fairview, TX Aug09. STORED

13494 42-93568 ATC – Accident 10Apr45 Admiralty Island, nr New Guinea.

13498 42-108965 1562 BU, APO 920 had a taxying accident at Hollandia Strip, New Guinea in Feb45. W/o?

13501 42-93574 ATC – Taxying accident 29Jan45 Garbutt Fld, Townsville, QLD.

13503 'RI-001' – believed preserved in Indonesia, one of two aircraft marked thus in Apr10. PRESERVED?

13505 42-93578 taxying accident at Tacloban, base was 1559 BU Biak Is.

13506 ZK-AMY to Southern DC-3 Limited, Christchurch, R23Feb07. Donated to Ashburton Aviation Museum Jun08 at Ashburton Apt. ACTIVE

C/n 13445 C-47A-DK N50CM of the Battelle Memorial Institute at Renton, Washington State, illustrating some air sampling equipment over the forward cabin. The photo was taken in March 1985. *(Peter Kirkup)*

13510 PI-C649 1968 register gives Palanan Logging, so sold to Commercial Air Tpt, not 'sold by'.

13513 42-93585 1 TCS – Landing accident 31Jan46 at Lipa A/fld, Philippines.

13516 42-93588 ATC – Accident 10Apr45, Biak, New Guinea. Probably sold as spares.

13519 42-93590 ATC - Crashed 21Dec44 Sterling Fld, Solomon Islands.

13521 ZK-BKD in use as winebar at Gisborne Mar07. DISPLAYED

13523 42-93594 was based at 1562 BU, Biak, New Guinea, SWPW ATC in May45.

13524 42-93595 ground accident at Biak, New Guinea while based there with 1562 BU in Jul45.

13525 42-93596 was with 1536 BU ATC at Hollandia strip, New Guinea Mar45.

13527 42-93598 1 TCS, 54 TCW – Ditched 09Feb46 1ml W of Dumog, Philippines.

13529 XW-PFX was probably not with Air America and was del to Xieng Khouang in 1967/68.

13530 42-93600 was based at 1379 BU Dow, ME in Dec45

13531 42-93601 was based at 1466 BU Ladd, AK in May45.

13537 42-93607 with 79 TCS Melun (A-55), France, in Jun45.

'607' was leased by the USAF to Air America in Jul66. It ran off the runway into a gulley on 22Mar68 at Gia, S Vietnam and was still there in 1972.

13538 42-108969 was with 5 FyG, Love Field, TX in Jan46.

13539 6837 SAAF – C-47-65TP i/s Sep08 at SAAF Cape Town, noted at Ysterplaat Sep10. ACTIVE

13540 6839 SAAF – C-47-65TP i/s Sep08 at SAAF Cape Town. ACTIVE

13541 ZS-CAI stored engineless at Wonderboom in Jan07, operational with Skyclass at Lanseria Sep08 and Apr09. ACTIVE

13543 VT-CYX was noted derelict at Yelahanka AB, nr Bangalore in 2007. DERELICT

13546 42-93615 – R Thai AF 615 29Aug46 – L2-1/90 [See c/n 9871]

13552 42-93620 – Soviet AF – Polish AF '1' SPL Presidential aircraft – SP-LCH etc.

13573 VT-CGQ was canx on 05Dec95. Noted damaged at Dharmastala Dec01.

13576 ET-AJG Relief and Rehabilitation Committee – Stored Addis Ababa, Ethiopia Feb03. STORED

13579 VT-CGR was canx 03Dec89.

13580 C-GJKM Buffalo Airways i/s Sep08. ACTIVE

13590 G-ALWC Les Ailes Anciennes, Toulouse, France, preserved Oct05. PRESERVED

13598 42-108975 was with 1536 BU APO 565 in Mar45. Accident in Philippines on 25Feb45.

13605 42-93668 – Taxying Accident 23Jan45, Sorido, SW Pacific.

13610 42-93672 base was Amberley, QLD, SW Pacific ATC in Apr45.

13612 'B-126' Chung Cheng Aviation Museum, Chiang Kai Shek Int Apt, Taiwan Jan99. PRESERVED

13615 42-93677 was with 1557 BU Brisbane in May45.

13622 42-93683 9 AF, 2 PFS (Jan45), 2 TCP (Apr45), based at Chartres (A-40), France.

13624 VH-ANW Blair Howe, preserved Aug03 Myalup, WA. PRESERVED

13625 42-93686 was based with 1562 BU Biak A/fld, New Guinea in Mar45.

13628 42-108978 India-China Wg (Jul45).

13630 42-93690 unit at Hassani was 1173 FMS in Aug50.

13635 42-93695 22 FyS Newcastle - Crashed 26Jul44 3mls S of Sedalia AAF, MO [EF].

13639 PK-GDH Sekolah Menengah Teknologi Penerbangan (Aircraft Polytechnic School), Jakarta, used as instructional airframe. Noted Sep08 and Apr10. STORED

13642 306 F A Hondurena noted at Tegucigalpa museum, Toncontin Nov07. PRESERVED

13643 42-93702 was attached to 310 TCS, 315 TCG Spanhoe, 9 AF in Feb45.

13645 '0-03704' Korean Aircraft Industries Collection. No recent observation.

13647 SE-CFR Flygvapen Museum, Malmslatt, preserved Jun05. DISPLAYED

13659 42-93716 303 BU Bremen AB, landing accident Bremen, Germany 19Aug47. Probable w/o.

13660 42-93717 304 TCS, AFE May46 – Sold to Aero American as N87627 in reclaimed state by 1961. After sale to Acme in dismantled state, this was scrapped by 1984.

13663 42-93720 9 AF 301 TCS in Nov44 - Crashed on take-off 15May51 at Giebelstadt, Germany, unit 36 ABG, Hq 12 AF based at Fürstenfeldbruck AB.

13664 42-93721 AFE, 323 TCS – Landing accident 15Mar46 Capodichino, Naples, Italy.

13665 42-93722 landing accident 04Feb53 Orly Airport, Paris.

13668 42-108982 9 AF, 32 TCS Mourmelon (B-44), France - Crash site quoted as 4mls E Shelf Moor, Glossop, Derbyshire.

13669 42-93725 AFE, 313 TCG, 48 TCS - Landing accident on 15Nov46 at Illesheim AAB, Germany.

13670 42-93726 crash date was 14Sep44.

13671 42-93727 with 12 TCS Tempelhof, Berlin Dec47.

13675 42-93731 was with 14 TCS, 61 TCG 9 AF, Abbeville (B-92), France in Apr45 - Lost at sea 10Sep45 6mls NW of Borinquen Fld, Puerto Rico, with 6 AF.

13678 N272R Kestrel Inc – To McCollough Holdings LLC, Parker, CO R06Jun06 – Lsd to Cascade Air, i/s Sep08 – Desert Air Transport Inc, Anchorage, AK 28May10. ACTIVE

13683 42-93738 10 AF, 11 CCS - Landing accident at Mu-Se, Burma on 07Mar45.

13688 42-108984 was with 315 TCS at Ledo in Jan45.

13690 42-93744 10 AF, 1 TCS, then 11 CCS – Accident date given as 28Aug45 at Szemao, China (See also c/n 13717).

13692 42-93746 was with 9 CCS in Nov44.

13693 42-93747 was with 10 CCS in Nov44.

13697 42-93751 10 AF, 11 CCS from 29Jul44.

13701 42-93754 3 PFS – Crashed 26Nov44 into Leith Hill, nr Coldharbour, Surrey.

13702 XA-FIR named "Juan Maria Salvatierra" with Trans Mar de Cortes – Then to F A Mexicana 1962/63.

13704 42-93757 10 AF, 11 CCS (Aug44).

13705 42-93758 10 AF, 12 CCS - cause of accident PE.

13706 42-93759 14 AF, 27 TCS, Chungking in Nov44.

13708 42-108986 11 CCS (29Apr44).

13709 42-93761 10 AF at time of accident.

13713 YU-ABB was damaged beyond repair in severe storm en route Sarajevo to Belgrade 12Sep67 and WFU.

Stored Belgrade Museum, without wings or titles Aug08-Sep10. DISPLAYED

13717 42-93769 10 AF, 11 CCS – Landing accident 28Aug45 Szemao, China. (See also c/n 13690)

13719 42-93770 20 AF, 22 ADG (Mar45).

13720 VT-AUT preserved by Skychef at Delhi-Palam Jan09. PRESERVED

13721 42-93772 10 AF, 12 CCS – Crashed 195mls SW Moran, India.

13722 42-93773 10 AF by Oct44.

13726 HS-TDA Thai Dakota Association, believed stored in Bangkok area. STORED

13727 CC-CBS preserved Lago Rapel, Chile 1995. No recent report.

13730 NC54091 Willis Air Service Inc. FAA card gives 42-93780, thus confirming this identity. It would seem the aircraft was, perhaps, repossessed by the USAF.

13734 42-93784 – Hit by C-47 42-92683 at San Giovanni, Italy 12Sep45.

13735 42-93785 fate as for 42-93784.

13739 42-93788 20 AF, 9 TCS – Taxying accident on Saipan on 16Dec45.

13740 S Vietnam AF C-47 '789' was badly damaged at Tan Son Nhut on 29Aug67 while with unit PD417. This may have been repaired and sold as 293789 Thai Police – Toc R Thai AF 21Sep70 – 62 Sq 19Jan72 – To JL-2 [AC-47] by Feb76 – Further mods by 01Apr77 – 42 Sq 25May77 – rn 402 Sq 01Oct77 – 603 Sq 21Nov83 – DBR Don Muang 08Deb88 – soc 31May88 – Pres. outside Wing HQ, Don Muang, Bangkok, Mar09. DISPLAYED.

13741 '0-93740' preserved National Infantry Museum, Fort Benning, GA Mar70. PRESERVED

13747 42-93796 Canadair – Taxying accident 18Jan46, Walnut Ridge, AR.

13749 93797 preserved Aug00 Norway Aircraft Collection, Gardermoen AFB. DISPLAYED

13752 '42-93800' preserved Bonanzaville FOE Aircraft Museum, West Fargo, ND Sep01. PRESERVED

13754 42-93802 9 AF, 12 TCS, Tempelhof AB – Crash-landed 12Jul47 4mls SSW Sangerhausen, Eisleban, E Germany [EF] [also given as Ober Roblingen]

13756 42-93804 HQ AAF Attache, Cairo, code 'X' - Crashed 20Mar47 SSW Dessie, Ethiopia. Not sold.

13757 N2VM C E Poindexter, Lone Wolf, OK, last reported stored Jun97

13763 42-93810 9 AF, 301 TCS, 473 ASG – Landing accident 17Nov45 1.5mls S Sarrable, France.

13764 42-93811 9 AF, 310 TCS at Spanhoe in Nov44.

13769 CR-LBK regd 1946.

13774 42-93820 12 AF, 7 TCS from Aug44.

13775 42-93821 based at Melun (A-55), France with 3 PFS - Landing accident 26May45 at Mannheim (Y-89), Germany.

13778 R Thai AF 19Dec58 L2-26/02 – 61 Sq 31Jan69 – W/o 05Apr79.

13784 XT-827 to B-827 CAT BMar55 – Op. as '827' in mid-60s. Shot down 11Jun67 on approach to Quang Ngai, S Vietnam – DBF.

13785 42-24414 5 AF, 27 ADG, 93 ADS – Crashed on take-off 12Mar45 Henderson Fld, Nadzab, Guinea.

13787 42-24416 13 DRS, 13 AF – Landing accident Tontouta, New Caledonia, 01Dec43.

13790 42-24419 10 AF, 1 TCS to (Sep44) - Accident report states Bhamo, Burma, which is near the border with Yunnan, China.

13795 42-30644 1 TCS (Dec43), 10 AF, 315 TCS (Mar45).

13798 N62CC Air Classics LLC, Sheffield, MA i/s Dec04 – Sold to Kenneth Richard Oddy, Orange Park, FL 18Jun10, regd 23Jul10. ACTIVE

13803 N345AB 1941 Historical Aircraft Group Museum, Geneseo, NY i/s May05 - 2010. ACTIVE

13804 43-30653 9 AF Hq, base Y-90 – Crash-landed 25Oct45, 12mls NE Dijon, France.

13806 43-30655 was with 1466 BU Ladd, ATC in Mar45.

13807 43-30656 was based with 1452 BU, Edmonton, Canada in Jul45 – 4149 BU Olmsted Jul46 – Take-off accident at Olmsted 15Dec48.

C/n 13816 C-47A-DL 0-30665 of the United States Army, named "Beulah". The photo was taken at Davis-Monthan AFB in March 1975 when the aircraft was in storage with code '4ZB026.' *(Doug Olson)*

13810 43-30659 - Crash-landed 03Apr44 at Mingan, QU, Canada [EF].

13815 43-30664 with 313 TCS, Pope, went missing 25mls E of Cape Fear, NC on 21Jul44 with two other C-47s of same unit.

13816 43-30665 ATC, 314 TCS Jun44. N47E Dynamic Aviation, Bridgewater Air Park, VA, i/s Apr04 – Dynamic Air Lease Inc, Bridgewater, VA R23Jul10. ACTIVE

13817 N63376 canx 13Oct61 – B-841 Air Asia B 09Oct61 – '6110' Naval Aux. Comm. Center (1964) – B-933 BJun67 – N11AF Continental Air Svces R02Feb74 – Lsd by Air Alliance to CASI – Sahakol Lsd Sep74 – Air Fast Services B1975 – David B Leib B09Apr79 – Air Fast leased to 1981.

13819 43-30668 was with 807 BU Bergstrom on 16Jan45.

13820 43-30669 had an accident 10 mls W of Pope AAF, NC. This may account for the undated 'Pope' entry. Sale via RFC to Pan American – no further history.

13825 43-30674 was with 805 BU Alliance in Jul/Aug44.

13826 43-30675 was with 807 BU Bergstrom in Jan45.

13827 43-30676 - Crashed 16Mar45 Mt Lewis, 10mls SW of Leeving, CA, op by 4127 BU. Wreckage not found until 23Sep45. Remains in situ 1960. Corrects page 452.

13828 43-30677 had an accident at Pope Fld, NC but was repaired.

13830 43-30679 was with 805 BU Alliance in May44.

13831 43-30680 was based with 805 BU, Alliance in May44, moving to George by Feb45.

13832 43-30681 crashed 15Jun45 in Idaho. Date may be a year out?

13834 43-30683 - Landing accident at Alliance 805 BU, NE on 24Jun44. It is not impossible that this was the cause of reclamation.

13836 49-2634 on dump at Sedes from 1994 to Nov07. DERELICT

13837 43-30686 – based at Smoky Hill 204 BU May45. CB-31 date of accident was 01Feb51 (not Jan).

13838 43-30687 - base 318 BU Lockbourne, OH – Crash-landed 21May46 Patterson Fld, OH [PE]

13839 43-30688 was at Sedalia in Apr44.

13840 43-30689 was with 301 TCS in Feb44.

N8187E was noted with Basler's at Oshkosh in Jul08-Jun10. STORED

13841 43-30690 was with 308 TCS in Feb44, and 805 BU George by Jan45.

13843 43-30692 was with 23 TCS at Pope in Jan45.

13844 43-30693 was with 1 TC, 807 BU Bergstrom in May44.

13845 43-30694 crashed at Lawson Fld on 08Mar45 with 811 BU Lawson TCC.

13846 43-30695 was with 805 BU Alliance in Jun44. To Philippine AF 1951.

13847 43-30696 was with 807 BU Bergstrom in Jan45.

13850 43-30699 was with 813 BU Sedalia in Mar45. 76-20 Malawi Air Wing i/s 1995. ACTIVE?

13851 43-30700 was based with 805 BU, George in May44.

13852 43-30701 crashed on 23Jan45 at #1 Ealson Aux Fld, IN while with 805 BU George.

13854 43-30703 unit was 810 BU Laurinburg in Jul45.

N705GB Atlantic Air Cargo, Doval, FL R13Oct06. ACTIVE.

13860 N293WM Wings of Eagles Museum, Batavia, NY preserved Dec96 – Rebuilt and test flown at Elmira-Corning Regional Apt, NY as 43-30709. ACTIVE

13861 TF-NPK actually in Flugfelag c/s, i/s Jul05. ACTIVE

13863 43-30712 807 BU Bergstrom from Aug44.

N19454 Cape Smythe Air Services to South Central Air, Kenai, AK Dec98. Ceased ops Jul99 and sold to Galaxy Air Cargo Inc, t/a Majestic Air Cargo, Anchorage, AK – Crashed at Eider Point, AK after t/o from Dutch Harbor, AK 23Jan01.

13868 43-30717 9 AF, 75 TCS quoted in accident report for incident on the Isle of Man in 19Feb44. 74 TCS may be wrong. 30717 Philippine AF stored from Jan80 at Manila.

13869 43-30718 had a take-off accident on 08Feb44.

13871 43-30720 crashed 17Oct44 off SE coast of England ex Welford.

13875 43-30724 crashed in Hungary 13Jun49.

13877 YSL-52 Turkish AF – Preserved Havacilik Muzesi, Yesilkoy Sep01. PRESERVED

13880 '315208' "Fassberg Flyer" preserved Luftbrücke, Fassberg, Germany Mar99. DISPLAYED

13881 43-30730 9 AF, 78 TCS in Apr44. In Jul45 it had moved to ATC Nashville.

13883 SE-CFP SAS c/s – i/s Stiftelsen Flygande Veteraner, Bromma Jun05. ACTIVE

13903 43-30752 5 AF, 21 TCS – Landing accident 01Dec43, Garbutt Fld, Townsville, QLD, hit C-47s 42-24227 & 43-30755.

13906 43-30755 5 AF 21 TCS hit by C-47 43-30752 01Dec43, Garbutt Fld, Townsville, QLD – repaired. XW-PFA was probably never with Air America, but Xieng Khouang.

13909 43-30758 was with 21 TCS in May44.

18901 XT-... Chennault & Willauer to Civil Air Transport as N8358C 19Dec49 – Canx 07Oct65 as permanently WFU. Probably remained in China, long before that date.

18905 42-100442 10 AF, 11 CCS on 05Aug44.

VT-AUM canx 26May94. Stored Magda Museum, Madhya Pradesh 2006 at Birla factory. PRESERVED

18907 42-100444 10 AF in Apr45.

18908 42-100445 10 AF, 9 CCS.

18913 42-100450 319 TCS, 10 AF – Taxying accident 22Jun45 Warazup, Burma. [Crashed 31Mar45 Comilla, India also reported, but unlikely]

18918 42-100455 crashed 12Mar45 in Pacific Ocean.

18920 42-100457 crashed 05Apr44 in India.

18921 42-100458 crashed 25Apr44 nr Tingpai, Burma according to Form 14.

18922 42-100459 with 420 BU March, 4 AF Dec45,

18923 ZK-CAW total time at retirement in 1985 was 56,282 hrs. It passed to MacDonalds who equipped it for further service at their restaurant at Tauhara, Taupo in 1990, where it was still giving good service in this role in Nov09. DISPLAYED

18925 42-100462 was with ATC on 28Dec44.

18933 42-100470 crashed with 33 TCS on 12Dec43 [SF]

18949 N99131 for Kanako read Kamaka – James C Petrides, Honolulu, HI R20Jan10. STORED

18951 42-100488 was at Pope in Apr44. 81 ABG – Crashed 06Dec51 20mls E of Marseille, France.

18952 42-100489 – was with 311 TCS Pope by Sep44 - Crashed 29Sep52 6mls SE of Newport, ME.

18953 42-100490 4149 BU Olmsted Apr46 - Crashed 07Sep48 28mls SE Edmonton, Alberta, Canada.

18955 42-100492 14 CCS crashed 02Jul44 1ml E of Syracuse Municipal Apt, NY.

18959 42-100496 crashed 24Nov43 (Correction).

18961 42-100498 was with ATC in Apr45 based in Labrador.

18962 42-100499 9 AF, BAD2 – Taxying accident 16Jun45 at Warton (582), Lancs [Hit by B-24 41-23737].

18965 42-100502 ditched 10Mar52 0.5ml SE of La Ciotat, France [EF].

18968 42-100505 9 AF, 72 TCS (Apr45).

18969 42-100506 AFE, 42 ARS, Stewart Fld – Hit trees 20May46 18mls SE Aachen, Germany. Landed Brussels, but DBR.

18970 42-100507 9 AF, 73 TCS Fulbeck Feb44 – 71 TCS, Mourmelon (A-80), France – DBR 09May45 in landing accident Ergolding (R-73), Germany?

18971 42-100508 9 AF, 76 TCS at time of accident.

18972 42-100509 9 AF, 96 TCS (Jul44).

18973 12-032 as '052', preserved as burger bar Eskisehir Havacilik Parki ve Tavyare Muzesi, Turkey. PRESERVED

18974 42-100511 - The date indicates crash was pre-delivery – so ATC.

18977 9Q-CYC Air Kasai, WFU Kinshasa, DR Congo Jul08 and May09. STORED

18983 42-100520 71 TCS, 434 TCG.

18984 N308SF Universal Asset Management, Memphis, TN, i/s Aug08. ACTIVE

18988 42-100525 79 TCS was based at Melun (A-55), France in Mar45.

18993 CP-1960 stored Trinidad, Bolivia Mar06 to May09 complete with engines and propellers. STORED

18995 42-100532 9 AF, 80 TCS from Melun (A-55), France – Crashed 02Apr45 Nidda (Y-87), Germany.

18999 '100536' R Thai AF L2-6/90 toc 06Nov46 – Tpt Sq 1 18Apr47 – VIP conv Jun67 – W/o Lopburi 17Jan85 – Soc 08Feb85 – Tail displayed at Don Muang, outside Dakota Sq hangar Mar 2009.

19000 YV-227C RACA stored Feb01. STORED

19006 OK-WDO – D-xxx Czech AF 1950 – 0543 Czech AF Jun57 – France. F-BTDC should read F-BTDC (1), to F-BRGP reserved Nov72. See c/n 26557 for F-BTDC (2)

19008 42-100545 9 AF, 81 TCS (Apr44), 80 TCS (Apr45).

19009 42-100546 was with 80 TCS, 9 AF base Melun (A-55), France in Apr45 – Crashed 12Apr53 Fire Island, Bethel, AK.

19010 42-100547 9 AF, 81 TCS Melun (A-55), France (Apr45).

R Thai AF L2-39/15 12Sep72 - TAC 16Nov72 – At Don Muang Oct81 to Jan84 - WFU by Apr91 – Derelict Aerothai apron, Don Muang – To 'Tango' apron mid-1995 – To Crown Prince Maha 1996 – Aerothai apron Jan99 – To R Thai AF Museum, Don Muang by Feb02-Nov09. DISPLAYED

19014 42-100551 8 AF, 81 TCS (01Feb44) pre-9 AF.

19015 42-100552 8 AF, 81 TCS (01Feb44) pre-9 AF.

19016 MM61775 Italian AF – Broken up at Pratica di Mare after 2001.

19017 42-100554 324 TCS Bovingdon Dec45.

19021 CX-BJG F A Uruguaya, display Apr08 as gateguard at Carrasco, Montevideo. PRESERVED

19022 42-100559 – Crashed 1ml NE Henry, NE (Sep45?)

19023 42-100560 forced landing 03May53 2mls W of Ostend, Belgium [EF].

19024 42-100561 82 TCS was based at Melun (A-55), France in Apr/May45.

19026 42-100563 listed as 8 AF, 82 TCS, but should have been 9 AF by Feb44.

19028 42-100565 8 AF, 82 TCS in Jan44.

19029 42-100566 was based at Eccles (548), 9 AF in Feb45.

'XB-GED' remains on dump at Tegucigalpa, Honduras Nov07. DERELICT

19033 42-100570 9 AF, 82 TCS in Mar44 and at time of crash.

19034 42-100571 9 AF, 82 TCS, Melun (A-55), France – Hit trees on approach 16Jun45, Thruxton, Wilts, England.

19038 42-100575 9 AF, 83 TCS, Voisins (A-58), France – Taxying accident 20Apr45, Meiseberg (R-31), Germany.

19041 42-100578 9 AF, 83 TCS, Voisins (A-58), France (Apr45).

19045 42-100582 9 AF 83 TCS, Voisins (A-58), France – Crashed 12May45 Bous (Saar), Germany.

19046 HR-ALD remained derelict at Tabatinga, Amazonas, Brazil in late 2006. DERELICT

19050 42-100587 10 AF, 315 TCS. Crash date 04Dec44.

19051 42-100588 10 AF, 1 TCS – [PE].

19052 1667 F A Colombiana BT-67 was i/s Jan02. ACTIVE

19054 2100591 BW-K WFU 26Jul56 – K-684 R Danish AF WFU 30Jul82 – Stored Duxford 24Oct82 – del ex Vaerlose as N3239T 15Aug83. On restoration 2005 Titusville and test flown there 23Jun09, i/s 2010. ACTIVE

19057 42-100594 1522 BU John Rogers Apt, HI Aug45.

19058 42-100595 ATC – Forced landing 22Jan44 Abeche, Tchad [EF] – recovered.

19062 XT—... Chennault & Willauer to Civil Air Transport as N8355C 19Dec49 – Canx 07Oct65. [See c/n 18901].

19066 N47060 '43-9095' N Illinois Aviation Museum, Rome, GA Jul08. Sold 08Oct10 to Basler Turbo Conversions LLC, Oshkosh, WI. STORED

19068 42-100605 landing accident 02Jun44 813 BU, Sedalia AAF, MO.

19070 42-100607 315 TCS by Aug44.

19072 42-100609 1 TCS, 10 AF Dec44.

19073 42-100610 315 TCS, 10 AF – Landing accident 30Jun44 Tingkawk Sakan, Burma (St30).

19075 42-100612 342 ASS 329 ASG, 10 AF Aug45.

C/n 18988 C-47A-DL 0-2100525 of the 27th Air Division, USAF Air Defense Command, taken in 1956. *(Doug Olson)*

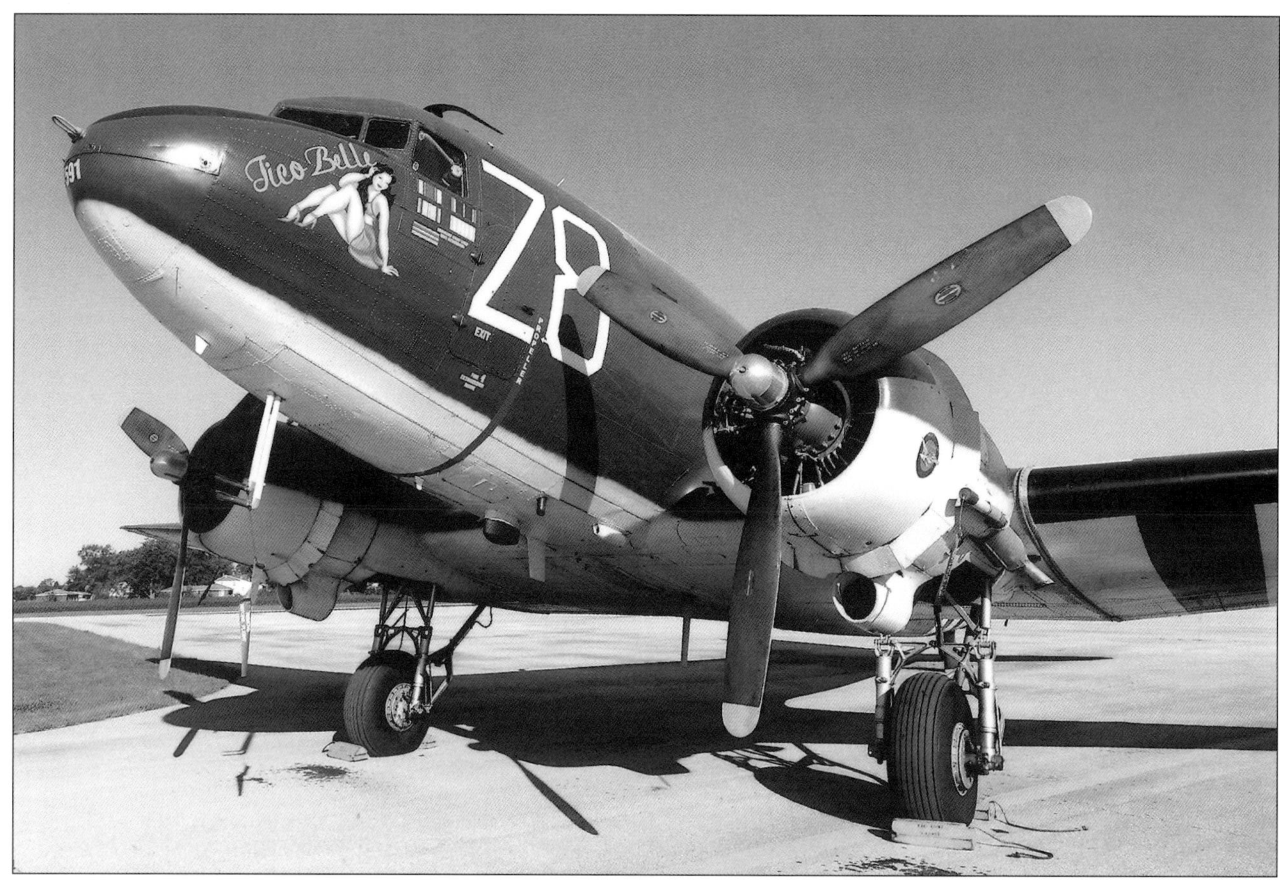

C/n 19054 N3239T in USAAF markings as '2100591' at "The Last Time Douglas DC-3 & C-47 Reunion" at Rock Falls, Illinois on 25 July 2010. (Ralph M Pettersen)

19093 42-100630 84 TCS, 9 AF – Mid-air collision 27Aug44 in France.

19096 42-100633 85 TCS, 9 AF – Landing accident 06Jun44, Welford Pk, Berks., on top of 42-24122.

19103 42-100640 94 TCS, 9 AF Feb45 – 484 ASG Erding (R-91), Germany, 9 AF, crashed 13Oct45 Huntingdon Warren, Hunts? [no mention of mid-air].

19104 42-100641 92 TCS 9 AF took part in ALBANY D-Day Jun44.
5R-MMB 'ZS-NZD' WFU at Ivato 1998. STORED

19107 42-100644 91 TCS, 9 AF May44.

19110 42-100647 10 TCS crashed 14Sep48 7mls NW Weimar, E Germany [EF].

19119 42-100656 86 TCS, 9 AF, landing accident 06Apr45 Voisins (A-58), France. Delete AA damage?

19121 42-100658 86 TCS, 9 AF 02Aug44. YV-226C WFU Feb01 Ciudad Bolivar. STORED?

19125 1670 F A Colombiana BT-67 i/s Jun00 with Esc. de Combate Tactico 113. This crashed on landing at Palanquero-German Olano AFB, Colombia on 18Feb09.

19126 42-100663 Pope May44, and 807 BU Bergstrom Nov.44.

19128 42-100665 80 TCS, 9 AF Melun (A-55), France Apr45.

19129 42-100666 S Vietnam AF unit PD415 was w/o at XS.782960 (map ref.?) on 25Oct67. Service with the Laotian AF seems unlikely.

19131 42-100668 Hq Sq 5039 ATG, Elmendorf AAC – Crashed 22Aug51 at Summit, AK.

19133 42-100670 79 TCS, 9 AF Melun (A-55), France Apr45 – Crashed 14Dec61 Santiago Peak, 10mls S of Corona, CA.

19136 42-100673 82 TCS, 9 AF Jun44 toApr45 Melun (A-55), France Apr45 – 79 FrS, Biggs (Sep46).

19138 42-100675 78 TCS, 9 AF – Taxying accident at Welford on 02Dec44 – too early for reclamation.

19146 42-100683 315 TCS, 10 AF 13Jan45 (error for 13Jun45?)

19149 42-100686 12 CCS, 10 AF Feb45.

19150 42-100687 27 TCS, 14 AF Jun44.

19154 42-100691 80 Repair depot Panagarh A/fld, India ASC?

19155 42-100692 27 TCS, 14 AF Oct44.

19157 42-100694 2 TCS, 10 AF Mar44.

19160 42-100697 315 TCS, 10 AF Aug44.

19161 42-100698 84 ADG Hq, 10 AF (Jan45).

19165 42-100702 12 CCS, 10 AF – Taxying accident 06May45 Shwebo, Burma.

19167 42-100704 10 AF on 19Oct44.

19168 42-100705 315 TCS, 10 AF – Landing accident 26Jun44 Moran A/fld, India.

19170 42-100707 315 TCS, 10 AF – Taxying accident Warazup, Burma 18Aug44.

19173 TZ-390 Mali AF BT-67 – i/s Bamako May05. ACTIVE

19194 MM61776 Museo Storico dell'Aeron. Militare Italiane, Vigna de Valle, preserved Oct08. PRESERVED

19195 42-100732 96 TCS – Hit ground 6mls from ALG (Adv Ldg Grd) Orleans (A-50), France [PE -Pitot cover in place].

19200 K-687 WFU 07Jan81 – Ferry to Billund 03Sep87 – Dansk Veteran Museum, preserved Jun06. DISPLAYED

19204 42-100741 was with 324 TCS, Bovingdon when it had an accident on 26Dec45. It had another accident in Germany on 10Mar46 which may have led to write-off.

19207 42-100744 75 TCS Baer 1 TCC Oct45 – Crashed Baer Fld, IN (Jul47?).

19208 42-100745 87 TCS, 9 AF Apr44.

19214 42-100751 88 TCS, Prosnes (A-79), France May45 - date for Kellogg an error, read 05Aug45.

19220 42-100757 88 TCS, 9 AF May44.

19221 42-100758 88 TCS, 9 AF, Prosnes (A-79), France – Landing accident 06Apr45 Gelnhausen (Y-67), Germany.

19223 42-100769 88 TCS, 9 AF May44.

19224 N96H fuselage stored Stapleton Apt, Denver, CO 2006. STORED

19227 N79017 BT-67 - canx 18Jul07 on sale as C-GAWI [Alfred Wegener Inst] to Triumph Airways Ltd, Oshawa, ONT and R31Jul07. Fitted with survey equipment for use in the Antarctic from Oct07. Del Nov 07. Regd to ALCI Aviation Ltd, Oshawa, ONT 13Dec07. Noted Oshawa Jul08 – Kenn Borek Air Ltd, Calgary, Alta R22Sep09. ACTIVE

19229 42-100766 89 TCS, 9 AF – Crashed 25Oct44 1.5mls N Guildford, Surrey.

19231 CX-BHR/T-521 preserved Museo Aeronautico, Montevideo, Uruguay 1980. DISPLAYED

19235 42-100772 89 TCS, 9 AF landing accident Short Bros, Rochester 12Oct44 – 913 AES, mid-air collision with F-6C 44-10887 27Jul45 Fürth (R-28), Germany – 9 AF, 10 PRG – Crashed on take-off 03Jan46 Fürth, Germany.

19236 CB-65 regd to Cia "Aramayo" de Minas ca Nov50 – Corp. Minera de Bolivia Oct52 – Rr CP-565 1953.

19239 42-100776 fatal accident 25Oct44 1.5mls N of Guildford, Surrey with 89 TCS, 9 AF but must have been repaired.

19245 42-100782 805 BU George Mar45.

19246 42-100783 crashed near Williams AFB, AZ on 01Oct53, and then rebuilt [EF].

19249 42-100786 805 BU George Sep45.

19250 42-100787 80 TCS, 9 AF at Melun (A-55), France (Apr45).

19251 PI-C141 1968 register gives owner as Juan Poasdas III, Malate.

19252 was suggested on p.465 of Vol 2, as PI-C184. However the latter was reported as w/o at Rangoon on 18Jan50. This is incompatible with sale as F-OAMU on 08Apr53, unless PI-C184 was repaired. Can anyone clarify?

19253 42-100790 9 TCS, 7 AF May45.

19255 42-100792 58 AsrG, 38 AES, 5 AF – Crashed 16Aug46 Itazuke.

19256 XT-817 CAT BJan52 – Rr B-817 – Stored Tainan 18Nov69 – To XU-AAE Khmer A/l 03Aug73.

19258 B-815 Air America i/s Apr60 – Crashed 27Dec63 35mls SW Songkhla, Thailand.

19267 42-100804 84 TCS, 9 AF, Voisins (A-58), France (Apr45) – 306 TCS, AFE 06Jul46.

19277 42-100814 9 AF, 1 TpG, 326 FyS R-45 – Take-off accident Aachen (R-40), Germany.

19279 42-100816 at A-7 3 FyG Romulus, ATC Aug45.

19281 42-100818 91 TCS, 9 AF, Chateaudun (A-39), France – Hit by C-47 43-15323 on 08May45 at Ergolding (R-73), Germany.

19286 N15MA remained in service with Florida Air Cargo in Feb10 – CofA revoked and to Skyway International LLC, Bay Harbor Islands, FL, R11Jun10. ACTIVE

19287 42-100824 92 TCS took part in ALBANY on D-Day Jun44 – Chateaudun (A-39), France, crashed 15May45 – Reported as tactical no 12 with Polish AF. Maybe it was repaired. Confirmation required.

19288 42-100825 93 TCS took part in ALBANY on D-Day Jun44.

2100825 Airborne Troop Museum, St Mère l'Eglise, preserved 1991. DISPLAYED

19289 42-100826 92 TCS took part in ALBANY on D-Day Jun44.

19291 42-100828 92 TCS took part in ALBANY on D-Day Jun44 – To 2100828 BW-O Norway – K-685 del Denmark 11Oct56 – WFU 29Jul82.

'348910' preserved Don F Pratt Memorial Museum, Ft Campbell, KY Jul08. DISPLAYED

19292 42-100829 357 FG, 364 FS, 9 AF, Neubiberg (R-85), Germany, crashed nr Cuneo, S of Turin, Italy 30Oct45. [Not YV-C-AMP]

19293 42-100830 92 TCS took part in ALBANY on D-Day Jun44.

19294 42-100831 92 TCS took part in ALBANY on D-Day Jun44 - 91 TCS Chateaudun (A-39), France (Apr45).

19295 42-100832 crash date was 04May44.

19296 42-100833 91 TCS, 9 AF at Chateaudun (A-39), France. Taxying accident 05Apr45 Giessen (Y-84), Germany and crashed 26Apr45 Orleans (A-50), France [EF].

19300 42-100837 93 TCS, 9 AF at Chateaudun (A-39), France Apr45.

19308 42-100845 430 FS, 474 FG, 9 AF Nice (Y-52), France Oct45.

19309 OH-LCD, Air Veteran o/y was restored to flying condition to go on display at Helsinki-Vantaa Jan06. ACTIVE

19310 42-100847 was actually for sale ex Phillips A/fld, Aberdeen Proving Ground, MD.

19311 42-100848 ferry by 94 FyS when it crashed on 22Feb44 destined for 313 TCG, 9 AF.

19313 N8348C canx 26Feb53 – CAT SA to Civil Air Transport 15Jun53 – N4884V R24Jun53 – 42-100850 USAF 09Jul53. Delete ref to CIA.

19316 42-100853 92 ADRS, 44 ADG, AFE – Take-off accident 15Mar46 Erlangen, Germany.

19318 42-100855 cause of crash [FP].

19319 42-100856 94 TCS, 9 AF, forced landing 23Dec44 Chilbolton, Hants [EF].

19320 N41, '315497' Alaska ANG, Kulis, displayed ANG Museum, Anchorage, AK Jul10. DISPLAYED

19321 42-100858 516 TRG – Taxying accident 29May46 Bovingdon. Repaired.

19324 42-100861 crashed 25Jan62 nr Wolf Creek, MT [SF].

19331 42-100868 301 ASrS, 473 ASrG Tempelhof R-95, Germany, W/o.

19335 YV-O-MC-1 preserved Nov08 Museo del Transporte, Caracas. PRESERVED

19336 42-100873 crashed 08Feb44 8mls W of Linton, TN [FP].

19340 42-100876 93 TCS crashed 11Mar44 Axford (437), England.

19341 42-100877 83 TCS crashed 11Mar44 [EF] – no location given. Repaired.

19345 N5831B Rr N473DC 14Jun06, Patrick Green, Liverpool, England, i/s. as '2100882'. ACTIVE

19347 42-100884 was noted at North Weald Jun07, in USAAF c/s coded L-D4. Based Dunsfold, Surrey as N147DC. ACTIVE

19348 MACR involved a crew member bailing out and being taken prisoner - FLC states to NC20961 Pan American 02Oct46 – Apparently never used by PanAm and as of 03Sep48 was at Brussels in non-flyable condition. US Regn Canx 17Sep48 as exported to Belgium (spares?).

19351 42-100888 hit Goddingston Hill, Swanage, Dorset on 26Jun44 and was condemned as salvage on 05Jul44. It is given in the 'book' as TS433, but that is also quoted for 43-15113 c/n 19579. The Air Ministry card actually shows 43-15133 for TS433, but '133 remained with the USAAF and USAF until 1970. The ARB gave c/n 19362 for G-ALLI, but that can be rejected as the dates are wrong. C/n 19579 went to Canadair, but what happened then is unknown. So, we have a mystery over G-ALLI c/n 19351 - did it serve with the RAF? After flying into a hill, survival seems unlikely! The TS4xx batch were rushed into RAF charge at very short notice to meet a need for C-47s with glider pick-up gear in the Arnhem campaign. The dates quoted must be suspect as they are almost certainly clerical entries of the date the transfer was notified. The RAF serial numbers were probably allocated in arrears.

19354 42-100891 45 DRS, 45 ADG, 9 AF Hanau (Y-91), Germany – Taxying accident 05Jul45, Gatwick, Surrey.

19356 42-100893 94 TCS, 9 AF Jun66.

19360 42-100897 78 TCS, 9 AF Bretigny (A-48), France Apr45.

19364 42-100901 95 TCS, 9 AF, take-off accident 06May45 Jarne (A-94), France.

19366 N141JR reported stored at Gainesville-Municipal in Oct07. To R F Diver, Crossroads, TX R01May08 [reported regn. pending 28Apr10]. At Valley View, TX noted Aug09 – Vintage Flying Museum, Fort Worth, TX D19Mar10. ACTIVE

19368 42-100905 wreckage was eventually found 10mls SW of Cherbourg. The MACR was for the immediate purpose of notifying next of kin.

19378 42-100915 AFE, IX AFSC crashed 04Oct46, 1ml SW Koge, Denmark [PE].

19380 42-100917 AFE IX AFSC, 43 AD, Erding – Crashed 09Aug46 Bovingdon, Herts [Control locks in place]. Clearly this was repaired after damage on 06Jun44.

19383 42-100920 96 TCS, 9 AF Jun44.

19385 42-100922 97 TCS 9 AF Apr44.

19387 42-100924 97 TCS when it crashed with a fuel problem. F-BFGG must be another aircraft.

19388 42-100925 crash site was Mt Manaugal.

19393 CR-AGD went direct to F A Portuguesa 6175, with Esq 801 in 1971. It was shot down by an SA-7 Grail missile on 06May74, leading to forced landing at Nacatari, nr Mueda. It remained derelict at Nacatari, Mozambique in Jun03. DERELICT

19394 N1944M to N1944M LLC, Wilmington, DE R09May08 – Rr N16005 02Dec08. Painted in American Airlines colour-scheme. ACTIVE

19400 100937 L2-48/18 R Thai AF – 62 Sq 28Nov75 – Crashed 15Mar78.

19401 42-100938 98 TCS, 9 AF, Orleans (A-50), France – Landing accident 25Jun45 Tille (A-61), France.

19403 42-100940 98 TCS, 9 AF Orleans (A-50), France, until Jun45.

19406 42-100943 4 TCS, 12 AF, crashed 01Jun44 Tingkawk Sakan (Stn30), Burma. (on TDY).

19410 42-100947 35 TCS, 12 AF 16Nov44.

19414 42-100951 51 TCS, 12 AF – Landing accident 14May45 Klagenfurt, Austria. W/o

19418 42-100955 accident Jan45 at Tarquinia AD, Civitavecchia, Italy, with 7 TCS, 15 AF.

19419 42-100956 35 TCS, 12 AF Jul44.

19420 4X-FNB preserved May00 IDF/AF Museum, Haifa AB. PRESERVED

19423 42-100960 304 TCS, St. André-de-l'Eure (B-24), France Jun45.

19426 305 F A Hondurena noted WFU at Tegucigalpa, Honduras Nov07. STORED

19427 42-100964 2 PFS, 9 AF crashed 12Nov44 3mls SE of Wallington, Surrey [Hit trees]?

19429 42-100966 landing accident 26Feb54 at Kadena, Japan.

19432 42-100969 10 AF Feb45 – Crash site was in Burma.

19433 HK-2664 SADELCA i/s Oct01. ACTIVE

19434 PH-PBA All Planes BV, Schiphol R24Apr06, i/s. ACTIVE

19445 WAA to RFC to NC19900 J P Riddle Co, Coral Gables, FL 01Feb46 – Pan American, Miami, FL 14Oct46 – CB-32 LAB 07Oct46.

19446 N471DK Basler Turbo Conversions, BT-67, was stored at Oshkosh in Jul08 – Under conversion as #49 Jul09-Jun10. STORED

19447 '2100984' fuselage stored at Pima County Museum, AZ. STORED

19452 N8352C canx 26Feb53 – CAT SA to Civil Air Transport 15Jun53 – N4883V 24Jun53 – USAF 09Jul53 – [Delete ref. to CIA].

19455 42-100992 9 TG, 7 AF, crashed 11Apr45 Okinawa.

19458 Delete all references to '43-15732' preserved at National Atomic Museum, Albuquerque, NM Oct02 and at Kirtland AFB, NM. The identity of this aircraft is unknown.

c/n 19458 (as N3433E) is the aircraft that was stored at Memphis IAP from around 1985 until 1999. The fuselage was stored in a field near Basler's at Oshkosh, WI in Jul10. STORED

19459 42-100996 805 BU George – Crashed 14Feb45 4mls SE Oblong, IL [EF].

19460 111 R Jordanian AF, preserved 2005 at Flugausstellung Junior, Hermeskeil, Germany. DISPLAYED

19461 42-100998 318 TCS, Camp Mackall 07Aug44 – 4 Prov, Pope, take-off accident 23May45 Knollwood, NC.

19462 42-100999 1 PTCG, Camp Mackall Sep44 – 2 PG, Pope Apr45 - 37 TCS Pope, CAF Sep45 – Crashed 18Jan48 on landing Andrews AFB, MD.

19463 42-101000 309TCS Alliance Feb44 – DBF 24Apr61 Pease AFB, NH.

19464 42-101001 190 FS Boise/Gowen – Forced landing 13Jan51 1ml SE Boise Air Terminal, ID [EF].

19472 42-101009 99 TCS, 9 AF Mar45.

19473 42-101010 99 TCS, 9 AF Dreux (A-41), France, crashed 26Jul45 Houdan, SW of Paris, France

19475 42-101012 45 ARS, AFE – Landing accident 14May47 Bremen AB, Germany. K-686 WFU 22Dec80, stored Vaerlose. Ferried to Duxford 15Feb84 as G-BLDI.

19486 42-101023 100 TCS, Dreux (A-41), France – Crash-landed 11May45 Merseberg (R-31), Germany.

19487 42-101024 100 TCS, 9 AF – Taxying accident 14Dec44 Aldermaston, Berks.

19492 42-101029 was diverted as NC20630 on 20Aug46 and regd to Pan American in 09Oct46 – Ferry permit for one flight Turin-Brussels May47 and sold to Panair do Brasil in Jul47 [As nothing more is known of this it seems likely it was used for spares]

19496 B-929 Air America B01Dec65 – Shot down by VietCong 14Jan66, 11mls N of Vi Thanh, Mekong River, S Vietnam.

19501 43-15035 302 TCS, 9 AF Nov44 – 100 TCS 24Dec44, hit by C-47 42-101024 on take-off from Aldermaston, Berks.

19502 43-15036 449 BS, 322 BG, 9 AF take-off accident. 27Aug45 at Hanau (Y-91), Germany.

19503 CS-DGA was stored from 1990 to 2008+ at Lisbon and painted as 'CS-TDA' for TAP Museum, Portela. It was never CS-EDA which crashed 12Apr59.

19511 43-15045 crashed 28Aug52 Toul-Rosieres (A-98), France.

19512 43-15046 92 TCS took part in ALBANY D-Day Jun44.

19513 YV-769C Servivensa, Puerto Ordaz, WFU Feb01.

19516 43-15050 324 TCS Bovingdon, Herts Dec45.

19517 43-15051 315 TCS, 10 AF.

19518 43-15052 1 TCS, 10 AF Nov44 – 12 CCS Tulhal Apr45.

19519 43-15053 1 TCS, 10 AF Aug44.

19520 43-15054 315 TCS, 10 AF, landing accident at Myitkyina, Burma 03Aug44.

19524 PP-PCM to LV-PJU ALA provisional regn. Reregd LV-FYI ALA.

19525 43-15059 – 5059 Czech AF Jun57 – wfu 14Oct60.

19526 43-15060 326 FyS, 1 TpG, 9 AF, (R-45), Germany - Crash-landed 31Jul45 1ml NW of L'Echelle, France.

19529 12-072 Turkish AF – Preserved Etimesgut Muzesi, Turkey Oct01. PRESERVED

19531 H-025 Turkish AF – Preserved Kayseri airfield Aug97. Noted there in March 09. PRESERVED

19534 43-15068 79 TCS, 9 AF, Melun (A-55), France Apr45.

19539 43-15073 – 71248 Yugoslav AF D11Apr73 (?) – 111 ppa Zagreb - wfu at Rajlovac, Sarajevo in damaged condition 1992 – Donated to D-Day Museum, Merville, France - D06Dec07 to Caen-Carpiquet for storage – '315073 9X-D' USAAF c/s. PRESERVED

19541 43-15075 9 AF, 91 TCS, Chateaudun (A-39), France – Damaged by 43-15323 (May45).

19543 43-15077 7 Ferry, Gore, MT in Nov44.

19547 43-15081 303 TCS St André-de-l'Eure (B-24), France – Take-off accident Tille (A-61), France 18May45.

19555 43-15089 crashed on take-off 11Mar44.

19556 43-15090 303 TCS, AFE, landing accident Feb46 Eschborn AAF, Frankfurt, Germany.

19557 43-15091 32 TCS, 9 AF Jan45.

19560 BT-67 C-FMKB lsd by National Science Foundation from Kenn Borek, damaged in take-off accident nr Mt Patterson, W Antarctica 19Dec07. Repaired using rear fuselage of N23SA Mar08. ACTIVE

19562 43-15096 11 TS crash-landed 05Jul48 6mls E of Wiesbaden, Germany

19570 43-15104 324 TCS, 9 AF Bovingdon, crashed 04Nov45 Schlatt, Germany.

19572 R Thai AF L2-7/90 after Tpt Sq 1 to FTS 15Feb61 and then 61 Sq. Conv TL-2 [not JL-2] by Dept of Aeron. Eng. post-26Jun67 – Royal Artificial Rainmaking Unit from 1991 – Then 46151 BT-67 toc 02Feb98 – Damaged at Phitsanulok ca 2003/04 – Remained WFU Apr06 unrepaired. STORED

19575 43-15109 128 ABG Truaux Fld, WI - Crashed 30Oct51 5mls NNW March AFB, CA.

19576 43-15110 1172 FM, Athens-Ellinikon, AFE - Crash-landed 24Dec50 5mls NW of Montaltodi di Castro, Italy [FP-BW]

19582 43-15116 7 TCS, 12 AF, forced landing Gaudo, Italy – Repaired – 14 TS mid-air collision 24Aug48 with 43-16036 nr Hanau, W Germany.

19586 43-15120 47 TCS, 9 AF, Achiet (B-54), France – Hit by taxying C-47 01Jul45 place unknown – W/o?

19588 43-15122 305 TCS, 9 AF, Nov44, mid-air collision with 43-15131 but repaired.

19593 43-15127 7 FyG ATC Gore Nov45.

XA-CEG Sonora Aero Transportes – Stored Nogales Mar08. STORED

19596 43-15130 crash site to read Rascafria, 30mls NW of Madrid, Spain.

19600 43-6050 Turkish AF – Sunk off coast as scuba-diving site 2009.

19601 43-15135 302 TCS, 9 AF Dec44.

19603 N89HA sold to Jorge C.Allala, Brownsville, TX 13Dec07. ACTIVE

19606 HK-3176 Alicol – on dump at Medellin-Enrique Olaya Herrera, Mar08. DERELICT

19607 43-15141 306 TCS, take-off accident 02May45 St André-de-l'Eure (B-24), France.

19608 43-15142 306 TCS, 9 AF, St André-de-l'Eure (B-24), France Mar45 – 14 TCS, AFE (Oct46 & Feb47).

19610 43-15144 4905 AMG Kirtland - Landing accident 01Jul51 0.5ml S of McGuire AFB, NJ [BW].

19618 43-15152 302 TCS, 9 AF, Villacoublay (A-42), France – Landing accident 09Sep45 Stuttgart (R-50), Germany.

19620 XT-... Chennault & Willauer to Civil Air Transport as N8349C 19Dec49 – Canx 07Oct65 as WFU. Remained in China.

19623 43-15157 1107 BU Walker ATC Jul45.

PK-OAZ had Philips Petroleum titles in Sep74. Stored at Jakarta-Halim Apt Oct06. Painted in Garuda c/s at Jakarta in Jul09 and displayed at Soekarno-Hatta Int Apt, Jakarta Apr10. DISPLAYED

19625 43-15159 91 TCS, Chateaudun (A-39), France 9 AF - Hit by C-47 43-15323 08May45 at Ergolding (R-73), Germany, W/o.

19628 43-15162 435 TCG when lost.

19632 9N-AAL was regd 12Sep63.

19633 43-15167 95 TS, 434 TG Stout - Landing accident at Lockheed Air Terminal Burbank, CA 03Dec45.

19640 43-15174 88 TCS, Prosnes (A-79), France.

19643 43-15177 was probably repaired after Mar44 accident.

19647 43-15181 crashed Mar44 200yd ENE of Waterway 313, Indian River, FL.

19649 43-15183 15 TCS, 9 AF Apr44.

19655 43-15189 crashed 29Aug48 Germany.

19661 HK-3292 Air Colombia, on overhaul at Villavicencio Jul08 – i/s Feb10. ACTIVE

19662 43-15196 crashed 19Jan54 0.5ml SE of Clinton, UT, before rebuild.

19663 43-15197 47 TCS, AFE, taxying accident Feb47 Tempelhof AB (R-95), Germany.

19666 43-15200 Museum of Alaska Transportation & Industry, Wasilla, AK. Preserved Sep01 to Jul10. PRESERVED

19667 RFC to Pan Am 10Oct45 – NC14283 – XH-SAA SAHSA R30Mar48 [del Jan52].

19668 43-15202 304 TCS, AFE (Feb46).

19674 575 F A Guatemalteca went to Basler to be converted to BT-67 and returned as TG-FAG-3/575. It was w/o 06Feb94 at Playa Grande, El Quiche.

19675 43-15209 78 TCS 29Aug44 – Crashed 03Oct57 nr Colesville, MD.

19677 43-15211 left Morrison, FL on delivery to 8 AF in England on 08May44 and reached 92 TCS, coded J8-B, at Balderton on 20May44. 92 TCS was part of 439 TCG, 53 TCW and 9 AF. On 28May the unit moved to Upottery, Devon and on 06Jun44 as chalk #47 it took part in ALBANY. Subsequently took part in re-supply missions. On 18Jul the unit moved to Orbetello, N of Rome, Italy, in preparation for the invasion of southern France as ANVIL/DRAGOON on 15Aug44. Paratroops were dropped and later gliders towed. On 08Sep44 a further move was made to Juvincourt (A-68), France, and on 17Sep flying from Balderton, UK the unit took part in MARKET. They returned to Lonrai (A-45), France on 28Sep44, moving to Chateaudun (A-39) on 06Nov engaging in re-supply missions and the Ardennes offensive in December. On 24Mar45, the unit took part in VARSITY and the Rhine Crossing. In May45 '211 helped with the repatriation of POWs, including French POWs to Le Bourget. '211 was transferred to 29 TCS, 313 TCG on 30May45 at Achiet (B-54), France, then to 70 FW Neubiberg, Germany on 05Dec45 and to 98 BW at Kitzingen (R-6), Germany on 26Jul45, moving on to 160 TRS, at Fürth (R-30) on 11Sep46; to 43 ADG on 20Sep46; to 28 ACRS on 03Dec46; to 45 ARS on 01May47, and to 85 ABG on 25Jul49, all at Erding. On 19Apr50 it moved to 61 ABG at Rhein-Main and then to 85 MG prior to transfer to Norway under MDAP on 20Nov50. It will be noted that the above dates and places do not always agree with those given in the book. No doubt there is some truth in both, but those from USAAF sources are likely to be on paper – as many, it will be noted, are 'beginning or end' of month. While in Denmark as K-683 '211 served with 721 Sq. It was leased for use in 'Bridge too Far' on 31Aug76 and painted as '337185' and 'KG912', but flown by Danish crews. It was WFU on 26Sep82 and flown to Florida in autumn 1983. Doan Helicopter bought N3239W on 05Sep88. By Sep89 the airframe time was 15,833:80! Wings Venture, CT B01Apr97 – Rr N1944A Apr92 – To UK 1999 – '211 restored to D-Day condition by Personal Plane Services, Booker, Bucks, UK. [Information courtesy of Tom Woodhouse, Personal Plane Services]. Based at Kidlington, Oxon Jul08. At Kemble, Glos 2010. ACTIVE

19685 PNC-0256 Policia Nacional de Colombia, BT-67 i/s Dec04 to Nov08. ACTIVE

19691 NC50311 sold by Rainbow to A J Williams in 1947 – DBR 01Sep50 in interior of British Guiana and rebuilt again as N50311 on 03Sep51 to A J Williams – VP-GAH ntu – Then VP-GAS.

19692 43-15226 6 AF crashed and DBF 16Aug45 Waller Fld, Trinidad.

19697 43-15231 13 AF Hq crashed 13Dec45 Mt Mandalgan, Negros, Philippines.

19699 43-15233 HqGp 14 Corps, Nichols Fld 13 AF Apr45.

19708 43-15242 6 ASG, 82 AES, 13 AF, crashed 05May46 Laoag AAB, Philippines [Blew tyre on landing]

19712 43-15246 544B Hq&HqS, 7 AF, mid-air collision 22May46 with 43-15247 Hawaii. Repaired after sale?

19713 43-15247 544B Hq&HqS, 7 AF – see above. Repaired.

19717 43-15251 43 TCS Aug44.

19718 43-15252 85 TCS, Voisins (A-58), France May45.

19721 N19721 E&L Leasing, Vichy, MO R07Dec05 – Derelict at Rolla National, MO by Apr09. DERELICT

19727 43-15261 78 TCS, Bretigny (A-48), France.

19729 43-6045 Turkish AF – Sunk 26Jan09 off coast at Akcakoca on Black Sea as scuba diving site.

19730 43-15264 78 TCS, 9 AF Feb45.

19733 43-15267 1402 BU Bovingdon Mar45.

19734 315268 Philippine AF, stored at Manila Jan80.

19735 43-15269 813 BU Sedalia, forced landing [EF] 3mls SW Salisbury, MO 23Jul44, but not w/o. 23Jul45 date probably wrong.

19737 43-15271 813 BU Sedalia Apr45 - then 439 TCG in Dec45.

19738 RP-C758 Avia Filipinas, stored Manila May03. STORED

19739 43-15273 crashed 01Mar53 Crabtree Creek State Park, 8mls W of Raleigh, NC.

19741 N842MB stored at Warner Robins Museum of Aviation, GA May07. Will be restored for display. The DBF report has to be taken with some caution (possibly just damaged). STORED

19747 43-15281 Pope Apr44.

19748 43-15282 316 BU crashed 07Jul48 Greenville AAF, SC.

19752 43-15286 75 TCS, crashed 03Oct46 10mls S of Columbus, Chatlahoochee, GA [PE]

19754 PH-DDZ All Planes BV, Schiphol R24Apr06. Remains in Martinair c/s in Mar09. ACTIVE

19755 6157 F A Portuguesa based at Portela 1961 to 1976 – BA1 Sintra as photo aircraft 1976 – Preserved Museo do Ar, Sintra. PRESERVED

19757 43-15291 82 TCS Feb45.

19759 NC50212 Rainbow to A J Williams R 1947, t/a British Guiana A/ws – Rr VP-GAF 15Sep50.

9Y-TDY was reported in use as a coffee bar at Georgetown, and on 07 Dec 2009 this was officially opened as the DC-3 Museum at Cheddi Jagan International Airport, Georgetown, Guyana. DISPLAYED

19760 43-15294 94 TCS, 439 TCG in Feb45.

19764 43-15298 crashed 20Jul44 North Front A/fld, Gibraltar.

19765 43-15299 7 FyG ATC Gore Aug45 - 65 FIS, crashed 12Sep50 Mt Susitna, 40mls WNW of Elmendorf, AK.

19767 43-15301 Forced landing 30Oct49 Tyndall AFB, FL [EF].

19769 43-15303 92 FyS crashed 22Mar44 Bowman AAF, KY [Spin]

19770 43-15304 9 AF Hq Nov44.

N47CR last reported in store at Opa Locka, FL in Mar99. No recent report.

19773 43-15307 was interned at Portela Apt, Lisbon on 12Apr44 – Dakota D-1 tested 28Apr44 from Sintra AB with Comando de Instrucao e Treino, Portela, Lisbon. Rn 6150 ca 01Oct56. W/o as described on page 480. Cause unknown.

19778 43-15312 59 TCS, 9 AF Sep44.

N301AK last reported Feb01 in derelict condition at Aruba Apt. DERELICT

19783 NC16815 WAA to AAXICO 09May46 – Cia Aereas Viajes Expresos (CAVE), Caracas, Venezuela prior to 06Aug48 – Regd in YV-C-Cxx series – YV-C-AMH LAV regd ca Feb49.

19784 43-15318 81 TCS, Melun (A-55), France, 9 AF Apr45 – 301 TCS, AFE – Forced landing 11Feb46 1ml SW Chattillon, Belgium.

19785 EC-ALC Iberia remained in service until Feb73.

19786 43-15320 87 TCS, Prosnes (A-79), France, 9 AF, landing accident 06Apr45, Gelnhausen (Y-67) nr Frankfurt, Germany.

19789 43-15323 94 TCS, Chateaudun (A-39), France – Hit five C-47s on landing 08May45 at Ergolding (R-73), Germany. 43-15159, 43-15351 & 42-100818 were destroyed but 43-15075 and 43-15351 of 91 TCS were repaired.

19791 415325 Philippine AF stored at Manila in Jan80. Probably scrapped.

19794 43-15328 2 TCP, Chartres (A-40), France, landing accident at Gablingen (R-77), Germany on 16May45.

19795 DO-5 Finnish AF – Used as instructional airframe from Nov77 at Utti AB. Fuselage only.

19796 43-15530 435 TCG, 9 AF Aug44.

19797 43-15331 3 FyG Romulus Nov45.

43-15331 Preserved since Apr64 at National Museum of Transport, St Louis, MO. DISPLAYED

19798 43-15332 crashed on take-off 09Aug44.

19800 N130D sold by McSwiggan to Gary F Quigg, Crawfordsville, IN R19Dec05 – Stored wingless at Punta Gorda, FL 12Mar07. Another report states moved from Charlotte County, FL to Punta Gorda-Shell Creek on 19Dec07, and still there, wingless in Feb10. DERELICT

19802 XA-HUF appears never to have been with Aerolineas Mexicanas.

19809 9Q-CSL was noted at Kinshasa in Dec03.

19811 43-15345 add 8 ARS Peterson Fld, CO Dec51. Crashed 09Sep58 on take-off Elmendorf, AK.

19816 43-15350 based at Mourmelon (A-80), France when in collision.

19817 43-15351 91 TCS, Chateaudun (A-39), France, 9 AF, hit by C-47 43-15323 on 08May45 at Ergolding (R-73), Germany.

19818 6158 F A Portuguesa D19May61 – By 1970 this was based at AB8 with Esq 801. It was used in Africa for defoliation spraying in 1973 – Left in Mozambique.

19819 43-15353 325 TCS, 1 TpG, (R-45), 9 AF, landing accident Hawkinge, Kent 31Oct45 – 306 TCS, AFE crashed 30Aug46 Furth AAB, Germany.

19823 43-15357 64 AACS, AFE – Take-off accident 23Feb47 Kaufbeuren AFB, Germany.

19825 43-15359 79 TCS, 9 AF (16Jun44), to 34 TCS Jun44.

19826 43-15360 35 TCS, 12 AF - Crashed 18Apr45 nr Ronda, Italy.

19830 RFC 25Sep45 – [user between 1945 and 1951 unknown] – N1555V regd 1952 – N1511V Lee Mansdorf Rr 18Feb52.

19833 43-15367 1 TCS, 10 AF (May44 & Apr45).

19841 43-15375 51 CTW, HqSq, AFE – Ground loop 13Sep46 Erding AB, Germany.

19844 43-15378 10 TCS, 12 AF Dec44.

19845 43-15379 reverted to USAF after NC36349. Crashed 29Apr52 off Cho-do Island, N Korea. (delete ref. to 24Sep44).

19849 43-15383 14 AF date of crash 15May44.

19851 43-15385 delivered by 5 FyS 12Apr44.

19854 43-15388 crash site was Li'Ping, China.

19856 43-15390 1333 BU Chabua, India Sep45.

19860 43-15394 taxying accident Karachi on 09Aug45. W/o.

19861 43-15395 2 TCS, 10 AF.

19863 43-15397 S&R 1352 BU Mohanbari AF Jun45.

19866 R Thai AF 61 Sq Aug58 – FTS 23Jan61 – 41 Sq 02Feb64 – 23 Sq 10Sep65 – 22 Sq 04Feb66 – 62 Sq 28Aug67 – Std Takhli 04Nov76 – Soc 31May88 due to corrosion – To Takhli for display.

19867 43-15401 16 CCS, 10 AF, take-off accident 14Sep45 Ledo AB, India.

19868 43-15402 India-China Wg until Dec44.

19889 43-15423 accident in the Philippines on 11Dec45 conflicts with being condemned in Jan45.

19903 43-15437 – c/n 15437 is listed as c/n for PI-C54. 15437 is also the first c/n for B-809 of CAT regd in 1950. 43-15437 and c/n 15437 seem to have become mixed, as the former was damaged at Clark AB in the Philippines in Jul45 with the parts possibly used to rebuild PI-C54.

19909 43-15443 6 CCS, 2 CCG, 5 AF in SW Pacific. Accident report suggests taxying accident 23Sep44, Kalaikunda B+2 with 10 AF, 319 TCS. There is obviously a mix-up in the paper work. It was not written-off, but went to Manila.

19919 was actually named 'Cook of the Walk'.

19923 43-15457 360 SrG, 5 AF, crashed 11Dec44 Kerowaggi, New Guinea. DBF.

19932 43-15466. As PI-C54 this has been quoted as c/n 15437 [see c/n 19903], which may have donated parts [?] to XT-543 "St Paul II" of Lutheran World Federation who earlier had XT-T72 c/n unknown, which crashed on 10Feb49 and was named "St Paul". It seems that XT-543 was reported as defected to communist China, but also, in an arrangement with CAT, was re-registered XT-811. The latter registration was canx on 23Jan50 when the agreement between CAT and Lutheran World Fedn. expired. This aircraft was then regd 13Jan50 as N8399C, which was possibly never applied to the aircraft. It was then sold to Capt William Dudding etc of International Air Transport on 28Mar50 and N8399C canx on 07Apr50. It was regd VR-HEX on 26Apr50. This was leased as B-809 to CAT on 01Nov50 and bought on 18Nov50. It is claimed this was sold by Air America Inc to VIAT [Vietnamese Air Transport] on 09Jun61. It was shot down in Ninh Binh Province over North Vietnam on 01Jul61 and parts are in the Air Defense Museum at Hanoi. [Any connection with c/n 15437 seems to be accidental – see c/n 26882 in Vol.2]

19933 43-15467 crashed 08Jul58 on take-off Tachikawa AFB, Japan.

19934 Nepal Airlines quote 9N-AAX ex VH-BUR.

19946 315480 Philippine AF – Stored at Manila Jan80. Probably scrapped.

19960 43-15494 12 TCS, AFE, landing accident 01Nov46, Munich AAF, Germany.

19961 TC-21 F A Argentina – Preserved Oct01 Museo Aeroespacial, Campo dos Afonsos, Rio de Janeiro. PRESERVED

19965 TA-05 Aeroparque Museum, Buenos Aires, preserved from Jul96 – Observed at Museo Nacional de Aeronautica Feb10. DISPLAYED

19968 43-15502 74 TCS Mourmelon (A-80), France.

19975 315509 preserved to 2010+ American Air Museum, Duxford. DISPLAYED

19976 '42-510' remained at USAF Museum, Hurlburt Field, FL in Dec02. PRESERVED

19977 R Thai AF L2-27/02 27Jan59 – 61 Sq by Nov59 – FTS 13Aug64 – 62 Sq 02Feb65 – Takhli for storage 23Sep76 – SOC by 14Aug81 Lopburi.

19978 315512 preserved Aug01 Evergreen Aviation Museum, McMinnville, OR. DISPLAYED

19980 NC50040 although crashed on 08Aug46 was not canx until 04Feb49.

19981 43-15515 was DBF in crash.

19982 43-15516 77 TCS, 9 AF, crashed on take-off 13Dec44 Welford Park (474), Berks.

19983 43-15517 was with ATC United A/l in Jun44. Accident in Tennessee on 06Feb46.

49-2637 Greek AF – Stored Feb01 Athens-Ellinikon.

19989 43-15523 Forced landing 25Jan45 Nashville Municipal, Apt, TN 205 BU. W/o.

C/n 19975 C-47A-DL G-BHUB painted as '315509' for the American Air Museum at Duxford, Cambridgeshire, England and photographed on 28th May 1983. This aircraft had appeared earlier in the Yorkshire Television series "Airline" as 'G-AGIV' and was formerly with the Spanish Air Force as T.3-29. (Jennifer Gradidge)

19990 43-15524 1 MAT ATC Stockton Fld Dec45.

19991 43-15525 had an accident in Pennsylvania on 05Feb46, before moving to RFC.

19996 43-15530 561 BU Rosecrans Aug45.

19998 43-15532 7 FyG Gore Feb45 – NC54334 to N54334 on 01Jan49 – L B Smith to Colombian Petroleum Co, New York – Rr HK-1504X 06May49 – [J M Davis suggests HK-1504E most unlikely as HK-1504X became HK-1504W on 13May49]

19999 N437GB to Atlantic Air Cargo Inc, Dora, FL R31Mar06. Immaculate Feb07. ACTIVE

20002 G-BGCG Tim Moor, Sky Sports Engineering – Stored 2008 Rotary Farm, Hatch, Bedfordshire, England. STORED

20004 43-15538 Biggs 235 BU, Dec44.

20007 43-15541 112 BU Westover Sep45.

TC-37 was reported under restoration at the Area Material museum, Rio Cuarto, Cordoba on 17Jan09. STORED

20012 VT-DTS Flytech Aviation Ltd, Secunderabad – Instructional airframe Feb96 to 2008. STORED

20013 43-15547 Corning is in IA not IO.

20015 43-15549 805 BU Alliance May44 – 805 BU George Oct44, crashed at George 12Oct44.

20017 N52935 G T Baker Aviation School, Miami, FL instructional airframe, 1986 onwards. PRESERVED

20018 43-15552 2 CCS Bowman Jul44 - 1 TC, 312 TCS, Pope, crashed 20Dec44 Pope Fld, Ft Bragg, Cumberland, NC. [Acft u/s].

20019 43-15553 805 BU George Mar45 - LN-IAT was named "Nordtind" with DDL – K-682 WFU 30Jul82 and stored Vaerlose – To OY-BPB Foreningen for Flyvende Museumsfly 25Jun92 – Painted in 1950s SAS c/s as "Arv Viking" 19Apr96 – To Military VIP c/s 17Oct97 – i/s 2010 Billund. ACTIVE

20021 43-15555 4032 BU St Paul Jul45.

20023 43-15557 341 BS, 97 BG Biggs AFB, crashed Aug50 3mls W of Walker AFB, NM.

20024 43-15558 813 BU Sedalia May44.

20025 insert after '559' Air America Lsd Jun66 – escaped from Saigon to Bangkok 23Apr75 – MAP – Surplus May75 – 559 R Thai AF toc 20Jan76 – 62 Sq 16Dec76 – Stored Lopburi Apr86 until May89 – SOC Apr91 and believed unmarked, displayed inside main gate Jan07-Mar09. DISPLAYED

20026 43-15560 2 CCS, Bowman – Crashed 16Jul44 Atterbury, IN.

20027 43-15561 2 CCS Bowman 07May44.

20029 43-15563 1 CCS Bowman Jul44.

20030 43-15564 810 BU Laurinburg 1 TCC, May45 – 814 BU Stout 1 TCC Sep45.

20031 530 F A Guatemalteca BT-67 was noted i/s Guatemala City, Feb06 and Jan10. ACTIVE

20034 43-15568 807 BU Bergstrom Jan45.

20040 43-15574 807 BU Bergstrom Aug44.

20041 43-15575 4 TCS, Pope, 1 TCC, May45 – 315575 was dismantled in May03 and trucked to the property of Jeff Green at Armadale, WA where it was intended to convert it into a studio – Western Oak Aviation Museum, Perth (Mar10). STORED

20044 43-15575 crashed 06Feb49 105mls NE of Ahwaz, Iran.

20045 43-15579 still displayed at March AFB in Feb08. DISPLAYED

20048 2040 crash location was Anajas, 100km W of Belem.

20051 'NZ3547'/ZK-BYF Gisborne Aviation Preservation Society, preserved in Mar07. DISPLAYED

20053 R Thai AF L2-18/00 61 Sq 14Sep57 – Missing 26Mar66 Laos.

20054 43-15588 Memphis 554 BU Feb45.

20055 43-15589 1 MATG Stockton ATC Jul45.

20056 43-15590 – Crashed Lambert Fld, MO 17May49.

20058 43-15592 805 BU George TCC Jan/Feb45.

20059 43-15593 crashed 16Aug56 landing at Elmendorf, AK.

20060 43-15594 crashed 29Jun55 Sitkinak Isle, 90mls S of Kodiak, AK.

20062 43-15596 1 MATG Stockton ATC Apr45.

20063 43-15597 1 MATG Stockton Dec45.

N135FS to G D Aircraft LLC, Atherton, CA R17Jan06 – Noted at San Juan, PR Feb10. ACTIVE

20064 43-15598 92 FyS – Take-off accident 12Aug44, Memphis Mun Apt, TN.

20065 43-15599 crashed 09Sep53 Greenland.

20066 43-15600 Hq 78 ABG, Hamilton landing accident 17Jun51 Offutt AFB, NE [EF].

20070 0-15686 Philippine AF stored at Manila Jan80.

20073 43-15607 813 BU Sedalia, crashed 26Jul44 3mls S of Sedalia AAF, MO [EF]

20080 N50034 was canx 10Jul50 – long after sale to Bolivia.

20082 46157 R Thai AF BT-67 #39 L2k-07/45 - Toc 29 May02 – i/s Dec05. ACTIVE

20088 43-15622 310 TCS, 9 AF Feb/May45.

20090 43-15624 4 FyG, 554 BU – Accident 6May44 on delivery.

20093 43-15627 310 FyS, 8 AF D22Apr44.

TC-33 F A Argentina – Preserved Museo Aeronautica da Baradadero Jan02. PRESERVED

20094 43-15628 72 TCS Mourmelon (A-80), France, crashed 16Apr45 Gotha, Germany, hitting 43-16037.

20096 43-15630 84 TCS Voisins (A-58), France Apr45.

20101 43-15635 preserved Jul08 St Louis National Museum of Transport, Kirkwood, MO. DISPLAYED

20105 43-15639 accident 02Feb46 TX. Then sold?

20106 43-15640 79 TCS Melun (A-55), France; DBR by explosion Melun 05Jun45.

20110 43-15644 301 TCS, 473 ASrG AFE – Taxying accident Bovingdon, Herts. (Feb46).

20111 6159 F A Portuguesa 19May61 – Esq 801 Mozambique in 1970, when it had loudspeakers for psychological warfare – To Mozambique as FP-502 1975.

20112 E-062 Turkish AF – Displayed Izmir Graziemir Jun01. DISPLAYED

20113 43-15647 32 TCS Frankfurt, Eschborn, AFE Jan46 – 14 TCS, premature gear retraction 15Oct46 at Rhein Main AAB, Frankfurt [PE].

20114 43-15648 S Vietnam AF was w/o while with LPD43 on 14Feb64. Map ref BS.285788 quoted.

20115 6095 Turkish AF was stored behind the 222 filo hangar at Kayseri Erkilet, Turkey in Mar09. STORED

20116 43-15650 94 TCS, Chateaudun (A-39), France, 9 AF – Landing accident May45 Cham (R-64), nr Regensburg, Germany.

20117 12-046 Turkish AF – Stored Feb96 Erkilet. STORED

20118 To Danish AF 25Oct56 – K-688 WFU 30Jul82 – Preserved as ZU-5 R Netherlands AF at Neth. A F Museum, Soersterberg Aug99 – Removed Mar10 for restoration, to return 2014. DISPLAYED

20127 43-15661 HqSq 7360ABG, Erding AB, Germany.

20131 43-15665 73TCS Reims (A-62), France, 9 AF Ice Station 3 is known as Fletcher's Ice Island. Crash date appears to be 22Oct52.

20132 43-15666 73 TCS, 9 AF 26Jun44.

20135 9N-AAO was regd 17Jul64.

20141 43-15675 73 TCS, 9 AF Aug44.

20142 43-15676 304 TCS, AFE – Mid-air collision with 42-93717 (which survived) 3.5mls NNE Heidelberg, Germany [PE].

20145 N574JB War Eagles Air Museum regd 10Apr87 i/s Oct04, Santa Teresa, NM. ACTIVE

20146 43-15680 813 BU Sedalia Nov44.

20148 43-15682 8 CCS, crashed 16Jul44 Cortland Municipal Apt, NY on take-off.

20153 43-15687 812 BU Pope Dec44 - 37 TS, 316 TG, Pope, Crashed 11Aug45 7mls SW Marietta, GA.

20157 43-15691 314 TCS Pope (28Nov44) - 131 FG, 110 FS, Bergstrom – Landing accident 27Mar51 1.75mls N of Matagorda AFB, TX [BW].

20158 'LV-ADF' Aerolineas Argentinas c/s preserved Aug05 Los Cerillos, Chile. PRESERVED

20160 N8328C canx 12Aug53 – N1797B CAT SA to TEMCO Acft Corp 09Dec53 and to Argentine Army.

20166 N839M was in service in Feb10 at LeHigh Acres, FL. ACTIVE

20171 43-15705 3 FyG Romulus AAF Oct45. HK-2820 operational Jul08 with Aerovanguardia at Villavicencio. ACTIVE

20173 6168 F A Portuguesa Esq 403, AB4 1964 to 1970 – Abandoned in Angola 1975.

20175 N145RD DC-3-65TP was flown regularly in 2006, i/s Jul09 with Baja Air, California City, CA. ACTIVE

20178 43-15712 61 AES, ATC Dec44.

20180 43-15714 1 OUT, 420 BU March Nov44. N100MA canx Nov10.

20185 43-15719 1 ITU Rosecrans, 1 TCC Mar45 (ie ex St Joseph).

20188 43-15722 591 BU Stockton AAF, ATC Oct45.

20189 43-15723 crashed 20Oct45 2mls S of Unnak, St Paul, AK at Ft Glenn on Amchitka Isle.

20190 43-15724 1452 BU Edmonton, Canada Aug45.

N95460 Brooks Fuel, stored in poor condition at Fairbanks, AK May99-Jul10. STORED

20193 43-15727 4 FyG Memphis, ATC Aug45. PP-AKA was not broken up but was preserved in 2005 at the Brazilian Army Parachute School with false markings as 'FAB 2017'. PRESERVED

20194 N63440 stored as '315728' Jul04 at Arlington, WA. STORED

20195 43-15729 3 FyG Romulus Oct45.

20197 N24320 preserved Museum of Mountain Flying, Missoula, MT, del 17Oct01. DISPLAYED

20198 43-15732 1452 BU Edmonton, Canada Oct45 – Shot down 11Feb62 at Bao Loc, Vietnam. This still does not account for the 21Aug63 date – possibly a 'book' entry.

20204 43-15738 11 AF Sep44.

20206 43-15740 1452 BU Edmonton, Canada Apr45.

2031 F A Brasileira, preserved 1995 Museu Aeroespacial, Brasilia. PRESERVED

20210 43-15744 561 BU Rosecrans Jul45.

20211 43-15745 ATC, 5 FyG, 21 TpS - Crash-landed 07Sep44 20mls S of Ottawa, Canada.

20213 43-15747 5 FyG Long Beach Jan45.

20214 43-15748 6 FyG, 4 AF Long Beach Nov44.

20215 N346K was acquired by Pacific Alaska in May 1972 – N33623 Dakota Aircraft Museum Inc, Mason, NH in Northeast A/l colours i/s Jun05, Nashua Boire Fld, NH. Stored at Mason A/fld, NH in Oct09. ACTIVE

20217 43-15751 9 FyS 08May44.

20218 43-15752 554 BU Memphis, ground collision 03Oct45 Memphis Mun Apt, TN

20219 43-15753 4 FyG Romulus Jul45 – 2 MATG Ft Dix, ATC Aug45.

20221 43-15755 594 BU, 3 MATW Topeka, ATC – Crashed 02Feb46 0.25ml from Lowry Fld, CO. [Another report states 4mls S of Lowry]

20222 43-15756 – Take-off accident 18Jan53 Kirtland AFB, NM.

20227 43-15761 ATC Anchorage 1470 BU (Apr45) – N91002 finally canx 06Apr49.

20228 43-15762 1452 BU Edmonton, Canada Sep45 – CF-ITH. The file on this aircraft states that this was to be registered CR-AGU on lease to ARTOP and later to VP-KLJ before return to CF-ITH. See also c/n 33325 Vol 2. VP-KJU is given as to CR-AGU. Comments please? CR-AGU would seem to have been ntu. C-FITH Stored Malta Aviation Museum, in poor condition Sep05 to 2010. STORED

20231 43-15765 crashed 18Jul60 NW of Valdosta, GA.

20232 43-15766 815 BU Malden, crashed 11Jan45 15mls E Dexter, MO. (1945?)

20233 43-15767 14 CCS, 10 AF, Syracuse – Crashed 07Jul44 Lake Oneida, 1ml SW of Constantia, NY [Ground collision]. This unit may be connected with 4 CCG which never operated C-47s in India. A later report gives 10 AF, 12 CCS, Missing China/Burma/India area. This may account for Apr45 survey.

20235 43-15769 805 BU George Mar45, 1107 BU Walker ATC Jul45.

20237 43-15771 crashed 04Oct44 Illinois.

20238 derelict May03 as N68363 [N786T ntu] San Juan, PR.

20242 43-15776 George Oct44, possibly crashed 19Oct44 George.

20243 43-15777 – crashed, details unknown.

C/n 20197 C-47A-DL N24320 operated by Johnson Flying Service from 1946 until 1954 as a 'smokejumper', ie for dropping firefighters by parachute. It force-landed in the Monongahela River in Pennsylvania on 22nd December 1954 and broke through the ice, drowning nine. Later the aircraft was salvaged and rebuilt and then sold to Evergreen, who continued to use it for 'smokejumping'. After storm damage in 1999, it was repaired for the Museum of Mountain Flying at Missoula in Montana in 2001. *(Doug Olson)*

C/n 20228 C-47A-DL C-FITH of Terra Surveys Ltd at Mount Hope, Ontario in September 1978. The aircraft was fitted with a tail-mounted magnetometer for mineral survey work and is currently preserved in the Malta Aviation Museum. During its years as a survey aircraft, C-FITH was overhauled on numerous occasions by the Malta-based MIACO company. (Jack McNulty)

20244 PT-KZF fuselage trucked to Appena Eco Park, Pacatuba, 30km from Fortaleza, Brazil on unknown date. To be used for educational purposes.

20246 43-15780 crashed 01May53, Elk Grove, Mt Prospect, IL 3mls from O'Hare Apt.

20251 43-15785 315 TCS, 10 AF 17May45.

20255 43-15789 9 CCS, 10 AF Jul44.

20257 43-15791 12 CCS, 10 AF, India Oct44 & May45.

20258 43-15792 9 CCS, 10 AF.

20259 43-15793 12 CCS, 10 AF.

20260 '7273' Chinese Nationalist AF stored Feb00. STORED

20262 43-15796 12 CCS, 10 AF 30Nov44.

20277 43-15811 1 CCS, 10 AF, Laohokow, China. It would seem that this survived the 27Oct44 accident.

20290 43-15824 317 TCS, 10 AF landing accident 04Jun45 Ledo AB, India.

20291 43-15825 317 TCS, 2 ACG Kalaikunda, India May45.

20294 43-15828 10 AF Jun45.

20297 43-15831 436 BS, 7 BG, 10 AF – Crashed 07Aug45 15mls SSW Lalminorhat, India.

20298 43-15832 10 AF (not 14 AF).

20300 43-15834 2 CCS, 10 AF – Crash date 12Jun45 at Yanglin Fld, China.

20302 43-15836 crashed 25Nov44 at Yazagyo, China.

20303 VT-AXC was present at Bombay, Santa Cruz in Sep74.

20312 43-15846 crashed 09Oct44.

20313 43-15847 1 CCS, 10 AF – Crash-landed 15Jun45 Luingshan, China – Repaired?

20316 43-15850 4 CCS, 10 AF – DBR 07May45.

20319 43-15853 3 CCS Myitkyina – Landing accident Chenkang, China 26Jun45 [EF].

20324 43-15858 3 CCS – Taxying accident Myitkyina Field Jun45.

20327 43-15861 3 CCS, 10 AF.

20333 43-15867 crashed in Cha Tien Shan, 30 mls SE of Taipei.

20339 43-15873 3 CCS, Indo-China ATC, Myitkyina Jul45 – Taxying accident 20Jul45 Nanning, China

20340 43-15874 328 TCS, 10AF – Take-off accident 07Oct45 Kunming, China.

20346 N8327C canx 22Jul53 – N1796B CAT SA 1953 – TEMCO Acft Corp. 09Dec53 – Canx 09Feb55.

20349 43-15883 2 CCS, 10 AF landing accident 13Jun45 Mytkyina North, Burma.

20350 43-15884 806 BU/2 CCS Baer Jul44.

20351 43-15885 2 CCS, 10 AF at time of crash.

20352 43-15886 2 CCS, 10 AF – Hit by C-46 44-78225 02Jul45.

20356 43-15890 2 CCS Bhamo A/fld, 10 AF, Burma – Taxying accident Bhamo 08Jul45.

20359 43-15893 2 CCS Bhamo A/fld, 10 AF, Burma – Taxying accident Bhamo 08Jul45. W/o and sold?

20363 VT-ATT – Crash due to [PE]

20366 43-15900 2 CCS, 10 AF 23Mar45.

20367 43-15901 1 CCS, 14 AF – Crashed 29Mar45 Alon, India Accident in Vietnam seems unlikely, as the country was still Indo-China at the time.

20372 43-15906 2 CCS, 10 AF – Take-off accident 04Aug45 Luliang Strip.

20373 43-15907 3 CCS, 10 AF Mar45.

20376 43-15910 1 CCS, 10 AF Sep45.

20379 43-15913 crash site was 100mls NW of Foochow, China.

20380 43-15914 crash site given as E of Tura, India.

20383 43-15917 10 AF in Sep44.

20385 43-15919 1 CCS, 10 AF based Chengkung.

20388 N8324C canx 12Aug53 – N1795B CAT SA – TEMCO Acft Corp 09Dec53 and to Argentine Army.

20390 7231 Republic of China AF Academy – Preserved Kangshen AB Aug00. PRESERVED

20395 43-15929 Mansfield AAF Oct44.

20397 43-15931 – 3801 TW Maxwell – Crashed 07Jan49 on approach to McChord AFB, WA near Elbe, S of Mt Rainier [PE].

20398 43-15932 48 ABG crashed 29Sep51 due to [BW].

20401 N33VW was also painted as '320401/C8 in Jul04. It was airworthy with Cavanaugh Flight Museum in Sep07 at Addison, TX, R29Jan09. ACTIVE

20408 43-15942 20 TCS, 6 AF – Take-off accident 23Aug45 Limatambo Apt, Lima, Peru

20412 43-15946 815 BU Malden Nov44 – Crashed 17Nov44 8mls NW of Malden, OK.

20414 2032 F A Brasileira preserved Feb01 Museu Belem. PRESERVED

20415 '949' Air America lsd Jul66, del Jun66 – Struck mountain and crashed 16Jan69 15.5mls SE of Hue Bai Apt, nr Da Nang, S Vietnam [BW].

20421 R Thai AF L2-40/15 toc 12Sep72 – TAC 16Nov72 – Fitted with cameras May76 – W/o Sahon Nakhon 23Sep76.

20426 N7 accident due to bad weather and pilot error.

20428 43-15962 24 TS Berry Fld, Jul44.

20429 43-15963 Nashville ATC 558 BU Apr45.

20431 43-15965 20 FyS Nashville Dec44.

20432 43-15966 5 FyG Love Jan46. HK-1175 Air Colombia i/s Villavicencio Jul08 & Feb10. ACTIVE

20435 NC16050 via WAA to J P Riddle Co 10Jun46 – Transcontinental, Rio de Janeiro 02Jun47 – US regn canx 27Apr48 as exported to Brazil but no registration known and probably direct to PP-SDD VASD.

20437 43-15971 550 BU Memphis Jun44.

20439 43-15973 552 BU Newcastle Jan45.

20440 43-15974 806 BU Baer Jul44.

20442 43-15976 20 Ferry Nashville Jul45.

20443 43-15977 1103 BU Morrison Dec44.

N230GB/'315977' Castle Air Museum, Atwater, CA preserved Sep01. PRESERVED

20444 N8021Z International Air, shows signs of N61724 on starboard side! This had no obvious connection with c/n 20444 – i/s Edinburg, TX Nov08. ACTIVE

20445 43-15979 20 FyS Nashville Dec44, 6 FyG Long Beach Aug45 - 5039 ATG, Elmendorf. [EF], and part crew bailed out 20mls E of Palmer, AK 26Aug51, pilot landed safely.

20447 43-15981 4 FyG Memphis Apr45.

20448 N838M Lee County Mosquito Control was in service in Feb10. ACTIVE

20449 43-15983 586 BU Cincinatti ATC Jan46.

20450 '984' probably 43-15984 S Vietnam AF was likely to have been written-off at Tan Son Nhut on 08Aug67 while with unit PD415.

20451 43-15985 805 BU George 1 TCC Jul45.

20455 N55U Bought by W F Remmert/Beldex ex Turkey 24Dec55, R24Dec56 – Remmert Werner R07Jun57 – Del ex Orly 14Jul57 as HI-40 – N55U canx 25Jul57 – Gift to Katanga KAT-40 Aug62 – Pilot unpaid so stole plane and was arrested in Luanda, before disappearing in S Africa.

20456 43-15990 1406 BU – Accident 05Sep44 St Mawgan, Cornwall – Repaired.

20460 43-15994 5039 ATG Elmendorf – Hit mountain 31Aug51 45 mls E of Platinum airstrip, AK [BW]

20461 43-15995 6 FyG Long Beach Oct45 – Crashed 03Jun57 0.25ml from McGrath airstrip, AK.

20463 43-15997 2 MATG Ft Dix, ATC Aug45.

20464 43-15998 449 FS Davis – Take-off accident 10Dec48 Thorobrough AFB, Canada.

20468 43-16002 16 FSS Ft Dix, Dec45 – Crashed 20Sep61 Oak Mountain, 5mls N of Chatsworth, CA.

20469 43-16003 21 FyS, Palm Springs in Feb45 – Stockton on 28Mar45 (not 44).

20471 43-16005 Boeing Fld Jan45.

20473 43-16007 3 FyG Romulus Oct45.

20474 49-2622 Greek AF was in service with 355/1 at Tanagra, the last active Dakota that saw service in Korea. Active in Sep08, but stored at Thessaloniki-Makedonia in Nov08 due to small fatigue cracks in wings. STORED

20475 43-16009 crashed 07Feb48 Alaska. Sold and rebuilt.

ZS-LVR Skyclass, Nelspruit R31Jul08. Moved to Rand on 23Aug08 for overhaul. ZS-regn canx 15Mar10 on transfer to 5H-LVR Indigo Air, regd Mar10. ACTIVE

20479 43-16013 delivered by 72 FyS 08Jun44.

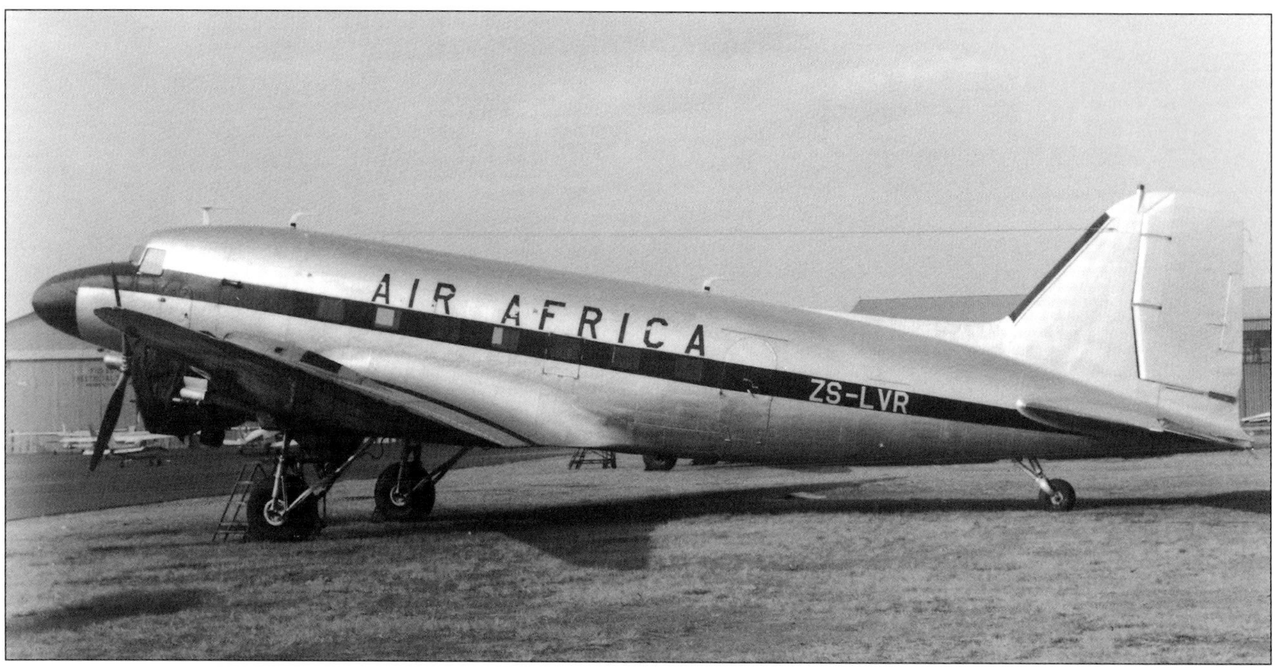

C/n 20475 C-47A-DL ZS-LVR in Air Africa colour-scheme, but owned by Bazaruto Air Charter. The photo was taken at Johannesburg-Rand Airport in May 1992 and the aircraft is still current as 5H-LVR. *(Andy Heape)*

20491 43-16025 321 TCS, 9 AF, Villacoublay (A-42), France – Crashed 10Nov45 Chezy-sur-Marne, France.

20493 43-16027 9 AF, 71 TCS – Take-off accident 04Apr45 Mourmelon (A-80), France.

20494 N142Z USDA Forest Service BT-67, i/s 2006. ACTIVE

20495 43-16029 74 TCS, 9 AF at Mourmelon (A-80), France Apr45. 60-059 Republic of Korea – Preserved Taegu Nov03. PRESERVED

20502 43-16036 7210 MSU – Mid-air collision 24Aug48 with 43-15116 nr Hanau, W Germany.

20504 43-16038 crashed 28Nov45 in France.

20507 TAM-38 F A Boliviana, BT-67. Fuselage stored Santa Cruz, El Trujillo Sep97. STORED

20510 43-16044 crashed 24Oct54 into mountain nr Limone Piemonte, Cuneo, Italy [PE]. Also reported crashed 40mls N of Monte Carlo.

20512 43-16046 14 TCS, AFE 24Dec46.

20513 43-16047 815 BU Malden – Crashed 13Dec44 2mls NE of Zelma, MO.

20514 43-16048 306 TCS, Metz (Y-34), France, 9 AF, Jun45.

20516 43-16050 72 TCS Feb46.

20517 43-16051 accident Germany 25Feb46.

20522 43-16056 811 BU Lawson TCC Jan45 – 10 ABG – Crashed 31Mar49 Pope AFB, NC [EF]

20525 43-16059 13 CCS, 4 CCG, Aug44 – 75 TCS Lawson Apr46.

20526 43-16060 crashed Delaware 05Nov44.

20528 43-16062 814 BU Stout Dec44 – Crashed 09Oct49 Isachsen Land, Ellef Ringnes Island, NWT, Canada - Wreck found May07.

20529 43-16063 810 BU Laurinburg Feb45, so date quoted should be 20Feb45.

N9141 fuselage was still at Muskogee Apt, OK in Nov05. STORED

20530 N8160Z fuselage stored at Naples, FL Feb01. STORED

20531 43-16065 AC-47 S Vietnam AF was written-off while with PD417 on 16Aug69 at map ref. WS 765136.

20532 43-16066 815 BU, Malden 61 TCW – Crashed 20Dec44 6mls S of Ironton, MO. [PE].

20535 43-16069 75 TCS, 316 TCG Lawson, TAC Apr46.

20536 N67588 Majestic Air Leasing Inc, Salt Lake City, UT from Feb88 – Op. by Majestic Airlines Inc from Feb88 to Jan96 when it ceased trading – Lsd to Galaxy Air Cargo Inc, Anchorage, AK Jul97 – Op by Majestic Air Cargo and crashed 24May98 at Point Mackenzie, AK on approach to Anchorage. Fuselage (less wings) towed to Anchorage Intl Apt and repairs commenced, but abandoned – Majestic Air Cargo ceased trading Jan01 – Returned to lessor and regd to associate Tammy Maxwell – WFU at Anchorage May98, but no longer there Jul10. Fate?

20537 43-16071 320 TCS, Roswell, NM, SAC – Landing accident Roswell, NM 14May46.

20538 43-16072 crashed on take-off 12Mar65 Marquette Apt, MI.

20543 43-16077 805 BU George Mar45.

20548 HK-3037 ARALL, Villavicencio, i/s Jul08 and Feb10. ACTIVE

20549 '083' Air America i/s by Jul66 ['Log Wr.Patt' is cover for Air America] – Escaped 29Apr75 from Saigon to Tainan, Taiwan – USAF surplus May75. Other reports of crash probably in error.

20550 N139JR stored engineless at Columbus, IN in Sep07 with Rhodes titles. STORED

20554 43-16088 814 BU Stout Jul45.

20555 43-16089 4149 BU Boeing Fld Nov45.
'PP-AVJ' on gate at Museu Aeroespecial in 2005. PRESERVED

20558 43-16092 801 BU, Laurinburg 1 TCC Apr45.

20560 '316094' Preserved Aug96-Jul03 Dakota Territory Air Museum, Minot, ND. PRESERVED

20562 43-16096 805 BU George, TCC Feb45

20564 43-16098 314 TCG Hq (Nov45).

20567 43-16101 281 BU Brownsville – Crashed 01Jul45 6mls E of Spring Lake, TX.

20568 43-16102 123 ABG, Godman AFB, KY, 9 AF – Crashed 28Jan51 Godman AFB, KY.

20574 43-16108 Yonton A/fld, 7 AF, China Nov45.

20577 43-16111 39 TCS, 5 AF – Landing accident 08Jul46 Kwangju strip, Korea.

20583 43-16117 5 AF (Dec44).

20584 43-16118 crashed 30Jan49 California.

20585 43-16116 crashed 12Dec55 on take-off from Smoky Hill, KS.

20587 6160 F A Portuguesa – Based at BA2 Ota and then AB1, where it remained as VIP aircraft until transfer to Guiné-Bissau.

20590 43-16124 805 BU George Mar/Apr45.

20591 43-16125 2 PTC Pope – Take-off accident 03Apr45 Pope – Possibly delayed cause of w/o?

20592 43-16126 805 BU George Jan45.

20594 43-16128 354 BU Rapid City, SD – Accident 5mls NE of Greeley, CO [BW]

20595 43-16129 805 BU George Feb45.

20596 43-16130 on display Nov06 at USAF Museum, Barksdale AFB, LA. DISPLAYED

20598 43-16132 815 BU Malden – Crashed 21Sep44 1ml N of Malden AAF, MS.

20600 43-16134 813 BU Sedalia Nov44. T.3-36 remained on display at Museo del Aire, Cuatro Vientos, Madrid in Nov06. DISPLAYED

20602 43-16136 was reported as 'Crash 17Feb54'. In fact this a/c was destroyed on the ground on the date given, at Doson Airfield, French Indo-China, when an ammunition truck was sabotaged. It had MATS titles and was involved with maintenance of C-47s and B-26s supplied to France under MDAP.

20604 CX-BKH/T-514 F A Uruguaya – Coleccion de la Base Aerea, Montevideo – Preserved at Carrasco AB Apr08. PRESERVED

20607 N54610 Vermont ANG Heritage Park, South Burlington, VT Sep01-Dec04. PRESERVED

20608 43-16142 S Vietnam AF unit LPD43, was written-off on 15Apr63 at Lien Khuong.

20609 43-16143 561 BU Rosecrans Nov44 – Crashed 11Nov44 14mls N of Glendale, CA.

20610 43-16144 George 805 BU Jan45 – Mid-air collision 04Mar45 with 42-24101 3mls N of Lawrenceville, IL.

20611 43-16145 crashed 24Sep55 3mls NE of Burns, WY.

20613 '147' to Air America 14Jun61 – in use in SE Asia to 1975 – Escaped 29Apr75 from Saigon to Bangkok – Sold by USAF May 75 - R Thai AF 62 Sq L2-53/19 20Jan76 – Conv TL-2 – Soc 14Aug81.

20614 43-16148 6 AF – Crashed 06Mar45 Avianca Fld, Bogota, Colombia.

20615 43-16149 556 BU, 6 FyG Long Beach Feb46.

20616 43-16150 4131 BU, Offutt, NE – Landing accident 30Sep46 Offutt Fld, NE.

20617 43-16151 61 TCW/815 BU – Crashed 25Dec44 Black Mesa Mtn, nr Quartzsite, AZ [PE].

20619 43-16153 accident 18Jan48 in Bolivia which probably led to sale.

20620 43-16154 4112 BU Olmsted – Landing accident 07Aug45 Olmstead Fld, PA.

20625 43-16159 shot down 05May68 at Pleiku, Vietnam.

20627 43-16161 1466 BU Ladd Jan45.

20628 43-16162 4136 BU Tinker Jul45.

20629 full serial for Libyan AF is '0-16163'.

20630 43-16164 2926 AMG Wright Patterson 23Oct50.

20634 43-16168 127 TG Sacramento AAF – Forced landing 22Oct45 Washington Natl Apt, DC [EF].

20636 43-16170 Indo-China, 84 ADG Hq (Nov44), 10 AF, 317 TCS 20May45.

20640 43-16174 crashed on take-off, Dinjan airfield, Assam.

20642 43-16176 3 CCS, 10 AF – Crashed on take-off 29Aug45 Luliang, China.

20643 43-16177 12 CCS, 10 AF, Tulihal 09Apr45.

20644 43-16178 319 TCS, 10 AF – Landing accident 18Feb45 Palel, India – ATC – Crashed 01Apr45 Kunming.

20646 43-16180 317 TCS, 10 AF, Ledo Jun45.

20649 43-16183 del. by 5 FyG, HqSq Dallas Jul44.

20651 43-16185 27 TCS, 10 AF – Crash site was 1ml S of Chanyi.

20654 43-16188 315 TCS, 10 AF Apr45.

20667 43-16201 Baer – Accident 29Oct44 at Baer, IN. This probably accounts for its relegation to instructional airframe.

20670 43-16204 360 SrG, 5 AF – Crashed 19Feb45.

20671 43-16205 360 SrG, 5 AF – Crash-landed 18Jan45 New Guinea.

20675 43-16209 313 BS, HQ Sq – Ran into ditch at Clark AAB, 21Sep46.

20676 43-16210 46 TCS 'X106' – Crashed on take-off 30Sep46 8 mls NW of Pusan, South Korea [PE].

20677 43-16211 1 TCS – Crashed 23Mar46 Banahao Mt, Philippines.

20679 43-16213 39 TCS, 317 TCG, 5 AF - Crash-landed 14Jun46 Kwangju Strip 3W, Korea [PE]. Delete ref to Belgian AF.

20681 9N-AAC regd 29Jul59.

20688 43-16222 crashed Jul49 Guam. (Anderson is Guam).

20691 was actually named 'Hustin Housier III'.

20711 43-16245 landing accident 24Aug52 Muir Fld, Indian Town Gap, PA.

20714 43-16248 805 BU George 1 TCC Dec44 and Mar45 – Ditched 27May45 0.75ml from Mayaguana Island, British West Indies.

20715 43-16249 crashed 12Jan52 135mls NNE Ladd AFB, AK. Sold.

20716 43-16250 555 BU 5 Ferry, Love Dec44 – 5 FyG Love Dec45.

20718 43-16252 1503 BU Hamilton Aug44 – Crashed 22Feb54 61.08N x 44.05W Greenland.

20721 43-16255 5 Ferry, Love Aug45.

C-GJDM reported derelict at Peterborough, Ont in Feb10. Engineless. DERELICT

20722 43-16256 crashed 28Feb49 Tierras Coloradas, Mexico. Also reported 75mls SW of Del Rio, TX.

20723 43-16257 crashed date also given as 10Mar52 at Offutt AFB, NE.

20725 43-16259 India-China ATC, 4 MS Feb45.

20726 43-16260 6 MMRS 1339 BU, Chengkung, Jul45.

20727 43-16261 1305 BU Dum Dum when it was lost.

20729 NC15709 via WAA to Howard J Korth, Miami Springs, FL 18Sep46 – To VASP 10Dec46 – US Regn Canx 07Jan47 as sold to Brazil.

20730 43-16264 del to R Hellenic AF Jun48. W/o at Elefsis on take-off.

20733 43-16267 crashed 21Mar48 Davis Pk, Cowlitz City, WA/ 11mls NE Woodland, WA.

20734 NC18664 European Div, ATC, War Dept – Canx 03Jan46 - 1408 BU Orly - Landing accident 17Jun46, Orly, Paris, France.

20736 43-16270 crashed 29May53 Itazuke, Japan.

20737 43-16271 1402 BU Bovingdon ATC – hit car while landing Bovingdon, Herts 12Aug45 – repaired.

20743 N236GB to Indiana Research & Rescue Inc, R18Sep08 – WFU Jul08 Cleveland–Burke Lake Front, OH for restoration. STORED

20749 43-16283 1 MATG Stockton, Nov45.

'20750' an aircraft with this c/n quoted is believed to be ex LAN-Chile, and is preserved at Santiago Intl. Apt.

20753 43-16287 1379 BU Dow, Jul45 – 6603 AMG – Crashed 16Jan51 Goose Bay, Newfoundland.

20764 to MAP 13Oct53 – Dept of Aeronautical Engineering 14Oct53 – R Thai AF 61 Sq 12Nov53 – 62 Sq – Std Takhli 21Sep76 – Army Mounted Infantry Battalion 1 by Mar82 – Soc May88, cause unknown.

20767 RP-C147 was noted WFU at Manila in Dec07 and Mar10, with Swiftair tail logo. STORED

20774 43-16308 Hq, Leyte AD, PASC – Take-off accident 05Jul46 Tacloban Airstrip #5.

20776 43-16310 Flt Test PASC – Landing accident 07Jun46 Baguio airstrip, Philippines.

20790 316324 Philippine AF stored at Manila Jan80.

20792 43-16326 – VR-SCB Malayan Airways should be deleted. Regd to South Eastern Airways Ltd, Singapore on 17Mar47, the aircraft was sold to Hindustan Airways, India in Nov47.

20794 R Thai AF L2-29/02 61 Sq 12Mar59 – Ran off taxiway into sea at Hong Kong 03Dec59 – rebuilt as VR-HFR May61 etc.

20796 43-16330 take-off accident 24Aug49 North Guam AFB, Guam.

20806 XT-20?- Chennault & Willauer – Civil Air Transport Inc as N8350C R19Dec49 – Rr N37800 [no date given] – Grand Central Aircraft Co, Glendale, CA B27May53 – Johnson & Johnson, New Brunswick, NJ, B22Oct53 – Rr N800J 20Aug59 – N8009 Rr 15Jan69 – Samual A. Tamposi & Gerald Q. Nash, Nashua, NH 22May69 – Munchen Nassau Trading Co, Hackensack, NJ 08Oct70 – East Hill Constr. Co., Hackensack, NJ, 04Nov70 – Tiburzi Tours Inc, Ft Lauderdale, FL – East Hill Constr. 12May71 – Tiburzi Tours – Club Passport Inc., 14May71 – Indiatlantic Trading Corp, Ft Lauderdale, FL 01Jun71 – Club Passport Inc – Hanscom Air Service Inc., Lincoln, MS B11Jun71 – Air Nashua B06Aug75 – Intl Shoe Machine Corp B09Jun78 – Classic Air Transport Inc, Lehighton, PA, B23Jan96 – Victoria Forest & Scout LLC, San Francisco, CA B23Jan96 - N877MG Rr 29Feb96 - John T Sessions Historic Acft Foundn, Seattle, WA R04Aug06. Restored to flying condition Victoria, BC Jun10. [Ownership of this aircraft is complicated by bankruptcy and court action in 1971-1975] ACTIVE [This aircraft has been quoted as c/n 4193. If it is assumed that this is a line number, then the c/n comes out as 20806 which tallies with its early history]

20813 43-16347 accident 10Feb46 Hawaii.

20814 '316348' Greek AF – Stored Sedes 1996. STORED

20817 43-16351 319 TCS, 10 AF – Take-off accident 14Jun45 Myitkyina Nth, Burma – Repaired. N8334C canx 22Jul53 – N1798B CAT SA 1953 – TEMCO Acft Corp 09Dec53 and to Argentine Army.

20819 43-16353 10 CCS, 10 AF Mar45 – Crashed 25Nov53 5mls S of Sirte, Libyan desert.

20820 43-16354 11 CCS, 10 AF – Landing accident 05Apr45 Mu-Se, Burma.

20823 K-16/OT-CWG Belgian AF – Preserved Musée Royale de l'Armée, Brussels since 1973. DISPLAYED

20825 43-16359 36 DRS, 10 AF – Crashed 27Jul45 Myitkyina, Burma.

20828 43-16362 crashed 14May49 Saudi Arabia.

20829 43-16363 11 CCS, 10 AF – Mid-air collision 20Sep45 Peishiyi, China.

20830 N102DH Asean Air, Manila – WFU at Manila from May03, still there Mar10. DERELICT

20832 43-16366 ATC 26 TS Rosecrans Aug44 – 561 BU Rosecrans Jan45.

20835 N2805J '43770/EN' American Flight Museum, i/s Jun08 Topeka, KS and at Gillespie, CA in Oct09 – 2010. ACTIVE

20836 43-16370 Take-off accident 23Mar49 Resolute Bay, NWT, Canada.

20838 43-16372 1 MATG Stockton Apr45.

20840 43-16374 1 MATG Stockton – Crash site 3mls N of Stockton, CA.

20841 43-16375 1 MATG Stockton Fld, Jun45.

20842 150187 (if correct) – Crashed 13Aug69 at Langanes, NE Iceland. Airframe used as a sheep shelter. DERELICT

20844 43-16378 44 ADG, AFE – Crashed 18Dec46.

20845 43-16379 4505 BU, Kelly Sep47.

3407 F A Dominicana, i/s San Isidro AFB May98 – ACTIVE (?)

20848 43-16382 308 AirWrXG, 59 RS, Fairfield – Landing accident 15Nov46 4mls SW Mills, CA.

20849 43-16383 Adm S.B. 561 BU Rosecrans Dec44 – Crashed 12May45 3.5mls SSW of Cordelia, CA [BW].

20852 43-16386 crashed 05Oct49 Mt Mitchell, 3mls WNW of Marion, NC.

20853 43-16387 7 Ferry, Gore Fld Jan45.

20854 43-16388 312 FyS, 8 AF – Hit B-17 on landing at Membury, Wilts 12Dec44.

20856 43-16390 S Vietnam AF was written-off at Kon Tum on 16Jul62 while with LPD1VT.

20861 43-16395 7 FyG Gore Nov44 – Gore 1455 BU – Wheels-up landing at Great Falls AAB, MT 25Jul46 – Repaired.

20862 43-16396 ditched in Atlantic Ocean, 380mls from Newfoundland 27Apr49 beside USCG cutter 'Sebago'. Sank, so not reclaimed.

20863 43-16397 26 TS, 561 TSG ATC (16Nov44) – 561 BU St Joseph Feb45 – 6147 TCS – Crashed 29Jan51 K-37 Taegu # 2 AB.

20865 N780T MBD Corp – Wfs Dec05 San Juan, PR – Moved to Restaurant Los Aviones as bar at Barranquitas, Puerto Rico as N780T. DISPLAYED

20871 43-16405 ATC – Taxying accident 17Mar45.

20873 43-16407 7 Ferry, Gore Fld – Crashed 25Nov44 2mls NW Blue Pounds, WI [BW]

20875 PNC-213 BT-67 r/n PNC-0213 in 2004 – Policia Nacional de Colombia i/s Nov08. ACTIVE

20876 316410 – Obock was in French Somaliland (as was – now Djibouti).

20880 43-16414 ATC Nigeria (Apr45).

20886 NC67125 Aviation Maintenance Corp, Van Nuys, CA.

20887 43-16421 1369 CWB – Ditched 28Jan46 off Formosa.

20888 43-16422 319 TCS, 1 ACG, 10 AF, Nov44 – Crashed 29Sep45 47mls S of Hsian, China.

20893 43-16427 20 AF, 1 ATS, 20 AF Nov44.

25225 43-47964 Philippine AF named 'Mamburao'. This was stored at Manila in Jan80, in protective black paint.

25226 43-47965 the Toledo crash was a landing accident only.

25236 43-47975 3 PFS crashed 26Nov44 Leith Hill, nr Coldharbour, Surrey.

25240 43-47979 crashed 12Mar57 Mt Yarigatake, Japan.

25242 43-47981 858 BS, 492 BG, 8 AF May/Jun45.

25247 43-47986 Hq 15 AF, Bari Apt, Mar45.

25249 43-47988 18 TCS, 12 AF, Italy, May45.

25255 43-47994 2 ERS, 13 AF – Crashed 05Jan46 2km off Gumab, Masbute Is, Philippines.

25263 43-48002 37 AwyD, 6 AF Jun45.

25264 43-48003 20 TCS, 6 AF, 21Jun45.

25267 43-48006 DBR.nat.phen = storm damage.

25269 43-48008 812 BU Pope, Dec44/Apr45.

R Thai AF 61 Sq 15Oct58 – 20 Sq 26Feb65 – 62 Sq 28Aug67 – Conv TL-2 Sep69 – Reverted to L-2 transport Jun88 – Royal Artificial Rainmaking Unit 1991 to 1995 – 46155 R Thai AF BT-67 L2k-05/42 D15Jan99 – i/s Dec07. ACTIVE

25271 43-48010 315 TCG, Pope Jul45

25273 62-357 F A del Peru, preserved Oct03 Museo del Peru, Las Palmas AFB, Peru. PRESERVED

25275 HC-SBS named "Star of Sangay" f/n 20, i/s with Shell 04Mar47. This is given as c/n 25272 in both indices! That crashed in September 1944

25278 YV-147C noted WFU at Ciudad Guayana, Venezuela Feb07 in Servivensa c/s. STORED

25291 KG747 actually crashed on 09Jun46 60mls N of Lagos. Oni is a river, but there is no indication as to whether the aircraft actually came down in or near the river.

25309 N2271C was stored at Lampang, 300mls N of Bangkok, Thailand in 1992 before it was ferried to Australia. Preserved Ipswich Amberley Aviation Museum Aug00. DISPLAYED

25311 6840 SAAF C-47-65TP display Ysterplaat Sep08. Flying Sep10. ACTIVE

25313 N173RD has Algonquin Airlines titles on the port side and Everlast on the starboard side. Owner Lance Toland flies it occasionally from Griffin, GA. Active May07. ACTIVE

25320 43-48059 1 TCC, Hunter 3 AF Jul45.

25321 43-48060 813 BU Sedalia Dec44.

25325 348064 Philippine AF stored at Manila Jan80 in black paint – To RP-C81.

25327 43-48066 was with 312 TCS, at Pope Fld, NC 18Sep44.

25328 43-48067 39 TRS, 412 FG March, Jun46.

25329 43-48068 4 TCG Bowman Aug44 – 60 BU Atlanta, crashed 18Nov45.

25330 43-48069 23 TCS, Pope Jan45 – Crashed 21Apr52 110mls W of Anchorage, AK.

25332 43-48071 37 TCS, 316 TCG Pope Jul45.

25336 43-48075 37 TCS, Pope 1 TCC Aug45.

25337 348076 Philippine AF, stored Jan80 at Manila in black paint.

25339 43-48078 4152 BU Clinton County, OH, AMC Sep46.

25341 N7AP Ohio University, i/s? Jul01. ACTIVE?

25344? 9T-PKB was noted at Lagos-Ikeja in May70.

25345 '084' was bailed to Air America in Jun66 at Tainan. It was stored at Saigon from 20Jun70 to May74 and escaped from Saigon on 29Apr75, crashing on landing at U Tapao R Thai Navy Base on that day. It was declared surplus in May75.

25346 43-48085 2750 ABG, Wright Patterson – Take-off accident 10Oct51 Robins AFB, GA.

25347 RP-C1352 noted derelict at Manila in Dec07 and again in Sep09. DERELICT

25349 43-48088 ETOU Wright ATSC Sep45.

25350 43-48089 104 BU crashed 06Aug46 1.5mls NNE of Commack, Suffolk, NY [PE].

25352 43-48091 landing accident 27Jan55 Niligata AB, Japan. Sold for rebuild.

25357 43-48096 75 TCS Lawson, Apr46 – ? 9T-PKE noted at Lagos-Ikeja in May70.

25358 43-48097 805 BU George Dec44 – Crashed 31May54 2mls from Duluth Airport, MN.

25359 0-48098 was on display at SAC Museum, Omaha, NE in Jun06. DISPLAYED

25360 43-48099 811 BU Lawson 1 TCC Mar/Jul45 – N64490 crashed 11Apr80 at Athol, ID.

25361 43-48100 314 TS, 349 TG, 1 AF, Pope, Nov44.

25362 '48101' probably escaped from Vietnam to U-Tapao in 1975 – derelict at U-Tapao by Oct97, still there in 2009. DERELICT

25363 43-48102 2472 RTC, Fairfax – Taxying accident 04Mar50 Fairfax – 303 TCS, Fairfax – Crashed 10Apr50 Fairfax Fld, KS [EF]

25368 RP-C1354 derelict at Manila Dec07 but stored in good condition Sep09 – STORED. The c/n was wrongly given on page 521 of Vol 2.

25372 N91260 was DBR late 1968 in a remote area of Ethiopia. 5Y-ACF was almost certainly ntu.

25395 43-48134 5010 ABG, Eielson AFB – Crashed 07Sep51 S of Moose Creek Bluff, 5mls SW Eielson AFB, AK [EF].

25400 43-48139 hit mountain nr Udine, Italy 03Dec61.

25401 43-48140 taxying accident 15Jul52 K-9 Pusan-East AB, Korea.

25402 43-48141 crashed 13Nov49 Iwojima.

25403 43-48142 1704 ATG, Travis, MATS – Crashed 26Dec51 48mls E Redding, CA

25404 43-48143 2 MATG Ft Dix Jan46.

25405 43-48144 2 MATG Ft Dix Dec45 – 558 BU Nashville ATC Dec45 – 6550 ASG Patrick – Crashed on take-off 22Dec51 1ml S of Nassau, Bahamas.

25409 117 F A Salvadorena, BT-67, i/s Mar02. ACTIVE

25410 43-48149 21 TS, 3 FyG, ATC Romulus Sep44. R Thai AF L2-21/00 to 61 Sq ca Nov57 – 62 Sq 01Apr69[i/s 1971/72] – Std Takhli 24Sep76 – 603 Sq 24Jul80 – W/o 28Feb84.

25412 43-48151 53 ES, Romulus Sep44.

25414 43-48153 4 FyG Memphis, ATC Jul45.

25415 43-48154 believed named 'Bessang Pass'[when?]. RP-C845 Victoria Air, Manila, i/s Jan01. NLR

25417 43-48156 2 MATG Ft Dix AAB Dec45.

25423 43-48162 1452 BU, Edmonton ATC Oct45 – 1452 BU Whitehorse ATC Nov45.

25425 540 F A Guatemalteca was i/s in Feb06 and Nov07, but WFU by Dec08 at La Aurora. DERELICT [J M Davis points out that there is no Museo de la FAG]

25430 43-48169 1536 BU Hollandia, New Guinea Apr/May45.

25432 43-48171 1559 BU Tacloban ATC Jul45.

25437 43-48176 1558 BU, ATC Feb45.

25443 1686 F A Colombiana BT-67, i/s Sep94. ACTIVE

25450 'D-CADE' Auto und Technik Museum, preserved Apr08 Sinsheim. DISPLAYED

25453 YU-ABI stored Jul08-Sep10 Belgrade, Serbia. STORED

25455 T-101 F A Argentina - Preserved Jul01 Ville Reynolds, Argentina. Reported to be displayed at new El Calafate IAP, SCZ. PRESERVED

25457 OO-SBD did become N3910A and was taken up, possibly just for a ferry flight from Brussels to Paris by a pilot with an American licence. Probably never carried marks.

25458 43-48197 crashed 10Nov44 Aldermaston, Berks – Repaired – 72 TCS, crashed wheels up 01Mar45 Aldermaston, Berks

25464 CR-821 Sri Lankan AF, Ratmalana Museum, preserved Jul01. PRESERVED

C/n 25450 The aircraft currently masquerading as 'D-CADE' at the Auto und Technik Museum at Sinsheim, southern Germany is modelled on Lufthansa's Dakota D-CADE (c/n 27108 - illustrated) which was one of three of the type which saw service with the airline between 1955 and 1960. (Ulf Boie)

25467 VT-CGA regn canx 03Sep93.

25474 43-48213 crashed 29Jul55 after take-off from Wheelus AB, Libya, 50mls off coast at Misurata in Mediterranean Sea.

25475 43-48214 306 FyS – Crashed 04Aug44 30mls NE Romulus AAF, MI [EF] – Repaired.

25480 YU-ABG parts preserved 1968 at Muzei Jugoslovenskoy Vazduhplonta, Surcin. PRESERVED

25482 N64784 Dream-Aire Inc, i/s Mar03 Bakersfield, CA. ACTIVE

25483 CF-FOL ran out of fuel and ditched in the Atlantic Ocean 17Nov72 [PE].

25484 KG807 reverted to 43-48223 which spun in at Carmeilles-en-Vallangou, nr Orly, Paris 03Mar45.

25485 N982Z Stan Brock, Knoxville, TN i/s Jul01. ACTIVE

25486 43-48225 45 ADG, Hanau (Y-91), Germany, 9 AF, landing accident 17Nov45 Auerbach, nr Nurnberg, Germany.

25487 43-48226 1562 BU Biak Island, ATC Jun45.

25488 43-48227 1562 BU Biak Island – Ground accident Biak Island 03Jul45 – probably w/o.

25489 43-48228 1559 BU Biak Island, Aug45. T-482 AURI, preserved Museum Pusat TNI-AU, Yogyakarta AB, Indonesia 1995. PRESERVED

25491 43-48230 1552 BU Finschafen, New Guinea May45. R Thai AF L2-15/96 Squadron 1 10Nov53 – SOC 16Jan57.

25494 43-48233 1562 BU Biak Island, ATC Jul45.

25495 VH-BAB/'348234' N Queensland Warbirds, Mareeba, QLD. Stored Jan05. STORED

25503 43-48242 unit was 1402 BU [FP].

25504 43-48243 crashed 30Jun48 Germany.

25505 43-48244 84 TCS, Voisins (A-58), France, 9 AF May45.

25507 43-48246 crashed on take-off 31Dec53 at Marks Fld, Nome, AK.

25508 43-48247 was named 'Vandra Min Vaq' with 27 TCG Jan to Aug 1945. Was with 211 FyS, 9 AF in Jul45?

25509 has been a mystery for many years after it was listed as being assigned to a secret project. Thanks to Karl Hayes' investigations this has now been identified as N61696. However, between Mar51 and May68 nothing is known of its operation. Since then it has continued to be used by various agencies. N61696 Southern Sky Inc, Dallas, TX Bill of Sale 05Jan68 – Aviation & Inland Marine Rentals Inc, Denver, CO B03May68 – World Aviation Services Inc, CofA 03Jun68, operating with Imperial Aviation on AUTEC contract (5459 fl hrs) – N6169H Rr Apr76 ntu – Aviation & Inland Marine Rentals, Rr N68071 04Aug76 – Benton Smith & Co, Houston, TX 04Oct82 – Tony Taylor (Taylor Avtech) B20Jan83 – N21669 Rr 25Jan83 – To Baslers Dec91 for conv. to BT-67 – Stevens Express Leasing Inc, Washington, DC 08May92 – later at Cordova, TN - N5156T Rr 10Aug92 – Flew to Luqa, Malta 1993 – N811RB Rr Jun98 – N845S Rr May2000. By October 2006 it had 19,524 flying hours. Stevens Express Leasing is claimed to be a CIA front company, Stevens just being a 'mail drop'. The aircraft is maintained by Aero Contractors, Johnston County Airport, Smithfield, NC and probably operates in Central and Northern South America, but what it does with its 'state-of-the-art' navigation and communications equipment remains a mystery. It is not for us to investigate further, but it is good to know that after 64 years' government service, it remains active. Delete N61696 from page 253 wanted list. ACTIVE

25515 DO-4 Finnish AF, Aviation Museum of Central Finland, Tikkakoski, preserved May82. PRESERVED

25516 9T-PKJ was noted at Lagos-Ikeja in May70.

25517 43-48256 12 TCS crashed 08Jul48 12mls NNE Wiesbaden, in Mt Taunus Range, Germany.

25519 43-48258 Hq ECAF, Stn 558 Poltava, Russia.

25521 43-48260 132 AACS, Orly. AFE Dec46.

25522 43-48261 – 6166 F A Portuguesa BA12 prior to 02May61 – BA9 in Jan69 – used for defoliation in Mozambique – Abandoned Guiné-Bissau.

25523 43-48262 323 TCS, AFE, premature gear retraction on take-off 01Oct46 at Ciampino Apt, Rome, Italy.

25526 43-48265 29 ADG Morton AFB Dec50.

25527 N10005 WFU in Feb01 and was to have been preserved but hurricane damage at LeHigh Acres, FL prevented this. It remained at LeHigh May08, but was dismantled and shipped to the Netherlands in May2009 where the nose is to be displayed at Museum 'Bevrijdende Vieugels' in Best.

25530 3404 F A Dominicana, preserved May98 San Isidro AFB, Dominican Republic. PRESERVED

25532 43-48271 crashed 15Dec59 on take-off Mahdia airstrip, Potaro District, British Guiana.

25533 43-48272 9 AF, 314 FyS, landing accident 29Oct44 Maupertuis (A-15), France.

25535 43-48274 accident 29May49 Alabama. Cause of w/o?

25537 43-48276 crashed 04Nov55 in Connecticut River, Smith Ferry, Holyoke, MA. Recovered and sold.

25538 43-48277 20 FyG Nashville ATC Feb/Jun45 – 554BU Memphis Dec45 – 1380 BU, Ft Pepperrel, Newfoundland; forced landing 02Apr47 Mingan AAF, PQ, Canada. Presumed reason for reclamation in July 1948. Page missing from report.

25541 9U-BAE Air Burundi – Derelict at Bujumbura 2001. DERELICT

25546 71254 Yugoslav AF 27Nov72 – 111 ppa Zagreb to Mar75 – YU-ABV Civil training centre – Canx 02Oct79. As DC-3-65TP – ZS-OJM Dodson Intl Parts, Wonderboom, R01Sep03, i/s 2006 and Apr09. [N330RD canx 20Jan09] – Intl Committee of Red Cross, i/s Afghanistan Jun09. ACTIVE

25553 TR-KBD Gabon AF – Gate guard at Libreville Apr97. PRESERVED

25554 43-48293 1134 SAS, Fornebu – Landing accident 23Feb51 Fornebu Apt, Oslo, Norway.

25555 43-48294 805 BU George Dec44.

25556 43-48295 3 MAT, 5 FyG, Romulus May45/Jul46 – Crashed 30Mar49 4.5mls SW Edgar Springs, MO. (28 ABG)

25557 43-48296 Lima, Peru – Crashed 10Oct47 40mls SSW Borja, Peru.

25558 43-48297 3905 BSS, 21 AD, Forbes, KS Feb51.

25559 43-48298 123 FBW – Crashed 08Apr51 on approach to Kanawha Apt, Charleston, WV [PE].

25561 43-48300 crashed 22Oct58 5mls S of New Cumberland, PA.

25562 348301 Philippine AF – Stored at Manila Jan80 – RP-C83/'48301' preserved Villamore AB, Philippine Republic Aug07. PRESERVED

25563 43-48302 1 MATG, Stockton Aug45.

25564 43-48303 Hq 1257 BU Marrakech, French Morocco – 1432 BU Euro ATC – Crashed 19Mar47 36.45N x 51.22E, 52mls W of Aq Qaleh, Iran [BW/PE].

25565 43-48304 1408 BU Rhein Main, 9 AF – Crashed 11Jan46 4mls S of Muennerstadt, Germany [EF]

25566 43-48305 807 BU Bergstrom – Crashed 08Sep44 1.4mls SW of Bergstrom, TX.

25569 43-48308 1304BU, ATC India Wg - Crashed 17May46 between Rangoon, Burma and Barrackpore, India [BW]

25570 43-48309 805 BU George Mar45.

25571 43-48310 was still with US Liaison Mission, Rabat, Morocco on 03Oct71.

RP-C1353 C R Miller, noted WFU Jan01 to Mar10 at Manila. DERELICT (NB: This is the correct c/n).

25576 43-48315 Wright ATSC – Crashed 25Dec45 Ontario, CA.

25579 6162 F A Portuguesa Esq 801 base AB8 Mozambique – DBR 08Jan74.

25580 43-48319 Tinker 4136 BU (Nov44).

25581 43-48320 127 BU McClellan, CA ATSC – Forced landing 0.5ml WNW Sanborn, CA.

25584 43-48323 4134 BU Spokane, Jun45 – 313 BU Hill Fld – Crashed 31Aug47 Rapid City AAF, SD.

25585 43-48324 S Vietnam AF unit PD415 reported badly damaged at Bien-Hoa on 08Oct65. This date is later than the date for the R Thai AF, so unlikely.

25593 43-48332 80 TCS Melun (A-55), France, 9 AF 13Apr45 – Crashed 13Apr45.

25608 CX-BHP F A Uruguaya, preserved Carrasco, Montevideo, Jul96. PRESERVED

25610 ZS-OJK to Dodson Intl Parts Inc Oct05 – i/s at Wonderboom Sep08-Jun09. ACTIVE

25612 C-GCXD was reported crashed on 23Mar95, but not a w/o – Reported engineless at Val d'Or in Oct07 – Logistique Opti-Nord Inc, Radisson, PQ R02Dec08 – No news of its current status. See c/n 27026. TT 22062 hrs. STORED

25615 CF-DTT – although this crashed in 1995 the 'wreck' was bought by Preferred Airparts LLH, of Kidron, OH and regd on 18May10 as N8610. Ferried Bangor-Stoltzfus 20May10. Reregd to Basler Turbo Conversions 27May10. In storage at Oshkosh, WI with Trans Fair titles, awaiting turbine conversion Jun10. STORED

25618 43-48357 75 TCS, Bretigny (A-48), France, 9 AF – Crash-landed 15Apr45 Eisfeld (R-8), Germany.

25629 Bu 17254 was SOC 04Aug69 – Missing en route Vina del Mar, Chile to Buenos Aires on that date, so never went to Cambodia.

25634 As N21769 this was acquired by Pacific Alaska in 1971 and re-registered N777DG (DG = Don Gilbertson). After lease to Pacific Galactic as N777PG it returned to Don Gilbertson and did not apparently use N777DG again as this was applied to an F-27. N777YA Bush Air Cargo, was returned to airworthy status at Anchorage in 2007, and was noted fitted with skis at Palmer, AK in 2009. ACTIVE

25641 EC-AQE cause of accident was error by student pilot.

25643 43-48382 crashed 26Jul49 Erding, Germany.

25644 D-20 Czech AF call sign OK-XAB – French AF

25646 43-48385 312FrS Villacoublay (A-42), France, ASCE – Ground accident 23May45 Stn 180, DBF.

25647 43-48386 crashed 30May55 La Luz Canyon, 10mls NE of Alamagordo, NM.

25649 43-48388 shot down 29Jul66 by a Mig-29 over Sam Neua in N Vietnam.

25653 43-48392 303 TCS, 9 AF, Feb45.

Czech D-24 to 8392 Jun57 – French AF.

25662 43-48401 crashed 16May49 3mls E of Roswell, NM [EF]

25666 43-48405 crashed 04Jan49 California [salvage date precedes this?]

25667 D-18 Czech AF 15Jul46 – 8406 Rn Jun57 – WFU 01Mar60 – OK-WZA Min Narodn Obrany; del to France by May61. PNC-0211 Policia National de Colombia, i/s Feb01. While loading at Medellin-Enrique Olaya Herrera Apt on 18Feb09 a smoke grenade was dropped and exploded. The aircraft was destroyed.

25669 43-48408 landing accident 11Jul53 K-40 Cheju-Do Island, Korea [Not shot down]

25674 R Thai AF L2-16/00 toc 16Apr57 – 61 Sq 15May57 – 22 Sq 10Sep65 – 21 Sq 04Feb66 – Conv TL-2 Observation Tpt Mar67 – 20 Sq 25Apr67 – 62 Sq 14Sep67 – Royal Artificial Rainmaking Unit 1991 to 1995.

46154 R Thai AF BT-67 L2k-04/41 D30Oct98 - i/s Aug09. ACTIVE

25676 43-48415 was 348415 at Kelly in Oct91 – As '43-201' was moved to Lackland AFB Traditions Museum, TX on 23Nov06. PRESERVED

25677 43-48416 4114 OS, 92 ABG, 15 AF Fairchild AFB – Take-off accident 22Jun51 Fairchild AFB, WA.

25679 2009 F A Brasileira preserved at Museu Aeroespacial, Campo dos Afonsos, Rio de Janeiro in 2005. PRESERVED

25685 2015 F A Brasileira was under restoration at Museu Aeroespacial, Campo dos Afonsos, Rio de Janeiro, in 2005. PRESERVED

25711 43-48450 12 AF, Italy (Dec44).

25713 43-48452 George 805 BU – Take-off accident 21Nov44 George Fld, IL [EF].

25715 43-6010 'I-TAK-096' Turkish AF, WFU in 1994, this was sunk in the sea off Bodrum, Turkey on 03Jul08 as divers' attraction.

25716 43-48455 1 MATG Stockton Apr45.

25717 43-48456 crashed 24Dec44 Welford Park, Berks.

25718 43-48457 7 MS, Carswell AFB, 8 AF – Crash-landed 10Feb50 Los Angeles Intl Apt, CA.

25720 N105CA still stored at Rickenbacker, Lockbourne, OH Apr08. STORED

25721 43-48460 crashed 03Sep54 190mls E of Thule AB, Greenland [BW].

25725 43-48464 9 ABG, HqSq, Fairfield – Crashed 11Mar50 5mls E Hot Springs, NM/ SW Hope [EF].

25728 43-48467 2759 ABG Muroc – Crashed 03Dec48 25mls E of Muroc, CA. Earlier salvage may be error.

25732 43-48471 crashed 18Feb68 Tan Son Nhut AB, Vietnam.

25734 43-48473 86 FyS, 27 ATG, 8 AF – Crashed 11Nov44 nr Conway, N Wales.

25737 '476', probably S Vietnam AF 43-48476, was damaged at Tan Son Nhut on 08Aug67, but repaired.

RP-C550 was i/s with Victoria Air in May07 and again in Sep09, but hit house on take-off from Manila, Philippines on 17Oct09. Fatal.

25738 43-48477 3310 MS, Scott AFB – Crashed 10Jun50 on take-off 6.2mls NE Tulsa, OK [EF].

25742 43-48481 21 TCS Ashiya AB, Japan Oct51.

25743 43-48482 21 TCS Ashiya AB, Japan – Landing accident 17Oct51 Ashiya AB.

25744 43-48483 6332 ABG, Kadena – Take-off accident 05Mar51 Kadena AB, Okinawa [DBF/EF]

25746 303 F A Hondurena noted WFU at Tegucigalpa, Honduras Dec07. STORED

25747 43-48486 8 AF, 311 FyS – Crashed 10Nov44, RAF Grove (519), Bucks, England.

25753 R Thai AF 492 L2-49/18 toc 14Nov75 – 62 Sq 29Dec75 – Soc 27Apr84 and stored Don Muang Nov85 – To Lopburi for display Nov88 to May03, when dismantled for transport to Oshkosh, WI and conv to Basler BT-67 – Parts used to build BT-67 conv #44 and toc 06Jul04 '46-158'. Although the data plate claims this to be c/n 34386 L2k-08/47, such conversions are based on a 'kit of parts, drawn from store after complete overhaul', so it must be accepted that the BT-67 is virtually a new 'composite' aircraft.

25757 2014 F A Paraguaya, stored Asuncion Apr00. STORED

25758 43-48497 54 TCS, 11 AF – Landing accident 21Apr45 Casco Cove, Attu, AK.

25759 43-48498 87 TpS, 9 AF – Crashed 28Sep44 RAF Grove (519), Bucks, England.

25762 43-48501 reported to have served with Khmer or Vietnam AF, but with MAP 11Apr68 and toc R Thai AF 501 May68, so former doubtful – L2-32/11 62 Sq 04Jun08 – 42 Sq 25May77 – Rn 402 Sq 01Oct77 – 603 Sq 21Nov83 – Stored Lopburi 22Oct86 – Tango Sq – Dumped Lopburi from about May89 – Nakhon Pathon by Dec07-Mar09. DISPLAYED.

25769 N56KS remained in store at Oshkosh in Jul08 – Cvtd to Basler BT-67 Jun10 for Bell Geospace. Canx 12Nov10 on export to Canada. ACTIVE

25771 N4994N EAS Inc regn canx 23May07 – Permanently retired at Houma, LA. STORED

25778 N132FS to GD Aircraft LLC, Atherton, CA 24Jan06. ACTIVE

25781 43-48520 75 TCS Bretigny (A-48), France, 9 AF Apr45 – Ditched 04Oct57 nr Iwojima.

25802 N90M of Outboard Marine was reregd as N90M on 14Jan71 prior to sale to C W Jones in 1971.

25806 'G-AMZZ' preserved Kuwait Science & Natural History Museum, Kuwait. PRESERVED

25808 HK-4045 ALCOM – Derelict Villavicencio Mar08 and Feb10. DERELICT

25810 N9986Q canx as permanently retired 18Sep09 – Derelict at Khartoum, Sudan. DERELICT

25820 43-48559 PASC – Crash-landed 13Sep46, Naha AB, Okinawa.

25824 Bu 17278 preserved 1994 Quantico Marine Corps Air-Ground Museum, Quantico, VA. PRESERVED

25834 43-48573 Base ops. FEAF – Take-off accident 12Mar46 Naha Fld, Okinawa [BW]

25844 43-48583 ATC – Landing accident 29Jun45 Cazes AB, Casablanca, French Morocco.

25850 43-48589 325 FyS, 9 AF Apr45 – Crashed 21Apr45 5.5mls E of Linz am Rhein, nr Bonn, Germany.

25852 43-48591 Shot down 02Oct67 at Hue City, Vietnam.

25854 43-48593 2527 BU South Plains Sep44 – 1304 BU Barrackpore 28Jan45 – India China ATC, 7 MS – 1348 BU Myitkyina – Crashed on take-off 06Feb45 Chanyi, China.

25857 43-48596 accident in Egypt 14May46 and then 'diverted', possibly as spares?

25861 43-48600 Prestwick, Stn 500 ATC – Crash-landed 30Apr45 Orly (A-47), Paris [an earlier accident or wrong date].

25863 43-48602 311 RW, 91 RS, 6 AF – Crashed 03Dec45 10mls SE Carlos Pellegrini, Argentina.

25864 43-48603 3 RS, 7 RG (Dec46) – Crashed 12Dec57 Hachioji, 25mls W of Tokyo, Japan (67 TRW)

25866 43-48605 27 ATG, 325 FyS, 9 AF – Take-off accident 25Nov44 Stn 385, England [EF]

25869 N47SJ noted at Edmonton in Aug06 – Gooney Bird Group Inc, Paso Robles, CA R19Jul07 – Noted Sep09-2010 in USAAF c/s as 348608 at Paso Robles, CA. ACTIVE

25873 43-48612 1258 BU Oran, ATC Sep45.

25874 43-48613 1408 BU, ATC – Taxying accident 11Jan46 Bromma Apt, Stockholm – Sold as SE-BBP.

25876 43-48615 1260 BU Casablanca, ATC May45.

25877 43-48616 501 ASrG (Feb47).

25879 43-48618 2527 BU South Plains – Landing accident 12Sep44 Idalou Aux Fld, South Plains, TX.

25883 43-48622 27 TCS, 10 AF – Hit by taxying C-87 44-39288 18Sep45 Kunming, China.

25884 43-48623 315 TCS, 10 AF – Landing accident 02Apr45, Kutkai, Burma.

25885 43-48624 crashed 22Sep48 Harmon Fld, Guam.

25886 43-48625 1 CCS, 14 AF – Take-off accident 28Jun45 Peishihyi, China.

25887 43-48626 2 TCS, 10 AF Nov44.

25888 N8335C Canx 22Jul53 – N68780 Southern California Acft Corp, Ontario, CA B28Jul54 – The Dow Chemical Corp, Freeport, TX B07Jan55 – N730D Rr 13Sep56 ntu – N81T The Dow Chemical Corp, Midland, MI Rr 19Feb57 – Commander Aviation Inc, Pontiac, MI B27Jan62 – The Trane Co, La Crosse, WI B29Jan62 – N1181T Rr 28Feb69 – Millardair Ltd B18Jun69 – To Canada – then as on page 539 Vol 2.

25889 43-48628 1 TCS, Base S7, 10 AF – Take-off accident at Lashio, Burma.

25892 43-48631 10 CCS, 10 AF Nov44 – 12 CCS Jun45.

25896 43-48635 1 TCS, 10 AF – Crash-landed 18Jan45 Ledo, India.

25897 43-48636 also quoted as crashed 35mls SW of Saravan, Laos on 05Feb73.

25899 43-48638 10 CCS, 10 AF Jan45.

25901 43-48640 4135 BU Hill, Sep46.

25917 43-48656 – This was restored to USAF at Fairey's, Nottingham on 30Jan55 – To 86 FIW, Landstuhl Jun55 and visited Dublin in Apr56 and again in Aug56. To 7030 SG Ramstein Jan58 and 1001 ABW Andrews May59. If it went to Greece it was later than this.

25928 9J-RDR front fuselage built into Apollo/Proteus building, Rand Apt, South Africa Mar08, still present Sep10.

25951 CP-2255 moved from Maracay to Cochabamba in Mar06. Owner Lineas Aereas Canedo. Remains as YV-912C in Caribbean Flights c/s, at Valencia Dec07. STORED.

25956 N51938 noted derelict at Vichy, MO in Apr09, following storm damage in 2008. DERELICT

25957 N8666 was named 'Tortola' while with British Caribbean.

25962 43-48701 S Vietnam AF unit PD817 was badly damaged on 17Sep71 at Da Nang. Possibly a w/o.

25964 N9923S noted at Oshkosh in Jul07 in MVA colours but no titles. Under conversion to BT-67 Jun10. STORED

25974 43-48713 Crashed 02Sep49 15mls W of Anchorage, AK.

25976 43-48715 76 TCS, 9 AF, Welford Nov44.

25977 N836M airworthy at LeHigh Acres, FL in Feb07. ACTIVE

25980 43-48719 76 TCS, 9 AF, Welford Nov44 – N68CW regd to Aviation Business Corp, St Louis, MO 15Nov07 – Preserved St Louis Bi-State Park, MO Jul08. PRESERVED

25981 43-48720 75 TCS Bretigny 16Apr45.

25982 43-48721 to RAF Trostan, 8 AF by Feb45 - 4121 BU Kelly, SAAMA, ATSC, accident Feb46 – 4505 BU Kelly – Crashed 08Sep47 4mls S of Larkspur, CO.

25984 43-48723 crashed 25Jun52 Mt Wilson, 5mls NE of Monrovia, CA.

25985 NC15817 via WAA to AAXICO 18Sep46 – To VASP 10Dec46 PP-SPV – NC15817 Canx 07Jan47. C/n given as 25958 in book. Delete, and correct index.

25986 43-48725 Landing accident 26May53, Talara, Peru [Ground loop]

25991 43-48730 319 TCS, 10 AF Jun45.

25995 43-48734 Bretigny (A-48), France Apr45.

25997 43-48736 Bovingdon ATC Mar45 – 15 TS, 61 TG, Rhein Main AB, Germany – Crashed 28Nov47 nr Trappa, 20mls SSW of Cuneo, Italy in the Maritime Alps [BW/PE]. Site also given as 5mls SW of Limone Piemonte.

26001 VH-PWN Discovery – Derelict Bankstown Mar04 – Moved by road Bankstown to Molong Jan10. DERELICT

26005 CF-QHY to First Nations Transportation Inc, Winnipeg, Man, R14Aug07 – FNT ceased ops 02Jul09 – Sioux Narrows Airways Ltd, Winnipeg, Man, R21Dec09. ACTIVE

26019 43-48758 crashed on take-off from Barrairas Apt on 17Nov57 [not on 23May58 apparently] and was declared unsafe and unrepairable. The wreckage was sold to Navegação Aérea Brasileira (NAB) as salvage; engines, control surfaces etc. replaced. Regd PP-NAR 07Aug58 and on 22Sep58 NAB attempted to fly the aircraft to Salvador. On take-off the centre section collapsed, the wings folded and the aircraft crashed.

26026 43-48765 crashed 03Jul53 in Canada, but repaired – Landing accident 14Apr55 35mls SE of Narsarssuak, Greenland.

26030 43-48769 80 Wg Hondo, Apr45.

26032 43-48771 86 TpS, 8 AF Feb45.

26033 43-48772 S Vietnam AF unit LPD43, written-off at Tan Son Nhut on 21Jan64.

26038 '48777' R Thai Navy – Derelict U-Tapao Oct97 to 2009. DERELICT

26040 43-48779 crashed 09Aug48 in Germany.

26041 43-48780 crashed 07Oct44 [EF].

26042 F-BIEE – Owner was Edwin P Wilson.

26043 43-48782 Greek AF crashed on Mt Mitsikeli near Ioannina on 09Jan70.

26044 HK-3199 was noted at Villavicencio with Aerovanguardia in Jul06 – Damaged in heavy landing at Araricura, Vaupes State 25May07 – Repaired at Villavicencio Oct07 - i/s Jul08 and Feb10. ACTIVE

26052 PP-PCL to LV-PJT ALA and then LV-FYH.

26054 N269LM was at Edmonton in Aug06 – To The American Foundation and broken up by Global Aircraft Industries on 16Sep08. Canx 18Nov08.

26055 43-48794 ATC – Landing accident 21Dec44 Bovingdon, Herts (112).

26064 43-48803 collided 10Jul53 with Norwegian F-84 1.5mls from Sola airfield, Norway.

26065 43-48804 US Embassy, Kastrup Apt, Denmark – Crash-landed 31 Jul47 Fornebu A/f, Oslo, Norway [EF]. This may have been confused with 348604 which went to Greece, but the accident report does not describe the damage incurred. Another entry suggests the aircraft was repaired.

26066 43-48805 98 TCS Orleans-Bricy (A-50), France May45.

26067 C-51219 Chinese Nationalist AF for VIP use – To Taiwan in 1949 – Was also '219', '7219' then '48806' – Preserved Chinese AF Museum, Kangshan AB, Taiwan Aug06. PRESERVED

26070 43-48809 91 TCS, Chateaudun (A-39), France, 9 AF May45.

26071 43-48810 8 WX, Albrook Fld, CZ – Take-off accident 09Oct47 Albrook [EF] (probably not repaired?).

26072 43-48811 Guam AD, Harmon Fld, 20 AF, Aug45 – PASC, take-off accident 08Aug46 Nichols Fld, Philippines.

26073 43-48812 316 TCS, 20 AF, Harmon/Guam Apr45 – Guam AD, 20 AF – Take-off accident Central Fld, Iwojima 09Jan46.

26075 43-48814 ATC May45.

26076 43-48815 56 ADG, 20 AF – Take-off accident 8mls NE Agana, Guam.

26087 6845 SAAF C-47-65TP – Display Ysterplaat Sep08. DISPLAYED

26095 ST-AHL Sasco Air Charter – Stored Khartoum Jun01. STORED

26108 N231GB Howe Bros, Wilmington, DE i/s Aug03. ACTIVE

26111 HK-3215 LACOL – Fuselage stored Villavicencio Jul08 – ALIANSA in Feb10. ACTIVE

26120 N40386 BT-67 to C-GEAJ Triumph Airways Ltd, Oshawa, Ont. R13Aug07. To ALCI Aviation Ltd., Oshawa, Ont R13Dec07 - Crash-landed 05Jan09 on 3200m mountain in Antarctica. Despite access problems was dug out of the snow after nearly a year buried. The engines and propellers were replaced and a/c ferried to Canada where it arrived on 21Dec09. Regd to Kenn Borek Air Ltd 01Oct09, for overhaul.

26125 43-48864 4 MMRS, 1340 BU Kunming ATC, Feb/Jun45.

26126 43-48865 R Hellenic AF del Jun48 – Crash-landed at Goura, SW of Korintos 10Dec48.

26127 Delete reference to NC19931 as this was c/n 25997.

26129 43-48868 accident 01Jul45 India.

26131 43-48870 crashed 07Oct52 0.5ml from Philadelphia, PA [EF].

26132 43-48871 7 PRG, 22 PRS, 8 AF (Nov44) – 381 ASrG, 7 PRG, Mount Farm, Oxon, Stn 234 Feb45.

26133 N211GB was noted active at LeHigh Acres, FL in Feb10. ACTIVE

26135 43-48874 S Vietnam AF unit PD415 was written-off on 06May68 map ref. XS.783953.

26137 '876' R Thai AF toc 15Sep57 – 61 Sq Oct57 – AC-47 23Mar77 – 62 Sq – 42 Sq 25May77 – rn 402 Sq 01Oct77 – 461 Sq 21Sep84 – 603 Sq 26Dec85 – Stored Apr86 – display Lopburi May89-May09. DISPLAYED

26138 N91289 was on display at Bellingham, WA in May85, devoid of markings.

26139 43-48878 44 ADG, B-53, 9 AF - Crashed 01Apr45 2.5 mls W of Wiesensteig, nr Stuttgart, Germany.

26140 43-48879 S Vietnam AF unit PD 415 was written-off on 24Oct71, map ref. CR. 045195.

26141 43-48880 302 TCS – Toul-Rosieres (A-98), France, 9 AF – Take-off accident 09May45, Toul-Rosieres (A-98), France.

26144 6163 F A Portuguesa BA12 Bissau – Left at Bissau 1975 – Regd in the CR-GBx series in 1979-83 – Apparently flown to Cape Verde and WFU.

26145 43-48884 1252 BU, ATC – Landing accident 03Jan46 Cabo Juby, French Morocco.

26146 43-48885 1856 AACS, Tinker AFB – Ground accident 19Jun50 Tinker AFB, OK.

26148 43-48887 1386 BU Meeks Fld Apr46 – Crashed 20Mar48 Canada.

26151 43-48890 310 FyS, 31 ATG, ASC – Taxying accident 05Dec44, sank into concealed foxhole at Hixon, Staffs [PE]. Presumably nosed over as pilot killed.

26152 43-48891 ATC Hq – Ground accident 27Nov45.

26154 43-48893 34 TCS, 51 TCG, 11 AF – Crashed 21Oct45 2mls E of Elmendorf AFB, Anchorage, AK [EF].

26155 43-48894 crashed 06Dec49 Germany.

26157 K-14 crashed 10Apr47 at St John's Town of Dalry in Dumfries, Scotland.

26158 PP-PCK to LV-PJV ALA and then to LV-FYJ.

26163 43-48902 58 G, ATC Feb47.

26164 43-48903 310 FyS, 9 AF – Crashed 04Mar45 Marone (Y-35), France.

26171 43-48910 crashed 07Feb48 Mt Page, 2mls SW of Saluda, NC [BW] – '43-48910' reported displayed at Ft Campbell, NY in Jul08. Is this a repaint? PRESERVED

26172 43-48911 76 TCS, Bretigny (A-48), France 9 AF, Feb/May45 – 6 RCF Elmendorf, AK – Landing accident 07Nov51 Elmendorf AFB, AK – Sold for spares.

26175 43-48914 76 TCS, 9 AF – Mid-air collision 26Nov44 2mls E of Liège (A-93), Belgium.

26176 43-48915 902 BU – Crashed on take-off 15Feb46 2mls E of Orlando, FL.

26178 315 F A Hondurena unconfirmed – noted at Tegucigalpa Museum Nov07. Painted as 'XH-TAZ' (painting funded by TACA). PRESERVED

26179 43-48918 99 TCS Dreux (A-41), France, 9 AF May45.

26181 43-48920 Forced landing at Suwon AB, Korea on 12Feb51. W/o.

26182 43-48921 crashed at Cam Ranh, Vietnam, following flare explosion on 26Apr67.

26184 43-48293 crashed 29Feb48 in British Guiana – probably sold and rebuilt.

26186 43-48925 crash site was Ban Phakat, Laos.

26187 43-48926 crashed on take-off 25Jan48 at Nome Airport, AK.

26189 43-48928 HqSq, 2918 AMG, Kelly Nov50.

26191 43-48930 Take-off accident 26Jul53 K-47 Chunchon, Korea. [not enemy action]

26193 N2568 82nd Airborne Division Museum, Ft Bragg, NC – Preserved Jun01. PRESERVED

26194 43-48933 48 TCS, Folkingham, 9 AF, Dec44.

26195 43-48934 97 ADS, AFE May/Jun46.

26196 43-48935 50 TCS, Mourmelon (B-44), France 9 AF - Crashed 06Apr45 20mls NW Limburg, Germany.

26200 43-48939 crashed 27May48 4mls S of Malingiuin, also 20mls SW of Baton Rouge, LA [BW]

26201 43-48940 3087 ABG, Griffiss – Crashed and DBF on take-off 23Mar50 Griffiss AFB, NY.

26204 43-48943 99 TCS, Toul-Croix de Metz (A-90), France, 9 AF – DBR landing 06May45 (R-69), Germany.

26206 43-48945 393 TS, 509 AG, Roswell AAF – Crashed 01Dec47 2.2mls N Herford, TX [FP]

26211 N834M Lee County Mosquito Control District, LeHigh Acres, FL i/s Feb10 - ACTIVE

26215 43-48954 2 ABG, Hunter - Take-off accident 31May51 Turner AFB, GA, DBF [This confirms that N7862B is not this aircraft]

26218 43-48957 as 'AF-957' preserved Jul08 Niagara Falls AFB Collection, NY. PRESERVED

26219 43-48958 crashed 18Dec52 19mls N of Guercif, French Morocco.

26220 43-48959 76 TCS, 9 AF Feb45.

26222 43-48961 Peterson AAF, 8 AF Aug45 – Crashed on take-off at Nha Trang AB 11Nov66.

26244 CS-AZL was stored at Perugia, Italy, for sale in 2005. STORED

26248 12949 CAF preserved CFB Winnipeg Heritage Park, Man. May08. PRESERVED

26252 KJ960 Greek AF, preserved at Tanagra AFB Museum, Tatoi Nov08. PRESERVED

26258 12-258 Turkish AF – Sunk off coast at Kasin, S Turkey, 27Jun09, divers' attraction.

26268 C-FTGI BT-67 ALCI Aviation, i/s Aug08. Used on geosurvey work in southern England and N Ireland 2008-2009. ACTIVE

26269 43-49008 3088 BU Holloman AB May50.

26270 43-49009 stored in South Vietnam AF c/s at Manila in Jan80. Presumably used by Philippine AF for spares.

26271 349010 escaped from Cambodia to Udorn, Thailand 1975 – R Thai AF 010 L2-46/18 toc 11Nov75 – 62 Sq 11Nov75 – 42 Sq 25May77 – rn 402 Sq 21Oct77 – 461 sq 21Sep84 – 603 Sq 26Dec85 – soc 23Apr91 – derelict Don Muang 1995 – on display Vietnam Veteran Museum, Surasri Army Camp, Kanchanaburi, Thailand. since at least Feb01 to Oct09 onwards. DISPLAYED

C/n 26244 C-47B-DK 9Q-CGW taken at Johannesburg-Rand Airport in August 1990. The aircraft was stored as CS-AZL at Perugia, Italy in 2005. (Andy Heape)

26273 '215061' preserved at Tinker AFB Heritage Park, OK in Nov06. PRESERVED

26275 43-49014 crashed into mountain 19Apr01 after take-off from Hong Kong.

26280 43-49019 crashed on take-off 18Sep69 McChord AFB, WA.

26282 43-49021 was shot down E of Bien Hoa, Vietnam.

26284 43-49023 crashed 19Oct59 at Thule, Greenland.

26285 43-49024 1173 FMG Athens Dec50.

26286 550 F A Guatemalteca, on dump at Flores Dec00.

26287 43-49026 87 TCS, Amiens (B-48), France 9 AF Jun45 – Accident was on 13Jul65 at Agordat, Ethiopia.

26289 43-49028 ATC – Landing accident 04Sep45 Chungking, China.

26291 43-49030 HqSq, McClellan AFB – Crashed 26Oct50 10mls NNW Truckee, CA. [Not div to MDAP]

26292 1654 F A Colombiana BT-67 – i/s Aug96. ACTIVE

26293 Bu 50765 crashed 13Feb45 in San Francisco Bay on take-off from Oakland, CA. [PE].

26296 43-49035 S Vietnam AF unit PD415, badly damaged 26Jul67 at Qui Nhon.

26299 N8383 SAGAT, preserved Turin Caselle – Restored May08 as 'I-LEON'. PRESERVED

26300 43-49039 6000 BSG Haneda AB, 5 AF – Take-off accident 08Nov51 Haneda AB, Japan.

26301 43-49040 20 ABG, Shaw AFB – Crashed 19Oct51 18mls NW of Miami Intl. Apt, FL [Fire]

26302 43-49041 3805 MS, 3901 M&S Maxwell AFB – Crashed on take-off 13Oct50 3mls W of St Claire, AL [EF, DBR]

26303 50767 crashed on landing 1/2Dec50 Hagaru-ri, Chosin Reservoir, N Korea [Not Japan].

26304 43-49043 ATD Quintero, Chile, landing accident 29Sep47 Los Cerrillos Apt, Chile.

26334 43-49073. Used by Soviet AF.

26338 43-49077 ATC, landing accident 03May45 Kano Apt, Nigeria.

26339 43-49078 919 AES, 501 ASrG – DBR 01Apr47 at Wiesbaden A/fld, Germany [PE].

26341 43-49080 accident 26Jul49 in Guatemala.

26342 43-49081 on display Luftbrücke Museum, Frankfurt, in Apr08. DISPLAYED

26343 HK-3993 SADELCA preserved Cali Alfonso Bon, La Aragon Museum Nacional de Transport Feb08. PRESERVED

26344 43-49083 312 SrG Hq, Nancy-Essey (Y-42), France Apr45 – Crash-landed 14Jul54 Komaki, Japan.

26345 43-49084 undershot runway 21Dec52 at Haneda AB, Tokyo [PE].

26348 43-49087 forced landing 11Aug49 7mls NE of Marion, FL [EF]

26354 43-49093 crashed 25Nov53 Camp A P Hill, Bowling Green, VA [EF]

26356 43-49095 probably escaped from Vietnam to U-Tapao in 1975 – derelict at U-Tapao Oct97 to 2009. DERELICT

26361 43-49100 310 FyS, RAF Grove, 9 AF Feb45 – Crashed due to instrument failure on 08Oct69.

26365 43-49104 1503 BU Hamilton ATC Oct45

26366 43-49105 5700 ABG, Albrook, CZ – Crashed on take-off 17Aug50 La Sabana, San Jose, Costa Rica – Reported as N75391.

26367 43-49106 was reported as going to NASA as NASA106 and also to Chinese Nationalist AF. It is now clear that it was 43-49526 c/n 26787 which was NACA 106. It was originally at Langley as '269' becoming NACA 106 probably on 02May50 (hence the 'Recl'), and then to NACA 501. NACA became NASA in 1958. Then as given.

26372 43-49111 Greek AF continues to be stored at Dekalia-Tatoi Nov07 and Nov08. STORED

26373 Bu 50776 although SOC 02Jan64 this was still operated by the Arctic Research Laboratory in May65.

26374 43-49113 5 HQ K-2 Taegu AB, Korea Jan51.

26375 43-49114 S Vietnam AF unit PD415 was badly damaged on 10Jun67 at map ref AR. 790890.

26379 43-49118 Hq & Hq Sq – Crashed 02Jan46 50mls N of Canton, China [BW].

26381 43-49120 1 CCS, 14 AF – Taxying accident 23Dec44 Yunnanyi, China.

26384 43-49123 54 TCS, 11 AF Feb45 – Crashed 13Sep49 Barter Island Stn, AK.

26385 43-49124 – Shot down at Quang Ngai, Vietnam. The date quoted is now 09Jan67.

26388 '43-49770' preserved Enlisted Heritage Hall, Gunter AFB, AL Sep01. PRESERVED

26391 43-49130 1537 BU, ATC – Crashed on take-off 19Jan46, Harmon Fld, Guam.

26397 43-49136 ATC, 1339 BU – Crashed on take-off 21Dec44 Hsian Apt, China.

26400 43-49139 1351 BU Tezgaon, India, Jul45.

26401 43-49140 India-China ATC – Landing accident 22Jun45 Tsingchen, China. Obviously found after 31Mar45.

26402 43-49141 334 TCS – Missing 02Nov46 Caribbean – as stated.

26404 43-49143 5900 ABS – Crashed 04Feb50 4mls NW of Roosevelt Roads, PR

26408 N151ZE was active as 'Bu 50783' – i/s American Airpower Heritage Flight Museum, Lancaster, TX Nov06 and Jun08. ACTIVE

26428 43-49167 ex KJ989 R Hellenic AF crashed 12Feb56 into mountains on Euboea Island, during supply drop.

26432 G-AMDB was WFU at Lympne, Kent in Dec67.

26438 ZS-NTD still stored at Lanseria in Jan07 in good condition. STORED

26439 ZS-OJI to N9562N Dee Cee Tres Sales & Leasing Corp (regn not applied to acft). At Caracas on 30Nov07. DC-3-65TP – YV2119. ACTIVE

26445 43-49184 – Crashed 20Jul53 12mls from Etah, Greenland.

26449 43-49188 R Hellenic AF – Shot down by 'friendly fire' during supply drop at Theotokos area of Grammos Mountains.

26452 D-25 visited Ringway in Aug47.

26456 H-008 Turkish AF – Display Yesilkoy Museum Sep01. PRESERVED

26462 43-49201 Crash site was at Duc Pho, Vietnam.

26463 43-49202 1571 BU, Manila, ATC Jul45 – 1115 SAR, Marietta AFB, GA – Landing accident 11Feb50 Atlanta Mun Apt, GA.

26467 '11843' Display Altus AFB Museum, Altus, OK Sep01. PRESERVED

C/n 26408 R4D-6S BuAer 50783/N151ZE of the Confederate Air Force in United States Navy colours found its way to Fairford, England in July 1985. (Jennifer Gradidge)

26471 South Vietnam AF escaped to U-Tapao, Thailand 1975 – '210' R Thai AF L2-41/18 toc 28Aug75 – 62 Sq 09Dec75 – i/s Jan81 to Nov85 – W/o Don Muang 21Jan92 – derelict at Don Muang until at least May97 – to Si Racha scrapyard by Mar00 to May10. DERELICT

26472 'KS.211', probably 43-49211 AC-47 unit PD817, was badly damaged on 09Jun73 at Quang-Ngai.

26474 349213 Royal Thai Navy used as guest house 2003, west of runway 01 threshold, U-Tapao Navy Base. DERELICT

26475 43-49214 4152 BU Clinton County, OH, AMC Sep46 - 9N-AAE Royal Nepal Airlines report regn date of 24Jul63 [Three years after delivery]

26476 South Vietnam AF '215' probably 43-49215 unit PD417 was badly damaged at Tan Son Nhut on 29Aug67 but repaired, and damaged again (as 43-49215) unit PD415 at Da Nang on 16Jul72.

26478 full serial for Libyan AF was '0-49217'. Then became Libyan Arab Air Force and 43-49217.

26480 ZK-DAK was repainted in RNZAF colours with false serial 'NZ3546' and in 42 Sq marks, i/s Ardmore, Auckland, in Nov08; i/s Wanaka Mar10. ACTIVE

26482 43-49221 ATC 21 FyS Palm Springs Feb45 – 5 FyS – Take-off accident18Oct45 Love Fld, TX.

26487 43-49226 503 BU Washington, DC – Accident 23Jan45 Reno, NV – 6600 ABG Pepperell – Crashed 28Feb52 Sydney Apt, Nova Scotia.

26488 43-49227 1562 BU Biak Is ATC – Taxying accident 10Apr45 Okinawa.

26489 43-49228 landing accident 26Mar45 4mls S Chanyi, China.

26491 43-49230 1339 BU Chenkung, China Mar45.

VT-CEB preserved at Vijayput Singhania Hospital, Thane, Mumbai Aug01. DISPLAYED

26492 43-49231 ATC, 4 MTS – Crashed 08Feb45 Mapientien, China [BW].

26494 43-49233 1365 BU Kunming AF, I-C Sep45.

26495 43-49234 India China ATC – Missing 19Mar45 Pachung, China.

26501 N99346 Fuselage stored at North Weald, Essex, UK May02 (registration not carried). DERELICT

26502 43-49241 India-China 4 MRS – Landing accident 19Mar45 Tengchung, China.

26509 43-49248 1452 BU Edmonton, ATC Sep45 – 1465 BU Great Falls – Crashed 19May47 5.5mls from Livingston, MT [Prop failure]

26511 HS-DOA Thai Army Aviation Center, Lopburi preserved Nov95-Mar09. DISPLAYED.

26513 43-49252 ATC – Landing accident 05Apr45 La Senia Fld, Oran, Algeria.

26514 43-49253 204 BU Smoky Hill, 2 AF May45 – Crashed on take-off 06Jul64 Westover AFB, MA.

26515 serial quoted as 43-9254 S Vietnam AF, may be this aircraft. It was written-off at Phu Bai on 23Nov65 with unit PD415. R Thai AF '349254 L2-42/18 62 Sq 09Sep75 – 42 Sq 25May77 – 402 Sq 01Oct77 – 461 Sq 21Sep84 – 603 Sq 23Jan85 – Royal Artificial Rain Making Unit 1991 to 1995 – BT-67 #33 46156 D16Mar99 L2k-06/42, i/s Aug09. ACTIVE

26516 43-49255 4019 OS 47 AD, Walker AFB – Crashed 17Oct51 0.5ml N of Kelly AFB, TX.

26519 43-49258 named 'Lady Helen' during Apr45 – 43 BS – Crashed 09Apr47 7mls SW of Bayer, San Antonio, TX.

26520 N8099 Auir Recovery Inc – Stored Opa Locka, FL Dec01. STORED

26522 43-49261 21 TCS, Ashiya AB, FEAF – Ditched 08Sep51 20mls E of Tsushima, Japan [EF].

26523 43-49262 was lost off the coast of Liberia on 04Dec45.

26526 43-49265 crashed 11Apr45 China.

26527 43-49266 crashed 11May51 17mls NE Felts Fld, WA.

26528 43-49267 343 BS, 98 BG, Spokane AFB – Crash-landed 17May50 1ml NW of Burley, ID [EF]

26529 43-49268 Shot down 13Mar66, SW of Da Nang, Vietnam

26531 349270 remained on display at USAF Museum, Grissom AFB, IN in Jul08. DISPLAYED

26539 43-49278 3498 SptS, 3499 MTG, Chanute AFB - Take-off accident 03Aug50 Decatur MAF, IL and DBF.

26541 319 F A Hondurena – i/s at Tegucigalpa Nov07. ACTIVE

26542 43-49281 on display Hill AFB Museum, UT Sep01. PRESERVED

26553 43-49292 35 BU Brooks CAF Apr46.

26557 French AF 349296 to F-BTDC (2) permit issued 21Nov72. Yugoslav AF 71255 was noted at Otacac in July 1978. Last reported in Aug09. STORED

26558 N514AC Southwind A/l, Port Isabel, TX Apr05 – For sale. STORED

26569 G-AMPY sold to RVL Aviation Ltd – Air Atlantique Ltd, Coventry, R13Jul07. I/s as KK116, but repainted as G-AMPY in Coast Guard c/s in 2009. STORED

26583 43-49322 USAF Museum, Minnesota ANG Museum, Minneapolis, MN – Display 2001. PRESERVED

26591 43-49330 Date of mortar attack now given as 16Mar68.

26592 7344 Chinese Nationalist AF – Preserved Taipei-Sung Shan, Taiwan. PRESERVED

26593 HK-1149 in SADELCA colours at Villavicencio in Dec06. In Aerovanguardia c/s when it crashed on 31Jul07 nr Puerto Concordia, Colombia – Substantially damaged, but repaired at San Jose del Guaviare – While flying with SADELCA the terrorist group FARC attempted to shoot the a/c down on 15Oct09, but it landed safely. ACTIVE

26597 349336 was on display at Octave Chanute Aerospace Museum, Rantoul, IL in Jul08. DISPLAYED

26602 43-49341 3502 BU Chanute ETTC Apr45.

C/n 26542 C-47B-DK N143Z of the United States Forest Service taken at Salt Lake City, Utah in September 1981. The aircraft served with the USFS from 1976 to 1984 and was then transferred to the USAF Museum who loaned it to the Hill AFB Museum as 43-49281. *(Dennis Goodwin)*

26604 43-49343 crashed 13Mar52 11mls SE of Bay Minette, AL [Fire]

26616 '2100972' was displayed in Transport Aircraft Museum, Charleston AFB, SC in Oct08. DISPLAYED

26625 'NE.364', possibly 43-49364 S Vietnam AF unit PD 415, was written-off at Lien Khuong on 31Dec65

26626 43-49365 Mod Center, Wichita, KS – Crash-landed 16Nov44 5mls S Placites, NM.

26632 43-49371 3515 MS (Nov50).

26633 43-49372 35 BU, Lockbourne AAB – Damaged on ground 01Apr46 Godman Fld, KY.

26635 43-49374 3505 BU Scott – Accident Jan45 (not -46).

26638 VH-PTE displayed at Stockyard Tavern, Moree, NSW from 1994. DISPLAYED

26640 A65-64 RAAF preserved Mulwala Returned Serviceman League, Mulwala, NSW 2005. PRESERVED

26641 CAF 12959 displayed at CFB Cold Lake Air Park, Alta Sep99. PRESERVED

26645 43-49384 Norton AFB – Crashed 10Jan51 235mls W of Albuquerque, NM [EF]. This was almost certainly after delivery to French AF, crew bailed out.

26647 43-49386 4197 BU Greenville AAF Dec45 – 102 ACS – Crashed 06Aug46 Spokane AAF, WA [Crew error].

26648 349387 Philippine AF, named 'The Pathfinder'. Noted at Manila Jan80.

26656 43-49395 Soviet AF to Aeroflot 14 TO, Yakutsk 1946.

26666 'TAM-01' TAM gate guard at La Paz AB, Bolivia Apr03. PRESERVED

26667 43-49406 11 TCS, 12 AF Pomigliano, Italy, Jan45. 6165 F A Portuguesa D02Jun61 – Esq 801 at AB8 Lourenço Marques – DBF in hangar fire at AB8 10May68.

26669 43-49408 crashed 29Apr56 Grenier Fld, Manchester, NH – Sold as wreck.

26674 43-49413 Hq Sq 136 ABG Itazuke, AB, Japan – Take-off accident 27Dec51 Itazuke AB, Japan.

26677 43-49416 crashed 24Oct48 Chanute AFB, IL [BW].

26679 43-49418 35 TCS Rosignano AD, Italy, 12 AF Feb45. R Thai AF L2-20/00 61 Sq 15Sep57 – JL-2/AC-47 Conv Sep67 – 62 Sq 06Nov67 – W/o Nakhon Phanom 13Dec67.

26696 XW-PAD Air America operation doubtful – with Air Laos from Mar60 (*Archive* for Spring 2007 gives a different version). XW-TAD is listed as crashed into Mekong River on 24Feb68 in bad weather. Was XW-PAD repaired after the shelling?

26700 43-49439 24 ATS Great Falls – Crashed 08Oct47 Sawmill Bay Airstrip, Canada – Sold.

26701 43-49440 6 OTG Charleston AAF, ATC Nov/Dec45 - 1414 ABG, Dhahran, Arabia – Crashed on take-off 19Oct50 Dhahran.

26703 43-49442 was on display at Robins AFB Museum of Aviation, GA in Dec02. PRESERVED

26704 XT-... Chennault & Willauer to Civil Air Transport as N8330C 19Dec49 – Canx 22Jul53 – N4661V B24Sep53. CC-CBW preserved Museo Nacional de Aeronautica de Chile, Los Cerillos Nov00. DISPLAYED

26705 43-49444 1455 BU Great Falls AAF, MT Dec45.

26707 MM61799 Italian AF – Fuselage at Roma-Guidonia Oct01. DERELICT

26709 43-49448 1339 BU Chungking Mar45.

26711 43-49450 6 MMRS, 1339 BU Chungking, China Feb45.

26716 N513GL stored on top of hangar at Zerniki-Gadki, Poland May08. STORED

26717 G-AMPP last used as 'KN491' in film at Berlin, parts moved to Olawa, Poland Feb05.

26718 N48211 preserved Southern Museum of Flight Foundation Inc, Birmingham, AL May02. PRESERVED

26720 7311 Yugoslav AF 111 ppa Zagreb – Surcin Aug69 – 71202 rs ca Jul71 111 ppa (Aug75) – later broken up.

26735 G-AMRA sold to RVL Aviation Ltd – Air Atlantique Ltd, Coventry R17Jul07. I/s Baginton Apr08-2010. ACTIVE

26740 KK156 Greek AF – Stored Tanagra Sep05-Sep08. STORED

26744 N300BF i/s with Basler Airlines in Jul10. This was reported to have rectangular windows, and never circular. In fact as the Turbo Express it did have rectangular windows, but when it became the prototype for the BT-67 it was fitted with round windows, as it was intended for freight work. More recently, rectangular windows have been refitted. ACTIVE

26747 43-49486 1340 BU Kunming AF, ATC Jun45.

26748 43-49487 accident 07Dec45 Formosa.

26749 43-49488 ATC, 5 MRS – Take-off accident 27Feb45 Chengkung, China.

26750 43-49489 ATC, 6 MSS – Crashed 08Feb45 near Peishyhi, China.

26751 43-49490 3705 BU Lincoln 15Oct45 – Crashed 1ml N of Bounville, OK [EF – crew bailed out – in view of later history, did this land itself!].

26753 43-49492 shot down at Tan Son Nhut, Phan Rang 17Dec65.

26757 43-49496 HqSq 2922 AMG, Hill – Landing accident 17May50 Lowry AFB, CO [BW].

26758 349497 stored at Manila in S Vietnam AF markings in Jan80 – Probably never op by Philippine AF.

26761 43-49500 S Vietnam AF 'ew' 415th Tpt Sq – Crashed 1969 – hit building.

26765 43-49504 2114 BU Chatham Apr45 – 307 F A Hondurena was damaged at Toncontin, Honduras on 14Oct70 – possible cause of demise? Remains on dump at Tegucigalpa Nov07. DERELICT

26766 43-49505 335 BU Dale Mabry 3 AF, Aug45.

26767 43-49506 was on belly at RAF Bentwaters, Suffolk on 11May63, so dismantled might be more correct.

26768 '315174' displayed at USAF Museum, Dayton, OH Sep01. DISPLAYED

26769 43-49508 8 ARS Peterson Fld, CO Oct51.

26770 43-49509 300 BU Langley – Taxying accident 09Dec47 Langley Fld, VA.

26776 43-49515 ground fire at Lod Airport, Israel 16May53.

26777 R Thai AF 516 L2-43/18 62 Sq toc 09Sep75 – 42 Sq 25May77 – rn 402 Sq 01Oct77 – 603 Sq 21Nov83 – to Police for display at least from Apr94 – 219789 [false marks] at Police Museum, Thanon Ram Intra, Don Muang Nov09. PRESERVED

26780 43-49519 S Vietnam AF unit LPD43 was written-off on 28Jan64 at Tan Son Nhut.

26784 43-49523 crashed 42mls NW of Nome, AK.

26785 349524 AC-47D preserved at Saigon with Vietnamese Peoples' AF 18Nov09. DISPLAYED

26786 43-49525 1406 BU St Mawgan, 9 AF 22Jan45.

26787 43-49526 display USAF Museum, Fairchild AFB Heritage Museum, Spokane, WA Sep01. PRESERVED

(See also entry for c/n 26367 above)

26788 43-49527 Hq 4 AF Hamilton – Crashed 15Apr51 6mls N Solano, CA.

26790 43-49529 57 ABG Elmendorf, AK – Landing accident 09Nov50 Kenai Apt, AK.

26791 43-49530 12 AF, 4 TCS, hit by 42-92683 while parked at San Giovanni, Italy 12Apr45.

26792 N215CM to American Aeronautical Foundation, Camarillo, CA D24Sep08. Under restoration 07May09. STORED

26794 CC-PLU was canx 08Mar06, delivered as LV-BEH 08Apr06 to Mendoza. Impounded there in Sep06 (paperwork problems). Engines were being run at Mendoza in Jul07. I/s Oct08. ACTIVE

26795 43-49534 crashed 25Jul48 Handjerystrasse, Schoenberg, Berlin – hit houses in bad weather (7150 CG Wiesbaden).

26796 43-49535 305 TCS, 492 ASrG, AFE – Mid-air collision with 42-93717 3.5mls NNE Heidelberg, Germany.

26800 MM61815 Italian AF – Was displayed at Ditellandia Air Park, Castel Volturno, Italy Apr01 but the collection has now been dispersed.

26801 43-49540 crashed 03Apr69 2mls NW of Sembach, Germany.

26802 43-49541 100 BU Mitchel, NY, ADC – Taxying accident 03Jul46 Marianna AAF, FL.

26804 43-49543 345 FG, 3AF Jun45.

26806 '545' R Thai AF L2-24/01 toc 15Oct58 – 61 Sq 01Dec58 – 23 Sq 11Dec63 – 21 Sq 10Sep68 – 23 Sq 04Feb84 – at Don Muang Nov85 – Display Lopburi 1989-Mar09. DISPLAYED

26807 43-49546 Shot down 15May66 at Ban Nampakhon, Laos. The remains were only found in 1999.

26809 43-49548 2926 BMG, EWM BA.3 Wright Patterson – Damaged Mar51.

26810 43-49549 crashed 06Mar55 Clinton, IA.

26814 43-49553 crashed 10Dec52 Humboldt Mountain Range, 15mls SSW of Wells & Elko, NV.

26815 43-49554 316 TCS, 7 AF (Jul45). N140JR was operated by Florida Air Cargo in Nov06 – Noted at Opa Locka, FL Feb09 & Nov10, engineless. STORED

26822 43-49561 Landing accident 11Aug51 K-8 Kunsan AB, Korea.

26823 was first registered N4667V to Trans Alaska A/l, Seattle, WA. Then NC79020. PP-VBK Museu do Armas, Vehiculos Motorizados e Avioes Antigos, Bebedouro, Brazil Nov95. PRESERVED

26829 43-49568 PASC – Taxying accident 21Mar46 Harmon Fld, Guam.

26831 '049570'/'D-7' – Stored Sungnam AB, Republic of Korea AF Oct01. STORED

26837 43-49576 322 TCS, ATC Kunming Mar45.

26839 43-49578 806 BU Baer Dec44 - 374 BS, 308 BG, 1 BT Rupsi A/fld, India Sep45.

26860 Greek AF KK169 continues to be stored at Dekalia-Tatoi Museum Nov08. STORED

26874 N229GB C of A still valid as such 28Dec06 – N68AH no longer used – Painted as Bu 50819 – i/s Mid-Atlantic Air Museum, Middleton, PA Dec06-Nov08. ACTIVE

26877 N400MF Missionary Flights & Services. Joined DC-3-65TP N300MF in Mar10 on supply flights into an airstrip in Haiti after severe earthquake. ACTIVE

26892 43-49631 332 TCS – Missing 18Jan47 Linfing, China.

26896 43-49635 5 M&MS, 1342 BU Peishi ATC Feb45 – Reported to have suffered a fatal landing accident on 05Jul45.

26902 R Thai AF L2-30/07 62 Sq 06Dec68 [UNO Korea] – JL-2 conv [AC-47] 62 Sq 23Sep70 – 42 Sq 25May77 – Rn 402 Sq 01Oct77 – W/o 09Aug83.

26903 Another composite 'RI-001' at Taman Mini-Indonesia Theme Park, nr Jakarta Apr10. Identity uncertain. DISPLAYED

26905 43-49644 ATC – Crashed 09Feb45 15mls NW Mangshih, India [conflict with MACR12038].

26906 N4662V first regd to Civil Air Transport Inc, N Hollywood, CA Aug53 B24Sep53 ex C.A.T. SA – Allied Acft Co B22Sep53 – Aviation Mart Co B16Dec53 – To CC-CBH.

26907 43-49646 accident report quotes 328 TCS, 10 AF.

26913 43-49652 landing accident 13Jun49 Kokunda A/fld, Palestine [Country quoted as IRZ]

26914 43-49653 6 MMRS, 1339 BU Chengkung Feb45.

26921 PP-VBN – Although this remained in VARIG c/s it was sold to a Brazilian entrepreneur at Mococa, Sao Paulo State in July 2005 for his private collection. Previously as PT-KZG it was used from 12Feb96 by WEEAIR "Carte Mohr" for sightseeing flights until stored at Blumenau from May97 and put up for sale. It is the last airworthy DC-3 in Brazil, based at Porto Alegre. ACTIVE

26939 43-49678 crashed 12Oct45 5mls ENE of Dum Dum, Calcutta.

26942 43-49681 3 Res, Misawa AB – Take-off accident 04Nov50 Misawa AB, Japan.

26943 43-49682 take-off accident 02Jun49 Campbell AFB, 13mls S Hopkinsville, KY.

26944 43-49683 India-China ATC – Crash-landed 23Oct45 Calcutta, India.

26957 43-49696 1342 BU Changi AB Mar45.

26958 CC-PJN Hernando Gallardo, i/s Oct97. ACTIVE?

26964 '349703' probably escaped from Cambodia, and first noted at Bangphra A/fld in Dec94, dismantled – Built into side of Royal Garden Plaza Hotel by Apr95 as though crashed. There in May10. DISPLAYED.

26965 43-49704 21 TCS, 374 TCG – Crashed 21Nov50 8mls SW Hyesaojin, Korea.

26966 43-49705 crashed 29Sep60 on take-off from Randolph AFB.

26968 43-49707 USAF Museum, North Dakota ANG, Fargo, ND display Sep01. PRESERVED

26980 EC-ASP stored on Madrid Airport dump since 1975. Derelict May05. DERELICT

26984 KK205 – After return to USAF on 13May48 this became R Belgian AF K-24 in Feb49, code CW-X and then OT-CNN. It went to France in Oct52. TN211 F A Congolaise i/s Apr96 – i/s?

26989 14+01 German AF – Preserved Deutsches Museum, Oberschleissheim, Germany Mar10. DISPLAYED

27002 6852 SAAF C-47-65TP i/s 35 sq Sep08. ACTIVE

27005 76-21 Malawi Air Wing was in use 1995. Now probably stored. STORED?

27011 43-49750 21 TCS, 374 TCG, Ashiya AB, Japan – Take-off accident 12Aug50 K-1 airstrip, Korea.

27012 43-49751 8 ABG Hq Sq Itazuke AB, Japan – Ground loop 12Apr51 Kimpo (K-14), Korea. W/o.

27013 43-49752 ATC Myitkyina, Indo-China – Crashed 19Jul45 Luliang, China.

27016 RP-C535 Victoria Air, i/s May03 – WFU at Manila Sep09.

27018 43-49757 46 ASG Kimpo AAB – Crash-landed 02Apr47 Itazuke AAB, Kyushu, Japan [PE/BW].

27022 43-49761 6 TCS, FEAF – Ground loop 15Jan46 Laoag AAF, Luzon, Philippines.

27023 43-49762 crashed 08Jun45, Mt Seriban, Mindanao, Philippines.

27026 C-FQBC of Nordair Quebec crashed on 30Mar95, canx 23Jun08. Wreck sold to Logistique Opti-Nord Inc, Radisson, PQ on 03Dec08. It may be assumed that the two wrecks will be rebuilt as one aircraft [see c/n 25612] STORED?

27032 43-49771 85 AMG, Hq Sq, Erding AB, Germany Mar50.

27034 43-49773 – possibly destroyed by storm at Dyess AFB, TX 01Aug62.

27038 43-49777 accident 11Mar46 in Italy.

27040 43-49779 crashed 09Dec47 in Turkey.

27042 R Thai AF L2-29/02 61 Sq 20Apr59 – W/o 03Sep64.

27043 43-49782 crashed 05Nov53 1.5mls N of Calhan, CO [EF]

27046 HC-AUP TAME – Fuselage derelict at Guayaquil May03.

27047 N376AS Frellum LLC, Darien, CT R18Apr07 – Lsd to Rhoades Intl. – for Missionary Flight and Services Inc, Fort Pierce, FL, R29Apr10 – N500MF reserved Jun10 & taken up 06Aug10. ACTIVE

27048 43-49787 accident 20Feb46 Italy. Sold and repaired.

27049 43-49788 8 TCS 12 AF – Landing accident 13May45 Klagenfurt, Austria. The report of a crash in West Irian, Netherlands New Guinea, on the same date must be an error. (43-49768?)

27052 43-49791 51 TCS 12 AF – Crashed 14Dec45 Heraklion Fld, Crete.

27053 43-49792 crashed 25Feb57 after collision with F-100 nr Itazuke, Japan.

27069 43-49808 3605 MS, Ellington AFB, TX - Take-off accident Aug50 Ellington AFB, TX [EF]

27074 43-49813 CF-GBJ – This is one of four C-47s registered for ferrying from Egypt to the RCAF. The four, CF-GBG/BH/BI & BJ were, hypothetically SU-AHP/HT/HU & HV. Thus, CF-GBJ may have been SU-AHV. These aircraft were rebuilt from aircraft nominally scrapped by the RAF (see also c/n 32843, 32963 & 33540)

27079 HK-2497 LANC – Derelict at Villavicencio Oct01. DERELICT

27080 N54602/'312061' i/s Empire State Aerosciences Museum, Schenectady, NY Apr04. ACTIVE

27085 Delete K-24 and OT-CNN [see c/n 26984] and insert K-25 del Feb49, code CW-T, CW-Y, then OT-CWK before passing to France in Sep52. 5Y-RDS DC-3-65TP noted under major overhaul at Lanseria in Jan07. ICRC i/s Lanseria Sep08. In Sep09 and Sep10 only the fuselage was noted. STORED

27098 It now seems likely this was Pakistan AF C-402 and was sold as a fuselage and spares to D W Connor, Karachi 11Mar52 – [Connor states he is a director of Lee Mansdorf] – N4724V Lee Mansdorf, Sun Valley, CA 10Feb53 – Canx 10Mar53. 2032 F A Paraguay – derelict at Asuncion Oct03. DERELICT

27099 6850 SAAF – was displayed at Emperor's Palace Casino, Johannesburg from May01 but believed no longer there. DISPLAYED?

27110 P2-ANQ Air Niugini Collection, Port Moresby – Mounted on pole 1978. DISPLAYED

27120 43-49859 Shot down at Phan Rang, Vietnam, date quoted as 15Feb67.

27121 N300MF Missionary Fellowship – I/s Nov04. Noted at Nassau on 09May09 & Ft Pierce, FL Nov10. ACTIVE

27123 43-49862 9 CCS, 10 AF – Landing accident 02Apr45 Hsipaw, Burma.

27127 A65-69 Deutsches Technikmuseum, General Steinhott Kaserne, Kladower-Damm, Berlin-Gatow, Preserved May08. PRESERVED

27130 VH-DNA reported to be airworthy with Discovery at Sydney-Bankstown in Jul07. Was to be used to scatter Al Bovelt's ashes – Moved by road Bankstown to Molong 17Dec09 – Presumably not airworthy. STORED

27131 VH-CIN Australian War Memorial, Canberra, ACT i/s 2001. ACTIVE

27132 43-49871 reported lost at sea on delivery 18Jan45. Conflict with book.

27137 N472DK Bought by Basler's 08Aug03, R06Feb06 – Cvtd BT-67 #46, sale reptd Jun06 to F A Colombiana as 1683. ACTIVE

27159 43- 49898 crashed 09Jul48 in Pennsylvania.

27162 43-49901 62 TCG Rosignano AF, MAAF Sep45.

27164 43-49903 crashed 05Feb65 9mls off Onna Point, Okinawa.

27168 43-49907 S Vietnam AF unit PD 415, badly damaged at Binh Thuy 26Jun71.

27171 349910 Philippine AF named 'Capiz'.

27172 349911 Philippine AF named 'Pag-asci', then 'Virac' and later 'The Airman'.

27173 43-49912 941 AES, 515 ASG, 12 AF – Crashed on take-off Mar45 Pomigliano, Naples, Italy.

27176 43-49915 6106 ABG Komaki AB, Japan – Crashed 26mls SE of Komaki AB.

27180 349919/'919' R Thai AF L2-25/01 toc 05Nov58 – 61 Sq 01Dec58 – FTS 20Aug63 – to AC-47 Sep67 – 62 Sq 06Nov67 – 42 Sq 25May77 – rn 402 Sq 01Oct77 – 603 Sq 21Nov83 – St Feb84 – 603 Sq 16May85 – soc 17Oct90 corrosion – Tango Sq Sep92 – derelict at Don Muang by 1994 – Si Racha scrapyard by Mar00-May10. DERELICT

27186 probably escaped from Vietnam in 1975 to U-Tapao – '2202' R Thai Navy – derelict at U-Tapao Jan00. DERELICT

27187 N12907/349926' preserved Carolina Aviation Museum, Charlotte, NC. ACTIVE

C/n 27187 Dakota IV N12907, formerly 12907 of the Royal Canadian Air Force and N92BF. The photo was taken at Oshkosh in August 1993, at which time the owner was the Fleming Corporation of Nashua, New Hampshire. The owner was proud to show the author the copy of the 1984 DC-3 book which he had on board! *(Jennifer Gradidge)*

27199 N148RD Dodson Aviation Inc was at Wonderboom marked 6853. Regd to Dodson International Parts Inc, Rantoul, KS 11Aug07 – Moved to Freeway airstrip by 18Feb10. STORED

27202 N133FS to GD Aircraft LLC, Atherton, CA R17Jan06 – i/s San Juan, PR Feb10. ACTIVE

27203 N47HL Commemorative Air Force, Burnet, TX noted i/s Nov06. ACTIVE

27204 43-49943 460 BU Hamilton – Taxying accident Davis Monthan 28Nov45 – to Hamilton after repair.

27213 43-49952 64 BU Andrews AFB – Crash-landed 21Jun47 Peterson Fld, Colorado Springs, CO [EF]. Date for Peterson post-accident, being 'on charge' there!

27214 43-49956 3008 BU Minter, CA Jan46.

27215 N9985Q finally canx 18Sep09 – Was used as a clubhouse in 1986, but no later news.

27218 N64766 Environmental Avn Service, Houma, LA i/s Feb10. ACTIVE

32529 44-76197 add 802 Smoky Hill (18Nov56), to 2314 ATS O'Hare 07Dec56.

N73CD transferred to PNC-0258 Colombian Police BT-67 by 02Jul06, i/s Jun08. ACTIVE

32539 44-76207 crashed 04May68 at Pleiku, Vietnam.

32541 1658 F A Colombiana BT-67 – i/s Jul02. ACTIVE

32542 44-76210 HqSq, 57 ABG, Elmendorf, AK – Landing accident 03Oct50 15mls SW of Elmendorf AFB, AK [BW]. Sold and rebuilt

32558 KAT-02 was captured by the United Nations at Elizabethville in Aug61 and was derelict by Jun63.

32561 After F-GCXP should be inserted G-BVRB Regd 27Jul94 to Aces High Ltd and then to F-GNRB, owner unknown. Preserved St Mère l'Eglise Oct06. PRESERVED

32562 44-76230 ENG Wright Fld – Crashed 27Oct45 3mls NW of Pennville, IN [EF].

32563 44-76231 North American Aviation, Burbank, CA – Crashed 05Apr47 5mls W of Decaturville, Decatur, TN [SF/PE].

32564 44-76232 72 ASS, 52 ASG, 10 AF – Missing 23Oct45 China-Burma-India.

32565 44-76233 2 CCS, 10 AF – Landing accident 24Jul45 Nanning, China (not Nanking).

32566 44-76234 10 CCS, 10 AF May45 – Ledo is in India, not China.

32567 44-76235 PCS, 1 TCC, ATC Feb45.

32569 44-76237 315 TCS Ledo, 10 AF Apr45.

32571 44-76239 PCS, 1 TCC, ATC Feb45.

32576 44-76244 35 BU Bolling Jun46 – 35 BU Mitchell – Crash-landed 15Jun47 Godman AAF, KY and DBF [PE].

32577 44-76245 2 TCS, 10 AF – Crashed on take-off 30Mar45 Shingbwiyang, Burma.

32578 N8331C CAT Inc canx 22Jul53 – TEMCO Acft Corp, Dallas, TX B09Dec53, R12Jan54 – Canx 09Feb55 and exported to Colombia.

32579 44-76247 11 CCS, 14 AF Jul45 – 332 TCS Nov46 – Crashed 03Mar54 Limestone AFB, ME.

32583 44-76251 11 CCS, 10 AF – Landing accident 04Sep45 Luliang, China.

32585 44-76253 12 CCS, 10 AF, accident 10May45 India.

32588 44-76256 N4663V Regd ca 22Jul53 – Humble Oil & Refining Co B19Nov53 – Rr N99H 10Apr56 – Edgar W Brown B03Jun70 – CRC Crose International B22Jan71 – Sank 19Feb71 Houston, TX.

32590 44-76258 HqSq 452 FBG, Nagoya, Japan. L2-10/96 R Thai AF served with 61 Sq post 12Nov53 – w/o details uncertain.

32598 44-76266 HqSq Hamilton, 4 AF – Crashed 30Dec51 on mountain 35mls N of Globe, AZ.

32605 44-76273 crashed 09Aug52 Texas.

32618 44-76286 1340 AB, Kunming, China Sep45.

32626 CP-2290 Air Beni – Stored Riberalta, Bolivia 2001-Jan10. STORED

32630 2010 F A Paraguaya – last reported Nov01.

32635 6854 SAAF C-47-65TP – i/s Cape Town Sep08. Stored Cape Town Sep 10. ACTIVE

32644 DC-3-65TP – ZS-MAP National Test Pilots School, stored at Lanseria in poor condition, in Jan07 – Regd to Marsess Mining Investments (Pty) Ltd 28Jan09 – At Rantoul, KS in May09 – N882TP National Test Pilots School, Mojave, CA R10Jul09. I/s Oct09. ACTIVE

32647 44-76315 crashed 23May49 1.5mls NE of Kimpo, Korea [EF].

32650 SA-R-1 Saudi Arabian A/l – Preserved Riyadh Museum Nov02. PRESERVED

32651 7039 Zimbabwe AF – Stored Wonderboom Nov04 (but not seen there Oct10). STORED

32653 44-76321 KN339 crashed 31May48 at Sedes, wheels up and DBR.

32658 '0-76276' preserved at USS Alabama Museum, Mobile, AL in Dec02. Damaged by Hurricane 'Katrina'? DISPLAYED

32662 44-76330 shot down 23Mar61 NW of Phon Savan, Vientiane, Laos.

32664 CU-T1559 [not CU-T1058] Aerotaxi, noted WFU at Havana - Jose Marti in May06. There is some confusion over this airframe as it was recently reported as c/n 11645. DISPLAYED

32668 VH-AGU Dakota Airways – Stored Morwell Sep01. STORED

32671 VH-HJT/A65-73 Aviation & Military Museum, Mareeba, QLD – Preserved Apr01. PRESERVED

32675 6155 F A Portuguesa del ca Apr61 Portela – Guiné & Cape Verde by Oct63 – Modified by OGMA 1965 as bomber with flare chutes – Guiné-Bissau AF 1977.

32676 44-76344 crashed 03Nov52 Pennsylvania.

32677 A65-78 preserved Nov01 RAAF Museum, Point Cook, VIC. PRESERVED

32698 44-76366 608 BU Aberdeen, MD – Crashed 11Dec47 5mls S of Memphis, TN.

32708 44-76376 Soviet AF – Probably Arctic Aviation in 1946.

32710 109 F A Salvadorena – noted at Ilopango Nov07. ACTIVE

32716 G-AMYJ preserved Dec01 Yorkshire Air Museum, Elvington, Yorks. PRESERVED

32721 43-76389 take-off accident 14May49 Chaklala Apt, Pakistan

32734 EC-BUG preserved Aug08 Salamanca-Matapan. PRESERVED

32738 44-76406 crashed off Drewin, nr Sassasdra, Ivory Coast. Cape Palmas was many miles away, in Liberia!

32744 44-76412 crash date 11May58 at Hal Far, Malta. With 20 FBW at time. Also quoted as 04May58 at Qrendi, Malta.

32745 44-76413/KN374 was flown to Brisbane to be used as spares, probably in 1946. It never returned to the USAF, but was sold as scrap. The fuselage is intact in the garden of Werner Kroll at Watts Bridge, QLD and carries the name 'Piccalilli Lil'. Mr Kroll bought the a/c in Mar04. DERELICT.

32750 '2102' R Thai Navy WFU by Oct97 – Restored by Jan03 – Stored U-Tapao Naval Base Oct07. DISPLAYED

32752 F-GEOA/'2108979' in museum at Albert, Somme in Jun07 and Oct09. DISPLAYED

32755 N60154 noted in camouflage c/s at Chino, CA in Feb08. DISPLAYED

32761 YV-911C based at Caracas, Venezuela, Rr YV1415 Sol de America and noted Mar06. I/s as YV-911C at Valencia in Dec07. ACTIVE

32764 476432 Philippine AF, stored Manila Jan80.

32771 44-76439 HqSq FEAF Haneda AB - Crashed 27Jul50 in the Pacific Ocean, about 10mls S of O-Shima Island, about 60mls ENE of Haneda AB.

32773 44-76441 ATC Jul45.

32775 44-76443 crashed 26Jan48 in Mediterranean en route Istres, France to Udine, Italy.

32777 44-76445 1107 BU Waller Fld, Trinidad Jun45. Landing accident 23Aug55 Osan (K-55), Korea (347 ABW).

32778 44-76446 crashed 23Dec48 Felts Fld, WA. Report at Spokane probably indicates remains stored there.

32779 44-76447 was with 8 ARS when noted at Dublin on 12Aug53.

32780 'CA6448' TAME, Guayaquil, fuselage stored Nov05. DERELICT

32782 44-76450 accident on 16Jan47 in Italy, but 'excl' 31Dec46. Repair at Naples?

32786 44-76454 S Vietnam AF, unit PD 415, badly damaged 31Jul68 Nha Trang.

32789 44-76457 Historic Aircraft Restoration Project, Floyd Bennett Fld, NY May01. PRESERVED

32794 44-76462 displayed as '293496' at USAF Museum, Pope AFB, NC Sep01. PRESERVED

32818 0-39103 painted as '43-010' NC-47K with mini-guns – Preserved at USAF Armament Museum, Eglin AFB, FL Sep01. PRESERVED

32820 G-AMSV to N347DK The Mustang Restoration Co., Coventry – Christy Keane R08Jan07 – Canx 06Feb07 - DC-3 Holdings Inc. R06Feb08 – Del 19Nov09 to Weston, Eire after storage since 2002. STORED

32823 44-76491 crashed 02Nov48 RAF Northolt, Middx. (Also quoted as crashed nr Wiesbaden!)

32825 N81952 noted stored at Wonderboom in Jan07, in SAAF c/s as 6874. Regd to Dodson International Parts Inc, Rantoul, KS 11Aug07 – To Freeway airstrip by 18Feb10. STORED

32828 G-ALXK was used by Starways between 25Aug61 and 25Nov61 in North-South colours after going to Starways for a check. North-South could not pay so the aircraft was used to 'fly-off' the amount due before return to Yeadon.

32834 476502 preserved Sep01 USAF Museum, McChord AFB, WA. PRESERVED

32837 4X-FNG Preserved Kibbitz Revivim Museum Dec08. PRESERVED

32843 KN417 – It is suggested that this was rebuilt in Egypt as SU-AHT and ferried to Canada as CF-GBH for RCAF 10916. (see also c/n 27074, 32963 & 33540).

CF-FTR to FNT – First Nations Transportation Inc, R01Dec06, i/s Winnipeg – Ceased operations Jun09 due to non-compliance of aircraft (no TCAS). Stored Gimli, Man Oct10. STORED

32844 ZS-OJE canx 2001 as sold in Congo, but this was regd in Jul02 still as ZS-OJE, to Aquarius Contracts, Lanseria. ACTIVE

32847 This is much more likely to be N8351C than a DC-4. C/n 10699 was C-54 0-272594 with 3902 Ops Sq at Offutt, NB ca 1960 so was USAF long after N8351C was registered. Hence, the 1984 DC-3 book is likely to be correct. Now what we do know:- C/n 16099 N8351C Chennault & Willauer sold to Civil Air Transport 19Dec49 – Canx 07Oct65 as PWFU – In fact defected to Peoples' Republic of China from Hong Kong in 1949.

32849 76517 L2-8/90 R Thai AF toc 06Nov46 – Transport Sq 1 as Royal aircraft – soc Apr91 – R Thai AF Museum by Feb94 – to Lopburi for restoration 2007 – To Tawee Wattana Palace. PRESERVED

32855 N116SA R Partyka, was stored at Texarkana, AR Nov06. STORED

32866 44-76534 was shot down at Hoi An, Vietnam on 29Mar67.

32872 D-CXXX Air Service Berlin carried the title 'Rosinenbomber' and was named 'Jack Bennett' after the late head of American Overseas in Europe. Sight-seeing flights were offered from various centres in Germany and it was until recently the only DC-3 carrying passengers on a daily basis in Europe. Crashed nr Selchow 19Jun10 on take-off from Berlin-Schönefeld. Probable write-off [EF]

32874 44-76542 crashed at Binh Thuy AB, Vietnam.

32877 P2-002 Papua New Guinea Defence Force, displayed 1994. DISPLAYED

32879 VH-NVD R A N Museum, Nowra i/s Sep05. ACTIVE

32883 VH-NVZ R A N Museum, Nowra i/s Sep05. ACTIVE

32884 VH-TMQ Air Nostalgia, Essendon, i/s Jan08 – Ceased operations 2009 – Bought by Australasian Jet in 2009. ACTIVE

32895 5W-FAA was delivered to Polynesian on 31May63 and returned to NAC in Sep68.

32897 N146RD DC-3-65TP was stored engineless at Mena, AR in Nov05. To Dodson International Parts Inc, Rantoul, KS R11Aug07 – Sold to Lee County Mosquito Control District, Ft Myers, FL R18May09, D15Jan10. ACTIVE

32906 44-76574 crashed 26Nov66 Tan Son Nhut AB, Saigon, S Vietnam [EF] (change of place and cause).

32914 N710Z/476582 was at Forbes Field Museum, Topeka, KS i/s Jun06. ACTIVE

32920 N131FS to GD Aircraft LLC R17Jan06 – i/s San Juan, PR Feb10. ACTIVE

32922 KN451 Preserved 2004 Greenwood Military Aviation Museum, Greenwood, Nova Scotia. PRESERVED

32935 T9-ABC Malta Aviation Museum, TaQali, Malta – Preserved Mar06-Sep08. PRESERVED

32938 44-76606 S Vietnam AF AC-47, unit PD 417, written-off Binh Thuy 05Sep69.

32944 44-76612 2530 BU Selman – Crashed 25Jul45 20mls NE of Tampa, FL.

32945 VH-BPN was noted at Sydney-Bankstown in Jul07, being restored for static display – Moved by road Bankstown to Molong 25Nov09. PRESERVED

32948 N467SP was noted i/s at Wilson, Nairobi in May06 and Oct10. ACTIVE

32950 44-76618 Crashed 02Nov48 25mls N of Muldrow, OK. (3705 BU)

32952 KN475 remains on dump at Sedes Nov07. DERELICT

32961 DC-3-65TP – ZS-OJJ was del to Camden, NSW, Australia on 05Oct06 – Regd to Dodson International Parts Inc, Rantoul, KS R11Aug07 (possibly flown to Australia as ZS-OJJ for use by ICRC?) – N8194Q canx 20Jan09, but it became ZS-OJJ in Jul08 – Damaged 08Jul09 Ottawa, KS – Noted at Rantoul, KS on Nov09. STORED

32963 KN485 – It is suggested that this was rebuilt in Egypt as SU-AHP and ferried to Canada as CF-GBG. The tie-up is conjecture (see also c/n 27074, 32843 & 33540)

32964 476632 Philippine AF stored at Manila Jan80 – also reported Laotian AF, possibly ex-Laotian.

32966 G-AMCA preserved Aviodrome, Lelystad, Netherlands Oct03 – Repainted as 'PH-ALR' in wartime KLM c/s. PRESERVED

32971 44-76639 27 ABG, Itazuke, Japan Jan51 – Landing accident 03Mar54 K-8 A/fld, Kunsan, Korea.

32974 N4039S Basler's – Stored Oshkosh 2002 but no recent reports. STORED?

32975 44-76643 was with Air Maintenance Section, 12 AF, Naples AAF, Italy on 17Jun46.

32982 44-76650 Hq Chio Lung Po AB, ATC Sep45.

32983 44-76651 FEA Com, Tachikawa, Japan – Landing accident 09Jul51 K-3 Pohang AB, Korea. [BW].

32986 44-76654 6 FrG Long Beach Apr45.

32988 CP-1419 was noted derelict at Cochabamba in Mar06 and Mar10. DERELICT

32992 VT-CYT Canx 25Jul86. Preserved Birla Museum, Pilani, India Dec01 to 2008. PRESERVED

32995 44-76663 crashed 10Jan62 1ml NE of Osan AB, Korea.

32998 44-76666 1809 AACS, HqSq, Nagoya AB, 5 AF – Ground loop 09Oct50 Seoul AFB, Korea.

33001 44-76669 3 CCS, 10 AF, amend cause to 'take-off accident' at Meiktila, Burma.

33003 44-76671 remained on display at Lackland Air Museum of History & Tradition, San Antonio, TX in Nov06. PRESERVED

33010 46159 R Thai AF BT-67 #42 toc 01Dec04. ACTIVE Jun09 [Although this aircraft is, according to the data plate, c/n 34349, it is almost certainly ex N2685W c/n 16262/33010 and is R Thai AF L2k-09/47.]

33012 44-76680 crashed 23Oct52 6mls NW of Pendleton Fld, OR.

33018 44-76686 S Vietnam AF mispainted 476886.

33024 DC-3-65TP N198RD was stored engineless at Mena, AR from Nov05-Aug09. To Dodson International Parts Inc, Rantoul, KS R11Aug07. STORED

33031 4X-FMJ/1442 Preserved Israel DF/AF Museum, Hatzerim, Dec08. PRESERVED

33032 N1350A '44-76700' E&L Leasing, Vichy, MO R07Dec05. ACTIVE

33046 N707BA Basler's stored Oshkosh Dec65 – To BT-67 Jul08 – To US Dept of State Air Wing, Patrick AFB, FL 06Nov08. Del to Tarin Kwot, Afghanistan 13Nov08. ACTIVE

33048 N8704/'476715' was i/s with the Yankee Air Museum, Belleville, MI as of 26Sep07. Noted at Detroit in Jul09-2010. ACTIVE

33049 N15SJ/476717 American Airpower Museum, Farmingdale, NY, D-Day c/s in 2010. ACTIVE

33053 C-GEAI BT-67 is named 'Lidia' – ALCI Aviation Ltd, Oshawa, Ont R13Dec07 – Kenn Borek Air Ltd, Calgary, Alta. R28Sep09. ACTIVE

33066 '476734' R Thai AF L2-37/14 62 Sq 07Apr71 – Conv JL-2/AC-47 by May72 – 42 Sq 25May77 – rn 402 Sq 01Oct77 – 603 Sq 21Nov83 – believed crashed in mountains nr Takhli in 1982 but presumably recovered and rebuilt or stored - WFU Lopburi by Feb84 – Wreck dumped by May89 at Lopburi and moved to Phuket early 2008 – Sunk as diving attraction about 1km off Bang Tao Beach, Chemg Talay, Phuket Nov08. Coded 'D2'.

33071 44-76739 delete ref. to US Navy – Crashed pre-delivery 11Apr45 12mls NE of Oklahoma City, OK [EF/SF].

33072 AF-103 Zambian AF – WFU at Zasti Sep08. STORED

C/n 33170 TC-47B-DK N57123. This photo, taken at Chandler Memorial, Arizona in March 1985, predates the information in volume 2 by five years. It is one of the aircraft used by the CIA for various clandestine missions and which was never listed on the official US Register. *(Peter Kirkup)*

33083 7301 Zimbabwe AF reported WFU. When?

33093 6156 F A Portuguesa D25May61 – Bissau 1964 to 1973 – Guiné-Bissau AF 1974-1979.

33094 44-76762 Soviet AF – Noted with '019' in 1951.

33095 9023 Japan MSDF, Kanoya AB Museum – Preserved Oct99. PRESERVED

33096 VH-EAE present at Illawara Museum, Illawara, NSW Sep05. DISPLAYED

33102 VH-OVM Shortstop Jet Charter, Essendon, VIC i/s Jan05. ACTIVE

33105 HK-2494 Sadelca – i/s Mar08 Villavicencio, Colombia. ACTIVE

33106 VH-EAF Illawara Museum, Illawara, NSW Sep05. STORED

33113 VH-SPY South Pacific Airmotive, i/s Jan02. ACTIVE

33119 F-BAIF was operated by Uni-Air by 12Oct72 at the earliest. Remained on display with Bevrijdende Vieugels, Best in Jun07 as '2100847'. Badly damaged 13Aug10 when became stuck under a motorway bridge during transport from Best to Valkenburg for use in the musical "Soldaat van Oranje". DISPLAYED

33123 N791HH to Martin Aviation Inc, R28Aug06, i/s Ephrata, WA – Moved to Lyon Air Museum, Santa Ana, CA and painted in USAAF c/s, coded W6-L. ACTIVE

33134 N8241T stored at Wonderboom in SAAF markings as 6846 Jan07 fuselage sold to Dodson International Parts Inc, Rantoul, KS R11Aug07. To Freeway airstrip by 18Feb10. STORED.

33135 5W-FAI of Polynesian returned to NAC on 29Feb72 (possibly not entering service with NAC until later).

ZK-AWP canx 21Nov05 on sale as A3-AWP to Peau Vava'u, Tonga. i/s Mar06 – WFU by 2007 but engines run Aug 2009. Flying again Aug10 with Chathams Pacific. ACTIVE

33146 KN452 Greek AF preserved at Sedes Nov07. DISPLAYED

33153 N56V Tillamook Air Museum, Tillamook, OR preserved Jan02. DISPLAYED

33158 44-76826 Soviet AF – Coded '007' in 1945.

33169 44-76837 Soviet AF – Code '13' with 19 otap GVF.

33170 N57123 at Falcon Fld, Mesa, AZ Apr05 in poor condition. Fuselage stored at Basler's, Oshkosh, WI Jun10. STORED

33174 N2271D remains dismantled at Ongkarak, Thailand 2008. DERELICT

33185 G-AMPO/'FZ625' displayed at RAF Lyneham, Wilts, Sep01-Jul10. DISPLAYED

33199 KN575 Greek AF remains preserved at Sedes Nov07. DISPLAYED

33201 N2298C Catalina Flying Boat Inc, i/s May08. ACTIVE

33202 44-76870 – Probably direct to GVF as CCCP-L3800 – Later to '800' GVF/Soviet AF c/s 1945.

33206 SX-ECF CAA HQ Athens Airport (old) Sep09. DISPLAYED

33211 N332RD stored engineless at Mena, AR from Nov05-Aug09. STORED

33213 N3753N D & D Aero, Rantoul, KS stored Jul03-Jul10. STORED

33216 N2312G/ '459838' display at Thurmaston, GA Sep08. To be overhauled. DISPLAYED

33220 7323 Yugoslav AF 111 ppa Zagreb (1969) – 71214 Yugoslav AF 111 ppa Zagreb (Jan70) – 71214 Muzej Yugoslovenskog Vazduhplovstva, Surcin Apt, Belgrade Jul08-Sep10. DISPLAYED

C/n 33222 C-47B 44-76890 of the Soviet Air Force on delivery to Russia in May 1945. Note the C-54D in the background.
(McDonnell Douglas via Mike Hooks, no.LK-Y2-1093)

33222 44-76890 Soviet AF – CCCP-L1027 (1945).

33232 N213GB engineless at Punta Gorda-Shell Creek Airpark, FL Feb10. STORED

33238 118 F A Salvadorena BT-67 noted at Ilopango, Salvador in Nov07. ACTIVE

33248 1681 F A Colombiana BT-67 i/s Sep94. ACTIVE

33251 N225GB canx 31May06, almost certainly scrapped.

33267 Bu 99844 crashed 10Mar67 nr Phan Rang, S Vietnam.

33277 YU-ABK – The forced landing was at St Florian, nr Linz (Std should have read St!). The extent of damage was uncertain, but engine failure the cause.

33282 116 F A Salvadorena BT-67 noted i/s at Ilopango, El Salvador in Nov07. ACTIVE

33286 KN630 – The wreck was only reached in Nov08 to remove bodies, in the foothills of Gua Musang district, en route Changi to Kota Baru.

33294 RP-C535 Victoria Air, i/s May03. This was reported as 476962 stored at Manila in Jan80. It would seem that RP-C535 had no connection with this airframe.

33297 VH-JXD B McDermott, Rupanyup, VIC. Stored Jul00. STORED

33300 VH-UPQ Discovery Air, Bankstown, NSW – Stored Mar04 – Donated to Australian Air Museum 16Feb09. STORED

33301 VH-MMD Australian Aviation Museum, Bankstown, stored – Preserved Dec99. DISPLAYED

33307 4X-FNZ Israel DF/AF Museum, Hatzerim Dec08. DISPLAYED

33310 44-76978 Crashed 09Jun45 in Brazil on delivery.

33313 DC-3-65TP - N81907 Dodson International Parts Inc, Rantoul, KS R15Aug07, but canx 20Jan09. Along with other Dodson-owned DC-3s, this remained in S Africa. Stored as ZS-OJL at Wonderboom Sep08 under conversion Sep10. ACTIVE

33315 ZK-BQK had 50,345 hrs at time of retirement to MoTaT, Auckland in Jul73 – on display, repainted Nov08. DISPLAYED

33316 ZK-AZL/'ZK-SAL' Preserved Clydesdale Agricultural Museum, Hamilton until closure. Stored Mystery Creek Events Centre Mar07. STORED

33317 KN633 – Substantial remains were found on 25Aug01 at crash site.

33330 44-76998 Soviet AF '26' – 19 otap GVF (Jun45).

33333 44-77001 Soviet AF – 19 otap GVF '7' white (Jun45).

33335 'KG374' RAF Museum, 'Cold War Hangar', Cosford, UK 2009. DISPLAYED

33345 N227GB/'315033' Commemorative Air Force, Great Lakes Wing, Gary, IN i/s Jan02. Under overhaul Lansing, IN Jul10. ACTIVE

33352 F-GIDK noted stored at Dinard, France in Jul07 – Overhauled Biscarosse-Parentis May10 – Reregd F-AZOX May10. Regd to Seine Aviation SARL, Caen-Carpiquet 07Jun10. ACTIVE

33353 PH-MOA cause of accident [PE].

33359 N34 FAA i/s Oshkosh, WI Aug10. ACTIVE

33368 N32AL B Porterfield, Kotzebue, AK i/s Jul07. Canx 20Oct08.

33375 N193RD was stored engineless at Mena, AR from Nov05 to Aug09. STORED

33379 N3455 had Arax titles in May73, while at Lagos-Ikeja. G-AMSN Aces High, North Weald, fuselage stored Oct01. DERELICT

33392 CX-BDB Museo Aeronautica El Cilindro, Montevideo, Uruguay, preserved Dec98. DISPLAYED

33393 HB-IRN Transport Museum, Lucerne, still present Nov09. DISPLAYED

33419 KP208 Following the closure of the Airborne Forces Museum at Aldershot, this was taken by road to North Weald on 28May09, where it was worked on. It was delivered to Merville Barracks, Colchester, Essex on 20Jan10 for display on a concrete platform with a D-day colour scheme, despite delivery just after VE-day, and reserialled 'KG374' to commemorate Flt Lt David Lord, VC. It carries the unit code 'YS-DM'. DISPLAYED

33426 44-77094 crashed 05Mar56 1000ft from top of Mt Fuji, Japan.

33436 G-ANAF to Air Atlantique Ltd, Coventry R13Jul07, i/s Apr08. Radome removed by late 2008. STORED

33441 N346AB Falcon Aero sold to Karl W Ritter, Fredericksburg, TX 29Mar07, i/s 2010. ACTIVE

33444 N99886 finally canx 17Sep09, but never carried regn as it was derelict as G-ANEG at Bahrain in 1982.

33445 ES-AKE returned to Vallentuna on 11Sep06. Re-regd 9Q-CUK by Apr07. ACTIVE

33448 77116 – as Rochefort was closed on 23Jun02, what has happened to this aircraft?

33460 A65-114 S Australia Historical Aviation Museum, Port Adelaide, SA – Preserved Nov01. DISPLAYED

33470 44-77138 1 TCS, 322 TCW, PAF - Crashed on take-off 3mls SW of San Jose, Philippines. Probably not taken up by Philippine AF.

33471 44-77139 PAC Liaison Sec XXIV Corps, 5 AF – Crashed 16Jul46 Saishu Is, Korea – DBF.

33478 N8190X C-47-65TP, remains stored at Wonderboom as SAAF 6865 in Jan07. Sold to Dodson International Parts Inc, Rantoul, KS R15Aug07. To Freeway airstrip by 18Feb10. STORED.

33484 R Thai AF '152' L2-44/18 toc 09Sep75 – 62 Sq 09Sep75 – 42 Sq 25May77 – rn 402 Sq 01Oct77 – 603 Sq 21Nov83 – soc 27Feb84 – Preserved at Phitsanulok AFB from about May96 to Mar09. DISPLAYED

33489 44-77157 USA Hq Flt, PASC – Take-off accident 07May46 Nichols Fld, Manila, Philippines [PE].

33492 44-77160 HqSq Haneda, FEHF Jan50.

33495 44-77163 ATC – Landing accident 05Oct45 Nichols Fld, Manila, Philippines.

33496 HC-AUT on display at Museo Aéronautico de la FAE, Quito in Apr07. DISPLAYED

33498 44-77166 15 FW, 5 AF – Landing accident 31Aug46 Okadama AB, Japan.

33499 555 FA Guatemalteca BT-67 – Stored (damaged) Santa Elena, 11Mar98. STORED

33532 ET-AHS Relief & Rehabilitation Committee, Addis Ababa – Derelict Feb03. DERELICT

33534 44-77202 1537 BU Harmon, ATC W Pac W – Missing 18Jul46 Philippine Is.

33535 44-77203 8 PAF – Ground accident 23May46 Nichols Fld, Manila, Philippines.

33537 44-77205 1553 BU, ATC – Crashed 09Feb47.

33540 KP238 was not scrapped but rebuilt in Egypt as 'SU-AHU' and sold as CF-GBI for ferrying to RCAF 10915. (see also c/n 27074, 32843 & 32963).

C/n 33335 Dakota C.4 KN645, painted as 'KG374' to commemorate Flt.Lt Lord, who won the Victoria Cross at Arnhem. This was one of the last Dakotas in service with the Royal Air Force. It was in the RAF Collection at Colerne from 1974 and was then moved to the RAF Museum at Cosford, where this photo was taken in June 1985. *(Jennifer Gradidge)*

33542 590 F A Guatemalteca BT-67 i/s Nov07 & Jan10. ACTIVE

33549 44-77217 5 AD Offutt – Take-off accident 03Jul51 Offutt AFB, NE [EF].

33552 N149RD remains stored at Wonderboom as SAAF 6890 Jan07. Sold to Dodson International Parts Inc, Rantoul, KS regd 11Aug07. To Freeway airstrip by 18Feb10. STORED

33556 CR-822 Sri Lanka Air Force Museum – Preserved Ratmalana Mar97-2010. PRESERVED

33557 KP255 Greek AF remains stored at Thessaloniki Nov07. STORED

33567 N115Z BT-67 USDA Forest Service, Boise, ID i/s Sep08. ACTIVE

33569 Confusion continues over this airframe which was broken up at Croydon in Jul53. Sold to Flabob Aviation Associates, Riverside, CA R20Feb07. [See c/n 9531]

33581 ZS-ASN BT-67 canx 06Jul07 as PR-MSY – Noted at Zambezi on 25Jul07 in Spectrum 2000 Microsurvey c/s – At Bogota Mar08 – Flew Las Palmas to St Johns, Newfoundland 13Mar09 – At Lanseria, RSA in Spectrem Air c/s 21Sep10. ACTIVE

33583 44-77251 330 TpS Antille AC – Crashed 04Jun46 5mls W of Isabela, PR [PE].

33584 44-77252 54 TCS – Taxied off embankment in high wind 21Apr47 at Amchitka, AK [This may not be the final accident]

33588 44-77256 FEAF Hq Sq – Ground accident 20Mar46 Kimpo AB, Korea.

33589 44-77257 crashed and DBF 09Mar52 Westover AFB, MA

33590 44-77258 ARP, CDC – Landing accident 11Oct46 Buenavista AB, Colombia.

33592 44-77260 crashed 16Dec48 8mls E of Suisun, CA [BW] (1702 ATG)

33593 44-77261 was lost on 30Apr51 S of Wonsan, in Korea.

33594 44-77262 crashed 05May49 in Trinidad, BWI.

33595 '263' S Vietnam AF AC-47 - probably 44-77263 – unit PD 817, written-off Phan-Rang, 11May73.

33596 '264' S Vietnam AF – probably 44-77264 – unit PD-716 – Badly damaged An-Thoi 26Jan73.

33597 44-77265 4 FyG, Memphis – Ground accident 25Oct46 Biggs Fld, TX.

33601 44-77269 HqSq, 18 ABG, K-10 Chinhae AB – Take-off accident 08Jul51 K-10 Chinhae, Korea [EF].

33604 see c/n 33213

33608 44-77276 6 WS, Albrook, CZ Sep47.

33613 N97H Stephen Hiller, Hayward, CA, i/s May05-2010. ACTIVE

33614 44-77282 crashed 19Nov48 near Georgetown, British Guiana (3018 ABG)

33620 44-77288 1504 BU – Crashed 22Mar47 7mls E of Fairfield AAB, Solano, CA [PE].

33621 44-77289 MAT 6 FyG Long Beach Dec45.

33623 44-77291 crashed 18Jan61 nr Resolution Island, NWT, Canada.

33624 44-77292 1225 ABG – Landing accident 28Mar50 Harmon AFB, Newfoundland

33626 TAM-28 F A Boliviano – Stored La Paz Oct97. STORED

34129 45-2545 – this may the aircraft that crashed on 26Apr63 nr Placitos, NM en route to Kirtland.

34134 45-876 6 FyG Long Beach ATC Dec45.

34138 45-879 crashed 21Nov55 Iceland.

34141 50882 R Thai AF 882 L2-51/19 toc 19Mar76 - 62 Sq 18Jul77 – SOC 04Apr91 and to Tango Sq – Dumped or preserved Lopburi pre-Apr98 to Jan00 – Allocated for conversion to Basler BT-67 25Sep01 but damaged in transit and replaced by c/n 20082. There is confusion over this airframe as the plate was checked at Oshkosh in 2005 and showed 45-883 when it ought to have been 45-882. The Douglas Acft Co plate states TP-67, serial 45-883 factory no 34141 – Replacements are available, so an error may have been made at some time. Stored at Oshkosh Jul05-Jul10, in damaged condition. STORED

34142 '0-50883' Air America Dec64 in USAF c/s – Ret to USAF by Jul70 and to R Thai AF L2-38/14 24Mar71 – 62 Sq 22Apr71 – Conv TL-2 Obs-tpt Apr72 – Wfu by Apr91 and std until 1994 – Royal Artificial Rainmaking Unit 1995/96 - Both this and 34141 were intended to be converted to BT-67 for R Thai AF, but neither airframe was suitable. Damaged in transit and remains stored Oshkosh Jul05-Jul10. STORED

34146 45-886 Hq & Hq Sq AKAC – Crashed 12Nov48 on take-off Eielson Fld, Alaska. Hit B-50.

34147 45-887 20 Ferry, Cincinatti Sep45.

34150 45-890 21 TCS, 374 TCG Tachikawa AB – Taxying accident 13Jul50 Taejon AB, S Korea.

34153 45-893 crashed 01Sep55 Skwentna, 65mls N of Anchorage, AK.

34154 N374AS K-Tech Yard, Davis-Monthan, dumped Aug00.

34155 45-895 crashed 04Feb54 Kesugi Ridge, Lake Curry, 65mls NE Anchorage, AK after in-flight explosion.

34177 45-916 with 3 BCS in Mar47.

34183 45-922 Civilian owner, Fargo Apt, ND – Crashed 08Dec45 12mls S of Billings, MT.

34185 45-924 accident 04Sep48 Lowry, CO.

34187 45-926 mid-air collision 04Apr52 5.5mls N of Brookley AFB, AL.

34189 N54599/'50928' MAPS Museum, Akron-Canton Regional Airport, OH Oct03. PRESERVED

34190 45-929 crashed 17Jun53 Korea.

34192 45-930 3 MATG ATC – Crashed 18Jul46 4mls NW of Goodland, Sherman, KS [BW?]

34193 45-931 173 BF Long Beach Sep51 – Crashed 04Dec51 10mls NE of Ontario IAP, CA.

C/n 34227 Dakota C.4 ZK-APK in service with New Zealand National Airways Corporation. Note the enlarged passenger windows and the "Skyliner" nomenclature used for the modified Dakotas. This aircraft is currently preserved at Wellington. (via Jennifer Gradidge)

34194 45-932 crashed 01Feb52 Korea.

34196 45-934 crash site on 21Oct68 was nr Ban Me Thuot, 110mls NE of Saigon (Central Highlands).

34201 45-939 11 WS Mar50. 45.039 S Vietnam AF unit LPD-43 – probably 45-939 – Written-off Hon Quan 15Jul64.

34202 N403JB Catalina Flying Boats Inc, i/s Apr09. ACTIVE

34203 45941 R Thai AF L2-11/96 61 Squadron 1953 and after return from Thai A/W in 1959.

34212 45-2554 VC-117B mid-air collision with B-25 24Aug48 5mls N of Newton, NJ. B-25 landed safely.

34213 45-950 S Vietnam AF unit PD415 – Badly damaged Long Thanh 09Aug72.

34214 45-951 has been with the Deutsches Technikmuseum since before May01 to Jun10. DISPLAYED

34217 45-954 1734 ATS Kelly – Crashed 26Apr50 2.5mls E of Leon Springs, TX.

34218 45-955 1730 ATG – Crashed 05May49 Hill AFB, nr Ogden, Utah.

34220 A65-124 Aviation Heritage Museum of Western Australia, Perth, WA – Preserved Feb01-2009. PRESERVED

34222 ZK-BBJ still derelict in UN marks Oct10 Mombasa, Kenya. DERELICT

34223 NZ3551 RNZAF Museum, Wigram, preserved Dec08. DISPLAYED

34225 ZS-LJI Wonderair DC-3-65TP – WFU May03. STORED

34227 ZK-APK preserved as restaurant at Mangaweka, NZ Nov86. Newly painted by Jun10. DISPLAYED

34228 AF-4775/'RI-001' FASI – I/s 2005 for skydiving, Pondak Cabe, Java. ACTIVE

34231 45-968 was on a demonstration flight for the Mexican AF when it crashed on 02Oct46 W of Sonora, Hermosillo, Mexico. It wore TTD-6005 on the fin.

34236 N8040L '0-50972' was noted derelict at Titusville, FL in 2005. Canx 28May09. Used for spares.

34259 '994' Air America Jun62 (approx) to May74 – Escaped from Saigon 29Apr75 to Bangkok – Surplus May75 – to R Thai AF L2-54/19 62 Sq 29Jan76 – Conv TL-2 – Soc 14Aug81.

34277 45-1011 561 BU, Ft Dix – Crashed 15Sep45 on take-off 1ml N of Kansas City, MO [EF].

34280 45-1013 Salvaged from Vatnajokull Glacier, Iceland 06May51, where it had crashed in a rescue attempt for DC-4 TF-RVC on 19Sep50 – Del to Blackbushe 8-9Nov51. Still i/s as EC-AHA with Iberia in Feb73.

34282 45-1015 57 ABG, Elmendorf, AK – Crashed 30Jan50 20 mls SSW of Whitehorse, NWT, Canada.

34285 PT-KUB Centro Contemporaneo de Technologia, Sao Paulo May08. PRESERVED

34286 N843DD canx 24Jan08 as permanently WFU. To Ron Hargrove, Florala, FL after 15 years' storage without wings. To be restored for preservation. PRESERVED.

34288 46152 R Thai AF L2-31/07 61 Sq 06Dec68 – Std Lopburi ca 1986 to May89+ – Royal Artificial Rainmaking Unit ca 1995 – Basler BT-67 D28Apr98 – Code 46152 L2k-02/41 – DBR nr Korat AFB 24Aug06.

34290 45-1023 HqSq, Eielson AFB – Take-off accident 06Mar50 Eielson AFB, AK.

34295 HK-3359 to Air Colombia 2002 – overhaul at Villavicencio Oct07 – Transamazonica, Villavicencio by Jul08. ACTIVE

34297 45-1029 1048 AES, 582 ASG, CDC Jan47.

34298 B-829 to Air Asia 1960(?) – To Xieng Khouang Air Tpt, Vientiane as XW-TFB 1970 – To Tri-9 Corp 1972/73 – Lane Xang Lsd Mar74 – Air Cambodge Lsd 1974 – Golden Eagle A/l, Phnom Penh Lsd 1974 – N48230 ntu.

34300 308 F A Hondurena, stored Tegucigalpa Mar02. STORED

34304 45-1036 Soviet AF – CCCP-L1058 Aeroflot (1945).

34306 45-1037 54 TCS - Crashed 08Apr47 Shemya, AK [Wind squall on landing] but repaired – Hq Sq Eielson AFB – Crashed 07Feb50 15mls NW of Pon Lake, Canada – Sold and rebuilt, but N7712B dubious as 45-1037 still existed, derelict, at Haines Jct in Feb02. DERELICT

34309 45-1040 6 RCU Elmendorf – Take-off accident 18Jan51 Ft Nelson, BC, Canada.

34314 45-1045 54 TCS, 11AF - Accident at Point Hope was on 20Nov45 – Landing accident 09Oct54 Ladd AFB, AK – Sold and rebuilt.

34317 45-1048 54 TCS – Crashed 03Sep46 40mls S of Big Delta, Rapids, AK [PE].

34325 0-51055 was reported crashed in Alaska on 11 Feb57. Probably recovered to 5039 ABW and assessed as not worth repair and sold to Sholton & Carson, who rebuilt it as N4788C. Then as follows:- B-879 Air America R17Aug64 – Air Asia R15Sep64 – "879" Lsd to Air Asia to Jun74 – China A/l B29Jun74 – WFU Mar77.

34327 'KJ.157' S Vietnam AF unit PD 817 – probably 45-1057 – Written-off 24Nov72 map ref. ZA.235425.

34330 45-1060 4 ADG Andrews – Crash-landed 10Dec47 nr Andrews Fld, MD [BW]

34335 45-1065 RCAF Rockcliffe – Crashed 28Mar50 9.5mls SE of Rockcliffe, ON, Canada. DBF

34336 45-1066 24TS, 22TG, Haneda AB – Crashed 30Nov47 60mls SSW of Tokyo, Japan.

34340 45-1070 1534 BU to read 1504 BU.

34341 45-1071 1504 BU Fairfield Sep45 – Landing accident 22Dec45 Fairfield-Suisun AAF, CA.

34344 45-1074 fuselage stored at Pima Museum Feb08. STORED

34348 45-1078 Johnson to read Johnston Is, Marshall Islands – Crashed 13Feb52 Mt Mauna Kea, HI.

34349 51079 – Khmer AF to '079' R Thai AF L2-47/18 toc 14Nov75 – 62 Sq 29Dec75 – 402 Sq 02Mar78 – 603 Sq 21Nov83 – Soc 07Sep89 due to corrosion – dumped at Lopburi since at least Jan99 – To Phuket 2008 and sunk Nov08 as 'D1' diving attraction off Bang Tao Beach, Chemg Talay, Phuket.

35350 stored as 51080 South Vietnam AF at Manila Jan80 – Probably used for spares by Philippine AF.

34352 45-1082 550 BU Memphis – Crashed 23Jun46 Memphis Mun. Apt. Shelby, TN [hit parked car, DBR].

34355 45-1085 3 MATW, Topeka, KS – Crashed 19Mar46 0.75ml S of Hobart Mills, CA.

34359 45-1089 FEA 31 TCS, Ashiya AB – Crashed 10Sep51 5mls SE of K-47, Chunchon AB, Korea.

34361 45-1091 4 FyG Memphis ATC Dec45. EC-CPO was painted as such in May05, in Museo Nacional de Aéropuertos, Malaga. DISPLAYED

34363 51093 R Thai AF 093 L2-50/19 toc 62 Sq 30May76 – Soc 15Jan87 and stored Lopburi until moved to Phuket early 2008 - Sunk as diving attraction coded 'D3' about 1km off Bang Tao Beach, Chemg Talay, Phuket Nov08.

34365 2023 F A Brasileira – Delete 'Cambirck' and insert 07Jun49 near Florianopolis, Santa Catarina, Brazil.

34368 N932H Basler Turbo Conversions LLC R10May06. At Oshkosh in Jul07 and in bare metal Jul08. Conv BT-67 #53 – To Airborne Support Inc, Houma, LA R22Jul09. ACTIVE

34369 45-1099 accident 19May55 Peru – rebuilt for F A Peruana.

34370 N814CL Clay Lacy Avn, in United colours, i/s Aug05 Van Nuys, CA. ACTIVE

34372 45-1102 date of loss also given as 12Apr72.

34375 45-1105 804 ABG Hunter – Take-off accident 28Jan53 Hunter AFB, GA [EF]. Remains probably rebuilt as N2025A. 5Y-BMB Skyways Kenya Ltd – Stored Lokichoggio Apr01. STORED

34376 2023 F A del Paraguay stored at Asuncion, less engines and outer wings. DERELICT

34378 N1944H regd to N1944H LLC, Wilmington, DE R12May08 – ERA Classic A/l 'Spirit of Alaska' – Offered for sale by Courtesy Aircraft at Rockford, IL – i/s Jul10. ACTIVE

34379 45-1109 crashed 11Jul60 10mls W of Quito, on Mt Pichincha [volcano]

34382 45-1112 5064 CWMTU, 5001 CG – Crashed 03May50 3mls N of Ladd AFB, AK.

34383 45-1113 US Embassy, Guatemala – Spun in 31Jan50 5mls N of La Tinta, Guatemala [PE].

34386 51116 R Thai AF L2-45/18 toc 62 Sq 12Sep75 – 402 Sq 21Oct77 – 461 Sq 21Sep84 – Soc 23Apr91 – To Tango Sq and stored Lopburi by Jan99 to Jan04 – Intended for BT-67 conv and to Oshkosh, but unsuitable and replaced by stock airframe – fuselage at Oshkosh Jul04. DERELICT

34390 45-1120 crashed 24Dec65 at Ban Bac, Laos.

34394 45-1124 crashed 01Dec52 Mt San Gorgonio, CA at 11,500ft – the wreck is still on the mountain and unless this was a data plate sale, there may be a problem here! HC-SJI must be another airframe.

34396 45-1126 5 AF, 21 TCS, Ashiya AB, Japan – Landing accident 24Aug50 K-10 Chinhae, Korea [not Nashiya]

34397 51127 R Thai Navy – Derelict U-Tapao Oct97 to 2009. DERELICT

34398 560 F A Guatemalteca BT-67 noted at Guatemala City in Nov07 and Dec08. Under repair at La Aurora Jan10. ACTIVE

34399 45-1129 accident 09Jan48 in Venezuela. Probably sold to government as was.

34403 45-1133 crashed at Ban Phan, Laos 05Feb69, but the remains were not located until October 1969.

34406 45-1136 USMAA – Landing accident 1947 40mls WSW of Managua – To Guatemala under ARP 10Dec46 and with F A Guatemalteca until at least end of 1956. (See also c/n 12297)

34408 45-1138 crashed 17Feb49 75mls SW of Salta, in mountains in NW Argentina. (Attaché)

34409 9Q-CAM Virunga Air Charter, Goma, remains at Goma in Aug09. STORED

42956 9N-AAB was regd 17Jul64.

42961 N3006 DC3 Entertainment, Aurora, CA i/s Feb04 - 2010. ACTIVE

42965 PJ-ALD was named 'Decla'.

42966 NC34970 Douglas Acft Co R23Nov45, M11Feb46 – Pacific Northern D19Feb46 – N34970 The Babb Co B17Mar59 – Caribbean Atlantic B31Jul59 – Interstate Air Services B10Jun68 – Canx as scrap 15Jul77.

42968 9Q-CUL remained in Rhodesia from Feb68 - therefore not F A Portuguesa 6169, which crashed on 31Mar73 at 13.30S x 19.03E [Cuito Cuanavale], Angola, but the c/n is unknown. This remains a mystery despite being quoted as 42968 on page 633 of Vol 2.

42978 7310 Zimbabwe AF – Stored Wonderboom Nov04. STORED

43079 YV-218C RUTACA – Stored Ciudad Bolivar Feb01. STORED

43082 N3749Q to Airplane On Line Sales Inc R03Oct06. DERELICT

43083 TP-0202 noted preserved at Mexico City Nov07. PRESERVED

43084 N683LS noted at Oshkosh Jul08-Jun10, engineless. STORED

43086 HK-2006 sold to Viarco – i/s Villavicencio Jul08, but forced landing at Teresita 'dirt strip', Colombia on 24Jan08 after hitting high ground on approach. No injuries. Repaired by early 2009 and in service with Aliansa – LASER in Feb10 named "Zeus". ACTIVE

43087 YV-609C Servivensa, stored at Canaima in Sep06. STORED

43159 N30TN DES LLC, t/a TransNorthern LLC, Wilmington, DE, i/s May05 – Parked Anchorage, AK Sep08, i/s May10 with additional 'Aleutian Air' titles for film work until Jul10. This is the only passenger DC-3 operating commercially on skis in the winter. ACTIVE

43301 N32TN was operated by TMF Aircraft, i/s Opa Locka in Nov06. At Opa Locka Dec07. ACTIVE

43302 N851M Airpower Inc, ferried to Anchorage, AK 03Jul07. To Smoki Foods Corp, R14Oct08. Regd to May Investments, Anchorage, AK 29May09 – Reregd N29TN 10Jul09, i/s with TransNorthern LLC Jul10. ACTIVE

43305 Bu 17177 K-Tech Yard – Stored Tucson, AZ 2001. STORED

43307 C-GJGQ to Victoria Airport Authority, Victoria, BC – Stored Feb08-Sep08. Being cut up Oct10.

43309 Bu 17171 crash-landed 24Nov73 on beach en route Hofa to Keflavik [PE/fuel problem]. Airframe at Solheimasandur, Iceland Aug08. DERELICT

43311 Bu 17150 stored at K-Tech Yard, Tucson, AZ May01. DERELICT

43312 N587MB continued in service with TMF at Opa Locka in Nov06. ACTIVE

43317 Bu 50823 is currently atop a building in Okinawa. STORED

43321 Bu 50835 'Iwakuni' was on display at Flying Leathernecks Avn. Museum, Miramar MCAS, CA in Oct03, with no sign of N835TD. DISPLAYED

43322 Bu 50821 was on display at Navy Aviation Museum, Pensacola, FL in Dec02. Still carried 'Rota' on fuselage. DISPLAYED

43324 N834D was at Cunningham Museum of Aviation, Tucson, AZ but later derelict Oct01. DERELICT

43325 HK-3586 LADU stored at Rio Negro, Medellin, Colombia Jun08-Sep10. STORED

43326 N5584N Air Power Yard, Davis Monthan, AZ – Stored Aug00. STORED

43330 C-GERD Air Dale – Stored K-Tech Yard, Tucson, AZ Aug00. STORED

43331 Bu 17160 K-Tech Yard, Tucson, AZ – Stored Aug00. STORED

43332 N99857 Preserved Wings over Miami Museum, New Tamiami, FL Dec01. Work started in 2009 in preparation for cargo work in Alaska, and delivered 04May09 to Palmer, AK for TransNorthern LLC. Reregd N27TN 03Aug10. ACTIVE

43334 N102BF Basler's – Fuselage marked '17216' stored Oshkosh Jul06-Jun10 in faded US Marines titles. STORED

43335 N505C was finally canx on 02Feb09 after damage by hurricane at Miami on 02Feb98.

43336 'N28BF' Basler's sold ex-Davis Monthan Mar94.

43342 N722NR Naval Arctic Research, China Lake – Stored 1998-Apr01. STORED

C/n 43342 C-117D N722NR of the Naval Arctic Research Laboratory, based at Barrow, Alaska. The photo was taken at Seattle-Boeing Field in July 1976, with the aircraft being stored at China Lake from 1998. *(Doug Olson)*

43343 Bu 17241 crashed 30Mar59 on take-off, Naples, Italy [EF].

43345 N321L Nord Aviation, Santa Teresa, NM i/s Apr03. ACTIVE

43348 Bu 12410 crashed 18Apr61 on take-off from Fallon, NV.

43352 N107BF Stored K-Tech Yard, Tucson, AZ Aug00. STORED

43354 C-GGKG R04Jun07 to TransNorthern & ferried to Anchorage 06Jun07. Canx 30May07 on sale in USA as N28TN to DES LLC, Wilmington, DE, t/a TransNorthern LLC 04Jun07. I/s Anchorage Sep08-Jul10. ACTIVE

43357 Bu 17196 probably crashed off Point Loma, CA after take-off from San Diego NAS – SOC 23Apr53.

43358 Bu 50812 stored K-Tech Yard, Tucson, AZ Aug00. STORED

43359 Bu 17281 – DBR 10Jul74 – Airframe in use Aug08 as summerhouse nr Hoffell, Lagofell, SE coast of Iceland. DERELICT

43360 N34AH Classic Air Transport, Las Vegas, NV i/s Jul05. ACTIVE

43361 N100BF remained in store at Oshkosh Jul08-Jun10. STORED

43362 Bu 99845 – Stored K-Tech Yard. Tucson, AZ Aug00. STORED

43363 Bu 50826 is coded 'CZ' at Pima Museum, AZ on display Oct05. DISPLAYED

43365 CP-2421 was active in Mar06 but for sale – To L.A. Canedo Oct08, i/s. ACTIVE

43366 C-GGKE was seized by local sheriff at Brantford, ONT – Dumped Aug08. DERELICT

43367 Bu 17284 crashed 28Dec69 into high ground Quang Tri Province, S Vietnam.

43369 N587LM was wingless and engineless at Opa Locka, FL in Nov06, but TMF Aircraft intend eventual restoration. STORED

43370 Bu 12428 stored K-Tech Yard, Tucson, AZ Aug00. STORED

43371 Bu 17097 stored K-Tech Yard, Tucson, AZ Aug00. STORED

43372 Bu 17287 stored K-Tech Yard, Tucson, AZ Aug00. STORED

43374 C-GDOG seized by local sheriff and dumped at Brantford, ONT Jun05. DERELICT

43375 N9796N Kamaka Air, Honolulu, HI i/s May04. ACTIVE

43378 HI-477CA stored May03 Isla Grande, San Juan, PR. DERELICT.

43379 Bu 17191 was moved 02Sep06 to Egil Olafsson Folk Museum, Hnjotar, NW Iceland – Noted Aug08. DISPLAYED

43380 Bu 50784 stored K-Tech Yard, Tucson, AZ May01. STORED

43381 N110BF stored K-Tech Yard, Tucson, AZ May01. STORED

43382 1685 F A Colombiana – Fuselage stored Villavicencio Sep99. DERELICT

43383 Bu 17149 – Stored K-Tech Yard, Tucson, AZ Aug00. STORED

43385 N9663N fuselage stored at Ft Lauderdale, FL Dec01, but removed by Oct07.

43386 N212DD D D Parts, Opa Locka, FL – Fuselage stored Opa Locka Dec01, but removed by Oct07.

43389 N105BF stored K-Tech Yard, Tucson, AZ Aug00. STORED

43391 Bu 17211 crashed 25Jul66 on take-off Da Nang, S Vietnam.

43393 N44GH was in RDS titles at Denton, TX in Sep06, owner Flight Data Inc. Denton, TX – WFU May08, but active in 2010. ACTIVE

43394 Bu 50808 stored K-Tech Yard, Tucson, AZ Aug00. STORED

43396 N106BF stored K-Tech Yard, Tucson, AZ Aug00. STORED

43399 Bu 12412 stored K-Tech Yard, Tucson, AZ Aug00. STORED

C-117D HI-466 was reported to be at Bonaire, Netherlands Antilles in 1987, but nothing has been reported since.

Much of the new data on USAAF/USAF C-47s and C-53s originates from Form 14 accident reports extracted and placed on the internet. This was supplied to Air-Britain by Matt Miller and thereafter transferred to this Update. Many of the accidents did not cause a write-off and have just been a source of unit details.

Most of the aircraft that served overseas during wartime changed units often but no details were reported to home authorities – there being more important uses for the limited communications of the era.

It is worthwhile summarising the various causes given on the aircraft cards for write-off. It has become obvious that these were often almost meaningless.

Cond usually meant an accident of some kind and in the final years of the war was often qualified by the addition of 'salvage'. Condemned just meant not fit for further service. Many aircraft, it is suspected, had minor accidents but spares were not available in the field to carry out repairs, so the aircraft was kept as a source of spares for other aircraft.

Excl or excluded from the inventory usually only came into use in 1945/46. Dates were frequently either 'end-of-month' or 'first-of-month', so a tidying-up exercise.

Recl or reclaimed referred to airframes that were used as spares sources after an accident, or were not considered worth overhaul. This was only used post-war and many aircraft stored at Davis Monthan were so designated. Sometimes they were rebuilt by a purchaser.

Salvage was often given as a fate when an airframe was condemned following an accident. There was a tendency for this to be used in 1945/46.

Survey was only given as a fate for accidents on the US mainland. A committee of three officers would be convened to see what could be learned from an accident and recommendations would be made as to retraining personnel etc.

Washout was used rarely, when an airframe was badly damaged, and not fit for repair.

If the reader finds some of the above Production List entries confusing, this is hardly surprising, as they have been compiled from a combination of official reports and observations. We have attempted to explain discrepancies, but this is sometimes impossible due to errors in the paperwork. Data plates can be changed, and often cannot be relied upon, and some airframes are hybrids due to parts of two or more airframes being combined on rebuild.

Abbreviations

AAB	Army Air Base
AAF	Army Air Force
AB	Air Base
ABS	Air Base Squadron
Acc	accepted
Acft	aircraft
ACG	Air Commando Group
ADG	Air Delivery Group
AES	Air Engineering Squadron
AF	Air Force
A/fld	airfield
A/l, A/ls	airline(s)
AS	Air Station
ASG	Air Service Group
ATC	Air Transport Command
ATG	Air Transport Group
ATS	Air Transport Squadron
Avn	aviation
A/w, A/ws	airway(s)
B	bought
BS	Base Squadron
BU	Base Unit
BW	bad weather
BoS	Bill of Sale
Canx	cancelled
CCS	Combat Cargo Squadron
CG	Cargo Group
Cmd	command
Co	company
Cond	condemned
Conv	conversion
Corp	corporation
Cr	crashed
c/s	colour scheme
csg	callsign
Cvtd	converted
D/del	delivered
DBF	destroyed by fire
DBR	damaged beyond repair
Def	defense/defence
Div	division
DPC	Defense Plant Corporation
DSC	Defense Supply Corporation
E	East(ern)
EF	engine fire/failure
FG	Fighter Group
FLC	Foreign Liquidation Commission
Fld	field
f/n	fleet number
FP	fuel problem
FS	Fighter Squadron
FyG	Ferry Group
FyS	Ferry Squadron
GVF	(Soviet) Civil Air Fleet
Hq	Headquarters
Intl	international
i/s	in service
km(s)	kilometre(s)
LLC	Limited Liability Company
Lsd	leased
Lsg	leasing
Ltd	Limited
ml(s)	mile(s)
Mod	modified/modifications
Mt	Mount/mountain
Mun	municipal
N	North(ern)
Natl	national
NLR	no longer registered
nr	near
Ntu	not taken up
Op	operated (by)
PE	pilot error
PRG	Photo Reconnaissance Group
PRS	Photo Reconnaissance Squadron
R/regd	registered
Ref	reference
Regn	registration
Rep	repossessed
Ret	returned
RFC	Reconstruction Finance Corporation
Rn	renamed or renumbered
Rs	reserialled
S	South(ern)
SF	structural failure
SOC	struck off charge
Sq	Squadron
SrS	Strategic Reconnaissance Squadron
Std	stored
t/a	trading as
TC	Transport Command
TCC	Troop Carrier Command
TCG	Troop Carrier Group
TCS	Troop Carrier Squadron
TDY	tour of duty
TG	Transport Group
TOC	taken on charge
TPG	Transport Group
TPS	Transport Squadron
TS	Transport Squadron
VVS	Soviet Air Force
W	West(ern)
WAA	War Assets Administration
Wfs	withdrawn from service
Wfu	withdrawn from use
w/o	written-off

Specific Soviet Air Force/GVF abbreviations are listed after the Li-2/PS-84 updated information to Volume II, Chapter 7 (to be found in Part III of this chapter)

Sometimes the significance of an abbreviation – as here "ANG" on the fin – is explained elsewhere on the aircraft, for example in the attractive titling on the roof of this smart Tennessee Air National Guard C-47A, 0-224105 (c/n 9967). *(Brian Stainer/APN)*

Part V – C-47/TS-62, c/ns unknown

CCCP-L918 TS-62 Aeroflot Yakutsk – To 14 TO 1949.

CCCP-L924 C-47 GVF, op by 2 ap 10 gatd. W/O 02Apr46 on flight from Tbilisi to Rostov-na-Donu when the crew decided to cut the route short and overfly the main ridge of the Caucasus. Aircraft entered cloud and crashed into the slope of Mt.Guram (northern Osetiya) at about 3,000 metres above sea level and 93kms to right of the prescribed flight path. All 5 crew and 2 pax killed. Wreck not found until 20Jul47.

CCCP-L929 TS-62 Aeroflot Yakutsk – To 14 TO 1949.

CCCP-L940 C-47 to '940' 18Mar45, reverted to CCCP-L940 in Jun45

CCCP-L943 TS-62 Aeroflot Yakutsk – To 14 TO 1949.

CCCP-L946 C-47 GVF, op by 10 gv.atd. W/O 05Nov46 on flight from Berlin-Schönefeld via Riga to Moscow-Vnukovo. Aircraft held in holding pattern at Vnukovo for two hours, then tried to land in thick fog. Aircraft had to go around, pulled up too steeply, stalled and crashed 600-700 metres from the landing "T". 13 killed.

CCCP-L952 C-47 Aeroflot Georgia. W/O 05Mar47 on flight from Tbilisi to Moscow-Vnukovo when the crew decided to cut the route short and overfly the main ridge of the Caucasus. Aircraft entered cloud and crashed into a mountain in the northern Caucasus. All 4 crew and 19 pax killed. Wreck not found until 20Jun47.

CCCP-L963 C-47 Aeroflot Azerbaijan. W/O 22Jan45 on a flight from Baku to Simferopol, on the Makhachkala-Grozny sector. Aircraft took off when weather conditions were below the minima, and missing the weather data for Grozny, crew followed a railway line, but got lost near Gudermes in fog and crashed into the slope of the Terski Kherbet mountain (nr. Cherviyonnaya in the Shelkovskaya district of the Grozny region). All 4 crew and 1 pax killed.

CCCP-L970 C-47 to '970' Jun46

CCCP-L976 C-47 to '976' Sep46

CCCP-L977 C-47 GVF. Noted in olive drab scheme with light grey undersides in 1951.

CCCP-L997 C-47 Aeroflot. W/O 18Dec47 on a test flight from Moscow-Vnukovo after overhaul by ARB-400 GVF, when the aircraft entered fog on the approach to Vnukovo, hit a hill with the starboard wing, nr km18 of the Kaluga highway (close to Tyoply Stan), hit a high-voltage power-line and crashed inverted.

CCCP-L1003 C-47 to '1003' Sep46

CCCP-L1005 C-47 to '1005' Apr46

CCCP-L1006 C-47 to '1006' Aug46

CCCP-L1008 C-47 to '1008' Sep46

CCCP-L1011 C-47 to '1011' Feb47

CCCP-L1013 C-47 Apr45

CCCP-L1015 C-47

CCCP-L1019 C-47 to '1019' Jan46

CCCP-L1020 TS-62 Aeroflot Yakutsk – i/s 06Jul50

CCCP-L1040 TS-62 Aeroflot Yakutsk – To 14 TO 1949

CCCP-L1042 C-47 to '1042' Nov45

CCCP-L1062 TS-62 Aeroflot Yakutsk?

CCCP-L1063 TS-62 Aeroflot Yakutsk – To 14 TO 1949.

CCCP-L1069 TS-62 Aeroflot Yakutsk – To 14 TO 1949

CCCP-L1074 May be C-47 or TS-62 – latter more likely if in same regn block as earlier TS-62s

CCCP-L1100 TS-62 Aeroflot Yakutsk – To 14 TO 1949

CCCP-L1204 C-47 Aeroflot Krasnoyarsk. DBR 22Apr47 on a flight from Kosisty to Khatanga when an engine failed and the aircraft made a forced landing in the tundra 180kms NW of Volochanka on the Taimyr peninsula, approx one & a half hours into the flight. All 5 crew and 28 pax survived the landing, but the captain and 8 others left the site 26Apr47 to seek help and were never seen again. The remaining 24 were rescued 11May47.

CCCP-L1209 TS-62 Aeroflot Yakutsk – To 14 TO 1949.

A number of C-47s were transferred from the Soviet AF to Aeroflot, Yakutsk in 1949. These were designated TS-62 [this is the version fitted with the ASh-62IR engines developed by Shvetsov from the M-25, licence-built Wright Cyclone SGR-1820-F]

Part VI – General Corrections

P.6:

With reference to the unsubstantiated story about Russian C-47s at Naples/Pomigliano, it is generally understood and accepted that all deliveries under Lend-Lease were made without payment and came to an end on 2nd September 1945. Russian aircraft all went via Great Falls, Montana to Ladd AFB, Fairbanks, Alaska, where they were handed over to Russian crews. See p.671. An answer to this story may be provided by Maurice Wickstead who has found that 32 war-worn C-47s and C-53s were awaiting collection at Capodichino by the newly-formed post-war Italian airlines in 1947/48. They were sold at $20,000 each, but needed major overhaul. Can anyone identify the source of the undated story that appeared in the book?

P.24:

The entry DC-2-253/C-41 c/n 2053 should read DC-**3**, not DC-2.

P.25:

The entry for DC-3-253A is incorrect as a line was missed out. The entries should read:

DC-3-253A c/n 2145, then
DC-3-269A Northwest Airlines c/n 2146

P.54:

Czechoslovakia – At the bottom the line should read 'Some of the missing C-47 c/ns …'

P.136:

Photo caption for 34911, c/n to read 26372.

P.139:

The photo shows a pre-war Japanese DC-3, but whether ex Douglas or J2D-3 built is unclear. It was never a C-47.

P.150:

Photo caption for the PA-NG C-47 0-3403 should be credited to the late Gene Sommerich.

P.193:

SISA must have been taken over by ALI in September 1949. See also p.332 which confirms this.

P.220:

Sivewright Airways never operated from Manchester/Barton, as the airfield was too short for safe DC-3 operation.

P.276:

TU-TIA – This aircraft was built from unused C-117A parts, the C-117D being the Super DC-3.

Photo page I:

PH-AJU was not used for spares by Marshalls of Cambridge, but Marshall Airways of Sydney, NSW, Australia.

Photo page XVII:

C-GWIR served with the 9th AF in Europe, not the 8th. The 8th only operated C-47s in N Africa, and looked after them at Burtonwood after their ferry flight. The 8th AF was split into the 8th, 9th and 11th Air Forces.

Photo page XXVI:

N47FL. This photo was taken by Jennifer Gradidge. The aircraft served with the RCAF until 1973 and was followed by a further 17 years with Canadian operators. It then passed via the USA to Spain to be operated for two years by AR Markt. When operations ceased EC-FIN was sold as N47FL prior to returning to the USA. It was photographed at Elstree, Herts on 01Oct95.

Photo page XXVII:

N96BF omitted from caption.

Photo page XXVI:

VT-CYG c/n 13019 was not returning to Great Britain. It was delivered direct to India via the S Atlantic.

Photo page XXXII:

PK-GDN was re-registered PK-NDD in 1969 with Merpati.

Photo page XXXIV:

N12RB. At the time this photo was taken only ten registrations had been carried.

Photo page XXXIX:

43-48415 was built as a C-47B, not C-47J. The –J and –M models were used by the US Navy – which this never flew with.

Photo page XXXIX:

OT-CND eventually found its way to F-ODHB and it was with these markings that it was shot down in error.

Photo page XLVII:

The caption should read 'Initially it was VQ-FBJ …'

Photo page LII:

The photograph of N32TN was taken by Michael Prophet.

Chapter 17
Miscellaneous Photo Gallery

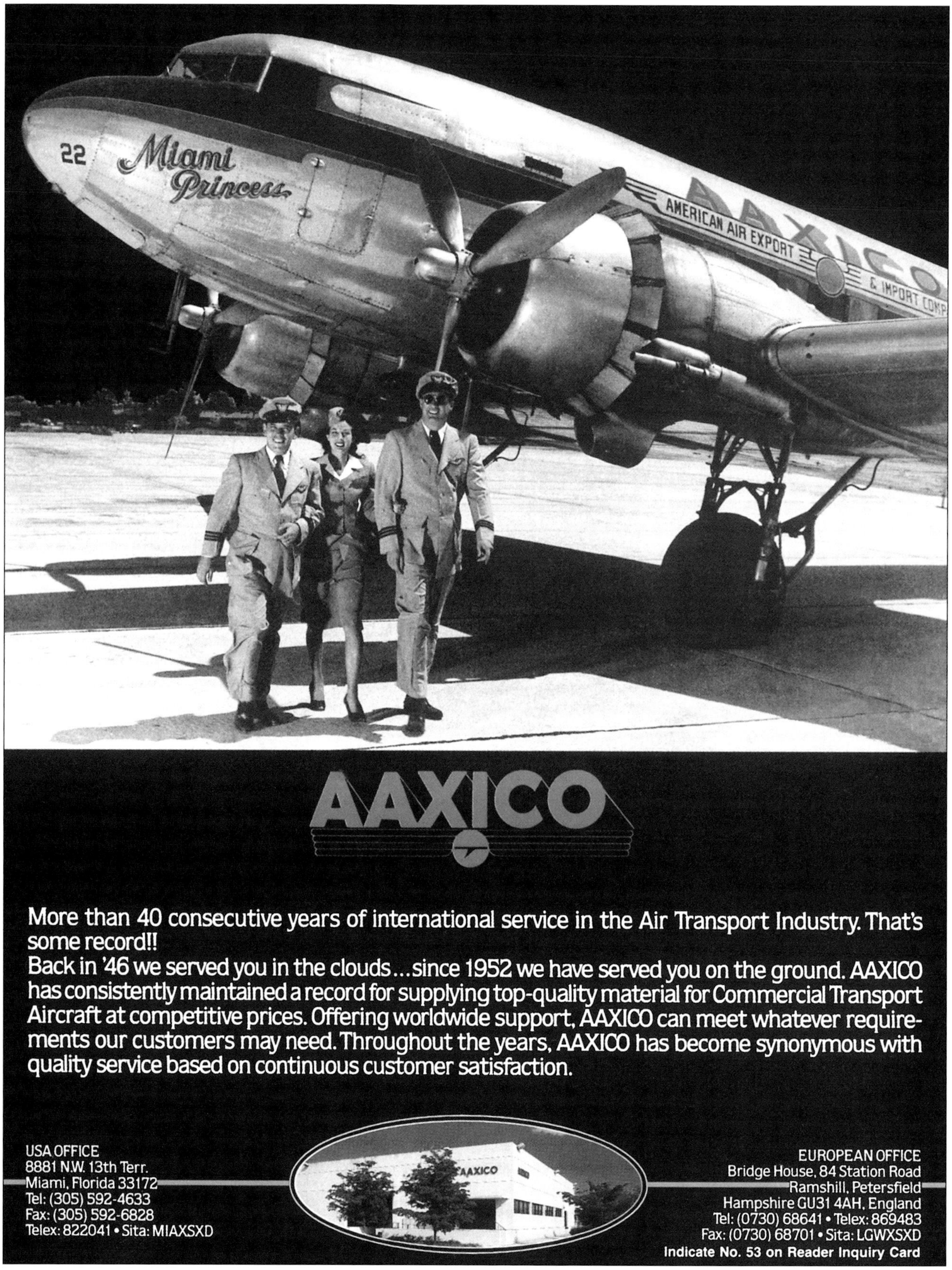

AAXICO

More than 40 consecutive years of international service in the Air Transport Industry. That's some record!!
Back in '46 we served you in the clouds...since 1952 we have served you on the ground. AAXICO has consistently maintained a record for supplying top-quality material for Commercial Transport Aircraft at competitive prices. Offering worldwide support, AAXICO can meet whatever requirements our customers may need. Throughout the years, AAXICO has become synonymous with quality service based on continuous customer satisfaction.

USA OFFICE
8881 N.W. 13th Terr.
Miami, Florida 33172
Tel: (305) 592-4633
Fax: (305) 592-6828
Telex: 822041 • Sita: MIAXSXD

EUROPEAN OFFICE
Bridge House, 84 Station Road
Ramshill, Petersfield
Hampshire GU31 4AH, England
Tel: (0730) 68641 • Telex: 869483
Fax: (0730) 68701 • Sita: LGWXSXD

Indicate No. 53 on Reader Inquiry Card

A 1940s photo used in a 1980s magazine advertisement: AAXICO – American Air Export & Import Company started cargo charter operations in 1945 with DC-3s and progressed to Curtiss C-46s and DC-6As in the 1950s (as AAXICO Airlines), before ceasing flying operations in the 1960s. Unfortunately no records of AAXICO's use of fleet numbers or individual aircraft names exist in the editor's files, so the DC-3 depicted remains unidentified.

Two early turbine-powered Dakota conversions: Seen above is the Dart-powered Dakota Freighter, one of two used by British European Airways for development work in connection with the introduction of the turbine Vickers Viscount during the years 1951 to 1953. Illustrated is G-AMDB (c/n 26432) "Claude Johnson" at Rolls-Royce's airfield at Derby (Rolls-Royce Ltd No.6747 via Mike Hooks). Seen below is the Dart-powered Conroy Aircraft Corporation's Turbo-Three which first flew in May 1969, using two Dart engines from an out of service Viscount. Their sole conversion N4700C (c/n 4903) is seen flying in formation with the company's "Stolifter" single-engined turbine development based on the Cessna 336 Skymaster. Their turbine-powered Dakota was later converted to fly with three PT-6A turboprops (Douglas Aircraft via PJ Marson).

Three pre-war European DC-2 operators: (top) Polskie Linie Lotnicze (LOT) – Polish Airlines SP-ASK (c/n 1377) taxying in snowy conditions (via Mike Hooks); (middle) Ceskoslovenska Letecka Spolecnost (CLS) – Czechoslovak Air Transport Company's OK-AIB (c/n 1582) illustrated on an official airline postcard at the company's base at Prague (Praha) Airport. (via Mike Hooks); and (bottom) Swiss Air Lines' HB-ITI (c/n 1321) unloading passengers and baggage at the old terminal of Zürich at Dübendorf. (Swissair Photo AG via Mike Hooks)

Two C-47s of the French Aéronautique Navale "36" (23936, c/n 9748) and "84" (18984 c/n 18984) are seen at an unknown location in France. The former aircraft reached the French from Czech Airlines, later becoming the well-known G-DAKK of British pleasure-flying fame, while the latter came from Piedmont Airlines in the USA, returning across the Atlantic after sale in May 1985. *(Stephen Piercey Collection)*

C-47 KAT-03 (c/n 32557) of the Katanga Air Force is seen with a Dove (left). The photo was taken probably in 1961, but no further details are available. *(Stephen Piercey Collection)*

This C-47 of the Mali Air Force (TZ-341 c/n 9644) was formerly operated by the French Air Force and then the French Ordre de Malte (Maltese Order) as F-BRAM in connection with Biafran relief flights. *(Stephen Piercey Collection)*

Extended nose EC-47 of the Força Aerea Brasileira (Brazilian Air Force) 2088 (c/n 34268) heads a line-up of Brazilian Air Force C-47s, date and location unknown. *(Neville Franklin Collection)*

Radar-equipped C-47 of the Colombian military airline SATENA serial 1127 (c/n 33038) is seen here in the later livery (a two-tone blue). This photograph was taken at Bogotá in the late 1970s. *(Stephen Piercey)*

One of the many schemes carried by Dakotas of the South African Air Force was an overall metal finish, as illustrated on 6820 (c/n 12115). This aircraft was photographed at Eastleigh Airport, Nairobi, Kenya in 1954. *(PJ Marson Collection)*

A smart Dakota of the Royal New Zealand Air Force, NZ3546 (c/n 33313), operated by 42 Squadron. The aircraft, formerly flown by New Zealand National Airways Corporation (NZNAC), was photographed in 1961, and was eventually withdrawn and sold via Comores to the South African Air Force twenty years later. *(PJ Marson Collection)*

One of a number of C-47Hs that the United States Navy flew on behalf of Naval attachés all over the world was this aircraft BuAer 17134 (c/n 12283) that was used by the Naval attaché in Indonesia. The attaché aircraft usually carried – as here - a large United States flag on the fin in place of the unit markings, with the titling "United States Naval Attaché to ..." on the nose. *(Brian Stainer/APN)*

Douglas R4D-8/C-117D Super Daks were based by the United States Navy in the United Kingdom for many years and were used mainly for communications duties. This example, 17211 (c/n 43391) with the "FT" code denoting FASRON-200, was photographed at its Blackbushe base in the late 1950s. *(Brian Stainer/APN)*

On this page we see three DC-3s from the United States airline scene of the 1950s: Transocean Airlines (TALOA – generally believed to be Transocean Airlines of Oakland) DC-3 N17314 (c/n 1924) was a former Transcontinental & Western Air (TWA) aircraft. Although Transocean owned a number of DC-3s, they were rarely seen with the airline's titles as the majority of the type were used for the development of services for new airlines abroad, for example Air Jordan and Iranian Airways. The DC-3 illustrated crashed in the USA in February 1959. *(Don Hannah Collection)*

Robinson Airlines operated DC-3s from 1948 until 1952, including this example N25676 (c/n 2214). Robinson Airlines became Mohawk Airlines in August 1952 and N25676 "Air Chief Niagara" was later sold for executive use. *(Don Hannah Collection)*

When Robinson Airlines became Mohawk Airlines in 1952, the emblem on the fin was taken over, as was the slogan carried on the side of the fuselage "Route of the Air Chiefs". N25671 (c/n 2211) "Air Chief Onondaga" was photographed in the early 1950s. *(Don Hannah Collection)*

Devlet Hava Yollari was the forerunner of Turk Hava Yollari – Turkish Airlines, which dates this photo of TC-TUG (c/n 20115), fleet number '56' to 1956 or earlier. After many years' service with the airline, the Dakota was transferred to the Turkish Air Force. *(Don Hannah Collection)*

Transadriatica operated Dakotas only from 1947 until January 1949, when the company was merged with Avio Linee Italiane (ALI). I-PADO (c/n 4329) was then sold in the Yemen, where it became the first airliner to be registered in the YE-series as YE-AAA. *(Don Hannah Collection)*

Royal Canadian Air Force Dakota 989 (c/n 33466) was operating on behalf of the United Nations Organization when this photo was taken around 1958. The aircraft flew with 115 Air Transport Unit and was later transferred to the Indian Air Force. *(Peter R March)*

Pan American World Airways transferred this DC-3 XA-GUF (c/n 1931) to its Mexican subsidiary Aeronaves de Mexico in the late 1940s and the aircraft was operated on the Mexican domestic network until the early 1970s. *(Don Hannah Collection)*

ALPA Air Taxis acquired this Dakota OB-T-1043 (c/n 12876) for charter flights in 1974. It would appear to have been intended as the operator's first aircraft, judging by the "No.1" on the fin but there is no record of any others. *(Brian Stainer/APN)*

Aerovias Q operated Dakotas mainly within Cuba, but also to the Caribbean area from 1946. CU-T2 (c/n 34289) was flown by the airline until 1955, when it returned to the USA. *(Don Hannah Collection)*

Air Carriers Ltd was a short-lived charter airline based in Hong Kong. Dakota VR-HEP (c/n 32530) was acquired from the China National Airlines Corporation in 1949, but crashed in January 1951. In the background an XT-registered Cessna of Civil Air Transport is just visible.
(Don Hannah Collection)

When South West Africa gained its independence from South Africa in 1978, the country was renamed Namibia. The local airline Suidwes Lugdiens/South West Airways was renamed Namib Air, and aircraft were mainly leased from South African carriers to operate domestic and regional services. This Dakota ZS-EDX (c/n 9452) was photographed at its home base Windhoek in August 1984. *(G le Roux)*

Sporting a much-used registration, Dakota VH-EAK (c/n 12872) was photographed in the early Qantas Empire Airways scheme and operated for the airline from 1946 until 1953, when it was sold to the Royal Thai Air Force, with whom it has since crashed. *(Don Hannah Collection)*

Early Airline Adverts for the DC-3

Seen on this page are three examples of early airline advertising for DC-3s:- American Airlines Airfreight services (October 1944), Trans-Canada Air Lines Aircargo (June 1948) and Air France passenger services from Birmingham (Elmdon) to Paris (1949).

American Airlines Introduces

Airfreight

A COMPLETELY NEW AIR SHIPPING SERVICE AT NEW, LOW COST

AIRFREIGHT, exclusive with American Airlines, is the answer to a long-standing need of regular, consistent shippers. It provides swift transportation of freight by air, over vast distances, *at rates low enough to make air shipping of profitable use in everyday business.*

AIRFREIGHT makes possible a new era of marketing and merchandising. It opens the way for expansion of markets and trading zones never before possible with other means of shipping. It offers a priceless opportunity for *new business.*

AIRFREIGHT will be available October 15, with pick-up and delivery in 43 American Airlines' cities, on a single document. By using coordinated trucking service between American's on-line cities and points not contiguous to these on-line cities, shippers everywhere will be able to obtain this swift, new air service.

AIRFREIGHT provides service from all points in the United States to Mexico City, Monterrey and any one of 40 off-line cities in Mexico.

AIRFREIGHT, not to be confused with Air Express, offers first-morning delivery over distances of 450 to approximately 1,500 miles, and second-morning delivery beyond. Rates are set according to four freight classifications depending on value, volume, density, perishability and fragility. Delivery and pick-up are included in the charges, but deductions are allowed where these services are not required.

AIRFREIGHT, by making it possible for our nation's business to ship in bulk by air, will contribute substantially to the war effort, in addition to providing the basis on which post-war air shipping will be built.

For complete information write

AIRFREIGHT Division, American Airlines Inc.
100 East 42nd Street, New York 17, N. Y.

AMERICAN AIRLINES *Inc.*

THE NATIONAL AND INTERNATIONAL ROUTE OF THE FLAGSHIPS

TCA
"AIRCARGO"
Trans-Canada's "Aircargo" service has now been extended to Boston, New York, Cleveland and Chicago. These are the first United States links with T.C.A.'s Canadian coast-to-coast, Newfoundland and Trans-Atlantic "Aircargo" services.
For quick-reference tariff and complete information, write or call your nearest T.C.A. "Aircargo" office.
BOSTON .... The Statler Hotel at 66 Arlington St.
NEW YORK .... 16 East 58th Street
CLEVELAND .... Arcade Union Commerce Bldg.
DETROIT .... 1253 Washington Boulevard
CHICAGO .... 75 East Monroe Street
SEATTLE .... 414 University Street
TRANS-CANADA Air Lines
LINKING UNITED STATES—CANADA—NEWFOUNDLAND—BRITAIN
PASSENGER • AIRCARGO
AIR EXPRESS • AIR MAIL

WINGED FEET

direct to Paris

from Birmingham

in a famous Douglas D.C.3 aircraft; thence to the Riviera, Corsica, Italy, Spain, Majorca or Switzerland. Ask your Travel Agent for details of Air France services from Birmingham, London, Manchester, Glasgow and Belfast.

Return fare Birmingham - Paris £18 . 0 . 0

AIR FRANCE

ELMDON AIRPORT, BIRMINGHAM. SHELDON 2441

A selection of the 27 aircraft that assembled at Rock Falls, Illinois (14 DC-3/C-47 and one DC-2 visible) on 25 July 2010 for "The Last Time Douglas DC-3 & C-47 Reunion", prior to flying on to Oshkosh, Wisconsin on 26 July 2010. *(Ralph M Pettersen)*

Appendix I
Survivors

In the 'First Seventy Years' a list of survivors by constructor's number was given, broken down according to whether the airframe was Active, Preserved or Derelict. This proved to be somewhat limiting as it took no account of the airframe that was stored and out of service for some time, but still capable of being overhauled for further service. No category has proved to be perfect as some preserved aircraft have flown again (and some listed as in museums are airworthy anyway). Even an aircraft quoted as derelict has been known to recover and fly again. This often depends on how the term 'derelict' is interpreted (see later). And, of course, two derelict airframes are sometimes merged into one airworthy frame.

The number of survivors has fallen since the text of the first two Volumes went to press in 2003, mainly because of the interpretation of the term 'Active'. However, further aircraft have been 'discovered' and have boosted the number. The US Register has proved to be particularly difficult to assess, as an aircraft may remain on the register regardless of its status until the owner applies to have it cancelled. Some aircraft are quoted as 'sold' but the new owner never registers that change because the aircraft was broken up or otherwise destroyed. We have, therefore, introduced a further category, that of 'Stored' when the aircraft is parked in the open, possibly with engines and control surfaces removed, but still largely intact. Stored aircraft often have parts removed to prevent damage by storm or vandalism.

Thus, the number of DC-3 airframes thought still to exist, has fallen from about 1,080 to about 991 in mid-2010, as well as nine DC-2s.

Some of the details given here rely on observations made by those who have visited airfields overseas – but unfortunately such observations are not always concise – so if there is some doubt, the entry may be downgraded

+ indicates 'turboprop conversion'.

ACTIVE AIRFRAMES

ACTIVE indicates that an airframe is airworthy or under overhaul to be made airworthy. Omitted are those airframes which come into the 'Stored' category and which are unlikely to fly in the near future. Museum exhibits which do fly are included here.

DC-2:-

1368, 1404

DC-3:-

1910, 1920, 1997, 2029, 2053, 2054, 2137, 2141, 2145, 2169, 2201, 2202, 2204, 2213, 2234, 2239, 3278, 3291, 3294, 4082, 4089, 4123, 4126.

4219, 4307, 4319, 4359, 4463, 4538, 4545, 4564, 4583, 4715, 4727, 4733, 4894, 4932, 4935, 6021, 6055, 6062, 6102, 6144, 6315, 6346, 7313, 9028, 9040, 9043, 9058, 9059, 9172, 9186, 9276, 9286, 9290, 9371, 9380, 9415, 9531, 9581, 9593, 9670+, 9700, 9766+, 9813, 9891, 9894, 9926, 9967, 9995, 10035, 10199, 10200, 10201, 11639, 11665, 11737, 11750, 11757, 11761, 11775, 11867, 11925, 11926, 11991, 12026, 12056, 12060, 12073+, 12106, 12107, 12160+, 12192, 12267, 12295, 12300, 12317, 12327, 12413, 12415, 12425, 12438, 12540, 12543, 12570, 12852, 12857, 12907, 12983, 13070, 13087, 13155, 13310, 13331, 13333, 13334, 13342, 13383, 13506, 13539+, 13540+, 13541, 13580, 13678, 13798, 13803, 13816, 13850, 13854, 13860, 13861, 13883, 18984, 19052, 19054, 19173+, 19227+, 19286, 19309, 19345, 19347, 19394, 19433, 19434, 19560, 19603, 19661, 19685+, 19754, 19999, 20019, 20031+, 20063, 20082+, 20145, 20166, 20171, 20175+, 20215, 20401, 20432, 20444, 20448, 20475, 20494, 20548, 20806, 20835, 20845, 20875+.

25269+, 25311+, 25313 , 25341, 25409+, 25443+, 25482, 25485, 25509+, 25546+, 25610, 25634, 25674+, 25753+, 25778, 25869, 25977, 26005, 26044, 26108, 26120, 26133, 26211, 26268+, 26292+, 26408, 26439+, 26480, 26515+, 26541, 26593, 26735, 26744+, 26794, 26874, 26877+, 26921, 26958, 26984, 27002+, 27047, 27080, 27121, 27130, 27131, 27137+, 27187, 27202, 27203, 27218.

32529+, 32541+, 32644, 32710, 32761, 32844, 32872, 32879, 32883, 32884, 32897, 32914, 32920, 32948, 32961, 33010+, 33032, 33046+, 33048, 33049, 33053+, 33102, 33105, 33113, 33123, 33135, 33201, 33238+, 33248+, 33282+, 33313+, 33345, 33359, 33441, 33445, 33542+, 33567+, 33581+, 33613, 34202, 34228, 34295, 34368, 34370, 34378, 34398+.

42961, 43086, 43159, 43302, 43312, 43332, 43345, 43354, 43360, 43365, 43375, 43393.

Indian AF IJ302

Total 281

PRESERVED AIRFRAMES

Whether a DC-3 is displayed under cover, in a museum, or in the open as part of a large collection, it is included here. Also there are some which are kept as 'gate-guards' to mark the entrance to a military establishment. However displayed, these aircraft are usually in good condition, complete with all externally visible parts – even if the interior is fairly bare. Those airframes kept in the open, are likely to suffer from the weather. A few aircraft have no data plate or this has not been examined so their identity is uncertain. They are listed at the end. While many listed here have not been reported recently, it is assumed that once they become a museum exhibit, they are still there.

DC-2:-

1286, 2072.

DC-3/C-47/C-53:-

1499, 1545, 1911, 1944, 1975, 1983, 1995, 1997, 2000, 2144, 2165, 2198, 2245, 2248, 3264, 3269, 3275?, 4120, 4129, 4201, 4236, 4260, 4280, 4282, 4306, 4347, 4380, 4423, 4479, 4563, 4579, 4664, 4666, 4705, 4824, 4828, 4830, 4865, 4877, 4900, 4968, 4978, 4979, 6007, 6179, 6223, 6261, 6314, 6338, 6355, 7347, 9041, 9358, 9414, 9525, 9530, 9551, 9578, 9619, 9628, 9664, 9836, 9911, 9914, 10132, 10156, 10239, 10253, 11645, 11664, 11722, 11747, 11762, 11837, 11906, 11928, 11973, 12205, 12248, 12251, 12253, 12254, 12256, 12303, 12386, 12449, 12478, 12486, 12490, 12494, 12498, 12542, 12586, 12647, 12679, 12683, 12686,12704+, 12715, 12719, 12792, 12830, 12832, 12937, 12950, 12970, 12975, 13004, 13009, 13028, 13050, 13073, 13084, 13142, 13227, 13296, 13319, 13373, 13399, 13448, 13468, 13503, 13521, 13590, 13612, 13624, 13642, 13645, 13647, 13720, 13727, 13740, 13741, 13749, 13752, 13877, 13880.

18905, 18923, 18973, 19010, 19021, 19194, 19200, 19231, 19288, 19291, 19320, 19335, 19420, 19460, 19529, 19531, 19539, 19623, 19666, 19755, 19759, 19797, 19866, 19961, 19965, 19975, 19976, 19978, 20007, 20025, 20045, 20051, 20093, 20101, 20112, 20158, 20193, 20197, 20206, 20390, 20414, 20443, 20495, 20555, 20560, 20596, 20600, 20604, 20607, 20750, 20823, 20865.

25273, 25309, 25359, 25450, 25455, 25464, 25480, 25489, 25515, 25527, 25530, 25553, 25562, 25608, 25676, 25679, 25685, 25762, 25806, 25824, 25980, 26067, 26087+, 26137, 26171?, 26178, 26193, 26218, 26248, 26252, 26271, 26273, 26299, 26342, 26343, 26357, 26388, 26456, 26467, 26491, 26511, 26531, 26542, 26583, 26592, 26597, 26616, 26638, 26640, 26641, 26666, 26703, 26704, 26718, 26746, 26768, 26777, 26785, 26787, 26800, 26806, 26823, 26903, 26968, 26989, 27099, 27110, 27127.

32561, 32650, 32658, 32664, 32671, 32677, 32716, 32734, 32752, 32755, 32789, 32794, 32818, 32834, 32837, 32849, 32877, 32922, 32935, 32945, 32966, 32992, 33003, 33031, 33095, 33096, 33146, 33153, 33185, 33199, 33206, 33216, 33220, 33301, 33307, 33315, 33316, 33335, 33392, 33393, 33419, 33448, 33460, 33484, 33496, 33556, 34189, 34214, 34220, 34223, 34227, 34285, 34361.

43083, 43317, 43321, 43322, 43363, 43379.

C/n unknown:- El Salvador 114, Greece 92613, 92626, 92632, 92641, Honduras 315, India IJ817, Indonesia RI-001, RI-001, RI-001, Israel 003, Myanmar UB736, Pakistan (unknown), Slovenia 71253, Thailand 979, 22246, HS-ISS, USAF '43-48910', Venezuela 4AT1, Yugoslavia 71203

Total 336

STORED AIRFRAMES

There are now many DC-3 airframes reported to be stored or withdrawn from use, but potentially capable of being made airworthy again if there was a demand. They are almost always parked in the open, perhaps weather-beaten, and usually lacking engines and/or control surfaces, but otherwise intact. It is often almost impossible to tell from airfield reports that an airframe is stored or perhaps derelict, unless there is some indication as to how long an airframe has been out of use, so this list has to be an approximation.

DC-2:-

1288, 1292, 1354, 1376.

VH-DNA (c/n 27130) of Dakota National Airways was used for pleasure flying for several years, but has now been withdrawn from use. The photo was taken at Sydney-Bankstown in March 2004. *(Al Bovelt)*

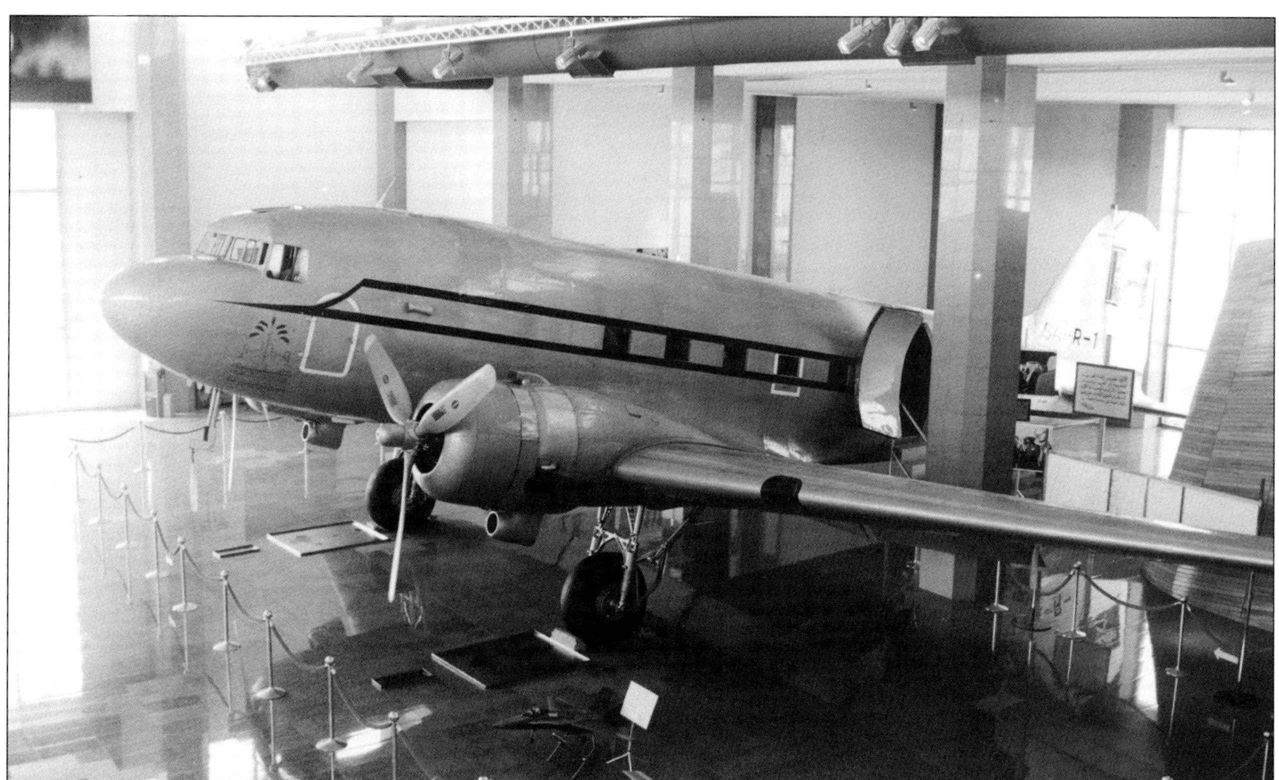

SA-R-1 (c/n 32650), ex HZ-AAX of Saudi Arabian Airlines, is preserved in the Royal Saudi Air Force Museum at Riyadh, where this photo was taken in November 2002. Note the engine nacelle mock-up. *(Leif Hellstrom)*

DC-3:-

1984, 1998, 2008, 2118, 2167, 2193, 2216, 2236, 2241, 2247, 4126, 4128, 4174, 4218, 4349, 4363, 4409, 4414, 4433, 4438, 4481, 4574, 4654, 4667, 4747, 4863, 6054, 6061, 6068, 6085, 6098, 6135, 6148, 6208, 6215, 6343, 6354, 7320, 7386, 9036, 9103, 9137, 9247, 9369, 9410, 9452, 9798, 9802, 9831, 9832, 9860, 10028, 11625, 11637, 11700, 11741, 11746+, 11986+, 11990+, 12004, 12064, 12090, 12115, 12150, 12166, 12172, 12287, 12363, 12369, 12445, 12471, 12524, 12557, 12580, 12582, 12591, 12596+, 12597, 12693, 12873, 12907, 12949, 12962, 13019, 13228, 13368, 13436, 13439, 13445, 13459, 13460, 13485, 13576, 13639, 13713, 13726, 13757, 13840.

18949, 18977, 18993, 19000, 19066, 19104, 19121, 19366, 19426, 19446+, 19447, 19458, 19503, 19572+, 19593, 19677, 19738, 19741, 19809, 19983, 20002, 20012, 20017, 20115, 20117, 20118, 20190, 20194, 20228, 20244, 20260, 20474, 20550, 20743, 20767, 20814, 20830.

25278, 25368, 25453, 25495, 25571, 25612, 25720, 25746, 25757, 25769, 25771, 25951, 25964, 26095, 26244, 26271, 26372, 26438, 26520, 26557, 26558, 26569, 26716, 26792, 26815, 26831, 26860, 27005, 27016, 27085, 27130.

32626, 32635+, 32668, 32750, 32820, 32825, 32843, 32855, 32974, 33024, 33072, 33106, 33119, 33211, 33213, 33232, 33294, 33297, 33300, 33352, 33375, 33436, 33448, 33478+, 33499, 33626, 34141, 34225, 34300, 34375.

43079, 43084, 43087, 43301, 43325, 43342, 43369.

c/n unknown: '0-315732'

Total 219

DERELICT AIRFRAMES

As we said in 'The First Seventy Years' we only included an aircraft in the 'derelict' category, when it was damaged, had many parts removed and was unlikely to fly again. Yet at least one aircraft did fly again, which shows how much one has to rely on a report on status. If one catches an airframe just after it has been stripped down for overhaul, it could well look derelict. Hence we should warn that inclusion in this section is no guarantee that the airframe is beyond hope of restoration – though some may be restored for display.

DC-2:-

1562

DC-3:-

1917, 1969, 2108, 2217, 4138, 4221, 4500, 4519, 4550, 4658, 4785, 4790, 4810, 4827, 4836, 4890, 4903, 4918, 6024, 6051, 6164, 6325, 6337, 7340, 9001, 9049, 9053, 9061, 9089, 9118, 9668, 9720, 9910, 9949, 9978, 10106, 10166, 10178, 11672, 11693, 11719, 11731, 11780, 11825, 11853, 12196, 12217, 12446, 12550, 12652, 12712, 12757, 12874, 13041, 13074, 13140, 13177, 13231, 13378, 13543, 13573, 13836.

19029, 19046, 19224, 19393, 19606, 19721, 19778, 19795, 19800, 20041, 20238, 20507, 20529, 20530, 20721, 20842.

25347, 25362, 25425, 25541, 25808, 25810, 25928, 25956, 26001, 26038, 26111, 26286, 26356, 26471, 26474, 26501, 26707, 26740, 26765, 26964, 26980, 27046, 27079, 27098, 27180, 27186, 27199.

32651, 32745, 32780, 32952, 32988, 33134, 33174, 33379, 33532, 33552, 33557, 34142, 34154, 34222, 34306, 34344, 34376, 34386, 34397, 34409.

42978, 43082, 43305, 43309, 43311, 43324, 43326, 43330, 43331, 43334, 43352, 43358, 43359, 43361, 43362, 43366, 43370, 43371, 43372, 43374, 43378, 43380, 43381, 43382, 43383, 43385, 43386, 43389, 43394, 43396, 43399.

Yugoslav AF 71212, 71245.

F A Colombiana 1660.

Total 164

Surviving airframes – as of October 2010: 991 DC-3s, 9 DC-2s

Apart from aircraft preserved in museums, indoors or out, no aircraft has been included in the above list if there has been no report of its existence in the past 10 years. As these lists rely, in the most part, on reports of observations by visitors to airfields etc., 'no report' may just indicate that no visit has been made. We have excluded aircraft sunk at sea to act as diver's attractions. There must be plenty of airframes lying on the seabed in a reasonably intact state. Preserved cockpits have also been omitted.

Below: This C-53 serial 41-20066 (c/n 4836) was flying from Perth in Western Australia to Broome, but got lost and crash-landed at Vansittart Bay, nearly 400 miles away on 26th February 1942. There were no casualties and the radio continued to work. Eventually QANTAS Short S23 "Corinthian" located the C-53 and picked up the crew. The airframe was salvaged to recover usable parts, the engines, control surfaces, etc, and the wreck was left to the elements, where it lies in situ to this day. The wreck has become a regular attraction for cruise ships, and Toby Gursansky visited the remains with his wife on 17th June 2008, and she was able to take this photo from the cruise ship's helicopter.
(Toby Gursansky)

Appendix II(a)
Civil Registration / Constructor's Number Cross-Reference

This registration index covers only those aircraft mentioned in the Update sections, whether the information is new or corrected. The constructor's numbers given are the 'corrected' numbers only.

Registration	*C/n*
AN-ASP	4519
AN-AWT	4174
A3-AWP	33135
"B-126"	13612
B-809	19932
B-815	19258
B-827	13784
B-829	34298
B-841	13817
B-879	34325
B-929	19496
B-933	13817
C-100	2012
C-101	1991
C-102	1989
C-104	1992
C-105	1989
C-503	10171
CB-32	19445
CB-35	4867
CC-CBH	26906
CC-CBJ	13296
CC-CBO (2)	6190
CC-CBW	26704
CC-CBX	13296
CC-CLDT	13296
CCCP-N328	9118
CCCP-N329	9024
CCCP-X361	4771
CCCP-H417	9357
CCCP-J500	9016
CCCP-L800	6228
CCCP-L801	6229
CCCP-L802	6233
CCCP-L806	6234
CCCP-L807	6237
CCCP-L809	6000
CCCP-L810	6001
CCCP-L811	6002
CCCP-L814	9017
CCCP-L815	9019
CCCP-L816	9021
CCCP-L817	6230
CCCP-L818	6235
CCCP-L819	9020
CCCP-L820	9116
CCCP-L821	9022
CCCP-L822	9440
CCCP-L823	9441
CCCP-L824	9612
CCCP-L825	9436
CCCP-L826	6236
CCCP-L827	9601
CCCP-L828	10007
CCCP-L829	4799
CCCP-L830	6025
CCCP-L831	9425
CCCP-L832	9115
CCCP-L833	11889
CCCP-L834	11885
CCCP-L835	9427
CCCP-L836	9852
CCCP-L837	9615
CCCP-L838	9431
CCCP-L839	9604
CCCP-L840	11893
CCCP-L841	11887
CCCP-L842	11895
CCCP-L843	9119
CCCP-L844	12230
CCCP-L845	12123
CCCP-L846	11939
CCCP-L847	12133
CCCP-L848	11952
CCCP-L849	12237
CCCP-L850	12390
CCCP-L851	11891
CCCP-L852	11941
CCCP-L853	12410
CCCP-L854	12225
CCCP-L855	12399
CCCP-L856	11962
CCCP-L857	12119
CCCP-L858	12030
CCCP-L859	11930
CCCP-L860	11935
CCCP-L861	12400
CCCP-L862	12136
CCCP-L863	12231
CCCP-L864	11950
CCCP-L865	12398
CCCP-L866	12601
CCCP-L867	12402
CCCP-L868	11944
CCCP-L869	12600
CCCP-L870	12707
CCCP-L871	12243
CCCP-L872	12405
CCCP-L873	12394
CCCP-L874	11969
CCCP-L875	11899
CCCP-L876	12224
CCCP-L877	12129
CCCP-L878	12797
CCCP-L879	12407
CCCP-L880	12802
CCCP-L881	12996
CCCP-L882	12884
CCCP-L883	12602
CCCP-L884	12703
CCCP-L885	12994
CCCP-L886	12997
CCCP-L887	13000
CCCP-L888	11879
CCCP-L889	12117
CCCP-L890	12127
CCCP-L891	9426
CCCP-L892	9854
CCCP-L893	13096
CCCP-L894	13097
CCCP-L895	13215
CCCP-L896	12883
CCCP-L897	12998
CCCP-L898	13002
CCCP-L899	11955
CCCP-L900	12029 (?)
CCCP-L901	12890
CCCP-L902	13001
CCCP-L903	13089
CCCP-L904	13090
CCCP-L905	13091
CCCP-L906	13094
CCCP-L907	11901
CCCP-L908	6231
CCCP-L909	13348
CCCP-L910	13216
CCCP-L911	13093
CCCP-L912	13353
CCCP-L913	13346
CCCP-L914	9598
CCCP-L915	13350
CCCP-L3800	33202
CCCP-L3803	12390
CCCP-L3831	9425
CCCP-L3867	12119
CCCP-L3881	12996
CCCP-L3894	13097
CCCP-4027	33222
CCCP-4058	34304
CF-BZI	13448
CF-CPY	4666
CF-CQT	9813
CF-CUE	12983
CF-DTB	12597
CF-DTD	12253
CF-DTH	12591
CF-FAY	4785
CF-FOL	25483
CF-FST	9041
CF-FTR	32843
CF-GBG	32963
CF-GBH	32843
CF-GBI	33540
CF-GBJ	27074
CF-GHX	11780
CF-IAE	4563
CF-ITH	20228
CF-JWP	9089
CF-LFR	13155
C-FMKB	19560
CF-NWU	6095
CF-OOW	13342
CF-PWH	2198
CF-QBC	27026
CF-QBI	6179
CF-QHF	13392
CF-QHY	26005
C-FROD	13028
CF-TDJ	6261
CF-TES	11906
C-FTGI	26268
CF-VQV	3264
CF-YED	4433
CF-YQG	4654
C-GAWI	19227
C-GCXD	25612
C-GDAK	2141
C-GDOG	43374
C-GEAI	33053
C-GEAJ	26120
C-GEKG	43354
C-GERD	43330
C-GGKE	43366
C-GJDM	20721
C-GJGQ	43307
C-GJKB	13383
C-GJKM	13580
C-GNTK	13149
C-GPNR	13333
C-GRSB	12295
C-GVKB	12300
C-GWIR	9371
C-GWZS	12327
CP-583	9668
CP-607	12570
CP-1128	1998

CP-1419	32988
CP-1960	18993
CP-2255	25951
CP-2290	32626
CR-ABJ	11699
CR-AFR	13018
CR-AGD	19393
CR-AGU	33325
CR-LBK	13769
CR-LDK	12445
CS-AZL	26244
CS-DGA	19503
CS-TAI	12060
CS-TDB	10033
CU-T144	4466
CU-P266	11684
CU-T1059	11645
CU-T1192	10028
CU-T1558	12445
CU-T1559	32664
CX-BDB	33392
CX-BHP	25608
CX-BHR	19231
CX-BJG	19021
CX-BKH	20604
C9-ATH	9410
C9-STF	12205
"D-CADE"	25450
D-CXXX	32872
D2-FDK	12445
EC-AHA	34280
EC-ALC	19785
EC-AQB	12844
EC-AQE	25641
EC-ASP	26980
EC-BUG	32734
EC-EJB	4479
EI-AYO	1911
ES-AKE	33445
ET-AGH	9501
"ET-T-1"	9628
F-AZOX	33352
F-AZTE	9172
F-BAIF	33119
"F-BBBE"	9172
F-BEIG	10253
F-BFGX	11722
F-BIEE	26042
(F-BLOZ)	13142
F-GDXP	32561
F-GIDK	33352
F-GNRB	32561
F-SEBE	13467
G-AGIZ	12075
G-ALLI	19351
G-ALWC	13590
G-ALXK	32828
G-AMCA	32966
G-AMDB	26432
G-AMHJ	13468
G-AMPO	33185
G-AMPP	26717
G-AMPY	26569
G-AMRA	26735
G-AMSN	33379
G-AMSV	32820
G-AMYJ	32716
"G-AMZZ"	12254
"G-AMZZ"	25806
G-ANAF	33436
G-APUC	12893
G-BGCG	20002
G-BHUA	9914
G-BLDI	19475
G-BVOL	9836
G-BVRB	32561
G-DAKK	9798
HB-IRN	33393
"HB-IRN"	4828
HB-ISB	4667
HB-ISC	9995
HC-ALD	19046
HC-ATG	12876
HC-AUP	27046
HC-AUT	33496
HC-BOT	9831
HC-SBR	12374
HC-SBS	25275
HC-SGG	9980
HC-SMB	1549
HH-CNE	11700
HI-40	20455
HI-477CA	43378
HK-122(2)	4414
HK-124	4349
HK-140	6354
HK-142	1957
HK-503	10171
HK-1149G	26593
HK-1175	20432
HK-1315	4307
HK-1514E	11741
HK-2494	33105
HK-2497	27079
HK-2663X	10201
HK-2664X	12352
HK-2665X	32540
HK-2666X	12352
HK-2820X	20171
HK-3006	43086
HK-3037	20548
HK-3176	19606
HK-3199	26044
HK-3215X	26111
HK-3286	6144
HK-3292	19661
HK-3293X	9186
HK-3348X	11775
HK-3349	11825
HK-3350	1969
HK-3359	34295
HK-3462X	11759
HK-3586X	43325
HK-3993	26343
HK-3994	4319
HK-4045	25808
HK-4189	4319
HK-4700	9700
HS-DOA	26511
"HS-ISS"	12832
HS-SAF	12150
HS-TDA	13726
HS-TDF	9414
HS-TDI	12246
"I-LEON"	26299
JZ-PDF	13334
LN-IAT	20019
LN-WND	11750
LV-ADF	20158
LV-FYH	26052
LV-FYI	19524
LV-FYJ	26158
LV-PJT	26052
LV-PJU	19524
LV-PJV	26158
LX-DKT	10253
N1XP	4733
N2VM	13757
N3BA(2)	12172
N7(1)	20426
N7AP	25341
N8WJ	9276
N10CR	4112
N11AF	13817
N12BA	10035
N15MA	19286
N15SJ	33049
N20TW	2236
N21BF	9832
N22RB	4926
N23AJ	9247
N23SA	4903
N26H	4871
N26MA	2169
N27TN	43332
N28AA	2239
N28BF	43336
N28TN	43354
N30TN	43159
N32AL	33368
N32MS	4978
N32TN	43301
N33VW	20401
N34	33359
N34AH	43360
N36AP	13439
N37FL	6343
N39DT	4871
N41(2)	19320
N41F	2184
N41HQ	2053
N43XX	11665
N44GH	43393
N44V(2)	4545
N47AZ	13019
N47CR	19770
N47E	13816
N47FJ	9053
N47FK	9700
N47FL	13087
N47HL	27203
N47L	7313
N47SJ	25869
N47TF	12317
N49AG	11737
N49FN	4179
N50CM	13445
N51D(2)	4550
N51F	6095
N53FN	4319
N53ST	9380
N55U	20455
N56KS	25769
N56V(1)	4900
N56V(2)	33153
N58NA	12970
N59NA	9043
N62BA	6095
N62CC	13798
N67K	7313
N68CW	25980
N72B	2250
N73CD	32529
N75T	12715
N79MA	4089
N81B	7382
N81T	25888
N84KB	9040
N85SA	11637
N87T	6148
N89HA	19603
N96H	19224
N97H	33613
N99	4574
N99FS	12425
N99H	32588
N100BF	43361
N100MA	20180
N101KC	11639
N101MX	2102
N102AP	2257
N102BF	43334
N102DH	20830
N103NA	9531
N105BF	43389
N105CA	25720
N106BF	43389
N107B	4082
N107BF	43352
N110BF	43381
N115NA	11625
N115SA	13310
N115Z	33567
N116SA	32855
N122CA	4827
N123DZ	12004
N129H(2)	4126
N130D	19800
N130Q(2)	11761
N131FS	32920
N132FS	25778
N133D	1499
N133FS	27202
N134D	11731
N135FS	20063
N136FS	10267

N137PB	4128
N138FS	9967
N139D(2)	2165
N139JR	20550
N140JR	26815
N141JR	19366
N142Z	20494
N143D	2054
N145A	6098
N145RD	20175
N146RD	32897
N147DC	19347
N148RD	27199
N149RD	33552
N150D(2)	4463
N151ZE	26408
N165LG	6314
N167BT	13383
N168LG	4089
N169RB	4939
N173RD	25313
N190BB	4369
N192RD	12115
N193DP	4433
N193RD	33375
N198RD	33024
N200MF(3)	9766
N200MX	4082
N207U	4984
N211GB(2)	26133
N212DD	43386
N213GB	33232
N213MA	7320
N215CM	26792
N220GB	4438
N224GB	12261
N225GB	33251
N226	6355
N227GB	33345
N229GB	26874
N230GB	20443
N231GB	26108
N236GB	20743
N242AG	12679
N242SM	4877
N243DC	9247
N269LM	26054
N272R	13678
N293WM	13860
N294R	2103
N300BF	26744
N300MF	27121
N301AK	19778
N305SF	6208
N308SF	18984
N321L	43345
N330RD	25546
N332RD	33211
N340EL	4110
N341A	2145
N341W	13041
N345AB	13803
N346AB	33441
N346K	6148
N347DK	32820
N353MM	11665
N364K	20215
N374AS	34145
N376AS	27047
N400BF	9415
N400MF	26877
N403JB(2)	34202
N408D	2247
N437GB	19999
N467SP	32948
N471DK	19446
N472AF	13485
N472DK	27137
N473DC	19345
N473DK	6223
N486C	6325
N489F	12269
N496	2270
N505C	43335
N513GL	26716
N514AC	26558
N574JB	20145
N583V	12369
N587LM	43369
N587MB	43312
N600NA	3291
N600RC	2193
N603MC	4932
N650K	13174
N683LS	43084
N700CA	12438
N705GB	13854
N707BA	33046
N710Z	32914
N715F	4129
N722NR	43342
N728G	4359
N730D	25888
N734H	4727
N737H	6062
N751A	12060
N760	3269
N763A	4894
N777DG	25634
N777PG	25634
N777YA	25634
N780T	20865
N781T	4306
N782T	4382
N783T	4219
N784T	6054
N784V	11664
N786T	20238
N791HH	33123
N800J	20806
N811RB	25509
N814CL	34370
N834D	43324
N834M	26211
N834TP	12590
N835TD	43321
N836M	25977
N837M	12524
N838M	20448
N839M	20166
N840MB	9670
N842MB	19741
N843DD	34286
N843MB(2)	13228
N844TH	13070
N845S	25509
N851M	43302
N872A	7403
N877MG	20806
N882TP	32644
N900	2165
N907Z	12300
N922CA	2204
N932H	34368
N941AT	12907
N943DJ	7313
N982Z	25485
N983DC	12267
N1000A	2184
N1010S	6097
N1181T	25888
X1331	1331
N1350A	33032
N1559K	4134
N1788B	1954
N1789B	2130
N1791B	2183
N1792B	2184
N1793B	4859
N1794B	7313
N1798B	20817
N1934D (DC-2)	1368
N1944A	19677
N1944H	34378
N1944M	19394
N1945	3294
N2025A	34375
N2028	6164
N2111M	4319
N2270M	10239
N2271C	25309
N2271D	33174
N2298C	33201
N2312G	33216
N2568	26193
N2647	4862
N2805J	20835
N3006	42961
N3239T	19054
N3239W	19677
N3455	33379
N3749Q	43082
N3753N	33213
N4003	11672
N4039S	32974
N4550J	6055
N4565L	2108
N4630V	4823
N4660V	13296
N4661V	26704
N4662V	26906
N4663V	32588
N4667V	26823
N4724V	27098
N4788C	34325
N4843N	1920
N4867V (DC-2)	1368
N4868V	11883
N4883V	19452
N4884V	19313
N4991E	12106
N4994N	25771
N5106X	9058
N5156T	25509
N5584N	43326
N5590C	12187
N5831B	19345
N5874V	7377
N6169H	25509
N7500A	11693
N7712B	34306
N8009	20806
N8021Z	20444
N8040L	34236
N8041C	13375
N8061A	6085
N8099	26520
N8160Z	20472
N8187E	13840
N8190X	33478
N8194Q	32961
N8194Z	12166
N8241T	33134
N8324C	20388
N8326C	13296
N8327C	20346
N8330C	26704
N8334C	20817
N8335C	25888
N8336C	7313
N8338C	2183
N8339C	2184
N8340C	2130
N8341C	2185
N8342C	1954
N8349C	19620
N8350C	20806
N8351C	32847
N8355C	19062
N8356C	4573
N8357C	6151
N8358C	18901
N8359C	2261
N8360C	2135
N8361C	4927
N8362C	4871
N8383	26299
(N8399C)	19932
N8563	9830
N8610	25615
N8666	25957
N8704	33048
N9141	20529
N9382	12331
N9562N	26439
N9663N	43385

Registration	c/n
N9796N	43375
N9838A	13139
N9891A	9891
N9923S	25964
N9985Q	27215
N9986Q	25810
N10005	25527
N11461	9750
N12907	27187
N12954	4996
N12978	4983
N13711 (DC-2)	1368
N14280 (DC-2)	1313
N14283 (3)	19667
N14291 (DC-2)	1351
N14636	13399
N14931	2118
N14937	4466
N14950 (DC-2)	1371
N14978 (DC-2)	1408
N15563	4941
N15577	4805
N15583 (1)	4867
N15587	4439
N15595	2246
N15709	20729
N15817	25985
N16001	1495
N16002	1496
N16003	1497
N16005 (1)	1499
N16005 (2)	19294
N16007	1549
N16017	1555
N16048 (DC-2)	1586
N16050	20435
N16070	1910
N16082	1949
N16094	1915
N16815	19783
N17091	6170
N17109	4999
N17313	1923
N17316	1931
N17323	1969
N17331	1917
N17333	1919
N17334	1920
N17397	11772
N17884	4538
N17890	7363
N18104	1952
N18106 (1)	1954
N18107	1955
N18109	1957
N18111	1983
N18113	1989
N18115	1991
N18116	1992
N18117 (1)	1993
N18121	1997
N18124	2000
N18141	2137
N18491	4955
N18639 (1)	4584
N18646	11684
N18648	4404
N18649	6068
N18664 (1)	20734
N18664 (2)	9980
N18775	4684
N18937	2012
N18951	2015
N19428	11648
N19454	13863
N19721	19721
N19900	19445
N19906	4747
N19912	11716
N19915	7347
N19919	4869
N19924 (2)	11762
N19930	6318
N19931 (1)	25997
N19931 (2)	26127
N19932	4928
N19934	4979
N19971	2261
N20630	19492
N20756	9223
N20956	10187
N20961	19348
N21669	25509
N21715 (1)	2130
N21728	2144
N21769 (2)	25634
N21782	2170
N21798	2202
N24320	20197
N25608	2183
N25609	2184
N25610	2185
N25623	3276
N25641 (2)	9059
N25646	2234
N25647	2235
N25649	2224
N25668	2241
N25673	2213
N25693	2266
"N28340"	2105
N28341	3278
N28394	3250
N28395	3251
N30088	6064
N33321	7391
N33324	1954
N33623 (2)	20215
N33632	4138
N33639 (2)	4085
N33644	4123
N34970 (2)	42966
N36349	19845
N37800	20806
N37906	12712
N39165 (DC-2)	1404
N40386	26120
N44587	12857
N44991	11706
N44995	11719
N45366	11757
N45398	4892
N45399	11629
N46877	9186
N47060	19066
N48211	26718
N49541	7340
N49543	11672
N49952	12680
N50039	10240
N50474	4563
N51938	25956
N52935	20017
N54091	13730
N54374	6177
N54599	34189
N54602	27080
N54610	20607
N54705	12844
N57123	33170
N57626	4564
N57850	9214
N59314	12363
N60154	32755
N60480	9530
N61696	25509
N61724	13176
N61981	2216
N63440	20194
N64490	25360
N64605	13227
N64766	27218
N64767	10199
N67125	20886/43086
N67136	6187
N67588	20536
N68363	20238
N68780	25888
N74589	9926
N75097	6151
N75391	26366
N79017	19227
N79044	9654
N81907	33313
N81949	12582
N81952	32825
N86553	4715
N86584	4935
N86593	11696
N86594	11664
N86596	4975
N87624	9147
N87625	4858
N87626	4988
N87627	13660
N87641	10193
N87642	11835
N87643	13060
N87745	6315
N88783	12785
N88874	12693
N90079	7392
N90830	13050
"N91008"	2245
"N91008"	6337
N91260	25372
N91289	26138
N91314	4538
N92578	9028
N95640	20190
N99131	18949
N99346	26501
N99857	43332
(N99886)	33444
OB-R-581	4830
OB-1756	13177
"OE-LBC"	13073
OH-LCD	19309
OH-LCH	6346
OH-VKB	1975
OK-AIH	1973
OK-AIZ (DC-2)	1564
OK-WCT	12611
OK-WDO	19006
OK-WZA	25667
OK-XAB	25644
"OK-XDM"	1995
OO-AWM	12318
OY-BPB	20019
"OY-DDA"	9664
PH-AJU (DC-2)	1288
"PH-AJU" (DC-2)	1286
"PH-AJU" (DC-2)	1404
PH-AKF (5)(DC-2)	1331
"PH-ALR"	32966
PH-ARS	2110
PH-DDZ (2)	19754
PH-MAG	12472
PH-MOA	33353
PH-PBA	19434
"PH-PBA"	9172
"PH-TCB"	9836
PI-C141	19251
PI-C149	4823
PI-C647	9786
PI-C649	13510
PJ-ALD (1)	42965
PK-GDH	13639
PK-IBA	12652
PK-OAZ	19623
PK-VDM	9551?
PP-AKA	20193
PP-ANN	1992
"PP-AVJ"	20555
PP-CBT	4968
PP-FBR	6015
PP-PAY (DC-2)	1351
PP-PCK	26158
PP-PCL	26052
PP-PCM	19524
PP-SDD	20435
PP-SPV	25985
PP-VBF	10156
PP-VBK	26823
PP-VBN (2)	26921
PP-YPU	12303

Registration	c/n
PR-MSY	33581
PT-BFU	2248
PT-KUB	34285
PT-KUC	4347
PT-KYZ	11837
PT-KZF	20244
PT-KZG	26921
PT-LGO	4433
P2-ANQ	27110
RP-C83	25562
RP-C147	20767
RP-C368	2217
RP-C535	27016
RP-C550	25737
RP-C758	19738
RP-C845	25415
RP-C1352	25347
RP-C1354	25571
SA-R-1	32650
SE-CFP	13883
SE-CFR	13647
SP-LCB (2)	12704
SP-LCC (1)	9903
ST-AHL	26095
SU-AHP	32963
SU-AHT	32843
SU-AHU	33540
SX-ECF	33206
TC-ALI	12830
TF-AVN	4363
TF-ISB	9860
TF-NPK	13861
TG-ASA	4369
"TG-CHP"	11741?
T9-ABC	32935
URSS-B (1)	2032
URSS-D	2096
URSS-L3403	2096
URSS-M	2031
URSS-M25 (DC-2)	1413
URSS-N	2033
URSS-P	6004
URSS-R	4765
VH-ABR	2029
VH-AEQ	6024
VH-AES	6021
VH-AGU	32668
VH-ANH	4120
VH-ANR	1944
VH-ANW	13624
VH-BAB	25495
"VH-BPA"	12187
VH-BPL	12873
VH-BPN	32945
VH-CDZ (DC-2)	1376
VH-CIN	27131
VH-CNS	9286
VH-DAS	6051
VH-DNA	27130
VH-EAE	33096
VH-EAF	33106
VH-EDC	12874
VH-EWE	6007
"VH-EWE"	13084
VH-HJT	32671
VH-JXD (2)	33297
VH-MIN	13459
VH-MMA	9593
VH-MMD	33301
VH-MMF	12540
VH-NVD	32879
VH-NVZ	32883
VH-OVM	33102
VH-PTE	26638
VH-PWN (2)	26001
VH-SBI	6122
VH-SBL	12056
VH-SPY	33113
VH-TMQ	32884
VH-UPQ	33000
VP-KJU	33325
VP-KLJ	20228
VQ-TAF	12550
"VR-HDA"	9525
VR-HDB	4423
VR-HEX	19923
VR-HFR	20794
VT-ATT	20363
VT-AUI	13231
VT-AUM	18905
VT-AUT	13720
VT-AXC	20303
VT-CEB	26491
VT-CGA	25467
VT-CGQ	13573
VT-CTV	10178
VT-CYG	13019
VT-CYT	32992
VT-CYX	13543
VT-DDW	9949
VT-DTS	20012
XA-BJI (DC-2)	1304
XA-BKQ (DC-2)	1408
XA-BKV (DC-2)	1599
XA-BLN	1989
XA-BLO	1993
XA-BLW	1992
XA-CEG	19593
XA-CIL	4218
"XA-CMA"	9276
XA-DOO (C-39)	2092
XA-FIR	13702
XA-FUV	3261
XA-FUW	3260
XA-GEV	7339
XA-GUF	1931
XA-GUX	4383
XA-HUE	12891
XA-HUF	19802
XA-ION	13378
XA-IUI	11719
XA-JEL	12990
XA-JUI ?	
XA-KIK	4369
XA-KTB	2118
XA-REP	9049
XA-RNF	12192
XA-ROM	12287
XA-RPN	2167
XA-UDY	12192
XB-EHX	4918
"XB-GED"	19029
XB-HED	1920
XB-JSJ	9276
XB-UNO	9276
XC-ABF	7377
"XH-TAZ"	26178
XT-817	19256
XT-827	13784
XT-T90	4871
XT-T91	2135
XT-T92	2261
XU-AAE	19256
XV-NIA	12832
XW-PAD	26696
XW-PFA	13906
XW-PFT	12539
XW-PFX	13529
XW-TFB	34298
YN-BVK	6215
YR-GAD (DC-2)	1378
YR-PAF	1986
YS-53C	6061
YU-ABB	13713
YU-ABE	12381
YU-ABG	25480
YU-ABI	25453
YU-ABK	33277
YU-ABU	12704
YU-ABW	11746
YV-C-AKE	4705
YV-C-AMH	19783
YV-O-MC-1 (1)	19335
YV-147C	25278
YV-201T	11775/10201
YV-218C	43079
YV-222C	7386
YV-226C	19121
YV-227C	19000
YV-426C	4093
YV-C-430	9061
YV-440C	2201
YV-500C	6135
YV-609C	43087
YV-610C	9894
YV-670C	13074
YV-769C	19513
YV-822C	9137
YV-911C	32761
YV-1179C	11775
YV-1415	32761
YV-1854	6135
YV-2119	26439
Z-WRJ	11989
ZK-AMY	13506
ZK-APK	34227
ZK-AWP	33135
ZK-AZL	33316
ZK-BBJ	34222
ZK-BKD	13521
ZK-BQK	33315
ZK-BYF	20051
ZK-CAW	18923
ZK-DAK	26480
"ZK-SAL"	33316
ZS-ASN	33581
ZS-BXF	12107
ZS-BXJ (2)	12413
ZS-CAI	13541
ZS-CRV	13331
ZS-DAK (2)	12073
ZS-DIW	11991
ZS-DRJ	12026
ZS-GPL	9581
ZS-JMP	2119
ZS-KEX	2008
ZS-LJI	34225
ZS-LVR	20475
ZS-MAP	32644
ZS-MFY	12073
ZS-MRU	4363
ZS-NTD	26438
ZS-NTE	11926
ZS-NZC	11726
ZS-NZD	19104
ZS-NZE	13368
ZS-OJD	4890
ZS-OJE	32844
ZS-OJI	26439
ZS-OJJ	32961
ZS-OJK	25610
ZS-OJL (2)	33313
ZS-OJM	25546
"4X-AES"	6223
5B-CAW	10106
5B-CBD	9623
5H-DAK	9581
5H-LVR	20475
5N-AAP	13304
5N-AAQ	9874
5W-FAA	32895
5W-FAI	33135
5Y-ACF	25372
5Y-BMB	34375
5Y-DAK (2)	12073
5Y-RDS	27085
9G-AAF	9407
9J-RDR	25928
9N-AAC	20681
9N-AAE	26475
9N-AAH	6216
9N-AAP	42956
9N-AAQ	9950
9N-AAX	25998
9N-AAY	19934
9Q-CAM	34409
9Q-CSL	19809
9Q-CTR	9452
9Q-CUK (2)	33445
9Q-CUL	42968
9Q-CYC	18977
9U-BAE	25541
9Y-TDY	19759
China #48	4852
China #49	4853
China #53	4904

Appendix II(b)

Military Serial / Constructor's Number Cross-Reference

Please note that only aircraft included in the Update to the Production listing are included here.

USAAF/USAF C-47 serials (including those taken over by other air forces) have been omitted from this cross-reference as they follow a logical order in line with the Construction numbers.
For full details, see pages 119-120 in Volume I of "The DC-1/2/3 – The First Seventy Years".

ARGENTINA

CTA-15	4664
ST-22	9578
T-101	25455
T-104	13373
TA-05	19965
TC-21	19961
TC-33	20293

AUSTRALIA

A30-9	1292 (DC-2)
A65-64	26640
A65-69	27127
A65-73	32671
A65-78	32677
A65-114	33460
A65-124	34220
N2-43	12542

BELGIUM

K-16	20823
K-24	26984
K-25	27085

BOLIVIA

TAM-01	26666
TAM-28	33626
TAM-38	20507

BRAZIL

2009	25679
2015	25685
2017	20193
2023	34365
2031	20206
2032	20414
2040	20048

CANADA

10916	32843
12928	13149
12949	26248
12959	22641
FZ576	12111
FZ658	12217
FZ671	12256
KG455	12490
KG587	13310
KG611	13370
KN451	32922

CHILE

121	13009
961	12937

CHINA (TAIWAN)

7219	26067
7231	20390
7273	20260
C-51219	26067

COLOMBIA

670	4824
1120	12446
1654	26292
1658	32541
1667	19052
1670	19125
1681	33248
1683	27137
1685	43382
1686	25443
PNC-213	20875
PNC-0211	25667
PNC-0213	20875

CONGO

TN211	26984

CUBA

203	4627

CZECHOSLOVAKIA

0543	19006
8406	25667
D-18	25667
D-19	12617
D-20	25644
D-24	25653
D-25	26452

DENMARK

K-682	20019
K-683	19677
K-684	19054
K-686	19475
K-687	19200
K-688	20118

DOMINICAN REPUBLIC

3404	25530
3407	20845

ECUADOR

CA-747	11747

EL SALVADOR

109	32710
116	33282
117	25409
118	33238
119	6204

FINLAND

DO-1	1354 (DC-2)
DO-3	1562 (DC-2)
DO-4	25515
DO-5	19795

FRANCE

12471	12471
77116	33448

GABON

TR-KBD	25553

GERMANY (WEST)

1401	26989

GREAT BRITAIN

DG476	1251 (DC-2)
FZ570	12105
'FZ625'	33185
'KG374'	33335
KG611	13370
KG747	25291
KG807	25484
KK116	26569
KN491	26717
KK205	26984
KN374	32745
KN417	32843
KN485	32963
KN630	33286
KN633	33317
KP208	33419
KP238	33540

GREECE

49-2615	12843
49-2617	4658
49-2622	20474
49-2625	4409
49-2637	19983
49-2638	9720
KJ960	26252
KK156	26740
KK169	26860
KN475	32952
KN542	33146
KN575	33199

GUATEMALA

3/575	19674
510	12196
530	20031
540	25425
550	26286
555	33499
560	34398
575	19674
580	9100
590	33542

HONDURAS

303	25746
304	12962
305	19426
306	13642
307	26765
308	34300
315	26178(?)
319	26541

INDIA

BJ496	12494
BJ764	12449
MI965	12819

INDONESIA

AF-4775	34228
AF-4776	13334
T-474	12719
T-482	25489
U-603	4500

ISRAEL

4X-FMJ/1442	33031
4X-FNB	19420
4X-FNG	32837
4X-FNL/04	12486
4X-FNZ	33307

ITALY
MM61775 19016
MM61776 19194
MM61777 9910
MM61799 26707
MM61815 26800
MM61826 4380
MM61895 6011

JAPAN
9023 33095

JORDAN
111 19460

KATANGA
KAT-02 32558
KAT-40 20455

KOREA
60.059 20495

MALI
TZ-390 19173

MALAWI
76-20 13850
76-21 27005

MEXICO
TTD-6005 34231
EATM-6041 9276
ETM-6046 12647
TP-0202 43083

NETHERLANDS
'ZU-5' 20118

NEW ZEALAND
'NZ3546' 26480
NZ3547 20051
NZ3551 34223

PAKISTAN
C-402 27098

PAPUA NEW GUINEA
P2-002 32877

PARAGUAY
2010 32630
2014 25757
2023 34376
2030 12557
2032 27098

PERU
62-357 25273

PHILIPPINES
30717 13868
415325 19791

POLAND
1 13552
2 13349
3 13348
8 13144
10 13217

PORTUGAL
6151 11765
6152 11668
6153 11675
6154 10049
6155 32675
6156 33093
6157 19755
6158 19818
6159 20111
6160 20587
6161 10076
6162 25579
6163 26144
6165 26667
6166 25522
6167 13018
6168 20173
6169 ? (see 42968)
6170 11698
6172 13140

SOUTH AFRICA
6811 11986
6814 11990
6825 12160
6828 12415
6832 12478
6837 13539
6839 13540
6840 25311
6845 26087
6846 33134
6850 27099
6852 27002
6854 32635
6864 12580
6865 33478
6866 12090
6876 12582
6877 11925
6884 12064
6885 12596
6886 12166
6887 12704
6890 33552

SPAIN
T.3-28 9914
T,3-36 20600
T.3-67 13375

SRI LANKA
CR-821 25464
CR-822 33556

SWEDEN
79001 9001
79002 9103

THAILAND
010 26271
079 34349
093 34363
152 33484
210 26471
545 26806
559 20025
615 13546
865 12498
876 26137
882 34141
883 9290
919 27180
2102 32750
2202 27186
40223 13112
45941 34203
46151 19572
46152 34288
46153 9290
46154 25674
46155 25269
46156 26515
46157 20082
46158 25753
46159 33010
76517 32849
212248 12248
L2-1/90 13546
L2-1/90 9871
L2-6/90 18999
L2-7/90 19572
L2-8/90 32849
L2-10/96 32590
L2-11/96 34203
L2-13/96 12872
L2-14/96 12667
L2-15/96 25491
L2-16/00 25674
L2-18/00 20053
L2-20/00 26679
L2-21/00 25410
L2-24/01 26806
L2-25/01 27180
L2-26/02 13778
L2-27/02 19977
L2-29/02 27042
L2-29/02 20794
L2-30/07 26902
L2-31/07 34288
L2-32/11 25762
L2-33/13 12487
L2-36/14 13112
L2-37/14 33066
L2-38/14 34142
L2-39/15 19010
L2-40/15 20421
L2-41/18 26471
L2-42/18 26515
L2-43/18 26777
L2-44/18 33484
L2-45/18 34386
L2-46/18 26271
L2-47/18 34349
L2-48/18 19400
L2-49/18 25753
L2-50/19 34363
L2-51/19 34141
L2-53/19 20613
L2-54/19 34259

TURKEY
12-046 20117
12-072 19529
12-258 26258
12-42 12949
42-6059 12757
43-6045 19729
6039 13436
6095 20115
E-062 20112
H-008 26456
H-025 19531
Ho-035 10132
I-TAK-096 25715
YSL-52 13877

URUGUAY
T-514 20604
T-521 19231

UNITED STATES (NAVY)
01981 4437
12410 43348
12412 43399
12417 9357
12418 9358
12428 43370
12436 9619
17094 11808
17097 43371
17149 43383
17150 43311
17160 43331
17171 43309
17177 43305
17191 43379
17196 43357
17203 13103
17211 43391
17221 13319
17241 43343
17254 25629
17278 25824
17284 43367
17287 43372
50767 26303
50776 26373
50784 43380
50808 43394
50812 43358
50821 43322
50823 43317
50826 43363
50835 43321
99844 33267
99845 43362

VENEZUELA
1840 12386

YUGOSLAVIA
7311 26720
7323 33220
71202 26720
71214 33220
71248 19539
71254 25546
71255 26557

ZAMBIA
AF-103 33072

ZIMBABWE
7039 32651
7301 33089
7310 42978